Friendship in Doubt

OXFORD STUDIES IN WESTERN ESOTERICISM

CHILDREN OF LUCIFER
The Origins of Modern Religious Satanism
Ruben van Luijk

SATANIC FEMINISM
Lucifer as the Liberator of Woman in Nineteenth-Century Culture
Per Faxneld

THE SIBYLS OF LONDON
A Family on the Esoteric Fringes of Georgian England
Susan Sommers

WHAT IS IT LIKE TO BE DEAD?
Near-Death Experiences, Christianity, and the Occult
Jens Schlieter

AMONG THE SCIENTOLOGISTS
History, Theology, and Praxis
Donald A. Westbrook

RECYCLED LIVES
A History of Reincarnation in Blavatsky's Theosophy
Julie Chajes

THE ELOQUENT BLOOD
The Goddess Babalon and the Construction of Femininities in Western Esotericism
Manon Hedenborg White

GURDJIEFF
Mysticism, Contemplation, and Exercises
Joseph Azize

INITIATING THE MILLENIUM
The Avignon Society and Illuminism in Europe
Robert Collis and Natalie Bayer

IMAGINING THE EAST
The Early Theosophical Society
Tim Rudbog and Erik Sand

MYSTIFYING KABBALAH
Academic Scholarship, National Theology, and New Age
Boaz Huss

SPIRITUAL ALCHEMY
From Jacob Boehme to Mary Anne Atwood
Mike A. Zuber

THE SUBTLE BODY
A Genealogy
Simon Cox

OCCULT IMPERIUM
Arturo Reghini, Roman Traditionalism, and the Anti-Modern Reaction in Fascist Italy
Christian Giudice

VESTIGES OF A PHILOSOPHY
Matter, the Meta-Spiritual, and the Forgotten Bergson
John Ó Maoilearca

PROPHECY, MADNESS, AND HOLY WAT IN EARLY MODERN EUROPE
A Life of Ludwig Friedrich Gifftheil
Leigh T.I. Penman

HÉLÈNE SMITH
Occultism and the Discovery of the Unconscious
Claudie Massicotte

LIKE A TREE UNIVERSALLY SPREAD
Sri Sabhapati Swami and Śivarājayoga
Keith Edward Cantú

Friendship in Doubt

Aleister Crowley, J. F. C. Fuller, Victor B. Neuburg, and British Agnosticism

RICHARD KACZYNSKI

OXFORD
UNIVERSITY PRESS

Oxford University Press is a department of the University of Oxford. It furthers the University's objective of excellence in research, scholarship, and education by publishing worldwide. Oxford is a registered trade mark of Oxford University Press in the UK and certain other countries.

Published in the United States of America by Oxford University Press
198 Madison Avenue, New York, NY 10016, United States of America.

Library of Congress Control Number: 2023056798

ISBN 978–0–19–769400–8

DOI: 10.1093/oso/9780197694008.001.0001

Printed by Integrated Books International, United States of America

Contents

1
THE AGNOSTICS

They called themselves Agnostics. Secularists. Atheists. Rationalists. Infidels.

In 1903, Aleister Crowley, J. F. C. Fuller, and Victor B. Neuburg—young, educated, and rebelling against their religious upbringing—matched the target demographic of the New Agnostics, the latest iteration of spiritual disbelief that had swept the Victorian era. As the older, more militant school steeped in upper-class intelligentsia, the New Agnostics fermented on the streets, appealing to younger or working-class activists. These punks, protesting the church's domination over civic life, shared their predecessors' goal: to "acquaint this audience with recent scientific discoveries," firm in the belief that "all natural phenomena were governed by fixed and uniform laws."[1] Attacking religion, promoting science, and advocating for social and sexual reforms often resulted in these provocateurs being jailed for blasphemy or obscenity, martyrs for the cause. Crowley, Fuller, and Neuburg joined this movement at the same time and, through it, met each other.

The general whose theories inspired the Blitzkrieg and the poet who discovered Dylan Thomas would seem, at first, to share nothing in common. Fuller is remembered as a military strategist and historian, a career officer who attained the rank of major general before retiring, involving himself in fascist politics, and even attending Adolf Hitler's fiftieth birthday party. Neuburg, meanwhile, was a slight and delicate bard who ran the Vine Press out of his aunt's country cottage in the 1920s and edited the *Sunday Referee*'s weekly "Poets' Corner" column in the 1930s. However, in their youth—Fuller was five years Neuburg's senior—they found common ground in England's Freethought and Atheist movements. Both contributed to the *Agnostic Journal* before meeting as students of that controversial and radical thinker Aleister Crowley. Together, the three of them dipped their toes into the river of nonconformity, delving into the mysteries of scientific

[1] Bernard Lightman, "Ideology, Evolution and Late-Victorian Agnostic Popularizers," in *History, Humanity and Evolution: Essays for John C. Greene*, ed. James R. Moore (1990; repr. Cambridge: Cambridge University Press, 2002), 292.

Friendship in Doubt. Richard Kaczynski, Oxford University Press. © Oxford University Press 2024.
DOI: 10.1093/oso/9780197694008.003.0001

occultism until, a mere seven years later, the tide carried them in different directions: Fuller into the military, Neuburg into poetry, and Crowley into ill-deserved notoriety.

This seminal period remains largely overlooked. While Fuller's biographers acknowledge that the occult supplied his military writings with a colorful metaphorical language, they gloss over these early years.[2] Neuburg's biographer seems so enamored of her subject that she blames Crowley for all of Victor's subsequent woes, a claim that casts her objectivity into doubt.[3] I excavated the information for this book during my research into Crowley's biography *Perdurabo*,[4] but that book did not allow the kind of deep dive that this focused volume undertakes. As we shall see, the few years spanning this threesome's burgeoning friendship would influence the rest of their lives.

The Birth of Secularism

The Industrial Revolution in England resulted in a prosperous middle class that enjoyed unheard-of mobility and cultural exchange with London thanks to a system of railways that connected once-remote areas of England. It was the era of Charles Darwin and Michael Faraday. Science brought progress, and science began to replace religion as the guiding principle of life. Activists increasingly called for the separation of religion from the civic life. Society's ills, they argued, stemmed from the pernicious influence of religion. As Bloom puts it, "Secularism was the 'religion' of the intellectual mid-Victorian."[5]

[2] The two principal biographies of Fuller are Brian Holden Reid, *J .F. C. Fuller: Military Thinker* (Basingstoke, UK: Macmillan, 1987); and Anthony John Trythall, *"Boney" Fuller: Soldier, Strategist, and Writer, 1878–1966* (New Brunswick, NJ: Rutgers University Press, 1977). For an appraisal of Fuller's later military thought, see Alaric Searle, "Was there a 'Boney' Fuller after the Second World War? Major-General J. F. C. Fuller as Military Theorist and Commentator, 1945–1966," *War in History* 11, no. 3 (2004): 327–357.

[3] Neuburg's only biography to date is Jean Overton Fuller, *The Magical Dilemma of Victor Neuburg*, rev. ed. (London: W. H. Allen, 1965; Oxford, UK: Mandrake Press, 1990). For a memoir by an acquaintance during Neuburg's later years, see Arthur Calder-Marshall, *The Magic of My Youth* (London: R. Hart-Davis, 1951). A brief biographical monograph was also issued as Victor E. Neuburg, *Vickybird: A Memoir by His Son* (London: Polytechnic of North London, 1983).

[4] Richard Kaczynski, *Perdurabo: The Life of Aleister Crowley*, rev. ed. (Tempe, AZ: New Falcon, 2002; Berkeley, CA: North Atlantic Books, 2010).

[5] Clive Bloom, *Victoria's Madmen: Revolution and Alienation* (Basingstoke, UK: Palgrave Macmillan, 2013), 9.

Early Secularists such as Richard Carlile (1790–1843) and George Jacob Holyoake (1817–1906) may have spearheaded the movement,[6] but Charles Bradlaugh (1833–1891),[7] with an "almost obsessive hatred of Christianity,"[8] directed Secularism into a brash militant force, intent on exposing the obvious and demonstrable errors of fact in religious claims. He supplanted the movement's leaders, founded the National Secular Society (NSS) in 1866, and adopted the *National Reformer* as the NSS weekly paper. Bradlaugh proved to be an effective spokesperson with formidable powers of persuasion, and he attracted promising supporters to his cause. These included George William Foote (1850–1915), founder of the *Freethinker* in 1881 and successor to Bradlaugh in 1890, and Annie Besant (1847–1933), who in 1907 would succeed Henry Steel Olcott as president of the Theosophical Society–Adyar. The movement was challenged by adherents of established religion, who branded these Secularists, atheists, and Freethinkers as infidels—a name they gladly embraced.

Despite the strident and even obnoxious tendencies of atheism's more extreme adherents, unbelief also spawned its share of moderates. Most prominent of these was middle-class scientific naturalist[9] Thomas Henry Huxley (1825–1895), who in 1869 introduced the term *agnostic*. Known as "Darwin's bulldog," his background helped bring the debate out of the ivory tower and to the masses. His term *agnostic* had the advantage of emphasizing what was actually knowable, thus avoiding the negative associations of terms such as *atheist*, *freethinker*, or *secularist*.

Fault lines soon formed in the militant camp when Bradlaugh brought the columnist "G. R." on to the *National Reformer*. "George Rex" was the nickname of George R. Drysdale (1825–1904), whose anonymous book *The Elements of Social Science*[10] proposed a medical argument in favor of regular sexual activity for both men and women, free of marriage and monogamy. He also called for widespread use of contraception, a contentious political

[6] Holyoake coined the term *secularism* in 1851. For an analysis of early Secularism from 1840 through 1870, see Shirley Annette Mullen, "Organized Freethought: The Religion of Unbelief in Victorian England" (PhD diss., University of Minnesota, 1985). For the later years of Secularism, see Edward Royle, *Radicals, Secularists and Republicans: Popular Freethought in Britain, 1866–1915* (Manchester, UK: Manchester University Press, 1980).

[7] For Bradlaugh's biography, see Bryan Niblett, *Dare to Stand Alone: The Story of Charles Bradlaugh* (Oxford, UK: Kramedart, 2011).

[8] Royle, *Radicals*, 91–92.

[9] This phrase is from Lightman, "Ideology," 285.

[10] See for example, A Graduate of Medicine [George Drysdale], *The Elements of Social Science; or, Physical, Sexual, and Natural Religion*, 4th expanded ed. (1854; repr. London: E. Trulove, 1861).

and legal issue. In 1877, Bradlaugh and Besant wrote a new introduction for the pamphlet *The Fruits of Philosophy*, which contained birth-control information, to which was appended new material by G. R., "widely known in all parts of the world as the author of the *Elements of Social Science*."[11] Bradlaugh and Besant were prosecuted under the Obscene Publications Act, along with NSS Secretary Charles Watts (1836–1906), who had published it. Watts pleaded guilty, claiming that he never read the pamphlet; he was let off with a suspended sentence and court costs. Bradlaugh and Besant, meanwhile, challenged the charge and went to trial; they were found guilty but later acquitted. In addition to bringing the concept of birth control to wider attention, the case spawned the procontraception Malthusian League[12] and framed Bradlaugh and his followers as "the Erotic School of Freethought."[13]

The mid-1880s were what Lightman has called "the heyday of Victorian unbelief."[14] The "New Agnosticism" that emerged at this time sought to educate people in "scientific unbelief" instead of targeting and offending the religious. Informed by Darwin's theory of evolution, it set gradual, incremental goals rather than seeking radical revolution. Important branches of this new generation emerged from the Watts-Holyoake camp. In the wake of the 1877 *Fruits of Philosophy* court case, Watts, Holyoake, and Foote seceded from the NSS to form the short-lived rival group the British Secular Union (BSU).[15] Watts also took over as editor of Holyoake's paper, the *Secular Review*.[16] Foote reconciled with Bradlaugh and returned to the NSS in 1881, starting his own journal, the *Freethinker*. Following Bradlaugh's militant lead in openly mocking Christianity, Foote soon found himself charged with two counts of blasphemy. Unlike the exonerated Bradlaugh, Foote was sentenced to one year in prison. As Crowley surmised of this phase of this movement,

> The army of Satan had, unfortunately, failed to keep discipline in the face of the enemy. The anti-Christians were in fact as prone to split up into sects as the non-conformists themselves. Bradlaugh's personality was big

[11] Charles Knowlton, Charles Bradlaugh, and Annie Besant, *Fruits of Philosophy: An Essay on the Population Question* (London: Freethought, 1877).

[12] F. D'Arcy, "The Malthusian League and the Resistance to Birth Control Propaganda in Late Victorian Britain," *Population Studies* 31, no. 3 (1977): 429–448.

[13] Charles R. Mackay, *Life of Charles Bradlaugh, M. P.* (London: D. J. Gunn, 1888), 29.

[14] Lightman, "Ideology," 285.

[15] The BSU operated until 1884.

[16] Foote and Holyoake had collaborated on the *Secularist: A Liberal Weekly Review* (1876–1877). They each went forward with their own magazines: Holyoake with the *Secular Review*, followed by Foote in 1881 with the *Freethinker*.

> enough to enable him to keep any differences that he may have had with Huxley in the background, but the successors of these paladins were degenerate. Mrs. Besant had broken away from atheism altogether; her hysteria handed her over from one strong influence to another as it appealed to her imagination. G. W. Foote, with the medal of his martyrdom glittering on his manly breast, marched monotonously against the mob of Christianity. He had suffered for the cause and was consumed by personal pride on that account.[17]

These events set the stage for two important new voices to emerge: William Stewart Ross and Watts' son, Charles Albert Watts.

Saladin and the *Agnostic Journal*

The BSU vacancy left by Foote was filled in 1882 by another NSS expatriate, William Stewart Ross (1844–1906), who had been editor of Bradlaugh's *National Reformer* since 1876. He was also the proprietor of his own publishing company, which was dedicated to publishing his Secularist writings under the pseudonym of "Saladin," after the formidable military commander who led the Muslim opposition against the Christian Crusades (see figure 1.1). The historical Saladin (An-Nasir Salah ad-Din Yusuf ibn Ayyub, 1137–1193) had been glorified in the eighteenth century by Gibbon and Lessing and popularized in the nineteenth by Sir Walter Scott's romance *The Talisman*.[18] With Arabic culture subsequently romanticized by Sir Richard Burton in *The Arabian Nights*,[19] Saladin came to represent more than just Scott's "noble savage"; he was the most famous historical Muslim, "a model of moderation, mercy, and what Westerners today understand as the values of chivalry."[20] Ross's pseudonym was no doubt a poke in the eye to the religionists

[17] Aleister Crowley, *The Confessions of Aleister Crowley*, ed. John Symonds and Kenneth Grant (London: Jonathan Cape, 1969), 538. As for that "medal of his martyrdom," see G. W. Foote, *Prisoner for Blasphemy* (London: Progressive, 1886).

[18] Sir Walter Scott, *The Talisman* (Edinburgh: Constable, 1825). This was the third volume in his Tales of the Crusaders series.

[19] Richard F. Burton, *A Plain and Literal Translation of the Arabian Nights' Entertainments, Now Entituled the Book of the Thousand Nights and a Night: With Introduction Explanatory Notes on the Manners and Customs of Moslem Men and a Terminal Essay upon the History of the Nights*, 10 vols. (Benares, India: Kama-Shastra Society, 1885).

[20] Aljouharah Bent Saleh Ben Abd-Arrahman Almayman, "Richard the Lion Heart and Salah Ad-Din Al-Ayyubi: A Historical Comparative Study" (PhD diss., Florida State University, 1993), 239.

Figure 1.1 Saladin (William Stewart Ross [1844–1906]), secularist author and publisher of the *Agnostic Journal*

who dubbed Secularists as "infidels";[21] an apt and potent symbol of the "New Agnostic" warrior. And wage war he did. Under his coeditorship of the *Secular Review*, the anti-Bradlaugh tone of the journal increased notably. Royle called him the "chief pin-pricker of Bradlaugh and Besant Bubbles"

[21] Much as Crowley, upon becoming British head of the Oriental Templars, chose (ironically enough) the name Baphomet after the idol that the original Templars were accused of worshipping and that the French antimasonic craze, led two decades earlier by Leo Taxil, associated with the devil.

The Agnostic Journal

AND ECLECTIC REVIEW.

EDITED BY SALADIN.

VOL. LVI No. 23. LONDON. JUNE 10, 1905. PRICE TWOPENCE.

Figure 1.2 The masthead for the *Agnostic Journal*

and "the self-conscious 'joker' in the pack of Secularist leaders."[22] Two years later, when the BSU folded and Watts reconciled with Foote and moved to Canada, Ross became editor and proprietor of the *Secular Review*.

Ross was a contradiction within the Secularist movement, considering faith and atheism to be equally problematic intellectual roadblocks to an understanding of spiritual truth. He preferred Huxley's *agnosticism*, but he breathed new meaning into term. As Bonnett writes, "In Ross's hands agnosticism was fashioned into something much more fiery. It was a bullish, evangelical project of radical investigation and critique. He delighted in flinging his irreverent opinions in the face of both the faithful and the faithless."[23] Rather than partner with atheists as Bradlaugh had, Ross made his bed with the Agnostics. In 1888, he changed his journal's name from the *Secular Review* to the *Agnostic Journal and Eclectic Review* (see figure 1.2). From that point, as Royle has put it, "Bradlaugh was to know no peace."[24] Undeterred by Foote's assertion that "the Agnostic is a timid Atheist,"[25] Ross fiercely criticized religion and Secularism alike in his *Why I Am an Agnostic*.[26] The dogma-free intellectual studies that he embraced ranged from transcendental Buddhism to hypnotism to the theosophical writings of H. P. Blavatsky (1831–1891). Thus, whereas Besant's conversion to theosophy in 1889 was promptly scorned by her former NSS colleagues, Ross opened the *Agnostic Journal* to contributions from theosophists and other spiritual researchers.

[22] Royle, *Radicals*, 31, 101.
[23] Alastair Bonnett, "The Agnostic Saladin," *History Today* 63, no. 2 (February 2013): 47–51.
[24] Royle, *Radicals*, 102.
[25] G. W. Foote, *Frederick Harrison on Atheism*, in *Flowers of Freethought: Second Series*, ed. G. W. Foote (London: G. Foote, 1894), 245.
[26] Saladin and Joseph Taylor, *Why I Am an Agnostic: Being a Manual of Agnosticism* (London: W. Stewart, 1888).

Despite an intense dislike of Besant stemming from the birth-control issue, Ross featured a front-page interview with Besant, including her portrait.[27]

Charles A. Watts and Rationalism: Into the Twentieth Century

Charles Albert Watts (1858–1946) was a second-generation Secularist with a front-row seat to his father's bitter ideological quarrel with the movement (see figure 1.3). He'd spent a dozen years as an apprentice in Holyoake's print shop. When the elder Watts moved to Canada, he left his printing company in the care of his son, whose experience with Holyoake allowed him to succeed where his father could not. As Cooke has observed, "Watts was not a titan, but unlike his predecessors, he understood intimately the processes, and the costs, of publishing as an industry."[28] In 1884, he began publishing books under his own imprint—including the *Agnostic Annual* (later the *Rationalist Annual*)—and in 1885, he launched *Watts's Literary Guide* (later the *Literary Guide and Rationalist Review*) as a platform to review and promote Agnostic literature (along with other literature of interest), printing "comprehensive summaries of books by leading thinkers, for those who could not afford to buy them."[29] This strategy was born of necessity: traditional distribution channels were hostile to anti-Christian literature, and "Watts frequently complained of periodicals refusing to place his advertisements."[30]

Watts simultaneously faced opposition within the Freethought movement itself. Whereas his publications appealed to both middle- and working-class audiences, the wealthy and established "rock stars" of the movement shied away from someone of such low social standing.[31] This prompted Watts to collaborate with other mavericks of the movement. As Cooke notes, "For ten or so years from its foundation in 1880, Watts & Co. survived by printing the

[27] Ajax Junior, "Theosophy and Secularism: An Interesting Interview with Annie Besant," *Agnostic Journal* 57, no. 5 (July 29, 1905): 65–67. This was followed in the next issue by an editorial response, wherein Ross took exception to her characterization of Agnostics. See Saladin, "Mrs. Annie Besant," *Agnostic Journal* 57, no. 6 (August 5, 1905): 83.

[28] Bill Cooke, *The Gathering of Infidels: A Hundred Years of the Rationalist Press Association* (Amherst, NY: Prometheus Books, 2004), 11.

[29] Cooke, *Gathering of Infidels*, 14.

[30] Cooke, *Gathering of Infidels*, 14.

[31] Cooke, *Gathering of Infidels*, 13, 22.

Figure 1.3 Charles Albert Watts (1858–1946), founder of the *Literary Guide and Rationalist Review*, Rationalist Press Association, and the Cheap Reprints series

various works of William Stewart Ross."[32] In addition, they collaborated on the *Agnostic Annual*, which was edited and printed by Watts but published by Ross from 1884 to 1896.

Although many writers have characterized the Secularist movement as largely played-out by 1900,[33] the uncertainty underpinning the first decade of the twentieth century created a climate ripe for the science-based moral philosophy of the New Agnostics. It began with the death of Queen Victoria in 1901, the end of an era and the beginning of a new one (albeit destined to be short: Edward VII reigned only until 1910). The end of the second Boer War in 1902 came not with the thrill of victory but with doubt about Britain's military prowess: despite vastly greater numbers and superior weaponry, the

[32] Cooke, *Gathering of Infidels*, 11.
[33] Cooke, *Gathering of Infidels*, 5.

Crown struggled to overcome the guerrilla tactics of the Boer insurgency. Birth rates were falling, a startling phenomenon that some blamed on social changes wrought by the women's movement. The Liberals' landslide victory in the 1906 elections crushed the ruling Conservative majority in the most stunning political reversal ever seen. And the church receded in importance in civil society.[34] Into these turbulent times the New Agnostic standard-bearers, Watts and Ross, marched boldly, playing major roles in bringing together Crowley, Fuller, and Neuburg.

In order to facilitate fundraising to bring his publications to the masses, Watts in 1893 set up the Rationalist Press Committee, subsequently incorporated in 1899 as the Rationalist Press Association (RPA). (Watts would come to prefer the term *rationalist* to *agnostic*, as the latter implied ignorance to some; also, *rationalist*'s more positive connotations avoided dividing religionists and nonreligionists, which was a frequent source of tension within the movement.[35]) According to the first memorandum of the RPA, "Rationalism may be defined as the mental attitude which unreservedly accepts the supremacy of reason and aims at establishing a system of philosophy and ethics verifiable by experience and independent of all arbitrary assumptions of authority."[36] The first book published by the RPA was Joseph McCabe's *The Religion of the Twentieth Century*, followed by McCabe's translation of Ernst Haeckel's *The Riddle of the Universe*.[37] The latter title enjoyed "the kind of success of which publishers dream,"[38] selling a hundred thousand copies by 1905 and netting the RPA a great deal of revenue, respectability, and recruits.

This success allowed the RPA to undertake in 1902 an audacious new venture: The Cheap Reprints series, the aim of which was to issue paperback reprints of freethought and rationalist classics for only sixpence. While it was not uncommon to publish bestselling novels as paperbacks, this was uncharted territory for serious nonfiction. Nobody believed that they would sell or that, if the books did sell, the books could be produced at that price point. But Watts knew his business, and, according to Cooke,

[34] For more on the social and political milieu of the Edwardian era, see Donald Read, ed., *Edwardian England* (New Brunswick, NJ: Rutgers University Press, 1982); and Simon Nowell-Smith, ed., *Edwardian England 1901–1914* (London: Oxford University Press, 1964).

[35] Cooke, *Gathering of Infidels*, 25.

[36] "First Principles of the R.P.A.," *Literary Guide and Rationalist Review* 128 (February 1, 1907): 25.

[37] Joseph McCabe, *The Religion of the Twentieth Century* (London: Watts, 1899); Ernst Haeckel, *The Riddle of the Universe at the Close of the Nineteenth Century*, trans. Joseph McCabe (London: Watts, 1899).

[38] According to Edward Royle, quoted in Cooke, *Gathering of Infidels*, 35.

"the first Cheap Reprint, T. H. Huxley's *Lectures and Essays*, sold out its first edition of 30,000 copies and a second edition of 15,000 in its first year alone."[39] The first five Cheap Reprints cumulatively sold one hundred fifty-five thousand copies in 1902 alone, and over the ensuing decade, the RPA would sell roughly four million of their Cheap Reprints.[40] Cooke writes, "The success of the RPA's endeavours, the Cheap Reprints in particular, took just about everybody by surprise. The publishing community was taken unawares that a substantial market existed for inexpensive works of non-fiction."[41]

These three Secularist journals of the early twentieth century—the old-school and more militant *Freethinker* and the friendly competitors of the New Agnostic movement, the *Agnostic Journal* (edited by Saladin) and the *Literary Guide* (published by Watts and the RPA)—would prove pivotal to the story of Fuller, Neuburg, and Crowley.

Enter J. F. C. Fuller

John Frederick Charles Fuller (1878–1966), nicknamed "Boney," was born in Chichester, West Sussex (see figure 1.4). He was the son of Rev. Alfred Fuller (1832–1927)—an Anglican cleric and the Rector of Itchenor—and Selma Marie Philippine *née* de la Chevallerie (*c.* 1847–1940), who was of French descent but raised in Germany. The family moved to Lausanne, but in 1889, when he was eleven, Fuller was sent back to England on his own to attend Fulmer House preparatory school in West Woking. While he was there, his parents settled at Sydenham Hill. In his letters home, he answered to "Fritz," the German form of his middle name; he would continue doing so until his mid-thirties[42] (coinciding with the Great War).

Fuller would later reflect that, by age five, he was already a heretic. He preferred reading to socializing, lacked discipline and focus, and considered art "one of the few things worth living for,"[43] carefully illustrating his letters with pen and ink drawings. In 1893, he attended Malvern School. He hated it and only remained there for two years before his grandfather in Leipzig

[39] Cooke, *Gathering of Infidels*, 43. See also Thomas Henry Huxley, *Lectures and Essays* (London: Macmillan and the Rationalist Press Association, 1902).
[40] Cooke, *Gathering of Infidels*, 39, 43.
[41] Cooke, *Gathering of Infidels*, 55.
[42] Trythall, *"Boney" Fuller*, 1.
[43] Trythall, *"Boney" Fuller*, 3; Reid, *J. F. C. Fuller*, 10.

Figure 1.4 John Frederick Charles Fuller (1878–1966)

suggested that he attend military school. Starting in 1895, Fuller spent two years at a "crammer" preparing for entrance exams to the Royal Military Academy Sandhurst. Although he passed the exam, he was nearly rejected because of his slight weight, and he entered on probation on August 30, 1897. Having a dreamy disposition that resisted the structure of the classroom, preferring the study of Home's *Tactics* to the prescribed reading of Clery's *Minor Tactics*.[44] This demonstrated what Reid has called the fundamental paradox of Fuller: "that he eventually excelled in a profession which ill-suited his temperament."[45]

He graduated the following year with a commission to the 1st Battalion (43rd) of the Oxfordshire Infantry. Spending the winter of 1898–1899 in Mullingar, Ireland, his reading included Scottish writers like Thomas Carlyle, Andrew Lang, and "Darwin's bulldog" Thomas Henry Huxley. A fellow

[44] Robert Home, *A Précis of Modern Tactics: Compiled from the Works of Recent Continental Writers at the Topographical and Statistical Department of the War Office* (1896; repr. London: HM Stationery Office, 1873); Sir C. Francis Clery, *Minor Tactics* (London: Kegan Paul, Trench, Trübner, 1890).

[45] Reid, *J. F. C. Fuller*, 10.

officer was so disturbed to see Fuller perusing *The First Philosophers of Greece* that he reported Fuller to the regimental surgeon![46] This did nothing to deter his reading in off-hours, and while stationed in South Africa during the Boer War in 1899, he read some two hundred different books on history, literature, evolution, religion, science, and philosophy. These included Laing's *A Modern Zoroastrianism*, Allen's *Evolution of the Idea of God*, Arnold's *Science and the Christian Tradition*, Wiedemann's *The Ancient Egyptian Doctrine of the Soul*, and—significantly—Saladin's *Why I Am an Agnostic*.[47] "I am a believer in Darwin and Evolution," Fuller declared at this time.[48] Decades later, he would recall in his memoirs,

> When I began to grow up, my scepticism quite naturally took an anti-religious form, and the reading of two books, one called *Modern Christianity a Civilized Heathenism*, and the other Winwood Reade's well-known *The Martyrdom of Man*, definitely turned me into an agnostic. Further, it should be remembered that this pronounced mental change coincided with the last lap of the great theologico-Darwinian controversy, and in consequence I soon became immersed in Huxley, Lecky, Samuel Laing and other rationalist writers. This, in turn, led to my first attempts in writing being heterodox.[49]

His self-confessed skepticism, Agnosticism, and Rationalism signaled his entry into the ranks of the infidels.

While stationed in Shimla, India, in 1903, he reached an intellectual turning point. His studies branched out to include Hinduism, including its sacred texts and its discipline of yoga, a subject still relatively unknown in the West.

> I met holy men, yogis, advanced radicals, for it would be a mistake to call them revolutionaries, and various members of the Arya Samaj. I studied

[46] Reid, *J. F. C. Fuller*, 9; Arthur Fairbanks, *The First Philosophers of Greece* (London: Kegan Paul, Trench, Trübner, 1898).

[47] Saladin was the publisher of the *Agnostic Journal*, to which Fuller would later contribute.

[48] Reid, *J. F. C. Fuller*, 11.

[49] J. F. C. Fuller, *Memoirs of an Unconventional Soldier* (London: Ivor Nicholson and Watson, 1936), 458–459. Henry William Pullen, *Modern Christianity, a Civilized Heathenism* (London: Simpkin, Marshall, 1872) was a dialogue expressing the author's clerical unbelief. William Winwood Reade, *The Martyrdom of Man* (London: Trübner, 1872) was a secular history of the Western world and critique of religion and its morality from the perspective of a social Darwinist.

> the *Vedas* and the *Upanishads*—in translations, of course—and took a deep interest in the Yoga philosophy. I soon discovered that, once its mystical jargon is set aside, it is little more than a system of self-control: the control of the body, of the instincts, and finally of mind and of soul. After a little practice I found it quite easy to cut out noises at will and to remain cool and collected in any set of circumstances. I make no claim to having been thrown into ecstasies or to have attained to supernatural powers; but having experimented with Yoga, what I do claim for it is: that intellectually it enables one to maintain a sense of proportion, and so release oneself from the thraldom of trivialities. It may be much more, yet this alone is no mean recommendation.[50]

He also began writing Swinburnian poetry. The biggest influences, however, came from two books in particular: Ellis's *Studies in the Psychology of Sex* and Carrington's *A Plea for Polygamy*.[51] Convinced that humanity needed to discard the "mystic fig leaf . . . and stand naked and sublime in all the glory and consummation of perfect Nature,"[52] Fuller took up sexual freedom as a rallying cry.

His next rebellion would prove harder to keep quiet. In 1904, his note from the Punjab, titled "A Barbaric Survival," appeared in the January 16 issue of the *Agnostic Journal*. It was a good place for an aspiring new talent to get started. Whereas the *Literary Guide* had a stable of established contributors like Charles Watts, Joseph McCabe, F. J. Gould, "Mimnermus," John M. Robertson, and G. J. Holyoake, the *Agnostic Journal* was open to new contributors.

Despite being twenty-five years of age, Fuller begged his mother not to tell his father about the article. It represented but the first step in an inevitable apostasy from his father's faith. Fuller would contribute many more pieces to the journal, his biting critiques adopting a tone which recalled Bradlaugh's virulent "crude anti-clericalism."[53]

[50] Fuller, *Memoirs*, 17–18.
[51] The third volume of Havelock Ellis's *Studies in the Psychology of Sex* appeared in 1903. Havelock Ellis, *Studies in the Psychology of Sex*, vol. 3 (Philadelphia: F. A. Davis, 1903). It offered an analysis of the sexual impulse, love and pain, and the sexual impulse in women. Other volumes dealt with topics such as the evolution of modesty and autoeroticism. Charles Carrington, *A Plea for Polygamy* (Paris: C. Carrington, 1898). Reid gives the author of *A Plea for Polygamy* as Huston, but I have been unable to trace any such title.
[52] Reid, *J. F. C. Fuller*, 13.
[53] Lightman, "Ideology," 287–288.

Figure 1.5 Victor Benjamin Neuburg (1883–1940)

Introducing Victor B. Neuburg

Another young writer had meanwhile found his way to the *Agnostic Journal*.

Victor Benjamin Neuburg (1883–1940) was the Jewish son of Viennese commission agent Carl Neuburg and his wife, Jeanette Jacobs, scion of a wealthy Highbury New Park family—the "Jacobs" in the firm Jacobs, Young and Co., Ltd., importers of cane, fibers, and rattans from China and the Far East (see figure 1.5). Theirs was an arranged marriage that did not take, and Carl abandoned his family in Islington shortly after his son's birth, forcing Jeanette to move back into the Jacobs family home, where Victor was raised by his mother and aunts.[54] He was a sensitive child and was already a vegetarian when attending the City of London School from 1896 to 1899.[55] It was

[54] The 1891 census shows Victor B. Neuburg, age seven, living at 123 Highbury New Park, in the London borough of Islington, with his grandmother Rebecca Jacobs and her three daughters, four sons, and two servants. In 1901, the household consisted of Rebecca; her two daughters and two sons; her grandson, Victor; and three servants.

[55] Fuller, *Magical Dilemma*, 93.

part and parcel of his open rebellion against the bourgeois stuffiness of his family. From school, he went into the family business, which, it soon became clear, did not suit him. In a nearby borough High Street bookshop, he spotted "a little paper that changed my entire life": the *Freethinker*.[56] It was one of the Freethought papers circulating at the time, extolling the virtues of an areligious and rational society. He also began reading one of its competitors, the *Agnostic Journal*.

Neuburg's first two published poems appeared in back-to-back issues of these journals, with "Only" appearing in the October 10, 1903, *Agnostic Journal*, followed by "Vale, Jehovah!" in the October 25 *Freethinker*. The latter renounced his Jewish faith and declared his atheism. Much like Fuller, Victor—or Vickybird, as his friends called him—wrote in the style of Swinburne. Also, like Fuller, he promptly became a regular contributor. He was forging a lifelong connection, for even though his contributions to the journal would end several years later, the last years of his life found him correcting proofs of the *Freethinker*.[57]

Recognizing that the family business did not suit Victor, his uncle Edward paid for him to go to Trinity College Cambridge. Passing examinations in Latin and Greek, he was admitted in the autumn of 1906 and read for a tripos in modern languages. While he was older than most of his classmates, he entered with an impressive body of published work courtesy of the *Agnostic Journal*.

Saladin's Illness and Death; the End of the *Agnostic Journal*

Ross began suffering from debilitating sclerosis, which impaired his ability to walk. By the end of 1905, he was bedridden and able to write only by using two fingers. Nevertheless, he continued to edit the *Agnostic Journal* from his bed until November 30, when he joined Holyoake and Watts as the third prominent Secularist to die in 1906. According to the *Literary Guide*, "Only the inner circle knew that he was ill, and even they were not aware that there was any imminent danger. As a matter of fact, the doctors in attendance anticipated that Mr. Ross would linger on for some months." Even to the end,

[56] Fuller, *Magical Dilemma*, 96.
[57] Neuburg, *Vickybird*, 3.

he wrote nearly "a third of the matter contained in each issue" of the *Agnostic Journal*.[58]

As the leader of a small group who opposed the "established" Secularism of Bradlaugh, Besant, and Foote, Ross's significance to the overall movement is debatable, but his vision of Secularism was indisputably a continuing presence for a quarter century through the *Secular Review* and *Agnostic Journal*. As W. B. Columbine wrote,

> Saladin was not a general in the main armies of Freethought. He was rather a brilliant guerilla leader, who surprised and bewildered the enemy by the swiftness of his attacks at all sort of unexpected points. . . . He was the zealous champion of truth, and he believed the Christian religion to be false. And thus he took delight in tearing the dogmas of Christianity to pieces, and in scattering them to the winds with the artillery of his fierce invective.[59]

Watts himself lamented, "We have lost a Chief whose name will live in our movement—a truly heroic soul, whose chivalry was almost incomparable."[60]

Ross's funeral took place on December 6, and he was laid to rest in Brookwood Cemetery with a copy of the *Journal*—"the number he edited [the] greater part of from his death-bed, only for it to contain his own obituary notice"—alongside his son, Bruno, who had predeceased him twenty-three years before.[61] Foote, at the request of the family, offered a stirring tribute. Foote wrote in the December 9, 1906 issue of *Freethinker*, "I fancy that he would have been well satisfied to know that his tomb might honestly bear the inscription, 'Here lies a soldier of Freethought.' That he was from first to last."[62]

Memorials poured onto the *Agnostic Journal*'s pages from Saladin's various admirers. Fuller wrote to the *Agnostic Journal* that

> his, indeed, was a great and glorious spirit; and, although Saladin is dead, I can but feel that he will always live in the hearts and minds of

[58] "Random Jottings," *Literary Guide and Rationalist Review* 127 (January 1, 1907): 8.

[59] W. B. Columbine, "The Passing of Saladin," *Literary Guide and Rationalist Review* 127 (January 1, 1907): 9.

[60] Quoted in Lightman, "Ideology," 290.

[61] "The Funeral of Saladin," *Agnostic Journal* 59, no. 24 (December 15, 1906): 369–370. The issue containing his death notice was published on December 8, 1906 (vol. 59, no. 23).

[62] Quoted in "Funeral of Saladin."

> those who knew him, and be to them as a guiding star of hope, lighting their rough path towards that goal which he fought so nobly and bravely to attain.[63]

Meanwhile, Neuburg and his mother donated one pound, nineteen shillings, and elevenpence three farthings to a fund for Mrs. Ross.[64] Both Neuburg and Fuller would pen tributes to Saladin in subsequent issues of the *Agnostic Journal*: the former contributed "Saladin: In Memoriam" to the December 15, 1906 issue, while Fuller's "Saladin" appeared in the following issue, on December 29.

The death of Saladin threw the *Agnostic Journal* into disarray. According to Jean Overton Fuller, "The Rev. Arthur Peacock . . . tells me that he understood from [regular contributor] Guy Aldred that Victor Neuburg was, in fact, Sub-Editor of the *Agnostic Journal*."[65] Although this was third-hand information, Fuller was of the opinion that Neuburg could well have succeeded Ross as editor of the *Agnostic Journal*. However, Neuburg had already gone off to Cambridge by this time. The May 4, 1907, issue contained a form asking subscribers to support the journal by committing to purchase shares of a possible limited liability company that would continue the journal. The form stated, "Upon the response received to this circular will depend the future of the *Agnostic Journal*."[66] (See figure 1.6.)

Around this time, Aleister Crowley and J. F. C. Fuller approached Ross's widow and executors with a proposal to purchase the *Agnostic Review* for £150. They did not consider the publication to be profitable but saw its readership as a pool of potential candidates for the new mystical society they were starting. Their offer was rejected.[67] Undaunted, Crowley would later go on to found his own journal, *The Equinox*, in 1909.

[63] Quoted in "Saladin: Extracts from Letters of Condolence," *Agnostic Journal* 59, no. 25 (December 22, 1906): 387.

[64] "Fund for Mrs. Stewart Ross," *Agnostic Journal* 59, no. 25 (December 22, 1906): 393.

[65] Fuller, *Magical Dilemma*, 98.

[66] "Important. Urgent," form tipped into the May 4, 1907, issue of the *Agnostic Journal* 60, no. 18, between pages 280 and 281.

[67] For Crowley's account, see "The Agnostic Journal: [An unpublished insertion to Crowley's *Confessions*]" in the anthology. Given Crowley's familiarity with Ross, it is easy to imagine, when the character of Saladin appears in Crowley's writings—as in his rituals, or the play *The Scorpion*—a layered symbolism that invokes, by that name, both the historic and contemporary opponents of Christianity. For an analysis of Crowley's use of Islamic figures and themes, see Marco Pasi, "Aleister Crowley and Islam," in *Esoteric Transfers and Constructions*, ed. M. Sedgwick and F. Piraino (Cham, Switzerland: Palgrave, 2021), 151–193.

Important. Urgent.

It is suggested that a Limited Liability Company be formed to carry on the Agnostic Publishing Business including *The Agnostic Journal*. In the event of such Company being formed, would you be prepared to take Shares therein? The Shares would be One Pound each, payable as follows: five shillings on application; five shillings on allotment, and the balance of ten shillings at a month's notice. Upon the response received to this circular will depend the future of *The Agnostic Journal*.

The filling in of this form is simply meant as a guide to the promoters of the proposed Company, and attaches no liability whatsoever.

In the event of *The Agnostic Journal* being floated as a Company, I would be prepared to take up Shares.

Name

Address

Kindly fill up this form and return to—

THE COMMITTEE, c/o MRS. STEWART ROSS,

30, Canterbury Road, London, S.W.

Figure 1.6 The desperate last gasps of the *Agnostic Journal*: readers were polled regarding their willingness to buy stock should the *Agnostic Journal* become a limited liability company

Response to the reader appeal to purchase shares in a limited liability corporation was also inadequate. In June 1907, the journal announced, "With next week's issue the publication of the *Agnostic Journal* must cease" (see figure 1.7).[68]

[68] "To Our Readers," *Agnostic Journal* 60, no. 23 (June 8, 1907): 353.

TO OUR READERS.

With next week's issue the publication of the *Agnostic Journal* must cease. We exceedingly regret to have to come to this decision, but no alternative remains. For months, nay, for years, it has been a hard struggle to keep our banner flying, and with Saladin's death, our difficulties have been considerably increased, and we feel that there is not any one to take his place. Friends far and near have offered help, but we regret to say the proffered help has not been sufficient to guarantee the floating of the *A.J.* as a Company. To all those who kindly promised to subscribe if the *Agnostic Journal* were turned into a Company, we heartily offer our sincere thanks.

Saladin has left a quantity of unpublished manuscripts, which may now never see the light.

It was proposed to issue a biography of Saladin; this, we regret, will have to be relinquished.

Figure 1.7 The notice appearing in the June 8, 1907, issue that the *Agnostic Journal* would cease publication

2
CROWLEY AND RATIONALISM

Aleister Crowley's first encounter with Rationalism likely happened shortly after he matriculated to Trinity College Cambridge, in October 1895. A nonconforming freshman, he preferred meals brought to his rooms instead of joining fellow students in the dining call, skipped Sunday services under the pretense that his familial Plymouth Brethren faith prohibited it, and so derided his political economy class that he stopped attending lectures. As Crowley recalled in his *Confessions*, his absence from class came to the attention of university authorities: "My tutor naturally called me to account, but by great good fortune he was a man of extraordinary ability—Dr. A. W. Verrall. He accepted my plea that my business in life was to study English literature. He was, indeed, most sympathetic."[1]

His "dear old tutor"[2] was Greek classics scholar, translator, and lecturer Arthur Woollgar Verrall (1851–1912), who was popular for his riveting lectures and passion for literature both ancient and modern (see figure 2.1). One student recalled that Verrall's occasional recitations from the classics "gave you a new idea of the importance of language and sound in poetry, by chanting Horace, Catullus, etc."[3] He took his tutoring responsibilities seriously and held dinner parties at his Selwyn Gardens home for his freshmen "two or three times a week," while "tennis and croquet parties on Tuesdays and Fridays were a regular institution of the May term. It was in this way, besides others, that he sowed the seeds of that affection which most of his men came to feel towards him."[4] Crowley likely enjoyed his hospitality, too.

Verrall rehabilitated the reputation of Greek tragedian Euripides at a time when he was widely considered inferior to Aeschylus and Sophocles. In so doing, Verrall introduced into classics the interpretive lens known as

[1] Aleister Crowley, *The Confessions of Aleister Crowley*, ed. John Symonds and Kenneth Grant (London: Jonathan Cape, 1969), 108.

[2] Aleister Crowley, "A Literatooralooral Treasure-Trove," *The Equinox* 1, no. 9 (March 1913): 59.

[3] M. A. Bayfield, "Memoir," in *Collected Literary Essays: Classical and Modern, with a Memoir*, ed. M. A. Bayfield and J. D. Duff (Cambridge: Cambridge University Press, 1913), xlii.

[4] Bayfield, "Memoir," xxxii.

Friendship in Doubt. Richard Kaczynski, Oxford University Press. © Oxford University Press 2024.
DOI: 10.1093/oso/9780197694008.003.0002

Figure 2.1 Arthur Woollgar Verrall (1851–1912), Aleister Crowley's "dear old tutor" at Trinity College Cambridge. (Photograph by Eveleen Myers *née* Tennant, © National Portrait Gallery, London.)

Rationalist Criticism.[5] He introduced this argument in his translation of *Ion* (1890) and fleshed it out in his literary tour de force, *Euripides the Rationalist* (1895).[6] Verrall asserted—in what Jenkins called a "sly, anti-religious interpretation"[7]—that Euripides was actually a Freethinker, and his portrayals of the Greek gods and oracles were satirical, intended to show audiences the folly of belief in superstition: "Euripides was a soldier of rationalism after

[5] For a modern scholarly analysis of Verrall and Rationalist Criticism, see James E. Ford, *Rationalist Criticism of Greek Tragedy: The Nature, History, and Influence of a Critical Revolution* (Lanham, MD: Lexington Books, 2005).

[6] Bayfield, "Memoir," lx; Richard Smail, "Verrall, Arthur Woollgar," in *Oxford Dictionary of National Biography*, September 23, 2004, https://doi.org/10.1093/ref:odnb/36646; A. W. Verrall, Ἐυριπιδου᾽ Ιων: *The Ion of Euripides with a Translation into English Verse* (Cambridge: Cambridge University Press, 1890); A. W. Verrall, *Euripides the Rationalist: A Study in the History of Art and Religion* (Cambridge: Cambridge University Press, 1895).

[7] Thomas E. Jenkins, "The 'Ultra-Modern' Euripides of Verrall, H. D., and MacLeish," *Classical and Modern Literature* 27, no. 1 (2007): 122.

the fashion of his time, a resolute *consistent* enemy of anthropomorphic theology, a hater of embodied mystery, a man who, after his measure and the measure of his time, stood up to answer the Sphinx."[8] How was Euripides allowed to spout such heresy? According to Verrall, Euripides wrote for two audiences at the same time, but only the intelligent would understand his ironic subtext; those who did knew what to expect when attending a play by Euripides: "If we wanted to find any sort of parallel in our own life, it must be by supposing that some eminent Positivist or Agnostic were appointed for one Sunday in every month, upon certain terms of reticence and discretion, to preach the sermon in Westminster Abbey."[9]

Expanding on this metaphor, Verrall lays to rest any doubt that he was speaking from the perspective of British Rationalism:

> Suppose that once a year that part of the inhabitants of London, which frequents the clubs and reads the magazines, were accustomed to assemble for the purpose of witnessing plays in which the stories of the Bible were presented. . . . And suppose it then given out that the management had decided to exhibit a play entitled (let us say) *The Herdsmen of Gadara* or *The Shimammite*, and written by Professor T. . . . . H. . . . . What sort of a piece would the audience anticipate, and what motive could they attribute to the author?[10]

His use of ellipsis is curious, given that Verrall names other professors and authors throughout his book. Not only does the pattern of ellipses fit the name of Thomas Huxley, but the man who coined the word *agnosticism* perfectly fits the analogy that Verrall is making. In his study of Rationalist Criticism, Ford acknowledges that "there is no necessary relationship between the tenets of philosophical rationalism and the type of close-reading techniques which characterize Rationalist Criticism, including ironicism and historicism. Nevertheless, these doctrines and techniques were in fact joined in Verrallian Rationalist Criticism."[11]

Verrall's overly ingenious interpretations of literature were criticized for eschewing simpler explanations and today are largely deprecated.

[8] Verrall, *Euripides the Rationalist*, 260.
[9] Verrall, *Euripides the Rationalist*, 81.
[10] Verrall, *Euripides the Rationalist*, 85.
[11] Ford, *Rationalist Criticism*, 115.

However, they were influential during his lifetime and certainly influential on Crowley. After going down from Cambridge (sans degree) in 1898, Crowley would follow Verrall's footsteps with the essay "William Shakespeare: An Appreciation." In the manuscript, its original title was "Shakespeare: Freethinker and Disciple of George Bernard Shaw."[12] Crowley admits in the essay, "To me it seems of immediate and vital importance to do for Shakespeare what Verrall has done so ably for Euripides."[13]

The Rationalist Press Association

Early in his writing career, Aleister Crowley (1875–1947; see figure 2.2) cast about for a way to get his poetry in front of the public eye: He self-published his first book, *Aceldama* (1989), along with several other small early pieces. Others he had printed by the Chiswick Press. These received little public attention. He turned to Kegan, Paul, Trench, Trübner & Co. for distribution of his books, such as *The Tale of Archais* (1898), *Jephthah and Other Mysteries* (1899), *Songs of the Spirit* (1899), *An Appeal to the American Republic* (1899), *The Soul of Osiris* (1901), *Carmen Saeculare* (1901), and *Tannhaüser* (1902).[14] This arrangement would prove to be unsatisfactory. As I have written in *Perdurabo*,

> Kegan Paul disappointed Crowley with slow sales and price reductions on his overstocked titles. Since 1902, only ten copies of *Tannhäuser* had sold, five of *Carmen Sæculare*, seven of *Soul of Osiris*, and two of *Jephthah*, *Appeal to the American Republic*, *The Mother's Tragedy*, *Tale of Archais*, and *Songs of the Spirit* had not sold at all. In May 1904, Crowley closed his account with the publisher.[15]

[12] Aleister Crowley, *The Sword of Song: Called by Christians the Book of the Beast*, ed. Richard Kaczynski (London: Kamuret Press, 2021), 391.

[13] Crowley, *Sword of Song* (2021), 226. Crowley was not the first to apply this interpretative lens to other authors. Ford notes that "Verrall himself applied his rationalist method to writers as diverse as Dante, the author of the Gospel of Luke, and Jane Austen" (Ford, *Rationalist Criticism*, 3). In this sense, Verrall had pointed the way. For an example of another author who followed suit, see H. W. Herrington, "Christopher Marlowe: Rationalist," in *Essays in Memory of Barrett Wendell* (Cambridge, MA: Harvard University Press, 1926).

[14] *The Archives of Kegan Paul, Trench, Trübner & Henry S. King, 1853–1912* (Hertfordshire, UK: Chadwyck-Healey, 1973).

[15] Richard Kaczynski, *Perdurabo: The Life of Aleister Crowley*, rev. ed. (Tempe, AZ: New Falcon, 2002; Berkeley, CA: North Atlantic Books, 2010), 131.

Figure 2.2 Aleister Crowley (1875–1947)

By this time, Crowley had already allied himself with the RPA, having become a member on May 14, 1903.[16] This was a year after the RPA made a splash with its Cheap Reprints series, republishing inexpensive editions of the works of Huxley, Haeckel, and Arnold. Perhaps this fabulously successful publisher of Agnostic literature would succeed where others failed.

In November 1903, Watts & Co. published Crowley's *The God-Eater* in an edition of three hundred copies on machine-made paper and two on Roman vellum. *The Star & The Garter* followed in a very small edition consisting of

[16] RPA Register of Members, courtesy of Bishopsgate Institute Library and Archives Manager Stefan Dickers, private communication, May 4, 2016. According to the *Literary Guide*, "Membership of the R. P. A. can be secured by payment of an annual subscription of not less than 5s., renewable in January of each year. In addition to receiving the literature of the Association, and acquiring a vote at all General Meetings, Members who are resident in the United Kingdom can borrow books from the Association's Lending Library through the post . . . or can resort to the Reading Room at Nos. 5 & 6, Johnson's Court; while Social Gatherings of Members and their friends are arranged from time t time." *Literary Guide and Rationalist Review* 106, supplement (April 1, 1905): 4.

only fifty copies on machine-made paper and, like *The God-Eater*, two on Roman vellum. Both books had green camel's-hair wrappers.

Response to *The God-Eater* was fairly negative. Even the *Scotsman*'s praise was backhanded:

> Symbolical poetry does not seem so soul-satisfying as the more substantial sort. John Gilpin, for example, or "Father, dear father, come home with me now," or "Good-bye, Dolly, I must leave you," or something of that kind, seems preferable, if only because more tangible, to such airy, misty, gleamy, glamorous, and ghostly things as this so-called tragedy of satire. The poem, which is in dramatic form, makes allusions to the researches into the origin of religion made by philosophers and inquirers like the writer of *The Golden Bough*, and its action represents how, working under the spell of the hag of eternity (as the principal lady of the piece is, more poetically than politely, called), a brother intoxicates his sister by giving her haschish to drink and then kills her, with the result that she comes to be worshipped as a goddess, and the brother, learning this, dies satisfied. Free is not the word for the treatment this theme receives. The piece goeth as it listeth, showing indeed a certain not uninteresting skill in the making of nebulous evations in speech, but never, as Hamlet might say, coming to Hecuba.[17]

The *Sheffield Daily Telegraph* was even more blunt:

> From the same publishers [Watts & Co.], got up in artistic form, with rough edges and broad margins, comes *The God Eater: A Tragedy of Satire*, by Aleister Crowley. So far as we can understand the story, which is almost unintelligible, it is about a brother who seeks to found a new religion, of which his younger sister shall be the goddess, and, in order to achieve that end, stabs her and eats her heart. It is simply loathsome and horrible.[18]

Owing to its limited print run, *The Star & The Garter* garnered no press attention whatsoever. As remarked in a later catalog, "The private edition of this wonderful poem sold out before publication, and there is not a single copy to be had at any price whatever."[19]

[17] "Poetry," *Scotsman*, November 23, 1903, 3.

[18] "Literary Notes," *Sheffield Daily Telegraph*, November 20, 1903, 3.

[19] Society for the Propagation of Religious Truth, *Excerpt A—from the Catalogue: The Works of Mr. Aleister Crowley* (Edinburgh: Turnbull and Spears, [1904?]). Although undated, this would appear to

Both these publications indicated that more of Crowley's works were in the pipeline. *The God-Eater* included among a list of works "by the same author" a selection of works "in preparation." This included *The Argonauts, The Sword of Song, The Lover's Alphabet,*[20] and *The Goetia of King Solomon.* Similarly, the "By the Same Author" page in *The Star & The Garter* listed *The Lover's Alphabet* as being "in preparation" (see figure 2.3).

The Sword of Song

As shown in figure 2.4,[21] Crowley's holograph title page for *The Sword of Song* indicates that he anticipated publication through the RPA. When that fell through, he was unable to find a publisher in the United Kingdom willing to handle the antireligious text, so he wound up having it printed in Paris.[22]

As a book initially intended for the RPA, *The Sword of Song* (1904) exemplifies many features consistent with the skeptical and rationalist mindset. The pair of poems forming the core of the book—"Ascension Day" and "Pentecost"—spoof Robert Browning's religious work *Christmas-Eve and Easter Day* (1850).[23] Whereas Browning examines Christian faith, Crowley critiques it. For example, he questions doctrines regarding the soul, prayer, and the Annunciation. He also questions how an omniscient God could create Satan or Judas, and how an omnipotent God could allow rampant pain and grief in the world. Finally, he recounts two years of childhood suffering and abuse at the hands of H. D'Arcy Champney's religious school.

be a very early SPRT catalog, circa 1904, as *The God-Eater, The Sword of Song, The Star and the Garter, The Argonauts*, and *Why Jesus Wept* are listed as "Recently Issued or in the Press." The latest of these titles, *Why Jesus Wept*, appeared in 1904.

[20] In his *Confessions*, Crowley writes of this book, "I began to write a set of lyrics to be called *The Lover's Alphabet*. This was to consist of twenty-six poems, associating a girl's name with a flower with the same initial from A to Z. One of my regular pedantic absurdities! Needless to say, it broke down. The debris is printed in my *Collected Works*, Vol. III, pp. 58 seq." Crowley, *Confessions*, 333. Crowley here refers to what his *Works* dubbed *Rosa Mundi and Other Love-Songs* (1905). Originally consisting of H. D. Carr [Aleister Crowley], *Rosa Mundi* (Paris: Ph. Renouard, 1905), when Crowley reprinted it in the third volume of his collected works, as was his wont, he appended various previously unpublished pieces. Poems 4–13 consisted of "Annie," "Brünnhilde," "Dora," "Fatima," "Flavia," "Katie Carr," "Norah," "Mary," "Xantippe," and "Eileen."

[21] Aleister Crowley, *Sword of Song* (MS.), courtesy of the Harry Ransom Center, University of Texas at Austin, 2021.

[22] For details, see Aleister Crowley, *The Sword of Song*, ed. Richard Kaczynski (London: Kamuret Press, 2021).

[23] Robert Browning, *Christmas-Eve and Easter-Day* (London: Chapman and Hall, 1850).

BY THE SAME AUTHOR.

[*Of* **Kegan Paul, Trench, Trübner & Co.,**
Charing Cross Road, W.C.

SONGS OF THE SPIRIT.
THE TALE OF ARCHAIS.
JEPHTHAH AND OTHER MYSTERIES, &C.
AN APPEAL TO THE AMERICAN PEOPLE.
THE MOTHER'S TRAGEDY, &C. (*Privately printed.*)
CARMEN SAECULARE.
THE SOUL OF OSIRIS.
TANNHÄUSER.

Also :
ACELDAMA. [*Out of print.*
BERASHITH. [*Out of print. Reprinted in* **"The Sword of Song."**
JEZEBEL AND OTHER POEMS. [*Out of print. Mostly reprinted in* **"The Soul of Osiris."**
SUMMA SPES. [*Out of print.*
AHAB. [*Of the* **Chiswick Press, Took's Court, E.C.**
(*As Editor*) **ALICE.** [*Out of print.*

In preparation :
THE ARGONAUTS.
THE SWORD OF SONG.
THE LOVER'S ALPHABET.
(*As Editor*) **THE GOETIA OF KING SOLOMON.**

Figure 2.3 Advertisement from *The God-Eater* (1903) for Crowley's other books, past and pending

The remainder of the book consists of supplemental texts, some labeled as appendices and some not. "Berashith: An Essay in Ontology" applies logic and mathematics to the religions of Buddhism, Hinduism, and Christianity. "Science and Buddhism" (including section 9, "Agnosticism") attempts to establish Buddhism as a scientific religion.

It overflows with mystical elements as well: "The Three Characteristics" is a short story in the style of a Buddhist reincarnation saga, while "Ambrosii Magi Hortus Rosarum" is a symbolic exploration of the tarot and the

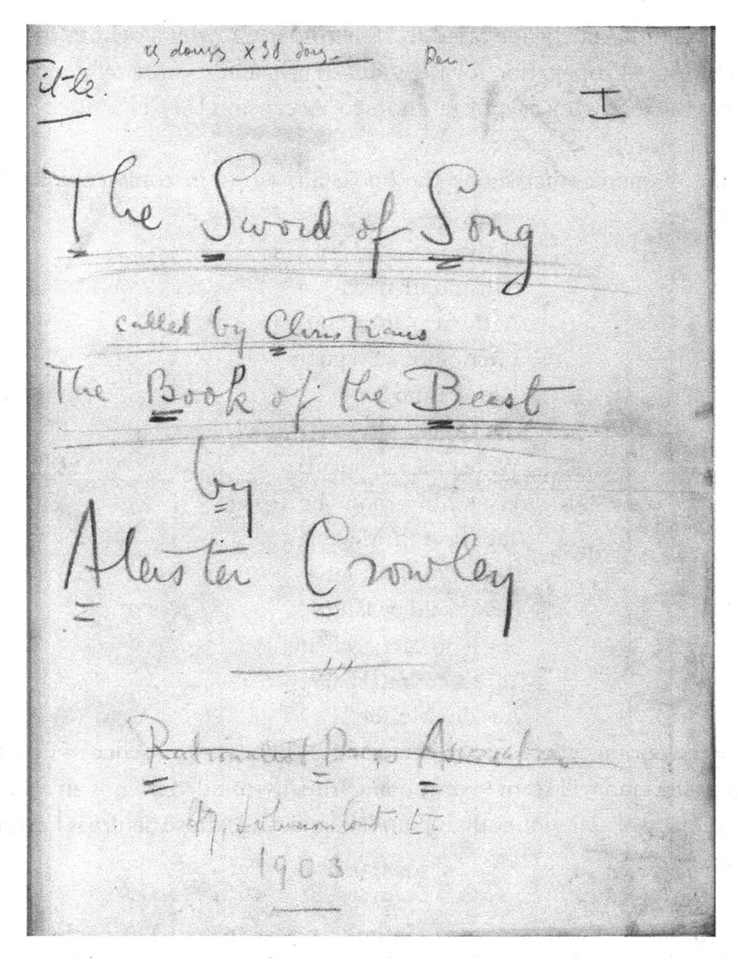
Title.

I

The Sword of Song

called by Christians

The Book of the Beast

by

Aleister Crowley

~~Rationalist Press Association~~

1903

Figure 2.4 The manuscript title page to *The Sword of Song* shows its intended publisher to be the Rationalist Press Association (later crossed out). (Image courtesy of the Harry Ransom Center; used by permission of Ordo Templi Orientis.)

Kabbalistic Tree of Life (offered as a spoof of *The Chymical Wedding of Christian Rosenkreuz*). The core of the book, the poems "Ascension Day" and "Pentecost," are also replete with references to occultism, theosophy, yoga, and mysticism, placing it at odds with its intended publisher, the RPA. The RPA declining to publish it may explain the book's dedication "to those FOOLS who by their short-sighted stupidity in attempting to boycott this book have witlessly aided the Cause of Truth."

The book ultimately appeared in 1904 under Crowley's own imprint, the Society for the Propagation for Religious Truth, and its only reference to the RPA was the following cryptic endnote to "Ascension Day":

> As the ex-monk (that shook the bookstall) wrote in confidence to the publisher:
>
> "Existence is mis'ry
> I' th' month Tisri
> At th' fu' o' th' moon
> I were shot wi' a goon.
> [Goon is no Scots,
> But Greek, Meester Watts.]
> We're awa' tae Burma,
> Whaur th' groond be firmer
> Tae speer th' Mekong.
> Chin Chin! Sae long.
> [Long sald be lang:
> She'll no care a whang.]
> Ye're Rautional babe,
> Aundra McAbe."
>
> Note the curious confusion of personality. This shows Absence of Ego, in Pali anatta, and will seem to my poor spiritually-minded friends an excuse for a course of action they do not understand, and whose nature is beyond them.[24]

The ex-monk is former Roman Catholic priest turned Rationalist Joseph McCabe, whose *Religion of the Twentieth Century* and translation of Haeckel's *The Riddle of the Universe* were the first two titles from the RPA's Cheap Reprints series that, indeed, shook the bookstall. His identity accounts for the exaggerated brogue and is confirmed by the "signature" in the last two lines of the poem. "Meester Watts" is of course Charles A. Watts. The poem itself begins as a riff on Crowley's "Summa Spes," with its opening line, "Existence being sorrow,"[25] paraphrasing the First Noble Truth of Buddhism. The poem refers to Crowley's 1901 trip to Ceylon (now Sri Lanka), during

[24] Aleister Crowley, *The Sword of Song: Called by Christians, the Book of the Beast* (Benares, India: Society for the Propagation of Religious Truth, 1904), 82.
[25] Aleister Crowley, *Summa Spes* (London: privately printed, 1903).

which he stayed with Allan Bennett and wrote the majority of *The Sword of Song*.[26] At this time, he embraced Buddhism, practicing yoga under the tutelage of several instructors in situ at a time when few Westerners understood either Buddhism or yoga. Yet, as Crowley explained his subsequent disaffection, "if he called himself a Buddhist, it was the agnostic and atheistic philosophy and the acentric nominalist psychology that attracted him. The precepts and practices of Buddhism earned only his dislike and contempt."[27]

After just a couple of years, Crowley's perspective changed dramatically. He experienced the revelation of *The Book of the Law* at Cairo. He grew dissatisfied with Buddhism. And magic—he was yet to begin spelling it "magick"—again proved alluring. His new perspective is reflected in the various essays added to the book when it was reprinted in the second volume of his collected *Works* (1906).[28] "Pansil" is a logical critique of Buddhism's precepts. In "After Agnosticism," Crowley notes in his opening paragraph, "after some years of consistent Agnosticism, being at last asked to contribute to an Agnostic organ, for the life of me I can think of nothing better than to attack my hosts!"[29] If the title of "After Agnosticism" itself was not telling enough, another of the added essays was the dialogue "The Excluded Middle; or the Sceptic Refuted." This dialogue, and its farcical twin, "Time," features a spirited discussion and meeting of the minds between Scepticus (the Agnostic) and Mysticus (the Mystic).

In both its original and expanded forms, *The Sword of Song* overflows with references to the Agnostic movement, including "Ingersoll's or Bradlaugh's pardie" ("Ascension Day," line 159), and (in "Time," pages 194 and 204) the "self-refuted Monism of Haeckel" and "Hume the Agnostic." He repeatedly cites Spencer's *First Principles* regarding causality and free will. As already mentioned, his essay "William Shakespeare: An Appreciation," added to the *Works* version, presents the bard as an Agnostic and was originally titled "Shakespeare: Freethinker and Disciple of George Bernard Shaw." Crowley even references his membership in the RPA when, in "The Creed of Mr. Chesterton," he writes (with a hint of pipe dream), "I trust I do not go too far, as the humblest member of the Rationalist Press Association, when I suggest

[26] For details, see Richard Kaczynski, "Editor's Introduction," in *The Sword of Song*, by Aleister Crowley, ed. Richard Kaczynski (London: Kamuret Press, 2021), ix–liv.

[27] Aleister Crowley, "The Temple of Solomon the King," *The Equinox* 1, no. 7 (1912): 362.

[28] Aleister Crowley, *The Works of Aleister Crowley*, vol. 2 (Foyers, UK: Society for the Propagation of Religious Truth, 1906).

[29] Crowley, *Sword of Song* (2021), 265.

that that diabolical body would be delighted to bring out a sixpenny edition of [*The Sword of Song*]."[30] Such an edition did not happen, and for a while Crowley considered issuing, on his own, a "cheap reprint" of "Ascension Day" and "Pentecost."[31] In "The Creed of Mr. Chesterton," Crowley also writes, "I regard Agnosticism as little more than a basis of new research into spiritual facts, to be conducted by the methods won for us by men of science. I would define myself as an agnostic with a future."[32]

Most notably, Crowley references Thomas Henry Huxley repeatedly. The essay "Science and Buddhism" is "inscribed to the revered Memory of Thomas Henry Huxley," while "The Three Characteristics" elevates him to the title of Huxlananda Swami. "Ascension Day" paraphrases Huxley's Romanes Lecture, *Evolution and Ethics* (lines 446–447), while "Pentecost" refers to the rational piano in Huxley's *Essays*. Throughout the text and its copious endnotes, Crowley either quotes from or alludes to passages in the books *Evolution of Theology*, *Man's Place in Nature*, *Hume*, *Science and Morals*, and *Christianity and Agnosticism: A Controversy* as well as the essays "Pseudo-Scientific Realism," "On Sensation and the Unity of the Structure of Sensiferous Organs," and "Hasisadra's Adventure." Crowley's *Works*-era addition to *The Sword of Song*, "Time," lauds Huxley as "at once the most and the least sceptical of philosophers."[33]

Lest there be any doubt that *The Sword of Song* was written from the mindset of (and later a reaction to) Agnosticism, he would later advertise this book in *The Equinox* as "the author's first most brilliant attempt to base the truths of mysticism on the truths of scepticism."[34]

A Parting of the Ways

Just as Crowley immersed himself in Buddhism as a new convert, only for his passion to fade, so too did his path now lead him away from the RPA. Was there a falling-out? A change in plans? Was Crowley engaging in wishful

[30] Crowley, *Sword of Song* (2021), 223–224.
[31] A draft prospectus for this proposed cheap edition is reproduced as part of Kaczynski, "Editor's Introduction," xxxvii–xl.
[32] Crowley, *Sword of Song* (2021), 221.
[33] Crowley, *Sword of Song* (2021), 204.
[34] This ad copy ran in most volumes of *The Equinox*, which was published biennially from 1909–1913.

thinking in his *Sword of Song* cover page? As he recounts in his *Confessions* without a hint of animosity,

> I had issued *The God-Eater* and *The Star & the Garter* through Charles Watts & Co. of the Rationalist Press Association, but there was still no such demand for my books as to indicate that I had touched the great heart of the British public. I decided that it would save trouble to publish them myself. I decided to call myself the Society for the Propagation of Religious Truth, and issued *The Argonauts*, *The Sword of Song*, *The Book of the Goetia of Solomon the King*, *Why Jesus Wept*, *Oracles*, *Orpheus*, *Gargoyles* and *The Collected Works*.[35]

Crowley took a leaf from Charles Watts & Co. and the Rationalist Press by creating his own publishing company. The name Society for the Propagation of Religious Truth (SPRT) was a swipe at the Society for Promoting Christian Knowledge, the same propaganda house that the RPA strove to challenge in the size and scope of its booklets and other literature, "inundating the reading public with material on agnosticism and evolution."[36] Crowley even copied the Cheap Reprints series strategy: "I printed a large edition of *The Star & the Garter*, and issued it at a shilling, with the idea of reaching the people who might have been unable to buy my more expensive books."[37] Crowley wasn't alone in modeling his publishing business after the RPA Cheap Reprints. We can also point to the Free Age Press (publishers and popularizers of Tolstoy) and even a large firm like Macmillan, in addition to SPRT. The RPA was flattered by such imitators, remarking,

> The success of the Rationalist Press Association is not to be measured only by the works issued from its own press. Other publishers, now discovering—contrary to their expectations—that there is a large reading public for serious literature at popular prices, are taking advantage of the enterprise of the "daring pioneers of Johnson's Court," and as a consequence dozens of sixpenny books, dealing with ethical, philosophical, and religious

[35] Crowley, *Confessions*, 406.

[36] Bernard Lightman, "Ideology, Evolution and Late-Victorian Agnostic Popularizers," in *History, Humanity and Evolution: Essays for John C. Greene*, ed. James R. Moore (1990; repr. Cambridge: Cambridge University Press, 2002), 291.

[37] Crowley, *Confessions*, 406.

problems, are to be seen on the bookstalls, with the imprint of the leading houses in the publishing world.[38]

First out of SPRT's gates, as Crowley noted, was *The Argonauts*, with press notices appearing around July 1904. The reprint of *The Star and the Garter* followed that fall, with Crowley's *Sword of Song* on its heels.[39] The latter received a glowing review from the *Literary Guide*, suggesting that Crowley's departure from the Watts & Co. stable was amicable:

> It is not easy to review Mr. Crowley. One of the most brilliant of contemporary writers, he surely bears the palm for eccentricity. In vigorous prejudice he rivals Mr. Swinburne. In obscurity of expression and abrupt transition from one idea to another he is a worthy disciple of Mr. Browning. The latter influence is probably as disastrous to the minor poet as that of Carlyle was to the ambitious prose writers of a bygone generation, and it is to be regretted that Mr. Crowley does not sedulously banish its traces from his verse and be content to rest on his own undoubted merits. It is not that this writer lacks individuality—of that quality he offers the most abundant evidence; but his mind appears to have an unduly close affinity to that which in Browning we find least admirable. Mr. Crowley's short poems in particular reveal the possession of a beautiful and genuine vein of poetry, which, like the precious metals, is at times scarcely discernable among the rugged quarts in which it is embedded. With this true poetic feeling, allied to remarkable learning, and with a pretty with of his own, Mr. Crowley is well-equipped for producing a work of permanent value. But his gifts are lavished with a hand so indiscriminate as frequently makes the judicious grieve. Good work is to be found in *The Sword of Song*, but there is even more which will arouse in the average reader (to whom, however, Mr. Crowley obviously does not appeal) no other feeling than one of sheer bewilderment. Sometimes an oasis of beauty will reveal the author's power to charm, the good-humoured egoism will tickle the fancy, the quaint allusiveness of his notes will raise the eyelid of wonder, while the crabbed involutions of style and the arrogant dogmatism will repel sympathy.

[38] "Random Jottings," *Literary Guide and Rationalist Review* 96 (June 1, 1904): 88.

[39] For an early press notice of *The Argonauts*, see "This Week's Books," *Saturday Review* 98, no. 2543 (July 23, 1904): 120. The "popular edition" of *The Star and the Garter* is mentioned in "This Week's Books," *Saturday Review* 98, no. 2551 (September 17, 1904): 374; this mention was followed by one of *The Sword of Song* in "This Week's Books," *Saturday Review* 98, no. 2556 (October 22, 1904): 528.

> Mr. Crowley's abilities deserve a more orderly and harmonious setting. As a specimen of his skill in rhyming we may mention that in one paragraph he manages to find syllables to rhyme with the names Euripides, Aristophanes, Æschylus, Sophocles, Aristobulos, and Alcibiades. We admire the cleverness of the feat, but the result is as far removed from poetry as a sack race is from ordinary running. With regard to the prose portions of the volume, the essay on "Science and Buddhism" reveals some penetrating touches; but we have to confess that the discourse on "Ontology" baffles our comprehension. The poetical epilogue is beautiful and contenting. A word of praise is due for the handsome style in which the volume is produced.[40]

In a similarly friendly gesture, the dedication of *Why Jesus Wept* (1904) bears a reference to Watts. Typical of Crowley's excess, this volume contained not one but five dedication pages: a *dedicatio minima* to Christ; a *dedicatio minor* to "My dear Lady S——," Kathleen Scott *née* Bruce, whom Crowley had been unsuccessfully pursuing; a *dedicatio major* to "My Friends," the "Eastern of Easterns," presumably including Allan Bennett; a *dedicatio maxima* to "my unborn child"; and a hostile *dedicatio extraordinaria* to literary critic G. K. Chesterton (1874–1936). The final dedication was the latest in a back-and-forth that began when the critic, reviewing *The Soul of Osiris*, teased that calling upon Egyptian gods such as Shu sounded like "an effort to drive away cats," and that Crowley would, in time, "work up from his appreciation of the Temple of Osiris to that loftier and wider work of the human imagination, the appreciation of the Brixton Chapel."[41] Taking exception to the pro-Christian sentiment of this otherwise positive review, Crowley responded in a footnote to *The Sword of Song*, "Mr. Chesterton thinks it funny that I should call upon 'Shu.' Has he forgotten that the Christian God may be most suitably invoked by the name 'Yah'? I should be sorry if God were to mistake his religious enthusiasms for the derisive ribaldry of the London

[40] "A Bewildering Poet," *Literary Guide and Rationalist Review* 102 (December 1, 1904): 188–189. Note that the excerpt of this review reprinted in P. R. Stephensen's *The Legend of Aleister Crowley*, 56, includes the following text, which appears nowhere in the original review: "'The Sword of Song' is a masterpiece of learning and satire. In light and quaint or graceful verse all philosophical states are discussed and dismissed. The second part of the book, written in prose, deals with possible means of research, so that we may progress from the unsatisfactory state of the sceptic to a real knowledge, founded on scientific method and basis, of the spiritual facts of the Universe." P. R. Stephensen, *The Legend of Aleister Crowley: Being a Study of the Documentary Evidence Relating to a Campaign of Personal Vilification Unparalleled in Literary History* (London: Mandrake Press, 1930).

[41] From the review appearing in the *Daily News*, June 18, 1901, quoted in Stephensen, *Legend*, 41.

'gamin.' "[42] Chesterton followed with a lengthy review of *The Sword of Song* under the headline "Mr. Crowley and the Creeds," which Crowley answered with the pamphlet "A Child of Ephraim."[43] Crowley concluded in *Why Jesus Wept* with this *dedicatio extraordinaria*: "You found your muddied oafs in Gods, ministers, passive resisters, and all the religious team—the 'Brixton Bahinchuts,' we might call them; while I, at once a higher mystic and a colder sceptic, found my Messiah in Charles Watts, and the Devil and all his angels."[44]

Other RPA-linked writers also took exception to Chesterton's religious advocacy. One particularly scathing review with the *Literary Guide* remarked that "His enormous ignorance is only equalled by his power of misstatement."[45] However, with *Why Jesus Wept*, the *Literary Guide* was more critical of Crowley than Chesterton ever had been:

> Mr. Crowley's latest volume is not only privately printed, but seems intended to be privately read. While those who can appreciate his peculiarities may peruse it with many an unholy chuckle, it is a work which, as far as pious innocence is concerned, should be kept strictly under lock and key. As on one page the date of the author's birth is followed by the text which forms the title of the book, the insinuation is as obvious as it is heterodox. The strange mingling of ribaldry, indecency, poetry, and wit could be perpetrated by no one but Mr. Crowley; and certainly no other author would issue, under his own name, such a ruthless violation of the conventionalities. It is possible that electric shocks of this nature may prove beneficial in some cases; but the display of Mr. Crowley's rampant virility does not always take a commendable turn, and many readers will regret that his genius is given so loose a rein. We may add that, on the score of good taste, the manner in which he advertises his wares is to be deprecated.[46]

[42] Crowley, *Sword of Song* (2021), 320.

[43] See the pamphlet G. K. Chesterton and Aleister Crowley, *Mr. Crowley and the Creeds: And, the Creed of Mr. Chesterton: with a Postscript Entitled, a Child of Ephraim, Chesterton's Colossal Collapse*, in Aleister Crowley, *Works*, vol. 2 (1906).

[44] Aleister Crowley, *Why Jesus Wept: A Study of Society and of the Grace of God* (n.p.: privately printed, 1904).

[45] A. W. Benn, "Mr. Chesterton's 'Orthodoxy,'" *Literary Guide and Rationalist Review* 150 (December 1, 1908): 185–186. For other reviews of Chesterton in the *Literary Guide*, see "G. K. Chesterton on Freethought," *Literary Guide and Rationalist Review* 95 (May 1, 1904): 66–67; "Mr. Chesterton at Large," *Literary Guide and Rationalist Review* 110 (August 1, 1905): 118–119.

[46] "Hinc Illæ Lachrymæ," *Literary Guide and Rationalist Review* 105 (March 1, 1905): 45.

The *Literary Guide* greeted Crowley's *Gargoyles* (1906)[47] with an equally unforgiving review:

> Many persons have wondered at the quaint heads, half human, half animal, which leer from the nooks and angles of Gothic cathedrals, and at the daring and irreverent spirit which seems to have animated the sculptors. These grinning monstrosities fitly symbolise the contents of Mr. Crowley's latest volume. But it is something more than the spirit of medievalism that he expresses. He is filled with the modern wonder at the marvellous, unintelligible world; the beauty, the mystery, the terror of life haunt and oppress him. He struggles against the horrors that attract him. He sings alike of the base and the beautiful, finding inspiration in the brutality of the flesh as easily as in the rapture of the soul, in the mockery of the real, and in the glory of the heavenly vision. "In these poems you shall hear the laughter of the gods and of the devils; understand their terrors and ecstasies; live in their heavens and hells." Readers who happen to be of a prudish turn should by all means avoid the poems of Mr. Crowley. One can picture Evangelical respectability recoiling from this little book with a horror surpassing that of the tramp condemned to a cold bath. The piety which thinks the mystery of existence explained by a copy-book precept will never understand a poet who probes the sores of the sinner with the callousness of a surgeon. Of ribaldry, wit, blasphemy, and indecency Mr. Crowley is usually lavish. He does not hesitate to wrote of things which Mrs. Grundy covers with a white sheet, and the strength and coarseness of his language are certainly appropriate to his subjects. It is true he damns uncleanness, though not without a certain smacking of the lips over its fascinations. Yet through all the poet's whimsicalities there gleam the rays of sweet and genuine poetry. His genius is unequal, rising easily to noble eloquence and descending with equal facility to the vulgar and the repulsive. Mediocrity is abhorrent to him; his rugged verse matches well the powerful and often profound daring of his thought. His knowledge of men, women, and things is "extensive and peculiar"; he writes strongly because he strongly feels. Mr. Crowley is frankly pagan, and goes out of his way to harrow the susceptibilities of the poor pietist; the reader is alternately delighted and irritated by having to balance striking merits against defects which the author's genius makes gratuitous.

[47] Aleister Crowley, *Gargoyles: Being Strangely Wrought Images of Life and Death* (Foyers, UK: Society for the Propagation of Religious Truth, 1906).

> We should be sorry to lose the strong individuality of Mr. Crowley's poems, but he would rise higher if he toned down the fleshly tints and fumigated the atmosphere of decadence with marks too many of his productions.[48]

As Crowley strayed further from Rationalism to explore magick, reviews by the *Literary Guide* became increasingly acerbic.

This doesn't seem to have been personal, as—unlike the *Agnostic Journal*—the scientific orientation of the *Literary Guide* was generally unreceptive to the occult. Of former Secularist Annie Besant's theosophy, the journal wrote, "we can neither accept the system of thought, nor rouse ourselves to any adequate interest in her presentation of it."[49] It referred to Spiritualism as "blind credulity on the one hand, and unscrupulous fraud on the other."[50] As for magic specifically, it opined,

> Belief in magic shows little sign of decay. Some of its varieties flourish openly, with merely a change of name; for we do not, at first sight, recognize that spiritualism is another form of necromancy, and that fortune-telling by cards is a kind of sortilege. . . . Every recipient of second-hand booksellers' catalogues must have noticed that they advertise a multitude of works on "occult science"; and there are some tradesmen who specialise in that department, and seem to find it very profitable. These "occult" works are not intended for the poor, for they are usually expensive: neither do they appeal to the ignorant, for many of them conceal their meaning in Latin and in Hebrew; they are evidently of interest to a comfortable and educated *clientele*. . . . Magic has always been a more or less illicit study, and, although there are few educated persons who will open avow their faith in it for fear of ridicule, yet the enormous success of clairvoyants, crystal-gazers, and other mystery-mongers, is a sufficient proof of the vast amount of latent belief that still exists in civilised mankind.[51]

This difference in worldviews set the stage for an inevitable parting of the ways.

[48] "Decadent Poetry," *Literary Guide and Rationalist Review* 134 (August 1, 1907): 123–124.

[49] "Mrs. Besant's Religion," *Literary Guide and Rationalist Review*, January 1, 1908, 139: 13. The *Literary Guide* also remarked, "We cannot really discover any advantage in Mrs. Besant's methods over the ordinary European methods of disciplining the mind and persuading to neighbourly consideration." "Mrs. Besant on Thought," *Literary Guide and Rationalist Review* 70 (April 1, 1902): 54.

[50] "The Secrets of the Spirits," *Literary Guide and Rationalist Review* 141 (March 1, 1908): 38.

[51] Chilperic, "Religion and Magic," *Literary Guide and Rationalist Review* 130 (April 1, 1907): 50–51.

3

THE PRIZE

When Crowley launched the Society for the Propagation of Religious Truth with its RPA-style "cheap reprints," the *Bookseller* noted:

> Mr. Crowley should be a happy man. His *Star and Garter*, which an accompanying leaflet describes as "the greatest love poem of modern times," was sold out before publication, necessitating a reprint that, as "popular" editions go, is an unusually handsome production. Moreover a prize is offered for an essay on the author's collected works, and the opportunity is announced as "the chance of the Geologic Period!"[1]

The *Manchester Courier*'s reviewer was less impressed, remarking of the contest, "This method of propagating minor poetry is not more remarkable than the publication of such poetry by the society."[2]

The competition for the best essay, hostile or appreciative, on Crowley's literary corpus came with a prize of £100 (equivalent to over £12,000, or over $15,000, today). Fortunately for prospective contestants, the ever-prolific Crowley, at the surprisingly early age of twenty-nine, had begun preparing his collected works in three volumes. For five shillings—half the retail price—prospective entrants could purchase a copy of volume one. He expected this first volume would be ready in December 1904, but it did not appear until early 1905, with the subsequent volumes following in 1906 and 1907 (see figures 3.1a–c and 3.2).

According to his *Confessions*, "I printed a leaflet and circularized the educated classes," targeting much the same audience as the New Agnostics. "The meat of the circular was the offer of one hundred pounds for the best essay on my work. The business idea was to induce people to buy my *Collected Works* in order to have material for the essay."[3] In addition to including the leaflet in copies of *The*

[1] "Short Notices," *Bookseller* 566 (January 5, 1905): 27. See also a similar but much earlier notice in "News of the Week and Notes," *Cambridge Review* 26, no. 639 (October 27, 1904): 20–21.

[2] "Books of the Day," *Manchester Courier and Lancashire General Advertiser*, November 18, 1904, 9.

[3] Aleister Crowley, *The Confessions of Aleister Crowley*, ed. John Symonds and Kenneth Grant (London: Jonathan Cape, 1969), 406.

Friendship in Doubt. Richard Kaczynski, Oxford University Press. © Oxford University Press 2024.
DOI: 10.1093/oso/9780197694008.003.0003

(a)

EVERYONE into whose hands this Pamphlet may come is sure to know somebody ambitious to make a name in Literature. Here is his opportunity. BEGINNERS with BRAINS have a better chance than professional critics who are perhaps palsied by prejudice.

THE CHANCE OF THE YEAR!

THE CHANCE OF THE CENTURY!!

THE CHANCE OF THE GEOLOGIC PERIOD!!!

Figure 3.1a Sample pages from the flyer for Crowely's essay contest

Star & the Garter, he also included it in other early SPRT titles, many of which were inexpensive reprints of his lackluster Kegan Paul titles. Crowley even gave out the contest entry form as a separate flier. As reported by *Truth*,

> "The Chance of the Year! The Chance of the Century!! The Chance of the Geologic Period!!!" Such is the announcement on a circular that has been widely distributed during the last few days, and appears to have been "dumped" wholesale upon the colleges of Oxford and Cambridge. . . . Strange to say, not one of the scores of people who have received the circular appear to know who Aleister Crowley is, or who the Society for Promoting [*sic*] Religious Truth are. . . . A suspicion naturally arises that the Society for the Promotion [*sic*] of Religious Truth and Aleister Crowley himself must be somewhat intimately connected. If that is not the case, perhaps one or other of them will explain the precise basis of the interest which the Society takes in this author's works.[4]

Although in his *Confessions* Crowley makes no pretense that the SPRT was anything other than his own publishing company founded specifically to

[4] "Entre Nous," *Truth* 57, no. 1466 (February 2, 1905): 270.

(ↄ)

A CAREER FOR AN ESSAY

THE SOCIETY for the PROPAGATION of RELIGIOUS TRUTH offer a Prize of ONE HUNDRED POUNDS for an Essay upon the WORKS of ALEISTER CROWLEY, under the following conditions:

1. The essay may be either hostile or appreciative.

2. In awarding the prize, the following essential points will be taken into consideration:

(*a*) Thoroughness of treatment.
(*b*) Breadth of treatment.
(*c*) Excellence of prose style.
(*d*) Originality.
(*e*) Scholarship.

3. As some of Mr. Crowley's works are rare or altogether out of print, it will not be necessary to deal with all of them, though to do so would naturally offer a better chance for the prize. The Works are being reprinted in a cheap form, and supplied to competitors at cost price. See the annexed form, which may be filled up if desired.

4. The rights of the prize essay are vested in the Society, **which undertakes to publish the winning essay at its own expense, on terms of half-profits.**

5. The competition is open to all the world. Competing essays must be written in English.

6. Essays may be sent in at any time up to August, 1905. The time may be extended if no suitable essay has been received up to that date.

7. Competitors will not be kept in suspense. Any essay sent in will be read at once, and returned within fifteen days if unsuitable. In case of any competitor requiring more time than that allowed, it is open to him to forward part of his MS. to the Secretary, when if his work shows promise of success, he will be accorded any reasonable time in addition to that above stated.

8. In the event of any essay being kept beyond the fifteen days, it should be

Figure 3.1b Sample pages from the flyer for Crowely's essay contest

publish his own works, at the time Crowley was cagier in his response to *Truth*. As the magazine subsequently reported,

> I have received a letter from Mr. Aleister Crowley . . . [explaining] that the Society for the Propagation of Religious Truth are his publishers, and that their interest in him is purely commercial. I cannot help thinking that Mr. Crowley would do well to restrain, if he can, the commercial enterprise of his publishers, for this method of advertising and stimulating sales, however suitable to soap or hair-wash, is hardly in keeping with the nature of

(c)

2

taken that its chances are considered worthy of more serious consideration: any essay so detained will in all events be awarded a small consolation prize.

9. The essay should extend to at least fifty pages of typed MS.

10. Only those essays that are typewritten will be considered.

11. The essays will be adjudicated upon by a member of the Society, and his decision will be final.

12. All essays should be sent by registered post: their receipt will be immediately acknowledged.

13. All essays should be forwarded without the name of the Author upon them, accompanied by a sealed envelope containing the name of the competitor, on the outside of which should be inscribed a motto selected by the competitor, and which motto should also appear upon the essay. These envelopes will not in any case be opened until the essays have been examined, and then only for the purpose of announcing the prizewinner, and communicating with him, or returning the rejected essays to their owners.

14. Should two essays appear of supreme and equal merit, the prize will be increased to one hundred and fifty pounds and divided between them.

15. Consolation prizes value under Ten Pounds, according to the merit of the MSS., may be awarded.

16. All communications should be addressed:

THE SECRETARY,
SOCIETY FOR THE PROPAGATION OF RELIGIOUS TRUTH,
BOLESKINE, FOYERS, INVERNESS,

who will be glad to answer any questions, or to supply books to competitors for the necessary study in case they do not already possess them.

Figure 3.1c Sample pages from the flyer for Crowely's essay contest

literary wares, and is likely to do more harm than good to the unfortunate author who is exploited in such a way.[5]

Crowley's letter did not stop there, however. As *Truth*'s article continues,

Mr. Crowley is a modest man, but also a little unreasonable. His modesty prompts him to confess that he is unknown, his unreasonableness leads him to impute this fact to me, because, though all his productions have been sent to TRUTH for review, none of them has ever received a notice. As a journalist I cannot afford to be modest; but when Mr. Crowley implies, as

[5] "Entre Nous," *Truth* 57, no. 1469 (February 23, 1905): 460–461.

THE WORKS OF ALEISTER CROWLEY

Extra Crown 8vo, pp. 300 circa, on India Paper

VOL. I. ACELDAMA TO TANNHÄUSER. Price 5s.

TO BONA-FIDE COMPETITORS ONLY [*Ready in December*

TO BE TORN OFF.

To THE SECRETARY, S.P.R.T.,
BOLESKINE, FOYERS, INVERNESS.

Sir,

I am desirous of competing for the £100 prize offered by the Society. Please furnish me with one copy of "THE WORKS OF ALEISTER CROWLEY," *Volume I., for which I agree to pay the sum of Five Shillings on delivery.*

Name ________________

Address ________________

Figure 3.2 Sample contest entry form from *In Residence: The Don's Guide to Cambridge* (1904)

he does, that a notice in TRUTH is the sole avenue by which an author can become famous, regard for strict veracity, which is another characteristic of journalists, compels me to observe that, though all the other journals in Britain may not be able to do as much for an author as TRUTH, yet, collectively, they can do something to make a man known.

Besides, it may be the fault of the reviewer quite as much as the editor of a paper if an author's works remain unnoticed. Not that I am going to blame my reviewer in this instance. After reading Mr. Crowley's letter, I caused search to be made among books which have not been noticed in TRUTH, and one of this gentleman's slighted volumes was brought to light. It was a little poem.[6] So far as I am a judge of the article, it was rather good poetry—of a sort. But if all the rest of the author's works are of the same sort, the reason why newspapers have not made the author famous is pretty simple and obvious. Judging by this sample, one would hardly select this gentleman's writings for special study at Oxford and Cambridge; and many

[6] Considering Crowley's works published up to February 1905, the "little poem" is most likely *The Star & the Garter*, which initially appeared in an extremely limited print run of fifty copies.

> people would be disposed to speak unkindly of a publishing firm whose commercial instincts led them to offer a prize with such an end in view. In this case the publishers style themselves the "Society for the Propagation of Religious Truth." That a body with this sanctimonious title should issue the particular work to which I have referred, and adopt this particular means of pushing the sale, is one of the strangest things I have heard of for a long while. The names of the parties forming this singular "society" deserve to be publicly known, and as Mr. Crowley is probably familiar with them, I suggest that he should favour me with the information.[7]

This prompted the following reply:

> Without Prejudice.
> From the S.P.R.T., Boleskine Foyers, Inverness.
> March 3, 1905.
> To the Editor of TRUTH,
> SIR,—Of the three volumes from Mr. Crowley's pen which we have issued hitherto, none can by any reasonable possibility be described as "a little poem." We are therefore completely at a loss to understand the allusions in your issue of the 23rd ult., a cutting from which has just reached us.
> We shall be glad if you will retract the statement that we are publishing, or pushing the sale of, any such volume as you describe.
> —Yours truly,
> THE S.P.R.T.[8]

The letter was curious. Its prefatory "Without prejudice" carried the implicit threat of legal action. Yet suspiciously it had been mailed from Camberwell—south London—rather than Foyers, where the SPRT was located. Furthermore, it wasn't even on company letterhead. When *Truth* replied asking if this was indeed Crowley's publisher, they received a more formal reply, this time on letterhead:

> SOCIETY FOR THE PROPAGATION OF RELIGIOUS TRUTH,
> Letters and Telegrams: BOLESKINE, FOYERS, is sufficient address.
> Parcels and Goods: INVERFARIGAIG PIER, LOCH NESS.

[7] *Truth* 57, no. 1469 (February 23, 1905): 460–461.
[8] Reproduced in "An Apostle of Religious Truth," *Truth* 57, no. 1482 (May 25, 1905): 1330–1331.

GENTLEMEN,—We are the publishers of the work you speak of.

The "Publisher's Note" was written by the Editor.

We have not laid the question of its propriety before anybody else.

We have severely reprimanded our Hon. Secretary for his most suspicious, if not actually criminal, conduct in attending to the correspondence of the Society during his absence in London, and beg you to accept our humblest apologies for the same.

A subscriber has called our attention to your description of our title as sanctimonious, which we should not ourselves have noticed, as we do not object to impoliteness, but only to perversions of fact. However, we volunteer the following explanation, as our more sensitive members resent your epithet:—

Religious Truth should be distinguished from Religious Folly and Religious Fraud. Further, it contains two elements: the negative and the positive. From the former standpoint we are agnostic;[9] from the latter, we hope to attain to spiritual fact by scientific method.

The first article of the memorandum of association, which is in course of preparation, contains words to this effect.

To call us sanctimonious, therefore, is as if a Tory paper complained of your Free Trade articles appearing "in a paper with this fine Protectionist title."

Pray reflect that at the present time opinions have such fundamental diversity that no abstract word has any signification out of its context.—We are, yours faithfully, THE S.P.R.T.[10]

Suspicion duly aroused by the first communiqué, *Truth* considered this reply skeptically:

This letter does not read precisely like a business communication from a firm of publishers; and it increased my desire to know more of this curious religious society, which is, from the negative standpoint of religious truth, agnostic. I therefore wrote again and asked the Society if I might have the name of the honorary secretary, and the individuals responsible for its management.[11]

[9] It is telling that Crowley in this letter identifies "Religious Truth" as being "agnostic."

[10] Reproduced in "An Apostle of Religious Truth," *Truth* 57, no. 1482 (May 25, 1905): 1330–1331.

[11] "Apostle of Religious Truth," 1330.

Mailed on March 30, this letter received no reply. Instead, in mid-April, the editorial offices at *Truth* received this reply:

April 20, 1905

SIR,—Having had no reply to our letter of nearly a month ago, we may, I suppose, take it that the incident is closed:—We are,

yours very truly,

THE S.P.R.T.[12]

Truth replied that, on the contrary, they had been awaiting a reply to its March 30 inquiry to the SPRT.

May 4, 1905

SIR,—Your letter, with a copy of one which miscarried, to hand.

We observe that your letter is said to be "in answer to" our last. As it consists only of a question, we will content ourselves with the observation that we have no branch in Ireland.

Before I can take myself the responsibility of forwarding your query to our head branch, through whom alone I can obtain authorisation to reply to it, I must ask your reasons for wishing to know. Should they appear to me to be of a satisfactory nature, I will at once forward your communication to India.

We beg to remain, yours obediently,

S.P.R.T.[13]

Truth elected to drop the matter, explaining to its readers the conclusions of its own research into the SPRT question:

> I have not thought it necessary to pursue this singular correspondence further, as it is evident to my mind that the writer is only playing the fool; and I therefore publish it as it stands up to this point, together with such information as I have of this interesting "society."
>
> It appears that Boleskine is the name of a house with a few acres attached to it, near Foyers, where Mr. Aleister Crowley has resided for the last two or three years. He is, I believe, the owner of the property. He is described

[12] "Apostle of Religious Truth," 1331.
[13] "Apostle of Religious Truth," 1331.

by those who know him as a gentleman of somewhat eccentric tastes and habits, particularly in the matter of dress. When he came to Foyers he adopted the name of MacGregor. This, however, does not seem to have been sufficiently distinguished, and he subsequently changed it for that of Lord Boleskine. He married about two years ago and his wife is, I suppose, Lady Boleskine. The Peer and Peeress are not very regularly in residence at the place, and have sometimes been absent for months at a time. No one else resides there. It is therefore pretty evident that the Society for the Propagation of Religious Truth, which is domiciled at Boleskine, is nothing more than an association of Crowley, MacGregor, and Lord Boleskine, with a possible addition of her ladyship. In other words it is simply one more of Mr. Crowley's aliases. It follows that when Mr. Crowley wrote to me from St. Moritz that the only relation between himself and the society was that of author and publisher, he was not telling the truth as ordinarily understood. As mentioned in one of the above letters, religious truth—which I suppose embraces all truth—contains two elements, the negative and the positive, and Mr. Crowley's statement about his publishers is evidently an example of the negative element. So also, I take it, is the suggestion in his last letter that the writer is merely the local representative of an organization with its headquarters in India, to which my communication will be forwarded in the event of its being deemed worthy of that honour. Separating for the moment the negative from the positive elements of truth in the whole correspondence, I conclude that Mr. Crowley, or Lord Boleskine, or whatever he wishes to call himself, is his own publisher, and that it is he, and nobody else, who is responsible for the distribution of the aforesaid advertisements of his works at Oxford and Cambridge in January last.

It is, of course, no reproach to any man to be his own publisher, especially if his works are of such a nature that no business firm would take the risk of putting them on the market. I do not, therefore, desire to lay any stress upon that point, nor upon the fact that in his character of a publisher Mr. Crowley assumes the designation of a "society." But it is a different matter when a gentleman who avows himself an agnostic, as I understand this gentleman to do in the above correspondence, assumes the title of a "Society for the Propagation of Religious Truth," and in that character offers to the public works of the nature of Mr. Crowley's. The particular volume to which reference has been made above is frankly and grossly immoral, and it speaks plainly enough for the tastes and opinions of the author. I gather that this gentleman is at war, not only with what is ordinarily known as religion,

> but also with what is ordinarily known as virtue; and when he masquerades as a propagator of religious truth, and in that character offers his works, including the one to which I have particularly referred, to young men at Oxford and Cambridge, with the stimulus of a £100 prize for the best essay on their contents, he is doing a very mischievous thing in a very dishonest way. While, therefore, Mr. Crowley is propagating the truth about religion, as he understands it, I think it desirable to propagate the truth about Mr. Crowley as I understand it. He is anxious for a notice, and here it is. As will be gathered from the letters given above, he is clever enough at handling his pen, and it is a pity that his talents are not employed to better purpose than he appears to have found for them at present.[14]

If *Truth* suspected that the SPRT was merely a sock puppet for Crowley, then *Longman's Magazine* was even more suspicious of his contest. As columnist Andrew Lang speculated,

> How does it work out as a commercial speculation? Say that I have written seventy works, and offer a prize of £100 for the best essay on them. Let us put the price at five shillings a volume. Competitors must each pay me three hundred and fifty shillings. That makes about £17 and some odd shillings; I am no mathematician, but it is thereabouts. Now, say that only five hundred persons are "ambitious to make a name in literature." Five hundred times £17 is £8,500, out of which I shall refund, as a prize, say, £150. I net £8,350: not bad. Mr. Crowley has only written nineteen books, not seventy, but there may be thousands of competitors for his prize; if so, whether Religious Truth is advanced or not, the pecuniary results will be gratifying. I expect to see this plan freely adopted by modern authors with a genius for advertisement.[15]

This critique, however, was unfair. It ignored the fact that entrants could purchase volume one of his *Works* at cost (as opposed to purchasing each individual title separately). Lang was furthermore wildly optimistic in suggesting that five hundred persons would enter the contest. As it turned out, it would garner only one entry: from J. F. C. Fuller. Fortunately for Crowley, it was effusive in its praise.

[14] "Apostle of Religious Truth," 1331.
[15] Andrew Lang, "At the Sign of the Ship," *Longman's Magazine* 45 (March 1905): 478.

The Star in the West

Fuller learned of this contest when he "saw an advertisement" while stationed at Lucknow.[16] Crowley's *Confessions* reports, "I had issued *The God-Eater* and *The Star & the Garter* through Charles Watts & Co. of the Rationalist Press Association,"[17] and word of the contest reached Fuller "through the Rationalist Press Association, to whose publications he subscribed."[18]

Fuller also may have recognized the author's name from the pages of the *Literary Guide*. Crowley had sent a letter to the editor in response to an article in the January 1, 1905, issue. Geoffrey Mortimer had presented two anecdotes: one of a fisherman-turned-Agnostic who gave up his career because no one wanted to risk being at sea with a nonbeliever, the other of an Agnostic lawyer who went with his family to church every Sunday lest his business suffer. While it is easy to punish and oppress a single dissenting voice, the author argued, it is harder to silence thousands.[19] In short, there is strength in numbers. The article prompted various responses, ranging from those who empathized with the lawyer—"do it to appease Mrs. Grundy"[20]—to those who were blatantly less conformist.[21] Crowley, of course, had a something to say on the topic of social conformity:

> Foyers, N. B., March 27th, 1905
>
> I feel obliged to say, with your permission, one word on this subject. It is my rule to blame nobody and has been ever since discovered (to my surprise and disgust) that I was not infallible. But it is a simple historical fact that the blood of the martyrs is the seed of the Church; and if a few murders can bolster up a mass of rubbish, as has been the case with such monstrosities as Baabism and Christian Science, to say nothing of more obvious ones,

16 Brian Holden Reid, *J.F. C. Fuller: Military Thinker* (Basingstoke, UK: Macmillan, 1987), 14.

17 Crowley, *Confessions*, 406.

18 Crowley, *Confessions*, 538.

19 Geoffrey Mortimer, "The Need of Intellectual Sincerity," *Literary Guide and Rationalist Review* 103 (January 1, 1905): 3–4.

20 G. D. B., "The Need of Intellectual Sincerity?," *Literary Guide and Rationalist Review* 104 (February 1, 1905): 30.

21 Further letters in response to "The Need of Intellectual Sincerity" appeared in Emilie F. A. Lamplugh and A.K., *Literary Guide and Rationalist Review* 105 (March 1, 1905): 45–46; G. Dawson Baker and Geoffrey Mortimer, *Literary Guide and Rationalist Review* 106 (April 1, 1905): 61–62; and Emilie F. A. Lamplugh, Geo. Caffrey, A.K., and Aleister Crowley, *Literary Guide and Rationalist Review* 107 (May 1, 1905): 78.

surely the truth may expect to reap an even greater benefit. The misfortune of sceptics is that they are sceptical. Let us go as readily to the stake for our disbeliefs as in old times people did for their beliefs, and our children and our children's children will be warmed by that fire. Latimer and Ridley did assuredly light a candle; we have a chance of installing an arc light.

So much for tactics. That a man who for any reason whatever lies to his own heart thereby injures himself is a truism which nobody, since the death of Socrates, has had the impudence to dispute.

> Let us not use words like cowards; who of us can assure himself that he is other?
> But there need be no doubt whatever as to the right course to pursue.
> Clive, for a trifling quarrel, was ready to say, with the bully's pistol at his forehead:—
> "Cheat you did, you knew you cheated, and this moment know as well.
> As for me, my homely breeding bids you—fire and go to Hell!"
>
> Aleister Crowley[22]

This letter appeared in the *Literary Guide* two months after the review of *Why Jesus Wept* and just before Fuller's first contact with Crowley in mid-1905.[23]

Learning of the contest, Fuller ordered a copy of Crowley's *Works* and, "on its arrival, I decided to try my luck."[24] Evidently delighted by Fuller's interest, Crowley mailed him copies of his other works, including the still-in-press volume two of his *Works*.

In a fateful turn of events, October 1905 found Fuller laid up for seventy days with a case of typhoid. It was so severe that on February 14, 1906, a medical board recommended eight months' leave.[25] He was discharged that April for a full year's sick leave. Fuller took advantage of his convalescence to write to Crowley. The response, dated August 8, 1906, gave them something in common:

22 "The Need of Intellectual Sincerity," *Literary Guide and Rationalist Review* 107 (May 1, 1905): 78.
23 Anthony John Trythall, *"Boney" Fuller: Soldier, Strategist, and Writer, 1878–1966* (New Brunswick, NJ: Rutgers University Press, 1977), 20. See also Aleister Crowley to J. F. C. Fuller, June 26, 1905, IV/12/1, papers of Major General John Frederick Charles (1878–1966), GB99, KCLMA Fuller, Liddell Hart Centre for Military Archives, King's College Library, London.
24 Reid, *J. F. C. Fuller*, 14.
25 After Fuller's military leave expired, he applied for and became adjutant of the 2nd South Middlesex Volunteers, got married, and moved into a modest home in Battersea.

> I am sorry to hear of your enteric fever, but fate has treated me even worse; for after a most successful trip through China without a day's illness for any of us, our baby girl died of that very disease on the way home.[26]

They arranged their first face-to-face meeting for mid-August at the Hotel Cecil,[27] where Fuller affirmed his interest in the essay competition. As they talked, they learned that they shared much in common: from attending Malvern and hating it to studying Hinduism and yoga in India and to their Secularist worldviews. According to Crowley,

> He was entirely at one with me on the point of my attitude to Christianity. We regard it as historically false, morally infamous, politically contemptible and socially pestilential. We agree with Shelley, Keats, Byron, Swinburne and James Thomson as far as they went. We agree with Voltaire, Gibbon, Strauss, Huxley, Herbert Spencer, Tyndall, J. G. Frazer, Ibsen and Nietzsche as far as *they* went. But we were absolutely opposed to any ideas of social revolution. We deplored the fact that our militant atheists were not aristocrats like Bolingbroke. We had no use for the sordid slum writers and Hyde Park ranters who had replaced the aristocratic infidel of the past. We felt ourselves to be leaders; but the only troops at our disposal were either mercenaries or mobs.[28]

They became fast friends and saw each other almost daily. Crowley's charisma nudged Fuller's interest in the occult toward passionate study. At this point, his contributions to the *Agnostic Journal*—which had been unsparingly critical of religiosity—took on an uncharacteristic spiritual reverence.

This transformation was neither easy nor sudden. Fuller's original competition essay contained only six of the seven chapters of the final product and "scrupulously avoided any reference to the magical and mystical side"

[25] Aleister Crowley to J. F. C. Fuller, August 3, 1906, IV/12/3, papers of Major General John Frederick Charles (1878–1966), GB99, KCLMA Fuller, Liddell Hart Centre for Military Archives, King's College Library, London.

[27] Aleister Crowley to J. F. C. Fuller, August 15, 1906, IV/12/4, papers of Major General John Frederick Charles (1878–1966), GB99, KCLMA Fuller, Liddell Hart Centre for Military Archives, King's College Library, London.

[23] Crowley, *Confessions*, 539.

of Crowley's work.[29] Crowley argued that any survey would be incomplete without considering their substantial influence. As he recalled,

> This got his goat; he was a friend of the late Saladin (Stewart Ross) and disbelieved most heartily anything connected with the occult science. We were both very stubborn about it and ultimately I lost my temper—one day I sent him a typescript of *The Book of the Law* which had at that time never been printed, with a rather sharp letter, with the deliberate intention of breaking off relations with him. My idea was that the book would disgust him with me so completely that he would send me to hell.
>
> What was my amazement when he replied a couple of days later, "Then there are Masters after all, there must be for these are the words of a Master."[30]

Crowley was dumbfounded. "It was as if I had sent a copy of *Tit-Bits* to the Archbishop of Canterbury, and he had reverently pronounced it to be the authentic Logia of 'our Lord.'"[31] Thus a seventh exhaustive and final chapter came to be written, nearly doubling the length of Fuller's essay. The resulting manuscript, *The Star in the West*, was a book-length work that shamelessly hailed Crowley's genius. Fuller's words weren't just sweet talk calculated to win the contest; he sincerely believed Crowley to be England's greatest living poet.

In retrospect, Crowley remarked, "I could have wished a more critical and less adoring study of my work"[32] but decreed the essay "a very complete and just exposition of my views."[33] When Fuller likewise looked back at the essay in hindsight, he expressed misgivings, seeing the book as "A jumble of undigested reading with a boyish striving after effect. Written in the execrable English of a public school educated subaltern."[34] At the time, however, Crowley was so pleased that he decided to publish it (see figure 3.3 for an example advertisement).

[29] Crowley, *Confessions*, 540–541.
[30] Aleister Crowley to David Curwen, December 5, 1945, in Aleister Crowley and David Curwen, *Brother Curwen, Brother Crowley: A Correspondence*, ed. Henrik Bogdan (York Beach, ME: Teitan Press, 2010), 84–85.
[31] Crowley, *Confessions*, 541.
[32] Crowley, *Confessions*, 544.
[33] Crowley, *Confessions*, 540–541.
[34] Inscription from J. F. C. Fuller to C. R. Cammell in *The Star in the West*, dated October 14, 1946, quoted in Charles Richard Cammell, *Aleister Crowley: The Man: The Mage: The Poet* (London: Richards Press, 1951), 34. Fuller also wrote to Cammell, "I have never re-read it since it was published, and do not expect to do so." Cammell, *Aleister Crowley*, 35.

Figure 3.3 A 1907 advertisement for *The Star in the West* from the newspaper *What's On*. (Image courtesy of Henrik Bogdan.)

Fuller's winning essay, weighing in at 328 pages, appeared in print in 1907 as *The Star in the West*. As Crowley explained in a letter to Montgomery Evans, "the book was, of course, intended purely for advertisement, though, incidentally, the title was meant as an antithesis to the *Star in the East*, which afterwards developed into the Krishnamurti foolishness."[35] The book was available in two editions. One was limited to one hundred copies signed by both Fuller and Crowley, bound in gilt-stamped white buckram (see figure 3.4). The standard issue was red cloth blocked in white. Both covers bore Crowley's latest device: his *lamen* (magical breastplate) as a *Magister Templi* or "Master of the Temple" ($8^{\circ}=3^{\square}$), the antepenultimate grade in his system of spiritual attainment. It consisted of a vesica piscis enclosing a sword thrust nearly to the hilt through the circumference of a crown, balancing on its tip a scale whose pans held the Greek letters alpha and omega. The lamen

[35] Aleister Crowley to Montgomery Evans II, December 25, 1926, Evans, Montgomery mss., Lilly Library, Indiana University, Bloomington, Indiana. While the phrase *star in the east* has Christian overtones, referencing the star that guided the Three Wise Men to Bethlehem to greet the birth of Jesus, it was also the name of an alchemical book: Arthur Edward Waite, *Azoth: Or, the Star in the East; Embracing the First Matter of the Magnum Opus, the Evolution of Aphrodite-Urania, the Supernatural Generation of the Son of the Sun, and the Alchemical Transfiguration of Humanity* (London: Theosophical Publishing Society, 1893). The Order of the Star in the East would be founded in 1911, after Theosophist Charles W. Leadbeater's 1909 discovery of the World Teacher Jiddu Krishnamurti. Although but fourteen years of age, Annie Besant became Krishnamurti's guardian and groomed him for his predestined role. The mission of the Order of the Star in the East was to prepare the world for this World Teacher. Crowley opposed the entire enterprise.

Figure 3.4 The gilt-stamped white buckram edition of J. F. C. Fuller's *The Star in the West* (1907), issued in a signed and numbered edition of one hundred copies. (Image courtesy of Clive Harper.)

also contained five *V*'s, which represented Crowley's motto as a Master of the Temple: "Vi veri vniversum vivus vici" (By the power of truth, I have conquered the universe). Shortly after the book's publication, Crowley mailed cards bearing this puzzling image with no explanation. Heads were scratched in response (see figure 3.5). As one recipient reported to the *Daily Mirror*,

> Two days ago I received the enclosed card anonymously, and just glancing at it briefly, thinking it an advertisement of some sort, I placed it on the

Figure 3.5 A *Daily Mirror* cartoonist's reaction to the V.V.V.V.V. postcard advertising *The Star in the West*

mantelpiece. Within a few minutes, disasters of a minor kind began to happen in my little home. First, one of my most valuable vases fell to the ground and was smashed to pieces. My little clock stopped—the clock was near the card—and then I discovered to my amazement that my dear little canary lay dead at the bottom of its cage![36]

[36] "Mystic Card: Household Mishaps Quickly Follow Receipt of Curious Missive," *Daily Mirror*, August 15, 1907, 4. This letter was sufficiently unusual for a lightly edited version to be reproduced in "Household Mishaps Quickly Follow Receipt of Curious Missive," *What's On*, August 31, 1907, 3.

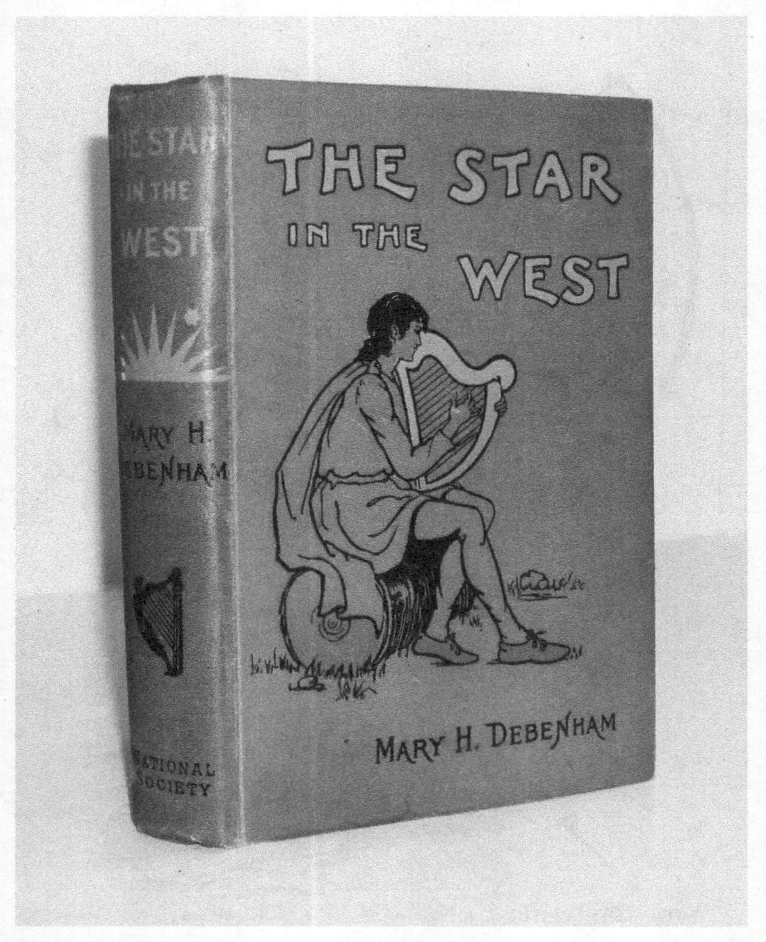

Figure 3.6 The "other" *Star in the West*, by Mary H. Debenham (n.d.) caused Fuller some embarrassment

Unfortunately for Fuller, *The Star in the West* also turned out to be the name of a recently published children's book by Mary Debenham (see figure 3.6).[37] While she was hardly the first one to use this title,[38] Fuller was sufficiently

[37] Mary H. Debenham, *The Star in the West* (London: National Society Depository, n.d.).

[38] See, for instance, Star in the West Lodge, *Complete Amendment of Rules of the "Star in the West" Lodge, No. 635, of the United Ancient Order of Druids, Taunton and West Somerset District* (n.p.: n.p. 1900); Polemus Hamilton Swift, *The Star in the West* (Cincinnati: Curts & Jennings, 1898); R. G. Loomis, *Washington: Star of the West: As Sung by Mr. Quale* (New York, NY: Charles Magnus, 1863); Philander Chase, *The Star in the West, or, Kenyon College in the Year of Our Lord, 1828* (Columbus, OH, 1828); and Elias Boudinot, *A Star in the West: Or, a Humble Attempt to Discover the Long Lost*

chagrined to apologize in the pages of the *Athenaeum*, London's premiere literary magazine, for any confusion:

> I exceedingly regret that through an unfortunate coincidence my recently published volume *The Star in the West*, a critical essay upon the writings of Aleister Crowley, bears the same title as a Welsh story for children by Miss Mary Debenham, already published by the National Society. But for the fact that my work was already printed and bound before my attention was drawn to this point, I would willingly have changed the title. However, with the courteous consent of both publishers, the title is retained; and I trust this letter will save booksellers any inconvenience that might have arisen from this similarity of the titles.[39]

Florence Farr's unsigned review in the *New Age* is a sometimes backhanded but mostly laudatory analysis of Crowley's body of work more than it is a review of Fuller's book, examining why it is that public opinion had united in denouncing Crowley. "Now this would be a remarkable achievement for a young gentleman who only left Cambridge quite a few years ago. It requires a certain amount of serious purpose to stir Public Opinion into active opposition, and the only question is, has Mr. Crowley a serious purpose?" Despite objecting to the fact that in Crowley's works "the organs of generation are always cropping up in unexpected places, such as in . . . Rosa Mundi's heart—which contains a symbol sadly out of place anatomically," she concludes that the opprobrium of public opinion "is only accorded to the most dangerous thinkers" and that Crowley is "a remarkable product of an unremarkable age."[40]

If the RPA's reception of Crowley's recent releases soured their cordial relations, then it threw down the gauntlet with the long, scathing review of *The Star in the West* in its November 1907 issue. The assault began with its first four words, which declared Crowley a "minor poet":

> Happy the minor poet who can secure so exhaustive an examination of his writings as that contained in this extraordinary volume. If we adopt the author's estimate, Mr. Crowley is no longer to be termed a "minor" poet,

Ten Tribes of Israel, Preparatory to Their Return to Their Beloved City, Jerusalem (Trenton, NJ: D. Fenton, S. Hutchinson, and J. Dunham, 1816).

39 "Literary Gossip," *Athenaeum*, no. 4159 (July 13, 1907): 44.

40 Anonymous [Florence Farr Emery], "Garter and Star," *New Age* 1, no. 18 (August 20, 1907): 282–283.

but stands in the ranks of the immortals. Captain Fuller, it is true, deals more in eulogy than in criticism, and would be a more convincing interpreter if he did not write as a Qabalist, an adept in ceremonial magic, occult Buddhism, and "all that sort of thing." His knowledge is weird and remarkable, his ethics unfettered by the shackles of convention, and his style frequently eccentric, sometimes in doubtful taste, and sometimes, like that of his master, rushing onward in a torrent of bold and magnificent images. Here, for instance, is a piece of "fine writing" which, of its kind, is excellent, though its meaning we presume not to fathom:—

> O, Dweller in the Land of Uz, thou also shalt be made drunken; but thy cup shall be hewn from the sapphire of the heavens, and thy wine shall be crushed from the clusters of innumerable stars; and thou shalt make thyself naked, and thy white limbs shall be splashed with the purple foam of immortality. Thou shalt tear the jeweled tassels from the purse of thy spendthrift Fancy, and shalt scatter to the winds the gold and silver coins of thy thrifty Imagination; and the wine of thy Folly shalt thou shower midst the braided locks of laughing comets, and the glittering cup of thine Illusions shalt thou hurl beyond the confines of Space over the very rim of Time.

After two or three pages of this the reader may well echo the chapter's concluding cry: "Wine, wine, wine"!

The first half of Captain Fuller's book is tolerably sober and often penetrative elucidation of the meaning of Mr. Crowley's fine poems. This we understand and like. It has certainly brought home to us more vividly the great beauty and insight of the poet's work. But in the latter part of the book, consisting of one long chapter entitled "The New Wine," and in which the philosophy of "Crowleyanity" is expounded at dire length, our admiration for Captain Fuller's judgment is somewhat abated. "Aleister Crowley," we are told, "is the artist Elias" of whom Paracelsus prophesied—

> The marvellous being whom God has permitted to make a discovery of the highest importance in his illuminative philosophy of Crowleyanity, in the dazzling and flashing light of which there is nothing concealed which shall not be discovered.
>
> It has taken 100,000,000 years to produce Aleister Crowley. The world has indeed labored, and has at last brought forth a man. . . . He stands on the virgin rock of Pyrrhonic Zoroastrianism, which,

> unlike the Hindu world-conception, stands on neither Elephant nor Tortoise but on the Absolute Zero of the metaphysical Qabalists. . . . And he shall be called "Immanuel"—that is, "God" with us, or, being interpreted, Aleister Crowley, the spiritual son of Immanuel whose surname was Cant.
>
> The author must have felt a good deal better after writing that.
>
> It is claiming much for Mr. Crowley that he embodies and completes the highest philosophy of Hume, Kant, Fichte, Schelling, and Hegel; that Crowleyanity is the scientific illuminism which reconciles the vision of God with the hard facts of natural law. But if the reader accepts this, he had better do so on the authority of the interpreter rather than on an intelligent understanding of the message, for at this he will have difficulty arriving. We frankly confess that this part of the exposition baffles our comprehension.
>
> The quaint symbolical frontispiece to the book is a sort of picture-puzzle to the uninitiated. Captain Fuller's task has apparently been a labour of love, and he has certainly expended great pains and ability in dragging Mr. Crowley up the steep slopes of Olympus.[41]

That the reviewer particularly objected to the book's treatment of Crowley's occultism (which had been written at Crowley's insistence) must have been especially galling.

Nevertheless, a third "popular" edition of *The Star in the West* appeared in 1908 from Bakunin Press, a far-left publisher named after Russian socialist revolutionary Mikhail Bakunin (1814–1876). Its founder, the young British anarchist Guy A. Aldred (1886–1963), was eight years younger than Fuller, but he was a peer of both Fuller and Neuburg through the pages of the *Agnostic Journal*. Much like them, he began writing letters to the editor and was soon contributing lengthy articles. Indeed, Aldred's was the lead memorial in the commemorative issue for William Stewart Ross. As Crowley recalled,

> The Reverend Guy A. Aldred . . . mixed up religious and political revolt like the Bolsheviks. In one sense the attitude is logical and it is certainly courageous.
>
> Fuller knew the animal and arranged with him to issue a cheap edition of *The Star in the West* with a preface of his "Alfred's" own, through the Bakunin Press.[42]

41 "Crowleyanity," *Literary Guide and Rationalist Review* 137 (November 1, 1907): 166.
42 Crowley, *Confessions*, 539.

This edition of *The Star in the West* was intended to make the book available to those who could not afford six shillings for the standard edition (again like the RPA Cheap Reprints series). In his introduction, Aldred raises and dismisses a theme common to reviews of Crowley, Fuller, and Neuburg—that "some of us may hardly concur in the extent of the sexual imagery employed alike by Captain Fuller and Mr. Crowley"—and instead praises the author's achievement:

> Captain Fuller's work is not alone an introduction to the works of the poet he interprets; not merely a poet's criticism of a poet; but an extremely erudite and mystically iconoclastic study of the morals and religion of a shallow civilization by a student of psychology and of classical mythology. Original alike in its conception and execution, . . . it has the singular virtue of being complete in itself, yet of making the reader long to study the original of which it is a master-study.[43]

Fuller's later political thinking would ironically wind up far right of Aldred's, but at this time they were both united in Agnosticism (see figure 3.7).

Aldred's memoirs make few mentions of this period, but he calls *The Star in the West* a "somewhat amazing book," "a study and a eulogy of the writing of Aleister Crowley," with whom he had an association and recalled as "strange genius . . . and very much a fool who maltreated his undoubted gifts." As for Fuller and his later politics, Aldred wrote, "He was much honoured in militarist circles although he remained an enemy of conscription. I recall him as a dapper young officer who lived in Battersea Bridge Mansions. The martinet that he became afterwards I did not know."[44]

Surprisingly for a book this specialized, a fourth edition was announced in the premiere (March 1909) issue of *The Equinox* as being "in preparation." *The Equinox* was an ambitious new biennial journal whose proprietor and main contributor was none other than Aleister Crowley. The aforementioned announcement repeated through the sixth issue (September 1911). Advertisements in the eighth through tenth issues of *The Equinox* proclaimed "fourth large edition now ready." While the book may have been printed, there is some doubt as to whether it was bound at the time, as Gerald

[43] Guy A. Aldred, "Introduction to All Friends of Freedom," in *The Star in the West: A Critical Essay upon the Works of Aleister Crowley*, ed. J. F. C. Fuller, 3rd ed. (London: Bakunin Press, 1908). Thanks to Keith Richmond and Weiser Antiquarian Books for assisting with this source.

[44] Guy A. Aldred, *No Traitor's Gait! The Autobiography of Guy A. Aldred*, 3 vols. (Glasgow: Strickland Press, 1955–1963), 2:413.

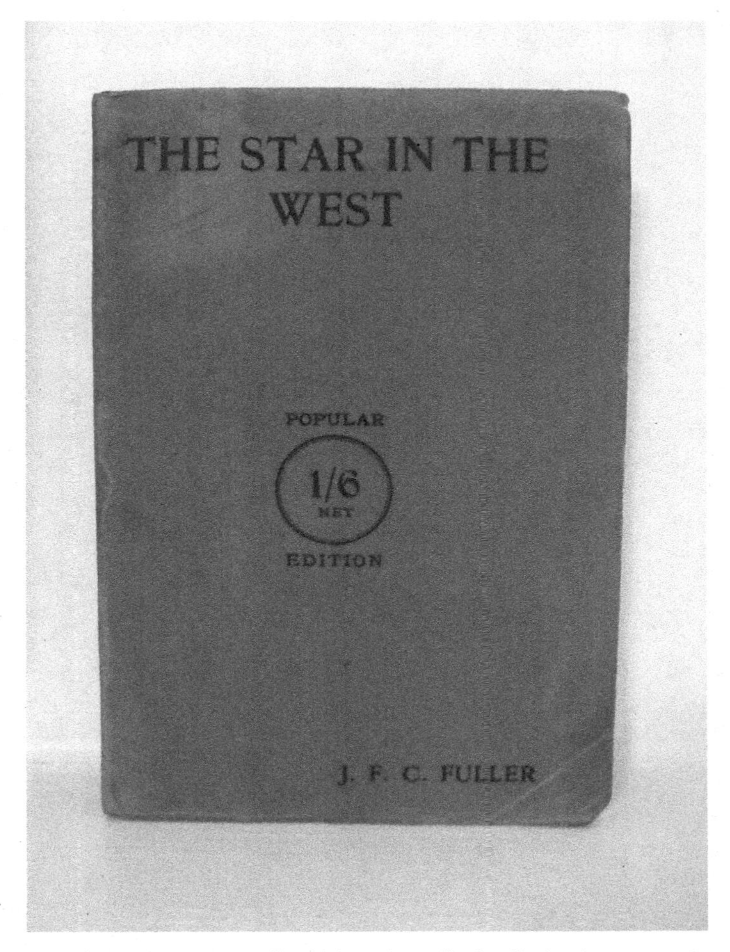

Figure 3.7 The Bakunin Press "popular edition" of Fuller's *The Star in the West* (1908)

Yorke noted that in the 1950s Fuller presented unbound sheets to Michael Houghton of the Atlantis Bookshop, who then had them bound and issued in blue boards with a vellum-like spine (see figure 3.8).

The Tiger Mahatma

After Swami Vivekananda represented India and Hinduism at the Parliament of the World's Religions in 1893, the runaway success of his book *Raja Yoga* (1896) lit the fire of yoga in the West. A string of yogis and gurus followed

Figure 3.8 The Atlantis Book Shop 1950s edition of *The Star in the West* made from unbound sheets of an earlier edition

his footsteps into Europe and America. Some were sincere teachers hoping to share their culture, while others were showmen looking to cash in on the craze. One of these purported masters was Mahatma Śri Agamya Guru Paramahamsa (b. *c.* 1841), notorious as the "Tiger Mahatma" for his contemptuous attitudes toward Western society and his ugly fits of uncontrolled anger (see figure 3.9).

His entrée to the West was accompanied by a beguiling origin story. As summarized by the *Detroit Free Press*,

Figure 3.9 The "Tiger Mahatma" Śri Agamya Guru Paramahamsa

He began to talk when he was 36 days old, and could read, write and make Hindoo music on a brass kettle at the age of 11 months, so Hindoo legends say. His parents began to instruct him in magic before he could walk. He early developed a faculty for hypnotism, hypnosis and metempsychosis. Mental telepathy came to him as an instinct, and while yet a child had solved the most profound esoteric secrets.[45]

[45] "Mental Marvel Just Arrived: Yogin, Loaded with Occult Knowledge, Hits New York and Stirs Things," *Detroit Free Press*, December 13, 1906, 14.

He had given up a vast fortune to spend two years living in a cave and five years in a Himalayan jungle, communing with nature.[46] He was ultimately recognized as an incarnation of Krishna and declared the chief mahatma of all India, a position comparable to the Pope and in which he was idolized by millions.[47]

Paramahamsa was possessed of immense strength and the ability to see remotely anywhere in the world, and he could make his heart stop on command. This latter talent he demonstrated to reporters, royalty, and others at various stops along his tour, including professors and doctors at Oxford and Cambridge such as Max Müller and J. Estlin Carpenter.[48] "As he sat in my study on the day of his first visit," Carpenter remarked, "he showed me that he could entirely suspend the normal circulation of the blood and the pulse ceased to beat as I laid my finger on it."[49]

On the strength of these claims, he became, for a while, a teacher not only to Ordo Templi Orientis forefather Carl Kellner (1851–1905)[50] but also to Crowley and Fuller. Like the Cambridge students who turned to Crowley, he, too, hungered for a mentor. Perhaps he was nostalgic for his days studying with Allan Bennett in Ceylon. Or maybe Paramahamsa's vocal disdain for Western culture and British norms appealed to the iconoclast in Crowley. Whatever the reason, in autumn 1907, he became one of the Tiger Mahatma's "cubs." Crowley attended a retreat in late September but couldn't focus on the tasks assigned to him. He also spotted errors while reading his new guru's book. Within two weeks, they had "a devil of a row"[51] during a meeting of students.

Convinced that the guru was a fraud, Crowley asked Fuller, well versed in yoga, to size him up. The colonel was already acquainted with the guru,

[46] "Seeking Recruits to Live the Simple Life: 'Tiger Mahatma,' in London, Would Show Wicked Britishers the Truth: Says That Unless Riches Are Used to Uplift Others, the Possessors of It Are a Burden to the Earth—Calls Americans 'Mad as March Hares'—Wants to Enlighten World," *Brooklyn Times*, December 6, 1906, 2.

[47] "The Chief of the Mahatmas," *Edinburgh Evening News*, October 14, 1903, 3.

[48] "Man Who Stops His Heart: A Mahatma Prophet Who Can Foretell Future Events," *Evening Telegraph*, October 27, 1903, 3; "Stopping the Heart by Will Power: Hindu Mahatma's Demonstration—Calls the English a 'Money-Grubbing Race'—Mostly 'Curiosity Seekers,'" *New York Times*, January 3, 1904, 23.

[49] "A Mahatma Stirs London: Crowds Going to Listen to Sri Agamya's Teachings: The First Genuine Mahatma to Visit the Western World, His Friends Say—Miracles Attributed to Him—Coming to America—His 'Parliament of Truth,'" *The Sun*, December 16, 1906, 4.

[50] See Richard Kaczynski, *Forgotten Templars: The Untold Origins of Ordo Templi Orientis* (n.p.: privately published, 2012), 80–86.

[51] Aleister Crowley to J. F. C. Fuller, September (October?) 1907, IV/12/11, papers of Major General John Frederick Charles (1878–1966), GB99, KCLMA Fuller, Liddell Hart Centre for Military Archives, King's College Library, London.

having read his *Sri Brahma Dhàra: Shower from the Highest*[52] and studied with him back in November 1906. Of these initial experiences, Fuller wrote in the *Agnostic Journal*, "As it happens, the Mahatma is a personal friend of mine. . . . The Mahatma does not claim any miraculous or occult power; he has denied such practices to me personally many times. He merely claims that his powers are a purer form of those natural forces which we all possess."[53] After that, the teacher went to America and Fuller "had almost forgotten about the Mahatma."[54] By the time he returned to England in the autumn of 1907, Fuller's attitude had soured. At Crowley's suggestion, he went to one of Paramahamsa's meetings, unable to disguise his disdain. Ninety minutes into the talk, the guru's famous temper boiled over at Fuller. "You pig-face man!" he cried out. "You dirty fellow, you come here to take away my disciples. . . . Crowley send this pig-one, eh?" Having had quite enough, Fuller ignored the outburst, calmly picked up his hat and cane, and exited the room. As he stepped out, Fuller remarked with doubtless unexpected fluency in Hindi, "Chup raho! Tum suar ke bachcha ho!" (Shut up, you are the son of a sow!). Through the closed door, he could hear another unseemly outburst of rage unfolding in the meeting room.[55] Paramahamsa's poor manners, misogyny, and temper were ultimately his undoing. Sailing from the United States to Paris, he repeatedly insulted fellow passengers to the verge of violence, causing the captain to threaten to arrest him if he did not desist.[56] Back in New York, his Parliament would be sued for $600 in back rent.[57] Then, on June 24, 1908, he was arrested in London on two charges of assaulting women who had answered his ad seeking a secretary.[58]

[52] Sri Agamya Guru Paramahamsa, *Śri Brahma Dhàrà: Shower from the Highest* (London: Luzac, 1905).

[53] J. F. C. Fuller, "The Successor of Samson," *Agnostic Journal* 60, no. 6 (February 9, 1907): 93. See "The Successor of Samson," in this volume.

[54] Sam Hardy [J. F. C. Fuller], "Half-Hours with Famous Mahatmas," *The Equinox* 1, no. 4 (1910): 284–290. See "Half-Hours with Famous Mahatmas, No. 1," in "The Successor of Samson," in this volume.

[55] Hardy, "Half-Hours," 289–290.

[56] "Hindu Mahatma Angers Americans: Passengers on the Kaiser Wilhelm der Grosse Arrive in Paris Very Indignant: Man Called Women "Pigs": Fight Imminent, Officer of Steamship Interferes and Prevents Throwing Man Overboard," *Indianapolis Star*, August 11, 1907, 18.

[57] "Sues for Expense of Tiger Mahatma: Treasurer of the Parliament of Infinite Wisdom Desires $600 Balance from Disciples," *New York Herald*, June 19, 1908, 10; "Says Morton Headed a Vedanta Society: Masseur Declares Financier and Other Social Leaders Studied under Yogi Paramahamsa: Mrs. Fish Interested, and So Was Emma Eames, Backman Says—He Is Suing Now for Back Rent," *New York Times*, June 19, 1908, 5.

[58] "To-Night's Story: 'His House Is Heaven'; Amazing London Scandal, Arrest of the Mahatma, French Girl's Remarkable Story," *Daily Mail*, June 24, 1908, 5; "A Strange Story: Serious Charge against a 'Holy Man of the East,'" *Western Gazette*, June 27, 1908, 2.

Sentenced to four months of hard labor, the Mahatma's tour of the West ended in ignominy.[59]

From Agnosticism to the A.·.A.·.

Another collegial relationship proved to be much more fruitful when Crowley chanced to reconnect with George Cecil Jones. When Crowley was a member of the Golden Dawn from 1898 to 1900, Jones had been his superior and one of the few members for whom Crowley had an abiding respect. Internal politics had disintegrated the London lodge to which they had belonged, and these two survivors—meeting years later—eagerly compared notes on where their spiritual journeys had taken them. Each surprised the other with how far he had gone on separate yet similar paths. Jones appears to have been of the opinion that Crowley had surpassed him and reached levels assumed to be unattainable by corporeal beings, as he declared, "How long have you been in the Great Order, and why did I not know? Is the invisibility of the A.·.A.·. to lower grades so complete?"[60] They decided to form a new school of occultism: a secret society to fill the void left by the demise of London's Isis-Urania Temple of the Golden Dawn, with a substantially expanded curriculum based on what they had discovered in the interim years.

For those with eyes to see, Crowley's next book, *Konx Om Pax: Essays in Light* (1907), was a calling card for the yet-to-be announced society. Its title was a phrase purportedly used in the Eleusinian Mysteries. This phrase, along with its Egyptian cognate *khabs am pekht* (light in extension), were familiar to both Crowley and Jones from the Golden Dawn's Neophyte initiation ceremony. Inside, the book is dedicated none too subtly

To all and every person
in the whole world
who is without the Pale of the Order;
and even to Initiates
who are not in possession of the Password
for the time being;

[59] "Hard Labour for the Mahatma: A Strong Rebuke from the Magistrate," *Irish Times*, July 9, 1908, 4; "Mahatma's Offences: Sentenced to Hard Labour," *Manchester Courier*, July 9, 1908, 8.

[60] George Cecil Jones to Aleister Crowley, *c.* December 10, 1906, quoted in *The Equinox* 1, no. 8 (September 1912): 47.

and to all those who have resigned
demitted,
or been expelled
I dedicate
this Revelation of the Arcana
which are in the
Adytum of God-nourished Silence.

Among the volume's varied contents is the mock-philosophical play *Ali Sloper*, which recounts a Christmas Day debate between "Bowley" and "Bones." The book's distinctive cover was designed by Crowley while on hashish, and it was executed by Fuller (see figure 3.10).

If Crowley no longer considered himself a Rationalist, it did not deter him from slipping further allusions to the movement into his subsequent work. His preface—referring to men "self-hypnotized into cataleptic trances"—quotes the phrase (without attribution) from Huxley's Romanes Lecture, "Evolution and Ethics."[61] Toward the end of part 3 of "Thien Tao" from *Konx Om Pax* (1907), Crowley writes about "The Manifesting of Simplicity" that "the instructed infidel shall no longer sneer at the church-goer, for he will have been compelled to go to church until he saw the good points as well as the bad; and the instructed devotee will no longer detest the blasphemer, because he will have laughed with Ingersoll and Saladin."[62] Finally, the subtitle of Crowley's *777* (1909) purports that the book—consisting of tables of correspondences between the Kabbalistic Tree of Life, tarot, astrology, color, mythology, and dozens of other categories—explicates a system of skeptical mysticism.[63]

In getting this new occult order rolling, Crowley and Jones needed a third. It was a tradition from the Golden Dawn's three founders—William Wynn Westcott, Samuel Liddell MacGregor Mathers, and William Robert

61 Thomas H. Huxley, "Evolution and Ethics: Delivered in the Sheldonian Theatre, May 18, 1893" (London: Macmillan, 1893), 18. Thanks to Krzysztof Azarewicz for sharing with me this observation from his annotated Polish translation of *Knox Om Pax*. Aleister Crowley, *Konx Om Pax*, trans. Krzysztof Azarewicz (n.p.: Lashtal Press, 2020).

62 Aleister Crowley, *Konx Om Pax: Essays in Light* (London: Walter Scott, 1907), 64. Robert Green Ingersoll (1833–1899), nicknamed "The Great Agnostic," was a prominent author in the American counterpart to the British Freethought movement.

63 [Praemonstrator Aleister Crowley], *777: Vel prolegomena symbolica ad systemam sceptico-mysticae viae explicandae fundamentum hieroglyphicum sanctissimorum scientiae summae* (London: W. Scott, 1909).

Figure 3.10 *Konx Om Pax: Essays in Light* (1907). (Image courtesy of Clive Harper.)

Woodman—which was itself a carryover from Masonry.[64] Fortunately, Crowley already had a third in mind. As he wrote in his *Confessions*, "There was besides such creative work and the editorial work which Fuller and I had undertaken on behalf of the Order, the task of reconstituting it in its original purity."[65] Thus, Fuller joined them in forming the A∴A∴, an order whose name is often understood as some variation of "Silver Star" in Latin

[64] Note, for instance, that the charters for the German group from which Ordo Templi Orientis emerged were similarly jointly issued to its three founders: Theodor Reuss, Franz Hartmann, and Henry Klein. For details, see Kaczynski, *Forgotten Templars*.

[65] Crowley, *Confessions*, 561.

(*argentium astrum*) or Greek (ἄστρον αργόν) but whose true name is revealed only to members. Its subsequent *libri*—lessons and other texts—would be issued under the imprimatur of the Praemonstrator, D. D. S. $7^{\circ}=4^{\square}$; the Imperator, Ol Sonuf Vaoresagi (I reign over you) $6^{\circ}=5^{\square}$; and the Cancellarius, Non Sine Fulmine (Not without thunder) $5^{\circ}=6^{\square}$: Jones, Crowley, and Fuller, respectively.

4
AGNOSTICS ON CAMPUS

According to Fuller, "I first met Victor Neuburg in 1906 at the house of Mr. William Stewart Ross, in Brixton."[1] While Crowley reports that the two met at Saladin's funeral,[2] it is unclear from Fuller's statement if this was indeed the occasion he spoke of, although Ross did die in November of that year. As frequent contributors to the *Agnostic Journal* (*AJ*), Fuller's and Neuburg's works occasionally appeared in the same issue.[3] Thus, by their 1906 meeting, they had both seen the other's name. On hearing that Neuburg was a Cantabrigian, Fuller remarked that his friend, the poet Aleister Crowley, had also attended Trinity College and was "from time to time, in the habit of visiting the university as he knew some of the undergraduates."[4] Neuburg was apparently already familiar with Crowley's work.[5] Based on this encounter, Crowley decided to look up Neuburg.

> Having to go to Cambridge one day on some business or other, I thought I would look the lad up. I was not sure of the name, and there were several similar "burgs" in the university register, but having drawn my bow at a venture, the first arrow struck the King of Israel between the harness at the very first shot.[6]

Crowley explained that he had read the undergraduate's poetry in the *AJ* and was interested in meeting its author because it showed evidence of astral travel. Neuburg's "A Recall" would have appeared in the most recent issue

[1] J. F. C. Fuller to Jean Overton Fuller, quoted in Jean Overton Fuller, *The Magical Dilemma of Victor Neuburg*, rev. ed. (London: W. H. Allen, 1965; Oxford, UK: Mandrake Press, 1990), 112.

[2] Aleister Crowley, *The Confessions of Aleister Crowley*, ed. John Symonds and Kenneth Grant (London: Jonathan Cape, 1969), 562.

[3] They first appeared together in the June 10, 1905, issue of *AJ*, to which Fuller contributed the essay "When It Was Dark," and Neuburg the poems "Three Earth-Notes." They subsequently coappeared in the following *AJ* issues: May 26, 1906, March 2, 1907, March 30, 1907, and May 18, 1907.

[4] Fuller, *Magical Dilemma*, 112.

[5] Crowley, *Confessions*, 562.

[6] Crowley, *Confessions*, 562. This quote references 1 Kings 22:34 (King James Version): "And a certain man drew a bow at a venture, and smote the king of Israel between the joints of the harness."

Friendship in Doubt. Richard Kaczynski, Oxford University Press. © Oxford University Press 2024.
DOI: 10.1093/oso/9780197694008.003.0004

of the *AJ*, and it indeed reads like an account of either a mystical vision or a fever dream:

> And so I rose, night-garmented, and sped
> Swift doorwards, with the angel at my side,
> And marvelled at the speed with which he led,
> Yet felt no speed,
> And he traversed much space and countries wide;
> Past myriad towns o'er which were stars thick-spread,
> He still did lead.
> And still I followed swiftly in his stride
> Over unshadowed lands;
> Then, by the yellow tide
> Of a broad hasting stream, he turned, and seized my hands.[7]

Steeped as Crowley was in the Golden Dawn's exercise of "rising on the planes," and given his own mystic visions up to that point, he naturally interpreted Neuburg's account in a similar light.

Neuburg's impressions of that first meeting are unknown. However, Crowley recalled it in his *Confessions*.

> He was an agnostic, a vegetarian, a mystic, a Tolstoyan, and several other things all at once. He endeavoured to express his spiritual state by wearing the green star of Esperanto, though he could not speak the language; by refusing to wear a hat, even in London, to wash, and to wear trousers. Whenever addressed, he wriggled convulsively, and his lips, which were three times too large for him, and had been put on hastily as an afterthought, emitted the most extraordinary laugh that had ever come my way; to these advantages he united those of being extraordinarily well read, over flowing with exquisitely subtle humour, and being one of the best natured people that ever trod this planet.
>
> But from the first moment I saw him, I saw far more than this; I read an altogether extraordinary capacity for Magick. We soon drifted into talking about the subject and I found that he already practised a good deal of spiritualism and clairvoyance.[8]

[7] Victor B. Neuburg, "A Recall," *Agnostic Journal* 60, no. 9 (March 2, 1907): 134. See "A Recall," in this volume.

[8] Crowley, *Confessions*, 562–563. Crowley's observations are supported by Neuburg's acquaintances, who also tend to remark on the disproportionately large size of his head, his peculiar

On April 4, during a reciprocal visit from Neuburg, Crowley tested him and concluded that he was a "clairvoyant—rather a good one."[9] In "A Fragment of Autobiography," Neuburg confirms Crowley's assessment:

> All my life I have had a power of vision: this was apparently a kind of Cosmic consciousness. It enabled me to see beauty everywhere, even in the most conventionally-unpromising places. It would come upon me quite suddenly and without warning. I would find myself in an ecstasy in which I could perceive things from an entirely new and transfigured point of view.
>
> I can best explain the kind of thing I mean by saying that I had a feeling of being identified with, and absorbed in, the universe: I became one with the Spirit of Nature. While I was in this state, the ordinary affairs of life had no importance for me at all: I was removed from the world in which they existed. There was only It, and It and I were one.[10]

From there they bonded across multiple roles. For Neuburg, Crowley became friend, ally, teacher, and lover. In the ensuing years, they traveled together to destinations like France, Spain, and Algeria. Crowley credited his benevolent influence for a profound transformation in the younger poet:

> He lost all his nervousness; he became capable of enduring great physical fatigue, of concentrating mentally, and of dismissing the old fads which had obsessed him. Incidentally, by removing his inhibitions, I released the spring of his genius, and in the next few years he produced some of the finest poetry of which the English language can boast.[11]

While Neuburg's friends and family perceived Crowley as a pernicious influence who had a baleful effect on their Vickybird, Neuburg was enchanted with his new comrade-in-arms.

hygiene and dress habits, and his startling laugh. See, for example, Arthur Calder-Marshall, *The Magic of My Youth* (London: R. Hart-Davis, 1951), 23–24.

[9] Aleister Crowley, diary entry, April 4, 1907, Aleister Crowley Collection, MS-01002, box 11, folder 5, Harry Ransom Center, University of Texas at Austin.

[10] Victor Neuburg, *The Magical Record of Omnia Vincam, a Probationer of A.·.A.·. in June 1909 O.S.*, June 30, 1909, box 15, folder 8, Aleister Crowley Collection 1889–1947, Harry Ransom Center, University of Texas at Austin. A typescript of this record is also preserved in NS92, Yorke Collection, Warburg Institute, London. An edition of seventy-five copies was released by 100th Monkey Press. Neuburg generally indents every sentence in his handwritten manuscript; editorial latitude is exercised here in grouping sentences together.

[11] Crowley, *Confessions*, 562–563.

Biographers of both Fuller and Neuburg have wrestled with the puzzle of how their subjects went from being radical atheists to students of a mystic society. Even Neuburg's son wrestled with this aspect of his father's past.[12] However, the Agnosticism of Saladin was not a rejection of spirituality but an attempt to understand the nature of spirituality without the dogma of either religion or atheism. Much like Saladin, Crowley drew on philosophy, psychology, and science. In this light, Fuller and Neuburg allying with Crowley was not so much a radical conversion as it was a sideways step onto a parallel track. Once Crowley opened the possibility of magick to them, it immediately seeped into their writing. Their contributions to the *AJ* and other subsequent writings are less polemical against Christianity and more celebratory of other spiritualties. This is the case with Fuller's "In the Temple of Isis" (with footnotes on the Kabbalah, Upanishads, Pythagoreanism, and Egyptian pantheons) in the September 29, 1906, issue of *AJ* and Neuburg's "Paganism and the Sense of Song" in the January 19, 1907, issue.[13]

Wild Honey

Around the time the *AJ* ceased publication in June 1907, Neuburg was pondering the poems he had contributed and decided to select the best ones for his first book, tentatively titled *Wild Honey* (see figure 4.1). The planned 1907 release by the Young Cambridge Press collected together twenty-three poems. Surviving page proofs indicate that Neuburg added revisions, extra verses, and introductions to the text.[14] Ultimately, the book did not appear until 1908, under the new title of *A Green Garland*. This slim volume of fifty-five pages reprinted roughly half of the poems that had appeared in the *AJ*—"scrupulously revised," as he put it in the colophon[15]—along with two new works, "A Song of the Promise of Dawn" and "A Leaf from Walt Whitman." Publication of *A Green Garland* by the Young Cambridge Press and Probsthain & Co. was financed by a wealthy fellow Trinity undergraduate whom Jean Overton Fuller identified by the last name "Schmiechen."[16]

[12] Neuburg, *Vickybird*, 4.
[13] See reproductions of Fuller's "In the Temple of Isis" and Neuburg's "Paganism and the Sense of Song," both in this volume.
[14] Lot 726/0303, Fonsie Mealy Auctioneers, accessed May 10, 2020, https://fonsiemealy.ie/auctions/lot-7260303/.
[15] Victor B. Neuburg, *A Green Garland* (Bedford, UK: Young Cambridge Press, 1908).
[16] Fuller, *Magical Dilemma*, 116.

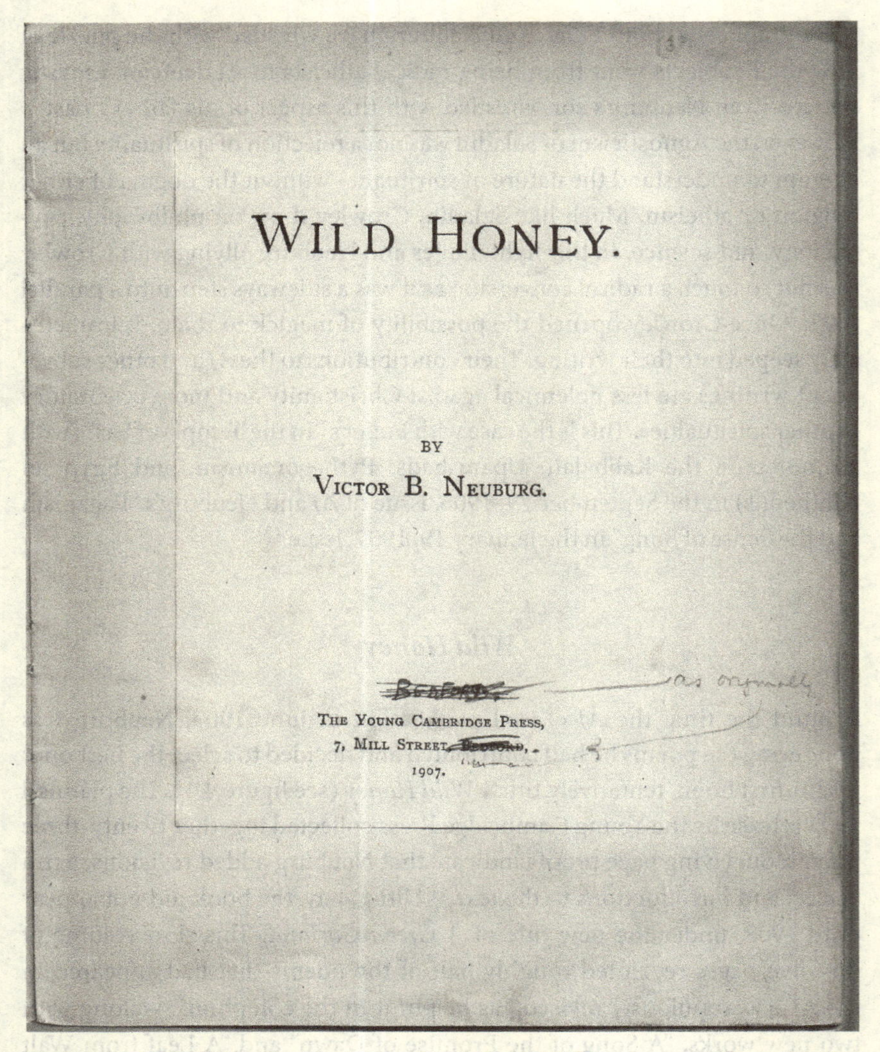

WILD HONEY.

BY

VICTOR B. NEUBURG.

~~BEDFORD.~~

THE YOUNG CAMBRIDGE PRESS,
7, MILL STREET, ~~BEDFORD~~,
1907.

Figure 4.1 Proof title page for Victor Neuburg's *Wild Honey*, with the author's notes. (Image courtesy of Clive Harper.)

The Cambridge University Calendar from 1906 to 1908 lists a Trinity student named Wilfred Schmiechen.[17] Wilfred Hermann Edward Schmiechen

[17] *The Cambridge University Calendar for the Year 1906–1907* (Cambridge, UK: Deighton Bell, 1906), 1012, 1161. Victor Neuburg appears on page 1144 of the same volume. By the 1908 volume, Schmiechen's name continues to appear, but Neuburg's is absent.

(1888–1957) was born in Kensington and while at Trinity befriended future legendary antiquarian book dealer Ernst Philipp Goldschmidt (1887–1954).[18]

Schmiechen had been around mystics and creative types his entire life. His mother Antonia Gebhard (1862–1930), hailed from a wealthy silk-manufacturing family that was very involved in occultism, with connections ranging from French occultist Éliphas Lévi to various German theosophists.[19] Antonia was also interested in spiritualism and the occult, and knew H. P. Blavatsky.[20] His father, Hermann (1855–1925), was an accomplished portrait painter; invited to London in 1883 by Queen Victoria, he became "a favorite portrait painter for British aristocracy."[21] Emigrating to South Kensington, London, they had four children together: Herbert (1884), Elsa (1886), Wilfred (1888), and Gerald (1893). Hermann joined the Theosophical Society (TS) on June 20, 1884, having begun painting his psychic impressions of the mahatmas, spiritual teachers, and collaborators who worked through Blavatsky: Koot Hoomi (figure 4.2)and Master Morya (figure 4.3). As Henry Steel Olcott recounted,

> Herr Herman Schmiechen, a very well-known German portrait-painter, domiciled in London, joined the Society and, to my great delight, at once agreed to have the inspirational test tried with him. . . . He began work on the 19th June and finished it on the 9th July. Meanwhile I visited his studio four times alone and once with H. P. B., and was enchanted with the gradual development of the mental image which has been vividly impressed upon his brain, and which resulted in as perfect a portrait of my Guru as he could have painted from life. . . . It was as clear a work of genius and proof of the fact of thought-transference as I can imagine. In the picture he has got all—the face, complexion, size, shape and expression of eyes, natural pose of head, shining aura, and majestic character.[22]

[18] Wilfred Hermann Edward Schmiechen birth record, Q2, 1888, Kensington, London, 1a: 155.

[19] For a detailed examination of the Gebhard family's Theosophical connections, see Birgit Liljestrom, "On the Quest for Olympus," *Farther In*, no. 2 (December 2021): 2–20.

[20] "Biography of Zachary Merton," Angus and Rosemary's Miscellany of Malvern (website), July 18, 2023, http://www.the-malvern-hills.uk/other_history_zachary_merton.htm; Jane Ridley, *The Architect and His Wife: A Life of Edwin Lutyens* (London: Chatto & Windus, 2002), 267.

[21] Massimo Introvigne, "Painting the Masters: The Mystery of Hermann Schmiechen" (paper presented at the meetings of the European Society for the Study of Western Esotericism, Riga, Latvia, April 18, 2015).

[22] Henry Steel Olcott, *Old Diary Leaves: The Only Authentic History of the Theosophical Society, Third Series 1883–1887* (London: Theosophical Publishing Society, 1904), 156.

Figure 4.2 Herbert Schmiechen's portrait of Koot Hoomi

These portraits quickly attained iconic status within the TS, and Hermann Schmiechen followed them with a portrait of Blavatsky herself in 1885.

In the late 1890s, Antonia Schmiechen began an affair with wealthy metal merchant and philanthropist Zachary Merton (1843–1915): Zachary abandoned his wife for Antonia around 1897, and in 1898 Hermann obtained a divorce on the grounds of adultery. Antonia and Zachary married soon thereafter, in 1899, and the Schmiechens' children would later take Merton's surname, "probably wisely deciding that German names would hinder their advancement in British society."[23] Antonia quit the TS, but after she was left widowed and rich in 1915, her friend Emily Lutyens "reconverted her and persuaded her to give her money to theosophy."[24] After the divorce, Hermann returned to Germany, where he became involved with the TS Lodge there; he

[23] "Biography of Zachary Merton."
[24] Ridley, *Architect*, 267.

Figure 4.3 Herbert Schmiechen's portrait of Master Morya

would later resign and become associated with Leopold Engel[25] (who, with Theodor Reuss, tried to revive the Illuminati Order, only to feud and wind up running competing branches). When he died in 1923, administration of his estate (£69) went to Wilfred.[26]

Despite Wilfred Schmiechen's patronage, *A Green Garland* was dedicated not to him but to H. W. Chetwin, a "close friend" whom Neuburg had met in a bookstore.[27] The United Grand Lodge of England contains a record for one Harry William Chetwin (b. *c.* 1878–1950), who became heavily involved in Freemasonry at age forty; his birth date would make him a contemporary of Neuburg,[28] Although they lived less than a mile apart, the nature of their relationship at this time remains unknown. However, Neuburg inscribed one of the

25 Introvigne, "Painting the Masters."
26 National probate calendar, Index of Wills and Administrations, England and Wales, 1924, p. 202.
27 Neuburg, *Vickybird*, 3.
28 With thanks to Diane Clements, director of the Library and Museum of Freemasonry, London.

forty deluxe copies of *Song of the Groves* (1921) "with the Author's love, to H. W. Chetwin, his oldest pal vii:xi:mcmxxi from me, Victor B. to thee, H. W. C."[29]

Reviews of *A Green Garland* in the *Times*, *Morning Post*, *Daily Chronicle*, and even *Freedom: A Journal of Anarchist Communism* (!) all characterized Neuburg as a poet of promise.[30] The book's central theme—as described by the *Occult Review*—is "the death of the old gods and the dawn of a new era when men shall stand alone."[31] The cautiously generous reviewer remarked, "Though imitative at present to a considerable degree, the writer undoubtedly possesses the temperament of a poet."[32] Others, however, were far less pleased with Neuburg's postreligious vision and his poetic temperament. In his review for the *New Age*, F. S. Flint wrote,

> Mr. Neuburg's gods are Youth, Truth, Progress, Love, and "Mighty Reason"; but he says that all the gods are dead. . . . Mr. Neuburg has more intellect than imagination, and the beauty of young summer, the heat of the sun, and the scent of blossoms stir him to sing rapturously, sometimes obscurely, of the Dawn and the Day, when life will not be sicklied o'er with the pale cast of other worldliness.[33]

Meanwhile, a fellow Cantabrigian wrote in the *Cambridge Review*,

> The author has not yet sufficiently assimilated all the poetry he has read. His style, generally quite promising, has occasional infelicities; and the thoughts and emotions seem to come from outside rather than from within. Mr. Neuberg [*sic*] must strive towards sincerity—that is, he must beware of

[29] Catalog listing by World's End Bookshop, London, accessed September 26, 2020, https://web.archive.org/web/20201201233806/https://worlds-end-bookshop.co.uk/products/neuburg-victor-benjamin-1883-1940.

[30] Reviews from the *Daily Chronicle* (May 13, 1908), *Morning Post* (May 21, 1908), *Daily Telegraph* (May 29, 1908), and *Times* (July 11, 1908) are quoted in an advertisement for *A Green Garland* in *The Equinox* 1, no. 1 (March 1909). See also "Literary Notes," *Freedom: A Journal of Anarchist Communism* 22, no. 231 (July 1908): 50. The latter review is perhaps unsurprising, considering that in 1908, Guy Aldred's Bakunin Press had released the third edition of Fuller's *Star in the West*. Neuburg may have been the beneficiary of an overlap between certain members of the anarchist and secularist movements.

[31] B. P. O'N., "Reviews," *Occult Review* 12, no. 3 (September 1910): 186–187. See, for instance, "Carmen Triumphans," in this volume, with lines (38–40) such as these:

> Yesterday gods! To-morrow, in their stead,
> Humanity shall guard the sacred Fane—
> The Trinity: Love, Life, Hope. The gods are dead.

[32] B. P. O'N., "Reviews," 187.

[33] F. S. Flint, "Book of the Week: Recent Verse," *New Age* 3 no. 11 (July 11, 1908): 212–213.

> gaining the whole world of modern emotions and losing his own soul; he must fast and study metre all the day; and he must abandon his agnosticism and pray without ceasing to Apollo, a difficult God. So, at length, perhaps the real flame will come.[34]

Notably, this first book from Neuburg contains at the back an advertisement for Crowley's *An Appeal to the American Republic*,[35] a testament to how intertwined their lives had already become (see figure 4.4).

The Pan Society

On behalf of his university poetry club, the Pan Society, Neuburg invited Crowley to speak at Cambridge University. As Crowley recalled, "Neuburg was the moving spirit of one of those societies which are always springing up in universities. They never take root; because death comes to all alike at the end of three years, so to speak."[36] Crowley's "First Missionary Journey," as he dubbed it, took place on Thursday, February 28.[37] The dons objected,[38] but Crowley nevertheless went to his alma mater, eager to connect with other students of like mind.

One of the students Crowley met during his addresses to the Pan Society was Norman Mudd (1889–1934), a freshman on a mathematics scholarship. A math person in a poetry club might seem incongruous, but as Mudd described himself,

> at the time I was quite young (18), utterly ignorant of the world, of bourgeois and rather unmanly upbringing, with a character entirely commonplace and devoid of any spark of the heroic. I was certainly gifted, creatively, with considerable mathematical talent (not however even approximating to genius) and on the receptive side with an unusual poetic sensibility.[39]

34 "List of Books Received," *Cambridge Review*, June 18, 1908, 29, no. 736: 463.

35 Aleister Crowley, *An Appeal to the American Republic* (London: Kegan Paul, Trench, Trübner, 1899).

36 Crowley, *Confessions*, 564.

37 Crowley, diary entries, February 28–March 3, 1907, Aleister Crowley Collection, MS-01002, box 11, folder 5, Harry Ransom Center, University of Texas at Austin.

38 Victor B. Neuburg to Aleister Crowley, January 28, 1907, IV/12/7, papers of Major General John Frederick Charles (1878–1966), GB99, KCLMA Fuller, Liddell Hart Centre for Military Archives, King's College Library, London.

39 Norman Mudd to Charles Stansfeld Jones, January 15, 1923, O.T.O. Archives.

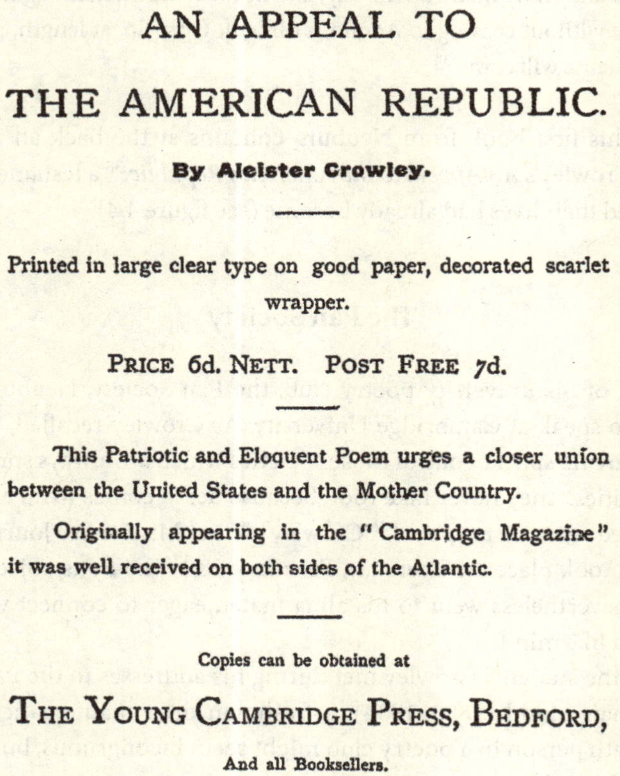

AN APPEAL TO

THE AMERICAN REPUBLIC.

By Aleister Crowley.

Printed in large clear type on good paper, decorated scarlet wrapper.

PRICE 6d. NETT. POST FREE 7d.

This Patriotic and Eloquent Poem urges a closer union between the Uuited States and the Mother Country.

Originally appearing in the "Cambridge Magazine" it was well received on both sides of the Atlantic.

Copies can be obtained at

THE YOUNG CAMBRIDGE PRESS, BEDFORD,

And all Booksellers.

Figure 4.4 Neuburg's *Green Garland* (1908) included this advertisement for Crowley's *An Appeal to the American Republic*

Mudd was the middle of three children born in Lancashire to schoolmaster William Dale Mudd and his wife, Emma. He attended Ducie Avenue School before earning a mathematics scholarship to Cambridge. Meeting Crowley and learning about magic was a turning point for the aspiring academic:

> My interest in the Great Work dates from Dec 1907 when I first met Crowley at Cambridge—thereafter enjoying, at intervals, for two years, his knowledge and conversation. There is no need for me to attempt to describe the

> effect which this meeting had upon me. I then understood for the first time what life was or might be; and the spark of that understanding has been in me ever since, apparently unquenchable. . . . During the years 1908.9, it had been customary, whenever Crowley came to Cambridge, for one of our circle at Trinity to put him up at the College and collect a company in our rooms to meet him, talk with him and listen to the papers he used to read to us.[40]

Neuburg fondly called Mudd "my friend and critic,"[41] and together they distributed copies of the popular edition of *Star in the West* on campus, promoting the work of both Fuller and Crowley.

The Cambridge University Freethought Association

Two other Trinity College students entered Neuburg's circle around this time. scholar and sportsman Kenneth Martin Ward (1887–1927) entered Cambridge in October 1906 on a physics and chemistry scholarship. His dress was as unconventional as his beliefs. Despite first-class marks in his mathematics tripos, a spiritual hunger led him to study literature, philosophy, and art. He chanced to meet Crowley while climbing at Wastdale Head in winter 1908 and was thereby introduced to Neuburg's Pan Society. The other was George Herne Saverie Pinsent (1888–1976), who—like Mudd—was attending Trinity College on a mathematics scholarship.[42]

Around early 1909, this group of students decided to form the Cambridge University Agnostic Association. The group's foundational meeting attracted twenty members and three associates, "the latter title acting merely as a curtain of protection to the timid."[43] At this meeting, the association's officers were determined to be Ward as president and Mudd as secretary, and the general committee included Pinsent and Neuburg, with "one to be elected."[44]

[40] Mudd to Jones, January 15, 1923, O.T.O. Archives.

[41] From Neuburg's dedication to Mudd of the poem "The Flowing Fire," in Victor B. Neuburg, *The Triumph of Pan: Poems* (London: The Equinox, 1910), 21.

[42] "Mr. Gerald Pinsent," *Times*, March 3, 1976, 16; "University Intelligence," *Times*, December 17, 1906, 7; "University Intelligence," *Times*, March 23, 1907, 14; "University Intelligence," *Times*, March 25, 1908, 14; "University Intelligence," *Times*, June 27, 1908, 14.

[43] Kevin Martin Ward to Aleister Crowley, n.d., OS EE1, Yorke Collection, Warburg Institute, London.

[44] Ward to Crowley, n.d., OS EE1, Yorke Collection.

The name of the treasurer is illegible: the handwriting looks like "Smeckin," which *might* be a misspelling of the name of Wilfred Schmiechen, the wealthy Trinity undergraduate who financed the publication of Neuburg's *A Green Garland* (1908), which would make sense for the role of treasurer.[45]

According to Cambridge University Freethought Association (CUFA) President Ward, "At the first meeting I read a paper on the objects of the Association etc., etc., and a discussion of the term 'agnosticism' in the matter of the evolution of its meaning. And in the light of present generally accepted significance, I suggested the title of 'Freethought Association.' This with the other alterations I have marked were passed by the meeting."[46] Thus the CUFA formed with the following rules, which explicitly referenced Huxley's Agnostic principles:

THE CAMBRIDGE UNIVERSITY FREETHOUGHT ASSOCIATION

RULES

1. This Association shall be called the Cambridge University Freethought Association.
2. Membership of the Association shall imply acceptance of the agnostic principle as defined by Prof. Huxley.

"Positively the principle may be expressed:—In matters of the intellect, follow your reason as far as it will take you, without regard to any other consideration.

And Negatively:—In matters of the intellect do not pretend that conclusions are certain which are not demonstrated or demonstrable."[47]

[45] An August 1924 diary entry by Mudd lends support to this theory. Listing potential recipients for his *An Open Letter to Lord Beaverbrook* (reproduced in "A Strange Epilogue," in this chapter), he groups together onto one line his CUFA contacts: J. F. C. Fuller, Victor Neuburg, G. H. S. Pinsent, and Wilfred Merton (a.k.a. Schmiechen). Norman Mudd, n.d., OS DD8, Yorke Collection, Warburg Institute, London.

[46] Ward to Crowley, n.d., OS EE1, Yorke Collection. The original TS rules, with the alteration of "Agnostic" to "Freethought," is preserved in OS EE1 in the Yorke Collection, Warburg Institute, London.

[47] From Thomas Henry Huxley's 1889 essay "Agnosticism," appearing, for example, in Thomas Henry Huxley, *Science and Christian Tradition: Essays*, Collected Essays, vol. 5 (New York: D. Appleton and Company, 1894), 209–262.

3. Any past or present member of the University shall be eligible for election to the Association. The minimum subscription shall be 2/6 per term.
4. The executive of the Association shall consist of the following officers to be elected annually:—
   a President
   a General Secretary
   a Treasurer
   a General Committee of 3 elected by the whole Association.
5. Honorary Vice Presidents and Honorary Members may from time to time be elected.
6. The Executive shall have power to call a general meeting of the members at one week's notice.
7. Names of persons desiring to become members of this Association shall be sent to the Secretary, who shall place those names before the members at the next general meeting.
8. Meetings for discussions and lectures shall be held at least four times during each term.
9. Matters of private business shall be transacted at the commencement of each meeting. For such matters two thirds shall constitute a majority.
10. Visitors may be admitted to any general meeting of the Association on application to the Secretary.

OBJECTS

The objects of the Association are:—

1. To establish the recognition of Huxley's Agnostic Principle as an essential condition of all intellectual progress.
2. To remove all disabilities attaching to freedom of thought and speech in the University.
3. To destroy the forces of superstition, obscurantism and theological dogmatism.[48]

[43] "The Cambridge University Freethoght Association," OS EE1, Yorke Collection, Warburg Institute, London.

Upon the CUFA's formation, Ward promptly sent Crowley an invitation to "come down and give us a stirring speech toward the end of the term"[49]—that is, the end of the Lent Term, which ran from January to March 1909. That the Freethought Association embraced Huxley's Agnostic principle, and invited Crowley as a speaker, shows that even as Crowley was launching the A.·.A.·. and *The Equinox*, he was willing to be associated with infidels and atheists.

Between the Pan Society and now the CUFA, Crowley's so-called Missionary Journeys to Cambridge had raised some red flags. As Crowley recalled,

> Now my connection with the Pan Society was of the slightest. I have merely been invited to read papers, I think altogether three times, on mysticism or kindred subjects. Nothing more harmless can be imagined, but the C.I.C.C.U. [Cambridge Inter-Collegiate Christian Union] went out of its mind. . . . In this instance the C.I.C.C.U. did not know or care what it was that I had read to the Pan society. They merely stated that I hypnotized the entire assembly and took a mean advantage of them. It did not matter to them that what I was supposed to have done is impossible in nature, at least to one of my very mediocre powers.[50]

Coincidentally, Trinity College "received one day a letter from somebody accusing him [Crowley] of paederasty and of being 'watched by the police of Europe' on that score."[51] Rumors of being watched by the police for moral turpitude had dogged Crowley since his Golden Dawn days[52] and in a climate in which one could be imprisoned—like Oscar Wilde had been—for gross indecency, this was most alarming. Dean Reginald St. John Parry (1858–1935) summoned the CUFA's secretary, Norman Mudd, to his office and demanded that Crowley's invitation be rescinded.

[49] Ward to Crowley, n.d., OS EE1, Yorke Collection.
[50] Crowley, *Confessions*, 564.
[51] John Symonds, *The Beast 666* (London: Pindar Press, 1997), 337.
[52] As a Cambridge undergraduate, Crowley had a romantic relationship with Jerome Pollitt (1972–1942), an actor and female impersonator with the Footlights Dramatic Club. Vague rumors of homosexuality followed Crowley: In January 1900, he received a letter warning him that the police were watching him and his Cambridge University flat at 67 Chancery Lane in relation to the "brother of a college chum." That same year, Crowley would be refused advancement into the Golden Dawn's Second Order because of rumors of "sex intemperance on Thomas Lake Harris lines in order to gain magical power—both sexes are here connoted." See Richard Kaczynski, *Perdurabo: The Life of Aleister Crowley*, rev. ed. (Tempe, AZ: New Falcon, 2002; Berkeley, CA: North Atlantic Books, 2010), 83. For more on Pollitt, see Aleister Crowley, *Early Poetic Works*, ed. Chris Giudice (London: Kamuret Press, 2018). Tabloids subsequently hinted at, or openly suggested, Crowley's homosexual leanings, which led to the *Jones v. the* Looking Glass libel suit. See Kaczynski, *Perdurabo*; Richard Kaczynski, *Perdurabo Outtakes* (Royal Oak, MI: Blue Equinox Oasis, 2005).

A series of telegrams and letters followed, with Mudd recounting his encounter with the dean in a letter to Crowley:

Dear Crowley,

I understand that Neuburg has written to you with characteristic vagueness about the combat we are about to wage. It falls to me to give an official account of the pretext for war and the preliminary movements.

On Thursday Jan. 28/09 I received a summons to wait on Rev. R. St. J. Parry Dean of Trinity, my tutor during my first term though not at present.

He made to me two demands:—

1. That I cease to distribute copies of a book called *The Star in the West* written by Captain Fuller on your work.
2. That the invitation sent to you by the C.U.F.A. be cancelled as he could not permit an Association in which Trinity men were concerned to extend an official welcome to men of evil repute.

(I, of course, am the Secretary.)
You will understand from this that

1. He has not read the book through.
2. That he had not read your works.
3. That he had not had the honour of your acquaintance.

The only explanation he could give of his demand was that the book was as filthy as its subject and author.

I pointed out of course that the Freethought question was not one I could settle myself and that I would bring it to the notice of the Committee, which he consents to see. I promised a reply in 24 hours.

The committee met the same evening and decided to interview the Dean the following day. Notices of an urgency meeting of the Association were then sent out and tactics discussed.

Free to cogitate I instant saw that the personal question must be shelved till the larger matter was settled. I accordingly wrote a letter to the Dean telling him what I thought of his soul and agreed not to distribute copies of *The Star in the West* without previously notifying him. (i.e., until I am free to fight him). I hope Fuller will not think I have betrayed him and will see that it was practically my only course. In any case it is only a waiting move & one cannot always attack.

The committee waited on him last night

1. To hear anything he had to say.
2. To inform him that the matter must go before the general meeting.
3. To give him the opportunity of saving his dirty soul by libelling you in plain terms before the Association.

He explicitly stated that he was afraid of libelling you by saying anything either vague or definite & that we must put his demand before the Association without explanation from him. He said he was acting on his own responsibility, whereat he was informed in polite terms that his insolence was if possible more patent than his cowardice.

To me at least he showed signs of caving in. He talked of not wishing to make the matter public in order that he might be free to withdraw if liked.

We shall of course force his hand by getting the Society to snub him, and then the pitched battle will commence. I foresee a scandal of the first magnitude which may result in a ditch death. We are at present the *enfants perdus* of the movement & shall probably have to play a lone hand. For the dons like loose shits fall away & will decompose under strain.

You will understand that the invitation to you and Fuller for the 14th still holds. I will let you know the decision of the Association anon. If anything unexpected befalls I will wire.

Your sincerely,
Norman Mudd

Kindly inform Fuller of the matter. I would write to him if I knew him better. Pay my humble respect to Mrs. Crowley.[53]

To help smooth over the situation, Crowley wrote to Fuller explaining, "Mudd had no choice about the ☆in the West: it was not a point to fight on. We shall win!"[54]

Whereas the students (along with Crowley) were eager for a fight, the dons and other CUFA supporters were less eager to challenge their dean. Foremost among the CUFA's allies was classics scholar Francis MacDonald

[53] Norman Mudd to Aleister Crowley, n.d. [January 30, 1909], OS EE1, Yorke Collection, Warburg Institute, London.

[54] Aleister Crowley to J. F. C. Fuller, n.d. [February 1, 1909], OS EE1, Yorke Collection, Warburg Institute, London.

Cornford (1874–1943), who had matriculated to Trinity College in 1893. In October 1896, he joined the Editorial Committee of the *Cambridge Review*, representing undergraduate opinion and, in 1899, took over as full editor.[55] During his tenure, the *Cambridge Review* covered university chess matches in which Aleister Crowley played and reviewed his books *The Tale of Archais* and *Songs of the Spirit*, opining,

> His work is redolent of blood and God and kisses, sharp swords, lilies and fire—all the furniture of mysterious eroticism. Fortunately Cambridge, among whose sons apparently Mr. Crowley is to be numbered, has produced better poets than him. But whatever his shortcomings, he is at least an original observer.[56]

Cornford was elected a fellow in 1899, appointed assistant lecturer in 1902, and became a full lecturer in 1904.

Intellectually, he joined Jane Ellen Harrison (1850–1928) and other like-minded classics scholars in what would become known as the Cambridge Ritualists, who sought to understand the underpinnings of classical Greek culture as found in ritual, and informed by the emerging fields of sociology and anthropology. These ideas led Cornford—much like his former mentor and now colleague A. W. Verrall—to reinvent the interpretation of Greek classics: in the pamphlet *The Cambridge Classical Course: An Essay in Anticipation of Further Reform* (1903), he encouraged shifting away from exclusively linguistics to a more holistic understanding of ancient Greek culture. The ideas of the Cambridge Ritualists evidently inspired Crowley: Ronald Hutton argues that the idea of a triune Maiden-Mother-Crone moon goddess is a modern invention, an outgrowth of ideas emerging from the Cambridge Ritualists and Aleister Crowley (whose "Invocation of Hecate" in *Orpheus* begins "O triple form of darkness! Sombre splendour! / Thou moon unseen of men!"[57]), and subsequently James G. Frazer, Margaret Murray, and Robert Graves.[58]

[55] Francis Cornford to Mary Emma Cornford, October 18, 1896, CORN/C/1/64, papers of Francis MacDonald Cornford, Trinity College Library; Francis Cornford to Mary Emma Cornford, June 5, 1899, CORN/C/1/132, papers of Francis MacDonald Cornford, Trinity College Library; Francis Cornford to Mary Emma Cornford, June 18, 1899, CORN/C/1/133, papers of Francis MacDonald Cornford, Trinity College Library.

[56] "The Paper-Knife: Short Notices," *Supplement to the Cambridge Review* 21, no. 520 (November 2, 1899): xvii.

[57] Aleister Crowley, *Orpheus: A Lyrical Legend*, vol. 2 (Boleskine, UK: Society for the Propagation of Religious Truth, 1905), 22.

[58] Ronald Hutton, "The Neolithic Great Goddess: A Study in Modern Tradition," *Antiquity*, March 1997, 3.

Cornford was also politically active. As an undergraduate, he advocated for university degrees for women. In 1904, he criticized the practice of compulsory chapel. And in 1908, his pamphlet *Microcosmographia Academia, Being a Guide to the Young Academic Politician*[59] would bring wider renown. From opposing compulsory chapel to satirizing university politics, he was a natural ally to the CUFA.

Other supporters of the CUFA included the following:

- **Vernon Henry Mottram** (1882–1976), who entered Trinity College in 1901 on a scholarship, taking a first class in the natural-science tripos in 1903 and 1905. In 1907, he was elected a fellow of Trinity College. He would remain at Cambridge until 1911, working on his research in nutrition and physiology. He served as the first president of the socialist Cambridge University Fabian Society in 1905 and 1906, through which he entered the Fabian circle of John Maynard Keynes and others who self-identified as gay, discovering his own inclinations in this direction. His political and sexual identities, in addition to the agnosticism to which he gravitated at this point, gave him much to empathize with in the CUFA's plight.[60]
- King's College economist **Hugh Dalton** (1887–1962), who was at Cambridge from 1906 to 1910 and succeeded Mottram as president of the Cambridge University Fabian Society for the years 1908 and 1909. This made him president during the CUFA snafu. As he recalled in 1951—after becoming a prominent politician—"At that time to be a Fabian was as far Left as you could go at Cambridge."[61] Interestingly, Cornford chaired and gave the opening speech at the November 27, 1908, joint meeting of the Cambridge University Fabian Society and the Cambridge Labour Representation Committee;[62] he would later sit on its committee. Similarly, in 1909, CUFA committee member G. H. S. Pinsent would serve as secretary of the Cambridge Fabian Society.[63]

[59] F. M. Cornford, *Microcosmographia Academica, Being a Guide for the Young Academic Politician* (Cambridge, UK: Metcalfe, 1908).

[60] *Cambridge University Reporter 1907–1908* (Cambridge: Cambridge University Press, 1908), 117; David F. Smith, "Mottram, Vernon Henry," *Oxford Dictionary of National Biography*, January 3, 2008, https://doi.org/10.1093/ref:odnb/31479.

[61] C. E. M. Joad, ed., *Shaw and Society: An Anthology and a Symposium* (London: Odhams Press, 1953), 250.

[62] "News and Notes," *Cambridge Review* 30, no. 744 (December 3, 1908): 134.

[63] Great Britain Fabian Society, *Twenty-Sixth Annual Report of the Fabian Society for the Year Ended 31st March, 1909* (London: Fabian Society, 1909), 22.

- A Cantabrigian named Campbell, who is harder to identify. This may be **Sidney George Campbell** (1875–1956). Entering Christ's College, Cambridge in 1808, he received a first class in the classics tripos in 1900 and 1901, his bachelor's degree in 1901, and his master's degree in 1905. He was elected a Cambridge fellow in 1902; by 1906, was a classics lecturer in epigraphy and dialects and assistant master at the Leys boarding school, Cambridge.[64] He appears in the *Cambridge University Reporter*'s "Electoral Roll of the University" as being affiliated with Christ's College and as an examiner for the classics tripos in 1908.[65] Campbell is mentioned in conjunction with fellow classicist Cornford, making this a reasonable identification.

These faculty and fellows appeared in Mudd's follow-up letter to Crowley, in which he supplied further details of the CUFA's loggerheads with Parry:

> I am writing immediately in order to clear up one or two things. I am not at all clear as to the order in which you received the note & telegram. I sent the letter on Saturday (I think, certainly not later) and the telegram at 5:15 on Sunday, after the meeting.
>
> I wrote the note when everybody seemed to be dropping away & the Dons threatened to resign if we decided to fight. I wanted you to oil your tools and be ready to hew them in pieces before mine eyes that I might paddle in their treacly guts.
>
> Cornford's change surprised us. He had in the interval between his first declaration & the meeting read *The Star in the West* and some of your work and many of his prejudices had disappeared.
>
> I should also mention that among the *bene meriti* are Mottram (Don) & Dalton (Fabian President). They had decided to fight with us when affairs seemed most serious & before the shit began to crumble.
>
> Spare these O Lord when thou smitest Sodom lest thy Sword of Song be stained with the blood of thy friends & become discordant.
>
> Unless the Dean is game which I doubt there is no need to wipe him out yet a bit. You can bide your time & then batter him with your club. The Sword is for gentlemen with guts.

[64] John Piele, *Biographical Register of Christ's College 1505–1905*, vol. 2, *1666–1905* (Cambridge: University Press, 1913), 825; *The Cambridge Yearbook and Directory* (London: Swan Sonnenschein, 1906), 115.

[65] *Cambridge University Reporter*, 188.

We had reckoned on the worst and were prepared to fight to the last ditch. Neuburg & Ward had determined if necessary to be sent down sooner than strike their flags. In the case of Pinsent & myself the final step was a matter of greater delicacy. We had of course interviewed the safe members & made quite sure of getting the meeting to defy Parry.

Well Cornford & Campbell turned up at the meeting & I reckoned on a preliminary fight with them. But it was not to be. It seems that Parry has interviewed them & considerably modified his position (the loose contemptible shit). He was no longer imperative. He did not object to your talking on magic. But he barred your sexual ethics. Of course we could not compromise even on this point although probably none of us had thought of it. We decided finally simply to send to him this resolution:—

"The Association having taken into consideration the request made to it by the Dean of Trinity regrets that it finds itself unable to comply with that request. It regards the right to invite down any person it thinks fit as essential to its principles & wishes to point out that its attitude towards any opinions advocated before it is purely critical." Proposed by Campbell. Carried unanimously.[66]

It was an amendment on my original motion that we had decided on, of which I enclose a copy.

It was presented officially to the Dean at 2 o'clock. It was at five o'clock that I sent the telegram. It was considered almost certain that the Dean would cave in at all points. I have not yet received his official reply but I understand that he has surrendered privately to Cornford.

When this is decided I propose to lay siege to the position I temporarily vacated. Thank God I had sense enough not to give up my flag. Neuburg I am afraid was rather tactless but he will recover it.

[66] A longer version of this resolution appears in Norman Mudd to Aleister Crowley, n.d., OS EE1, Yorke Collection, Warburg Institute, London:

> That this Association having taken into consideration the demand by the Rev. the Dean of Trinity does not feel itself justified in casting a slur upon the names of gentlemen who have already honoured its members by addressing them; and against whom nothing definite is alleged save unpopularity in certain quarters. The Association wishes it to be distinctly understood that its attitude toward the doctrines of any person who addressed it is purely critical.
>
> It further wishes to point out that the freedom to invite down any gentleman it thinks fit is a fundamental principle of its constitution from which it can under no consideration depart.
>
> The Association must always regret circumstances which compel it to differ from gentlemen for whom it feels great respect, but in the absence of any specific charges it considers the course adopted to be the only honourable one.

> You can't pull my leg about the London do. Understand that we have you up now whatever happens. Nevertheless I wish you joy in your London venture.
>
> I will let you know anything that happens.
>
> Neuburg sends his love to you & Mrs. Crowley.
>
> And I?, well I am no beadsman masters
> I am none of your friars & fasters
> I take my joys as they come to me
> So I again send my greetings to you and my respects to Mrs. Crowley.
>
> Yours,
> Norman Mudd
>
> I think I can shame some Dons into coming to hear you & Fuller. It is important that Cornford should meet Fuller whom he seems to think a misfit. Give him my greetings when you see him.[67]

CUFA President Ward offered a few additional details absent from Mudd's account:

> Cornford 2 or 3 days ago said that he agreed on the principle as if it had been anyone else but you, he would agree to fight—but as things were, he was afraid he would have to withdraw his name if it came to fighting.
>
> Today he acknowledged that he had not read anything of yours when he spoke to N. Mudd on the subject—but since them he had perused *The Star in the West* which had greatly changed his opinion [. . . W]hen Mr. Cornford said this I got up & mentioned that it was precisely that work which the dean had put forward as a sufficient reason to keep you out of Cambridge!! Rather Humorous! Cornford himself considered it frightful "balderdash," but he said that the balderdash seems to be chiefly the writer's & not yours.[68]

The letters from Ward to Crowley at this time are addressed cryptically to "Alice," and signed "Katie" or "Kate."[69] What it means in this context is

[67] Norman Mudd to Aleister Crowley, n.d. [February 1, 1909], OS EE1, Yorke Collection, Warburg Institute, London.

[68] Kenneth Martin Ward to Aleister Crowley, n.d., OS EE1, Yorke Collection, Warburg Institute, London.

[69] A handwritten note on one of these letters by Gerald Yorke states that the author is "probably V. Neuburg," but the handwriting clearly matches Ward's.

unclear, but later at the Abbey of Thelema (1920), Crowley would occasionally refer to himself as Alys when exploring his gender identity.[70]

Buoyed by this apparent victory over the dean, Mudd was soon sending enthusiastic notes to Crowley, signed "Yours →∞." One read, "Neuburg and I smote the humbugs before we left about *The Star in the West*. They have capitulated, we are free, so I again am glad."[71] Another read, "Have you any more copies of the cheap editions of *The Star in the West* and *The Star & The Garter* for distribution? We can spread them in Manchester. There are many who are thirsty for the wine. . . . Send also along with them some *Equinox* prospectuses."[72] The sense of victory, however, was short-lived.

Crowley's *Confessions* add additional details to the saga, although their timing relative to the course of events is unclear. As he recalled,

> The Senior Dean of Trinity, the Rev. R. St. J. Parry, started to make trouble. I went to see him and asked him what accusations he had to make against me. He merely became confused, tried to bluster, would not commit himself, and finally said that he had given orders that I was not to be admitted to the precincts of the college. On the following morning I waited in the Great Court for him to come out of chapel and called him a liar to his face in front of everybody. It then began to dawn upon him that he had no power to exclude me from Trinity, I being a life member of the college. He summoned the president, secretary and treasurer of the society, and threatened to send them down. But as it happened they none of them belonged to Trinity[73] and he had no more power over them than he had over the Queen of Madagascar. He must have been a really exceptional fool, even for a don, not to have found out such essential facts before entering upon his campaign.[74]

These actions must have complicated the negotiations between the CUFA and the University and possibly even precipitated what happened next. One day, Parry summoned Mudd to his office. The dean, Crowley reports,

[70] See Aleister Crowley, *The Magical Record of the Beast 666*, ed. John Symonds and Kenneth Grant (Montreal: Next Step, 1972), 191, 230, 247, 266, 296.

[71] Norman Mudd to Aleister Crowley, n.d., OS EE1, Yorke Collection, Warburg Institute, London.

[72] Norman Mudd to Aleister Crowley, n.d., OS EE1, Yorke Collection, Warburg Institute, London.

[73] Crowley is wrong here: Mudd, Neuburg, and Pinsent were all enrolled at Trinity College.

[74] Crowley, *Confessions*, 564–565. Crowley also referred to the dean as a "Parry-litic liar" in the course of a book review. Aleister Crowley, "Reviews," *The Equinox*, 1, no. 4 (1910): 239–240.

> ultimately resorted to the meanest possible course of action. He . . . threatened a man named Norman Mudd, whose parents were poor and without influence, with the loss of his mathematical scholarship. Only after I had left the battlefield to seek other victories did he succeed in bullying Mudd into resignation from the society by frightening his father. Mudd gave his promise to have no more to do with it—and promptly broke it.[75]

Parry's threat would have effectively ended Mudd's dream of pursuing an academic career, as his parents were already several hundred pounds in debt with college expenses and in no position to afford tuition. Mudd was effectively cut off at the knees.

> The miserable truth is that through my own personal cowardice, I chose the chance of a congenial worldly career before what I knew to be the highest thing that ever had or ever could come into my life. Or, to put it otherwise, I knowingly and deliberately betrayed the one thing by which I could really live, from base fear of worldly consequences. I will not now describe either the outward humiliation that was then put upon me, nor the hell of shame and remorse and miscellaneous damnation in which I agonised for months, nor yet the weak attempts I made to save some shreds of my self respect.[76]

Furthermore, Parry also revoked Crowley's privilege, as a former student, to visit the campus. Ward—once again writing as "Kate"—clarified to Crowley, "College ground is private property. There is no possibility of your doing anything legally."[77] Crowley responded to this latest development by asking the Master of Trinity College to intervene:

> Dear Master,
>
> For three years you stood to me *in loco parentis*, and that I was a worthy child is evidenced by the fact that I never suffered rebuke or punishment from any of the College Authorities.
>
> To that paternity I now appeal for justice in the following circumstances.

[75] Crowley, *Confessions*, 565.
[76] Mudd to Jones, January 15, 1923, O.T.O. Archives.
[77] Kenneth Martin Ward to Aleister Crowley, n.d., OS EE1, Yorke Collection, Warburg Institute, London.

Since leaving Cambridge in 1898 I have travelled all over the world on one single business, the search for Truth.

This truth I believe that I have found: it may be stated in the thesis following:

By development of will-power, by rigorous self-control, by solitude, meditation and prayer, a man may be granted the Knowledge and Conversation of his Holy Guardian Angel; this being attained, the man may safely confide himself to the Guardianship: and that this attainment is the most sublime privilege of man.

It seemed to be a prime duty to tell others of the results of my search; and I naturally began in the University, and especially in the College which had sheltered me for those three years, to which I look back with greater pleasure than to any other part of my career.

To my surprise, I found myself regarded with great suspicion by some of the College Authorities. They even used methods which seemed to be at the same time high-handed and underground. In particular, the Revd. St. J. Parry endeavoured to poison the minds of some of my friends by insinuating certain things against me. But as he was afraid to say what these dreadful accusations were, his interference was useless to his purpose. I confronted him, ready to defend myself against any accusations and to make clear the purity of my intention, or even to give him an undertaking to fulfil any request of his that I could conscientiously comply with; but he refused to discuss the matter, and I regret to say that he so far forgot his obligations to God as to lie to me, and that I so far forgot my duty to him as to tell him that he lied.

The matter then lapsed, and I continued my teaching. The campaign of anonymous and whispered slander, however, continued. This term I learn that the College Council have ordered the doors of the College to be shut against my gallant friend Captain J. F. C. Fuller and myself, that any member of the College found in communication with me will be expelled forthwith, that no member of the College may belong to any society with which I am in any way connected—measures, in short, savouring alike of panic and of the Inquisition.

That you, dear Master, can be a consenting party to such measures is unthinkable.

I have always been refused to be heard in my defence, or even to hear of what nature are the accusations against me. However, some indications of their nature has leaked out. They are as false as they are abominable; could

I track their author he would assuredly receive a sentence of some years' imprisonment at the hands of His Majesty's Judges, who hear evidence, and judge according to its weight, without fear or favour.

But the Council of Trinity College prefers the methods of the Council of Ten.

I here profess myself willing and anxious to submit myself to the judgement of any tribunal public or private that you may nominate, provided that I am allowed to obtain legal advice and representation, and that the ordinary Rules of Evidence are maintained.

I ask that, should my character be cleared, the Council of the College will rescind its Order; and promise that in the other event I will cease all relations with undergraduate members of the College.

Awaiting with the utmost hope and confidence a favourable reply from your justice and paternal affection.

I beg to subscribe myself, dear Master,
Yours faithfully,
Aleister Crowley[78]

The matter apparently ended there.

As for the CUFA, it appears to have kept a low profile since its inception: News of its formation was not reported in the *Cambridge Review*, nor did any of meetings or lectures appear in the weekly Cambridge calendar.[79] Information on its activities consequently remains scarce, particularly after Crowley's disinvitation as a speaker. This incident, however, was not the end of the CUFA. A few months later, Cornford reached out to philosopher, Agnostic, and RPA supporter Bertrand Russell on behalf of the CUFA, inviting him to do a public lecture:

Dear Russell,

The Committee of the Cambridge Freethought Association have asked me to ask you if you would be willing to give a public lecture here next term.

[78] Quoted in Symonds, *Beast 666*, 337–338.

[79] The weekly calendar in vol. 30 of the *Cambridge Review*—which covers October 1908 through June 1909—lists a wide range of meetings and lectures sponsored by the Cambridge University Additional Curates' Society, Anti-Female Suffrage Meeting, Antiquarian Society, Association for Women's Suffrage, Chemical Club, Christian Social Union, Church Society, Classical Society, Cricket Club, Drawing Society, Fabian Society, Free Trade Association, Free Church Societies, French Society, Inter-Collegiate Christian Union, Liberal Club, Mathematical Club, Musical Society, Nonconformist Union, Philological Society, Philosophical Society, Student Volunteer Mission, and Theological Society.

They are mostly undergraduates (Kenneth Ward, James Ward's son is president) with a few dons; and their objects are to promote freethought & such things. I sympathise with their wanting Freethinking people to make rather more show than they do here. Various Religious Societies organize public lectures (The Romans have a course going on now, proving the existence of God & Freewill & all that, to considerable audiences) and the Infidels remain silent. Also I don't want this Association to be down to getting as lecturers atheists & the blatant & ignorant sort.

I wish you wd come & tell them that the existence of God can't be proved like a proposition in Euclid from Aristotelian premisses—or some other trite but unknown or neglected truth of that kind.

Yours,
Frn Cornford[80]

Psychologist and philosopher James Ward (1843–1925) was a professor of mental philosophy and logic at Trinity College. As Russell would recall about his former teacher, "For James Ward . . . I had a profound respect and a considerable affection. He was my chief teacher in philosophy and, although afterward I came to disagree with him, I have remained grateful to him, not only for instruction but for much kindness."[81] Both Ward and Russell, along with A. W. Verrall, were members of the secret society, the Cambridge Apostles. James Ward's books *First Principles of Psychology* and *Naturalism and Agnosticism* played a large role in shaping Kenneth Martin Ward's thinking (and Freethinking). In short, Cornford was asking Russell to do a favor for his favorite teacher's son.

To drive home his point, Cornford included page 96 from the November 11, 1909, issue of the *Cambridge Review*. He placed an *X* beside the headline "Lectures on Christian Evidence," adding the note, "This is the kind of thing. Frn Cornford." The article opens, "The second of the lectures on Christian Evidence was given in the Victoria Assembly Rooms, on Saturday, Nov. 6th. There was again a very good attendance." According to the article's lecture summary,

[80] Francis Cornford to Bertrand Russell, November 15, 1909, doc. 048541, box 5.09, RA1, Bertrand Russell Archives, McMaster University, Hamilton, Ontario. A TS transcription of this letter is preserved as Francis Cornford to Bertrand Russell, November 15, 1909, CORN/G/17, papers of Francis MacDonald Cornford, Trinity College Library, Cambridge, UK.

[81] Bertrand Russell, *Portraits from Memory and Other Essays* (New York: Simon & Schuster, 1956), 64.

> Either the cause of this universe and of the order in this universe is contained within itself, or it is not. If it is contained within the universe itself then we are logically led on to pantheism. If, however, it is outside of the universe, then we are bound to admit some form of theism. Beyond these two there was, logically speaking, no third alternative. There is no possible solution except either pantheism or theism. Agnosticism offered no solution at all, it is merely the despair of ever reaching a solution.

Given the existence of proofs "that the universe depends on something outside itself," the speaker argued, this proves that God exists. This was the sort of logical fallacy that Cornford hoped Russell could counter. There is no record of Russell's response or of his speaking before the CUFA. However, a few years later when Russell ran afoul of Cambridge University over his pacifist stance toward the Great War, and he was dismissed from his Trinity College lectureship, Cornford would be one of the fellows fighting for his reinstatement.

From there, the CUFA vanishes from available records. In his *Confessions*, Crowley notes the phoenix-like appearance of a successor group:

> An imitation society called the Heretics, who had been trying to run with the hare and hunt with the hounds like the Rationalist Press Association, had melted away into the thinnest kind of mist at the first intimation from the authorities that their exceedingly mild programme of half-baked infidelity was displeasing to the powers that were.[82]

Crowley's account is ungenerous toward the group which succeeded his associates' CUFA. In 1909, then student Charles Kay Ogden (1889–1957) founded the Cambridge Heretics Society, "a society in the radical/rationalist tradition" for "students and other intellectuals that challenged traditional and religious authorities."[83] It operated until 1932, and over the years its members and lecturers included such luminaries as Rupert Brooke, Francis Darwin, Roger Fry, J. B. S. Haldane, Jane Harrison, John Maynard Keynes, G. E. Moore, Eileen Power, Bertrand Russell, Lytton Strachey, Rebecca West,

82 Crowley, *Confessions*, 565.

83 "Heretics," Cambridge University Library, accessed September 26, 2021, https://www.lib.cam.ac.uk/university-archives/glossary/heretics; "Cambridge Heretics Society," *Literature and Science in Modern Britain*, accessed September 26, 2021, https://carihovanec.com/litsci/people.php?person=31.

Ludwig Wittgenstein, and Virginia Woolf.[84] G. H. S. Pinsent's cousin, David Pinsent, was a member.

A Strange Epilogue

Echoes of these connections and parallels—James and Kenneth Ward, Bertrand Russell, the CUFA, and Russell and Crowley both having their separate falling out with Cambridge University—would resurface in 1924.

Having capitulated to Dean Parry's ultimatum, former CUFA secretary Mudd received his degree[85] and became a professor at Grey University College in Bloemfontein, South Africa. Yet he was haunted by shame and spiritual emptiness. He even lost his passion for mathematics. As he recalled of "my exile in South Africa (I deliberately chose to start a new life there, away from the old memories)[,] . . . nothing has ever had the same power to paralize and demoralise me as the letters of welcome and encouragement which I began to receive from him [Crowley] at the beginning of 1921. They were in effect direct accusations against which I had no possible defense."[86] The path to reopening communications with Crowley was torturous. Mudd took a sabbatical to track down his old spiritual mentor, the only person whose writings made sense of the world. "I was unable during 1920 to get into touch with him by correspondence—all the old addresses having become useless in the confusion caused by the war."[87] After false leads took him to London and Detroit, he eventually reunited with Crowley at his Abbey of Thelema in Cefalù, Italy. In the ensuing years, he would be an important, and sometimes vexing, presence in Crowley's life.[88]

Crowley and the Abbey's other residents became the target of a series of tabloid stories that publisher P. R. Stephensen called "a campaign of personal vilification unparalleled in literary history."[89] Among these stories—peppered

[84] "The Cambridge Heretics," *Humanist Heritage*, accessed September 26, 2021, https://heritage.humanists.uk/the-cambridge-heretics/.

[85] The *Manchester Guardian* noted that former Ducie scholar Norman Mudd appeared in a list of wranglers in the Cambridge mathematical tripos (i.e., he received first-class honors in his senior exams). "Ducie Avenue Schools," *Manchester Guardian*, June 17, 1910, 5.

[86] Mudd to Jones, January 15, 1923, O.T.O. Archives.

[87] Mudd to Jones, January 15, 1923, O.T.O. Archives.

[88] For more on Mudd, see Kaczynski, *Perdurabo*.

[89] P. R. Stephensen, *The Legend of Aleister Crowley: Being a Study of the Documentary Evidence Relating to a Campaign of Personal Vilification Unparalleled in Literary History* (London: Mandrake Press, 1930).

with falsehoods, rumor-mongering, and innuendo—was the headline that branded Crowley "The Wickedest Man in the World."[90] Crowley deplored these articles. What he objected to most of all, however, was the claim that he had been imprisoned in the United States for sexual indecency, a variation on the rumor that dogged him in various guises since he was placed "in coventry" at boarding school, fed only bread and water until he confessed to misdeeds of which he was never even accused. Yet his deep-seated aversion to defending himself before a magistrate, coupled with his belief that he lacked the necessary funds to prevail in a lawsuit against the deep-pocketed Lord Beaverbrook, led Crowley simply to fume from Cefalù.

Mudd dutifully transcribed Crowley's objections to several articles.[91] This provided an opportunity for Mudd to defend Crowley more vigorously than he had done with Parry back at Cambridge. Returning to Chelsea to raise funds and awareness, Mudd wrote *An Open Letter to Lord Beaverbrook*. Around August 1924, he had the pamphlet printed in Paris, then he returned to London with the goal of trying the case in the court of public opinion, forcing the paper's publisher (Beaverbrook) to issue a retraction. To this end, Mudd sent letters to a host of Crowley's past acquaintances, along with prominent officials and campaigners for social justice. Among them were George Bernard Shaw, Arnold Bennett, Miguel de Unamuno, and Emma Goldman.

Thus, on September 14, 1924, Mudd wrote to Russell:

> Dear Sir,
>
> I have the honour to invite your attention to the enclosed pamphlet, and to appeal for your help in insisting on the open discussion of this atrocious state of affairs. The last of my own resources have been exhausted in the printing of this statement, and I need at the moment financial backing to get it circulated to some three thousand persons and institutions to whom the cause of liberty and the honour of English letters still have some meaning. But still more I need that some few persons of public standing, who can command publicity, should force this matter on the public conscience of the English people.
>
> I am sure that this latest and foulest attempt to blackjack a great English poet will arouse your fierce indignation. Will you help me, in any way you can, to vindicate the cause of truth and justice against these venomous curs

[90] "The Wickedest Man in the World," *John Bull*, March 24, 1923, 10.

[91] These notes are preserved among the newspaper clippings that constitute NS 88, Yorke Collection, Warburg Institute, London.

who care nothing for the highest interests of humanity except to defile and destroy them?

Yours faithfully,
Norman Mudd[92]

Russell received several letters in response to his reply. Crowley forwarded a letter from Marian K. Clark, chief investigator with the Bureau of Industries and Immigration, who attested,

> The letter accompanying the enclosure contained a copy of an open letter from Professor Mudd to Lord Beaverbrook with the subject matter of which you are doubtless familiar. I may speak authoritatively on the falsity of the second accusation contained in the *Express* article, during the entire period that Sir Aleister passed in this country such an indictment much less a conviction could not under any possibility have escaped my attention in my official position, which brought me into most intimate relations with the Courts as well as the U.S. Department of State in all matters affecting alien residents in the State of New York.[93]

In forwarding this statement to Russell, Crowley also wrote the following:

> Dear Sir,
>
> A copy of your letter to Mr. Norman Mudd & one of Mrs. Clark's to Mr. Otto H. Kahn reached me by the same post.
>
> The letter should, I trust, cover the former. Mrs. Clark was Chief Examiner of Immigration & Labour N. Y. during my stay in U.S.A.
>
> It is perhaps little to my credit that I lived for 5 years amid that Gilbertian legislation without arrest; but I did. I was very prominent in public life all the time and after America came in,[94] was actually working for the Dept. of Justice. (Not in a striped suit, though!)
>
> What amazes me is that there are still men of intelligence who at least toy with the proposition "In a given newspaper article, some statement is probably approximate to some fact."

[92] Norman Mudd to Bertrand Russell, September 14, 1924, 710.053359, Bertrand Russell Archives, McMaster University Library, Hamilton, Ontario.

[93] Marian K. Clark to Otto Kahn, September 3, 1924, 710.051657, Bertrand Russell Archives, McMaster University Library, Hamilton, Ontario.

[94] That is, into the War.

We picked out the conviction lie as the simplest to disprove: the articles are a jumble of incoherent nonsense. "So she went into the garden to cut a cabbage to make an apple pie of . . . &c—&c" is really the logical style.

As to the actual evidence, the S. E., on the challenge of the pamphlet, have only to publish the date and place of the conviction. Which is absurd. I am asking you to take up this matter not on any ground of personal justice to me, but as a lever to overthrow the whole Babel-tower of irresponsible clamour—such as worked such mischief in the War, and is still the most evil force in modern life.

Yours very sincerely,
Aleister Crowley[95]

Mudd also replied to Russell in a rambling, disjointed, and not entirely convincing letter.[96]

Upon receiving the letters from Mudd and Crowley, Russell agreed that "Dr. Crowley . . . seems to show that he is in a position to establish the falsehood of the libel. Of course, I can see your difficulty. Other things which are true would be brought out, and would prejudice a narrow-minded jury." He suggested that if a major newspaper were to run a letter asserting that the *Sunday Express* had lied, the paper would be forced to take legal action: "For this purpose, you must find the right editor. I don't see what I can do to help you, I know nothing about Dr. Crowley, but should be glad to see the Beaverbrook press shown up."[97] Much as he apparently did with the CUFA's invitation in 1909, Russell kept his distance. The *Open Letter* failed in its goal of forcing a retraction. Thus, the Crowley-CUFA-Russell connection resolved into silence. Meanwhile, Crowley again "left the battlefield to seek other victories."

[95] Aleister Crowley to Bertrand Russell, n.d. [September 1924], 710.048743, Bertrand Russell Archives, McMaster University Library, Hamilton, Ontario.

[96] Norman Mudd to Bertrand Russell, September 20, 1924, 710.053360, Bertrand Russell Archives, McMaster University Library, Hamilton, Ontario.

[97] Bertrand Russell to Norman Mudd, September 29, 1924, OS E21, Yorke Collection, Warburg Institute, London.

5
BORROWED INFLUENCES

The Agnostics' enduring influence on Crowley is obvious through the names he continued to mention in his later works, decades after his brush with the movement. For instance, in *Magick in Theory and Practice* (1929–1930), Crowley directs students to study Herbert Spencer's *First Principles* (calling it "the Classic of Agnosticism"), *The Essays of Thomas Henry Huxley* ("masterpieces of philosophy, as of prose"), and the *Essays of David Hume* ("the Classic of Academic Scepticism").[1] Meanwhile his *Confessions* (1929) makes several references to prominent persons in the movement. E. S. P. Haynes—who advocated for the reform of divorce laws in the pages of the *Literary Guide*[2]—is recalled as "the lawyer . . . who had so elegantly and adroitly arranged the details of my divorce"[3] and who "told me that [*Rosa Decidua*] was the most powerful thing he had ever read."[4] Crowley includes the leaders of the NSS among writers historically accused of blasphemy when he remarks, "The people who persecuted Byron, Shelley, Darwin, Bradlaugh and Foote smiled amiably at the much more outspoken blasphemies of Bernard Shaw."[5] And elsewhere, contrasting skepticism and experience, he muses,

> One of my difficulties was that my senses told me that the archangel Gabriel existed exactly as they told me that Ernst Haeckel existed; in fact, rather

[1] The Master Therion [Aleister Crowley], *Magick in Theory and Practice* (Paris: Lecram Press, 1930), 211.

[2] E. S. P. Haynes, "The Reform of the Divorce Laws," *Literary Guide and Rationalist Review* 167 (May 1, 1910): 80.

[3] Aleister Crowley, *The Confessions of Aleister Crowley*, ed. John Symonds and Kenneth Grant (London: Jonathan Cape, 1969), 538.

[4] Crowley, *Confessions*, 536. *Rosa Decidua* was issued in an edition of only twenty copies to mark the occasion of his divorce from Rose Kelly. It was the final of the four "Rosas" that Crowley wrote for his wife, the first three being *Rosa Mundi*, *Rosa Coeli*, and *Rosa Inferni*. Aleister Crowley, *Rosa Decidua* (n.p.: privately published, 1910); Aleister Crowley, *Rosa Mundi* (Paris: Phillipe Renouard, 1905); Aleister Crowley, *Rosa Coeli* (London: Chiswick Press, 1907); Aleister Crowley, *Rosa Inferni* (London: Chiswick Press, 1907).

[5] Crowley, *Confessions*, 726. Charles Bradlaugh was the founder of the National Secular Society; G. W. Foote belonged to the NSS, split from the group in 1877 to form the British Secular Union, then reconciled with Bradlaugh to become NSS vice president in 1882.

Friendship in Doubt. Richard Kaczynski, Oxford University Press. © Oxford University Press 2024.
DOI: 10.1093/oso/9780197694008.003.0005

> more so. I had accepted Haeckel on mere hearsay. Why should I doubt Isis, whom I had seen, heard, touched; yet admit Ray Lankester, whom I hadn't?[6]

Whatever doubts he may have harbored regarding Haeckel's existence, Crowley dedicated a letter in *Magick without Tears* (1954) to the biologist.[7]

The following section looks beyond such passing references to more substantive ways in which Crowley echoed the Secularist movement.

The Method of Science

In addition to finding inspiration for a publishing model in the RPA's Cheap Reprints series, Crowley also appears to have brought much of the Rationalist ethos into his developing spiritual worldview, particularly into the A.·.A.·.. One can almost imagine Crowley squinting at the New Agnosticism through his Golden Dawn goggles and slapping on a coat of dispensationalism.

For instance, the motto of *The Equinox*—"The Method of Science, the Aim of Religion"—and Crowley's term for his evidence-based approach to magick as "Scientific Illuminism" both recall the RPA definition of *rationalism* as "the mental attitude which unreservedly accepts the supremacy of reason and aims at establishing a system of philosophy and ethics verifiable by experience and independent of all arbitrary assumptions or authority."[8] The fundamental premise underlying Agnosticism was to develop a moral system that is informed by the most up-to-date scientific knowledge: "Modern science could present an integrated and rational world view, encompassing every realm of thought"[9]

None of this precluded for the New Agnostic the possible existence of a deity—"The Unknowable"—beyond the boundaries of knowledge. Indeed, some Agnostics "celebrated evolution as a manifestation of the powers of the Unknowable"[10] and even "claimed a deeper insight into the nature of things

[6] Crowley, *Confessions*, 363.

[7] The commonly-available edition edited by Israel Regardie retitles letter 27 as "Structure of Mind Based on That of Body," but the original Thelema Publishing Company edition of 1954 gives the full title as "Chapter XXVII: Structure of Mind Based on That of Body (Haeckel and Bertrand Russell)." Published posthumously, these letters comprising *Magick without Tears* were written in the 1940s.

[8] "First Principles of the R. P. A.," *Literary Guide and Rationalist Review* 128 (February 1, 1907): 25.

[9] Bernard Lightman, "Ideology, Evolution and Late-Victorian Agnostic Popularizers," in *History, Humanity and Evolution: Essays for John C. Greene*, ed. James R. Moore (1990; repr. Cambridge: Cambridge University Press, 2002), 292.

[10] Lightman, "Ideology," 294.

than clergymen could attain, but at the same time they assumed the role of interpreters of God's inscrutable ways. Their theodicy was, ironically, less secular in its appeal."[11]

In 1889, Huxley ridiculed Laing's *Agnostic Problems* (1887) for attempting an Agnostic "creed."[12] Yet that is literally what Crowley did with the Creed in his Gnostic Mass:

> I resolved that my ritual should celebrate the sublimity of the operation of universal forces without introducing disputable metaphysical theories. I would neither make nor imply any statement about nature which would not be endorsed by the most materialistic man of science.[13]

Thus we find in Crowley's Gnostic Creed such lawyerly language as "And, forasmuch as meat and drink are transmuted in us daily into spiritual substance, I believe in the Miracle of the Mass."[14]

Evolutionary theory was particularly important to the New Agnosticism, not only for its materialistic application but also for its metaphorical power. As Lightman notes, "Evolution, according to Ross, could be described legitimately as 'the upward passing through karma to Nirvana.' . . . Watts shared Ross's interests."[15] Similarly, Thelema is arguably also Darwinian: those who discover and do their Will have the selective advantage of "the inertia of the universe to assist him,"[16] while those who act otherwise will constantly be swimming against the flow. As Lightman observes, "The political creed of Darwinism could only be 'Individualism.' "[17] Or, as Crowley might say, "Every man and every woman is a star."[18]

Application of scientific principles to religion predates the RPA, of course. Indologist Max Müller (1823–1900), compiler of the fifty-volume *Sacred*

[11] Lightman, "Ideology," 297.
[12] Lightman, "Ideology," 303.
[13] Crowley, *Confessions*, 714.
[14] [Aleister Crowley], "Ecclesiae Gnosticae Catholicae Canon Missae," *The International* 12, no. 3 (1918): 70–74; repr. "Ecclesiae Gnosticae Catholicae Canon Missae," *The Equinox* 3, no. 1 (1919): 247–270; repr. The Master Therion [Aleister Crowley], "Ecclesiae Gnosticae Catholicae Canon Missae," *Magick in Theory and Practice* (Paris: Lecram Press, 1929–1930), 345–361.
[15] Lightman, "Ideology," 301.
[16] Crowley, *Magick in Theory*, xv. Crowley follows this statement with the following Darwinian illustration: "The first principle of success in evolution is that the individual should be true to his own nature, and at the same time adapt himself to his environment." Crowley, *Magick in Theory*, xv.
[17] Lightman, "Ideology," 296.
[18] *Book of the Law*, vol. 1, p. 3.

Books of the East (*SBE*) series so esteemed by Crowley,[19] advanced the phrase "Science of Religion" in his 1870 book *Introduction to the Science of Religion.*[20] However, he did not apply the scientific method to the experience of religion but advocated for comparative religion as a social science. This message dovetailed with that of Swami Vivekananda (1863–1902), whose 1896 book *Raja Yoga* is regarded "one of the most important foundational documents in the history of modern, transnational yoga" and whose runaway success established Vivekananda as "the first teacher of yoga in the West."[21] This was also the year that Vivekananda met Müller. The yogi's interfaith message complemented the philologist's notion of the "Science of Religion." Thus Vivekananda used scientific language to promote the understanding of religion, particularly Hinduism.[22] Rambachan summarizes Vivekananda's position this way:

> The system of *rājayoga*, based primarily on the *Yoga-sūtras* of Patañjali, is proposed, by Vivekānanda, as a method for enabling us to attain direct perception of religious truths. It is declared to be "as much a science as any in the world," with its unique methods for producing results when properly applied. In particular, he contends that *samāddhi*, the culminating experience of the Patañjali system, is the self-valid and authoritative source of all religious knowledge. It confers a certainty comparable to that attained in the physical sciences.[23]

Recognizing Vivekananda's enormous influence, scholars have offered varying assessments of his "scientific" claims. Koppedrayer characterizes

[19] Friedrich Max Müller, ed., *The Sacred Books of the East*, 50 vols. (London: Oxford University Press, 1879–1910).

[20] Friedrich Max Müller, *Introduction to the Science of Religion: Four Lectures Delivered at the Royal Institution in 1870* (London: Spottiswoode, 1870).

[21] Debra Diamond and Molly E. Aitken, *Yoga: The Art of Transformation* (Washington, DC: Smithsonian Institution, 2013), 96. Incidentally, while Vivekananda's *Raja Yoga* was taking the English-speaking world by storm, in this same year the "spiritual father" of Ordo Templi Orientis presented a paper on yoga at the Third International Congress for Psychology in Munich. See Carl Kellner, *Yoga: Eine Skizze über den psycho-physiologischen Teil der alten indischen Yogalehre* (Munich: Kastner & Lossen, 1896); Richard Kaczynski, *Forgotten Templars: The Untold Origins of Ordo Templi Orientis* (n.p.: privately published, 2012), 80–86; Karl Baier, "Yoga within Viennese Occultism: Carl Kellner and Co.," in *Yoga in Transformation: Historical and Contemporary Perspectives*, ed. Karl Baier, Philipp A. Maas, and Karin Preisendanz (Göttingen, Germany: Vienna University Press, 2018), 387–438.

[22] Vivekananda, *The Science and Philosophy of Religion: A Comparative Study of Sankhya, Vedanta, and Other Systems of Thought* (Calcutta: Udbodhan Office, 1903).

[23] Anantanand Rambachan, "Swāmī Vivekānanda's Use of Science as an Analogy for the Attainment of *Mokṣa*," *Philosophy East and West* 40, no. 3 (1990): 332.

Vivekananda not as scientific per se but as using science as an effective metaphor: he bridged the cultural and religious gap between himself and his Western audience by presenting Hinduism in terms of "19th century Western preoccupations and sensitivities . . . characterized by a hybridity that drew upon the language of science, rationality, and universalism."[24] In Rambachan's more critical view,

> [Vivekananda's] parallels are possible only through a radical simplification of the scientific method. In describing "experience" as the common basis of knowledge in religion and science, he overlooks the complexity of the process through which knowledge is gained in the sciences. The scientific technique is even further simplified in the interests of superficial similarities.[25]

Ultimately, the approaches of both Müller and Vivekananda were founded in *essentialism*—that is to say, in distilling religion (as a singular concept, as opposed to multiple "religions") to its noumenal, experiential essence—rather than in applying scientific principles to its study.[26]

Nevertheless, both figures were immensely influential on Crowley's circle. The list of "Books for Serious Study" in *Magick in Theory and Practice* includes several titles from Müller's *SBE* series,[27] and T. W. Rhys David's volumes in the series framed Crowley's earliest psychological thinking about various yogic states of consciousness.[28] Fuller also mentions Müller in his 1907 letter to the editor of the *Agnostic Journal*.[29] And while Neuburg mentions neither Vivekananda nor Müller, his "Fragment of Autobiography" shares their perspective in expounding on his clairvoyant abilities:

> In some parts of the world—in India especially, I believe—the phenomena accompanying this religious experience are scientifically studied and

[24] Kay Koppedrayer, "Hybrid Constructions: Swami Vivekananda's Presentation of Hinduism at the World's Parliament of Religions, 1893," *Religious Studies and Theology* 23, no. 1 (2004): 8.

[25] Rambachan, "Swāmī," 340.

[26] Thomas J. Green, *Religion for a Secular Age: Max Müller, Swami Vivekananda and Vedānta* (New York: Routledge, 2016). See, in particular, chap. 2, "The Science of Religion and the Religion of Science."

[27] These are *The Yi King*, *The Tao Teh King*, *The Upanishads*, *The Dhammapada*, and *The Questions of King Milinda*. Crowley, *Magick in Theory*, 209–210. See also "VII. A Course of Reading," in [Aleister Crowley], "Liber E vel Exercitiorum sub figurâ IX," *The Equinox* 1, no. 1 (March 1, 1909): 23–34.

[28] See Aleister Crowley, *The Sword of Song: Called by Christians the Book of the Beast*, ed. Richard Kaczynski (London: Kamuret Press, 2021).

[29] See "The Successor of Samson."

> tabulated. I can say from personal experience that there is the utmost need for some such scientific study in the West,—if possible of an entirely non-religious, and above all nonsectarian nature. An excellent beginning in this work is Professor William James' *Varieties of Religious Experience*.[30]

Crowley likewise lauded Vivekananda as "certainly the best of the modern Indian writers on Yoga."[31] *Raja Yoga* occupied a spot on Crowley's recommended or required reading lists throughout his lifetime.[32] The fall 1910 issue of *The Equinox* includes Fuller's fulsome review of Vivekananda's *Bhakti Yoga*:[33] "If Swami Vivekânanda was not a great Yogi he was at least a very great expounder of Yoga doctrines. It is impossible here to convey to the reader a just estimate of the extreme value of this book. But we can say that this is the best work on the Bhakti-Yoga yet written."[34] This, incidentally, was the same issue of *The Equinox* in which Fuller published an extensive account of yoga. If Vivekananda's attempts to paint yoga in scientific terms was an oversimplification, his idea that spiritual practice was scientific in that it produced predictable and reproducible results resonated profoundly with Crowley's concept of Scientific Illuminism.[35]

Phallicism

In its 1909 review of the RPA Annual, *The Equinox* wrote, "Of all the lame ducks that crow upon their middens under the impression that they are

[30] Victor Neuburg, *The Magical Record of Omnia Vincam, a Probationer of A.·.A.·. in June 1909 O.S.*, June 30, 1909, box 15, folder 8, Aleister Crowley Collection 1889–1947, Harry Ransom Center, University of Texas at Austin.

[31] Aleister Crowley, *Magick without Tears* (Hampton, NJ: Thelema, 1954; repr. St. Paul, MN: Llewellyn, 1970), 421.

[32] *Raja Yoga* first appears in "VII. A Course of Reading" in Crowley, "Liber E," 23–34. Crowley and Desti include *Raja Yoga* in a list of books that "a student must possess." Frater Perdurabo and Soror Virakam [Aleister Crowley and Mary Desti], *Book 4*, pt. 1 (London: Wieland, 1912), 45. Issues 7–10 of *The Equinox* (i.e., 1912–1913) included a preliminary page of Official Announcements that declared "a Student of the Mysteries . . . must possess the following books," the second of which was *Raja Yoga*. It appears again among the "Books for Serious Study" listed in Crowley, *Magick in Theory*, 209–210. Crowley also recommends the book in Crowley, *Magick without Tears*, 493.

[33] Swâmi Vivekânanda, *Addresses on the Vedânta Philosophy*, vol. 2: *Bhakti Yoga* (London: Simpkin, 1896; repr. 1901; Calcutta: Udbodhan).

[34] J. F. C. F., review of "Bhakti-Yoga," by Swami Vivekânanda, *The Equinox* 1, no. 4 (September 1910): 24.

[35] For a detailed examination of Crowley's scientific approach to magick, see Egil Asprem, "Magic Naturalized? Negotiating Science and Occult Experience in Aleister Crowley's Scientific Illuminism," *Aries* 8 (2008): 139–165.

reincarnations of Sir Francis Drake, I suppose that the origin-of-religion lunatics are the silliest."[36] Despite this disparaging remark, Crowley closely followed writers on the origin of religion. Many of the authors he frequently cited would be familiar to readers of the *Literary Guide*, having been repeatedly referenced in its pages. While Crowley may have encountered these writers outside of the *Literary Guide*, this nexus of common interests and influences is nevertheless significant.

Foremost among these is social anthropologist James George Frazer's (1851–1941) monumental study of comparative mythology, *The Golden Bough: A Study in Magic and Religion*. Issued as two volumes in 1890 and followed by a three-volume edition in 1900, a third expanded edition appeared as staggering twelve volume set over the years 1906 to 1915.[37] The *Literary Guide* announced this new edition with great excitement and supplied readers with frequent updates about new volumes in this eagerly anticipated series.[38] *The Golden Bough*'s influence on Crowley cannot be understated: Frazer's thesis about the worship and sacrifice of a solar king or dying and reviving god runs throughout Crowley's writings. His Gnostic Mass is heavily influenced by this idea, as is his play *The Ship*,[39] from which the Gnostic Mass draws its anthem. After the final volumes of the expanded edition appeared in 1915, Crowley penned a series of short stories inspired by the myths explored by Frazer, later published in the *International*.[40] Finally,

[36] "Reviews," *The Equinox* 1, no. 2 (September 1909): 386.

[37] J. G. Frazer, *The Golden Bough: A Study in Comparative Religion*, 2 vols. (London: Macmillan, 1890); J. G. Frazer, *The Golden Bough: A Study in Magic and Religion*, 3 vols. (London: Macmillan, 1900); J. G. Frazer, *The Golden Bough: A Study in Magic and Religion*, 12 vols. (London: Macmillan, 1906–1915).

[38] "Random Jottings," *Literary Guide and Rationalist Review* 110 (August 1, 1905): 124; "'Golden Bough' Lectures," *Literary Guide and Rationalist Review* 118 (April 1, 1906): 53–54; "Adonis, Attis, Osiris: A New Work by the Author of 'The Golden Bough,'" *Literary Guide and Rationalist Review* 125 (November 1, 1906): 164. The *Literary Guide* announced that the awaited third edition of *The Golden Bough* would be broken up into a series of monographs with the series title *The Golden Bough*. "Random Jottings," *Literary Guide and Rationalist Review* 138 (December 1, 1907): 184. See also "Random Jottings," *Literary Guide and Rationalist Review* 151 (January 1, 1908): 8; "Random Jottings," *Literary Guide and Rationalist Review* 163 (January 1, 1910): 8; "Random Jottings," *Literary Guide and Rationalist Review* 168 (June 1, 1910): 88; "Random Jottings," *Literary Guide and Rationalist Review* 189 (March 1, 1912): 37; and "Random Jottings," *Literary Guide and Rationalist Review* 209 (November 1, 1913): 168.

[39] Saint Edward Aleister Crowley, 33°, 90°, 96°, X°, P.G.M., U.S.A., etc. etc. etc., "The Ship: A Mystery Play," *The Equinox* 1, no. 10 (September 1913): 57–79.

[40] Mark Wells [Aleister Crowley], "The Burning of Melcarth," *International* 11, no. 10 (October 1917): 310–312; Mark Wells [Aleister Crowley], "The Hearth," *International* 11, no. 11 (November 1917): 334–338; Mark Wells [Aleister Crowley], "The God of Ibreez," *International* 12, no. 1 (January 2, 1918): 19–24; Barbey de Rochechouart, "The Mass of Saint Sécaire," trans. Mark Wells [Aleister Crowley] *International* 12, no. 2 (February 1918): 42–46; Mark Wells [Aleister Crowley], "The King

The Golden Bough makes Crowley's recommended reading lists in the blue *Equinox* (1919) and in *Magick in Theory and Practice* (1929–1930): in both places he calls it "the Text-Book of Folk Lore. Invaluable to all students."[41]

A related writer on comparative religion was not only championed by the *Literary Guide*, but also published by the RPA (see figure 5.1): Rationalist and future Member of Parliament John Mackinnon Robertson (1856–1933). His *Pagan Christs: Studies in Comparative Hierology* (1903)[42] argues—according to the *Literary Guide*—that the drama of "the Last Supper, Passion, Betrayal, Trial, Crucifixion, and Resurrection . . . 'is demonstrably (as historic demonstration goes) a symbolic modification of an original rite of human sacrifice, of which it preserves certain verifiable details.' "[43] In other words, Christianity is but an amalgam of earlier pagan myths, an argument that sat neatly beside Frazer's trope of the "Corn King." Crowley cites *Pagan Christs* several times. The earliest mention occurs in his satirical dialogue "The Excluded Middle," which first appeared in the second volume of his collected *Works* (1906) as an addendum to *The Sword of Song*. Robertson appears among numerous citations, all offered without comment or explanation, in the footnote to the first word of the dialogue, "Well." *Pagan Christs* was next offered as an alternative to the "rite" theory put forth in Ralph Shirley's *The New God and Other Essays*, reviewed in the March 1911 issue of *The Equinox*.[44] Crowley offers a more substantive reference in his essay "The Revival of Magick," in which he writes,

> J. M. Robertson goes further, and says that the story of the Last Supper, Trial and Crucifixion of Christ is not a history but a scenario. Nor is this view confined to rationalists and anthropologists of the type of Spencer, Frazer, and Grant Allen; many Christian mystics uphold it, and say that

of the Wood," *International* 12, no. 4 (April 1918): 99–102; James Grahame [Aleister Crowley], "The Old Man of the Peepul-Tree," *International* 12, no. 4 (April 2, 1918): 107–110. A republication of these stories was planned by Mandrake Press in 1930, but it never advanced beyond proof stage. These stories, along with two that were unpublished at the time, were later collected as Aleister Crowley, *Golden Twigs*, ed. Martin Starr (Chicago: Teitan Press, 1988). They also appear in Aleister Crowley, *The Simon Iff Stories & Other Works*, ed. William Breeze (Ware, UK: Wordsworth Editions, 2012).

41 Aleister Crowley, "Curriculum of A∴A∴," *The Equinox* 1919, 3, no. 1 (1919): 22; Crowley, *Magick in Theory*, 211.

42 J. M. Robertson, *Pagan Christs: Studies in Comparative Hierology* (London: Watts, for the Rationalist Press Association, 1903).

43 "Beloved Gods," *Literary Guide and Rationalist Review* 86 (August 1, 1903): 116–117.

44 "Stop Press Reviews," *The Equinox* 1, no. 5 (supplement, March 1911): 177); Ralph Shirley, *The New God and Other Essays* (London: Rider, 1911.

PAGAN CHRISTS:

STUDIES IN COMPARATIVE HIEROLOGY.

UNDER the above heading THE RATIONALIST PRESS ASSOCIATION, LIMITED, will shortly publish a new work by Mr. J. M. ROBERTSON. The volume is designed to complement and complete the author's undertaking in *Christianity and Mythology*. That was a mythological analysis, introduced by a discussion of the rationale of mythology; the present volume aims at a constructive historical synthesis of Christian origins, introduced by a discussion of the rationale of religion as it is variously presented by Mr. Frazer, Mr. Jevons, and other writers.

The central feature of the book is the claim to show (1) that the Gospel story of the Last Supper, Passion, Betrayal, Trial, Crucifixion, and Resurrection is visibly the transcript of a Mystery Drama, and not primarily a narrative proper; (2) that the story is thus neither a normal fiction nor a collected tradition, but (3) the reduction to narrative of a dramatic rite of annual mock-sacrifice, developed from an original annual rite of actual human sacrifice. Mr. Grant Allen, in his *Evolution of the Idea of God*, affirmed the last part of the thesis on general grounds of analogy. Mr. Robertson has undertaken to trace so far as may be the historical process in Judaism and other Semitic cults, and by demonstrating the existence of the Mystery Drama has placed the theory on a definite documentary basis. At the same time, he traces through Judaism the institution of a Eucharist partaken of by twelve priestly persons presided over by a Christos or Anointed One.

In rebuttal of the assumption that there must have been a historical Teaching Jesus, Mr. Robertson (1) points to the evidence for the hypothesis that an ancient God Jesus underlay the myth of Joshua; and devotes a section to (2) the general evolution of the Teaching God in the different religions of antiquity, and of (3) the Logos idea in particular, showing it to be common to the systems of India, China, Egypt, and Babylon, and probably original in the last-named. He undertakes to show, further, that Buddha and Manichæus are probably, like Zarathustra, mythical personages created by the religious imagination on different lines of mythopoiesis.

Two of the four parts of the book are given to the foregoing subjects. The third and fourth parts consist of greatly expanded revisions of his studies of the Mithraism and the Religions of Ancient America, which first appeared as lectures in "The Religious Systems of the World." In the former is traced in close detail the evolution of a cult of a Pagan Christ which was long the chief rival of Christianity, and from which Christianity copied some of its leading rites and symbols; while the fourth and concluding section exhibits the manifold development in pre-Christian America of the principles of human sacrifice which, probably originating in Central Asia, were in Asia Minor and Syria gradually reduced to the form of the Christian Mystery-Drama as aforesaid.

The volume is copiously "documented" throughout, the author's purpose being to give exact evidence for every step in the constructive theory.

To all who subscribe in advance (with remittance) the price of "Pagan Christs" will be 7s. 6d. carriage paid. After publication the price will be 8s. 6d. net, or including carriage 9s.

A specimen page of the work is attached, with a Subscription Form.

AGENTS OF THE RATIONALIST PRESS ASSOCIATION, LIMITED:
WATTS & CO., 17, JOHNSON'S COURT, FLEET STREET, LONDON, E.C.

[P.T.O.

Figure 5.1 Subscription form for Robertson's *Pagan Christs* from the 1903 *Literary Guide* (included in either the April or May issue)

their reverence for the Logos is not lessened but increased by the identification of the legend of His life and death with that of the Cosmos.[45]

Crowley again cites Frazer, Robertson, and colleagues in *The Gospel According to St. Bernard Shaw*, written at the same time as his "Golden Twigs" short stories:

[45] The Master Therion [Aleister Crowley], "The Revival of Magick, Part 1," *International* 11, no. 8 (August 1917): 248.

> Suppose that the whole story of the Crucifixion is not a record of fact, but the scenario of a sacred drama or ritual of initiation. Have we any grounds for making such an assumption? The reader must be referred to Dr. J. G. Frazer, Herbert Spencer, Grant Allen, and J. M. Robertson for the general analogy between the crucifixion story and those of Egypt, India, Mexico, Peru and a dozen other places. But Mr. Robertson argues the case specifically in this matter of "Unity of Time." He shows how absurd it is to suppose that the Procurator held his courts at midnight: all Eastern cities being still after sunset, except on certain festivals, for festival purposes of music and dancing. He shows how incident is crowded upon incident, without reason, all with the evident necessity of getting the drama confined to a given number of hours. It is impossible to quote his proof in detail, for it is as elaborate as it is cogent.[46]

Finally, Crowley again cites both Frazer and Robertson in *Magick in Theory and Practice* to support his assertion that the formula of IAO (exemplified by the Egyptian figures of Isis, Apophis, Osiris) "applies to those of Jesus Christ, and of many other mythical god-men worshipped in different countries."[47] Linking the central Christian drama to the pattern outlined by Frazer is an essential concept in Crowley's magical worldview.

Rounding out Crowley's origin-of-religions worldview is the literature on phallicism, which proliferated in the Victorian era into the early twentieth century. I have written elsewhere on how the Freud-like conclusion that all ancient religious symbols fundamentally represent the power of sexual reproduction and how this idea dominated Crowley's magical thought.[48] It turns out this literature was also popular among Secularists.

This literature emerged from a sincere desire to understand ancient religious imagery, whose eroticism was often at odds with Christianity's puritanical form in the West. Early examples include Richard Payne Knight's

[46] Aleister Crowley, *The Gospel According to St. Bernard Shaw* (Barstow, CA: Thelema, 1953), 214. This was originally intended to be published as part of the second issue of *The Equinox*, vol. 3. Although printed, Crowley could not raise the funds to pay for both the printing and the binding, and the sheets were eventually destroyed. See Richard Kaczynski, *Panic in Detroit*, rev. exp. Blue Equinox centennial ed. (n.p.: privately published, 2019). The text was posthumously published in 1953 and again reissued as Aleister Crowley, *Crowley on Christ*, ed. Francis King (London: C. W. Daniel, 1974).

[47] Crowley, *Magick in Theory*, 29.

[48] Richard Kaczynski, "Continuing Knowledge from Generation unto Generation: The Social and Literary Background of Aleister Crowley's Magick," in *Aleister Crowley and Western Esotericism*, ed. Henrik Bogdan and Martin P. Starr (New York: Oxford University Press, 2012), 141–180.

(1751–1824) work on the worship of Priapus, inspired by his collection of explicit Greek antiquities, and César Famin's (1799–1853) illustrated tome about the Museum of Naples's "secret cabinet" of erotic *objects d'art* unearthed at Pompeii.[49] Before long, other writers began to argue that these sexual symbols and rituals had been subsumed unwittingly into modern Christianity;[50] this idea was especially embraced by the Victorian anti-Catholic movement, also popular in British Protestant circles. For these authors, here was damning evidence that the idolatrous Catholic Church was perpetuating a damnable secret doctrine.[51] For the Secularist, this literature allowed the inspiration for religion to be shifted from a supreme being to the biological impulse to perpetuate the species. And if it caused readers to question the religious symbols of the dominant religions of the era, then so much the better. Thus, we find none other than G. W. Foote's Progressive Publishing Company releasing an edition of *Bible Studies: Essays on Phallic Worship and Other Curious Rites and Customs*, by fellow Freethinker Joseph Mazzini Wheeler.[52] Interest in these writers extended beyond the *Freethinker*, and included the *Literary Guide*.

A major voice of this school of thought was James George Roche Forlong (1824–1904), author of works such as *Rivers of Life* (1883) and *Short Studies in the Science of Comparative Religions* (1897).[53] He was an "old subscriber to, and staunch practical supporter of, the RPA"[54] as well as an Honorary Associate member. He was also a reader of the *Agnostic Journal*, having even contributed a letter on the study of non-Christian martyrdom.[55] When his

[49] Richard Payne Knight, *An Account of the Remains of the Worship of Priapus: Lately Existing at Isernia, in the Kingdom of Naples* (London: T. Spilsbury, 1786); Colonel Fanin [César Famin], *Peintures, bronzes et statues érotiques du cabinet secret du Musée Royale de Naples* (Paris: n.p., 1832).

[50] See, for example, Thomas Inman, *Ancient Pagan and Modern Christian Symbolism Exposed and Explained* (London: self-published, 1869).

[51] See, for example, Alexander Hislop, *The Two Babylons: Their Identity, and the Present Antichrist Also the Last* (Edinburgh: W. White, 1853). Hislop's second edition, published in 1858, was retitled *The Two Babylons: Or the Papal Worship Proved to be the Worship of Nimrod and His Wife*. See also Investigator Abhorrens, *Idolomania: Or, The Legalised Cross Not the Instrument of Crucifixion: Being an Inquiry into the Difference between the Cross Proper and the Symbol of Heathen Processions* (London: E. Wilson, 1858).

[52] Joseph Mazzini Wheeler, *Bible Studies. Essays on Phallic Worship and Other Curious Rites and Customs*, with a preface by G. W. Foote (London: Progressive Publishing, 1892). Thanks to William Breeze for pointing out this edition.

[53] J. G. R. Forlong, *Rivers of Life, or Sources and Streams of the Faiths of Man in All Lands; Showing the Evolution of Faiths, from the Rudest Symbolisms to the Latest Spiritual Developments. With Maps, Illustrations, and Separate Chart of Faith Streams* (London: n.p., 1883); J. G. R. Forlong, *Short Studies in the Science of Comparative Religions: Embracing All the Religions of Asia* (London: B. Quaritch, 1897).

[54] "Random Jottings," *Literary Guide and Rationalist Review* 95 (May 1, 1904): 72.

[55] (Major General) J. G. R. Forlong, "Non-Christian Martyrdom," *Agnostic Journal* 52, no. 8 (February 21, 1903): 127.

FAITHS OF MAN: A Cyclopædia of Religions. By the late Major-General J. G. R. FORLONG, F.R.A.S., F.R.S.E., &c. 3 Vols. Rl. Octavo. Quaritch, 1906. £5 5s.

"A noble effort to meet a want that is being felt day by day with increasing urgency.......In this object he has admirably succeeded. But he has left us also a monument of a charming personality......the pioneer movement in a department of scientific inquiry that is of the first importance to mankind."—Dr. T. W. Rhys Davids.—*Journal of Royal Asiatic Socy.*

"There are about three thousand articles in these three volumes....... The book is not only erudite, but thoroughly modern, and is simply indispensable for a comprehensive knowledge of religions. The author was no ordinary man......in writing this book he has reared a fitting memorial to a most genial, sincere, and inspiring personality."—Rev. Dr. J. Glasse.—*Review of Theology and Philosophy.*

"It is almost an unique circumstance that one man should have possessed the ability, the time, the money, and the inclination necessary to carry out such labour; and the volumes now published will form a standard source of information for the increasing circle of those who are interested in the comparative study of human beliefs......the reader of this Cyclopædia cannot fail to recognise that the author was a man of truly religious nature, of fine tolerance, and of earnest desire to learn and maintain truth."—*Blackwood's Magazine*, April, 1906.

"The book is clearly of an erudition immensely wide.......conveniently arranged for purposes of reference of facts, and points of recondite learning, concerning religion in general, and Oriental religions in particular."—*Scotsman*, May 5th, 1906.

"It is altogether a remarkable book, and will be found extremely useful by all students of religion.......This book is the crowning glory of a most industrious, strenuous, and devoted life."—*Dundee Advertiser*, April 12th, 1906.

Figure 5.2 Advertisement in the *Literary Guide* for *Faiths of Man* (1907) by J. G. R. Forlong, whom Crowley would declare a Gnostic Saint

encyclopedic three-volume *Faiths of Man* was released posthumously in 1907, the *Literary Guide* advertised it prominently (see figure 5.2).[56]

Other books dealing with phallism covered by the *Literary Guide* include J. B. Hannay's *Christianity: The Sources of Its Teaching and Symbolism* (1912),[57] Dupuis's *Natural Religion* with its "astronomical theory of religious

[56] Advertisement in *Literary Guide and Rationalist Review* 127 (January 1, 1907): 15.

[57] "The Lingam Cult," *Literary Guide and Rationalist Review* 205 (July 1, 1913): 111; James B. Hannay, *Symbolism in Relation to Religion, or Christianity: The Sources of Its Teaching and Symbolism* (London: Kegan Paul, Trench, Trübner, 1912).

creed,"[58] and the late-life works of poet Gerald Massey (1828–1907), a "militant Freethinker . . . [who] spent half of an unusually long life in showing the mythical nature of the Christian religion."[59] His late-life works *A Book of the Beginnings* (1881), *The Natural Genesis* (1883), and *Ancient Egypt the Light of the World* (1907)[60]—each title sprawling over two volumes—caused consternation among Rationalists for their focus on Egyptology and occultism—similar to the reaction to Crowley's spiritual path. While one reviewer lamented the author's "misdirected efforts,"[61] others read these works more sympathetically.[62]

Crowley and company were familiar with both Forlong and Massey. In a book review in the September 1910 *Equinox*, Fuller wrote that Churchward's *Signs and Symbols of Primordial Man* "is in every sense a great book, and, by the way, it forms an excellent seventh volume to Gerald Massey's monumental work."[63] In his *Gospel According to St. Bernard Shaw*, Crowley quipped, "It is indeed a triumph for Solar-Phallic worship to add to the names of General Forlong, Sir Richard Burton, Sir R. Payne Knight, Messrs. Hargrave Jennings, Godfrey Higgins, Gerald Massey and Theodor Reuss the name of Bernard Shaw!"[64] Crowley similarly wrote in *Magick in Theory and Practice* about solar-phallism that "the subject is too abstruse and complicated to be discussed in detail here. The student should consult the writings of Sir R. Payne Knight, General Forlong, Gerald Massey, Fabre d'Olivet; etc. etc., for the data on which these considerations are ultimately based."[65]

[58] "The Sun-Christ," *Literary Guide and Rationalist Review* 156 (June 1, 1909): 95; F. J. B. [from Charles Francois Dupuis], *Natural Religion; Or, the Secret of All the Creeds* (London: Pioneer Press, 1908).

[59] Mimnermus, "Book Chat: An Appreciation of Gerald Massey," *Literary Guide and Rationalist Review* 138 (December 1, 1907): 187–188.

[60] Gerald Massey, *A Book of the Beginnings: Containing an Attempt to Recover and Reconstitute the Lost Origines of the Myths and Mysteries, Types and Symbols, Religion and Language, with Egypt for the Mouthpiece and Africa as the Birthplace* (London: Williams and Norgate, 1881); Gerald Massey, *The Natural Genesis, Or, Second Part of a Book of the Beginnings, Containing an Attempt to Recover and Reconstitute the Lost Origins of the Myths and Mysteries, Types and Symbols, Religion and Language, with Egypt from the Mouthpiece and Africa As the Birthplace* (London: Williams and Norgate, 1883); Gerald Massey, *Ancient Egypt: The Light of the World; a Work of Reclamation and Restitution* (London: T. Fisher Unwin, 1907).

[61] "Egypt and Christian Origins," *Literary Guide and Rationalist Review* 140 (February 1, 1908): 21–22.

[62] George St. Clair, "Gerald Massey's Last Book," *Literary Guide and Rationalist Review* 141 (March 1, 1908): 43. See also "Random Jottings," *Literary Guide and Rationalist Review* 144 (June 1, 1908): 88.

[63] Page 341 in J. F. C. Fuller, "The Big Stick," *The Equinox* 1, no. 4 (September 1910): 341; Albert Churchward, *The Signs and Symbols of Primordial Man: Being an Explanation of the Evolution of Religious Doctrines from the Eschatology of the Ancient Egyptians* (London: Sonnenschein, 1910).

[64] Crowley, *Gospel*, 193.

[65] Crowley, *Magick in Theory*, 193.

Crowley, however, was a bigger fan of Forlong, not only claiming him as a member of "the constituent originating assemblies of the O.T.O."[66]—Ordo Templi Orientis, the quasi-masonic occult organization of which Crowley would later become British and, even later, international head—but also canonizing him as a saint in the Gnostic Mass.

Saints and Other Gnostics

Forlong is but one writer with the dual distinction of being a Gnostic saint, and frequently appearing in the *Literary Guide*. The *Guide* also lauded German philosopher Friedrich Nietzsche (1844–1900) as a "fantastic genius,"[67] an "original and forceful spirit,"[68] "the most interesting philosophic writer since Schopenhauer," and "the most iconoclastic of philosophers. He is the unmasker of current ideals, he is the mocker of existing moral standards, he is the breaker of the most cherished images."[69] Even more floridly, he was described as "the last bar in the great revolutionary music which has lasted since the days of Dante and Boccaccio."[70] Mentions of Nietzsche in the *Literary Guide* are far too numerous to catalog here.

He was also the subject of Crowley's essay "The Vindication of Nietzsche."[71] Crowley not only canonized him as a Gnostic saint but

[66] L. Bathurst, "Liber LII: Manifesto of the O.T.O.," *The Equinox* 3, no. 2 (1919): 195–206. If Crowley preferred Forlong, his student and one-time secretary Kenneth Grant (1924–2011) drew heavily from Massey's works in his nine-volume *Typhonian Trilogies* (1972–2002), in which Grant expounds his reinvented vision of Thelema. See Christian Giudice, "Gerald Massey's Influence on Kenneth Grant's Idea of the Typhonian Tradition," in *The Servants of the Star & the Snake: Essays in Honour of Kenneth and Steffi Grant*, ed. Henrik Bogdan (London: Starfire, 2018), 63–74; and Manon Hedenborg White, *The Eloquent Blood: The Goddess Babalon and the Construction of Femininities in Western Esotericism* (New York: Oxford University Press, 2020), 162–163.

[67] "Nietzsche Again," *Literary Guide and Rationalist Review* 75 (September 1, 1902): 141.

[68] "Superman," *Literary Guide and Rationalist Review* 124 (October 1, 1906): 150–151.

[69] Mimnermus, "Book Chat: Fitzgerald—Nietzsche—Etc.," *Literary Guide and Rationalist Review* 156 (June 1, 1909): 93.

[70] "The Spirit of Nietzsche," *Literary Guide and Rationalist Review* 137 (November 1, 1907): 165–166. For some of the multitudinous mentions of Nietzsche, see, for example, "The Ethics of Nietzsche," *Literary Guide and Rationalist Review* 143 (May 1, 1908): 76; "The Awakener," *Literary Guide and Rationalist Review* 146 (August 1, 1908): 117–118; "The Will To Power," *Literary Guide and Rationalist Review* 147 (September 1, 1908): 140; "Nietzsche for the Multitude," *Literary Guide and Rationalist Review* 148 (October 1, 1908): 150; "Nietzsche," *Literary Guide and Rationalist Review* 150 (December 1, 1908): 188; "Nietzsche as Moralist," *Literary Guide and Rationalist Review* 152 (February 1, 1909): 29; "The Author of Zarathustra," *Literary Guide and Rationalist Review* 152 (February 1, 1909): 31; "Random Jottings," *Literary Guide and Rationalist Review* 156 (June 1, 1909): 88.

[71] This essay, dating from the start of the Great War, was intended for Crowley's collection *The Giant's Thumb*, which never moved past proof stage owing to a fire at the printer's. It remained

elevated him even further, declaring, "Nietzsche may be regarded as one of our prophets."[72]

French satirist Francois Rabelais (1494?–1553) is another prophet-saint of Thelema lauded in the pages of the *Literary Guide*.[73] His classic pentalogy *The Life of Gargantua and Pantagruel* (*c.* 1532–1564) describes the Abbey of Thélème, which was governed by a sole law: "Do what thou wilt." While the Law of Thelema of *The Book of the Law* differed from that of Rabelais, there was sufficient resonance to recognize him as a saint in the Gnostic Mass, for Crowley to dub his commune in Cefalù "the Abbey of Thelema," and to acknowledge Rabelais as a significant precursor in the essay "Antecedents of Thelema" (1926).[74]

Not a Gnostic saint but nevertheless a prominent writer on Gnosticism, George Robert Stow Mead (1863–1933) also deserves mention here. His scholarly writings were frequently reviewed by the *Literary Guide*, which is notable given his association with H. P. Blavatsky and the Theosophical Society.[75] Since Crowley admired Blavatsky but disdained most other theosophists, *The Equinox* subjected Mead to some ribbing in its book review pages.[76] Nevertheless, when mentioning "the Papyrus of Bruce" in *The Sword of Song*,

unpublished until it was released as a separate essay in 1979 by England's Morton Press. *The Giant's Thumb* page proofs were eventually published as a facsimile edition in 1992 by J. D. Holmes.

[72] Crowley, *Magick without Tears*, 217.

[73] "Book Chat," *Literary Guide and Rationalist Review* 145 (July 1, 1908): 107.

[74] Although unfinished and unpublished in Crowley's lifetime, it has been published posthumously. See, for example, Aleister Crowley, *The Revival of Magick and Other Essays*, Oriflamme 2, ed. Hymenaeus Beta and Richard Kaczynski (Tempe, AZ: New Falcon in association with Ordo Templi Orientis International, 1998), 162–169.

[75] "Though there is nothing specially original in his work, his review will be of use." "A Theosophist's View of Biblical Criticism," *Literary Guide and Rationalist Review* 72 (June 1, 1902): 93. The *Literary Guide* later wrote, "We value his scholarship, but we cannot pretend to admire the very obscure reflections which Mr. Mead devotes to the Religion of Mind." "A Gnostic Primer," *Literary Guide and Rationalist Review* 129 (March 1, 1907): 45. See also "Hermes Trismegistus," *Literary Guide and Rationalist Review* 127 (January 1, 1907): 6–7; "Mr. Mead's Scholarship," *Literary Guide and Rationalist Review* 174 (September 1, 1908): 140.

[76] When the scholarly esoteric journal *The Quest* launched in 1909 with Mead as its editor, *The Equinox* reviewed it, writing, "We note, however, with satisfaction that one of the contributors, a Mr. G. R. S. Mead, is a B.A. This sort of boasting is perfectly legitimate." "Reviews," *The Equinox* 1, no. 2 (September 1909): 390. In the next issue, Crowley followed up with the following: "We beg to apologise for having referred in our last number to G. R. S. Mead, Esquire, B.A., M.R.A.S., as Mr. G. R. S. Mead, B.A. B.A. (Baccalaureus Artium) is indeed the proud distinction awarded to our brightest and best intellects. M.R.A.S. does not mean Mr. Ass; but is a mark of merit so high that dizzy imagination swoons at its contemplation. We grovel." "Reviews," *The Equinox* 1, no. 3 (March 2, 1910): 326. Considering that Mead's work—scholarly but not academic—holds up well against his contemporaries' work, these remarks are unkind, particularly considering Crowley left Cambridge without completing his BA.

> Crowley refers to the *Codex Brucianus*, Bruce MS 96 in Oxford's Bodleian Library. As this Gnostic text was unavailable in English at the time, Crowley may be echoing references to it in G. R. S. Mead, *Fragments of a Faith Forgotten: Some Short Sketches among the Gnostics Mainly of the First Two Centuries. A Contribution to the Study of Christian Origins, Based on the Most Recently Recovered Materials* (London and Benares: Theosophical Publishing Society, 1900).[77]

Also, when writing about "energized enthusiasm" in *Magick in Theory and Practice*, Crowley refers readers to Mead, writing, "The earliest and truest Christians used what is in all essentials this method. See *Fragments of a Faith Forgotten* by G. R. S. Mead, Esq. B. A., pp. 80–81."[78]

A Familiar Voice

Crowley peppers his vocabulary with terminology popular in Secularist circles, including *superstition*, *freedom*, *slave*, and *infidel*.[79] The similarities are even more striking with certain Secularist-friendly organizations. Take, for instance, the Theistic Church in Piccadilly, which advertised, "Religion without superstition and strictly reasonable, being based on facts, is taught by the Theistic Church."[80] This sounds very similar to Crowley's assertion that Gnostic Mass could be "endorsed by the most materialistic man of science."[81] The founder of the Theistic Church, Charles Vosey (1828–1912), was a priest who, after being condemned for heterodoxy, split from the Church of England and formed his own church based on Freethought and pure theism. In 1903, Vosey befriended anarchist, communist, and Bakunin Press founder

[77] Aleister Crowley, *The Sword of Song: Called by Christians the Book of the Beast*, ed. Richard Kaczynski (London: Kamuret Press, 2021).

[78] Crowley, *Magick in Theory*, 131. In the section being referenced, Mead deals with "Sacred Dancing" abetted by singing hymns and drinking "nectar."

[79] See, for example, Thomas Hayes, "The Word 'Infidel,'" *Literary Guide and Rationalist Review* 108 (June 1, 1905): 94.

[80] Classified advertisement, *Literary Guide and Rationalist Review* 91 (January 1, 1904): 14. Another classified ad in the *Literary Guide* read, "Persons seeking a reasonable religion free from superstition, and based on the facts of the higher nature of man, are invited to apply for Literature (sent gratis and post free)." Classified advertisement, *Literary Guide and Rationalist Review* 90 (December 1, 1903): 191. In fairness, the Theistic Church advertised widely, including in the *Times*.

[81] Crowley, *Confessions*, 714. For the full quote, see the section "The Method of Science" in this chapter.

Guy Aldred. Aldred described Vosey's faith as "anti-Christian theism" in that "Christianity was an organized Atheism, an expression of man's disbelief in God the Father. He denied Christ to elevate God."[82]

The echoes of other rationalists are even greater in Crowley's encounter with Freemasonry—and his subsequent embrace of what Ellic Howe has dubbed "fringe masonry."[83] While living in Paris, Crowley took his three Craft degree initiations at Anglo-Saxon Lodge No. 343, an English-speaking lodge popular among expats, in the fall of 1904.[84] The Grand Orient of France did not require its Masons to profess belief in a supreme being; such belief, however, was one of the nonnegotiable "landmarks" of Freemasonry, with the result that French Masons were not recognized by the United Grand Lodge of England. Crowley was apparently unaware of this distinction. Thus, when he moved back to London and attempted to attend lodge, he was surprised and more than a little disgruntled to be refused entry. As a reader of the *Literary Guide*, Crowley would undoubtedly have noticed periodic discussions of whether Freemasonry was compatible with Rationalism.[85] One correspondent, writing in the May 1, 1906, issue, related a notable experience as a Rationalist candidate:

> A friend asked me to join his lodge. I consented, mentioning that I was an Agnostic, which he said was no obstacle. I attended to be initiated, and, following certain fantastic preliminaries, I was ushered blindfolded to the hall where the lodge was sitting. After a question as to age I was asked: "In all cases of difficulty and danger in whom do you put your trust?" A friendly bystander prompted me to answer: "In God." I declined, and asked them to define what they meant by "God." This seemed to cause some dismay, and I was requested to retire. Subsequently I was told that I could not be admitted.[86]

[82] Guy A. Aldred, *From Anglican Boy-Preacher to Anarchist Socialist Impossibilist* (London: Bakunin Press, 1908), 26–27.

[83] Ellic Howe, "Fringe Masonry in England 1870–85," *Ars Quatuor Coronatorum* 85 (1972): 242–280.

[84] Martin Starr, "Aleister Crowley: Freemason!," *Ars Quatuor Coronatorum* 108 (1995): 150–161.

[85] One correspondence included the following issues of the *Literary Guide*: *Literary Guide and Rationalist Review* 117 (March 1, 1906): 46; *Literary Guide and Rationalist Review* 118 (April 1, 1906): 62; *Literary Guide and Rationalist Review* 119 (May 1, 1906): 78. A later letter was published as W. Oppenheim, "Freemasonry and Oath-Taking," *Literary Guide and Rationalist Review* 171 (September 1, 1910): 144.

[86] J. H. Munday, "Freemasonry and Rationalism," *Literary Guide and Rationalist Review* 119 (May 1, 1906): 78.

Crowley could hardly have missed adding this anecdote to his own experience in the "atheistic" French lodge.

Even more remarkable is the following letter, dated to within six months of OTO being chartered in the UK with Crowley as its Grand Master:

> London, December 4, 1912.
>
> One of the most potent forces in political and social reform has always been the "secret" or "semi-secret" society. I need only refer to Jesuits and the Vehm-Gericht. Unfortunately, these societies have generally been on the side of reaction; it has even occurred that revolutionary bodies have stagnated and become the engines of oppression. A most striking example of this is to be found in Freemasonry.
>
> It was Freemasonry that destroyed the Bourbons at the end of the eighteenth century, and the temporal power of the Church in France at the end of the nineteenth; and it is Freemasonry which to-day defends France against all those forces which ambitious intrigue can bring about.
>
> In England, however, the Grand Lodge broke off relations with the Grand Orient of France some forty years ago, and the English Freemason is to-day one of the strongest supporters of dogmatic religion. This attitude has resulted in an intense bigotry and intolerance. Freemasonry was supposed to be an "Universal Brotherhood"; but the English Grand Lodge now refuses to tolerate the vast majority of other Freemasons; it has even broken off relations with those bodies which maintain its own dogmas.
>
> The general idea appears to be that anyone living outside England is "a dirty foreigner"—certainly immoral, and very probably an atheist. It has consequently become impossible for anyone of advanced or even liberal views to belong to the body; this although Charles Bradlaugh was a Freemason!
>
> It is a very great pity that this should be so, for the system of Freemasonry—I speak here only of the three Craft Grades—is a most admirably solemn and picturesque dramatic representation of the mysteries of birth, life, and death; it, moreover, enshrines a school of ethics and of manners which merits all possible praise; and this is specially useful at the present moment, when the tendency to be casual and slipshod is so strongly marked.
>
> Those Freemasons who hold these views have consequently obtained warrants from the highest authorities to establish a new body. The rituals have been purged of the crude theological conception which satisfied

> commonplace minds in an age when Huxley was still unborn; and I wish to call the attention of advanced thinkers to this movement, believing that their adhesion will help towards the organisation of those forces which are opposed to dogma. This movement is in sympathy with all the leading bodies of Freemasons on the Continent, and with two of the principal rites in America. Women as well as men are admitted. Readers of the *Literary Guide* who wish further information should apply to me at 93 Chancery Lane, W.C.
>
> Arundel Del Ré.[87]

The similarity to OTO in those last two paragraphs is head-spinning. Unsurprisingly, much as we find a link to the Theistic Church via Guy Aldred, there is also a connection to Aleister Crowley here.

Arundel del Re (1892–1974) was a "romantic Irish-Italian,"[88] standing just under six feet tall with auburn hair, with gray eyes and a fair complexion.[89] Hibberd has described him evocatively as "tall and slim, with dark hair cut long by English standards and a face more pale and dreamy than seemed usual for an Italian."[90] His exuberant exploration of the world around his Florence birthplace brought him into contact with a range of English poets, authors, artists, art critics, philosophers, socialists, and free thinkers who made annual sojourns to Florence for work or pleasure.[91] Among these, in November 1910—when del Re was around age eighteen—was poet Harold Monro (1879–1932), who took him on as a protégé. After their first meeting, as del Re recalled,

> I saw Monro almost every day. He became quite naturally and without any intention on his part, my teacher. . . . His friendship was a liberal education in the truest sense of that much abused term, for the privilege of which I can never be sufficiently grateful. Strange as it might seem Monro did not fill me with any ambition to become a poet, probably because of the very high standard he always kept before me, but rather with that of learning to interpret and criticize it.[92]

[87] Arundel del Ré, "Freemasonry," *Literary Guide and Rationalist Review* 199 (January 1, 1913): 16.
[88] Dominic Hibberd, *Harold Monro: Poet of the New Age* (New York: Palgrave, 2001), 3.
[89] Passenger lists of vessels arriving at New York, New York, 1897–1957, microfilm, T715, Records of the Immigration and Naturalization Service, National Archives, Washington, DC.
[90] Hibberd, *Harold Monro*, 81.
[91] Arundel del Re, "Georgian Reminiscences: I," *Studies in English Literature* 12, no. 2 (1932): 322–331.
[92] Del Re, "Georgian Reminiscences: I," 326.

Hibberd calls Monro's book of poems *Before Dawn* (1911) a manifesto for a time "when men and women would be true to the earth and would shape their own destinies, free from the shackles of religion, sexual taboos, respectability, and conformism."[93] Determined to breathe life into this vision, Monro returned to London in September 1911 with del Re "as his chosen helper."[94] The protégé was also slated to be assistant editor and reviewer for Monro's newly founded journal, *The Poetry Review*.[95] As del Re recalled those short, hectic months prior to the first issue appearing in January 1912,

> My own part in all this turmoil was a very modest one, consisting chiefly in sending out prospectuses, addressing envelopes, typing letters to likely contributors and subscribers and touting for advertisements. . . . From nine-thirty in the morning until five or six in the evening, I sat in our offices on the top floor of 93 Chancery Lane.[96]

Monro's efforts to reinvigorate modern poetry didn't stop there. His *Georgian Poetry* anthologies (1912–1922), with their "truly phenomenal sales,"[97] promoted and defined the "New Poetry" school that emerged during the reign of King George V;[98] in 1913, he opened the Poetry Bookshop in Bloomsbury.

The *Poetry Review* was the connective tissue to Crowley. How is unknown, but the editorial address at 93 Chancery Lane seems an evocation, 93 being the numerical values of the Greek words *thelema* (will) and *agape* (love) in Crowley's magical system, and a different Chancery Lane—the one in Cambridge—being the location of Crowley's rooms while attending Trinity College a dozen years before. As del Re noted, "After the review came to be known the office had frequent visitors."[99] Whether Crowley was one of those

[93] Dominic Hibberd, "The New Poetry, Georgians and Others: *The Open Window* (1910–11), *The Poetry Review* (1912–15), *Poetry and Drama* (1913–14), and *New Numbers* (1914)," in *The Oxford Critical and Cultural History of Modernist Magazines*, vol. 1: *Britain and Ireland, 1880–1955*, ed. Peter Brooker and Andrew Thacker (Oxford: Oxford University Press, 2013), 177.

[94] Del Re, "Georgian Reminiscences: I," 331.

[95] For a detailed account of the *Poetry Review* and its successor, *Poetry and Drama*, see Hibberd, "New Poetry."

[96] Arundel del Re, "Georgian Reminiscences: III," *Studies in English Literature* 14, no. 1 (1934): 30.

[97] Arundel del Re, "Georgian Reminiscences: II," *Studies in English Literature* 12, no. 3 (1932): 465.

[98] Published by Harold Monro and edited by Edward Marsh, five volumes were published between 1912–1922, covering the years 1911–1912, 1913–1915, 1916–1917, 1918–1919, and 1920–1922. According to del Re, the Georgians freed modern poetry "from the dead hand of tradition, to make it accessible to a wider public and to train the latter to pay some attention to poetry and to distinguish between genuine inspiration and mere album-verse." Del Re, "Georgian Reminiscences: I," 329.

[99] Del Re, "Georgian Reminiscences: III," 31.

visitors, or del Re had reached out to him as a potential advertiser, or Crowley and Monro had overlapping literary circles, in the end Crowley's works appeared in the *Poetry Review*: his *High History of Good Sir Palamedes*[100] and the September 1912 issue of *The Equinox* (number eight) were reviewed by Monro in the September 1912 *Poetry Review*.[101] Reciprocally, one presumes, the same September 1912 issue of *The Equinox* carried an advertisement for the *Poetry Review*. Crowley's poem "Villon's Apology" subsequently appeared in the next quarterly issue of the *Poetry Review*.[102] In 1913, Monro launched *Poetry and Drama* as a quarterly successor to the *Poetry Review*. In the second issue, del Re—who had gained notice for his critique of Ezra Pound[103]—reviewed Crowley's *Book of Lies*.[104]

Each copy of *Poetry and Drama* came with a ticket for free admission to hear Monro, with his "soft yet clear, musical voice,"[105] deliver twice-weekly poetry readings at the Poetry Bookshop. Monro's assertion that the modern poet "had a duty to give expression to the ideas and feelings of the new age that was dawning, 'an age in which man must finally cast off worn-out beliefs and meaningless traditions and begin to live life more joyously and rationally,'"[106] comported with Aleister Crowley's idea of a New Aeon. Thus, it's no surprise that poetry recitations at the bookstore included work by Crowley on at least two occasions in its inaugural year: February 12 and November 14, 1913.[107] In addition, Monro once "alarmed one Georgian supper party by introducing Aleister Crowley, who was a poet as well as a notorious satanist but not the sort of man that the others knew or wanted to know."[108] As Edward Marsh, who attended this supper party recalled, "We quaked and cowered like Tweedledum and Tweedledee under the shadow of the

[100] Aleister Crowley, *The High History of Good Sir Palamedes, the Saracen Knight and of His Following of the Questing Beast* (London: Wieland, 1912). *High History of Good Sir Palamedes* was reprinted as a separate volume from its first appearance as a special supplement to *The Equinox* 1, no. 4 (September 1910).

[101] Harold Monro, "Review of The High History of Good Sir Palamedes, by Aleister Crowley, and *The Equinox*: March, 1912," *Poetry Review* 1, no. 9 (September 1912): 436–439. The *Poetry Review* (later renamed *Poetry and Drama*) also advertised in *The Equinox*.

[102] Aleister Crowley, "Villon's Apology (on Reading Stevenson's Essay)," *Poetry Review* 1, no. 12 (December 1912): 540. This poem appears to be a reaction to Robert Louis Stevenson, "François Villon: Student, Poet, and Housebreaker," *Cornhill* 36, no. 212 (1877): 215–234.

[103] Eric Homberger, "A Glimpse of Pound in 1912 by Arundel del Re," *Paideuma: Modern and Contemporary Poetry and Poetics* 3, no. 1 (1974): 85–88.

[104] Arundel del Re, "Reviews," *Poetry and Drama* 1, no. 2 (June 2, 1913): 253.

[105] Del Re, "Georgian Reminiscences: I," 324.

[106] Joy Grant, *Harold Monro & the Poetry Bookshop* (Berkeley: University of California Press, 1967), 25.

[107] Hibberd, *Harold Monro*, 123, 135.

[108] Hibberd, *Harold Monro*, 107.

Monstrous Crow. It was the Satanist Alistair [*sic*] Crowley; and for once in my life I felt I had been in the presence of Evil with a capital E."[109]

Arundel del Re's reminiscences of the Georgian period contain but one reference to Crowley. He recalls Epstein's controversial sculpture for Oscar Wilde's grave at Père Lachaise:

> It so outraged the bourgeois morality of the French public that it was hidden for some time under a vast tarpaulin. Finally a compromise was reached and a huge bronze fig-leaf was screwed over the offending parts until it was surreptitiously removed by Aleister Crowley who turned up one night at the Café Royal in London with it hanging by a piece of red ribbon like an apron round his neck—a gesture which must have tickled Wilde's sense of humour could he have but known of it.[110]

And yet this passing mention belies a deeper connection between them. A surviving dues statement indicates that del Re progressed to the IV° in the early days of M.·.M.·.M.·. (Mysteria Mystica Maxima, Crowley's British branch of O.T.O.), which he must have joined around this time, when he was in his early twenties (see figure 5.3).[111]

Del Re obtained a scholarship to the University of London, earning his bachelor's degree in 1917 and his master's in 1921 in medieval and modern languages.[112] He would go on to a distinguished academic career, teaching at Oxford University, the University of Tokyo, Nanzan Catholic University, and Victoria University. After World War II, he worked with the Asiatic Society,[113] was an advisor to the Education Division of Civil Information and Education in Japan,[114] and also participated in the Tokyo Amateur Dramatic Club, with which he appeared in productions of *The Play's the Thing*, *The Madwoman of Chaillot*, and *The Glass Menagerie*.[115] He later lived in New Zealand but

109 Edward Marsh, *A Number of People* (London: William Heinmann, 1939), 367.

110 Del Re, "Georgian Reminiscences: II," 468.

111 Aleister Crowley papers, collection identifier 02310, Pennsylvania State University Libraries Archival Collections, University Park, PA. The United Grand Lodge of England has no record of del Re in their membership records, which indicates that he apparently initiated through these OTO grades rather than "affiliating" to his equivalent degree in Freemasonry.

112 University of London, *The Historical Record (1836–1926)* (London: University of London Press, 1926), 150, 281.

113 "Sir Alvary Gascoigne Asiatic Society Head," *Pacific Stars and Stripes*, January 14, 1948, 4.

114 Esther Crane, "Old Japan Hands," *Pacific Stars and Stripes*, February 22, 1948, 6.

115 "Stillwell Slates Molner Comedy," *Pacific Stars and Stripes*, June 9, 1949, 2; "Shaw Elected Dramatic Prexy," *Pacific Stars and Stripes*, June 23, 1949, 2; Esther Crane, "Audience Impressed with

O.T.O.

M∴ M∴ M∴

(Cheques to be made payable to
G. M. COWIE,
14 Glenisla Gardens, Edinburgh.)

33 AVENUE STUDIOS, (76 Fulham Road,)
SOUTH KENSINGTON, S.W.
Tel: 2652 Kensington.

The Grand Treasurer General begs to remind

Bro∴ Del Re

that the following dues are now immediately payable:

	Fee. (payable before taking degree.)	Annual Subscription (Payable March 1st.) (If a Br. in good standing takes a new degree he pays with his fee £1 1s. (P.R.S. £3 3s.) for extra subscription.)
Minerval	£1 1 0	
I°	1 1 0	£1 1 0
II°	1 1 0	2 2 0
III°	1 1 0	3 3 0
L. of P.	1 1 0	—
IV°	2 2 0	× 4 4 0
C.P.I.	1 1 0	—
L.K.E.W.	1 1 0	—
V°	3 3 0	5 5 0
Senate	2 2 0	—
VI°	5 5 0	6 6 0
G.I.C.	5 5 0	7 7 0
P.R.S.	5 5 0	8 8 0
Arrears £12.12 VII°	10 10 0	11 11 0

Total £16"6"0 Received with thanks,

Grand Treasurer General.

Figure 5.3 M∴M∴M∴/O.T.O. dues notice for Arundel del Re. (Aleister Crowley papers, collection #2310, Special Collections Library, Pennsylvania State University; used by permission of Ordo Templi Orientis.)

moved to Australia around 1968 (around age seventy-six), where he died, in Victoria, in 1974.[116]

'Madwoman,'" *Pacific Stars and Stripes*, October 26, 1949, 2; "Nagoya Show Set," *Pacific Stars and Stripes*, October 29, 1952, 7.

[116] Arundel del Re appears in the Australian electoral rolls in 1968; his death is recorded in the Victoria, Australia, death index, 1836–1988, Victorian Registry of Births, Deaths, and Marriages, Melbourne, Australia.

6
CROWLEY VERSUS THE RATIONALIST PRESS ASSOCIATION

Having panned *The Star in the West* six months earlier, the *Literary Guide* damned *Konx Om Pax* with faint praise.

> Frankly speaking, we do not know what to make of Mr. Crowley. We feel that ordinary rules of criticism are inapplicable to a writer of so marked an individuality. Mr. Crowley submits to conventions, and laughs consistency to scorn. Fleshly and spiritual by turns, he deifies that which the Philistine abominates, and mocks at the objects of the common adoration. He is a grovelling decadent, yet a lofty idealist. He revels in unclean innuendoes, and sings like a lark at the gates of heaven. In his latest work insight and wit go side by side with savage grossness that revolts and a triviality that is tedious. *Konx Om Pax* is the apotheosis of extravagance, the last word in eccentricity. A prettily-told fairy-story "for babes and sucklings" had "explanatory notes in Hebrew and Latin for the wise and prudent"—which notes, as far as we can see, explain nothing—together with a weird preface in scraps of twelve or fifteen languages. A clever piece of fooling called *Ali Sloper; or, The Forty Liars*, is sadly vulgarised by a sort of play-bill, which has neither wit, sense, nor relevancy. The best poetry in the book is contained in the third section—*The Stone of the Philosophers*. Here is some fine work, but so mingled with prurience and puerility as to dash our admiration. Altogether, Mr. Crowley has produced a singular volume, attesting alike his poetic genius and his lack of sober judgement.[1]

[1] "A Wandering Star," *Literary Guide and Rationalist Review* 143 (May 1, 1908): 76–77. Note that P. R. Stephensen, in *The Legend of Aleister Crowley*, attributes the following review, which does not match the quote from the "Wandering Star" review, to the *Literary Guide*: "Verbal fireworks. A wild and wasteful heterogeneous collection of weird words . . . Still, one cannot but admire the author's oftimes skilful jugglery with words and his kaleidoscopically changing humour, even though one deplores his prodigality." P. R. Stephensen, *The Legend of Aleister Crowley: Being a Study of the Documentary Evidence Relating to a Campaign of Personal Vilification Unparalleled in Literary History* (London: Mandrake Press, 1930), 68.

Friendship in Doubt. Richard Kaczynski, Oxford University Press. © Oxford University Press 2024.
DOI: 10.1093/oso/9780197694008.003.0006

The once-amicable relationship between Crowley and the RPA was disintegrating. Hints of this falling out appear in P. R. Stephensen's account of the critical reception of Crowley's works, *The Legend of Aleister Crowley*. In this book, Stephensen remarks that *Why Jesus Wept* "was too much even for the supposedly 'emancipated' *Literary Guide*," and when it came to *Konx Om Pax*, "the *Literary Guide*, beginning, no doubt, to be more afraid of Crowley than of the legitimate antagonists of the Rationalist Press Association, spoke under a strange reserve."[2] One wonders to what degree he was echoing the sentiments of Crowley, whose works Stephensen had contracted to publish through his Mandrake Press. However, it is fair to say that Crowley's shift from Agnosticism to occultism went somewhere the *Literary Guide* could not follow.

This mutual repudiation unfolded for all to see in the pages of both the *Literary Guide* and Crowley's new semi-annual literary and occult journal, *The Equinox* (see figure 6.1). As he did previously with G. K. Chesterton, so did Crowley—and, by proxy, J. F. C. Fuller—ratchet up the broadsides against the entire Agnostic movement. *The Equinox*'s premiere issue (March 1909) contained the first installment of "The Temple of Solomon the King," a serialized magical biography of Crowley compiled by Fuller, which in subsequent issues would draw heavily from Crowley's diaries and reproduce many of the Golden Dawn's initiation ceremonies and instructional papers. Part one was a florid preamble to the series, all in Fuller's words. Consisting of several sections that included such subtitles as "The Bankrupt, or the Atheist," "The Prude, or the Rationalist," and "The Wanton, or the Sceptic,"[3] Fuller pulled no punches in describing Crowley's personal evolution.

> For ten years he had been a sceptic, in that sense of the word which is generally conveyed by the terms infidel, atheist, and freethinker; then suddenly, in a single moment, he withdrew all the scepticism with which he had assailed religion, and hurled it against freethought itself; and as the former had crumbled into dust, so now the latter vanished in smoke.
>
> In this crisis there was no sickness of soul, no division of self; for he simply had turned a corner on the road along which he was travelling and suddenly became aware of the fact that the mighty range of snow-capped

[2] Stephensen, *Legend*, 58, 68.
[3] [J. F. C. Fuller], "The Temple of Solomon the King," *The Equinox* 1, no. 1 (March 1909): 161.

Figure 6.1 One of fifty copies of the deluxe edition of issue 3 of *The Equinox* (1910), bound in white buckram. (Image courtesy of Clive Harper.)

mountains upon which he had up to now fondly imagined he was gazing was after all but a great bank of clouds. So he passed on smiling to himself at his own childlike illusion.

Shortly after this he became acquainted with a certain brother of the Order of A.∴A.∴; and himself a little later became an initiate in the first grade of that Order.[4]

[4] Fuller, "Temple," 157.

Writing in his *Confessions* twenty years later, Crowley would offer a more nuanced account of the intellectual transformation that began in 1905 with his experience of "the Ordeal of the Abyss."

> I was in no way apostasizing from my agnosticism in looking for a universe of beings endowed with such qualities that earlier observers, with few facts and fewer methods of investigation and criticism at their disposal, called "gods," "archangels," "spirits" and the like.
>
> I began to remember that I was myself an initiate, that the Great Order had given me the Cabbala as my working hypothesis. I now found that this doctrine satisfied perfectly my science, my skepticism and my soul. It made no pretense to lay down the law about the universe. On the contrary, it declared positively the agnostic conclusion of Huxley. It declared reason incompetent to create a science from nothing and restricted it to its evident function of criticizing facts, so far as those facts were comprehensible by it.[5]

D'Amico's summary of this era in cultural history shows that Crowley was not alone in his dilemma, even if he blazed a unique trail.

> In late Victorian and Edwardian England, the rise of rationalism and scientific naturalism had not managed to establish a system of values strong enough to replace Christianity, which was undergoing a deep crisis caused by Darwinism and positivism. The result of this impasse left many unsatisfied with both religion and science. Christianity had been dismissed as irrational, but science alone did not manage to satisfy the spiritual exigencies of the individual. It was in this spiritual gap that psychic research, spiritism, occultism, theosophy, and oriental philosophy gained ground in Europe. Crowley was not immune to this wind of change.[6]

If there was any doubt that Crowley had left the fold, it would have been dispelled by the issue's special supplement—an extract from the magical record of Frater O.·.M.·.—which included a scathing "Confession of St. Judas

[5] Aleister Crowley, *The Confessions of Aleister Crowley*, ed. John Symonds and Kenneth Grant (London: Jonathan Cape, 1969), 511.

[6] Giuliano D'Amico, "Aleister Crowley Reads *Inferno*: Towards an Occult Reception of Strindberg," *Scandinavian Studies* 84, no. 3 (2012): 335.

McCabbage" (a short parody of the Nicene Creed at the expense of Joseph McCabe).

The *Literary Guide* panned the issue as "expensively printed lunacy, astrology, etc. in oriental-occidental jargon."[7]

The second (September 1909) issue of *The Equinox*—which published the preliminary initiation rituals and magic of the Golden Dawn—also returned the favor of a harsh review, striking hard and low with its take on the *Literary Guide*: "The Rationalists have created man in their own images, as dull simpletons."[8] In addition, in the second installment of "The Temple of Solomon the King," Fuller offered this critique of Freethought:

> To a child who has never seen a monkey, monkey is outside the circumference of its knowledge; but when once it has seen one it is mere foolishness for other children to say: "Oh no, you didn't really see a monkey; such things as monkeys do not exist, and what proves it beyond all doubt is that we have never seen one ourselves!" This, it will be seen, is the Freethinkers' old, old conclusive argument: "There is not a God because '*we*' have no experience of a God." . . . "There is not a South Pole because we have not trudged round it six times and cut our names on it with our pocket-knives!"[9]

Of this issue of *The Equinox*, the *Literary Guide* wrote,

> The singular periodical known as *The Equinox* appears to have Mr. Aleister Crowley as its leading spirit, and we fancy his hand may be detected behind more than one signature in the present issue. However that may be, the contents of this beautifully produced but wildly eccentric work baffle any review from the Rationalist standpoint. Some fine poetry of the daringly volcanic order is contributed by Mr. Crowley himself; but the bulk of the matter is such a phantasmagoric hodge-podge of Oriental mysticism, cabbalism, astrology, magic, delirium, esoteric Buddhism, and the occult generally (all apparently coming under the euphemism "spiritual experience"), that we are fain to retire crestfallen from the critical arena, and confess that even the dimmest comprehension of the whole business is beyond our reach. We admire the vigour and

7 "Also Received," *Literary Guide and Rationalist Review* 155 (May 1, 1909): 79.

8 "Reviews," *The Equinox* 1, no. 2 (September 1909): 387.

9 [J. F. C. Fuller], "The Temple of Solomon the King," *The Equinox* 1, no. 2 (September 1909): 297.

raciness of much of the writing, while privately questioning the sanity of its perpetrators.[10]

The third (March 1910) issue of *The Equinox* ran stinging reviews of *The R. P. A. Annual* and Joseph McCabe's *The Martyrdom of Ferrer*.[11] The *Literary Guide* reciprocated with one last review of *The Equinox*, titled "Occultism Rampant."

> Why *The Equinox* is published and who reads it are mysteries to us. The present number contains two fine vivid poems by Mr. Victor Neuburg, but the bulk of the contents will strike the uninitiated as weird and clotted nonsense. Certain R. P. A. publications are noticed, and the editor prints an apology for "Honest Reviews." These are probably honest; they are certainly valueless, and the apology was needed.[12]

If the *Literary Guide* had washed its hands of Crowley, Crowley was nowhere near finished. He responded directly to that review with his own review of the *Literary Guide* in the fourth (September 1910) issue of *The Equinox*:

> We regret that the R.P.A. disliked our reviews of their sewage. The said reviews were, however, written by one of the most prominent members of their own body. Rather like Epaminondas and the Cretans!
>
> Anyhow, the *Guide* has wittily retorted on us that our reviews are "valueless." What a sparkler! What a crusher![13]

The issue also featured hostile reviews of Charles A. Watts's other publications.

Next came *The World's Tragedy* (1910), a bitter autobiographical critique of religion, society, and various villains who plagued Crowley's early life. The introduction revealed the real-life identities of the book's various characters, including the following: "I cannot pretend to remember exactly who 'sat' for the ox and the ass, though the names of Charles Watts and Joseph Mc. Cabe somehow instinctively suggest themselves in this connection."[14]

10 "A Literary Curiosity," *Literary Guide and Rationalist Review* 161 (November 1, 1909): 176.
11 "Reviews," *The Equinox* 1, no. 3 (March 1910): 317–318.
12 "Occultism Rampant," *Literary Guide and Rationalist Review* 168 (June 1, 1910): 96.
13 A. C. [Aleister Crowley], "The Literary Guide," *The Equinox* 1, no. 4 (September 1910): 24.
14 Aleister Crowley, *The World's Tragedy* (Paris: privately printed, 1910), xxxv.

In the fifth (March 1911) *Equinox*, "An Essay upon Number" contained a short rant about different kinds of atheists, beginning with

> the mere stupid man. (Often he is very clever, as Bolingbroke, Bradlaugh and Foote were clever.) He has found out one of the minor arcana, and hugs it and despises those who see more than himself, or who regard things from a different standpoint. Hence he is usually a bigot, intolerant even of tolerance.[15]

Astonishingly, Crowley would reach out to Charles A. Watts in 1913, asking the *Literary Guide* to include a notice of his ninth (and penultimate) issue.

> Charles Watts. Literary Guide. 17 Johnson's Court, Fleet Str.
>
> My dear Watts
>
> I am enclosing you a literary article which I think might conceivably suit the *Guide*. We printed the Poem of the Athan[asian] Creed in No IX of *The Equinox*. Have we sent you a copy for review? Will you notice at least that poem, even though the rest of the Number should not appeal to you. Hoping you are well, I am Yrs ever.[16]

Crowley's poem "Athanasius Contra Decanum" is indeed peppered with references to the Athanasian Creed (a.k.a. Quicunque Vult), the first Christian text to state the equality of the Holy Trinity. Taking his fourth stanza as an example:

> He got through "neque confundentes"
> Gay as a boy in his twenties.
> With sang-froid mingled with afflatus,
> He gladly uttered "Increatus."
> "Immensus" and "omnipotens"
> Were meant to his "divinior mens."

[15] Fra. P. [Aleister Crowley], "An Essay upon Number," in [J. F. C. Fuller], "The Temple of Solomon the King," *The Equinox* 1, no. 5 (March 1911): 109. Tory statesman Henry St. John Bolingbroke (1678–1751) was an Enlightenment-era deist whose opposition to priestcraft and the notion of divine revelation caused him to be occasionally classed as an atheist. See Shinji Nohara, "Bolingbroke and His Agnostic-Rational View of the World: Searching for the Religious Foundation of the Enlightenment," *Kyoto Economic Review* 80, no. 1 (June 2011): 103–118.

[16] Aleister Crowley to Charles Watts, 1913, letter 61, pt. A, NS12, Yorke Collection, Warburg Institute, London.

"Tamen non tres dii" he smiled,
"Sed unus Deus," suave and mild;
Reciting thus the Creed verbatim
To "Quia, sicut singillatim."
He slapped his venerable femur:
"Religione prohibemur."[17]

However, the poem is not actually about the creed so much as it is sometimes clever and sometimes strained rhyming couplets attacking Rev. Reginald St. John Parry, the dean of Trinity College who had barred Crowley from speaking there.[18] Indeed, the poem's title translates as "Athanasius against the Dean." No review or notice would appear in the *Literary Guide*.

Undeterred, Crowley would follow up later that summer by submitting an article for publication.

My dear Watts,

I wrote you enclosing an article. I have not had a reply, and would like to know what you think about it. I am also sending you a story which I think you might like for the *Agnostic Annual* or whatever you call it,[19] as I suppose it is too long for the Guide. I think that it should meet with your approval whimsiest (? T) moral approval (? T). Please let me know as soon as you can what you will do in the matter.

Yours rationally,
Aleister Crowley[20]

Although no such paper appears to have been published, some laudatory reviews of Crowley appeared not long afterward. In a review of the January 1914 *English Review*, the *Literary Guide* remarked that "in 'The City of God,'

[17] Aleister Crowley, "Athanasius Contra Decanum," *The Equinox* 1, no. 9 (March 1913): 263. In this stanza, Crowley's quotes the original Latin of such passages as "Neque cofundentes personas" ("Neither confounding the Persons"—that is, of the Trinity) and "Increatus Pater, increatus Filius, increatus [et] Spiritus Sanctus. Immensus Pater, immensus Filius, immensus [et] Spiritus Sanctus" (The Father uncreated, the Son uncreated, and the Holy Spirit uncreated. The Father unlimited, the Son unlimited, and the Holy Spirit unlimited).

[18] See "A Strange Epilogue" in chap. 4, in this volume.

[19] Crowley is referring to the *RPA Annual and Ethical Review*, formerly known as the *Agnostic Annual*.

[20] Aleister Crowley to Charles Watts, July 3, 1913, letter 28, pt. B, NS12, Yorke Collection, Warburg Institute, London. In the transcript of this letter, typed from a shorthand notebook, the typist has indicated some uncertainty about "whimsiest" and "approval."

Mr. Aleister Crowley blazes forth the splendours of Moscow in a characteristic whirl of gorgeous imagery."[21] Later that year, the journal wrote of the October *English Review* that "Mr. Aleister Crowley's poem, 'To America,' is, in our judgment, one of the finest things he has written."[22] Apparently all was forgiven.

[21] "The English Review," *Literary Guide and Rationalist Review* 212 (February 1, 1914): 32.
[22] "Thoughts on the War," *Literary Guide and Rationalist Review* 221 (November 1, 1914): 175.

7

FULLER & NEUBURG AFTER THE *AGNOSTIC JOURNAL*

When the A∴A∴ officially opened its doors to new members, Victor Neuburg was the first to apply (see figure 7.1).[1] He signed his Probationer's Oath on April 5, 1909, in the presence of Frater Perdurabo (Crowley) and took the magical motto "Omnia vincam" (I will conquer all). It was the end of the 1909 Easter Term at Cambridge. Although he received third-class honors in his exams, Neuburg did not attend the graduation ceremony. As he noted in his *Magical Record*,

> At the time of my acceptance as a Chela into the A∴A∴ I was basically employed in working for my Final at Cambridge, and having but three weeks wherein to do practically two years' work, everything other than Academic study had to be temporarily abandoned. The only magical practice performed during these three weeks, and during the examination (which lasted one week), was that of the Banishing Ritual of the Pentagram, which up to this time has been regularly performed by me. . . . I was successful, by the way, in my examination, and am entitled to an honours degree, which I shall, however, not take, having no use for it, and being unable to afford the twelve pounds (or guineas) which it costs.[2]

On June 16, he left Cambridge, "which I have now quitted in all probability for ever"[3] for a ten-day magical retirement at Boleskine, Crowley's house in

[1] Although Neuburg's Probationer Oath is hand-numbered "3," that is because Crowley and Fuller, as part of the governing triad, were numbers one and two, respectively. As Keith Richmond puts it, "Indeed when the first number of *The Equinox* came out in March 1909, the Order had only three 'signed up' members: Crowley himself and his acolytes J. F. C. Fuller and Victor B. Neuburg." See Keith Richmond, "Discord in the Garden of Janus: Aleister Crowley and Austin Spare," in *Austin Osman Spare: Artist–Occultist–Sensualist*, ed. Geraldine Beskin and John Bonner (Bury St. Edmunds, UK: Beskin Press, 1999).

[2] Victor Neuburg, *The Magical Record of Omnia Vincam, a Probationer of A∴A∴ in June 1909 O.S.*, June 18, 1909, box 15, folder 8, Aleister Crowley Collection 1889–1947, Harry Ransom Center, University of Texas at Austin.

[3] Neuburg, *Magical Record*, June 18, 1909.

Friendship in Doubt. Richard Kaczynski, Oxford University Press. © Oxford University Press 2024.
DOI: 10.1093/oso/9780197694008.003.0007

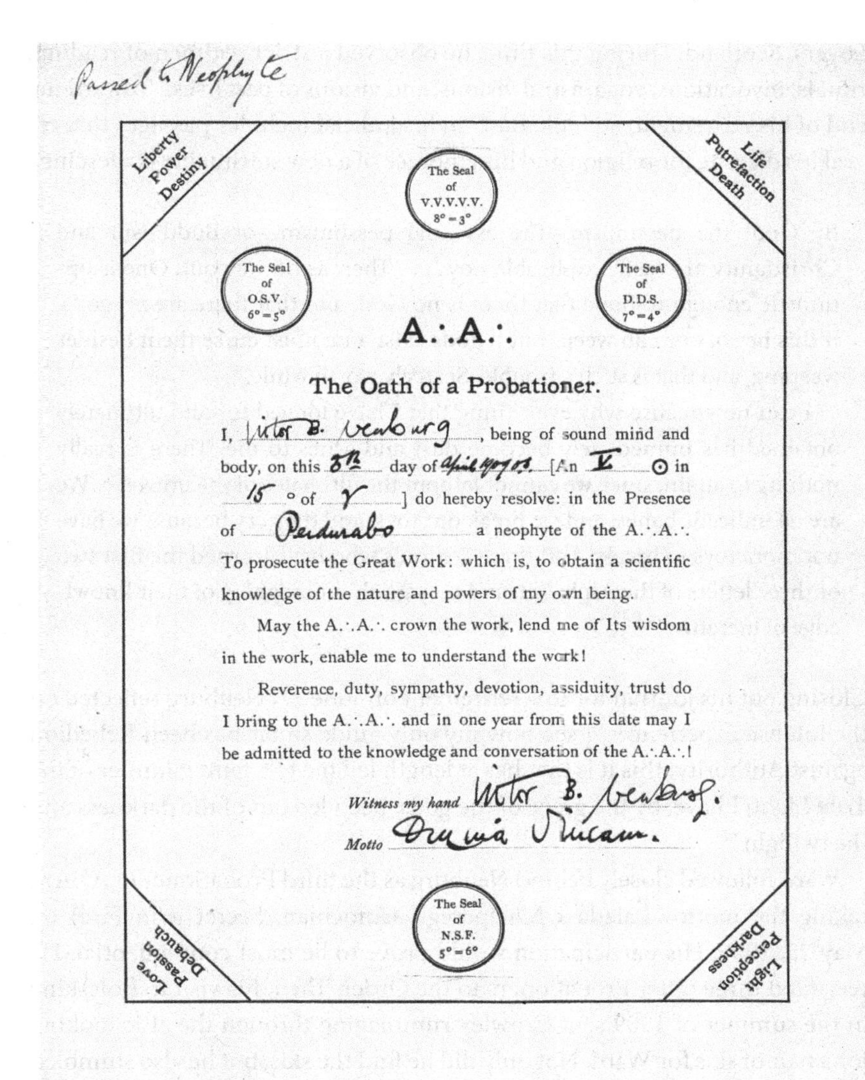

Passed to Neophyte

Liberty Power Destiny

Life Putrefaction Death

The Seal of V.V.V.V.V. 8° = 3°

The Seal of O.S.V. 6° = 5°

The Seal of D.D.S. 7° = 4°

A.·.A.·.

The Oath of a Probationer.

I, Victor B. Neuburg, being of sound mind and body, on this 5th day of [illegible] [An V ☉ in 15 ° of ♈] do hereby resolve: in the Presence of Perdurabo a neophyte of the A.·.A.·.

To prosecute the Great Work: which is, to obtain a scientific knowledge of the nature and powers of my own being.

May the A.·.A.·. crown the work, lend me of Its wisdom in the work, enable me to understand the work!

Reverence, duty, sympathy, devotion, assiduity, trust do I bring to the A.·.A.·. and in one year from this date may I be admitted to the knowledge and conversation of the A.·.A.·.!

Witness my hand Victor B. Neuburg.

Motto Omnia Vincam.

Love Passion Debauch

The Seal of N.S.F. 5° = 6°

Light Darkness Perception

Figure 7.1 Victor Neuburg's Probationer Oath. Although numbered "3" in the upper right corner, Neuburg was actually the first A.·.A.·. Probationer: numbers one and two were Crowley and Fuller, respectively. Fuller crossed through the date fields on his form, while Crowley backdated his to 1904 and indicated that he took the oath in the presence of Frater 'OY MH (himself!). (Aleister Crowley papers, collection #2310, Special Collections Library, Pennsylvania State University; used by permission of Ordo Templi Orientis.)

Foyers, Scotland. During this time, he observed a strict regimen of reading, rituals, invocations, yoga, astral visions, and visions of past lives.[4] Toward the end of his retirement, an "epic rant" in his journal includes passages that reveal his distaste for religion and his embrace of a new spirituality coalescing:

> By God! the pessimism—the essential pessimism—of Buddhism and Christianity are easily explicable now. . . . There is no way out. One is optimistic enough to hope that there is no God, and that there are no gods. If this be so, one can weep. But if gods exist, one must curse them besides weeping, and that is such a trouble. Scarcely worth while.
>
> I can now realise why everything that I have longed for and ultimately obtained has immediately become dust and ashes to me. There is really nothing to attain, since we cannot fathom the ultimates of the universe. We are all imbecile babes, and we break our toys, and they cry because we have not more toys to break. And there are fools who have learned the first two or three letters of the Alphabet, and they go about bragging of their knowledge of literature![5]

Closing out his journal for this retirement on June 27, Neuburg reflected on the intense experience: "I see how my only guide so far has been Rebellion against Authority; this it is that has at length led me to a faint glimmer of the True Light; I have, by the grace of the gods, been led out of the darkness and the twilight."[6]

Ward followed closely behind Neuburg as the third Probationer in A∴A∴, taking the motto "Laiada I Maelperegi" (Enochian, Secret is/in Fire) on May 25, 1909. His participation would prove to be most consequential. He recruited three other Probationers to the Order. Then, his visit to Boleskine in the summer of 1909 sent Crowley rummaging through the attic looking for a pair of skis for Ward. Not only did he find the skis, but he also stumbled upon the manuscript, presumed lost, of *The Book of the Law*. This coincidence was so significant that Crowley took it as a sign from the gods, placing the text at the foundation of his system of magick.[7] Between the CUFA and

[4] For details, see Jean Overton Fuller, *The Magical Dilemma of Victor Neuburg*, rev. ed. (London: W. H. Allen, 1965; Oxford, UK: Mandrake Press, 1990).

[5] Neuburg, *Magical Record*, June 25, 1909.

[6] Neuburg, *Magical Record*, June 27, 1909.

[7] As for Ward, according to his mother, "he became distrustful of the honesty and character of a certain prime leader of the 'côterie,' a man of brilliant gifts and powerful personal attraction." Having decided to break away from this circle of friends, in 1911 he welcomed the opportunity of a professor

A.·.A.·., 1909 was a period of youthful experimentation for Ward and his friends. This was plain even to his mother—who was also his biographer—who recalled that even after this time, he could not,

> he averred, exactly regret some of these "sad and bad" experiments, for they "opened his eyes to so much."
>
> Some of them certainly were more foolish than anything else, and consisted in eating hashish, hypnotizing themselves, and each other, and practising what they called magic.[8]

Important as Ward's presence was, it was ultimately brief. As Crowley noted on Ward's Probationer's Oath, "Underwent Vision of the Demon Crowley at moment of passing to Neophyte."[9] In Crowley's parlance, the "Vision of the Demon Crowley" referred to a predictable pattern among his students in which the teacher is demonized; in response, they either persevere through the vision to glimpse the truth on the other side, or they succumb to the vision and flee. Ward chose the latter, pursuing a career in Burma.

The Equinox

While Fuller understood that the journal was primarily a platform for Crowley to publish his "own works rather than a review,"[10] it was nevertheless open to other contributors. The spring 1909 debut issue, for instance, included short stories by Frank Harris and Lord Dunsany.

Given the CUFA's promotion of *The Equinox*, CUFA members unsurprisingly appear in its early issues. Neuburg's poem "The Lonely Bride" was the first of multiple pieces to grace the pages of *The Equinox*.[11] Throughout the first eight issues, he would also contribute "The Lost Shepherd" (#2), "An Origin" (#3), "The Coming of Apollo" (#3), "Inst Naturae Regina Isis" (#4), "The Gnome" (#4), "The Agnostic" (#4), "In the Temple" (#4), "A Nocturne"

of mathematics position at Rangoon College. See Mrs. Ward, *Memoirs of Kenneth Martin Ward* (London: Simpkin Marshall, 1929), 48.

[8] Mrs. Ward, *Memoirs*, 48.

[9] Signed oaths of the Probationers of the Argentum Astrum, Aleister Crowley Papers, 02310, Penn State University Libraries Archival Collections, University Park, Pennsylvania.

[10] Quoted in Brian Holden Reid, *J .F. C. Fuller: Military Thinker* (Basingstoke, UK: Macmillan, 1987), 18.

[11] Victor B. Neuburg, "The Lonely Bride," *The Equinox* 1, no. 1 (March 1909): 95–97.

(#5), "The Autumn Woods" (#6), "Three Poems" (#8), and "The New Evelyn Hope" (#8).[12] He also advanced to subeditor of the journal in March 1912, a position he held for the journal's last four issues.

Pinsent's poem "The Organ in King's Chapel, Cambridge" appeared in issue two; the poem would be included, alongside pieces by Crowley and Neuburg, in the 1913 anthology *Cambridge Poets 1900–1913*.[13]

Although he prudently kept his major contribution to *The Equinox* anonymous, Fuller compiled, edited, and penned the first four installments of "The Temple of Solomon the King." Crowley described the "gargantuan preface" in the first issue as "a series of sublimely eloquent rhapsodies descriptive of the various possible attitudes towards existence."[14] Of the subsequent installments, Crowley had equally high praise:

> Though his tendency to burst out into ecstatic rhapsodies resulted in disordering the proportions of its events, in the main his task was admirably accomplished, and there are passages of astonishing sublimity, not only in the matter of language but in that of thought. His point of view was indeed more subtle and profound than he himself realized. I am sure that many passages of this book will stand among the greatest monuments of English prose extant.[15]

If Crowley was unreserved in his praise, then he was even more exuberant about Fuller's *The Treasure-House of Images*, which Imy has called "a deeply eroticized exaltation of faith, ritual, and devotion."[16] It appeared as a special supplement to the third issue of *The Equinox*.He reached his high-water mark

[12] Neuburg's contributions to *The Equinox* are as follows: Victor B. Neuburg, "The Lonely Bride," *The Equinox* 1, no. 1 (March 1909): 95–97; Victor B. Neuburg, "The Lost Shepherd," *The Equinox* 1, no. 2 (September 1909): 131–136; Victor B. Neuburg, "An Origin," *The Equinox* 1, no. 3 (March 1910): 115–118; Victor B. Neuburg, "The Coming of Apollo," *The Equinox* 1, no. 3 (March 1910): 281–284; Victor B. Neuburg, "Inst Naturae Regina Isis," *The Equinox* 1, no. 4 (September 1910): 21–23; Victor B. Neuburg, "The Gnome," *The Equinox* 1, no. 4 (September 1910): 236–238; Victor B. Neuburg, "The Agnostic," *The Equinox* 1, no. 4 (September 1910): 274; Victor B. Neuburg, "In the Temple," *The Equinox* 1, no. 4 (September 1910): 352; Victor B. Neuburg, "A Nocturne," *The Equinox* 1, no. 5 (March 1911): 121–124; Victor B. Neuburg, "The Autumn Woods," *The Equinox* 1, no. 6 (September 1911): 149–152; Victor B. Neuburg, "Three Poems," *The Equinox* 1, no. 8 (September 1912): xxxvii–4; and Victor B. Neuburg, "The New Evelyn Hope," *The Equinox* 1, no. 8 (September 1912): 250–252.

[13] G. H. S. Pinsent, "The Organ in King's Chapel, Cambridge," *The Equinox* 1, no. 2 (September 1909): 162, repr. G. H. S. Pinsent, "The Organ in King's Chapel, Cambridge," in *Cambridge Poets 1900–1913: An Anthology*, ed. Aelfrida Tillyard (Cambridge, UK: W. Heffer, 1913), 157.

[14] Aleister Crowley, *The Confessions of Aleister Crowley*, ed. John Symonds and Kenneth Grant (London: Jonathan Cape, 1969), 603.

[15] Crowley, *Confessions*, 544.

[16] Kate Imy, "Fascist Yogis: Martial Bodies and Imperial Impotence," *Journal of British Studies* 55 (April 2016): 331.

with *The Treasure-House of Images*. Formally, this is the most remarkable prose that has ever been written. Each chapter of the main part of the book contains thirty sections, and each section has the same number of syllables. Each of these chapters hymns the sign of the Zodiac and in each section that sign is modified by another sign. It is the most astonishing achievement in symbolism. But this is not all. There is a chapter containing one hundred and sixty-nine cries of Adoration, which is, as it were, a multiplication of the previous chapters and a quintesentialization of them. To this day we chant these Adorations to the sound of the tom-tom and dance to the music, and the effect is to carry away the performer into the sublimest ecstasy. It possesses all the Magick of oriental religious rites, such as those of the Sidi Aissawa, but the rapture is purely religious. It is not confused with eroticism, and that although many of the symbols are of themselves violently erotic.[17]

An example of Fuller's writing, which Crowley praised so highly, is instructive:

1. O Thou snow-clad volcan [*sic*] of scarlet fire, Thou flame-crested pillar of fury! Yea, as I approach Thee, Thou departest from me like unto a wisp of smoke blown forth from the window of my house.
2. O Thou summer-land of eternal joy, Thou rapturous garden of flowers! Yea, as I gather Thee, my harvest is but as a drop of dew shimmering in the golden cup of the crocus.
3. O Thou throbbing music of life and death, Thou rhythmic harmony of the world! Yea, as I listen to the echo of Thy voice, my rapture is but as the whisper of the wings of a butterfly.[18]

Having contributed an anonymous book review to the second issue,[19] Fuller went on to pen several for the third and fourth issues, some unsigned and others signed under such varied names as J. F. C. F. (or just F.), Antoinette Bouvignon, Bathshebah Tina, Methuselah, A. Quiller (or A. Q.), Alicia de Gruys, H_2S, B. Rashith, Vishnu, and Elias Ashmole.[20] To the fourth issue he also contributed "Half-Hours with Famous Mahatmas," under the

[17] Crowley, *Confessions*, 544.

[18] [J. F. C. Fuller]. "Liber DCCCCLXIII—the Treasure-House of Images," *The Equinox* 1, no. 3 (supplement, March 1910): 10.

[19] "*Comte's Philosophy as Rectified by Schopenhauer* by M. Kelly," *The Equinox* 1, no. 2 (September 1909): 385–386.

[20] Fuller's reviews in the March 1910 issue of *The Equinox* include F., "*Scientific Idealism* by W. Kingsland," 285–286; Antoinette Bouvignon, "*The Cleansing of a City*," 312; J. F. C. F., "*Matter, Spirit, and the Cosmos* by H. Stanley Redgrove," 313; Bathshebah Tina, "*The Maniac: A Realistic Study*

pseudonym Sam Hardy, and "The Eyes of St. Ljubov," coauthored under his given name with George Raffalovich.

Neither were Fuller's contributions to *The Equinox* merely literary, as he also contributed most of the illustrations to its issues (see figures 7.2–7.6).[21] Crowley remarked that "his draughtsmanship, within certain limits, was miraculously fine"; while the human figure was his Achilles heel, "his geometrical work is almost inconceivably perfect."[22] Thus *The Regimen of the Seven* appeared in the first issue as a full color plate prepared by London engraver Carl Hentschel. Other works included *Adonai ha Aretz* (which, being a human figure, Crowley called "lamentable"), *The Sigils of the XXII*, *The Four Great Watch-Towers* ("superb"), *The Yogi (Showing the Cakkras)*, *A Vision of Golgotha (The Crucifixion of Fra. P.)*, and the ornamental letters for the *Alphabet of Daggers* and the *Enochian Alphabet* ("altogether beyond me to appreciate").[23]

Not only was Fuller's work being published, but the exercise improved his writing considerably. As Crowley noted, "He loved a sentence so much that he could not persuade himself to finish it, but his images are more vivid and

of Madness from the Maniac's Point of View," 314; Methuselah, "*Self Synthesis: A Means to Perpetual Life*, by Cornwell Round," 315; F., "*The Case for Alcohol: Or, the Actions of Alcohol on Body and Soul* by Robert Park, M.D.," 315–316; J. F. C. F., "*An Interpretation of Genesis* by Theodore Powys," 316; "*The R. P. A Annual*, 1910," 316–317; "*The Martyrdom of Ferrer* by Joseph McCabe," 317; "*The Hand of God* by Grant Allen," 317; "*Evolution from Nebula to Man* by Joseph McCabe," 317; A. Quiller, "*History of Chemistry* by Sir Edward Thorpe and *History of Astronomy* by George Forbes," 319; and A. Quiller, "*The Open Road*," 326. Fuller's reviews in the September 1910 issue include A. Quiller, "*The Literary Guide*," 332–334; Alicia de Gruys, "*With the Adepts* by Franz Hartmann," 334–335; H2S, "*History of Chemistry* by Sir Edward Thorpe," 335; B. Rashith, "*History of Old Testament Criticism* by Archibald Duff, D. D.," 335–336; Vishnu, "*The Sacred Sports of Siva*," 336; Elias Ashmole, "*Ritual, Faith, and Morals* by F. H. Perrycoste," 336; F., "*The Ancient Constitutional Charges of the Guild Freemasons* by John Yarker," 336; A. Q., "*Paganism and Christianity*," 336; A. Quiller, "*The White Slave Traffic*," 336–338; J. F. C. F., "*The Cannon: An Exposition of the Pagan Mysteries Perpetuated in the Cabala as the Rule of All the Arts.*," 339–340; J. F. C. F., "*Kant's Ethics and Schopenhauer's Criticism* by M. Kelly," 340–341; and J. F. C. F., "*The Signs and Symbols of Primordial Man* by Albert Churchward," 341–343. Note that A. Quiller (Fuller) should not be confused with A. Quiller Jr. (Crowley).

[21] Notable exceptions are the artwork of Austin Osman Spare, which illustrates, for example, page 140 of "A Handbook of Geomancy," *The Equinox* 1, no. 2 (September 1909): 137–161. He also contributed two diagrams to "The Temple of Solomon the King": Austin Osman Spare, "Diagram 33: The Garden of Eden," *The Equinox* 1, no. 2 (September 1909): 275; and Austin Osman Spare, "Diagram 51: The Fall," *The Equinox* 1, no. 2 (September 1909): 283. The first two examples are in Spare's distinctive style, while the last illustration bears the artist's initials.

[22] Crowley, *Confessions*, 544.

[23] The works of J. F. C. Fuller mentioned appear in the following issues of, *The Equinox*: *The Regimen of the Seven*, *The Equinox*, 1, no. 1 (March 1909), facing p. 89; J. F. C. Fuller, *Adonai ha Aretz*, *The Equinox*, 1, no. 4 (September 1909): facing p. 114; J. F. C. Fuller, *The Sigils of the XXII*, *The Equinox*, 1, no. 7 (March 1912): facing p. 70; J. F. C. Fuller, *The Four Great Watch-Towers*, *The Equinox*, 1, no. 7 (March 1912): between pp. 234–235; J. F. C. Fuller, *The Yogi (Showing the Cakkras)*, *The Equinox*, 1, no. 4 (September 1910): facing p. 90; J. F. C. Fuller, *A Vision of Golgotha (The Crucifixion of Fra. P.)*, *The Equinox*, 1, no. 8 (September 1912): facing p. 32; J. F. C. Fuller, *Alphabet of Daggers*, *The Equinox*, 1, no. 5 (supplement, March 1911): facing p. 46; J. F. C. Fuller, *Enochian Alphabet*, *The Equinox*, 1, no. 7 (March 1912): facing p. 238.

Figure 7.2 Fuller's illustration *The Regimen of the Seven*, which accompanied "The Chemical Jousting of Frater Perardua" in *The Equinox* issue 1 (1909)

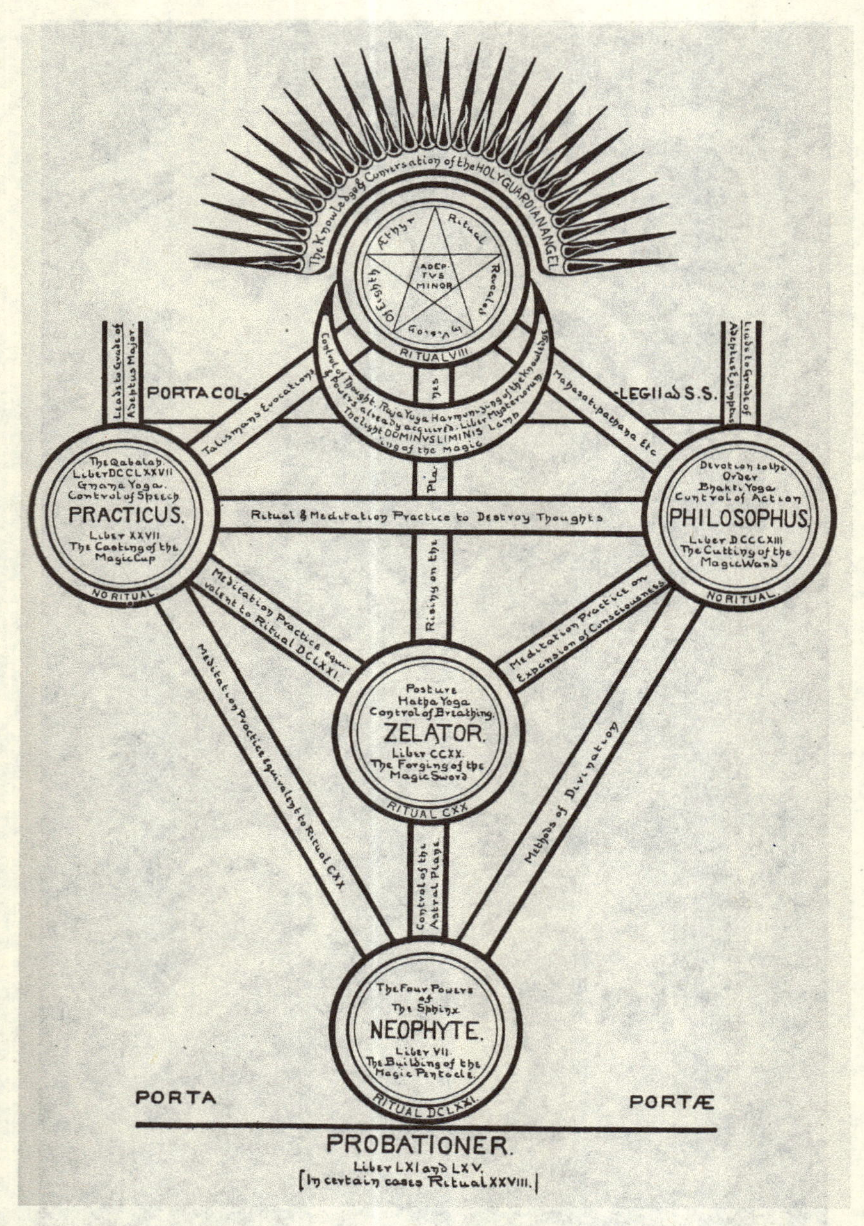

Figure 7.3 Fuller's *The Slopes of Abiegnus*, which accompanied Crowley's "Liber XII vel Graduum Montis Abiegni: A Syllabus of the Steps upon the Path" in *The Equinox* issue 3 (1910)

DIAGRAM 86.
The Flashing Figure of Adonai-ha-Aretz.

Figure 7.4 Fuller's *Adonai-ha-Aretz* from *The Equinox* issue 4 (1910)

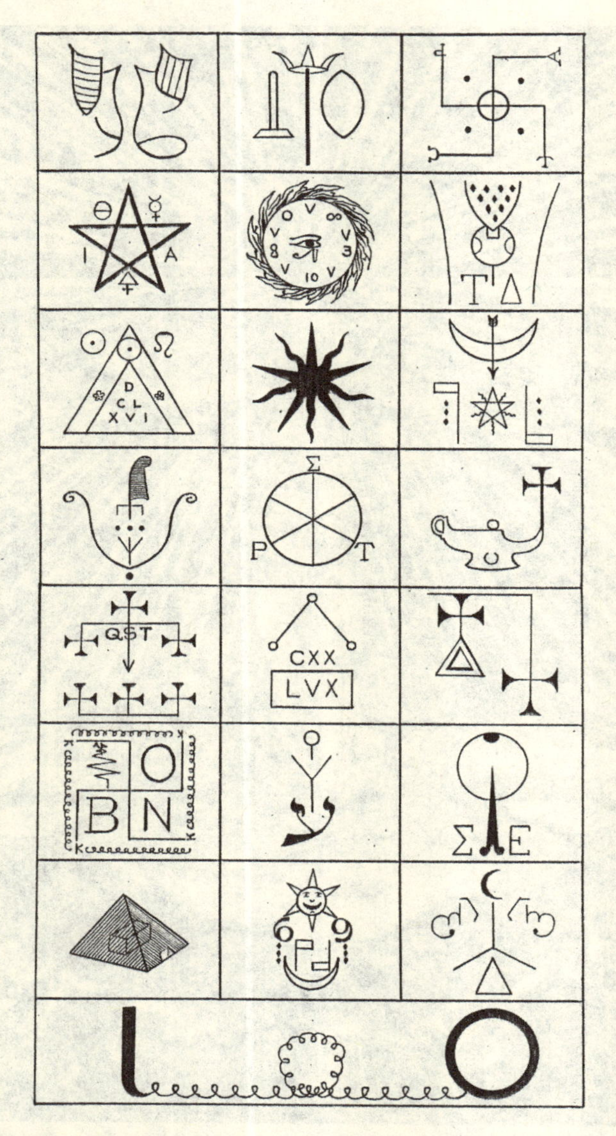

Figure 7.5 Fuller's illustration, which accompanied Crowley's "Liber Arcanorum" in *The Equinox* issue 7 (1912): "Liber XXII Domarum Mercurii cum Suis Geniis."

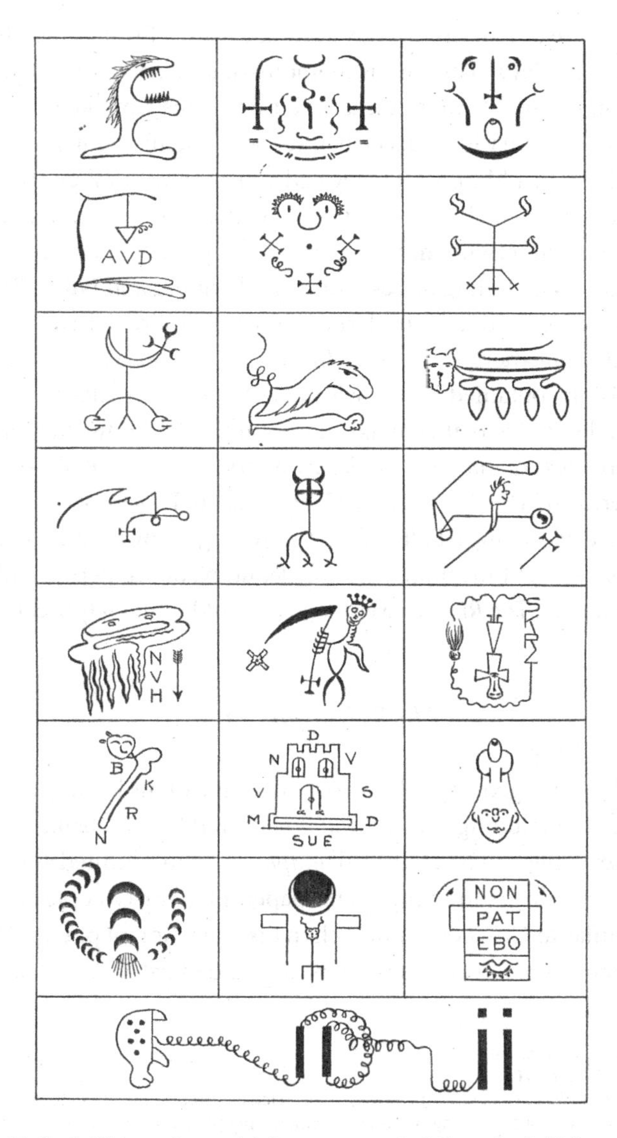

Figure 7.6 Fuller's illustration, which accompanied Crowley's "Liber Arcanorum" in *The Equinox* issue 7 (1912): "Liber XXII Carcerorum Qliphoth cum Suis Geniis."

virile than those of any writer I have ever known."[24] Even Fuller's biographer conceded, "Crowley's claim in his memoirs that he had taught Fuller how to write was an exaggeration, but it is true that by the time he began to circulate articles to military journals he had served a useful, if unusual, literary apprenticeship."[25] In addition, Crowley had a surprising number of connections with military men, and he provided Fuller with an introduction to Lieutenant Colonel F. N. Maude, who thereafter "acted as a kind of intellectual mentor."[26]

In addition to including pieces written by Neuburg and Fuller, *The Equinox* also chronicled the mystical undertakings of their circle. Issue five included as a special supplement the text of *The Vision and the Voice*, the record of a series of visions obtained by Crowley and Neuburg in Algeria by using the Enochian calls of Elizabethan magicians John Dee and Edward Kelly. Issue six contained the text of *The Rites of Eleusis*, a series of seven plays—one for each planet—performed by the A.'.A.'. at Caxton Hall in London on seven consecutive Wednesday evenings; Fuller, despite advising Crowley against this undertaking, even brought his mother to the debut. Neuburg performed as one of the cast members. The *Rites*, as we shall see, would ultimately break the circle.

The Triumph of Pan

Crowley also arranged to publish works by some of his leading and more literary students, including George Raffalovich and Victor Neuburg.[27] In 1910, *The Equinox* published Neuburg's *Triumph of Pan* in a limited and numbered edition of 220 copies on antique-laid paper, plus thirty copies on Japanese vellum. Similar to Crowley's approach in his collection of poems *The Winged Beetle*, which appeared at this time, Neuburg dedicated each poem making

[24] Crowley, *Confessions*, 544.

[25] Reid, *J. F. C. Fuller*, 20.

[26] Reid, *J. F. C. Fuller*, 20. Lieutenant Colonel Frederick Natusch Maude (1854–1933) and Captain Fuller were but two of a surprising number of military people connected with Crowley. These included Commander Guy Montagu Marston of the Royal Navy, who hosted Crowley's Bartzabel Working at his Dorset home; Everard Feilding, an A.'.A.'. member who during World War I served as a lieutenant in the Naval Censors' Press Bureau; Captain Guy Gaunt, naval attaché to Washington, to whom Crowley says he reported his counterespionage activities in America; Major Robert Thompson Thynne, who in 1930 would invest £1,000 in the limited liability corporation that took over the ailing Mandrake Press, publisher of Crowley's books at the time; and possibly even Admiral Roger Keyes, to whom Crowley sent a copy of Liber Oz in 1941. Richard Spence argues that Crowley was a long-time operative in the British intelligence community. Richard Spence, *Secret Agent 666: Aleister Crowley, British Intelligence and the Occult* (Los Angeles: Feral House, 2008).

[27] Crowley also helped Eugene Wieland set up Wieland & Co. to publish *The Equinox* and other works by Crowley. The only non-Crowley work produced by this imprint, in fact, was the 1911 publication of *The Whirlpool* by Wieland's wife, Ethel Archer.

up *The Triumph of Pan* to friends and acquaintances, including many members of the A.·.A.·. and its extended circle (see figures 7.7 and 7.8). Some of these met with nonplussed responses. As Fuller recalled,

> I have no idea why VN dedicated ["The Sacrifice"] to me, and on re-reading it can see no reason why he should have. This applies to most of the dedicatees, many of whom I knew. It would seem that he dished out the dedications in a haphazard way, including as many of his friends as there were poems.[28]

Both Charles Richard Cammell and Edward Noel Fitzgerald had annotated copies of the book with notes on the various dedicatees, such as "Dolly was a *fille de joie*, formerly a chorus girl" and "Nora was a tart VBN met one night in Bournemouth."[29] Thus, while Neuburg found himself the dedicatee of "The Garden of Janus" in Crowley's *Winged Beetle*[30] (the volume as a whole is dedicated to Fuller[31]), he returned the favor by dedicating "A Dialogue," "The Coming of Apollo," and the "Epilogue" to Crowley.

Advertisements for the book quoted its glowing reviews, but the book also garnered unflattering words from well-regarded corners. For instance, *Light*, a journal of "psychical, occult, and mystical research," declared that

> *The Triumph of Pan* is a gorgeous rhapsody, very eloquent but very highly coloured . . . Still, on the whole, we cannot help regretting that such splendid powers of imagination and expression are flung away in such literary rioting.[32]

The *Academy* did not warm to the poetry's rapturous tone, commenting wryly,

> When, dipping into Mr. Neuburg's *Triumph of Pan*, we glimpsed the word "phallic," and caught him asking a lady for "purple kisses," we began to be suspicious of him. He is far too fond of verse that is odorous of eroticism,

[28] Letter of J. F. C. Fuller to Jean Overton Fuller, quoted in Fuller, *Magical Dilemma*, 154–155; see also "The Sacrifice" in Neuburg, *Triumph of Pan*, 35–36.

[29] Fuller, *Magical Dilemma*, 154–155.

[30] "The Garden of Janus" appears in Aleister Crowley, *The Winged Beetle* (n.p.: privately printed, 1910), 35–44.

[31] "The Convert" appears in Crowley, *Winged Beetle*, 102, dropping Fuller's name into these oft-quoted lines while also demonstrating the proper pronunciation of Crowley's surname: " 'Where are you going, so meek and holy?' 'I'm going to temple to worship Crowley.' 'Crowley is God, then? How did you know?' 'Why, it's Captain Fuller that told us so.' 'And how do you know that Fuller was right?' 'I'm afraid you're a wicked man; Good-night.' "

[32] "Notes by the Way," *Light* 31, no. 1566 (January 14, 1911): 1.

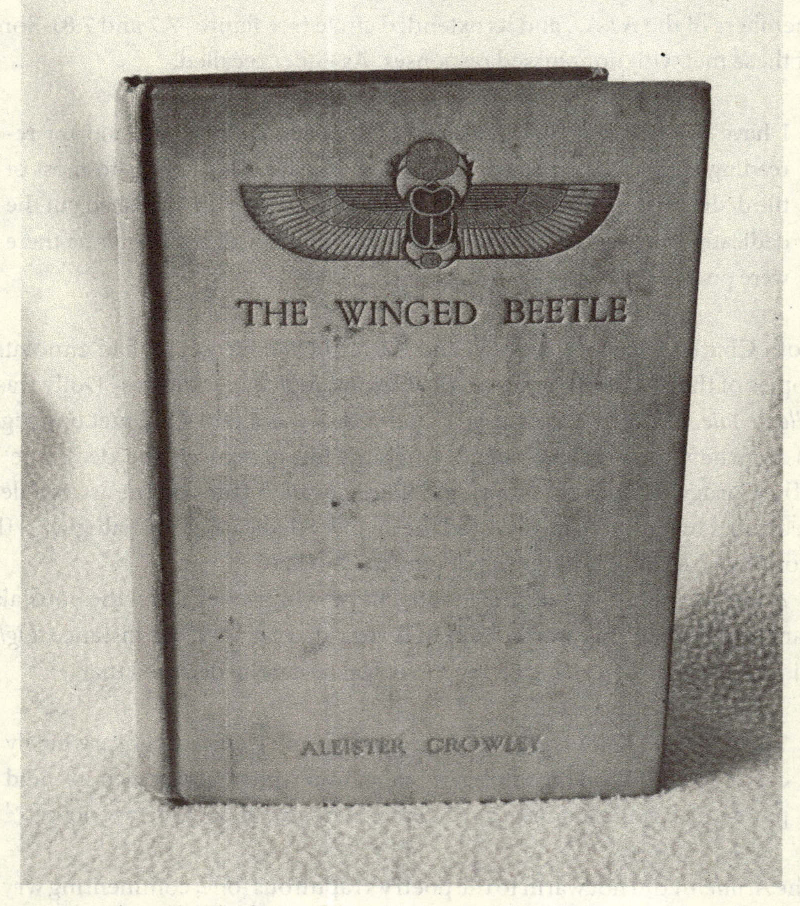

Figure 7.7 The individual poems in Aleister Crowley's *The Winged Beetle* (pictured here) and Victor Neuburg's *The Triumph of Pan* were dedicated to various acquaintances. (Image courtesy of Clive Harper.)

> of words such as "obscene," "slime," and of maltreated adjectives. . . . Altogether, Mr. Neuburg is hardly the sort of person we should care to meet on a dark night with a knobby stick in his hand.[33]

[33] "Reviews: Current Verse and Poetry," *Academy* 80, no. 2018 (January 7, 1911): 8.

Figure 7.8 The individual poems in Aleister Crowley's *The Winged Beetle* and Victor Neuburg's *The Triumph of Pan* (pictured here) were dedicated to various acquaintances. (Image courtesy of Clive Harper.)

The *Athenæum* offered a similar, but less amusing, critique:

> Though by no means deficient in originality, vigour, or imaginative power, his verse is too often cumbered with the fantastic symbols of a species of erotic mysticism, into which we feel no desire to probe. . . . It is difficult to believe that the persons to whom certain poems are inscribed will experience any very lively gratification at the compliment.[34]

[34] "Book Review," *Athenæum* 4356 (April 22, 1911): 442.

The *English Review* damned him by association, noting that "Mr. Neuburg is apparently a disciple of Mr. Crowley" and asking pointedly, "Would not 'The Crowning of the Beast' have been an explanatory sub-title?"[35] The *Co-Mason* was perhaps most constructive in noting,

> The work of this new minor poet shows as yet, more promise than fulfillment, for though there are many beautiful passages in the volume which give hope of something very fine in the future, we feel that the writer still needs to cultivate a greater terseness of diction, and also that he must rid himself of the habit of using the familiar but euphonious rhymes, that suggest echoes of the haunting melodies of Swinburne and of Wordsworth.[36]

Of all the reviews, perhaps the most notable is that by budding author Katherine Mansfield (1888–1923), who wrote for *Rhythm* magazine (see figure 7.9). She admitted that Neuburg "has something of the poet's vision, delighting in simplicity and sensuality which is born of passionate admiration," but she went on to opine,

> Mysticism is perverted sensuality; it is "passionate admiration" for that which has no reality at all. It leads to the annihilation of any true artistic effort. It is a paraphernalia of clichés. It is a mask through which the true expression of the poet can never be discerned. If he rejects this mask Mr. Neuburg may become a poet.[37]

Nevertheless, she thought enough of Neuburg's work to ask her editor and future husband, John Middleton Murry, for more information about Neuburg and his lover, Crowley. She would go on to meet the latter at a party where Crowley led the attendees on a drug-induced exploration of their inner selves.[38]

The final issues of *The Equinox* featured full-page advertisements for "Mr. Neuburg's New Works in Preparation." Titles included *Sonnets from the Spanish: A Contribution to the Personal Note in Literature*; *The New Diana: A History, with Other Poems, and Some Translations*; *The Changeling: A Fairy*

[35] "Book Notices: Poetry and Drama," *English Review* 8 (April 1911): 181.
[36] A. O., "Book Reviews," *Co-Mason* 3 (1911): 73–74.
[37] K. M., review of "The Triumph of Pan," *Rhythm* 2, no. 2 (July 1912): 70.
[38] Richard Kaczynski, *Perdurabo: The Life of Aleister Crowley*, rev. ed. (Tempe, AZ: New Falcon, 2002; Berkeley, CA: North Atlantic Books, 2010),259.

Figure 7.9 Author Katherine Mansfield (1888–1923) reviewed *The Triumph of Pan* for *Rhythm*

Play; *Rosa Ignota: An Essay in Mysticism*; *Heine's Lyrisches Intermezzo: A Complete Translation, with a Prose Preface*; and *Songs of the Decadence: New Lyrics*. While *Rosa Ignota* ran in the final issue of *The Equinox*,[39] these other works never appeared in Neuburg's lifetime.[40] However, Neuburg's works through *The Equinox* found an admirer in author and mystic Aelfrida

[39] Victor B. Neuburg, "Rosa Ignota," *The Equinox* 1, no. 10 (September 1913): 135–198.
[40] For a modern publication of one of these works, see Victor B. Neuburg, *The New Diana* (n.p.: 100th Monkey Press, 2012).

Tillyard (1883–1959), who included seven of his poems in her anthology *Cambridge Poets, 1900–13*, including two pieces that were published there for the first time.[41] Tillyard also became enamored of Crowley, briefly becoming one of his students.[42]

Writing years later, Crowley recalled Neuburg's poetry in glowing terms: "He had an extraordinary delicacy of rhythm, an unrivalled sense of perception, a purity and intensity of passion second to none, and a remarkable command of the English language."[43] In addition, he remarked, "He possessed the magical gift of conveying an idea of tremendous vividness and importance by means of words that are unintelligible to the intellect."[44]

Backing Away

Fuller and Neuburg, along with several other members of Crowley's inner circle, began distancing themselves from their controversial master for assorted reasons. One major fault line resulted from performances of *The Rites of Eleusis*: Publisher West F. de Wend Fenton, fearing that Crowley sought to introduce unwholesome pagan creeds to the God-fearing people of England, ran a series of attacks on Crowley in his tabloid the *Looking Glass*. "Many of my friends took fright and urged me to bring a lawsuit for libel," Crowley recalled. "Fuller, in particular, to my great surprise, was almost dictatorial about my duty."[45] Crowley's friends were disappointed by his refusal to defend himself and them.

When one of these articles accused George Cecil Jones of homosexuality, however, Jones did sue for libel. Once again, Crowley did not offer to testify on his friend's behalf; that being the case, Jones wasn't about to ask. Fuller was consequently the only witness to defend Jones. As Crowley put it, "Fuller had spoken up with soldierly straightforwardness."[46] The closing statement in this case from the defense could only have struck a nerve with the army man:

[41] They are included in the anthology: see "Seascape" and "Serpens Noctis Regina Mundi," in this volume. For their original publication, see Aelfrida Tillyard, ed., *Cambridge Poets, 1900–1913* (Cambridge, UK: W. Heffer, 1913).

[42] For a detailed biography of Tillyard, see Sheila Mann, *Aelfrida Tillyard: Hints of a Perfect Splendour; a Novel Biography* (n.p.: Wayment Print & Publishing Solutions, 2013).

[43] Crowley, *Confessions*, 562–563.

[44] Crowley, *Confessions*, 563–564.

[45] Crowley, *Confessions*, 638.

[46] Crowley, *Confessions*, 642.

> You have seen Captain Fuller. He is proud of knowing Mr. Aleister Crowley; . . . he is an admirer of his works. . . . Crowley stands as a man about whom no words of condemnation can be strong enough. That is the man of whose friendship Captain Fuller is proud.[47]

The jury ruled in favor of the *Looking Glass*. Incredibly, their decision was based not on any facts about Jones but on the conclusion that Crowley was a man of "notoriously evil character" and that if people drew false conclusions about Jones for being friends with such a man, then it served him right.[48] On the heels of this decision, Jones terminated his association with Crowley.[49]

This incident planted in Fuller's mind the very real concern that his name could well surface next in the papers, jeopardizing his military career. Imy suggests that a significant factor in Fuller distancing himself was the sexual relationship between Crowley and Neuburg, whom Fuller played a role in introducing. The legal jeopardy of bisexuality had lurked in the background of Crowley's life since his Golden Dawn years, and the tabloids chased after rumors as far back as his undergraduate days. Imy proposes that Crowley's relationship with Neuburg—whom Crowley's wife Rose disparagingly called "Newbugger"[50]—was a bridge too far for Fuller, whose politics and beliefs were moving away from his "youthful interest in undermining English sexual orthodoxy."[51] Discarding the "mystic fig leaf" in favor of free love was one thing, but being embroiled in a homosexual scandal would be a career-killer.

Crowley could tell something was up: "Fuller had begun to behave in a totally unintelligible way. It was all so subtle that I could not put my finger on a single incident. It was a mere instinct that something was wrong."[52] Concluding that he could no longer risk being associated with *The Equinox*,

[47] "Jones v. *The Looking Glass*: Verdict for *The Looking Glass*; Official Transcript of Evidence," *Looking Glass* 32, no. 1 (May 6, 1911): 4–7; repr. "Jones v. *The Looking Glass*: Verdict for *The Looking Glass*; Official Transcript of Evidence," in Richard Kaczynski *Perdurabo Outtakes*, Blue Equinox Journal 1 (Troy, MI: Blue Equinox Oasis, 2005), 113–136.

[48] For a detailed account and documentation of this case, see Kaczynski, *Perdurabo Outtakes*.

[49] He would, however, continue to administer the trust fund set up for Crowley's daughter, Lola Zaza.

[50] Tobias Churton, *Aleister Crowley, the Biography: Spiritual Revolutionary, Romantic Explorer, Occult Master—and Spy* (London: Watkins, 2011), 142.

[51] Imy, "Fascist Yogis," 331. Imy's suggestion that Fuller was referring to Crowley when he condemned "an unnamed 'potent but middle-class Magician—St. Shamefaced Sex,'" in "his 1925 study, *Yoga*" (Imy, "Fascist Yogis," 330) overlooks that this passage originally appeared in *The Equinox* vol. 1, no. 4, as part of Fuller's laudatory magical biography of Crowley. In context, Fuller in that passage appears to be attacking repressive middle-class attitudes toward sex.

[52] Crowley, *Confessions*, 635.

the man whom Crowley considered his best friend wrote to him on May 2, 1911, calling him a coward for not defending either himself or Jones and ending their friendship.

Crowley's bitter response in the spring 1913 issue of *The Equinox* hinted at how deeply all this hurt him. He pointed out that de Wend Fenton, publisher of the *Looking Glass* newspaper that prompted all this trouble, had been fined over £91 on six charges of sending obscene matter through the mail. He smugly reported that his former Golden Dawn mentor MacGregor Mathers—who testified against Crowley in the *Jones v. the* Looking Glass trial—had been "reduced to beggary, his only remaining capital, his brain, in a state of hopeless decay."[53] Finally, Crowley warned students about Fuller:

> The Chancellor of the A.·.A.·. wishes to warn readers of *The Equinox* against accepting instruction in his name from an ex-Probationer, Captain J. F. C. Fuller, whose motto was "Per Ardua." This person never advanced beyond the Degree of Probationer, never sent in a record, and has presumably neither performed practices nor obtained results. He has not, and never has had, authority to give instructions in the name of the A.·.A.·..[54]

This statement may seem puzzling given that Fuller constituted part of the governing triad of A.·.A.·. and appeared under the college's imprimatur on its various *libri* from this period as "N.S.F., 5°=6▫ Cancellarius" (*Non sine fulmine*, "Not without a thunderbolt"). However, the degree (5°=6▫) was honorary to accompany the role of Chancellor, which he filled administratively, and not as recognition of attainment to the corresponding grade of Adeptus Minor. Indeed, like the vast majority of Probationers (0°=0▫) in the A.·.A.·. during the *Equinox* years, Fuller never advanced beyond that introductory degree. Nevertheless, during his tenure, Fuller did act as introducing Neophyte (1°=10▫), witnessing the oath of eight Probationers.[55] This role

[53] [Aleister Crowley], "Editorial," *The Equinox* 1, no. 9 (March 1913): 5.

[54] [Aleister Crowley], untitled, *The Equinox* 1, no. 9 (March 1913): ii. This comment against Fuller was prompted when Crowley discovered that Charles Stansfeld Jones (1886–1950)—who became an A.·.A.·. Probationer on December 24, 1909, with Fuller as his superior—was still working with Fuller despite the captain having parted with Crowley.

[55] Fuller, under his 0°=0▫ motto of "Per Ardua," also witnessed the Probationer Oaths of Richard Noel Warren (June 17, 1909), Arthur de la Pereira (December 4, 1909), Charles Stansfeld Jones (December 24, 1909), Charles Hugh Davies (January 11, 1910), Henry John van Ginkel (February 26, 1910), Wallis Ken Sanderson (March 23, 1910), Harold J. Lloyd (April 15, 1910), and Herbert Close (June 6, 1910).

was typically filled by Crowley. The last of these eight Probationers, Herbert Close, would remain Fuller's lifelong friend.[56]

Neuburg—no doubt because of the emotional entanglement with his master—was slower to reach a parting of the ways. But by the conclusion of *The Paris Working*—a series of invocations of the gods Mercury and Jupiter through sex magick[57]—Neuburg wearied of the demands of being in a relationship with the boundary-pushing Aleister Crowley. Putting some distance between himself and his lover, Neuburg summered at a cottage in Branscombe, South Devon, with friends who were former disciples of Crowley: Olivia Haddon and Vittoria Cremers. A season of listening to their grievances changed his opinion of his estranged master. It arguably poisoned his relationship with Crowley. Busy with his writing and other students, Crowley didn't notice the distance at which Neuburg had placed himself. Then that fall, when Neuburg returned to London, he tendered his resignation and renounced his magical oaths.[58]

Another traumatic life event closely coincided with Neuburg's break with Crowley. He had been having an ongoing affair with *Rites of Eleusis* actress Jeanne Heyse (1890–1912), who went by the name Ione de Forest. Neuburg dedicated "Sigurd's Songs," a poem cycle in *The Triumph of Pan*, to her. On December 22, 1911, she married Wilfred Schmiechen,[59] Neuburg's friend and fellow student from Trinity who had financed *A Green Garland*. In addition to being Neuburg's benefactor, he was also credited with financially rescuing the Chiswick Press, which printed Crowley's early works. Schmiechen had by this point, owing in part to growing anti-German sentiment preceding

[56] Herbert H. Close (1890–1971) contributed the poem "Memory of Love" to *The Equinox*. Herbert H. Close, "Memory of Love," *The Equinox* 1, no. 7 (March 1912): 291. Other poetry of his from this period appears in the collection *The Religion of Love, Mirth & Gaeity* (Cambridge, UK: R. I. Severs, 1912), variously signed as H.C., Meredith Starr (his pseudonym), and Frater Superna Sequor (his probationer motto). Under his pen name Meredith Starr, he contributed over 120 poems, articles, and reviews to *The Occult Review* between 1910 and 1931.

[57] For *The Paris Working*, see Aleister Crowley, Mary Desti, and Victor B. Neuburg, "Liber CDXV: Opus Lutetianum, the Paris Working," in *The Vision and the Voice, with Commentary and Other Papers: The Collected Diaries of Aleister Crowley, 1909–1914 e.v.*, ed. Hymenaeus Beta, *The Equinox* 4, no. 2 (York Beach, ME: Weiser, 1998), 343–409.

[58] Fuller claims that Crowley responded to Neuburg's resignation by ritually cursing him. Fuller, *Magical Dilemma*, 222. This assertion is highly suspect, as Crowley does not discuss cursing in any of his writings, and it does not appear to be part of his magical practice. Furthermore, Neuburg's later treatment of Crowley hardly sounds like the reaction of a victim to the person who cursed him.

[59] Marriage record, Q4, 1911, St. George Hanover Square, 1a: 1083, GRO. It appears to have been a civil marriage, as the space for recording the officiating church is crossed out and the location given as "The Register Office." The witnesses were Jeanne's older sister, Kathleen, for the bride and Zachary Merton for the groom.

World War I, adopted his step-father's surname of Merton.[60] Despite the good deeds of his friend, Neuburg continued his affair with Heyse. This led Merton, six months into his marriage, to separate from her and, on June 4, 1912, to file for divorce, naming Neuburg in the complaint.[61] Merton's petition provided a laundry list of infidelities including, for example:

5. That since the date of the said marriage the said Jeanne Merton has on divers occasions the dates of which are unknown to your Petitioner committed adultery with Victor Benjamin Neuburg at No. 1, Rossetti Studios, Flood Street, Chelsea, in the County of London,[62] and at No. 3, Radnor Street, Chelsea, in the County of London[63] and at divers other places which are unknown to your Petitioner.
6. That on and between the 21st day of May, 1912, and the 26th day of May, 1912, the said Jeanne Merton committed adultery with the said Victor Benjamin Neuburg at the Hotel des Ecoles, Rue Delambra [*sic*] Montparnasse Paris in the Republic of France.
7. That on and between the 26th day of May, 1912, and the 1st day of June, 1912, the said Jeanne Merton committed adultery with the said Victor Benjamin Neuburg at No. 1, Rossetti Studios, Flood Street, Chelsea in the County of London.
8. That on and between the 1st day of June, 1912, to the date hereof the said Jeanne Merton committed adultery with the said Victor Benjamin Neuburg at No. 3, Radnor Street, Chelsea in the County of London.

Jeanne appeared on June 12 to give an affidavit supporting Merton's petition. The co-respondent, Neuburg, did not make an appearance. In his stead, he sent Frederick Freke Palmer (d. 1932), a solicitor who "had a fashionable practice and was lauded as 'an expert divorce practitioner,'"[64] to appear on his behalf on June 13.

[60] "Schmiechen . . . changed his name in the anti-German atmosphere of the Great War to Wilfred Merton." "Goldschmidt, Ernst Philip (1887–1954)," Christie's (website), March 21, 2005, http://www.christies.com/lotfinder/lot/goldschmidt-ernst-philip-seventy-five-4458354-details.aspx?from=searchresults&intObjectID=4458354&sid=589d6f06-625d-4772-8069-60cc22cbf4b9.
[61] Divorce court file 2768, appellant Wilfred Merton, respondent, Jeanne Merton, corespondent, Victor Benjamin Neuburg, J77/1080, National Archives, Kew, UK, 1912.
[62] This was the address of Jeanne Merton's flat, into which she moved after separating from her husband.
[63] At the time, 3 Radnor Street (now Radnor Walk) was part of Radnor Studios, popular artist studios in Chelsea.
[64] Andrew Rose, *The Woman before Wallis: Prince Edward, the Parisian Courtesan, and the Perfect Murder* (New York: Picador, 2013), 165.

On August 2, at her flat in Rossetti Studios, Chelsea, twenty-one-year-old Jeanne Merton shot herself in the heart with a revolver. The coroner ruled her death a suicide "while temporarily insane."[65] Despite the circumstances of her divorce and the fact that she had been talking for months about committing suicide, biographers have claimed that Neuburg blamed her suicide on some supernatural influence by Crowley. Calder-Marshall, however, offers an alternative take: a lovers' spat, in which Neuburg walked out, took place earlier on the day of her suicide, and Neuburg felt so responsible for her death that he placed his writing career on hold and, when he finally revived it, published his works through the Vine Press either anonymously or pseudonymously. Even this story, however, ignores the fact that Neuburg indeed published poetry under his own name in the 1920s and, in the 1930s, worked for the *Sunday Referee*.[66]

65 Death record, Q3 1912, London, 01A, 391, GRO.

66 Examples of Neuburg's signed publications include V. B. N., "Two Poems," *Pine Cone: Official Quarterly of the Order of Woodcraft Chivalry*, October 1923, 14; Victor B. Neuburg, "Advent," *Pine Cone*, January 1924, 5–6; and Victor B. Neuburg, "Birth Song," *Occult Review* 42 (July 1925): 12–13. See "The Victor Neuburg Bibliography Project," The 100th Monkey Press (website), accessed May 10, 2020, https://www.100thmonkeypress.com/biblio/vneuburg/texts/texts.htm.

8
LIFE AFTER CROWLEY

Having disentangled himself from Crowley without becoming the object of society gossip or newspaper slander, Fuller prospered in his military career. In 1912, he applied to the Staff College, a military academy for experienced officers; he failed the examination on his first try but got in the following year. During World War I, he invented artificial moonlight (using searchlights to provide illumination similar to that of a full moon to facilitate nocturnal operations), and his planning of tank attacks in 1917 and 1918 convinced him that mechanized warfare was the best strategy to reduce casualties. He became increasingly interested in the idea of a fully mechanized army and collaborated in the 1920s with B. H. Liddell Hart (1895–1970) to expand it further. His dogged insistence on mechanization as the path forward made him unpopular with his peers, as did his assertion that the Great War was won out of luck more than strategy. To Fuller, after World War I the failure of the military to learn any tactical lessons marked "a return to mediæval witchcraft."[1]

Appointed commander of the Experimental Force at Tidworth in 1927, he balked at having command of several infantry units, as well. A new commander replaced him, and Fuller was subsequently offered no other significant positions in the military. He was nevertheless promoted to major general in 1930.

His writings at this time veered from far right to a full-throated embrace of fascism. As Gat's examination of Fuller's politics makes clear, Fuller had already been writing "in a Nietzschean vein that Christianity, democracy, and socialism were the enemies of the forces of life and of true morality. . . . What the world needed was authority. The masses had to be controlled by the intelligent minority and by some mystical ideal. It was no accident that Fuller joined the Fascists when the party was established."[2] His book *The Dragon's*

[1] J. F. C. Fuller, *Memoirs of an Unconventional Soldier* (London: Ivor Nicholson and Watson, 1936), 493.

[2] Azar Gat, *Fascist and Liberal Visions: Fuller, Liddell Hart, Douhet, and Other Modernists* (Oxford: Clarendon Press, 1998), 36. See also Mason W. Watson, *"Not Italian or German, but British in Character": J. F. C. Fuller and the Fascist Movement in Britain* (honors thesis, College of William

Friendship in Doubt. Richard Kaczynski, Oxford University Press. © Oxford University Press 2024.
DOI: 10.1093/oso/9780197694008.003.0008

Teeth (1932) baldly proclaimed, "That the race is deteriorating there is no doubt."[3] Foreshadowing today's great-replacement theory, Fuller complained not only about the birthrate of "degenerate stock" outpacing healthy breeds at a rate of seven to four but that "everything possible is done to foster these stocks and reduce their death-rate. . . . The will of man can change all this. It can enforce segregation, sterilization and the lethal chamber. It can insist on birth-control, it can insist upon no vote without work and no relief except in kind."[4]

He butted heads with the War Office over the content of his book *War and Western Civilization* (1932),[5] which they thought could undermine British international legitimacy. He was also asked to rewrite sections of a book that subsequently appeared in 1936, *Generalship*.[6] Consequently, in 1933, his name was added to the list of retired soldiers.

Relieved of military constraints, he joined Sir Oswald Mosley's (1896–1980) British Union of Fascists (BUF) in 1934, as well as the far-right Nordic League. He served as the BUF military spokesman, contributed regularly to its journal, and even ran for Parliament as the BUF candidate. "With his newfound flexibility," Imy recounts, "he wrote one of the most famous anti-Semitic diatribes in 1935, entitled 'The Cancer of Europe' in *Fascist Quarterly*."[7] According to Gat, Fuller's article "blamed the Jews, portrayed as a meta-historical force, for a thousand years' Manichaean struggle to destroy Christian civilization. Quoting from the Cabbalist book *The Zohar* and from the prophets, Fuller claimed that the Jews were materialists and anti-spiritualists, successively using magic, money, and psychoanalysis to further their cause."[8] In his memoirs, published the following year, Fuller celebrated the dictators of his lifetime, calling upon readers to "look at the galaxy of

and Mary, Williamsburg, VA, May 2012, https://digitalarchive.wm.edu/handle/10288/16695; and Christian Giudice, "The Beast and the Black Shirt: J. F C. Fuller's Ties to the British Union of Fascists and the German N.S.D.A.P." (paper presented at the Rutgers University Libraries and Academia Ordo Templi colloquium "The Soldier and the Seer: J. F. C. Fuller, Aleister Crowley, and the British Occult Revival," Rutgers University, New Brunswick, NJ, June 23, 2014).

[3] J. F. C. Fuller, *The Dragon's Teeth: A Study of War and Peace* (London: Constable, 1932), 13.

[4] Fuller, *Dragon's Teeth*, 13–15.

[5] J. F. C. Fuller, *War and Western Civilization 1832–1932: A Study of War as a Political Instrument and the Expression of Mass Democracy* (London: Duckworth, 1932).

[6] J. F. C. Fuller, *Generalship: Its Diseases and Their Cure; a Study of the Personal Factor in Command* (Harrisburg, PA: Military Service Publishing, 1936).

[7] Kate Imy, "Fascist Yogis: Martial Bodies and Imperial Impotence," *Journal of British Studies* 55 (April 2016): 341. See also J. F. C. Fuller, "The Cancer of Europe," *Fascist Quarterly* 1, no. 1 (1935): 66–81.

[8] Gat, *Fascist and Liberal Visions*, 19.

the dictators—Lenin, Stalin, Pilsudski, Kemal Ataturk, Mussolini, Hitler. Not men of the study, but of the forge; blacksmiths of a return to manliness."[9]

Although many of the British military reforms for which Fuller advocated went unrealized, his ideas for mechanized warfare on both land and air influenced the German military in the lead-up to World War II. As the only Englishman invited to Adolf Hitler's fiftieth birthday party in 1939, he observed a massive military parade, which included a panzer tank division. Reputedly, Hitler remarked to Fuller, "I hope you are pleased with your children," to which the retired general replied, "Your Excellency, they have grown up so quickly that I no longer recognize them."[10]

Fuller's association with the BUF ended in May 1940 when the organization was banned by the British government. Although remarkably not imprisoned like Mosley and the other members of his circle, Fuller was placed under observation. His fascist sympathies—evinced through his participation in the BUF, his ongoing calls for a British peace settlement with Hitler, support for the regimes of Italy and Spain, and the fascist ideals expressed in his books—further undermined his standing among his military peers.[11] His nickname "Boney" became a term of derision. During World War II, rather than being asked to serve again, as his retired peers of comparable military rank had been, he was under surveillance, and his name on a list of British subjects "likely to be of potential assistance to the enemy."[12] Fuller's career as a military theorist was over.[13]

Whatever controversies and resentments Fuller may have fostered with his embrace of fascism, he reinvented himself after World War II and was ultimately recognized as the foremost military historian of his generation, if not of all time.[14] His three-volume *A Military History of the Western World* stands as his greatest achievement.[15] In 1963, the Royal United Service Institution

[9] Fuller, *Memoirs*, 476.

[10] For this oft-repeated tale, see, for example, H. B. B.-W., review of "Machine Warfare," *Royal Engineers Journal* 56 (1942): 342.

[11] David H. Zook Jr., "John Frederick Charles Fuller: Military Historian," *Military Affairs* 23, no. 4 (Winter 1959–1960): 185–193.

[12] Leo McKinstry, *Operation Sea Lion: The Failed Nazi Invasion that Turned the Tide of the War* (New York: Overlook Press, 2014), 174–176.

[13] Alaric Searle, "Was there a 'Boney' Fuller after the Second World War? Major-General J. F. C. Fuller as Military Theorist and Commentator, 1945–1966," *War in History* 11, no. 3 (2004): 327–357.

[14] Such, at least, is the opinion of Zook. See Zook, "John Frederick Charles Fuller," 192.

[15] Issued from New York by Funk & Wagnalls, *A Military History of the Western World* appeared in three volumes: *From the Earliest Times to the Battle of Lepanto* (1954), *From the Defeat of the Spanish Armada, 1588, to the Battle of Waterloo, 1815* (1955), and *From the Seven Days Battle, 1862, to the Battle of Leyte Gulf, 1944* (1956).

bestowed upon him the Chesney Memorial Medal for his contributions to military science. He died three years later in Cornwall. Eleven years after Fuller's 1996 death, the *Times Literary Supplement* celebrated its seventy-fifth anniversary with the piece "Reputations Revisited," naming Fuller as one of the most underrated writers of the past seventy-five years. Robert Lowell said he was "as good in his way as Bertrand Russell."[16]

The Science of War

Fuller wrote voluminously on military history and strategy, with forty-five books to his credit in addition to his many articles and lectures. The first of these, *Hints on Training Territorial Infantry*[17] appeared shortly after his split with Crowley. Throughout his career, Fuller carried the influence of his early years with Crowley and the New Agnostics. He reached back to his agnostic years, for "the ideas and vocabulary of Spencer, Darwin, James, and Pearson in formulating his evolutionary scheme of military development."[18] And, as Reid points out, "though he abandoned magic for ever after 1911 he never shook off its vivid vocabulary. His writings are littered with occult analogies."[19]

As we shall in the next section, Fuller did not abandon magic at all, which may account for its vocabulary and imagery seeping into his military writings. His *Reformation of War* (1923)—written "for civilians, who pay for their alchemy and mysteries"[20]—uses the magic wand as a metaphor not once but twice. Early in the book, he writes, "Nations must either move or perish, they dare not wait for miracles to reincarnate them, for to wait is to paralyse the will to act. This will is the true wand of the magician, that sceptre of common-sense which rules the orb of human reason."[21] He returns to this metaphor halfway through the book when he says, "There is nothing too

[16] "Reputations Revisited," *Times Literary Supplement*, no. 3906 (January 21, 1977): 66.

[17] J. F. C. Fuller, *Hints on Training Territorial Infantry: From Recruit to Trained Soldier* (London: Gale & Polden, 1913).

[18] Gat, *Fascist and Liberal Visions*, 39.

[19] Brian Holden Reid, *J .F. C. Fuller: Military Thinker* (Basingstoke, UK: Macmillan, 1987), 19–20. See also Anthony John Trythall, *"Boney" Fuller: Soldier, Strategist, and Writer, 1878–1966* (New Brunswick, NJ: Rutgers University Press, 1977), 242; Rich Stowell, "J. F. C. Fuller: Heretic, Mystic, and War Scientist," *My Public Affairs*, December 2014, https://medium.com/my-public-affairs/j-f-c-fuller-heretic-mystic-and-war-scientist-da348ec2c0e8.

[20] J. F. C. Fuller, *The Reformation of War* (London: Hutchinson, 1923), xii.

[21] Fuller, *Reformation of War*, 5.

wonderful for science—we of the fighting services must grasp the wand of this magician and compel the future to obey us."[22] Fuller dedicates *India in Revolt* (1931) to the goddess Kali, and his introduction, "India and the Gods," situates modern-day India in the context of millennia of the Hindu faith.[23] His 1932 history of war and peace, which devotes six pages to the subject of magical attack,[24] strikingly compares the soldier to a magician:

> The professional soldier is a pure military alchemist, he dabbles in tactical and strategical magic, fashions charms and pentacles, burns incense before training manuals, and when on the battlefield, if he has ever studied military history, conjures forth the ghostly theories of past masters of war in order to solve the problems which there confront him.[25]

However, Fuller's debt to New Agnosticism and Scientific Illuminism is best illustrated by his self-proclaimed magnum opus, *The Foundations of the Science of War*. Secularism called for governing civic life on scientific facts instead of religious dogma; Crowley applied the method of science to the practice of magick, and Fuller did so with his book: "In a small way I am trying to do for war what Copernicus did for astronomy, Newton for physics, and Darwin for natural history. . . . My book is the first in which a writer has attempted to apply the method of science to the study of war."[26] In this text from Britain's top military mind, Fuller sought to lay out an all-encompassing military framework to scientifically guide combat strategy.

Unfortunately, his prose was abstruse, and the book was ruthlessly discredited and disputed.[27] Military historian Brigadier General Sir James Edward Edmonds (1861–1956) "ridiculed the whole idea of a science of war," while Field Marshall Sir Archibald Amar Montgomery-Massingberd (1871–1947) quipped, "I hope someone will stop him making such an ass of himself."[28] Of Fuller's attempt to be the Copernicus, Newton, or Darwin

[22] Fuller, *Reformation of War*, 184. Fuller also quotes this passage, without attribution, in Fuller, *Memoirs*, 456.

[23] J. F. C. Fuller, *India in Revolt* (London: Eyre and Spottiswoode, 1931).

[24] Fuller, *Dragon's Teeth*, 144–149.

[25] Fuller, *Dragon's Teeth*, 275.

[26] Colonel J. F. C. Fuller, *The Foundations of the Science of War* (London: Hutchinson, 1926).

[27] Brian Holden Reid, *Studies in British Military Thought: Debates with Fuller and Liddell Hart* (Lincoln: University of Nebraska Press, 1998), 74.

[28] Reid, *Studies*, 38; Reid, *J. F. C. Fuller*, 87. Montgomery conceded that after seeing the reviews, he had not actually read Fuller's book on the ground that "it would only annoy me!" Reid, *J. F. C. Fuller*, 87.

of military science, the *Saturday Review* remarked, "He has come nearer the achievement of Spinoza, who took the Elements of Euclid as his literary model in a treatise on ethics, and thereby effectually succeeded in limiting the number of his readers."[29] The *Aberdeen Press*, while disappointed, offered a kinder take: "The fruit of 15 years of thought, observation, and experience, this book contains a vast deal of information which cannot but be of great service to military students, although one can hardly say that it is likely to be the last word on the subject with which it deals."[30] While the merits and demerits of the text from a military standpoint are well documented,[31] its agnostic and magical references call for further examination.

The first chapter, "The Alchemy of War," equates the contemporary study of war with alchemy "not because alchemy was utterly absurd, but because it was an art without a science. In alchemy what do we find? A false classification of real facts combined with inconsistent sequences."[32] Facts about war, he argues, can be put to good use through "The Method of Science," the title of his second chapter (partially echoing the motto of *The Equinox*). Here, Fuller cites the man who coined the term *agnosticism*, writing, "All that I have said is included in Huxley's definition of science, namely, 'organized common sense.' "[33] Fuller later recommends other leading agnostic thinkers:

> If the student has little time at his disposal for this study, I can recommend, besides Spencer's *First Principles*, the works of David Hume, four volumes, and, if these be found too long, then Thomas Huxley's essay on "Hume," which is a masterpiece of clear thinking. To read Huxley alone is a valuable training.[34]

These works by Spencer, Hume, and Huxley also appear in Crowley's "Curriculum of A.·.A.·.."

His next chapter, "The Threefold Order," introduces readers to what Welch calls the "triadic mysticism" of Hegel's dialectics[35] but what may just as easily

[29] "The Science of War," *Saturday Review of Politics, Literature, Science and Art* 141, no. 3678 (April 24, 1926): 544.

[30] "Science of War," *Aberdeen Press and Journal*, April 17, 1926, 2.

[31] Reid, *Studies*, 33–48.

[32] Fuller, *Foundations*, 23–24.

[33] Fuller, *Foundations*, 37.

[34] Fuller, *Foundations*, 195n1.

[35] Michael Welch, "The Science of War: A Discussion of J. F. C. Fuller's Shattering of British Continuity," *Journal of the Society for Army Historical Research* 79, no. 320 (2001): 320–334.

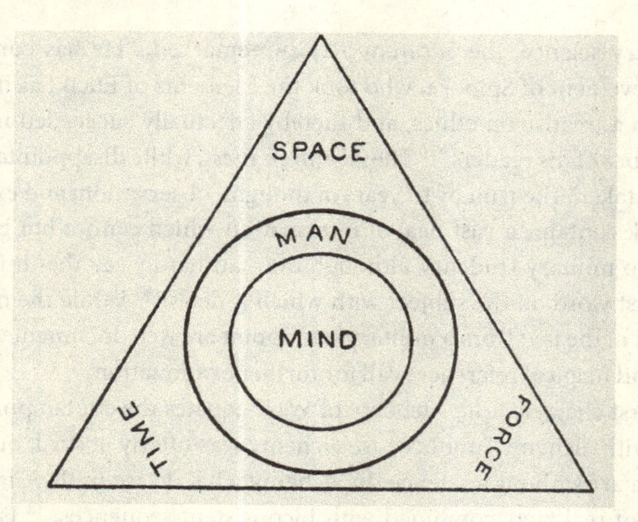

Figure 8.1 This illustration from Fuller's *Foundations of the Science of War*, (1926) p. 176, bears a striking resemblance to the *Triangle of Art* from Crowley's *Goetia*

reflect triads in occult topics near and dear to Fuller, such as the Kabbalistic Tree of Life, the three gunas in yoga, the three Fates in Greek mythology, the triple form of Hecate, and so on. Indeed, Hegel's concept of thesis, antithesis, and synthesis presents but another expression of the perennial wisdom that runs throughout Crowley's work. For instance, in the "Cry of the 22nd Aethyr," he says that the mystical formula of ARARITA[36] is used "to equate and identify every idea with its opposite; thus being released from the obsession of thinking any one of them as 'true.' "[37] This inclusion of Hegel within the context of harmoniously balancing polar opposites appears in Fuller's writing as early as 1907's *The Star in the West*, where he lists "the Favashi of the Zoroastrian, the Tree of Knowledge of Babylonia and Genesis, the Light and Darkness of Isaiah, the Yakheen and Boaz of Solomon, the Unique Athanor of the Qabalist, the Balance of Hegel."[38]

[36] In Kabbalah, ARARITA is a mystical name of God, formed from the *notariqon* (acronym) of the Hebrew phrase אחד ראש אחדותו ראש יחודו תמורתו אחד (*Achad Rosh Achdotho Rosh Ichudo Temurato Achad*), which is translated, in esoteric circles, as "One is His Beginning; One is His Individuality; His Permutation is One."

[37] Aleister Crowley, *The Vision and the Voice*, ed. Israel Regardie (Dallas: Sangreal, 1972), 74.

[38] Capt. J. F. C. Fuller, *The Star in the West: A Critical Essay upon the Works of Aleister Crowley* (London: Walter Scott, 1907), 169.

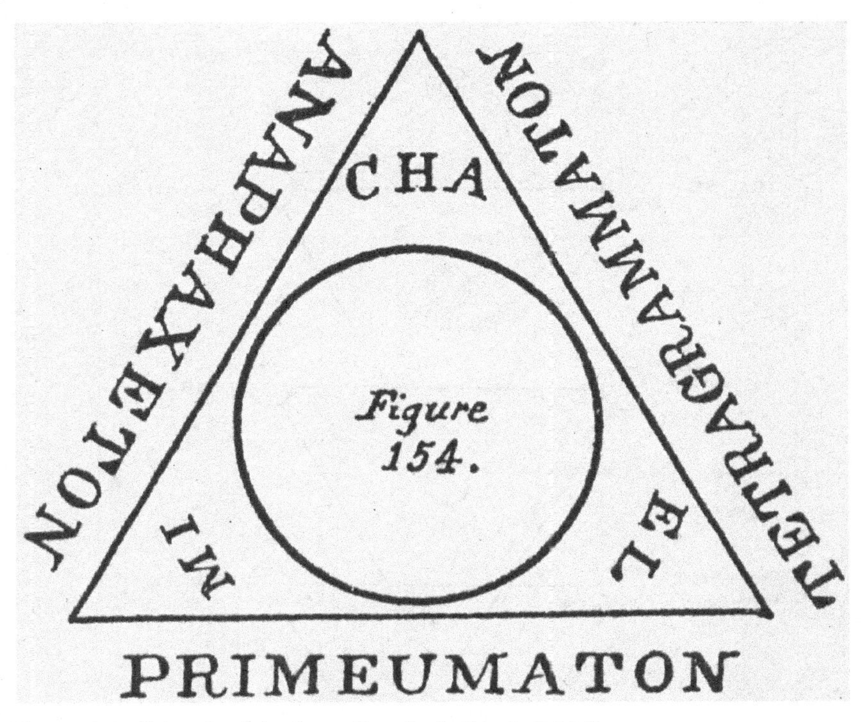

Figure 8.2 *Triangle of Art* from Crowley's *Goetia* (1904)

Much as Welch sees *The Foundations of the Science of War* through a Hegelian lens, so Pellegrini sees it from the perspective of Spencer. Fuller's chapter on "The Law of the Economy of Force" not only quotes from Spencer's *First Principles*, it treats force as the animating principle of Fuller's martial philosophy of war. Pellegrini argues, further, that Fuller's frequent reliance upon a triplicate order also derives from Spencer. For example, Fuller's triplicity of space, time, and force appears to draw upon the third chapter of *First Principles*, titled "Space, Time, Matter, Motion, and Force." In Fuller's division of the mind into knowledge, faith, and belief, Pellegrini sees an expansion of the two major subdivisions of *First Principles*: the knowable and unknowable.[39]

Regardless of the source—Hegel, Spencer, Crowley, or all three—triadic ideas permeate Fuller's magnum opus. Early on in his chapter on "The Threefold Order," he writes,

[39] See Robert P. Pellegrini, *The Links between Science, Philosophy, and Military Theory: Understanding the Past, Implications for the Future* (Maxwell Air Force Base, Alabama: Air University Press, 1997), 29–38.

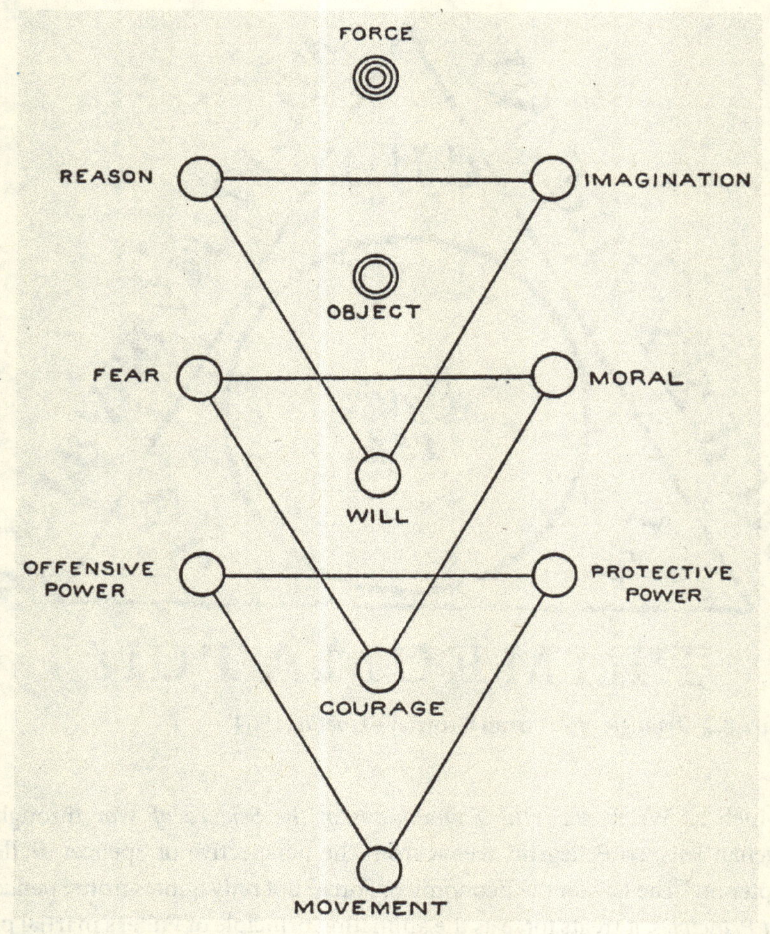

Figure 8.3 This illustration from Fuller's *Foundations of the Science of War* (1926) is one of several that are configured like the Kabbalistic Tree of Life

> Not only do we live in a three-dimensional world, but we think three dimensionally and our thoughts reflect a threefold order. We sense ourselves as mind, body, and soul, and the world as force moving through space. We talk of God, Nature, and man; all our religious ideas are ultimately based on a trinity, as are those of all but the crudest of cults.[40]

[40] Fuller, *Foundations*, 51.

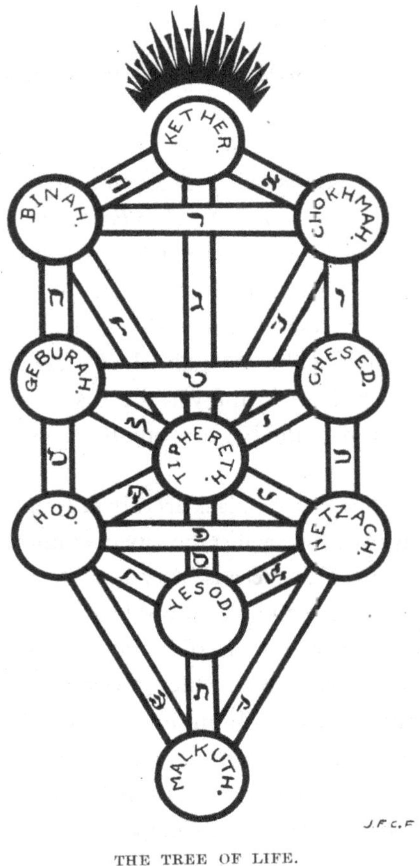

Figure 8.4 *The Tree of Life*, by Fuller from his *Yoga: A Study of the Mystical Philosophy of the Brahmins and Buddhists*, 1925

This chapter's threefold typologies of the organization, nature, and activities of man (as well as the threefold nature of war) includes diagrams reminiscent of the *Goetia*'s Triangle of Art (see figures 8.1 and 8.2).

Furthermore, on page 211, in his chapter on "The Principles of War," Fuller's diagram of "The General Relationship of the Elements of War" is clearly modeled on the Kabbalistic Tree of Life, as is his similarly structured diagram of the "General Relationship of the Principles of War," on p. 222 (see figures 8.3 and 8.4).

Occult Writings

Contrary to Reid's contention that Fuller abandoned magic altogether after 1911, his fascination with the occult continued. This was consistent with the significant overlap of the far right with mystic circles of the day.[41] Over the years, Fuller wrote books and articles on occult subjects. In 1921, he contributed the article "The Black Arts" to *Form*, the short-lived art magazine operated by former Crowley associate and *Equinox* illustrator Austin Osman Spare (1886–1956). Spare would even contribute striking artwork to accompany the article (see figure 8.5). The text would be reprinted in the 1926 *Occult Review*. Although published a decade after parting with Crowley, Fuller's words fittingly apply to the false charges of black magic to which Crowley was, and would be, continually subjected:

> Thus history will tell us that the black arts are in reality but a revolt against convention, an insurrection against the satiety of images, a war against accepted words. They are black because they are unknown, evil because they unfrock the commonplace and take bread from the mouths of mumbling priests. Sometimes these arts are terrible and infernal, sometimes they are sublime and celestial, but always are they powerful, compelling hostility or allegiance. Separating the goats from the sheep they sound a "Deus Vult" and emblazon a new crusade: a crusade against ignorance and oppression, which, like a living wind, raises the dust of the unconscious and casts it mote by mote into that beam of light which we call the intelligence of man.[42]

While it is well documented that Gerald Gardner paraphrased extensively from Crowley's writings in the rituals of his witchcraft revival, this article's influence is acknowledged less frequently. As Fuller writes,

> In the Middle Ages of Christian rule did once again the spirit of man break the shackles which bound it, and it broke them by an alliance with Satan. Mad, if not insane, would the sorcerer creep forth to some heath or grove far away from monastery or church, and, bereft of his senses through the gloom of those desolate places, would he shriek to the stars:

[41] Gat, *Fascist and Liberal Visions*, 18; Nicholas Goodrick-Clarke, *The Occult Roots of Nazism: The Ariosophists of Austria and Germany, 1890–1935* (Wellingborough, UK: Aquarian Press, 1985; repr. New York: NYU Press, 1993).

[42] J. F. C. Fuller, "The Black Arts," *Form* 2, no. 1 (November–December 1921): 57–66; repr. J. F. C. Fuller, "The Black Arts," *Occult Review* 43, no. 1 (January 1926): 227–236.

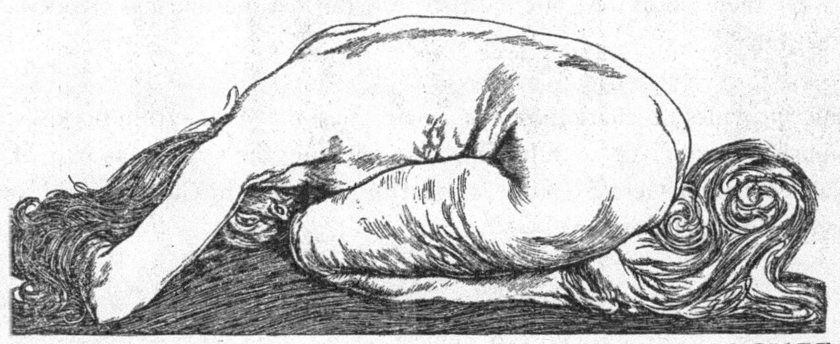

ARETHUSA *BY AUSTIN O. SPARE*

THE BLACK ARTS

BY J. F. C. FULLER

AN is human and a mystery; herein is to be sought all our sorrows, all our joys, all our desires, all our activities. Man is a troublesome creature, inwardly troubled by his consciousness, outwardly troubled by the unconscious, the things which surround him, the "why" and "wherefore" of which fascinate his mind and perplex his heart. We cannot fathom the origin of life nor can we state its purpose; we can but judge of it by inference, and inferences, if we probe them deeply, dissolve into an unknowable œther, an all pervading miracle. Yet, such as these shadows are, we follow them, and as day creeps out of night so does the conscious emanate from out the vast and formless body of that unconsciousness which softly enfolds us in its gloom.

SOME lie still in the coffin of existence; these are the human sheep who, where the grass of life is green, browse peacefully and, where it is dust, die or bleat helplessly to others. These others are those who tear their shrouds and hammer at the lid, with bleeding brow loosen the nails of oblivion, and, through the chinks between mind and soul, peer into the beyond.

FOLLOW me, cries the priest, the king, the lawyer and the physician, and the human flock follows. Herein is to be revealed a mystery; not of the seeing leading the blind, for all are ultimately sightless, but of a spirit intangible, mysterious, which impels gross human flesh to flow onwards in streamlets and rivers to some unknown and seemingly unknowable sea. This impulse towards movement, whether it be

57

Figure 8.5 Fuller's article "The Black Arts" (with accompanying illustration by Austin Osman Spare) appeared in the November/December 1921 issue of *Form*

> "Eko! eko! Azarak. Eko! eko! Zomelak!
> Zod-ru-kod e Zod-ru-koo
> Zod-ru-koz e Goo-ru-moo!
> Eo! Eo! Oo . . . Oo . . . Oo!"

Though the words be different, it is the same chant of the Assyrian seer, for it is the conjuration of freedom, freedom which was to beget the arts and sciences of to-day, that consciousness which, though latent, was unconscious when these words were uttered. They were the love murmurings of a new betrothal.[43]

Fuller provides no citation for these mad cries; they come from no known published source. Yet decades later, the opening line appears as part of a witches' chant in Gerald Gardner's ritual for Samhain (the Gaelic festival corresponding to Halloween):

> Eko, eko, Azarak
> Eko, eko, Zomelak
> Bazabi lacha bachabe
> Lamac cahi achababe[44]

The source for Fuller's chant was apparently his fertile imagination. Support is lent to this conclusion by the fact that much of this article seems to be a fantasy, a prose poem, or meditation on principles rather than a recitation of historical facts. Thus we find Fuller telling a fable about the vampire Elerion and the boy Zoodrillgoo encountering a witch chanting, "Thrice I passed the withered ash; Thrice I smote the hawthorn tree . . . ," while his tale of the Black Mass is an extended quote not from some ancient source but his preface to "The Temple of Solomon the King".[45] It therefore appears that Fuller was another of the various sources that Gardner drew from when composing his Book of Shadows.

A few years later, Fuller published his book-length study of *Yoga* (1925; see figure 8.6).[46] It was a slightly revised reprint of his lengthy installment on the subject from *The Equinox*'s "Temple of Solomon the King"[47] with all references to Crowley's diaries and practices omitted. Rather than use his

[43] Fuller, "Black Arts."

[44] Ronald Hutton, *The Triumph of the Moon: A History of Modern Pagan Witchcraft* (Oxford: Oxford University Press, 1999), 231–232. The last couplet of Gardner's quatrain, not appearing in Fuller's original, is drawn from the diabolical conjuration in the thirteenth-century miracle play *Le Miracle de Théophile*: "Bagahi, Laca, Bachahé, / Lamac, Cahi, Achabahé, / Karrelyos, / Lamac, Lamec, Bachalyos, / Cabahagi, Sabalyos, /Baryolas, / Lagozatha, Cabyolas, / Samahac et Famyolas, /Harrahya." Rutebeuf, *Le Miracle de Théophile*, act I, scene IV, lines 160–168.

[45] [J. F. C. Fuller], "The Temple of Solomon the King," *The Equinox* 1, no. 1 (March 1909): 186–187.

[46] J. F. C. Fuller, *Yoga: A Study of the Mystical Philosophy of the Brahmins and Buddhists* (London: William Rider, 1925).

[47] [J. F. C. Fuller], "The Temple of Solomon the King IV," *The Equinox* 1, no. 4 (September 1, 1910): 41–196.

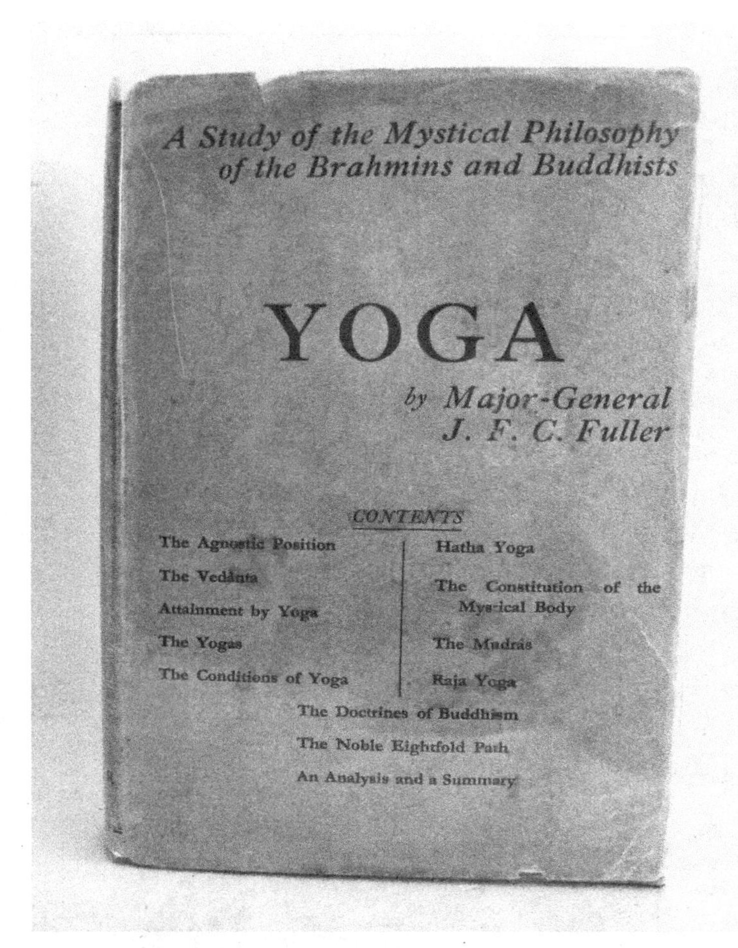

Figure 8.6 Fuller's book *Yoga* (1925) was a lightly edited outtake from his "Temple of Solomon the King" series in *The Equinox* (1910)

illustrations from *The Equinox*, Fuller supplied five new images, including one that reproduced his original version of *The Yogi* (see figures 8.7–8.10).

According to Trythall, Fuller "regarded himself as a working yogi, he told Starr at the time, a searcher after Truth which, like an onion, had many layers. All roads led to Truth and he had chosen War simply because he was a soldier."[48] Meredith Starr was the pen name of Herbert Close, a former A.·.A.·.

[48] Trythall, *"Boney" Fuller*, 107.

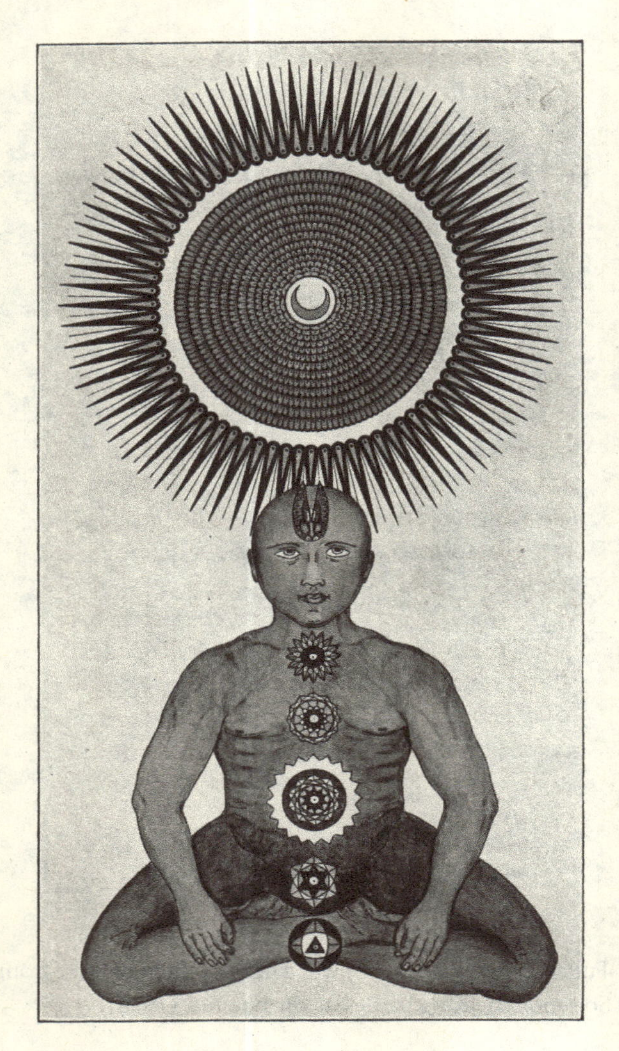

DIAGRAM 83.
The Yogi (showing the Cakkras).

Figure 8.7 Fuller's original picture of *The Yogi* from *The Equinox* (1910)

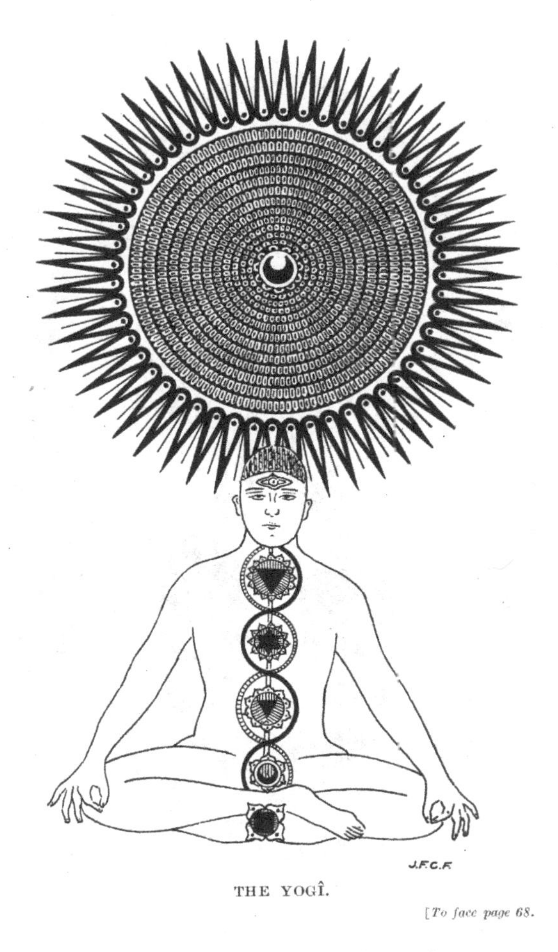

Figure 8.8 Fuller's redrawn picture of *The Yogi* from *The Equinox* (1910) for the reprint of his book-length essay as *Yoga* (1925)

Probationer under Fuller and a lifelong friend. He reviewed the book enthusiastically in the *Occult Review*:

> Many volumes have been penned about Yoga, but there is more sense in this little book of 140 pages than in most of them combined. Colonel Fuller has the rare gift of concentration, and concentration, when equilibrated, results in lucidity of vision. . . . As Col. Fuller shows by cross-references to the Quabalah and Western Magic, there are many close parallels in Eastern

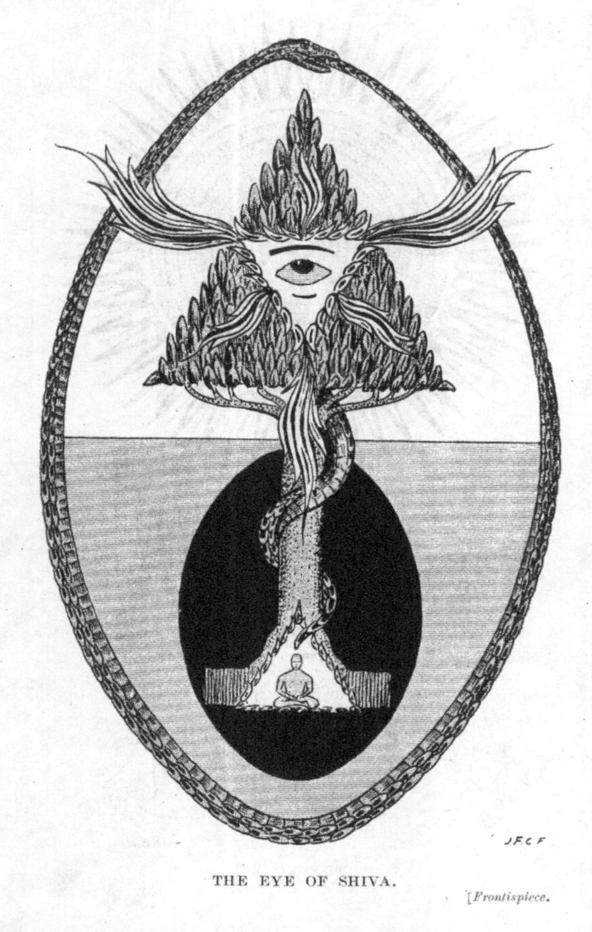

Figure 8.9 Illustration by Fuller for *Yoga* (1925): "The Eye of Shiva."

> and Western Methods. . . . This book is a ringing call to work. The only knowledge worth having is the fruit of personal attainment.[49]

The *Scotsman* concurred, albeit in more restrained tones: "Mr. Fuller, of course, writes from the standpoint of an enthusiast, but of a well-informed enthusiast, and he succeeds in holding the attention even of those who may not be in sympathy with his ideas."[50]

[49] Meredith Starr [Herbert H. Close], "Reviews," *Occult Review* 41, no. 6 (June 1925): 402.
[50] "Theological Works," *The Scotsman*, May 21, 1925, 2.

Figure 8.10 Illustration by Fuller for *Yoga* (1925): "The Bôdhi Satva."

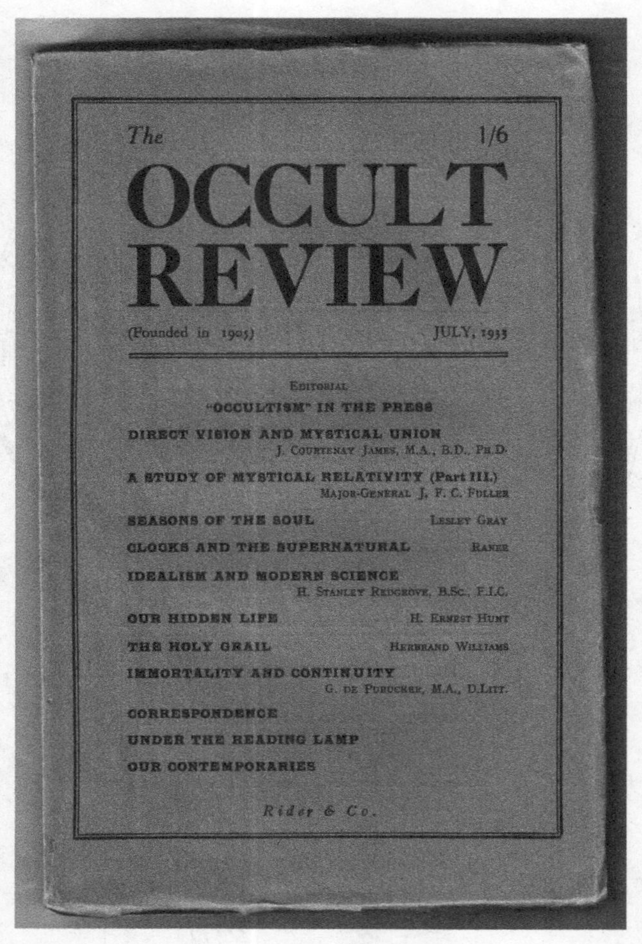

The 1/6

OCCULT
REVIEW

(Founded in 1905) JULY, 1933

EDITORIAL

"OCCULTISM" IN THE PRESS

DIRECT VISION AND MYSTICAL UNION
J. COURTENAY JAMES, M.A., B.D., PH.D.

A STUDY OF MYSTICAL RELATIVITY (Part III.)
MAJOR-GENERAL J. F. C. FULLER

SEASONS OF THE SOUL LESLEY GRAY

CLOCKS AND THE SUPERNATURAL RANEE

IDEALISM AND MODERN SCIENCE
H. STANLEY REDGROVE, B.SC., F.I.C.

OUR HIDDEN LIFE H. ERNEST HUNT

THE HOLY GRAIL HERBRAND WILLIAMS

IMMORTALITY AND CONTINUITY
G. DE PURUCKER, M.A., D.LITT.

CORRESPONDENCE

UNDER THE READING LAMP

OUR CONTEMPORARIES

Rider & Co.

Figure 8.11 The July 1933 *Occult Review* with the concluding installment of Fuller's "A Study of Mystical Relativity"

In 1933, Fuller published a three-part article in the *Occult Review* that argued that the theory of relativity—with time as the fourth dimension—had paved the way for a new understanding of cosmogenesis that reconciles science and religion, which was particularly suited to the emergent new spirituality of the twentieth century (see figure 8.11):

> The conflict between science and religion is, I believe, nearing the end of its last lap, and that the race will be won by neither, but by both in a stupendous spiritual revival, a revival which will change the world more completely

> than Christianity changed it after the fall of the Roman Empire, or rational thought changed it after the Reformation. What these changes will be it is as impossible to foresee as it would have been to have foreseen the existing world of science a hundred years ago. . . .
>
> Is there, then, no death, and is immortality with us now? Is the "I" within me both birthless and deathless? The mystical union of science and religion answers "Yes," and the courtship which alone can lead to this union is that the method of science, that search after truth, be applied to spiritual ends as it has been to physical ends. Once science struggles through the gloom of alchemy and astrology, but it had the courage to struggle through darkness towards light. To-day religion is in eclipse and it also must have the courage to struggle, to probe into the world within, as science has probed into the world without. When it does so, then, I think, we shall find that this world is not as it at present seems—a conflict between fears, but a harmony full of hope, and hope is fear reversed.[51]

Two decades removed from his association with Crowley (and four decades before Fritjof Capra's *Tao of Physics* compared quantum physics to Eastern mysticism),[52] Fuller's words resonate with those same ideals that unified them as idealistic young men at the turn of the century: ushering in the dawn of a transformative New Aeon, one as revolutionary as the Christianity that reshaped the world after the Roman Empire; exploring how "the method of science" can serve the aim of religion, as *The Equinox* proclaimed; and examining how, through this new understanding of the world, we can conquer death[53] and "fear not at all."[54]

Fuller followed these articles with *The Secret Wisdom of the Qabalah* (1937; see figure 8.12).[55] Trythall points out that this was foreshadowed a

[51] Major-General J. F. C. Fuller, "A Study of Mystical Relativity: (III) The Unity of the Material and Spiritual," *Occult Review* 58, no. 1 (July 1933): 18–21. See also Major-General J. F. C. Fuller, "A Study of Mystical Relativity: (I) The Question of Symbols," *Occult Review* 57, no. 5 (May 1933): 306–312; and Major-General J. F. C. Fuller, "A Study of Mystical Relativity: (II) The Source of Mystic Power," *Occult Review* 57, no. 6 (June 1933): 370–377.

[52] Fritjof Capra, *The Tao of Physics: An Exploration of the Parallels between Modern Physics and Eastern Mysticism* (Berkeley, CA: Shambhala, 1975).

[53] Crowley writes, "93 is the number of the word of the Law—Thelema—Will, and of Agape—Love, which indicates the nature of Will. It is furthermore the number of the Word which overcomes death, as members of the degree of M.·.M.·. of the O.T.O. are well aware." The Master Therion [Aleister Crowley], *Magick in Theory and Practice* (Paris: Lecram Press, 1929–1930), 48–49.

[54] *Book of the Law* 3:17.

[55] J. F. C. Fuller, *The Secret Wisdom of the Qabalah: A Study in Jewish Mystical Thought* (London: Rider, 1937).

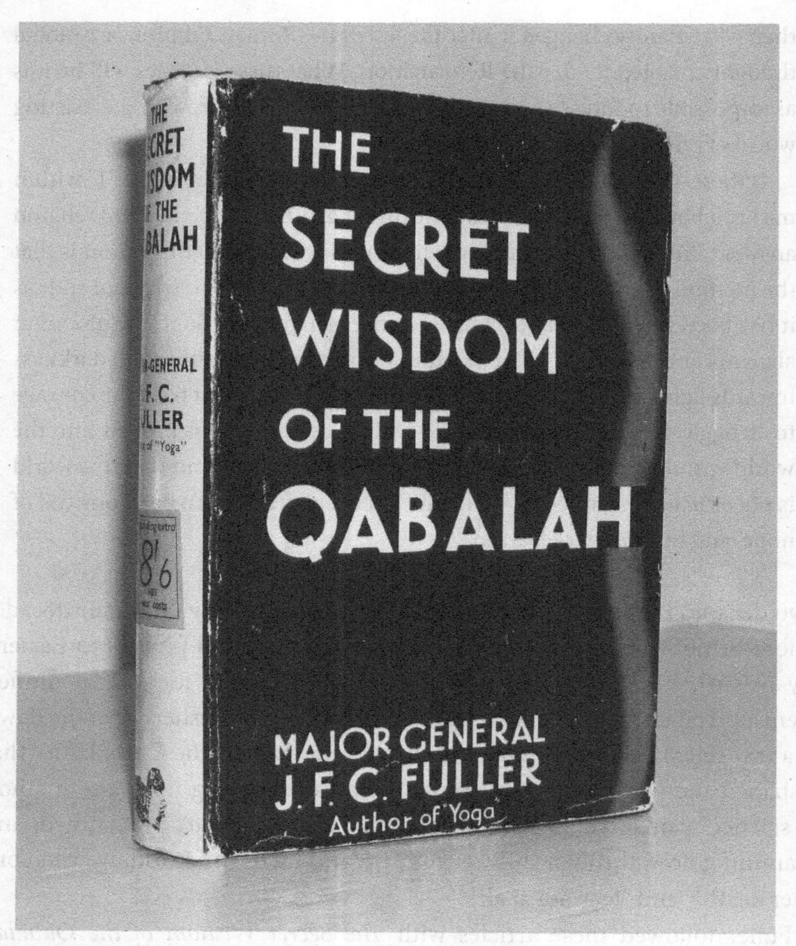

Figure 8.12 J. F. C. Fuller's *The Secret Wisdom of the Qabalah* (1937)

year earlier in Fuller's *First of the League Wars*, wherein Fuller asserted that Judaic law took on two forms, "the written and the oral, the latter the reverse of the former, Satanic as opposed to God-like. This was 'the key to the hidden wisdom in the Hebrew Qabalah.'"[56] The *Times of India* lamented that "Fuller's little book is extremely hard reading and is not meant to convey enlightenment to the masses," while the *Theosophical Forum* noted that Fuller draws insufficiently from original source documents and that his "speculative

[56] Fuller, *First*, 132. See also J. F. C. Fuller, *The First of the League Wars, Its Lessons and Omens* (London: Eyre and Spottiswoode, 1936); and Trythall, *"Boney" Fuller*, 201.

study" leads to "questionable conclusions and inaccuracies."[57] Nevertheless, in 1937 the publisher Gnosis, in Amsterdam, contracted with Fuller to produce Dutch translations of both works, which appeared in 1939.[58] An English rerelease happened not long after.[59]

Finally, in the 1940s, Fuller contributed another three articles to the *Occult Review*, reflections on wars both past and present that meld military and occult thinking in a way only Fuller could have penned.[60] Using language remarkably similar to Crowley's conceptualization of θελημα or "will," Fuller viewed warfare as a clash between wills of the opposing generals, each striving to impose his will on the other and thus "entering the world of magic."[61] Using a similar logic, Fuller also argued that propaganda is also a form of magic and that Nazi Minister of Propaganda Joseph Goebbels (1897–1945) was therefore a magician.[62]

Victor Neuburg's Later Years

Victor Neuburg, by contrast, publicly expressed little interest in magic or occultism after parting with Crowley. He contributed only once to the *Occult Review*: 1925's "Birth-Song."[63] Instead, his interests and pursuits were literary. In 1917, he contributed the column "Recent Verse" to the *New Age*, the same journal for which Katherine Mansfield was a writer.[64] During World War I, he served briefly as a private in the Royal Army Service Corps. As a clerk stationed in France, he was tasked with lighting the office fire each day but more often than not was found reading the newspaper with which he was provided rather than using it to kindle the fire.[65]

57 H. D., "Hebrew Mysticism," *Times of India*, February 12, 1937, 6; G. Barborka, "Book Reviews," *Theosophical Forum* 10, no. 3 (March 1, 1937): 233.

58 A copy of the contract is preserved in the J. F. C. Fuller Papers, box 4, MC1250, Special Collections and University Archives, Rutgers University, New Brunswick, New Jersey. The Dutch translations are J. F. C. Fuller, *Yoga: Een studie van de mystieke wijsbegeerte der brahminen en boeddhisten*, trans. J. H. W. Boelens (Amsterdam: Gnosis, 1939); and J. F. C. Fuller, *De verborgen wijsheid van de Kabbala: Een studie in de Joodse mystiek* (Amsterdam: Gnosis, 1939).

59 J. F. C. Fuller, *The Secret Wisdom of the Qabalah. A Study in Jewish Mystical Thought* (London: Occult Book Society, n.d.). Although undated, Weiser Antiquarian dates this publication to circa 1940.

60 Major General J. F. C. Fuller, "Magic and War," *Occult Review* 69, no. 2 (April 1942): 53–54; Major General J. F. C. Fuller, "The Attack by Magic," *Occult Review* 69, no. 4 (October1942): 125–126, 124; Major General J. F. C. Fuller, "The City and the Bomb," *Occult Review* 71, no. 1 (January 1944): 10–12.

61 Fuller, "Magic and War," 53. See also Reid, *J. F. C. Fuller*, 19–20; and Trythall, *"Boney" Fuller*, 221.

62 Trythall, *"Boney" Fuller*, 221.

63 Victor B. Neuburg, "Birth-Song," *Occult Review* 41 (June 1925): 352–353.

64 V. B. N., "Recent Verse," *New Age* 21, no. 6 (June 7, 1917): 134–135.

65 Victor E. Neuburg, *Vickybird: A Memoir by His Son* (London: Polytechnic of North London, 1983), 5.

Figure 8.13 Vine Cottage in Steyning (on the right side of the road)

Discharged in autumn 1919, he lived in his Aunt Ti's (Theresa Royce *née* Jacobs) cottage, Vine Cottage, in Steyning, Sussex. As Rupert Croft-Cooke put it, "After demobilization he persuaded his family to give him the means to do what he had always wanted—set up a hand printing-press. They gave him the use of Vine Cottage in Steyning, which belonged to one of them, bought him the press and made him a small allowance."[66] It was here, with the financial assistance of his aunt, that he started the Vine Press as a small, independent publisher of his own poetry along with works by friends and fellow literati (see figures 8.13–8.15).

Hopper conjures an outré image of the Vine Press, a labor of love quite different from a major publisher: "There wasn't much to it. A hand-cranked printing press and a unique typeface, set in a room in a cottage, turned by Neuburg and his wife."[67] This Mrs. Neuburg was Kathleen Rose Goddard, whom Victor married in 1921; their son, Victor E. Neuburg, was born in 1924. The "typeface," designed by Neuburg, was a "quaint and not unattractive type . . . carefully designed . . . with the ornate capitals, the linked double *o*'s and the little curve joining *s* to *t*"[68] (see figure 8.16). Neuburg tapped local talent to flesh out his publications. This included woodcut illustrations—a hallmark of

[66] Rupert Croft-Cooke, *The Glittering Pastures* (London: Putnam, 1962), 88.
[67] Justin Hopper, *Obsolete Spells: Poems and Prose from Victor Neuburg and the Vine Press* (London: Strange Attractor, 2022), 20.
[68] Croft-Cooke, *Glittering Pastures*, 98.

Figure 8.14 Detail of Vine Cottage in Steyning showing Vine Press signage

Vine Press titles—by three local brothers, Dennis, Percy, and Eric West.[69] Other illustrations were provided by artists like Beatrice Linda Stanbrough, who did the cover to *Swift Wings*, and Eve Rice, who made woodcuts for the book *Before the Storm*; the Vine Press even offered pens by inventor Merton Davis.[70] All these production choices reflected Neuburg's character, as captured by McNeff:

> Neuburg does not recant or foreswear the magic of his youth. He does not turn Catholic or take up golf. He publishes books that reflect his love of local lore and landscape. . . . [He is] a warm, flawed human being who works tirelessly to better the lot of others, especially fellow artists, and keeps faith with the magical, free-spirited royal road of his youth.[71]

Victor and Kathleen Neuburg together operated the press machinery, and "contemporaries commented that the couple seemed at their happiest while

[69] In 1931, Dennis (1893–1979) and Percy (1898–1989) would purchase the 64 High Street stationer, bookseller, and newsagent business of retiring Reg Bateman and began operating under the name "D. & P. West Library." The business still operates today as West Printing Works Ltd., now on its third generation of family ownership. See "Dennis & Percy West," Sussexpostcards.info (website), accessed September 26, 2020, http://www.sussexpostcards.info/publishers.php?PubID=385; and "About Wests!," Wests Printing (website), accessed September 26, 2020, https://web.archive.org/web/20180902000827/http://www.westsprinting.co.uk/about.htm.

[70] Hopper, *Obsolete Spells*, 40; Princess Ouroussoff, *Before the Storm: Four Tales of Old Russia* (Steyning, UK: Vine Press, 1925).

[71] Richard McNeff, foreword to Hopper, *Obsolete Spells*, 14–15.

Figure 8.15 Vine Press advertisement from the December 1922 *Bookman's Journal*

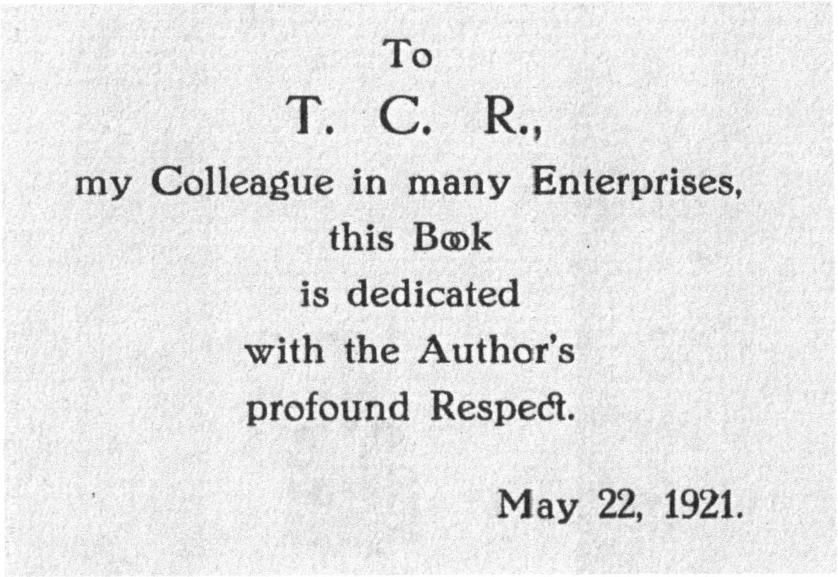

To
T. C. R.,
my Colleague in many Enterprises,
this Book
is dedicated
with the Author's
profound Respect.

May 22, 1921.

Figure 8.16 The dedication from *Songs of the Groves* (1921), illustrating the font Neuburg designed, showing ligatures (between *c* and *t*) and linked double *o*'s

printing and cutting pages, often late into the night."[72] The finished sheets were bound into books by Kensett of Brighton. Owing to the bespoke nature of the press, it produced only eighteen titles during its existence from 1920 to 1930[73] (see figures 8.17–8.20 for the titles featuring Neuburg's works and figures 8.21a–c for examples of his advertising circulars).

The Neuburgs hosted artists, musicians, and writers at the cottage, including composer Peter Warlock (Philip Heseltine, 1894–1930), who in 1923

[72] Hopper, *Obsolete Spells*, 41.

[73] These titles were Gabriele D'Annunzio's broadsheet *Appeal to Europe* (translated by Hayter Preston), 1920; and the following books: *Lillygay: An Anthology of Anonymous Poems*, 1920, edited by Victor B. Neuburg; Victor B. Neuburg's *Songs of the Groves: Records of the Ancient World*, 1921; Victor B. Neuburg's *Swift Wings: Songs in Sussex*, 1921; Rupert Croft-Cooke's *Songs of a Sussex Tramp*, 1922; Victor B. Neuburg's *Larkspur: A Lyric Garland*, 1922; Ernest Osgood Hanbury's *Night's Triumphs: Songs of Nature*, 1924; Princess Ouroussoff's *Before the Storm: Four Tales of Old Russia*, 1925; Gerard Durani Martineau's *The Way of the South Wind*, 1925; Gerard Durani Martineau's *Teams of Tomorrow*, 1926; Alfred de Musset, Henrietta Tayler, Constance Tayler, and Miron Grindea's *The White Blackbird*, 1927; *Wot's the Game? (England's Post-War Book)*, 1928, in verse and by Billy Muggins writing pseudonymously; *Seven Years*, 1928, poems by Shirley Tarn (pseudonym of Victor B. Neuburg; Vera Gwendolen Pragnell's *The Story of the Sanctuary*, 1928; Ernest Osgood Hanbury's *Poems: A Memorial Volume*, 1928; *Day of Life*, 1929, by Rold White (Harold Dinely Jennings White); Ethel Archer's *Phantasy, and Other Poems*, 1930; and *Twain One*, 1930, by Rold White (Harold Dinely Jennings White). See Hopper's *Obsolete Spells* for a history and anthology of these works.

Figure 8.17 A selection of Victor Neuburg's Vine Press titles: *Lillygay* (1920)

set four selections from *Lillygay* to music, including the Neuburg-penned "Rantum Tantum."[74] Sixteen years later, composer Roger Quilter would likewise set "Trollie Lollie" from *Larkspur* to music.[75] By the end of the decade, however, the Neuburgs grew estranged, the Vine Press folded, and Vickybird soon took up with his new love, Runia Tharpe, moving in with her in London.[76]

[74] Peter Warlock, *Lillygay* (London: J. & W. Chester, 1923).
[75] Roger Quilter and Victor B. Neuburg, *Trollie Lollie Laughter* (London: Ascherberg & Hopwood, 1939).
[76] For a contemporary reviewer's reaction to these books, see Wilfred G. Partington, "Mystery Books," *Bookman's Journal and Print Collector* 7, no. 18 (March 1923): 183–184. For a modern

Figure 8.18 A selection of Victor Neuburg's Vine Press titles: *Songs of the Groves* (1921)

In 1929–1930, Neuburg intersected in curious ways with London's short-lived Mandrake Press. Founded in 1929 by Edward Goldston and P. R. Stephensen, this small press published literary luminaries such as D. H. Lawrence, Liam O'Flaherty, and Rhys Davies. However, it is arguably best known for inking an ambitious publishing contract with Aleister Crowley, setting out to rehabilitate his literary reputation. Consequently, in 1929 the press brought out Crowley's

appreciation, see Justin Hopper, "O Sunny Hour! Toward the Centenary of the Vine Press," *Rituals and Declarations* 1 (Winter 2019–2020): 62–69.

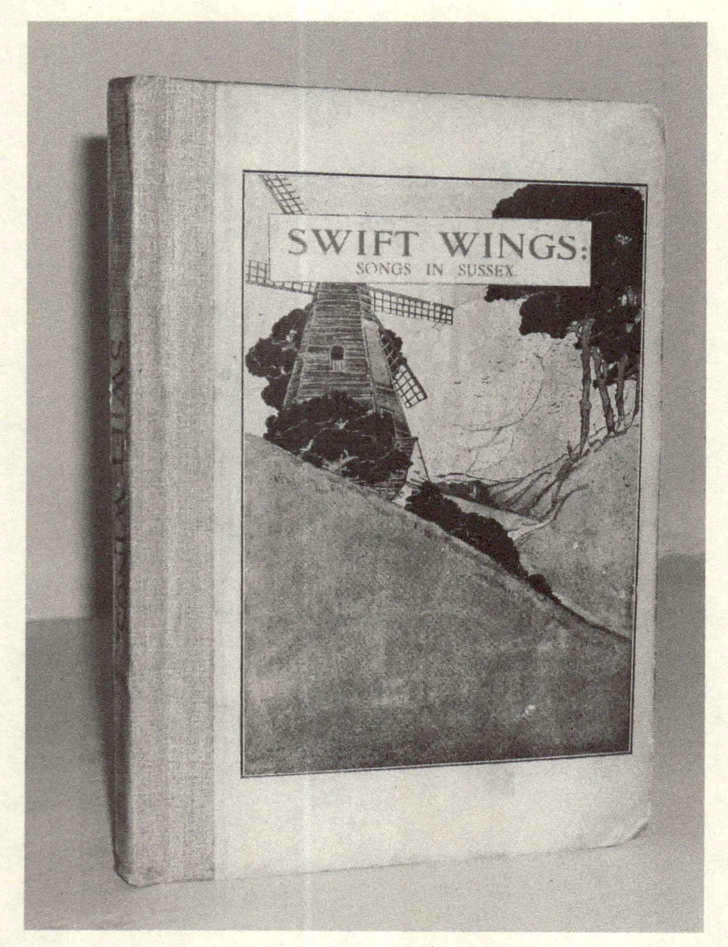

Figure 8.19 A selection of Victor Neuburg's Vine Press titles: *Swift Wings: Songs in Sussex* (1921)

short-story collection *The Stratagem and Other Stories*, his supernatural novel *Moonchild*, and the first two of six projected volumes of his autohagiography, *The Spirit of Solitude*. Stephensen himself—with Crowley's personal secretary, Israel Regardie, helping by compiling Crowley's press cuttings—added to this output with *The Legend of Aleister Crowley*, arguing that Crowley was a man of great poetic and spiritual gifts who had, for the past twenty years, been the victim of unprecedented vilification in the yellow press.[77]

[77] Aleister Crowley, *The Stratagem: And Other Stories* (London: Mandrake, 1929); Aleister Crowley, *Moonchild: A Prologue* (London: Mandrake Press, 1929); Aleister Crowley, *The Spirit of Solitude: An Autohagiography: Subsequently Re-Antichristened the Confessions of Aleister Crowley* (London: Mandrake Press, 1929); P. R. Stephensen, *The Legend of Aleister Crowley: Being a Study of the Documentary Evidence Relating to a Campaign of Personal Vilification Unparalleled in Literary History* (London: Mandrake Press, 1930).

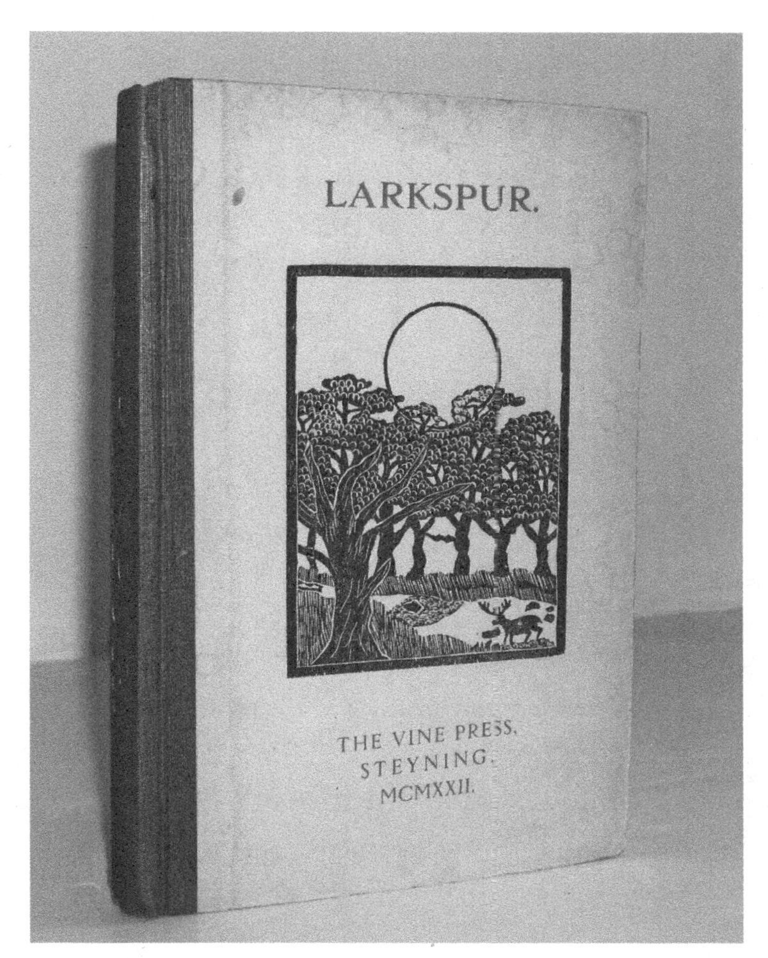

Figure 8.20 A selection of Victor Neuburg's Vine Press titles: *Larkspur* (1922)

Neuburg's composer friend Peter Warlock was Stephensen's drinking buddy and consequently also had a book with Mandrake Press. Published under the pseudonym Rab Noolas, *Merry-Go-Down* was an anthology of writings about "gorgeous drunkards through the ages," from Genesis to James Joyce.[78] It also included Neuburg's poem "Sick Dick, or The Drunkard's Tragedy" from *Lillygay*.

When Mandrake ran into financial straits in early 1930, another of Neuburg's friends, surgeon-turned-psychoanalyst Grace Pailthorpe (1883–1971) helped fund the limited liability corporation that was taking over Mandrake. While this "press syndicate" was largely funded by friends and

[78] Rab Noolas [Peter Warlock], *Merry-Go-Down: A Gallery of Gorgeous Drunkards through the Ages* (London: Mandrake Press, 1929).

(a)

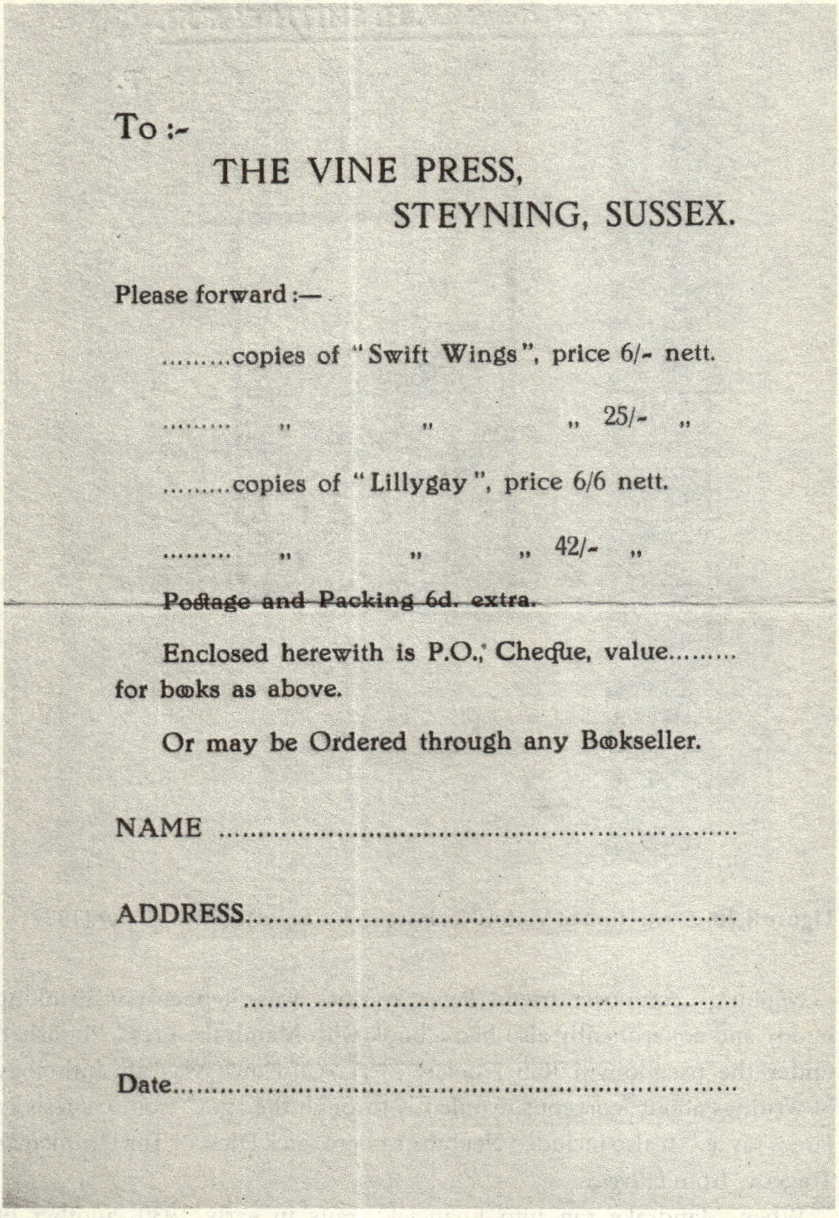

To :-

THE VINE PRESS,
STEYNING, SUSSEX.

Please forward :—

.........copies of "Swift Wings", price 6/- nett.

.... " " " 25/- "

.........copies of "Lillygay", price 6/6 nett.

.... " " " 42/- "

Postage and Packing 6d. extra.

Enclosed herewith is P.O.; Cheque, value.........
for books as above.

Or may be Ordered through any Bookseller.

NAME ....

ADDRESS...

....

Date..

Figure 8.21a Vine Press prospectus for *Swift Wings: Song of Sussex* (1921)

(b)

THE VINE PRESS, STEYNING, SUSSEX.

SUSSEX POEMS.

The Vine Press has pleasure in announcing that

SWIFT WINGS:

SONGS IN SUSSEX,

By the Editor of "LILLYGAY",
is Now Ready.

The Edition is limited to Five Hundred and fifty numbered copies.
Price Six Shillings, nett.

There are forty De Luxe copies on large hand-made paper.
Price Twenty-five Shillings, nett.

Figure 8.21b Vine Press prospectus for *Swift Wings: Song of Sussex* (1921)

(c)

May be obtained through W. H. SMITH & SON.

THE VINE PRESS, STEYNING, SUSSEX.

Price Seven-and-sixpence in Boards.

SONGS OF THE GROVES:

Records of the Ancient World.

By the Editor of "Lillygay" and the Author of "Swift Wings."

This Volume, of about 160 pages, contains, among other unusual Poems, Plato's Love-Song, entirely new versions of "The Wooing" of Theocritus and of "The Vigil of Venus," and a prose Apologue, "The Garden of Pythagoras." All the Poems are entirely unexpurgated.

The printing is of the calibre that has already rendered the productions of The Vine Press famous among Artists and Book-lovers.

The edition is limited to Five Hundred and Fifty numbered copies: there are also Forty copies printed upon large hand-made paper.

The cover is designed and cut by Dennis West, and the covers of the De Luxe copies will be hand-coloured by the same Artist.

This is the most important Work yet Issued from the Vine Press.

The De Luxe issue, perhaps the most exquisite example of modern book-craft, is Three Guineas nett: Thirty-five copies will be for sale, of which Ten will be bound in full parchment. The Price of these latter copies may be obtained upon application to the Publishers.

May be obtained through W. H. SMITH & SON.

P.

To:-

THE VINE PRESS,
STEYNING, SUSSEX.

Please forward :—

.........copies of "Songs of the Groves," price 7/6 nett.

.... " " " *(De Luxe)*, " 63/- "

.........copies of "Swift Wings," price 6/- nett.

.... " " " *(De Luxe)*, " 25/- "

.........copies of "Lillygay," price 6/6 nett.

.... " " " *(De Luxe)*, " 42/- "

Postage and Packing 9d. extra. Two copies and upwards sent post free.

Enclosed herewith is P.O., Cheque, value......... for books as above.

Or may be Ordered through any Bookseller.

NAME..

ADDRESS..

....

Date.................................

Figure 8.21c Vine Press prospectus for *Swift Wings: Song of Sussex* (1921)

followers interested in bringing out Crowley's books, she contributed with the understanding that they would also publish her book on the reform of juvenile-delinquency treatment, *What We Put in Prison*.[79] The new Mandrake Press Ltd. went into liquidation by the end of the year, before they could publish Pailthorpe's book. *What We Put in Prison* would finally appear in 1932 through Williams and Norgate. Indicating no hard feelings, she mentioned Mandrake Press in her acknowledgments. In the meantime, on July 22, 1931, Pailthorpe formed the Association for the Scientific Treatment of Criminals. The inaugural meeting took place at Runia Tharpe's home, with Tharpe and Neuburg serving as honorary secretaries. Neuburg took his role seriously, regularly attending meetings through July 27, 1932, when its name changed to the more familiar Institute for the Study and Treatment of Delinquency.[80]

Neuburg's literary fate changed dramatically when he came to the attention of maverick London newspaper the *Sunday Referee* in spring 1933. Its new editor, Mark Goulden, had galvanized the paper's reputation by recruiting an illustrious team of columnists, including Aldous Huxley, Bertrand Russell, Walt Disney, Compton Mackenzie, and Constant Lambert. Its literary editor, Ted Hayter-Preston, was an old acquaintance of Neuburg. Back in 1911, Hayter-Preston had wandered into the Secular Society on Farrington Road with a book of Ezra Pound's poetry under his arm; G. W. Foote and others there remarked on the book, saying that if he liked modern poetry then he needed to meet Victor Neuburg. They subsequently met and became friends.[81] Coincidentally, Hayter-Preston was also Neuburg's sergeant in France during his military service. Goulden recalled Neuburg joining the *Sunday Referee*:

> It seemed that Arthur Calder Marshall—just down from Oxford—had told Hayter-Preston that their mutual friend, Victor Neuberg [*sic*], appeared to be in pretty poor shape. This distressed Hayter-Preston—he was in Victor's debt and had a deep affection for the gifted but unrecognised writer.
>
> Preston, who was my Literary Editor, wondered if I could give Neuberg a job on the *Sunday Referee* and I readily agreed to meet Neuberg. As a

[79] See Richard Kaczynski, *Perdurabo: The Life of Aleister Crowley*, rev. ed. (Tempe, AZ: New Falcon, 2002; Berkeley, CA: North Atlantic Books, 2010),446–449.

[80] Lee Ann Montanaro, "Surrealism and Psychoanalysis in the Work of Grace Pailthorpe and Reuben Mednikoff: 1935–1940" (PhD diss., University of Edinburg, 2010), 43–44; Jean Overton Fuller, *The Magical Dilemma of Victor Neuburg*, rev. ed. (London: W. H. Allen, 1965, 256–259.

[81] Fuller, *Magical Dilemma*, 162–163.

> result of the interview Neuberg became Poetry Editor of the paper and it was decided to allocate him a weekly column within which he would conduct a poetry competition, publish some of the entries (with his own comments) and award prizes. I paid him a pathetic pittance for the work[82] but he was nevertheless overjoyed at the prospect of "working in Fleet Street." He told Hugo Manning it was the first money he had ever earned and the spiritual harvest the position was to bring him was beyond measure!
>
> The Poets' Corner made its first appearance in the *Sunday Referee* on 9 April 1933 and it was an instant success. Suddenly Victor, now a member of the same editorial staff as the Sitwells, Aldous Huxley, Bertrand Russell, Constant Lambert, Richard Aldington, etc., had become a power![83]

The Poets' Corner was a huge success. To expand its appeal, Neuburg—who had by that time sifted through some three thousand entries[84]—suggested that every six months they publish a book of poetry by whoever sent the best submissions during that time period. Goulden agreed and also offered to put up a cash prize. As he recounted,

> Much of the work sent in was often in handwriting difficult to decipher. One such was a poem beginning "That sanity be kept . . . ," which came from an unknown in South Wales, signed Dylan Thomas. It got the weekly prize. Another from the same source beginning "The force that through the green fuse drives the flower" impressed Neuberg [*sic*] even more and his comment was, "This is a large poem, greatly expressed . . . it is cosmic in outlook."[85]

"That Sanity Be Kept," with commentary by Neuburg, appeared in the September 3, 1933, Poets' Corner. With these contributions, Neuburg believed that they had "found a genius"[86] and nominated Dylan Thomas (1914–1953) as the winner of their second half-yearly prize.[87] After Goulden, Neuburg,

[82] According to Fuller, Neuburg asked to be paid two pounds a week, which was "the standard wage in those days for a typist." Fuller, *Magical Dilemma*, 227.
[83] Mark Goulden, *Mark My Words! Memoirs of a Journalist/Publisher* (London: W. H. Allen, 1978), 176.
[84] Goulden, *Mark My Words*, 178.
[85] Goulden, *Mark My Words*, 178.
[86] Goulden, *Mark My Words*, 179.
[87] The first-prize volume was Pamela Hansford Johnson, *Symphony for Full Orchestra* (London: Sunday Referee, 1934).

and Hayter-Preston interviewed the young poet to satisfy themselves, they concurred that this was no literary hoax. Thus, Thomas's first book, *18 Poems*, was sponsored by the *Sunday Referee*.[88] In later years, poet Dame Edith Sitwell (1887–1964) would remark that "Mr. Mark Goulden and Mr. Victor Neuberg [*sic*] invited the boy Dylan Thomas to London and to these gentlemen we must be ever grateful. They were indeed good friends to him."[89]

After discovering Dylan Thomas, Neuburg regaled him with stories of his exploits with Crowley. In 1935, Thomas wrote to A. E. Trick, "I must tell you one day, if I haven't told you before, the story of how Aleister Crowley turned Vicky into a camel."[90] This tale seems to have grown in the retelling so that by the time it was recounted by Thomas's biographer Constantine FitzGibbon, Crowley had not only turned Neuburg into a camel but sold him to the Alexandria Zoo, "where he languished for several years"![91] Thomas is remembered as repeating these tales in pubs that he visited. Once, in 1941 or 1942, when someone asked if he had ever seen a ghost, he reportedly replied, "No, but Aleister Crowley appeared in my bathwater once."[92]

On February 21, 1935, Neuburg and Tharpe attended a fateful party at Pailthorpe's Dorset Square home with Reuben Mednikoff (1906–1972)[93] in tow. He was a commercial artist fascinated by surrealism, and Neuburg had published his poems "Acquiescence" and "Tradition" in the Poets' Corner.[94] Although Pailthorpe was more than twenty years his senior, she and Mednikoff soon became inseparable: he introduced her to surrealism

[88] Dylan Thomas, *18 Poems* (London: Sunday Referee and the Parton Bookshop, 1934).

[89] Goulden, *Mark My Words*, 180.

[90] Dylan Thomas to A. E. Trick, 1935, in Paul Ferris, ed., *The Collected Letters of Dylan Thomas* (London: J. M. Dent, 1985), 194.

[91] Constantine FitzGibbon, *The Life of Dylan Thomas* (Boston: Little, Brown, 1965), 95.

[92] Andrew Sinclair, *Dylan Thomas: No Man More Magical* (New York: Holt, Rinehart and Winston, 1975), 27.

[93] Although Mednikoff's date of death has been reported as being anywhere from 1971 to 1975, the year 1972 is given by the Tate. See Michel Remy, "Lives of the Artists Grace Pailthorpe and Reuben Mednikoff," Tate (website), October 6, 2018, https://www.tate.org.uk/tate-etc/issue-44-autumn-2018/lives-of-the-artists-grace-pailthorpe-reuben-mednikoff-michel-remy. According to England & Co. Gallery, Mednikoff legally changed his name to Richard Pailthorpe, and he and Grace settled in Hastings, where they died. See "Reuben Mednikoff," England & Co. Gallery (website), accessed January 30, 2021, https://www.englandgallery.com/artists/artists_group/?mainId=167&media=Paintings. A death registry for Richard Pailthorpe of Hastings in spring 1972 appears in the UK General Register Office, England and Wales Civil Registration Indexes, 5h, p. 1012. Similarly, Richard Pailthorpe appears in the National probate calendar, Index of Wills and Administrations, England and Wales, 1972, p. 296 (probate date September 20, 1972).

[94] Reuben Mednikoff, "Acquiescence," *Sunday Referee*, October 1, 1933; Reuben Mednikoff, "Tradition," *Sunday Referee*, December 2, 1934. Both poems are reproduced in Montanaro, *Surrealism and Psychoanalysis*, 63.

and encouraged her to paint and write poetry, while she taught him the psychoanalytic interpretation of art. According to the Tate Modern, "They were to become among the most intriguing and controversial figures in the history of surrealism."[95] André Breton, leader of the Surrealist movement, called them "the best and most truly Surrealist" of living British artists.[96]

When the couple exhibited, as part of the 1936 International Surrealist Exhibition, critic and Poets' Corner alumnus Brian Crozier particularly praised Mednikoff's *Darts* "for its paranoiac tenseness of colour-expression."[97] This review appeared in *Comment*, a journal launched by Tharpe and Neuburg as a replacement for the Poets' Corner. Neuburg's column had ceased in November 1935 after a reorganization of the newspaper. As Crozier put it, "a lowbrow businessman bought the *Sunday Referee* and The Poets' Corner vanished from its pages."[98] To fill the void, Neuburg and Runia started their own weekly literary paper, running from December 1935 until January 1937. Crozier credited the paper for launching his journalistic career and that of other aspiring writers. The journal was certainly a friends-and-family affair. Mednikoff designed the magazine's masthead, and he and Pailthorpe were frequent contributors.[99] Mednikoff, however, ruffled some feathers when his sketch *Victor B. Neuburg Reading Swinburn* [*sic*] appeared in the January 1936 launch issue of *Janus*, a competitor to *Comment* (see figure 8.22). Any misgivings must have been short-lived, however, as *Janus* only endured for two issues.

By the end of the decade, Neuburg took ill with tuberculosis. As his son recalls, "Never robust, he simply fell way from life, lacking the will to go on. After a long illness he died on 30 May 1940."[100]

As Thomas's principal patron and champion, Neuburg had the dubious distinction of starring in Dylan Thomas's roman à clef, *The Death of the King's Canary*, a murder mystery that parodies the thin field of modern British poets. The first chapter of this collaboration with John Davenport depicts

[95] Remy, "Lives of the Artists."
[96] Quoted in "Reuben Mednikoff"; and Catherine Milner, "The Eeriest Couple in Art: Grace Pailthorpe and Reuben Mednikoff," *Sunday Telegraph*, January 18, 1998, repr. Catherine Milner, "The Eeriest Couple in Art: Grace Pailthorpe and Reuben Mednikoff," Artcornwall.org, accessed January 30, 2021, http://www.artcornwall.org/profiles/Pailthorpe_and_Mednikoff.htm.
[97] Brian Crozier, *Comment*, June 20, 1936; quoted in Montanaro, *Surrealism and Psychoanalysis*, 122–123.
[98] Brian Crozier, *The Other Brian Croziers* (Brinkworth, UK: Claridge Press, 2002), 10.
[99] Clippings can be found in the Grace Pailthorpe/Reuben Mednikoff Archive, GMA A62, Scottish National Gallery of Modern Art, Edinburgh, UK.
[100] Neuburg, *Vickybird*, 8.

Figure 8.22 Reuben Mednikoff, *Victor B. Neuburg Reading Swinburn* [*sic*], *Janus*, January 1936, p. 27

the prime minister having to select a new poet laureate after reviewing the contenders' works, thus providing the framework for presenting a series of poems that lampoon the style of Thomas's lesser contemporaries. The resulting newly minted poet laureate, Hilary Byrd, is a send-up of Victor Neuburg: the character's name references Neuburg's nickname, Vickybird; we are told that the poet was educated at Trinity; and, lest there be any doubt, Hilary uses one of Neuburg's neologisms:

> Sometimes I wonder why my bad verse should have been chosen in the teeth of such strong opposition. As I look round this room I can see so clearly many of you whose claim is even greater than mine, who may say "I, or I, or I, have written more unutterable *ostrobogulisms* even than yourself. Mine should be the prize!"[101]

The *Oxford English Dictionary* entry for *ostrobogulous* credits Neuburg with creating the word "to designate something that is slightly risqué or indecent." The term was seeped enough into the English language that Affleck Graves even authored a children's book titled *Ostrobogulous Pigs* (see figure 8.23).[102]

Curiously, *The Death of the King's Canary* also contains an apparent parody of Aleister Crowley. The character of the Black Master makes his entrance as one of the poet laureate's many banquet guests:

> Everyone at the table stopped quarrelling and stared at the Black Master. Ancient blessings and curses poured from his lips. He clapped his huge hands in a forgotten rhythm, and brought a glass ball from his pocket.
>
> He looked like an absconding bank manager.[103]

Later he is described as a "gross, decaying figure of the sage,"[104] and the way he addresses Byrd/Neuburg is quite telling: "Hail, neophyte." The Black Master speaks lines like "Miss Boylan is perhaps not altogether familiar with esoteric phenomena" and "The way to the truth is hard. He who would attain the ultimate vision must be prepared to suffer. He who would be immune from desire must experience all desires."[105] Seeing as Neuburg *was* a Neophyte in the A.·.A.·., and Crowley is often perceived (rightly or wrongly) as a hedonist, the Master is a clear caricature of Crowley, the Master Therion.

Although Dylan Thomas conceived of his book in 1938 and began work on it with Davenport in 1940, the book was unprintable so long as the parodied poets were still alive. It would remain unpublished until 1977.

[101] Dylan Thomas and John Davenport, *The Death of the King's Canary* (New York: Viking Press, 1977), 99; emphasis added.

[102] Affleck Graves, *Ostrobogulous Pigs* (London: Faber & Faber, 1952). For another example of Neuburg's neologisms, see Crozier, *Other Brian Croziers*. Crozier recalls that Neuburg "was in constant good humour and cracked harmless little jokes (such as RTK for 'round the corner')." Crozier, *Other Brian Croziers*, 9.

[103] Thomas and Davenport, *Death*, 94–95.

[104] Thomas and Davenport, *Death*, 122.

[105] Thomas and Davenport, *Death*, 121–122.

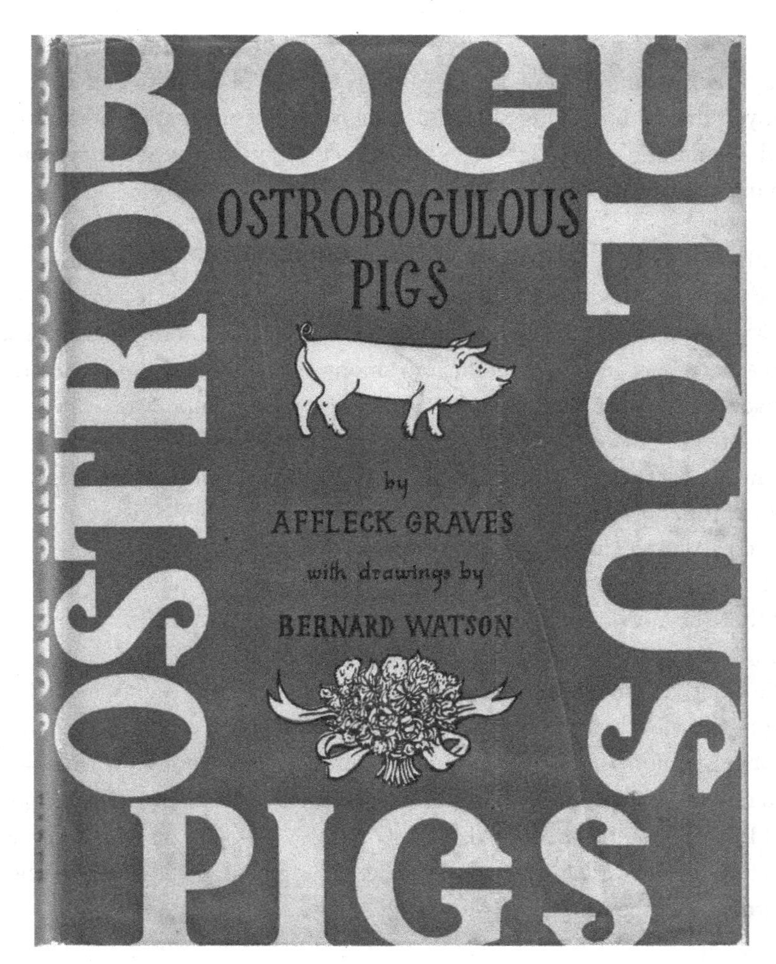

Figure 8.23 Affleck Graves's *Ostrobogulous Pigs* (1952) drew the first word of its title from one of Neuburg's neologisms

Neither Gone nor Forgotten

Despite parting with Crowley in the early 1910s, the paths of Neuburg and Fuller continued to intersect with that of their former friend and colleague.

Neuburg's connections with the Mandrake Press might explain his subsequent review of Stephensen's *Legend of Aleister Crowley* in the August 24, 1930, *Freethinker*. Much as Crowley's former Golden Dawn colleague Florence Farr did with *The Star in the West*, Neuburg's review started with an observation of British society's tendency "to single out an object of hatred," invoking the likes of Byron, Shelley, Carlile, and Bradlaugh as having "enjoyed the favour of this distinguishing mark of approbation at the stone-filled hands and patriotic voices of their grateful fellow-countrymen."[106] Moving on to Crowley himself,

> Although in some respects he was perhaps "not quite nice to know," as the slang phrase goes, we do not think that it is quite fair to charge him with murder, cannibalism, black magical practices, moral aberrations, treachery, druggery; as is the custom amongst the cunninger and more degraded jackals of Fleet Street. . . . Crowley is at least as important a figure as the late D. H. Lawrence and Mr. James Joyce, both unquestionably men of genius; and when we remember the kind of thing said about these artists in our cheaper prints, we hesitate to acquiesce in the Sunday Newspaper verdict on Aleister Crowley.[107]

Lest there be any doubt of his objectivity, Neuburg closes with,

> We ourselves differ profoundly on many points—on most points, indeed—from Crowley; but we do not see why he should not have a fair show; this notice therefore is written solely in the interests of fair play, by one who is in no respect a follower or partisan. It is a plea for ordinary human toleration, addressed by a Freethinker to his fellow Freethinkers. . . . This work, now in course of publication, is, in our considered judgment, the greatest autobiography that the world has ever seen.[108]

These are hardly the words of a shattered shell of a man, as Neuburg has often been depicted after parting with his former master.

Crowley's magnum opus, *Magick in Theory in Practice*, appeared shortly thereafter. Although printed in Paris by the Lecram Press in 1929, the book was not completed and sent to subscribers (or available to the general public) until 1930. Neuburg gave it a positive review in the *Referee*, calling it "witty, erudite, profound, and accomplished," and championing Crowley as "a

[106] Victor B. Neuburg, "The Legend of Aleister Crowley: A Fair Plea for Fair Play," *Freethinker* 1, no. 34 (August 24, 1930): 538–539.
[107] Neuburg, "Legend."
[108] Neuburg, "Legend."

master, at any rate, of prose; his power of expression is as near perfection as that of any author I have read."[109]

> THE MASTER MAGICIAN
>
> *Magick.* By the Master Therion.
>
> The writer, the Master Therion, is the Bad Boy of British Journalism—Aleister Crowley. This wicked man (*vide* the Press, *passim*) has produced a work that is witty, erudite, profound, and accomplished. . . . For once Mr. Crowley may be treated fairly critically, and without the rancour that is born of the over-payment of the professional scurrility-mongers of Grub-street. Much of this author's extreme unpopularity is due, beyond dispute, to his persistent habits not merely of explosive violence of expression and passionate assertiveness; habits not merely stupid, but dull as fireworks in sunlight. . . . The writer's accomplishment is patent; he is a master, at any rate, of prose; his power of expression is as near perfection as that of any author I have read.

Crowley called it a "wonderful review."[110]

In a final, postmortem coincidence, toward the end of his life Crowley would meet the writer John Symonds. This man gained Crowley's confidence enough to be listed as the O.T.O. contact address in *Olla* (1946) and charged with helping Crowley's lifelong friend Louis Wilkinson with sorting out the Beast's literary effects. He would also write a scathing and sensational biography after Crowley died in 1947, *The Great Beast*.[111] At the time when they met, Symonds was living at 84 Boundary Road, Hampstead, the same house where Victor Neuburg had died in 1940.

As for Fuller, Trythall reports that "between 1921 and 1924 Crowley pestered him with letters and blandishments all of which Fuller outwardly resisted."[112] And while it never came to pass that his former association with Crowley would adversely affect Fuller's military career, this association would indeed rear its head in his retirement. When Fuller became Oswald Mosley's right-hand man in the British Union of Fascists, he stepped into an ugly rivalry with the Imperial Fascist League. This group dug into

[109] Victor B. Neuburg, "The Master Magician," *Sunday Referee*, October 9, 1932, 4.

[110] Aleister Crowley, diary entry, October 9, 1932, NS20, Yorke Collection, Warburg Institute, London.

[111] John Symonds, *The Great Beast: The Life of Aleister Crowley* (London: Rider, 1951).

[112] Trythall, *"Boney" Fuller*, 107.

Fuller's past and in its paper, the *Fascist*, ran the attention-grabbing headline "Amazing Exposures of Mosley's Lieutenant: General Fuller Initiated into Aleister Crowley's (Beast 666) Occult Group"[113] (see figure 8.24). It quoted *The Star in the West* and Crowley's later denunciation of Fuller in *The Equinox*, and it implied that Fuller was somehow exerting "control of Kosher fascists" through "secret Jewish occult societies."[114] Fuller was outraged (especially, one might imagine, given his strident anti-Semitism) and contacted his solicitor to prepare a writ for libel. As he saw it, the so-called notorious activities of which *The Fascist* was accusing Crowley all happened after Fuller's exit. His solicitor reviewed Crowley's more controversial works dating to Fuller's association with him—used to devastating effect in the *Jones v. the* Looking Glass case—and advised Fuller against taking action. He said that if the *Fascist* continued its attacks, Fuller could pursue a criminal suit.[115] The *Fascist*'s publisher, Arnold Spencer Leese, claimed victory and asserted that Fuller dropped his case because "I had so much ammunition concerning him."[116] The simple truth of the matter, however, was that this story, starved of any attention, never gained traction, and the *Fascist* quickly moved on to other attention-grabbing conspiracies.

At about this same time, Crowley was in the midst of a libel suit of his own. He was suing Constable and Co., the publisher of his former student, the artist Nina Hamnett (1890–1956). Her book *Laughing Torso* claimed that the locals in Cefalù, Sicily—where Crowley had established a spiritual retreat dubbed the Abbey of Thelema—believed that Crowley was practicing black magic there.[117] Crowley objected to the term *black magic*. Seeking three character witnesses for his case, he went with the most respectable names he knew: popular science author J. W. N. Sullivan (1886–1937), fantastic fiction author J. D. Beresford (1873–1947), and Major General J. F. C. Fuller. Having terminated their friendship because Crowley would not come to the defense of George Cecil Jones against the *Looking Glass*, Fuller must have found it richly ironic that Crowley was now asking Fuller to defend him in

[113] "Amazing Exposures of Mosley's Lieutenant: General Fuller Initiated into Aleister Crowley's (Beast 666) Occult Group: Control of Kosher Fascists," *The Fascist* 72 (May 1935): 1.
[114] "Amazing Exposures," 1.
[115] Stanley Passmore to Sir Oswald Mosley, May 27, 1935, Oswald Mosley papers, XOMN/B/7/4, Special Collections Department, Birmingham University, Birmingham, UK.
[116] Arnold Spencer Leese, *Out of Step: Events in the Two Lives of an Anti-Jewish Camel Doctor* (Guildford, UK: n.p., 1951).
[117] Nina Hamnett, *Laughing Torso: Reminiscences of Nina Hamnett* (London: Constable, 1932).

THE
FASCIST 1D.

THE ORGAN OF RACIAL FASCISM
ESTABLISHED 1929
PUBLISHED BY: THE IMPERIAL FASCIST LEAGUE

No. 72. MAY, 1935 Editor & Director: ARNOLD S. LEESE

AMAZING EXPOSURES OF MOSLEY'S LIEUTENANT

General Fuller Initiated into Aleister Crowley's (Beast 666) Occult Group

CONTROL OF KOSHER FASCISTS

MAJOR General J. F. C. Fuller, who writes the only 'anti-semitic' article in Mosley's *Fascist Quarterly*, is now known to have been initiated into the Probationer Degree (for which an oath is necessary) of the "A.A." (Atlantean Adepts), an occult society whose nominal head, at the time of his initiation, was the notorious Aleister Crowley.

In Fuller's book, *The Star in the West*, appear the following remarks, under the heading—"CROWLEYANITY."

"God will permit a discovery of the highest importance to be made, it must be hidden till the advent of the artist Elias. Thus prognosticated Paracelsus, and further that divine philosopher predicted: And it is true there is nothing concealed which shall not be discovered: for which cause a marvellous being shall come after me, who as yet lives not and who shall reveal many things.

"And I for one take it that the prophecy has been fulfilled. **Aleister Crowley is the Artist Elias, the marvellous being whom God has permitted to make a discovery of the highest importance in his illuminative philosophy of Crowleyanity,** in the dazzling and flashing light of which there is nothing concealed which shall not be discovered. . . .

"It has taken 100,000,000 years to produce Aleister Crowley. The world has indeed laboured, and has at last brought forth a man. . . .

"**And as the doctrine taught by Jesus Christ became known as Christianity, so let this theurgy, as expounded by this marvellous being, be known as Crowleyanity** or in other words, according to the mind of the reader, Pyrrhonic Zoroastrianism, Pyrrhonic Mysticism, Sceptical Transcendentalism, Sceptical Theurgy, Sceptical Energy, Scientific Illuminism or what you will; for in short it is the conscious communion with God on the part of an Atheist . . ."

(The heavy type used above is our own).

However, Fuller seems to have quarrelled with Crowley, for in *The Equinox*, October, 1913 (Crowley's paper), there appeared the following announcement:—

"The Chancellor of the A.A. wishes to warn readers of the *Equinox* against accepting instruction in his name from an ex-Probationer, Captain J. F. C. Fuller, whose motto was *Per Ardua*."

Previous to this (September, 1910), Fuller had written an article jointly with one George Raffalovich (a Jew) in *The Equinox*, entitled 'The Eyes of St. Ljubov.'

Fuller's latest book on *Yoga* (1933), refers to "two great Western occultists, Abramelin the Mage and Eliphas Levi."

The Fascist has always warned its readers against Jew-controlled "Bastard Fascist" movements, designed to bring Fascism into disrepute, and furnished with heavy funds from anonymous sources. We should like to know how many more of Mosley's officials have been, or are, members of secret Jewish occult societies. For Crowley's link with Judaeo-Freemasonry, see our pamphlet "Freemasonry" p.p. 13 and 16.

ALEISTER CROWLEY

In case any of our readers have forgotten the nature of Aleister Crowley, we reprint a few extracts from *Light Bearers of Darkness*, by 'Inquire Within.'

". . . In 1905 Crowley went to India . . . In November of that year he was in Calcutta, and his night-prowling in the bazaars ended in such serious trouble that he, his wife, and young child left precipitately . . . In 1922, we hear of him in his 'Abbey' at Cefalu, Sicily, to which, according to the *Sunday Express*, . . . he enticed a brilliant university man of 22 and his young wife, and there, after going through unspeakable horrors, the young man died . . . Crowley was cleared out of Sicily by the Italian Government . . . and only recently (April 1929) was he asked to leave France on the score of his immoral cults and practices."

God Save the King!

The Jubilee is an expression of Loyalty and Gratitude, gratitude too often from those who have prospered exceedingly. In all revolutions these "grateful" Shylocks are the first to organise that Bolshevism prepared by Judaeo-masonic politicians around Royalty! "Confound their politics," we pray, and God "frustrate their knavish tricks!"

England's Loyalty can only spring from the bond of Aryan Blood, Aristocracy should lead—it has begun to betray us. Our Aryan loyalty is to His Majesty and to no Judaeo-masonic Government.

"May He defend our laws,
And ever give us cause
To sing with heart and voice:
God Save the King."

The I.F.L. will "Keep Troth" to the last man.

THE GENESIS OF UNITY

France to Italy:—Leave Hungary alone, and you may have a free hand in northern Africa, and may even be helped to get Palestine later on. *May we rely on your support?*

France to Yugo-Slavia:—We have called Italy off and will guarantee your present frontiers. *May we rely on your support?*

France to Russia:—During your threatened war with Japan we guarantee you a free western frontier, and that Britain will close her financial market to Japanese loans. *May we rely on your support?*

France to Britain:—We know you are nervous about the continued attacks on your currency—do what we want and you may fear no longer. *May we rely on your support?*

Britain to Russia:—Britain, France, Italy, and Yugo-Slavia, and the rest of Europe outside Germany, want you in the alliance against Germany; we guarantee you a free western frontier, and also new and cheaper credits, and facilities to compete on better terms with our own Dominions. *May France rely on your support?*

"*Russia*" *to Britain*:—We who murdered his kinsman, we who are destroying the image of God wherever it is found raise our glasses and say "God Save the King!"

All in Chorus. Hail Judah!

Time, and Jewish wire-pulling, have brought strange bed-fellows. For just how long Italy will be content to keep her fingers out of Central Europe, Soviet Russia [illegible] and the ordinary people of Europe fail to grasp the true significance of it all, we will not essay to prognosticate. It is clear, however, that this gimcrack structure of lies cannot endure; meantime, the hand of friendship proffered by Herr Hitler is still studiously ignored, and the arms keep piling up.

THE IMPERIAL FASCIST LEAGUE ORGANIZATION

The work of the League now necessitates a concentrated organisation of members' activities and it is now decided that as, after the period of three months' probation, any new member can apply to join the Imperial Fascist Guard, which has Active and Political Sections, all appointments and promotions in the I.F.L. will henceforth be made through the Imperial Fascist Guard.

A Women's Section of the League will now be organised.

Books Received

(These are not stocked by the I.F.L.)

LE JUIF: Poison Mortel, by J. Boissel. 3 francs. From Rif, 4, rue Ferou, Paris VI[illegible]. Useful information about the French aspect.

HITLER'S WONDERLAND, by M. Fry (John Murray, 1934) [illegible].

THE MYSTICAL QABALAH, by D. Fortune (Williams and Norgate, 1935), [illegible].

THE WAGE DOLLAR MONEY SYSTEM, by H. M. Hallam.

The last three will be dealt with in some detail in the [illegible] issue of *The Fascist*.

ATROCITIES TO ORDER

IT is becoming more difficult for the Jew-run Press to find new scares and tales of terrorism to stimulate the flagging anti-German feeling. [illegible]

Figure 8.24 The lead story in the May 1935 *Fascist* exposed Fuller's former connection to Crowley

court against Constable and Co. Predictably, Fuller—along with the other two—declined.

Fuller would hear again from Crowley a decade later. This time, Crowley had published a card bearing what he described as his "war aims." Published on the winter solstice of 1941, its official title was *Liber Oz*, and it described in words of one syllable the fundamental rights of humankind according to *The Book of the Law*. The reverse of the card reproduced an image from the newly completed *Thoth Tarot*: fifty with *The Devil* and two hundred fifty with *The Aeon* (see figure 8.25). As a symbolic gesture to affirm his intention, he sent cards to figureheads representing various walks of life in such fields as literature, journalism, medicine, and art. The recipients included Fuller as a representative of the army.[118] There is no record of Fuller responding, nor is it likely that Crowley anticipated a reply. For him, sending out the cards was a magical gesture, and he looked forward to and anticipated a revolution in nine months. On the fall equinox of 1942, the Manhattan Project began.

Although Fuller never communicated with Crowley after their split, it would be wrong to conclude that Fuller disdained or harbored adverse feelings toward his one-time friend. Quite to the contrary, the enthusiasm he once expressed in *The Star in the West* seems to have settled into his heart. According to Reid, even though he didn't publicly give these opinions voice, Fuller claimed that "the most extraordinary genius he ever knew was Crowley."[119] Fuller also maintained in pristine condition all the books, letters, and ephemera that he had gathered during his association with Crowley. Over the years, he continued to collect Crowleyana and also the works of his former Probationer (and Crowley's heir apparent), Charles Stansfeld Jones. When, toward the end of his life, Fuller decided to sell off the bulk of this comprehensive collection through bookseller Keith Hogg, he wrote a foreword to the catalog in which he declared, much as he did in his "Career of an Essay" moment with *The Star in the West*, that Crowley "remains one of the greatest of English lyric poets."[120]

[118] For an exhaustive history and analysis of *Liber Oz*, see Frater Orpheus, *On the Rights of Man: A Commentary on Liber Oz* (n.p.: n.p., 2019).

[119] Reid, *J. F. C. Fuller*, 14.

[120] J. F. C. Fuller, "Aleister Crowley 1898–1911: An Introductory Essay," in *Bibliotheca Crowleyana* (Tenterden, UK: Keith Hogg, 1966), 8. See "Aleister Crowley 1898–1911," in this volume.

Liber LXXVII

Oz:

"the law of
the strong:
this is our law
and the joy
of the world."
AL. II. 21

"Do what thou wilt shall be the whole of the law."
—*AL. I. 40.*

"thou hast no right but to do thy will. Do that, and no other shall say nay."—*AL. I. 42-3.*

"Every man and every woman is a star."—*AL. I. 3.*

There is no god but man.

1. Man has the right to live by his own law—
   to live in the way that he wills to do:
   to work as he will:
   to play as he will:
   to rest as he will:
   to die when and how he will.

2. Man has the right to eat what he will:
   to drink what he will:
   to dwell where he will:
   to move as he will on the face of the earth.

3. Man has the right to think what he will:
   to speak what he will:
   to write what he will
   to draw, paint, carve, etch, mould, build as he will.
   to dress as he will:

4. Man has the right to love as he will:—
   "take your fill and will of love as ye will,
   when, where, and with whom ye will."—*AL. I. 51.*

5. Man has the right to kill those who would thwart these rights.
   "the slaves shall serve."—*AL. II. 58.*

"Love is the law, love under will."—*AL. I. 57.*

Figure 8.25 *Liber Oz* (1941), a copy of which Aleister Crowley sent to J. F. C. Fuller (art by Frieda Lady Harris)

Conclusion

Fuller and Neuburg, despite parting ways with Crowley in the early 1910s and pursuing different paths in life, periodically returned to their shared interests in their writings. Over twenty years after they parted, Neuburg defended Crowley in the press as a poet and occultist, and he even reached out to him briefly after the publication of *Magick in Theory and Practice*. While Fuller never again contacted Crowley, he wrote occasional books and articles on esoteric topics and preserved until late in life his keepsake first and rare editions of Crowleyana (which ultimately found their way into the Humanities Research Center at the University of Texas at Austin).

Given the enduring impact of the few short years of their mutual friendship, it is instructive to look back on the earliest writings of Fuller, Neuburg, and Crowley. Gat writes,

> Fuller's literary remains held at Rutgers University include what appears to be his first substantial military work, a typescript of a book, *The Foundation of an Imperial Army*, composed in 1910–11. Written in a vague, semi-mystical, and somewhat tiresome style, it was never published and has remained unknown. It is a good catalogue of Fuller's intellectual makeup and roots.[1]

If so, then it is doubly true that the Agnostic writings of Fuller, Neuburg, and Crowley from even earlier years reflect their intellectual makeup and roots. These writings, the majority of which are reprinted here for the first time, hopefully provide a starting point from which to understand the trajectory of the intellectual and spiritual lives of all three men.

British Secularists—whether identified as Agnostics, Freethinkers, infidels, or any of the other terms they embraced—provided more than just the common cause that initially brought Fuller, Neuburg, and Crowley

[1] Azar Gat, *Fascist and Liberal Visions: Fuller, Liddell Hart, Douhet, and Other Modernists* (Oxford: Clarendon Press, 1998), 20, 36.

Friendship in Doubt. Richard Kaczynski, Oxford University Press. © Oxford University Press 2024.
DOI: 10.1093/oso/9780197694008.003.0009

together in the foundational years of the new religious movement of Thelema. For instance, the Agnostic dream of an evidence-based society, rather than one governed by religion and superstition, became, in Crowley's mind, "The Method of Science, the Aim of Religion." The RPA's successful Cheap Reprints series duplicated the popularity of religious publishers, thus inspiring Crowley to form his own self-publishing company, the Society for the Propagation of Religious Truth, to likewise beat the Society for Promoting Christian Knowledge at their own game.

The Agnostics and early Thelemites also shared a deep well of intellectual communality beyond mere surface similarity. This obviously included prominent Agnostic authors like Huxley and Spencer. But it also included the organizers who promoted these thinkers in their journals: Foote's *Freethinker*, Watts's *Literary Guide and Rationalist Review*, and especially Ross's *Agnostic Journal*—in which Fuller was so prolific, where Neuburg was not only a frequent contributor but also subeditor, and whose editor's pen name Saladin was pregnant with meaning in Crowley's lifelong work to oppose, and move beyond, the social influence of Christianity, never mind serving as an inspiration to launch his own literary review journal, *The Equinox*. Even more than that, however, the Agnostics promoted works by lay-authors in the emerging fields of anthropology and comparative religion: Frazer, Forlong, Robertson, and others. The intellectual underpinning of such writers is clear not only in the early works of Crowley, Fuller, and Neuburg but in later recommended-reading lists for prospective students of magick, which are dotted with these influential authors' works.

From the examination in these pages, the previously invisible hand of British Agnosticism, and its child Scientific Illuminism, remains clear even in the later writings of our principal figures. These ideas continued to influence Crowley's writings and schemes throughout his life. They permeated J. F. C. Fuller's military philosophy, from the Darwinian evolution of martial strategy to his liberal use of occult language. Even Neuburg, despite his intimate parting with Crowley, continued to call for people to give his former guru's ideas a fair airing, regardless of who he was as a person.

British Agnosticism must therefore be recognized as a formative influence on Western esotericism, particularly the Scientific Illuminism promoted by Aleister Crowley and his peers. For much as magick and Thelema have inspired the subsequent trajectory of Western esotericism—from Gardner's Wicca, to LaVey's Satanism, to the 1970s' chaos magic—so did its founders find inspiration in Agnosticism. The Secularist issues that Crowley, Fuller, and Neuburg confronted remain especially relevant today, in a world where political discourse is riven by partisan divides—at turns anti-intellectual or antireligious—over whether public policy should be determined by scientific evidence or sincerely held beliefs. The words of Crowley, Fuller, and Neuburg may well provide an opportunity to learn from the past rather than repeat it.

Acknowledgments

This book grew out of primary research that I had done for the revised and expanded edition of *Perdurabo: The Life of Aleister Crowley*. Unable to leave well enough alone and simply refer to unspecified Secularist writings (as did previous biographers of Crowley, Neuburg, and Fuller), I tracked them all down for a proper footnote. This book grew out of that one footnote. For that, I must thank everyone at North Atlantic Books who gave me the opportunity to revisit *Perdurabo* and make it into the book that I had always wanted it to be. My gratitude extends to Oxford University Press for supporting this publication.

I'd also like to thank the following individuals for their help: William Breeze for his encouragement, pointers, and research assistance along the way; Clive Harper for numerous photographs of first editions from his collection, and bibliographic information on Neuburg from his *Various Bibliographic Notes* (Fine Madness Society, in preparation); Keith Richmond for providing me with Guy Aldred's introduction to the popular edition of *Star in the West*, and ultimately hooking me up with my own copy of the book; Tony Iannotti for help with Fuller's *Occult Review* articles; and Krzysztof Azarewicz for sharing an observation from his Polish translation of Crowley's *Konx Om Pax*.

Thanks also to the many institutions without whose help or access this book could not have been written. This includes the Library of Congress, Rutgers University Library's Archives and Special Collections, Liddell Hart Military Archives at the University of London, and the Metzger-Aeschbach archive in Switzerland. I am particularly grateful to the following individuals who went above and beyond: Sheryl Adams, Library of Congress; Diane Clements, Library and Museum of Freemasonry; Tommy Nixon, University of North Carolina's Davis Library; Sandra Stelts, Pennsylvania State University Libraries' Special Collections; and Bridget Whittle of McMaster University's Archives and Research Collections.

Finally, I'd like to give a shout-out to J. D. Holmes and the Sure Fire Press, who invited me to write a brief introduction to their reprint of Fuller's *Bibliotheca Crowleyana* back in 1989. Thirty-five years later, I have come full circle.

Friendship in Doubt. Richard Kaczynski, Oxford University Press.
DOI: 10.1093/oso/9780197694008.003.0010

ANTHOLOGY OF PRIMARY TEXTS BY ALEISTER CROWLEY, J. F. C. FULLER, AND VICTOR B. NEUBURG

Editor's note: These works are reproduced faithfully in the manner in which they originally appeared. A handful of typographical errors have been silently corrected. This includes instances in which quotations from another text contain errors: quotes have been corrected to match the source being cited. Some stylistic changes (such as not italicizing "ibid.") were made for consistency with editorial notes and modern typographical conventions. Bylines have been moved to the beginning of each work for clarity.

The poems that Neuburg reprinted in *A Green Garland* served as a guide for correcting obvious typographical errors in the originals. Otherwise, minor changes to punctuation and capitalization to the poems as they appeared in *A Green Garland* are not followed in this anthology in order to keep the versions presented here faithful to the originals. Neuburg's more substantive revisions to wording, however, are noted in editorial comments.

Only[1,2]

Victor B. Neuburg

ONLY a mother with wistful eyes
  Watching enraptured her baby's face.

[1] *Agnostic Journal* 53, no. 13 (October 10, 1903): 238. A month prior to the appearance of this, Neuburg's first published poem, he received encouragement in the *Agnostic Journal*, presumably in response to an earlier submission. See "To Correspondents," *Agnostic Journal* 53, no. 10 (September 5, 1903): 153, which includes the statement (misspelling his name), "V. B. Newburg.—At your age you promise well."

[2] Another poem by this title appeared in the *Agnostic Journal* six months earlier: W. Luther Longstaff, "Only," *Agnostic Journal* 52, no. 15 (April 11, 1903): 236. Whether this inspired Neuburg or is a coincidence is unknown. Both poems, however, feature lines of nine syllables. For example, Longstaff's first two lines run: "ONLY her flow'r-face under the sky, / Under the shadows, under the sun!"

Only a glance of divine surprise,
    Only a lowly child of the race.
Ah! The Gods have no joy so rare
    As that of the mother! What power to lift
Has that scrap of flesh minus teeth and hair,—
    Only the token of Love's ripe gift!

. . . . . .

Only a prayer for a little bread,
    Only a mother in anguish wild,
Only a poor little drooping head,—
    Only a tiny, dying child!
Only a question hard and stern,
    "Where's your ring? Not got one? Go!"
Only the fierce despairing burn
    That only cast-out women know.

Only a narrow priest of the Lord,
    Only an outraged glance of hate,
Only a bitter, damning word,—
    Only a warning that comes too late.
Only a glance at the sky above,
    Only a cry from a mother torn;—
"Why, O God, was I made to love?
    Why, O God, was my baby born?"

Only a leap in the water dark,
    Only a gurgle, only a rise;
Only the trees the spot to mark,
    Only the witnessing star-strewn skies.
Only the river's patient song,
    Only a throbbing resting-place.
Only, only a nation's wrong,
    Only, only a world's disgrace!

Vale, Jehovah![3]

Victor B. Neuburg

I THROW off the yoke of my people,
I doff the white scarf of the Race.
My temple has fallen; its steeple
Has cast a long shade on my face.
The temple's red idol, Jehovah,
Has fallen in ruins: his state
Is finished and shattered and over
For me. I am proud in my gait.

No longer by legend and chanting
The priests shall endeavor to stay
My footsteps. Who heeds their weak ranting,
When, despite them, there dawns the world's day?
What if in the Race I *was* born?
To me that's no reason why I
Should cling to a faith that I scorn,
When my birthright's the infinite sky!

I leave the worn path I was led in,
To turn wheresoever I will,
And find fairer valleys to tread in,
And breathe on some purer-aired hill.
Behind me, more faintly, more pleading
I hear yet priests' voices. They say:
"Jehovah, our God, lieth bleeding—
His life ebbeth slowly away."

I heed not the fools who would warn me
(With threats)—Give me bribes (prayers)—to stay.
And if, as they say, the world scorn me,
'Twill only be mad, as are they!

[3] *Freethinker* 23, no. 43 (October 25, 1903): 684.

Poor, perishing, priest-propped Jehovah,
The days of thy blood-deeds are dead;
Thy yoke I for ever throw over!
Good-bye! My farewell has been said.

A Song of Dawn[4]

Victor B. Neuburg

'MID the ponderous roar of the breakers free, and the gingle[5] of laughing spray,
The jolly old sea-god's daughters fair carol to rising day.
I hear them above the sea-blast wild; beyond the water's bourn
There floats the song: "Behind is daylight, and ever beyond is morn!"

I stood by the wet-lipped, sea-woo'd shore; the waters played light at my feet,—
The weary day was dead, and the breathing of life was calm and sweet;
Stilled for a space was the striving of men, and over the silver bay
There came the echo: "The day dawns ever, and ever beyond is day!"

Out on the hills the tinkling sheep-bells ring up the inclines steep;
The sun-rise over the tinted meadows arouses the world from sleep,
Above the noise of the cities' roar is the cry of nature borne:
"Beyond, beyond lies daylight ever, and ever beyond looms morn!"

To greet the stars I wander forth,[6] and to bid the day good-bye;
The trees upon the hill-tops bare grow dark as the day doth die.
The world-twins, light and shadow, together mingle and clash in strife;
For life is born of the striving of twain, so shadow and light make life.

A sun-beam flooding a chamber with light; a moon-path illuming the sea;
The cry of the gulls as they endlessly circle; the skirl of the wind through a tree;

[4] *Agnostic Journal* 53, no. 18 (October 31, 1903): 284; repr. in *A Green Garland*.
[5] This word is "splash" in *A Green Garland*.
[6] In *A Green Garland*, the first half of this line becomes "I wander forth to greet the stars."

The ceaseless bustle of feverish men 'neath the star-light's quiet scorn;—
All these are echoes of parting daylight—are tokens that herald the morn.[7]

A Barbaric Survival[8]

J. F. C. Fuller

Sir,—Why should the British Army be compelled to pray by vote? Surely this is but a barbaric survival of intolerant times which we might do well to dispense with.

In the King's Regulations for the Army,[9] the following religions are laid down as sufficiently comprehensive for the intellectual powers of British officers and men—*vide* section 694: A soldier is to be classified under one of the following denominations:—

Church of England;
Presbyterian;
Wesleyan;
Other Protestant (not included in the foregoing);
Roman Catholic;
Jew.

On the face of it absurdity smiles satirically enough. Half-a-dozen puny squabbling sects of the crucified Galilean, half-a-dozen sects of the

[7] *A Green Garland* adds a new final stanza:

And above the warring of races and creeds, and the crash of the gods as they fall,
To the skies there rises an echo high above the outer wall.
And ever a few shall hear that echo,—from Earth's green bosom 'tis drawn,—
Behind, behind lies daylight ever, and ever beyond is dawn.

Amusingly, this appears to restore a stanza originally omitted by the *Agnostic Journal*. See "To Correspondents," *Agnostic Journal* 53, no. 18 (October 31, 1903): 281. There, Ross writes, "V. B. N.—*Dawn* will not rhyme with *drawn*." Neuburg's objection was answered in "To Correspondents," *Agnostic Journal* 53, no. 20 (November 14, 1903): 313, with Ross reiterating, "V. B. N.—No aural ingenuity can rhyme *drawn* with *dawn*."]

[8] *Agnostic Journal* 54, no. 3 (January 16, 1904): 45–46. While this is Fuller's first piece in the *Agnostic Journal*, it wasn't his first attempt. The February 7, 1903, issue's section "To Correspondents" contains the following note from the editor: "J. F. C. Fuller.—Smart; but marred by false rhymes" (p. 89). Fuller was undeterred by this rejection, although it would be nearly a year before his first piece was published. His first example of verse—"Sadness"—would appear the following month (February 1904).

[9] Great Britain, *The King's Regulations and Orders for the Army: (Provisional Edition) 1904* (London: HM Stationery Office, 1904).

gaberlunzies and throat-slitters of Constantine and Henry, out of an almost infinite number of philosophies, systems and religions. What a farce! and savoured too with a soupçon of "Shunyism." Poor old Yahveh, you once walked and talked with us in the prestine garden of Eden, when man was without knowledge and fig-leaves; and now your name scarcely echoes in our thoughts. Are we too knowing, or are we too occupied with our broadcloth and pipeclay sartorial voluntaries of that Adamic figment? Too knowing perhaps, but not brave enough to own it, and cast off these glittering trammels of infant thought and a barbaric age. A Sanger's circus, a Tussaud's show,[10] as we hideously howl with the former, so do we look stupidly mute with the latter, and like the old gentleman in the "Topper," wag our heads vacantly from side to side in rhythmic cadence to the inane.

Voluntary church attendance in civil life is and has been for a long time now a recognized thing; why in the army should we not be equally tolerant and have voluntary church parades? If it be necessary that the men of a regiment should turn out especially smart once a week, it matters little whether this parade is held on a Sunday or a week day, but it matters a great deal if they are forcibly driven to church as sheep to a pen, and for a rotten system of lies too.

From the point of view of a tolerant Freethinker, the question resolves itself thus: If the men truly believe, they will go to church, parade or no parade, if they can; if they do not, what good does it do them to be driven there?

From the narrow parsonic view compulsory church attendance means a full church, and a respectable palliation for the existence of the parson. A voluntary attendance would mean an empty church, and a slump in parsons, who would then have to seek some more honest employment to make ends meet. Christ and his father have really very little to do with the matter nowadays. They, however, form an excellent stalking-horse whereby one's bread may be buttered. I, for one, do not altogether blame the beetles when looking at them critically, for bread is indispensable, though Christ is not. I do not blame them any more than I blame the prostitute or the thief for indulging in a nefarious and injurious means of making a livelihood. I pity them for falling so low, poor victims of an effete and corrupt age; but I strongly object having to associate with them, and so too do I strongly object to have

[10] "Lord" George Sanger (1825–1911) famously ran circuses and other shows throughout England in the latter half of the nineteenth century until his retirement in 1905 (the year after this article was published). Anne-Marie "Marie" Tussaud (1761–1850) was a French artist renowned for her wax sculptures and for the world-famous Madame Tussaud's wax museum that she founded in London.

forcibly to associate with and support the State-paid "effigies" of Christ, and be deafened by their howling rant and humbug.

For centuries were we cramped by the platitudes and sophistries of dogmatic ignorance and theological intolerance; for centuries with our wings clipped and maimed we crawled through the foul and dismal swamps of the "Dark Ages," but those balmy days of ignorance and torture are past and gone, and with them should pass this petty annoyance, this "barbaric survival" of compulsory church attendance in the British Army.—Yours truly,

Punjab, India,
December 24th, 1903

Ego[11]

Victor B. Neuburg

Oh, I have sung, in the mother-tongue, of atom and beast and fowl;
The croak of a frog in a northern bog, and the jungle-panther's howl,
And I have seen the shifting scene, 'twixt hell and heaven whirled;
The lust of hate hath swayed my fate, and the love-flag's been unfurled.

As I wander now by a cliff's steep brow, to gaze at the yearning sea,
Or trace the path that the star-course hath, an echo comes back to me:
Oh, I've wandered afar from home, and ever rising higher;
I feel the sea and the stars in me 'mid the passion glow of fire.

And though I wander afar alone, and seek for the path I know,
The cold stars gleam across my dream, and dazzle me as I go:
The struggle of men athwart my ken comes hard in the light of day,
And how can I go when the earth calls so, and Humanity bars the way?

Oh, I have sung, in the mother-tongue, of atom and beast and fowl;
The croak of a frog in a northern bog, and the jungle-panther's howl:
And far away there looms the day: the gods' own gate of peace
Stands firm and clear in the outer sphere, to hasten the soul's release.

[11] *Agnostic Journal* 54, no. 7 (February 13, 1904): 107.

Sadness[12]

J. F. C. Fuller

SADNESS of heart is but a yearning for
That which no longer is, but having been,
Is gone, and past, vanished for evermore
Into the darkness, from this little scene,
In which our puny lives make up the part
Of One who lies beyond "The Knowable,"
Bidding us hither come, or hence depart,
According to His will inscrutable.
We dance our round of sorrow or of joy,
Like a pith ball rul'd by electric laws,
Then we depart, we, poor frail human toy,
And solve, or solve not, the great Primal Cause,
Making a little void by one soul less,
Causing, perchance, a world of loneliness.

Strong-Heart[13]

Victor B. Neuburg

STRONG-HEART, Strong-heart, I found you in the days of long ago;
The wind was whistling through the pines, the sky was all aglow.
The red sun sank behind the hills, a breeze came from the west;
All nature was at peace, Strong-heart, and then I was at rest.

Strong-heart, Strong-heart, I never knew, till you had left my side,
The meaning of the living Space, nor how the world was wide!
A melody of endless life through all the breezes blew;
I send my soul among the stars, and it returned to you.

[12] *Agnostic Journal* 54, no. 7 (February 13, 1904): 110.
[13] *Agnostic Journal* 54, no. 9 (February 27, 1904): 130. Elsewhere in this same issue, Ross chides, "V. B. N.—Kindly correct proofs in normal way. See *First Step in English Composition*, which our publishers would send you, post free, for 9d." See "To Correspondents," *Agnostic Journal* 54, no. 9 (February 27, 1904): 137.

I found you on the dewy moors, in the bright haze's sheen;
I lost you in the summer days, when all the woods were green.
The earth sent forth her scented breath; as at her breast I lay,
I caught your voice, Strom heart, and heard anew the sound of day.

And as the summer faded, and the earth her mantle doffed,
The winter crept upon the land the summer had left soft:
The branches of the pines stood bare against the faded sky,
And when the earth was all ahush, I knew that you were by.

The stars have echoed earth's love-song; the wondrous Song of Life
Is deeper than the depths of love, above the sound of strife;
All nature sings a passion-song that echoes my desire:
You come to me, Strong-heart, in wind and rain and sea and fire.

The winter's blast is passing now: the summer's song is done;
And now there is no land of joy to greet the rising sun.
Cities have sprung upon the land where once the song of birds

Filled all the sky with music, echoing to Nature's words.
Strong-heart, Strong-heart, I have not sought for you, I know, in vain,
For I have learned the song of life, and echoed the refrain.
And you have found the hidden land whence love came creeping low;
Your voice comes to me softly from the days of Long-ago.

Pillow Fighting, B.C.[14]

J. F. C. F.

Sir,—"Wherefore thus saith the Lord God: Behold, I am against your pillows, wherewith ye there hunt the souls to make them fly, and I will tear them from your arms, and will let the souls go, even the souls that ye hunt to make them fly" (Ezekiel xiii., 20).

How one can hunt souls with pillows and make them fly is a piece of hypermental gymnastics quite beyond my powers, and if any reader of the "A. J." can inform me on the subject I shall be very much obliged.

[14] *Agnostic Journal* 54, no. 9 (February 27, 1904): 142.

In my time I have hunted with the pillow, but that was in my early school-days, which reminds me of one very famous hunt, deeply impressed on my brain, and other parts of my anatomy. It happened thus. One evening one of the boys had left our dormitory for some purpose or other, when there was a general exclamation of, "Pillows!" I seized mine, upon which my youthful head was wont to repose (and which, curiously enough, had nothing whatever to do with armholes) and crept to the door. A few minutes after the handle turned, and the door opened. I struck out wildly, a candle flew into the air (but no soul), a scream, a body obliquely posed, and a thud. And, verily, I say unto you, lo and behold, it was the MATRON.—Yours truly,

Punjab, India

Credone?[15]

To My Friend F. A. C. S.[16]

Victor B. Neuburg

When that I think what I, a Man, have known,—
How little is the space in life for trust,—
Well do I know that I must fight alone,
A worm within an acreage of dust.
What if I sing the song that you would sing?
I only sing, good friend, because I must!

Credit me not! What I have done I've done
Because a voice in me its song did raise:
Because I am a mote by the red sun
That's swayed, I give an echo to my days.
So closely am I compassed all about,
I have no room for blame, no place for praise.

[15] *Agnostic Journal* 54, no. 11 (March 12. 1904): 173.

[16] Frederick Augustus Carlton Smith (1884–1966) was a schoolmate of Victor's at the City of London school and a future solicitor. He would have been in law school at the time this poem was published. For Fred's recollections—fifty years on—of his old "school chum," see Jean Overton Fuller, *The Magical Dilemma of Victor Neuburg*, rev. ed. (London: W. H. Allen, 1965; Oxford, UK: Mandrake Press, 1990),104–105. See also Census of England and Wales, 1911, South Mimms, Middlesex, England, Class RG14, Piece 7136, Schedule Number 164.

Only I live; why that I live, I know
    What you know—nothing! Shall I be afraid
When the Night calls me forth? And when I go,
    I shall but pass into the red sun's shade.
I need no God to call me to his arms;
    I am a Man, and ask no being's aid!

That which I've left undone, I could not do,
    Nor know I shame! No fear has made me bow!
Only I love one here and there, and who
    Shall live but in the ever-living Now?
A worm, and yet a god! In joy and pain
    I keep my feet, and bear an open brow!

And old Time calls! His mouthpiece is the earth;
    The earth upholds me with her echo-song:
A chant of Death, a love-song then of Birth—
    The world is wide enough, and life is long!
Be fearless, Brother! Fear nor Man nor God,
    But stand alone, and so you shall be strong!

March Twentieth

Many Happy Returns[17]

Victor B. Neuburg

BOLD prophet of the glorious To-be!
    Slayer of Gods! Son of the living Morn!
All hail! We circle you about, and we
    Will shield you from the chill of the world's scorn!

A million greetings from the men unborn
    Resound through us; the lying priests shall know

[17] *Agnostic Journal* 54, no. 12 (March 19, 1904): 182. William Stewart Ross, editor of the *Agnostic Journal*, was born on March 20, 1844.

The echo of your thund'ring battle-horn
In days that lie beneath the present's snow!

Days warm with love, and brilliant with the light
That Science bears around her radiant head,
Shall put the darkly-vested priests to flight,
When the false gods lie still, and cold, and dead!

Brave-hearted Chief! We, of the younger men,
Bow low in reverence to that mighty sword!
We kiss the hand that wields the drastic pen;
We love the smiter of the tyrant Lord!

To you we bow! To you, with one accord,
We chant the saga of the conquered God:
What nobler chief can this old world afford
Than Saladin, who broke Jehovah's rod?

Greeting to Saladin! Priest-hated Chief,
Noble and true, take this unworthy lay!
O hater of the lying, sham, Belief,
Joyous and keen be this, your natal day!

And we who watch, and aid in the great fray
That's waged betwixt red gods and earth, sweet green
Come forward with a wreath of living bay,
And cry "Long life! All hail to Saladin!"

To Count Tolstoy[18]

V. B. Neuburg

DEAR TOLSTOY, there's no doubt I shalt agree
With all you say when I am ninety-one;

[18] *Agnostic Journal* 54, no. 17 (April 23, 1904): 259. Remembered for penning such classics as *War and Peace* (1869) and *Anna Karenina* (1877), Leo Tolstoy (1828–1910) converted to Christianity late in life and embraced a path of nonviolence, ascetic renunciation, and sexual abstinence. The last idea clearly did not sit well with a just-twenty Neuburg. At the time when Neuburg wrote this poem,

But as I'm only twenty now, you see,
(And young at that!), I mean to have some fun!

I will not crush my nature 'neath my heel
To please a problematic tyrant God;
Great Cæsar! Tolstoy! I'm a *man*, and *feel*,
Perhaps I shan't when I'm beneath the sod!

What shall Achievement's glittering heights afford?
Thence come an echo with each scented breeze,
But never have I heard your ghostly Lord:
I serve not ghosts. It's men that I would please.
Doubtless, when I am old, I'll be as thou;
But now? I happen to be *living* now!

A Song of Freedom[19]

Victor B. Neuburg

FORWARD! Beyond lies freedom! Cast behind
The dying gods! Pale in the dawning light,
Their mangled limbs sway flapping in the wind;
Together, freed, women and men shall know
Beauty: a day of toil; a starry night;
The wonder of the endless ebb and flow.

Has heaven barred its portals? Then the earth
Shall wider be when men at length are free!
Fair Science, mother-like, awaits the birth
Of the new Man, and, by the open grave
Of all the gods together huddled—see!
The banner of Humanity shall wave!

Tolstoy was prominent in the press: he was promoting forthcoming religious books on theology and publishing articles such as Count Leo Tolstoy, "Detached Thoughts on Religion," *The Independent* 55, no. 2962 (October 8, 1903): 2377–2380; and Leo Tolstoy, "Tolstoy on the Orthodox Religion of Russia," *American Monthly Review of Reviews* 29, no. 3 (March 1904): 344–345. "Tolstoy on the Orthodox Religion of Russia" also appeared in *American Israelite*, April 14, 1904, 3.

[19] *Agnostic Journal* 54, no. 20 (May 14, 1904): 307; repr. in *A Green Garland*.

A nobler earth! A vista unexplor'd!
How weak the moaning of the dying gods
Where Beauty is the queen, and Love is lord!
Methinks the earth spins faster, and the stars
Echo her song of freedom! The fierce rods
Of priests are turned to hollow-sounding bars!

Onward! Ah! who shall stay the splendid tide
Of freedom? Who shall mar the World to be?
As on the flood the clear-eyed prophets ride
With arms extended to the stars, a song
Of freedom floats over the eager sea:
"The dawn approaches, though the night was long!"

Love! Freedom! Beauty! They are almost won!
A struggle with the dying powers that be—
A leap into the glory of the sun!
Fearless we stand and watch the dawning day—
A day when life shall rise unawed and free,
To greet the promises of gentle May.[20]

Carmen Triumphans[21]

[Verses in Honour of the Freethought Congress to be held in Rome in September, 1904.][22]

Victor B. Neuburg

[20] In *A Green Garland*, this line becomes "To chase the specters of the night away."

[21] *Agnostic Journal* 55, no. 7 (August 13, 1904): 102; repr. in *A Green Garland.* In the following issue, Ross commented, "V. B. NEUBURG.—Meritorious and opportune. We know of no lady from England who is to attend the International Freethought Congress at Rome." See "To Correspondents," *Agnostic Journal* 55, no. 8 (August 20, 1904): 121.

[22] The International Freethought Congress was held in Rome on September 20–22, 1904, featuring addresses by prominent Freethinkers like Ernst Haeckel, G. J. Holyoake, G. W. Foote, and Charles Watts. Thousands of delegates attended from around the world. The irony of the first Freethought Congress meeting so near the seat of the Vatican was not lost on the attendees. The *Literary Guide* called it "a triumphant success as an international demonstration of the progress of Rationalism. The English press, for decency sake, has been forced to publish some account of the Congress, though the information it has vouchsafed to its readers has been meagre and often misleading." "Random Jottings," *Literary Guide and Rationalist Review* 100 (October 1, 1904): 152.

SEVEN-HILL'D Rome[23] has reigned; to-morrow Truth
Shall flaunt her pennons from a thousand hills!
And we, the heirs of Science, strong in youth,
With steadfast eye, and heart that gladly thrills,
Acclaim the dawning light that slowly fills
The world with wonder. As the daylight grows
Our shout is raised, then suddenly it stills
Its thunder, for the first faint tint of rose
Brings heart-ease to the world, in promise of repose!

Yesterday Rome! To-morrow's sun shall rise
Upon a world transformed from Night to Day;
We rise to greet the sunshine, and our eyes
Are shaded from the glory far away.
Our herald tongues, entranced, give forth a lay
Of Spring and green and bursting buds—a world
Sweet with the songs of birds, and fragrant hay
From waving fields to strong-drawn waggons hurled—
A vision of the New, the Banner wide unfurled.

Yesterday Rome, where Bruno's ashes[24] gave
A fragrance that remains to this wide morn.
Mind-free, he died to spurn the name of slave,
Leaving his heritage to men unborn.
To-day we laugh the pious priests to scorn;
To-day the doctrines of old Rome are dead
To all the noblest! The pale Christ forsworn
Has given to men a stronger hardihead:
Godless, the world by Men shall still be onward led!

Interestingly, the congress included an address given by "a representative of the Grand Orient Masons, the highest Masonic body in the world, whose work reaches to the ninetieth degree." J. B. Wilson, an American delegate to the congress, includes the assertion that "masonry is as old, almost, as the history of man. Like all religions, it is founded on Phallic and Solar worship." J. B. Wilson, *A Trip to Rome* (Lexington, KY: J.E. Hughes, 1905), 162.

[23] The *Septem Montes Romae*, or "Seven Hills of Rome," refers to the hills in the heart of Rome within the borders of Servian Wall (i.e., the Aventine, Caelian, Capitoline, Esquiline, Palatine, Quirinal, and Viminal Hills).

[24] The Inquisition accused Italian philosopher and cosmologist Giordano Bruno (1548–1600) of heresy, ultimately burning him at the stake and scattering his ashes in the Tiber. In the nineteenth century, Bruno, much like Galileo, was taken up as a martyr for Freethought and science.

Yesterday Rome! To-day the dawn of Truth
Scorches her banners, and her towers nigh fall
At the glad cry of Day and Strength and Youth—
A world emancipate—a clarion-call
From out the depths. And now, to Love's wide hall
Troop men and women freed; with eyes aglow
They watch the sunrise by the outer wall,
Where swift the living waters ebb and flow—
Where melts the rising sun Religion's chilling snow.

Yesterday Rome! To-morrow Truth shall reign!
Yesterday gods! To-morrow, in their stead,
Humanity shall guard the sacred Fane—
The Trinity: Love, Life, Hope. The gods are dead.
From out the darkened past the dawning red
Flushes the world anew; the Day shall be
The promise fulfilled, that every age has fed
With heroes' blood—the promise of the Free,
Rising beyond the hills—THE NEW HUMANITY.

O for the Dawn beyond the Seven Hills,
That shews their darkness in the world's fierce Day!
The heart of Man now half-unconscious thrills
With growing sense of Dawn, and turns away
From all the idols with the feet of clay
Set up by Rome, for the new Dawn doth bring
The promise of Love—of Life that makes no stay,
But, ever-renewed, brings echoes from the Spring,
And, mindful of the earth, takes ever upward wing.

Yesterday Rome! To-morrow Truth! A song
Resounds throughout the earth, as widely blows
The breeze of Dawn Rome's darkened ways along,
Bringing the scent of hawthorn and of rose,
Of Winter mirth, of frozen lakes and snows,
Of Autumn forests, and of Summer trees
Shading the meadows—of a Life that glows

With Human love—of[25] Human hearts at ease.
And who shall stay the dawn, and who shall still the breeze?

Flash out, O Sun, widely upon the Morn!
Let our wild shouts be echoed in the wide!
Let priests and gods be scorched in the world's scorn,
Or sink, all useless, in the flowing tide!
To-morrow! Ah, to-morrow we will ride
Adown the path of Life, to eager fling
Laurels to dreamers of the Dawn, who died
To give us this new Life, this nobler Spring.
Forward, in joy, we ride; the REIGN OF MAN we sing!

The Pagan[26]

Victor B. Neuburg

MAIDENS' lips all glowing,
Ruby wine light flowing—
These were mine, and for my task
Nothing more 'twas mine to ask;
Now a little leap
Into the darkness whence I sprang;
A last farewell to those who sang;
Then to fall asleep.

I ask no priest to seal my lips,
Nor prayer to mar my going;
As the final moment slips,
Nothing I am owing.
Life was good and Love was fair:
Earth, sea, sky, and ambient air—
Farewell! I am going—*there*,
In the current's flowing.

[25] In *A Green Garland*, "love—of" becomes "love, with."
[26] *Freethinker* 24, no. 34 (August 21, 1904): 541.

Shall the stars the brighter be
  If he who loved them weepeth?
Shall the earth the lighter be
  When he who trod it sleepeth?
Not my going forth is vain,
  Nor was my coming hither;
Not vainly I expended pain,
  Asking *whence* and *whither*.

Lived I well my round of days,
  Felt the sunlight gleaming.
Wandered in the misty haze,
  Now and then, a-dreaming.
Sang my song and drained my glass
Over many lands did pass;
Leaving earth I know no fear,
Feel no bridge, 'twixt *there* and *here*.

Twilight falls upon the earth,
  Night is calm, night is deep.
Just a path to death from birth,
  Then a sleep, then a sleep.
With a laugh I turn to go—
Where the silent waters flow—
Where the stars are all aglow. . . . . .
  Can I weep? Can I weep?

Maidens' lips all glowing red,
  Golden days of youth—
Thro' a silver path proud led,—
The good green earth with white sap fed,
Autumn woods with brown cones spread,
Green sea, with foam-encrested head,
A darkened sky the pale stars thread,—
  Thus arrayed is Truth.

Sun and stars and gentle moon,
  Unto ye a long farewell;

Trackless paths shall make my shoon
'Twixt heaven's lonely road and hell.
With laughing lips in summer days
Pæans in the green earth's praise
Sang I joyous, drained my glass,
Laughed farewell. And now I pass.

Between the Spheres[27]

V. B. Neuburg

Still warm from the earth, from the whirling earth, I sing;
Widely-expanded, in œther I wander in awe;
Drops of light, dazzling, around me I fling
As I turn. I am near the hidden heart of the Law.

The passing from Earth, from Earth, my home, seems, ah
So far in the darkness: scarce know I now that I dwelt
Below, with dazèd[28] brow, in that whirling star.
I watch it—an emerald stone in the sun's wide belt.

And lips touch my hair—strange lips, unhuman and soft:
I am among the ones I knew. . . I would sleep . . . I would sleep.
No pain I know . . . now . . . but it seems[29] that oft
I could laugh and laugh . . . and then I cannot . . . I weep.

I have forgotten . . . I am afraid . . . A voice calls to me from the wide.
. . . I cannot stir . . . What is it I fear? . . . The sphere widens: here is one I know.
He takes me forth gently . . . I am by his side.
Together we will seek . . . It is over . . . let us go.

27 *Agnostic Journal* 55, no. 15 (October 8, 1904): 232; repr. in *A Green Garland.*
28 This word is changed to "fevered" in *A Green Garland.*
29 In *A Green Garland*, "it seems" changes to "I feel."

Beetledom Dying[30]

Victor B. Neuburg

SIR,—Is not this fine? It is from *The Daily Telegraph* of December 17th, 1904:

UNIVERSITY OF BERLIN.
From Our Own Correspondent.
BERLIN, Friday.

"The year book of the University of Berlin gives statistics which shew that this institute is the largest in the world. The number of matriculated students at present attending lectures is 7,774. The lectures on theological subjects are the worst attended of any. There are altogether only 335 divinity students in the university. The faculty of law has 2,756 students, that of medicine 1,111, and philosophy 3,572. In addition to students from every German state the Berlin University contains 413 Russians, 130 Austrians, 102 Swiss, 81 Hungarians, 39 British, 35 Roumanians, 25 Bulgarians, 24 French, and smaller numbers from every other European country, including Turkey and Montenegro. America sends 123 students, Asiatic lands 37, Africa 8, Australia 3. In addition to the matriculated students, 1,330 persons have received permission to attend the lectures. It is curious to note that the decline in the number of theological students is not confined to Berlin University, but is observed in every other German seat of learning. This decline has been so rapid during the past ten years as seriously to alarm the leaders of the Church. Since 1895 the decrease has been nearly fifty per cent. Two reasons are given for this: First, the superior attractions offered by commerce and industry since Germany became a great manufacturing country, and, secondly, the decay of belief, mainly owing to the destructive criticism of the Bible and religions dogmas by the professors of the modern liberal school."

[30] *Agnostic Journal* 55, no. 27 (December 24, 1904): 414.

I was immensely relieved on finding this after nearly three columns of "Do we believe?"[31] Bravo, Haeckel.[32] —Yours truly,

From India[33]

J. F.C. F.

On Sunday, the 20th of November last,[34] there was a great bustle amidst the good missionaries of this country; their wives donned their best frocks, and their children had their faces scrubbed, and all toddled off to church post-haste, with their hands full of bibles and prayer-books, and their brains full of—well, nothing in particular. There was a hurry, a skurry, a kneeling, a mumbling, and then a great prayer arose for "the conversion of India," and the Unchangeable was besought to change, as if the Omnipotent needed the adulations of man, or could act only when propitiated by the supplications of that microbic grub, *homo sapiens*.

Once Christians prayed against the "horrid comet," and the "dire eclipse"; they still sometimes pray for rain, but not quite so confidently as in former

[31] On September 29, 1904, the *Daily Telegraph* caused a stir when it printed a letter by "Oxoniensis" with the heading "Do We Believe?" Over the next three months, the newspaper was deluged with letters, only a fraction of which they had room to print, about readers' religious faith or lack thereof. This correspondence was soon collected and republished as W. L. Courtney et al., *Do We Believe? A Record of a Great Correspondence in "The Daily Telegraph," October, November, December, 1904* (London: Hodder and Stoughton, 1905). Meanwhile, the Rationalist Press Association quickly assembled an analysis organized around various themes in the correspondence, published as John Allan Hedderwick, *Do We Believe? An Analysis of a Great Correspondence* (London: Watts, 1904). Callum Brown reports that only 54 percent of readers of the column professed a Christian faith, triggering an existential crisis for a readership that regarded Great Britain as a Christian nation. See Callum G. Brown, *Religion and Society in Twentieth-Century Britain* (Harlow, UK: Pearson Longman, 2006), 1.

[32] A popularizer of Darwin's work in Germany, professor of zoology Ernst Haeckel (1834–1919) coined the phrase "ontogeny recapitulates phylogeny" for his own since-disproven theory of recapitulation.

[33] *Agnostic Journal* 56, no. 1 (January 7, 1905): 7. Two issues later, the editor published the following brief remark: "J. F. C. F., Lucknow—Your cordial letter cheers us. We feel deeply grateful to you for your enthusiastic and disinterested hostility to Priestcraft. We have instructed our publishers to write to you and do what they can to support you in the Cause." See "To Correspondents," *Agnostic Journal* 56, no. 3 (January 21, 1905): 41.

[34] Several missionary groups cooperatively designated November 20, 1904, as a "Day of Prayer for India." This was the seventh such annual observance held on the third Sunday in November. Fuller's article quotes from a list of "subjects we would suggest for prayer" circulated by the signatories of this call to prayer. See, for example, "Current Mission News: Day of Prayer for India, November 20, 1904," *Harvest Field* 25, no. 11 (November 1904): 433–435; and Rev. W D. Clarke, "The Native Church in Madras," *Church Missionary Review* 55 (October 1904): 743–746.

days, and still sometimes for wealth. I once met a certain proselyte Jew who in prayer promised the Lord that he would turn a Christian, if on the following morning he found a £5 note under his pillow. Next day he awoke extra early, and placing his hand under his pillow, lo and behold, drew forth a nice crisp fiver! But prayer is not always so accommodating; people understand comets and eclipses nowadays, and no longer treat them with prayer; they are beginning to understand the weather, and with the barometer and the aneroid prayer for rain is going out of fashion. So now they pray for the conversion of the "heathen," which nobody quite understands; let it be hoped that they may soon pray for a little common sense and, further, that it may be granted them. Now for the prayer for India, and some proposed emendations of my own:—

"That we all may be one in Christ Jesus."

That all men may be one in Human Brotherhood.

"That the Church may be quickened to realize the high responsibility and happy privilege in extending everywhere the Kingdom of her Saviour."

That the Church may be quickened to realize her false position in following Christianity; and the impossibility of attempting to sit on both sides of a fence at the same time.

"That confession may be made for sin, and the grace of true penitence granted."

That missionaries may be imbued with more honesty, and try a more useful occupation.

"That thanksgiving from hearts full of gratitude may abound for blessings spiritual and temporal, received during the past year."

That men, instead of thanking some divinity for plague, famine, and misery, may put their shoulders to the wheel and fight them, not on their knees but on their feet.

"That our Rulers may legislate and govern in the fear of the Lord."

That our Rulers may legislate and govern for the greatest welfare of the many to the least detriment of the few.

"That the European community of India, if careless and indifferent, may be convicted of sin; if striving to live a Christian life, may witness by word and example to the saving power of Christ."

That the European community of India, if careless and indifferent, may be meted out justice; if striving to benefit the country, may be rewarded with affection.

"That Europeans in Government and railway service, in the army, in mercantile and professional pursuits, on tea estates, and coffee plantations, in mines, mills, camps, and out-of-the-way places, in colleges, schools, and hospitals, may fear God always, be victors in temptation, and exercise themselves unto Godliness."

That Europeans in Government, etc., etc., may treat those under them with kindness as well as justice, and exercise themselves unto humanity.

"That the Indian Christian Church may adorn the doctrine of Jesus Christ in all things, and may under the Holy Spirit endeavour to win their fellow-countrymen to the truth as it is in Jesus."

That the Indian Christian Church may reverence the original possessors of the land, and not steal away their children, or pervert their wives; and endeavour to win their fellow-countrymen by a little human kindness and less "divine love."

"That all churches may experience days of refreshing, so that there may be a great revival."

That all churches may be blessed with a little more common-sense.

"That all those engaged in mission work—evangelistic, educational, medical, industrial, etc., may be filled with the spirit of Christ and be fully consecrated."

That all those engaged in mission work, etc., etc., may be filled with the spirit of Truthfulness, and be a little more manly.

"That Hindus, Mohammedans, and others who are convinced of the truth of the claims of Jesus Christ may be given courage to confess him in baptism."

That Hindus, Mohammedans, and others may adopt as their rule of life "Be thyself, imitate no one whomsoever; thou canst not possibly be anything so great as thine own true self"; and try to leave this world a little better than you found it.

"That caste may be broken down, idolatry abolished, prejudices overcome, and all false views of God and religion dissipated in the light of the glory of God manifested in Christ Jesus."

That caste may be broken down, idolatry abolished, prejudices overcome, and all false views of God and religion dissipated in the light and glory of Reason manifested by Nature through man.

"That the compassion of Christ may be realized by the afflicted of the land stricken by famine, plague, leprosy, or other dread disease."

That men may not be so blasphemous as to impute the evils that they themselves bring on this world to a supposed personal and loving deity, or to a malignant fiend.

"That God's mercy may be vouchsafed to the womanhood of India, women in zenanas, widows, girls in homes and schools, and all sorely tempted or tried."

That God may not be mocked by being supposed to allow or disallow temptations and trials, and that the womanhood of India, etc., etc., may lead noble and honourable lives, diffusing happiness, tenderness, affection and love on all around them.

And that missionaries may read more diligently a work called the "New Testament," wherein they will find that a certain Jesus Christ, whom they profess to worship, taught as follows:—

That those who were reviled should be blessed (Matthew v., 11); that we should sell all, and distribute it to the poor (Matthew xix., 21); that we should desert all and follow him (Matthew xix., 29). He reproved the rich, stating that it was harder for a camel to go through the eye of a needle than for a rich man to enter the kingdom of heaven (Matthew xix., 24), and even bade him who had two coats to impart to him who had none (Luke iii., 11), and in solemn tones uttered, "Woe unto you that are rich; for ye have received your consolation" (Luke vi., 24). "Ye cannot serve God and Mammon"; and yet this latter is exactly what the Christian missionaries in India are trying to do, "whose God is their belly, and whose glory is their shame, who mind earthly things" (Philippians iii., 19).

A Lullaby[35]

Victor B. Neuburg

THE wind has freshened the night;
The rain has freshened the sea;
The clouds are purple and white.
Dawn is a dream: unknown
It dwells in the heart of thee;
Dawn is thine own, thine own.

Night is silver and grey;
Golden is dawn, and red—
Who has lovèd the day,
Who has dreamed in the night,
Never the dark shall dread,
Never shall fear the light.

[35] *Agnostic Journal* 56, no. 2 (January 14, 1905): 20; repr. in *A Green Garland*.

So sing your song and depart,
Leaving the air right sweet;
And bear a gentle heart
Back to the night, and, when
Dusk and day-dawn meet,
You never shall wake again.

Be still. The dawn shall rise
Over your bended head,
Over your downcast eyes.
Ye thought the song was done?
Ye thought the day was dead?
. . . But how of to-morrow's sun?

Nor life nor death I know,
Save only as one, as one;
Never the life shall go,
Nor ever shall death depart;
Never the song he done,
Never be stilled your heart.

A breeze has stirred the night—
Dream on, dream on; be still.
Await the dawning light.
Your eyes shall know the day,
The dawn your heart shall fill,
When night is vanished away. . . .

The Silent Gods[36]

Victor B. Neuburg

O SILENT GODS! What path has led ye far beyond our ken?
O silent gods! What word has fed the hearts and brains of men?

[36] *Agnostic Journal* 56, no. 3 (January 21, 1905): 36.

We dream, and dreaming die; we live, and living seek to find
The answer. Give us speech—oh, give, ye gods, if ye be kind!
For we are sick of dreaming, and the way is dark and far,
And we hate the showy seeming, and we seek the things that are.
O silent gods! We live and die, we dream and wake; we go
Where all the dead years' harvests lie, where glistens last year's snow.

O silent gods! We think we live; we know that we must die:
And ye, who have so much to give, heed not the dreamers' cry.
We dream so fairly! Do we wake where all our dreams are true?
Oh, say, ye gods! and shall we take the answer back to you?
For we are sick of dreaming, and the night is deep and chill;
And we know the dawn is gleaming far beyond the darkened hill,
And we catch the breath of morning, far away, beyond our ken:
O gods! Say, are ye scorning the eager eyes of men?

O silent gods! To ye the skies, to ye the stars, have speech;
To ye the morning open lies; to ye the echoes reach.
No answer may we find, no voice comes downward to our star:
We wonder if the worlds rejoice, we wonder if ye are.
For we are sick of seeking, and the road is bleak and cold;
We are weary of vain speaking, of the idle legends told.
We need no priests, no altars but the open heath we need;
Will ye answer—our voice falters—oh, if ye be gods indeed?

Divine, and Other Carnage[37]

J. F. C. F.

"O all ye Beasts and Cattle, bless ye the Lord: praise him, and magnify him for ever."[38] So says the Canticle, and so whines John Smith; but the cattle and beasts which are devoured by this psalm-singing image of God have little to thank John Smith for, and still less the Lord their creator, through whose goodness and divine irrascibility their progenitors were once upon a time

[37] *Agnostic Journal* 56, no. 15 (April 15, 1905): 229–230.
[38] From the canticle "Benedicite, omnia opera Domini," used in the Roman Catholic *Liturgy of the Hours*, Church of England *Book of Common Prayer*, and Lutheran hymnals.

nearly all drowned; and at another time, in order to prove that he was "I AM THAT I AM," afflicted with loathsome plagues and diseases.

Samson, who was a chosen vessel of the Lord, and who judged Israel for twenty years, was an arch-destroyer of innocent men and women. One day, in order to justify his own negligence towards his wife, he tied burning lire-brands to the tails of three hundred foxes; and burnt his neighbours' corn, which so pleased the Lord that he "came mightily upon him," and the usual holocaust was the result. David—that man after God's own heart and ancestor to the pig-drowner—felt no qualms whatever, when, on one of his ruthless raids, he houghed the horses of a thousand chariots. But little else could be expected from followers of the bloody Jahveh, who at one moment, in a passion, would shout, "I will smite every horse with blindness," and at another smack his chops over roast oxen and sheep:—

> "The sword of the Lord is filled with blood, it is made fat with fatness, and with the blood of lambs and goats, with the fat of the kidneys of rams; for the Lord bath a sacrifice in Bozrah, and a great slaughter in the land of Idumea."—Isaiah xxxiv., 6.

Thus was it in those days when the Lord spoke face to face with man, but now that he does not even condescend to show him his back parts, customs are changing. We no longer hough our opponents' horses, though we are cruel enough in all conscience; we no longer settle our family bickerings as Samson did his, for it we did we should have to face the "Society for the Prevention of Cruelty to Animals," and yet we are still brutal enough, as will shortly be shown, and this, too, after nigh two thousand years of Christianity. In more Christian days he had bull-baiting, bear-baiting, cock-fighting, and other forms of manly (!) sport; even nowadays, in one of the most Christian countries, and, consequently one of the most cruel, we have thumb-screws and bull-fights; but, generally speaking, less Christ, less cruelty, less redemption, less bloodshed.

Listen, O Lord, to the following, for it will bring back to thy nostrils the sweet savour of those halcyon days when thy friend Solomon, son of Uriah's wife—hem!—slew before thee "two and twenty thousand oxen, and an hundred and twenty thousand sheep" (1 Kings viii. 63). "He that killeth an ox is as if he slew a man," ranted another of thy chosen ones (Isaiah lxvi. 3). Contradiction? Oh, dear, no? "And he said, Take now thy son, thine only son, Isaac . . . and offer him there for a burnt offering" (Genesis xxii. 2). "Then the Spirit of the Lord came upon Jephthah" (so Jephthah's daughter went into the mountains and bewailed her virginity, and after two months returned to her father) . . . "who did with her according to his vow" (Judges xi. 29, 38, 39). Holocausts of men were quite as frequent as those of oxen, were they not, O Holy One? Read that sacred work penned by the Ghost, peruse Leviticus xxvii. 28, in conjunction with Joshua vi. 17; Jeremiah vii. 30, 31; Ezekiel xx. 25, 26; Micah vi. 7; also Exodus xiii. 12; I Kings xviii, 19; II Samuel xxi. 8; and I Samuel xv. 1–8; in which latter case, O Lord, so fierce was thine anger with thy servant Saul, that, for sparing one human being alive, thou transferred his throne to that foreskin-cutting traitor, David. *Ergo*:—"He that killeth a man is as if he slew an ox." Verily, verily have I spoken, THOU ART WHAT THOU ART,—Jehovah the Bloody. For one moment, O Holy One of Israel, allow thy servant to withdraw thy attention from the counting of the hairs of our heads and the lifeless bodies of dead sparrows, and let him read to you a line or two out of the *Lancet*:—"It is estimated that between three million and four million cattle are taken to the Chicago stockyards annually. The number of hogs is set down at from seven million to eight million, and there are some three million to four million sheep . . . the greater proportion, from two-thirds to three-quarters of these animals, is killed on the spot."—*Lancet*, Jan. 7, 1905, p. 50.[39]

Some ten million animals or more slaughtered on the spot. Why Solomon in all his glory never slew like this. Eight million hogs, O righteous One; why thy virgin born son only slew two thousand, "for his mercy endureth for ever!"

J. Smith feeds on J. Christ, apparently a most unsatisfying dish, for it has often to be supplemented with other aliments, such as Chicago pork. Before he could eat Christ, Christ had to be crucified, to satisfy the vengeance of his loving father; before he can masticate pig, pig has to be brutally done to death, to satisfy the greed of some avaricious and time-serving pork butcher. O Lord, thou didst redeem the world by the blood of thy only son, when a little more bread-and-butter was all the world needed; and so it would, no doubt, interest you to know how J. Smith, pork butcher, redeems his extravagance, gluttony, sensuality and greed, by the death of pigs. You chose crucifixion as a suitable expedient. J. Smith chooses as follows:—

"At the Chicago stockyards I was first taken to see the killing of pigs and found that outside the big factory buildings there are long, inclined, boarded

[39] Special Sanitary Commissioner, "Chicago: The Stockyards and Packing Town; Insanitary Condition of the World's Largest Meat Market," *Lancet* 1, no. 4245 (January 7, 1905): 49–52.

> passages, up which the animals are driven. Thus the pigs are brought up to the height of the second floor. As they enter the main building each pig is caught by one of the hind legs. With rope and loop-knot and hook it is slung up, the head downwards and the neck exposed, at a convenient height for the slaughterer to strike. With great rapidity the suspended pigs are pushed on to a sort of passage about four feet broad where their throats are slashed open as they pass along. These rows of hanging pigs struggle violently, throwing out torrents of blood. Both sides of this death passage to the height of five feet are thickly caked with the blood of thousands of healthy and unhealthy pigs. Within less than a minute the dying pig reaches a long tank full of scalding water and in this the palpitating body is thrown, though life is probably not yet quite extinct."—*Lancet, Jan.* 14, 1905, p. 120.[40]

Does this please you, O Lord, or would you prefer the pigs to be consumed away while they stand upon their feet, their eyes consuming away in their holes, and their tongues in their mouths, as thy servant Zechariah has it?

"Pigs, only pigs," you say, not your department—belongs to the virgin-born. Well, listen to this, then:—

> "Thus, for instance, I saw bullocks slaughtered in the following manner. The animals are brought up to a huge building which looks more like a lofty prison than a slaughter-house. As they approach the outer wall men strike them on the head with a mallet. Then a sort of wooden partition gives way and lets the half-stunned animals fall into the basement of the building beyond. As they come tumbling in men seize their hind legs, affix ropes, and they are strung up to some machinery above that moves them along with their heads hanging downwards. Sometimes, however, and before this can be done an animal jumps up and rushes about. It has then to be shot at the risk of the bullet striking an onlooker. When I inquired why a leather gear was not affixed to the bullock's head with a nail so placed in it that, however clumsy the stroke given, it would cause the nail to penetrate the brain and instantly kill the animal, I was told that such a process would take far too much time. Indeed, so great is the hurry that the unfortunate animals are frequently not given time to die. First, they are dropped into the building,

[40] Special Sanitary Commissioner, "Chicago: The Dark and Insanitary Premises Used for the Slaughtering of Cattle and Hogs—the Government Inspection," *Lancet* 1, no. 4246 (January 14, 1905): 120–123.

> though some of them may be insufficiently stunned. Then, when strung up, the machinery carries the living animal forwards and men have to run after it to cut its throat, while others follow with great pails to catch the blood; and all this without interrupting the dying animal's journey to the part of the factory where the next process of manufacture begins. Sometimes the cattle are struck down and stunned more quickly than the men can pick them up and cut their throats, so they are left to live some time suspended in the air by their hind feet. The machinery carries forwards the animals that are hooked on to it regardless of their agony. On they go from stage to stage of manufacture and the men have to keep pace with them whether dead or alive. Quickly the throats are cut, no time can be lost to let the animals bleed, a man with a pail must walk by their side to catch the blood. Much of the hot blood is spilt over the man or over the floor; that does not matter so long as a small section of a minute is economised."—*Lancet, Jan.* 14, 1905, p. 121.[41]

Oxen, only oxen; a mere trifle is it, after the slaying of young men and maidens, of old men, and they that stoop with age, after slaughtering infants and ripping open women who are with child? Yes, truly it is! Thou hast dashed the child to pieces before the eyes of its mother, and hast thrust the wife into the arms of her ravisher, thou has drenched the world with blood. "The sword without a terror within" has been the motto, and that of thine accursed church. Thy arrows are drunk with human blood, and thy sword surfeits with human flesh and bone. What is an ox to thee that it should suffer. Even for nineteen hundred years thou and thy pig-drowning son have been unto us as a lion, and as a bear bereft of her whelps. Thou has rent the caul of our hearts, and torn us as the wild beast of the fields in thy wrath. Deep have we drunk of the cup of thy fury; it is time to dash it to the ground, with the cup of redemption, symbols of an untutored age. Let him who will shout adulations to thy name, let him who will sing. "O all ye beasts and cattle bless ye the Lord: praise him, and magnify him for ever;" but thy days are numbered, and the roar of the lion, the bellowing of the bull are over; alone in the hours of the breaking dawn the ass brays, fit emblem of fools and folly.

[41] Special Sanitary Commissioner, "Chicago: The Dark and Insanitary Premises," 121–122.

My Homeland[42]

(FROM THE GERMAN OF A. DE NORA)

V. B. Neuburg

"Himmel und Erde feiern
Dich, Du Land der Bayern!
O wie bist Du schön!"

Over thy glistening snows
The heavens are gold and blue;
Over thy lakes there glows
The fleecy clouds' light hue:
Heaven and earth give greeting,
In thee, Bavaria, meeting;
Oh, how fair art thou!

From the heat of the mowing
Streams the scent of the hay;
Over the corn ripe-growing
Lingers the breath of Day.
Heaven and earth give greeting,
In thee, Bavaria, meeting;
Oh, how fair art thou!

Happy the men thou dost raise,
Whom thy green vigour fills;
They are keen as thy harvest days,—
Strong as thy swelling hills!
Heaven and earth give greeting,
In thee, Bavaria, meeting;
Oh, how fair art thou!

[42] *Agnostic Journal* 56, no. 18 (May 6, 1905): 279; repr. in *A Green Garland*. De Nora's poem had appeared in the influential German arts journal *Jugend* only the year before. See A. De Nora, "Mein Heimathland," *Jugend* 2, no. 27 (June 21, 1904): 556. A. De Nora was the pseudonym of German doctor and poet Anton Alfred Noder (1864–1936). The German tercet at the beginning is from the original German, repeating at the end of each stanza. This translation marked the start of a passion for Neuburg. In the coming years, the *Agnostic Journal* would also print Neuburg's translations of Rehtz, Hugo, Heine, Goethe, Eichendorff, Rückert, and Froissart.

Saladin[43]

(A translation of the verses, in German, by Alfred Rehtz, in the *Agnostic Journal* for April 29th, 1905.)

Victor B. Neuburg

DARK visions once overcast
The good green earth we tread,
And the slaves of the clinging Past
Wandered, blind and unled.

And every man his heart
Must in that crowd enfold,
Nor from the path depart
His fathers trod of old.

And here and there a light
'Twas given one to find,
But the crowd knew but the night,
And scorned him, being blind.

For men had dwelt in the dark
For æons, and, fearing it bright,
Hated the glittering spark,
And mocked, in their hatred of light.

But torches were kindled, and they
Who bore them persisted, and then
The Temple of Folly soon lay
In dust at the feet of men.

And before an army vast,
A hero, with banner unfurled,
Rises: with challenging blast
He wakens the sleeping world.

[43] *Agnostic Journal* 56, no. 19 (May 13, 1905): 295. Alfred Rehtz (1875–1954) was a German poet and Freethinker.

"From Faith's hard fetters be free!"
How the dark, dark shadows are seen
To flee from the light.! And we
Cry, "Lead us still on, Saladin!"

To Shelley[44]

[*Shelley was born at Field Place, Horsham, Sussex.*][45]

Victor B. Neuburg

RADIANT son of the South, whose fingers
Strayed in love o'er a heart-strung lyre,
The glamour of Summer's veil still lingers
Over the hills of thy native shire,
Sweetest of all our country's singers,
Whose voice was flame, and whose eyes were fire!

The wind on the heath thy words still carries
Over the valleys and hills thou didst know:
Still the song of the springtide tarries,
Wrapt in the rivers and mountain-snow,—
Still the gorse on the hill-side marries
The summer sky to the earth below

Hawthorn buds in the lanes are springing;
The chestnuts rustle in living green:
Still are the sky-larks upward winging
Over the fields where thou hast been.
Still the wild sea her spray is flinging,
Glittering greenly in sunlight sheen.

Brother and bard, thy voice's thunder
Changed the grey sky of the past to white:

[44] *Agnostic Journal* 56, no. 20 (May 20, 1905): 317; repr. in *A Green Garland*. The great English Romantic poet Percy Bysshe Shelley (1792–1822) was highly regarded by both Neuburg and Crowley.
[45] This note is not present in *A Green Garland*.

Still we listen in pain and wonder—
    Still we weep in our hearts' delight
When the golden sun at eve goes under
    The earth's red rim at the touch of Night.

Over the hills the stars are gleaming,
    In silver moonlight the hamlets sleep;
The gulls in the darkness have ceased their screaming,
    And silence reigns, and the night is deep,
And dawning lies in the land of dreaming,
    Where thou didst wander, where thou didst weep.

Dawn's noblest singer,—the earth that bore us
    Sang the wide songs that thou didst sing—
Still we join in the earth's deep chorus,
    Still the echoes we outward fling.
Still the pathway lies far[46] before us,
    But Love the portals shall wider swing!

Pure in passion, with lustless longing
    For love, thou hast sung of another race,
Who, in the bosom of Earth, are thronging
    To come to light, and to see her face:
In the years to be, who loves by wronging
    Shall burn in the fires of his own disgrace.

Singer of Freedom, by Love had'st thou being!
    Singer of Love, thou by Freedom hast won!
Freedom and Love shall each other be freeing
    In Earth's greener years, 'neath a kindlier sun.
Who that doth sing from his heart is not seeing
    The dawn that shall rise when the night shall be done?

Our songs shall rise as the dawn grows whiter,
    Our hearts shall throb with the promise of Day;

[46] *A Green Garland* omits this word.

'Neath skies more deep, and in sunlight brighter,
With gold-strung[47] lyres we will go our way.—
Take thou this lay of a dawning lighter,
A song of the springtide, of Sussex in May.

The Swan-Song[48]

Victor B. Neuburg

Oh! for a passionless dawn, love and regret far away—
Oh! for a passionless dawn over a wind-stilled bay,
For the stars are my masters in fire, and "love" breathes the passionate sea,
And ever her current flows higher, and ever it flows to me.[49]

And I was lost in the dawn: I wandered alone in the night
Over a pathless lawn, and the stars were wan and white;
I heard the Naiads sing to the moon, and the wildering pipes of Pan;
Encircled in flame each wild note came, and maddened I turned and ran.

And so I reached the depths of hell, and lay in a rut to die,
But I heard the waters rise and swell, and the night-wind rushing by;
And the salt spray touched my lips, and straight I rose in my pain and hied
All eager and swift to the mystic Gate, and there I was shut outside.

Ah! but I heard the passion-song of a world of death and birth,
And the day was hot, and the night was long over the good green earth;
And when men heard my lays, they stayed, and scattered a meed of praise,
But I turned again from the haunts of men, to seek the nobler days.

And so I trod the mountain path, in the heat of a new-born day,
But[50] mount and morass, by field and rath, I took my lonely way;[51]

[47] This becomes "golden" in *A Green Garland.*

[48] *Agnostic Journal* 56, no. 21 (May 27, 1905): 325; repr. in *A Green Garland.*

[49] *A Green Garland* puts this verse in the past tense, changing "becomes" to "were," "breathes" to "breathed," and both occurrences of "flows" to "flowed."

[50] The errata slip in *A Green Garland* indicates this word should be "By."

[51] In *A Green Garland,* this line becomes "By field and fallow, by road and rath, I took my lonely way:".

And heaven all around me lay, but ah! I knew not then,
And I came at the close of a summer's day back to the haunts of men.

So now I long for a passionless dawn, and the calm of the great unknown;
With a last glance over the darkened lawn, now fare I forth alone.
The silent path before me lies, and the night is still and deep;
Ever a star is before my eyes, and I lay me down to sleep.

When It Was Dark[52]

J. F. C. F.

"When It Was Dark."[53] Such is the title of a story written by Mr. Guy Thorne, and boomed by the Bishop of London. Though late in the day—my only excuse is, I am not a new-novel reader—I think a few words might be said about this book, which evidently was intended as an attack on Freethought and Agnosticism. The story is briefly this.

The two villains, Constantine Schuabe, and Robert Llewellyn; a millionaire Agnostic Jew, and a sensual scientist, carry out between them a forgery, which takes the shape of proving that Christ never rose from the dead—a proof that neither agnostic nor scientist would need; Llewellyn goes to Palestine, and has the following inscribed in a certain tomb in Jerusalem:—

> "I, Joseph of Arimathæa, took the body of Jesus, the Nazarene, from the tomb where it was first laid and hid it in this place."[54]

Gortre, a youthful clergyman, virile and virtuous, and who is in close communion with the celestial regions, smells a mundane "rat"; he also rescues Gertrude Hunt, ballet-dancer, and kept mistress of Llewellyn, from her evil surroundings. He is a curate to the Rev, Father Ripon, a gentleman of erratic speed and forgetfulness, who seems never to remember the

[52] *Agnostic Journal* 56, no. 23 (June 10, 1905): 353–354.
[53] Guy Thorne [C. Ranger Gull], *When It Was Dark: A Story* (London: Greening, 1903). In subsequent reprinting, the subtitle became "The Story of a Great Conspiracy." For details on this author, see David Wilkinson, *"Guy Thorne": C. Ranger Gull; Edwardian Tabloid Novelist and His Unseemly Brotherhood* (High Wycombe, UK: Rivendale Press, 2012).
[54] Thorne, *When It Was Dark*, 181. This sentence is set in uppercase letters in the novel.

conventional hours for meals, and whenever he starts hanging a pair of crimson curtains, a gift from his sister, has a sudden call and rushes out to save a soul instead. The other characters are less important, and are chiefly employed in drinking beverages, ranging from a *Vermouth sec* to black currant tea.

The thunderous news breaks; the churches empty, crime increases fifty per cent., criminal assaults *two hundred per cent.*, consols fall to 65, India in mutiny, America in civil war, the world ablaze; all is rapine and murder, and it is of this scene that the Bishop of London has the impertinence to preach: "It paints, in wonderful colours, what it seems to me the world would be if, for six months, as in the story it is supposed to be the case, owing to a gigantic fraud, the Resurrection might be supposed never to have occurred."[55]

Gertrude now bestirs herself, and once again sacrificing her honour, falls into the arms of Llewellyn with a "kiss me, Bob."

"Dear, old Bob," she cried; "clever, old Bob, you're the best of them all. What have you done this time? Tell me all about it."[56] (Romans iii., 7.)

And he tells her all.

Thus Christianity, which originated in an illegitimate, was kicked into the world by a brutal murderer, and reformed by an incestuous Bluebeard, and saved by a harlot. *Hoi polloi!* What a rabble we must be!

Another character now enters more forcibly on the scenes; this is a Mr. Spence of the *Daily Wire*. He is sent by the editor of that paper to Palestine, and there discovers a certain Greek, Ionides, associate of Llewellyn in the forgery; and for the greater glory of God, threatens to shoot him—(Luke xix., 27)—if he do not at once reveal all. He reveals all. And, as speedily as the world swallowed the "not risen" sprat, it now gulps down the "is risen" whale; most men, apparently, being from the author's point of view, fools—as well as in that of Tam Carlyle.

The end now speedily approaches, and the villains turn "green grey," "pendulous," and "flabby."[57]

[55] From the syndicated column "Sunday Reading: Witnesses for Christ" by the Rt. Rev. A. F. Winnington Ingram, D.D., Bishop of London. It appeared, for example, in the *New Zealand Herald*. A. F. Winnington Ingram, *New Zealand Herald* 41, no. 12657 (September 10, 1904): 4. The quote appeared on the cover of subsequent editions, and was also used in advertisements for the book.

[56] Thorne, *When It Was Dark*, 255.

[57] Thorne, *When It Was Dark*, 361.

Llewellyn, dying, hears the Christian mob crashing at his door, when at the psychologic moment—

The door opened silently: Lady Llewellyn came swiftly into the room.
She wore a long white robe. Her face was lighted as if a lamp shone behind it.
In her hand was a great crucifix which was wont to hang above her bed.
When Christ died and bade the dying thief ascend with him to Paradise, can we say that His silence condemned the other?[58]
Her face was all aglow with love.
"Robert," she said. Her voice was like the voice of an angel.
Her arms are round him, her kisses press upon him, the great crucifix is lifted to his dying eyes.
A great thunder on the stairs, furious voices, the tide rising higher, higher.
Death![59]

Shilling shockers! One villain dead; and we trust Lady Llewellyn's fate was not that of Hypatia, as Christian mobs are not given to discriminate.

Now, let us turn to the other. We are introduced to a party of young and giggling Christian maidens, who are paying a visit to the lunatic asylum, where, now, Mr. Schuabe is residing as a drivelling idiot.

"On a bed lay the idiot. He had grown very fat, and looked healthy. The features were all coarsened, but the hair retained its colour of dark red. He was sleeping."
"Now, Miss Clegg, ye'd never think that was the fellow that made such a stir in the world but five years since. But there he lies. He always eats as much as he can, and goes to sleep after his meal."
"He's waking up now, sir. Here Mr. Schuabe some ladies have come to see you."
It got up with a foolish grin, and began some ungainly capers.
"Thank you, so much, Mr. Pritchard," the girls said, as they left the building. "We've enjoyed ourselves so much."
"I liked the little man with his tongue hanging out the best," said one.
"Oh, Mabel, you've *no* sense of honour! That Schuabe creature was the funniest of *all!*"[60]

[58] No. But only that he was a liar, for he did not go to Paradise [original note].
[59] Thorne, *When It Was Dark*, 374–375.
[60] Thorne, *When It Was Dark*, 389–390.

How sublimely Christian! And if Mr. Constantine Schuabe were only a living character, what a chance for the Torrey–Alexander–Agnostic–Conversion–Mission *Limited*.

Dean Gortre marries Helena, the daughter of his former vicar, a Mr. Byars, and with a shout of "Christ is risen!" we end "*the most daring and original novel of the century*."[61]

Now, the whole point of this story is, I presume, this:—To show the awful cataclysm that would befall this poor world, were the Resurrection of Christ proved false. But, as it has never yet been proved true, we have our doubts. Those who have read Saladin's "Did Jesus Christ rise from the Dead," can have none, neither can any of those who have carefully and frankly studied the Bible; but people, at least Christian people, do not read the Bible; they only possess it. Only last Sunday (Easter), I listened to a servant of the Lord reading out of that Holy Book, how the Lord smote the firstborn of Egypt, and bid the Israelites steal their neighbour's goods, and how a stupendous crowd left Egypt at a stupendous pace in a single night; and, looking carefully at the faces of the numerous women, kind-hearted mothers and affectionate wives: did I see horror, or even a smile? Oh, dear no! Placid vacuity and contentment, simple empty idiocy of expression; for the word of the Lord was being read to them—that was all.

But this book, after all, can do but little harm to Rationalism, and it cedes more than most of its uncritical readers have probably imagined. First it cedes this:—That Christ was never a Reality, but only a more or less amiable idea. What is real is real, and cannot be unreal. We know that the sun exists, but we are not sure of all its mysteries, and if some of our present ideas concerning it, are, in the future, proved wrong, we, as the great Marcus Aurelius did, will accept the new and more correct theories in the place of the old ones; and, curious to say, the sun will, however, still shine. Not so with Christ and the Christians. For if Christ were a reality, it would make but little difference whether the resurrection were proved true or not; for the resurrection is not Christ, but only—if we may so call it—an appendage of Christ's. But Christians will not accept this; and so Christ not being a reality, but becoming an idea, a very different aspect settles over the question. If we

[61] This was the claim of the book's publisher, Greening & Co. It is arguably true: according to Claud Cockburn: "*When It Was Dark* was one of the most significant works of the Edwardian and early Georgian eras." Claud Cockburn, *Bestseller: The Books That Everyone Read, 1900–1939* (London: Sidgwick and Jackson, 1972), 19.

break the end off a Rupert drop, the Rupert drop ceases to exist as such;[62] so with the Christ idea; deprive it of one of its many appendages, and at once Christendom wails that her saviour is being destroyed, the shattered bauble falling derisively at her feet.

A Rupert drop is only a Rupert drop with an unshattered tail, and Jesus is only a Christ with an impossible resurrection—How divinely true! Mr. Thorne, we sincerely thank you for this piece of information.

The Old Mysticism rose
With a fulness of heart,
And with a fulness of mind,
Mr. Thorne 't will depart.

Three Earth-Notes[63]

Victor B. Neuburg

I.—Even-Tide

Within a narrow coombe betwixt dark hills
That greenly rise, steep-browed, on either hand,
A little pausing, as the sunset fills
With silence this lone spot in a fair land—
A little lingering on yielding sand,
That, from the sea-ebb's tiny streams and rills,
Is soft and pliant 'neath a white sky spanned
With fleecy clouds—the sleepy birds' last trills
On darkening tree-tops—and the clay is dead:
The sun-light all is faded from the skies,
And, as the star-light to the night is wed,
Are hushed the notes of all the melodies
That brought bright tears into thy brighter eyes.
All songs are sung, and all the legends said;
For Day is joyous, but the Night is wise,
And silence reigns over the path we tread.
Darkness enfolds the dawn, for all the day is sped.

[62] A Prince Rupert's drop, or Dutch tear, is the result of dripping molten glass into cold water, producing a bulbous end of toughened glass with a long, thin, and fragile tail.
[63] *Agnostic Journal* 56, no. 23 (June 10, 1905): 358.

II.—Night

O million worlds that flash and roll and beam!
  O silent sea with voiceless longing dumb!
O pines whose odour mingles in my dream
  Of nations dead, of empires yet to come!
  O nightingales, white-voiced! O murmured hum
From the deep grass! O silver winding stream
  That over the white pebbles sings! O gum
That floods with life the trees!—What wide eyes' gleam
Touched all with life? The nightingale may sing,
  The stars roll on to destiny, the sea
Still throb in eager pain, while Night doth bring
  The words of life together—but for me
  The wrappings of the Night hold still in fee,
In songs that thrill with joy, in words that sting,
  A song of life—of life forever free
To scan the skies; with ever-rising wing
To merge into the wide, to pierce the outer ring.

III.—The Song

Deep-drunken of the morn methought I lay,
  Nor knew of light till half the day was gone;
But passing footsteps led my thought away,
  The murmur of strong voices drew me on.
  Then heard I, "*Hard the armour is to don.*
And hard to wear all through the burning day,
  But, at the end, the crown is set upon
His head, who laughed when all the world cried 'stay!'"
Straightway I followed. In the day's fierce gold
  I gazed enraptured down the roadway wide,
Whence came the echo of the song that rolled
  In silver cadences. With swinging stride
  I fast pursued the singer in my pride,
To know the song whose echo e'en could hold
  Me thralled, and many there I passed had died
In the pursuit. But still the song is trolled,
And still will I pursue, until the tale be told.

The Fugitive[64]

[*Sixteenth Century*]

Victor B. Neuburg

Ah! I can linger now,
    Here, 'mid the darkling trees;
The hair is hot on my brow,
    And oh! my aching knees!
God! I can scarcely stand—
    Oh! Let me sleep! Let me sleep! . . .
Are they watching on either hand? . . .
    Oh! how the path was steep!

We broke and fled, and then
    They chased us for miles, and we—
Fifteen hundred men—
    Made way right heartily;
And for seven miles I've run,
    And the stones have cut my feet:
Ah! but the chase is done
    Now, and the rest is sweet.

I can hear water there—
    There, by the cutting; maybe
I might for a moment dare,
    Without letting the devils see:
I'm parched and sick and done,
    And I'd give my soul for a drink;
For a moment I might run
    There, by the river's brink,

And drink, and drink, and drink;
    And then sleep till the light, . . .

[64] *Agnostic Journal* 56, no. 24 (June 17, 1905): 381; repr. in *A Green Garland*.

God! how the blood did stink! . . .
  God! But the stars are bright!
Oh! let me sleep, and forget!
  Ah! this is good—to be
Out of the blood and sweat,
  Under this wide oak tree! . . .

They killed my brother; he lies
  Under the burning stars;
There's a glaze upon his eyes,
  And his arms are rigid bars.
I know! For, before I ran,
  I stumbled across him; I kneeled,
And, . . . oh! but it does a man—
  Seven miles off the field . . .

And there was blood on his brow,
  And his locked teeth grinned at me;
And his eyes! I can see them now!
  Ah! but the wind is free
Over my brow; 'tis[65] good
  To sleep out under the trees,
Here, on the skirt of the wood—
  Here, with the blessèd breeze.

Seven miles I've run! . . .
  Oh! let me sleep, now wake
But to greet the rising sun,
  Onward my way to take.[66]
A breeze has sprung from the south,
  The night is calm and deep;
The moonlight kisses my mouth . . .
  Oh! let me sleep! Let me sleep! . . .

[65] Becomes "it's" in *A Green Garland.*
[66] In *A Green Garland*, this line becomes "To see the morning break."

Contempt of Court[67]

Letter to the Editor

J. T. [sic] C. FULLER.

Sir,—A few weeks ago a certain prisoner in the dock at Leeds, on being awarded eighteen months' hard, became most irate, and drawing a black bottle from his pocket, hurled it at the Recorder, Mr. Tindal Atkinson, K.C.; who being moved in—or by—the spirit, changed the sentence to five years' penal servitude. Mr. Atkinson was probably unaware at the time, that Eleazer, one of the Lord's chosen and servant of Sarai—that naughty darling who captivated the heart of King Abimelech when an innocent little dear of 90—committed a similar contempt of court. The following might interest him:—

> Upon one occasion Sarai sent her servant Eleazer to Sodom to enquire concerning the welfare of Lot and his family As he entered the city, Eleazer observed a Sodomite fighting with a stranger whom he had defrauded, and who, running to Eleazer, implored him for assistance.
>
> "What art thou doing to this poor man?" said Eleazer to the Sodomite; "shame upon thee to act in this manner towards a stranger in your midst!
>
> And the Sodomite replied:
>
> "Is he thy brother? What is our quarrel to thee?" and picking up a stone, he struck Eleazer with it on the forehead, causing his blood to flow freely in the street. When the Sodomite saw the blood, he caught hold of Eleazer, crying:
>
> "Pay me my fee as a leech; see, I have freed thee of this impure blood; pay me quickly, for such is our law."
>
> "What!" exclaimed Eleazer, "thou hast wounded me, and I am to pay thee for it?"

[67] *Agnostic Journal* 56, no. 25 (June 24, 1905): 398. A surprising scene unfolded at the Leeds Recorder's Court on the morning of April 12, 1905: John Jones, a nineteen-year-old miner who pleaded guilty to stealing from a wholesale tobacconist, was sentenced to eighteen months in prison. In response, Jones pulled a quart-sized wine bottle from his breast pocket and hurled it at the recorder, Tindal Atkinson. With typical British unflappability, the recorder called out "Mind! Mind!" as he lowered his head and dodged the projectile. When the prisoner remarked that he wished he had brought a pistol instead—"You would not have been here to give any more sentences, you old villain!"—Tindal changed the sentence to five years. As Jones was led away, he cried out, "You're a toff!" See "Recorder Attacked in Court: Prisoner Throws a Glass Bottle at the Bench," *Nottingham Evening Post* 8306 (April 12, 1905): 4; "A Costly Shot: Prisoner Throws a Bottle at the Recorder," *Western Times* no. 17402 (April 13, 1905): 4; "Bottle Thrown at Recorder: Exciting Scene at Leeds," *Manchester Courier* no. 15111 (April 13, 1905): 8.

This Eleazer refused to do, and the Sodomite had him brought into the court, and there, before the judge, reiterated his demand for a fee.

"Thou must pay the man his fee," said the judge, addressing Eleazer; "he has let thy blood, and such is our law."

Eleazer paid the money, and then lifting up the stone he struck the judge heavily with it, and the blood spurted out in a strong stream.

"There!" exclaimed Eleazer, "follow thy law and pay my fee to this man; I want not the money," and he left the court-house. *The Talmud (Polano's translation).*[68]

—Yours truly,
Lucknow, 11 May, 1905

A Lyric[69]

[*After Victor Hugo*][70]

V. B. Neuburg

Ah what if I hear
    The wood-birds rejoice?
That bird is most clear
    Who sings in thy voice.

What if the stars shine,
    Or they hide from the skies?
The brightest is thine,
    In the light of thine eyes.

Doth April renew
    With blossoms the earth?
What sweeter e'er grew
    Than in thy heart hath birth?

[68] Hymen Polano, trans., *The Talmud: Selections from the Contents of That Ancient Book, Its Commentaries, Teachings, Poetry and Legends; Also, Brief Sketches of the Men Who Made and Commented Upon It* (London: F. Warne, 1890), bottom of form 48–49.

[69] *Agnostic Journal* 57, no. 2 (July 8, 1905): 28.

[70] Prolific Romantic poet and writer Victor Hugo (1802–1885) is considered one of the best French writers.

This singer of lire—
This day-star aflame—
This flower of desire—
Oh! love is its name.

The Garden of Youth[71]

Victor B. Neuburg

O haunted garden of eternal youth!
O darkling avenues of fir and pine!
O sunlit lawns! O fountains clear as truth!
O singing air! O life of sparkling wine!
A voice comes chanting slowly, "All is mine";
A million ears are strained to catch the lay;
A song floats upward in a curling line,
Breathing of roses, poppies, odorous hay,
And all the stars of night, and all the lore of day.

I would the gods would whisper, "This is thine:
In every heart to plant a flower of May;
To bring each lip a measure of bright wine;
To teach each listening ear a roundelay."
Yet is there not, methinks, a perfect Way:
Each man a separate path must seek and tread.
No voice may mimic the red notes of Day;
No man the stars can summon overhead,
And so I sing, forlorn, to living and to dead.

To-night, the wind shall play among the trees,
To-night, still waters shall reflect the sky,
To-night, the moon shall shine o'er distant seas,

[71] *Agnostic Journal* 57, no. 14 (September 30, 1905): 214. When reprinted in *A Green Garland*, the stanzas were given Roman numerals.

To-night, shall men be born, and men shall die.[72]
Over waste lands shall rise a bitter cry:
"O Death! sweet Death! let me but hear thy wings!"
But Death, unseen, unheeding, shall pass by,
And bitter eyes shall seek the soul of things
Vainly. The Root is hidden by sharp-pointed stings.

O Garden of Youth Immortal! Were it well
To dwell forever in thy sheltering shade?
Or were it good to seek the heaven and hell
That men have sought and loved,—have marred and made?
The sun that warms the garden, many-rayed,
Beats down upon our heads; with dazzled eyes
We see, and, seeing partly, unafraid,
We shelter in our bosoms living lies,
And they ward off the sun of Truth that never dies.

Thy statue, Hebe, in the varying light
Of cypress dark, and gleaming laurel, stands;
A jar of sparkling water, crystal-bright,
Is highly poised within thy strong white hands:
Oh! we are bound to thee with many bands;
O Hebe! Thou our dark world shalt redeem!
Pour out, pour out, over the thirsty sands
Of this, our age, a long unyielding stream—
The water of Life and Youth, the sad world's fairest dream.

Close not the portals! Let the sunlight stream
Through widened gates on to the outer bar;
Beyond, though all be darkened as a dream,
Shines every man's effulgent guiding-star.
Onward, through forest, and o'er ford, the Car
Of Progress wends towards the light, and we,
Glancing within, where our time's heroes are,

[72] In *A Green Garland*, these two lines change to "To-night, the moonlight over wide stretch'd seas / Shall rouse the slumb'rous earth with melody."

Give cheer and jest, and, with our minstrelsy,
Make light the way, and, toiling, make the pathway free.

The world has thrilled beneath the songs of men,
The nations have arisen but to die,
But a wild poet with an eager pen
The unforgotten thunders of the sky
Hears, and the cleansing lightning sees fly,
And straightway song, that evermore shall free
The hearts of men in death or triumph-cry,
Brings earth and sky and market-place and sea
Into the world unknown, that yet men know shall be!

O earth unborn that all the bards have sung!
O youth unplumbed that all the bards have known!
Thy note shall spring upon the new world's tongue;
The earth to be shall make you all its own.
Gaze clown, O Hebe! from thy starry throne,
Look up, O bards unknown of the new Day;
It cannot[73] be that one should sing alone,
The divine Impulse striving to obey,
That comes with dawn anti youth—that grows with love and May![74]

O Garden of Youth Immortal! In thy shade
Has this, my song, been woven of air and light;
And at thy portal stand I unafraid,
For bear I not a fire-brand for the night?
And shall my lyre not serve when day is bright
Over men's heads? Ah! Hebe! 'Tis to thee
I owe my song: let now thy linger white
Point out the path the world shall tread to me.
Farewell, O Garden of Youth, for now my steps are free.

[73] This becomes "may not" in *A Green Garland.*

[74] These last two lines in *A Green Garland* become "That one alone should journey on the way / That leads unto the heights where Freedom holds her sway."

Bible Science[75]

J. F. C. F.

"... 'Tis an unweeded garden,
That grows to seed; things rank and gross in nature
Possess it entirely." HAMLET (Act i., 2).

IN the year of our Lord 1432 there arose a grievous quarrel among the brethren over the number of teeth in the mouth of a horse. For thirteen days the disputation raged without ceasing. All the ancient books and chronicles were fetched out, and wonderful and ponderous erudition, such as was never before heard of in this region, was made manifest. At the beginning of the fourteenth day, a youthful friar of goodly bearing asked his learned superior for permission to add a word, and straightway, to the wonderment of the disputants, whose deep wisdom he sore vexed, he beseeched them to unbend in a manner coarse and unheard-of, and to look into the open mouth of a horse to find answer to their questionings. At this, their dignity being grievously hurt, they waxed exceedingly wroth; and, joining in a mighty uproar, they flew upon him and smote him hip and thigh, and cast him out forthwith. For, said they, surely Satan hath tempted this bold neophyte to declare unholy and unheard-of ways of finding truth contrary to all the teachings of the fathers. After many days of more grievous strife the dove of peace sat on the assembly, and they as one man, declaring the problem to be an everlasting mystery because of a grievous dearth of historical and theological evidence thereof, and so ordered the same to be writ down.[76]

[75] *Agnostic Journal* 57, no. 15 (October 7, 1905): 225–226; *Agnostic Journal* 57, no. 16 (October 14, 1905): 253; *Agnostic Journal* 57, no. 17 (October 21, 1905): 269; *Agnostic Journal* 57, no. 18 (October 28, 1905): 276–277; *Agnostic Journal* 57, no. 19 (November 4, 1905): 300–301; and *Agnostic Journal* 57, no. 20 (November 11, 1905): 308–310. Ross may have acknowledged receiving this submission when he wrote "Lieut. J. F. C. Fuller.—Safely to hand, and shall have best attention." "To Correspondents," *Agnostic Journal* 57, no. 11 (September 9, 1905): 169.

[76] This quote—sometimes attributed to Francis Bacon—is said to be taken from the record of a Franciscan friary, but it appears to be an urban legend originating in the early twentieth century. This story appears in print for the first time in 1901 in two sources: Dr. Jacobus X***, *The Basis of Passional Psychology: A Study of the Laws of Love in Man and the Lower Animals* (Paris: Charles Carrington, 1901), 2:iv; and *Monthly Journal of the International Association of Machinists* 13, no. 3 (March 1901): 129–130. Both sources identify the passage as an "extract from the chronicle of an ancient monastery."

The above is an extract from the chronicle of an ancient monastery—but it is really more; for it is an extract from the very life history of that great unprogressive organization, the Christian Church. Wherever she become supreme, there Reason, like the young neophyte, was cast out forthwith; whenever a new idea arose, it was attributed to a Satanic snare; common-sense was declared unholy, and judgment an unheard-of way of seeking Truth, both contrary to all the teachings of the fathers and to the word of God; for Faith walked hand in hand with Ignorance, and Cruelty licked the leprous heels of Superstition.

And why? Because, as long as the world was maintained in ignorance, as long as her eyes were blinded by outward power, and her mind cramped by inward fear, the Church could reign supreme. Ignorance, to her, spelt salvation, and knowledge whispered death; for, as R. G. Ingersoll rightly said: "Just in proportion that the human race has advanced the Church has lost power. There is no exception to this rule."[77] And she knew this full well. "Believe or perish!" was her motto and her precept; and those who refused to believe and lick her festering sores, perished, and perished in the most horrible manner, for in one art alone did she attain perfection, and that one art was the art of torture.

"From the third to the thirteenth century, in Christian countries, instruments of torture were the only invention." But, in spite of the rack and the boot, the stake and the wheel, and a thousand other refinements of devilry, noble souls struggled onwards, and the rushlight of Science, though all but extinguished for a thousand years, yet flickeringly burnt, destined, one day, to burst forth into that glorious and resplendent sundawn which has, to-day, all but dried up the fœtid swamps and stagnant mires of those dark and dismal ages; putting Ignorance and Fear to flight, and opening the eyes of mankind to Truth, Liberty and Reason.

"Modern civilization," writes Huxley, "rests upon physical science; take away her gifts to our country, and our position among the leading nations of the world is gone to-morrow; for it is physical science that makes intelligence and moral energy stronger than brute force."

> The whole of modern thought is steeped in science; it has made its way into the works of our best poets, and even the mere man of letters, who affects to ignore and despise science, is unconsciously impregnated with

[77] From Ingersoll's lecture "Thomas Paine: With His Name Left Out, the History of Liberty Cannot Be Written," published in Robert Green Ingersoll, *An Oration on the Life and Services of Thomas Paine, at Fairbury, Ill., on the Evening of January 30th, 1871* (n.p.: n.p., 1871).

> her spirit and indebted for his best products to her methods. She is teaching the world that the ultimate court of appeal is observation and experiment, and not authority; . . . she is creating a firm and living faith in the existence of immutable moral and physical laws, perfect obedience to which is the highest possible aim of an intelligent being.[78]

But the Church has never thought so, or rather has never dared to acknowledge that she has; and, thinking it wiser to leave such men alone, turns her attention to the poor heathen"; quietly picks to pieces their creeds, pointing out a fault here, and a mistake there, sweetly unconscious that she herself in doing so, is but taking one more step towards the brink of that dark precipice, called destruction.

A Christian writer remarks:—"The word Creator in English strictly means *one who calls things into existence out of nothing*. In this sense of the word, according to Hinduism, there is no creation. God is indeed called *Sarva-Karia*, 'maker of all'; but this does not mean that He is the *Creator*. No Hindu sect believes God to have created anything. According to the Naàya School, the *paramanus*, the atoms of the earth, water, fire, and air, gods, animals, and plants are all uncreated, self-existent and eternal . . . "[79]

Here Hinduism and its conception of the Cosmos—whatever other faults it may possess—stands head and shoulders above that of its Christian antagonists; for it is based not only on a sound scientific theory, but on an immutable law of Nature, the law of the conservation of energy and matter, which lays down that neither energy nor matter can be created or destroyed, although their form may change. How grandly does this conception stand forth, when contrasted with the puny and impossible Christian doctrine: "That God, infinite in power and wisdom, has always existed, and that the universe, and all that it contains, was called into being by Him out of nothing."[80] But, to digress no further from our subject, let us now turn to the Bible, where we shall find that the first astonishing scientific argument it has to offer is that of the Creation.

78 Thomas Henry Huxley and Robert Hebert Quick, *Lectures Addressed to Teachers on Preparation for Obtaining Science Certificates, and the Method of Teaching a Science Class: Lecture IV on Zoology; Delivered at the South Kensington Museum, 14th May 1860* (London: George E. Eyre and William Spottiswoode, 1860), 14.

79 "Revival and Reform of Hinduism," p. 104. The Christian Literature Society for India [original note]. John Murdoch, *Letter to His Highness the Maharaja Bahadur of Darbhangah on the Revival and Reform of Hinduism* (London: Christian Literature Society for India, 1901), 104.

80 "Revival and Reform of Hinduism," p. 105 [original note].

This myth is far too well known to make it necessary here to enter into detail. The Almighty having physically rolled up his shirt sleeves, creates "the heaven and the earth" out of a pre-supposed nothing (Gen. i., 1), and this magnificent something is "without form and void" (Gen. i., 2); after which he manufactures "light" (Gen. i., 3, 5); a firmament (Gen. i., 7); and shouts to the earth to bring forth grass, and grass is brought forth (Gen, i, 11; but suddenly remembers he has forgotten to make the sun and the moon and the stars *also*, which he thereupon flings into space like a handful of small change (Gen. i., 16); and then setting to work like a forty horse-power donkey-engine, he creates everything in the fish line, from a sea-snail to a whale—detail! the latter not happening to be a fish—and in the fowl line, from a canary to a dodo (Gen. i., 20, 21; then creeping things and beasts, caterpillars and elephants, higgledy-piggledy. topsy-turvy, upside-down, and downside-up (Gen. i., 24, 25); and sweating like a hog, blowing like a grampus, conflabberated, buffled, and flummosced, he bungles on, and in his *own* image—my friends, strike your head seventy-seven times seven on the ground—produces man (Gen. i., 27). "Thus the heaven and the earth were finished, and all the host of them." After which, as postscript comes, second creation (Gen. ii., 4); rain (Gen. ii., 6); a second edition of man (Gen. ii., 7); also one of beasts and fowls (Gen. ii., 19); and last, but not least, Janet, her own sweet self (Gen. ii., 22), notwithstanding the fact that she had already been created.

But what a detail is this, whether a person has one birthday—creationday we mean—or two when compared to that momentous question: When did the Creation take place? Many students spent their lives in attempting to solve this problem of problems, but none succeeded until a great light arose, and Dr. John Lightfoot, Vice-Chancellor of the University of Cambridge, declared, and proved, beyond all possible manner of doubt, that the world was created by the Trinity on October the 23rd, 4004 B.C, at 4 o'clock in the morning! So at 4 a.m. on the 23rd of October, 4004 B.C., this little world of ours came into existence, and on the 26th—hour not stated—*the stars also*; and from the amount of misery, crime, and cruelty, that the Lord has since been pleased to permit, it would not have been a bad thing for many of us, had it gone out of existence half an hour later, that is at 4.30 a.m., notwithstanding the fact that "God saw everything that he had made, and behold it was very good."

Thus had the splendid legend of antiquity been twisted into a farce by latter-day credulity, till such men as "Copernicus, Kepler, Galileo, Descartes, and Newton arose; and when their work was done the old theological conception of the universe was gone. 'The spacious firmament on high,' 'the crystalline spheres,' the Almighty enthroned upon 'the circle of the heavens,' and with his own hands, or with angels as his agents, keeping sun, moon, and planets in motion for the benefit of the earth, opening and closing the 'windows of heaven,' letting down upon the earth 'waters above the firmament,' setting his 'bow in the clouds,' hanging out 'signs and wonders,' hurling comets, casting forth lightnings to scare the wicked, and 'shaking the earth' in his wrath: all this has disappeared."[81]

All this, which was borrowed from the Assyrians, Babylonians, and Egyptians, from Persia, Chaldea, and India; these old world myths, which we have learnt to despise, not through any fault of their own, but through the fault of an interested church who used them and abused them, forcing them down the throats of her subjects long after they had become unpalatable and indigestible to the age. Those:—

> "Thoughts that great hearts once broke for, we
> Breathe cheaply in the common air."[82]

Geography

THE earth is known by actual measurement to be about 8,000 miles in diameter, to be spheroidal, etc., etc. And for these, and all other great natural discoveries, we have to thank Science, and in no way Christianity, whose followers have exerted every power possible to crush out scientific knowledge and scientific progress, enthroning in their place those infantine ideas contained in that sacred word of God, the Bible, in which the world is considered as a kind of flat *plaque* suspended in the infinite (Job xvvi., 7). In the beginning it was "without form and void" (Genesis i., 2), but it soon assumed a more definite shape, and is stated to have possessed corners. "And after these things I saw four angels standing on the four corners of the earth" (Revelation vii., 1). That it was not considered spheroidal is mentioned time after time. Christ himself saw all the kingdoms of the earth

[81] "Warfare of Science and Theology." Andrew White. Vol. i., p. 15 [original note]. Andrew Dickson White, *A History of the Warfare of Science with Theology in Christendom* (New York: D. Appleton, 1896; repr. 1905).

[82] James Russell Lowell (1819–1891), "Masaccio: In the Brancacci Chapel," lines 25–26.

"from an exceeding high mountain" (Matthew iv., 8), which, impossible as it would have been even were the world as flat as a pan-cake, was infinitely more so seeing that it is a globe. The ends of the earth are also frequently mentioned (Isaiah xl., 28 and xli., 5, 9; xliii. 6; xlv., 22), which would not have been the case had these old writers considered it to have been of spherical form. Four winds blew upon it, from the four quarters of heaven (Jeremiah xlix., 36). It was stationary, and immovable (Psalms xciii., 1, and xvi., 10); below it is Hell (Revelation xx., 13; Amos ix„ 2); and somewhere above it was Heaven (Matthew xxviii., 2; Luke iii., 22; Amos ix., 2), and Heaven was separated from the terrestrial regions by a kind of crystalline dome or firmament (Genesis i., 6, 7; Psalms xix., 1; Daniel xii., 3; Job xxiv., 18; Ezekiel i., 22; x., 1). This firmament was supported on pillars (i. Samuel ii., 8; Job ix., 6; xxvi., 11), and possessed windows through which the rain fell (Genesis vii., 11; viii., 2; ii. Kings vii., 2; Isaiah xxiv., 18; Malachi iii., 10), for it separated the waters above from those on the earth (Genesis i., 7; Psalms cxlviii., 4). This extraordinary cosmos was in no way governed by natural laws, for fancy reigned supreme, and what was unseen was unknown, and what was unknown appertained to the mystic Jahveh, who could do what he liked, change rain into dust (Deuteronomy xxviii., 24), or dust into lice (Exodus viii., 16); withhold rain (ii. Chronicles vi., 26; Jeremiah iii., 3; Amos iv., 7; Zechariah xiv., 17); listen to people's prayers for it (i. Samuel xii., 17; i. Kings viii., 35, 36), and cause it to fall (i. Kings xviii., 1; Ezekiel xxxviii., 22). His chosen people, a horde of semi-civilized savages, were his only thought: what were the laws of Nature as compared to their wants; if a sea or river hindered their progress miraculously they were divided (Exodus xiv., 21; ii. Kings ii., 8, 14), if they were thirsty water flowed from the solid rock (Numbers xx., 8, 11), and if they were an hungered heavenly food shot from the skies (Exodus xvi., 14, 15). At times he would supply some special favourite with a wonderful and inexhaustible, if modest, dish (i. Kings xix., 5, 6; i. Kings xvii., 14, 16; ii. Kings iv., 4, 6); or calm a storm to enhance his, or their, safety (Matthew viii., 24, 26); and walk on the waves (Matthew xiv., 22, 36); rise from the dead (Matthew xxviii., 2, 6); float upto heaven (Luke xxiv., 39. 51); to test their faith and establish their salvation. He would do more-for was not he the great God of Unreason—destroy the world by a flood (Genesis vii), or threaten to reduce it to ashes (Luke xvii., 29, 30); in his wrath he would shake the kingdoms of the earth (Isaiah xxiii., 11; Jeremiah x, 10; Joel iii., 16; Haggai i., 6), it would reel at his anger like a drunken man (Isaiah xxiv., 20); he would dry up the sea, and the rivers (Isaiah l., 2; li., 10; Ezekiel xxx., 12); cause the mountains to tremble, and cast them down (Habakkuk iii., to; Zachariah xiv., 4; Ezekiel xxxviii., 20); nay more, he would turn the very world upside down (Job xii., 15; Isaiah xxiv., 1); despicable toy! empty out the seas, and the rivers (Isaiah xix., 5, 6); and ultimately in his frenzied fury upheave and break it all up (Job ix., 5, 12; Isaiah xxiv., 19; Psalms xviii., 7, 15).

> Then the earth shook and trembled; the foundations also of the hills moved and were shaken, because he was wroth. There went up a smoke out of his nostrils, and fire out of his mouth devoured: coals were kindled by it. He bowed the heavens also, and came down: and darkness was under his feet. And he rode upon a cherub, and did fly: yea, he did fly upon the wings of the wind. He made darkness his secret place; his pavilion round about him were dark waters and thick clouds of the skies. At the brightness that was before him his thick clouds passed, hail stones and coals of fire. The Lord also thundered in the heavens, and the Highest gave his voice; hail stones and coals of fire. Yea, he sent out his arrows, and scattered them; and he shot out lightnings, and discomfited them. Then the channels of water were seen, and the foundations of the world were discovered at thy rebuke, O Lord, at the blast of the breath of thy nostrils.[83]

Astronomy

Galileo and Copernicus knew a great deal more about the heavens than Jesus ever did, and Jahveh, his father, cannot be mentioned in the same breath with such men as Herschel and Ross.[84] To justify our saying so, let us turn once more to the infallible book, Word of God, and cheque-book of his priests, and this is what we find:—

The sun was but a subordinate administration to the needs of the earth, and served to illuminate her as a candle lights a room. The world was the *magnus opus*, the sun, moon, and stars but small attributes scattered in the firmament by the hand of God. The sun came into existence on the fourth

[83] Psalms 18:7–15.

[84] Sir William Herschel (1738–1822) was the British astronomer who discovered the planet Uranus. His son, Sir John Herschel (1792–1871), was a founder of the Royal Astronomical Society in 1820 and served three terms as its president, in the 1820s, 1830s, and 1840s. Irish amateur astronomer William Parsons, 3rd Earl of Rosse (sometimes spelled "Ross"), in 1845 built the world's largest telescope, known as the Leviathan of Parsontown, which led to his discovery of the spiral structure of galaxies.

day (Genesis i., 16), some twenty-four hours after the Almighty had seen the grass grow, and pronounced it "good"; it was made "to rule the day," and the lesser light, the moon, "to rule the night." He made the stars, *also*; mere specks of light that, on the opening of the sixth seal, were to fall down from on high. "And the stars of heaven fell upon the earth, even as a fig tree casteth her untimely figs, when she is shaken of a mighty wind" (Revelation vi., 13[85]).

The universe was measured out by God "with a span" (Isaiah xl., 12), and the heavens were stretched out by his almighty hand (Isaiah xliv., 24; xlv., 12; li., 13; Jeremiah li., 15; Zechariah xii., 1). They would open sometimes, and a vision of the beyond would appear (Genesis xxviii., 12); they would sing in joy (Isaiah xlix, 13); similarly, as in anger, the stars would fight against mankind (Judges v., 20); and display dire portents to the dismay of all (Jeremiah x., 2). "And there shall be signs in the sun, and in the moon, and in the stars; and on the earth distress of nations, with perplexity; the sea and waves roaring" (Luke xxi., 25). The very air containing them was the habitation of the fiend, and the sporting-ground of his demons (Ephesians ii., 2); from whose dread powers mankind was only protected by the clanging of the holy church-bell. The end of the heavens was to be as wonderful as their beginning; for, as they had been measured with a span, and stretched out by the hand of God, so were they to be rended asunder (Isaiah lxiv., 1); rolled up as a scroll (Isaiah xxxiv., 4; Revelation vi., 14); and vanish like smoke (Isaiah li., 6).

The sun, as we have seen, was but the earth's lamp, and the moon her night-light; they rose and set, revolving round the *magnus opus*. At times, the effulgent one would stand still, and look on at the petty crimes of men (Joshua x., 13), bidden by man to do so: "Sun, stand thou still upon Gibeon; and thou, Moon, in the valley of Ajalon" (Joshua x., 12); or would travel backwards along its course to guarantee the efficacy of a fig poultice: "And Hezekiah wept sore . . . . And Isaiah said, Take a lump of figs. And they took and laid it on the boil, and he recovered. And Hezekiah said unto Isaiah, What shall be the sign that the Lord will heal me? . . . And Isaiah the prophet cried unto the Lord: and he brought the shadow ten degrees backward, by which it had gone down in the dial of Ahaz" (ii. Kings, xx., 3–11; Isaiah xxxvi., 8).

[85] Light travels at 184,000 miles a second. Sirius, the brightest of the fixed stars, is 393 times greater than the sun, the sun being 880,000 miles in diameter. Light travelling from Sirius to this world at the above rate would take nearly twenty years to reach this earth, and the light we now see from some of the stars of the eighteenth magnitude can hardly have left them less than two thousand years ago [original note].

Sometimes, again, the celestial bodies would burst forth into increased splendour, the light of the moon being as the light of the sun, and the brilliancy of the sun being increased seven-fold, "as the light of seven days" (Isaiah xxx., 26); but, usually, it was the reverse—the sun, the moon and the stars were more prone to frown than to blush; for Jahveh was a stern God, a God of wrath rather than a God of laughter. The doom of Babylon was an important event in the life history of the celestial constellations, "For the stars of heaven, and the constellations thereof, shall not give their light; the sun shall be darkened in his going forth, and the moon shall not cause her light to shine" (Isaiah xiii., 10); but perhaps not so important as we might think, as this turning down of the lamps of the heavens was almost as frequent as the turning down of the lamps of the earth (Isaiah lx., 19, 20; Ezekiel xxxii., 7, 8; Mark xiii., 24; xv., 33; Matthew xxiv., 29; Acts ii., 20). Sometimes the darkness was incomplete and distributed in mystic patches, as it was once in the land of Egypt; "And the Lord said unto Moses, stretch out thine hand toward heaven, that there may be darkness over the land of Egypt, even darkness which may be felt. And Moses stretched forth his hand toward heaven; and there was a thick darkness in all the land of Egypt three days: they saw not one another, neither rose any from his place for three days: but all the children of Israel had light in their dwellings" (Exodus x., 21, 23). But generally it was opaque, horribly opaque, as it will be in the day when the Lord will come, "As a thief in the night; in which the heavens shall pass away with a great noise, and the elements shall melt with fervent heat; the earth also, and the works that are therein, shall be burned up." "And we cannot altogether blame the moon for being confounded, and the sun for being ashamed" (Isaiah xxiv, 23) at the Lord's senseless destruction of earth, sun, moon, and the stars also, all of which he created in some 144 hours, pronouncing them to be "very good."

Such is biblical astronomy—a mass of myth, fable, and fiction; of wandering stars that point out the obscure birth-places of a carpenter's son (Matthew ii., 2, 9); of blood red moons (Revelation vi., 12); of mystic heavenly voices (Mark ix., 7); and of talking clouds (Exodus xxxiii., 9, 11; Numbers xii., 5, 6). *Sancta simplicitas!*[86] forgive thou our unbelief!

[86] *Sancta simplicitas*—literally, "holy simplicity"—ironically indicates naivete and credulousness. Czech religious reformer and condemned heretic Jan Hus (1369–1415) uttered the phrase when, while being burned at the stake, an old peasant added wood to the fire.

Biology and Physiology

MAN most certainly is a curious animal, and his alleged origin in no way belies his character. God scraped together a few handfuls of dust, and, lo and behold, there was man (Genesis ii. 7); a rib extracted, and, "Abracadabra!" a woman stood smiling by his side (Genesis ii. 21, 22). These were our first parents, and, as the world in those days was not over-crowded, we are told they lived to quite abnormal ages (Genesis v.), evidently so that they might populate it (and prepare a good round holocaust for the flood). The human body was, in fact, entirely differently constituted. Now we should miss our dinner if we had to go without it, and a day or two without a sip of water would be more than a mere joke; but in those days it was nothing for an old man of eighty to walk up a bleak mountain and fast forty days on the top of it (Exodus xxxiv. 28), to inspect the hindquarters of the Deity (Exodus xxxiii. 23), to hew "tables of stone" (Exodus xxxiv. I, 4), and to chisel ten commandments on them; and then, at the end of it all, to carry this load of paving stones to the bottom of the mountain. This was even a greater feat than that of Elijah, who, though he went without food for as long a period, had a better start, seeing that, instead of dining off the sight of the Lord's hindquarters, he took a good round meal of angels' food (I. Kings xix. 6–8); or even that of the divinity himself, who, at any rate, acknowledged that, after his economical menage, he was "an hungered" (Matthew iv. 2). But this ability of dispensing with food was by no means the only peculiarity of the human body. Nowadays strength is usually to be found in the fitness of the biceps and other muscles; then, certain people carried it in the length of their hair. A certain gentleman of solar reputation was gifted this way (Judges xvi. 17), and, possessing greater strength than wisdom, he lost his eyesight with his locks (Judges xvi. 19, 20). A few other points worth noting, as regards the physiology of the human species, are:—Death was unknown before Adam ate the pippin (Genesis iii. 3; I. Corinthians xv. 21; Romans v. 12), but it soon made itself manifest under Jahveh and his bloodthirsty crew (Genesis vi. 5, 7; II. Chronicles xiii. 17). But the human frame in those days was very tough (I. Samuel xv. 7, 8, 20 I. Chronicles iv. 43 Numbers xxxi. 7, 9, 17, IS; Judges vi. 1, 5) in fact, not only did men resemble the proverbial cat that has nine lives, but dead men were known to wink the other eye (II. Kings xix. 35); and a valleyful of dry bones to come together, and live, and stand upon their feet—what a hunt there must have been for metatarsals!—"an exceeding great army" (Ezekiel xxxvii. 1–10); and graves to open, the dead they had contained "went into the holy city, and appeared unto many" (Matthew xxvii. 52, 53). How pleased, in some cases, the many must have been! Incidentally, Enoch and Elijah never died (Genesis v. 24; II. Kings ii. 11); Lazarus and Christ, etc., etc., rose from the dead (John xi. 44; Matthew xxviii.); Jonah for three days defied the digestive juices of a whale's belly (Jonah i. 17); Moses described his own death (Deuteronomy xxxiv. 5, 6); and Lot's wife, instead of changing into carrion, changed into salt. As Birth is quite as natural as Death, so being born, in many cases according to the Bible, is as biblical dying. Adam never had a mother—did he have a navel?—(Genesis i. 27; ii. 7); Eve's parents consisted of a rib (Genesis ii. 22); Ahaziah was two years older than his own father (II. Kings viii. 26; II. Chronicles xxi. 19, 20; xxii. 1, 2); Joseph had two fathers (Matthew i. 16 Luke iii. 23) to make up for the lack of them in his son; but anon a virgin could become a mother (Matthew i. 22, 23); a son could he his own father (John x. 30); also as old as his own father (John i. 1, 14; iii. 16). But let us hurry on, for we are beginning to trespass on the domains of the most unphysiological body that ever blessed (?) this earth with his presence, "Our Lord and Saviour (*sic*) Jesus Christ."

Some nineteen hundred years ago a Jewish girl, by name Mary—a female barber by repute—lived at Nazareth in Galilee. One day an angel called on her, and having seated himself on the "barber's chair"—which Messrs. Farmer and Henley[87] inform us is a synonym of "strumpet," because common to all comers—said: "The Holy Ghost shall come upon thee, and the power of the highest shall over-shadow thee" (Luke i. 28–35); and, if the Koran is to be believed, Gabriel—for that was the name of this angel—must have been a most deceitful young man, and very much of a type with a certain young hero of whom Boccaccio relates, "right pleasantly with joyaunce and jollity,"[88] for the result of this unexpected introduction was that, though still a virgin, Mary became pregnant (Matthew i. 18), and was placed, to say the least, in a rather awkward position with her mundane husband, Joseph

[87] John Stephen Farmer and William Ernest Henley, *Slang and Its Analogues Past and Present: A Dictionary, Historical and Comparative, of the Heterodox Speech of All Classes of Society for More Than Three Hundred Years, with Synonyms in English, French, German, Italian, Etc.*, 7 vols. ([London]: privately printed, 1890–1904).

[88] Giovanni Boccaccio, *Les cent nouvelles nouvelles: Suivent les cent nouvelles contenant les cent histoires nouveaux, qui sont moult plaisans à raconter, et toutes bonnes compagnies* (Cologne: Pierre Gaillard, 1701). A more contemporary edition was released as Robert B. Douglas, *One Hundred Merry and Delightsome Stories: Right Pleasaunte to Relate in All Goodly Companie by Way of Joyance and Jollity: Les Cent Nouvelles Nouvelles* Now First Done into the English Tongue (Paris: Charles Carrington, 1899).

the carpenter, who, humanly credulous of so untoward an occurrence, "was minded to put her away privily" (Matthew i. 19); but, after dreaming about angels and ghosts in a divine nightmare, was bidden by a heavenly hen not to consider his innocent darling as a mere mundane night bird, but as a celestial pigeon fancier, and ultimately changed his mind (Matthew i. 20). This Joseph in every way was a most suitable father (?) for his future son (?), the latter's remarkable deficiency in parentage being quite balanced by the former's superabundance (Matthew i. 16; Luke iii. 21); and, as like produces like, these two phenomenal parents produced a most phenomenal child. They called him Jesus (Matthew i. 21), evidently because it had been predicted that he should be named Emmanuel (Matthew i. 23). His father, as we have seen, was the Holy Ghost, and yet he claimed regal descent through his other father, Joseph (Matthew i. 16). He did more. He claimed he was his own father (John x. 30); more still, that he was the creator of his mundane father himself—in other words, his grandfather (John i. 1, 14); but this was tar too simple, for he went a step further still—or others did it for him—and asserted that he was not only God the Father, but God the Holy Ghost, and God the Son, all at the same time (I. John v. 7). Such are some of the assertions of this supreme corn-cutting-bunion-curer. His life in no way belied his extraordinary nativity; for he could walk on water without sinking (Matthew xiv. 22–36); ride an ass and a colt at one and the same time (Matthew xxi. 7); see round the globe (Matthew iv. 8, 9); drive devils out of men (Mark i. 34; Luke viii. 2), and into pigs (Mark v. 2–13); jump to heaven without gravity affecting him in the least (Mark xvi. 19); descend into hell (Acts ii. 31; and the Apostles' Creed), and yet at the same time keep an appointment with a thief in paradise (Luke xxiii. 43). His body was a kind of walking pharmacopoeia; his spittle cured blindness sometimes when mixed with clay (John ix. 6), sometimes without (Mark vii. 33); his name drove devils into fits (Acts xvi. 18); and at his word the dead rose (Luke vii. 11, 17; John xi. 1–54); lepers were cleansed (Luke xvii. 12–19); the crooked became straight (Luke xiii. 10–21); and the paralysed took up their beds and walked (Matthew ix. 6, 7). As a doctor, this wonderful thaumaturgus completely eclipsed Esculapius, and has put Mother Seigel[89] in the shade; his prescriptions were perfect, but he forgot to leave them behind him. Besides

[89] Mother Seigel's Curative Syrup was a line of tonics manufactured in New York and London by A. J. White Limited, which purported to "restore tone and efficiency to the stomach, liver, and kidneys impaired through worry, overwork, climatic changes, unhealthy atmosphere in factory or office, disease or any other cause" (*The Mercury*, September 19, 1902, 2).

this, he could turn water into wine (John ii. 7–9); wine into blood (Mark xiv. 23, 24); bread into flesh (Mark xiv. 22); and a few sprats into a fishery (Matthew xv. 34–39; xiv. 17–21). He was altogether the most wonderful being and the most astounding personality that ever trod earth, or water. Ultimately, he died by being nailed to a cross (Matthew xxvii. 35), or by being hung on a tree (Acts v. 30)—some say a cabbage stalk—and to show his utter contempt at so ungodlike an ending, with feline promptness he rose again (Matthew xxviii. 1–6), and with a hypergymnastic spring vanished in the clouds (Luke xxiv. 51); where he is at present sitting on the right hand of God (Mark xvi. 19), girt round the paps with a girdle (Revelation i. 13), his hair woolly and white as snow, his eyes as flames of fire, and his feet like unto brass (Revelation i. 14, 15). There he sits, surrounded by thunder and lightning (Revelation iv. 5), glass seas, and beasts full of eyes (Revelation iv. 6), and 144,000 virginal elders all singing "Ta-ra-ra-ra-boom-de-aye." No, no! I mean, "As it were a new song" (Revelation xiv. 3). Before him lies a mystic book, written within, with advertisements on the back page, just like the *A[gnostic].J[ournal].* (Revelation v. 1), and sealed with seven seals. There he waits for the awful day when the stars like green figs will fall to the earth (Revelation vi. 13), when in his wrath he will cast "the fearful, and unbelieving, and the abominable, and murderers, and whoremongers, and sorcerers, and idolaters, and all liars"—Torreyites, etc.—into "the lake which burneth with fire and brimstone" (Revelation xxi. 8). "The grace of our Lord Jesus Christ be with you all. Amen" (Revelation xxi. 21).

Pathology and Medicine

In all primitive societies pathology and medicine have been treated as a superstition, rather than as a science. A person falls ill, he is at once considered as possessed by the evil one; he is cured, the evil spirit has left him. This precept the Christian Church has ever buoyed up, considering—

> To follow foolish precedents and wink
> With both our eyes, is easier than to think.[90]

[90] From William Cowper "Tirocinium," in *The Task, a Poem. To Which Are Added an Epistle to Joseph Hill, Esq., Tirocinium; or a Review of Schools, and the History of John Gilpin* (London: Printed for J. Johnson, 1785), 293–341. This lecture is dedicated "to the Rev. William Cawthorn Unwin" with the date November 6, 1784, but it was published the following year.

And these foolish precedents are found in that inspired work the Bible, where prayer is more mighty than physic (Il. Chronicles xvi. 12); and where faith takes the place of the surgeon's scalpel (Acts xiv. 9, 10; iii. 16; Mark v. 34); where quackery of the most absurd kind is expounded; where leprosy is cleansed by a priest taking two birds, killing one in a vessel over running water, and then baking the living bird, and cedar wood, and scarlet, and hyssop, and dipping them into the blood of the bird that was killed over the running water, and Sprinkling "upon him that is to be cleansed from his leprosy seven times, and shall pronounce him clean, and shall let the living bird loose into the open held" (Leviticus xiv. 5–7). Who would attempt such a cure nowadays? Yet this is the very word of very God. All the birds that ever were, if killed over running water or not, would not cure a single leper, or add one single phalange to his fingerless hands. But, then, leprosy in those days seems to have heed an unusually extraordinary disease, curable by more ways than one, such as scrubbing the body seven times in the Jordan (II. Kings v. 14). This cure was connected with a particular form, that form of leprosy caught through greed of money—a disease that should be most prevalent at the present time (II. Kings v. 23–27). Another very infectious form was that caught whilst fumigating the Lord's house, when it generally attacked the forehead (II. Chronicles xxvi, 17–20. A little later on, touching seems to have supplanted wringing birds' necks and scrubbing, as an efficient cure (Matthew viii. 3; Mark i. 41; Luke v. 13). Touching was also considered an estimable cure for a disease known as "the king's evil." William the Third is said to have touched a patient, saying to him, "God give you better health and more sense." And most physicians, I think, would say the same to-day, if a toeless leper appeared and said, "Touch me, so that my flesh may come again like unto the flesh of a little child." Sometimes the mere act of speaking cured this incurable disease. Jesus Christus Thaumaturgus by word alone was successful enough to cleanse Len at one appointment (Luke xvii. 13, 14), which more than usual successful treatment the Roman "Lancet" and the Grecian "Medical Times" never deigned to notice. Contemptible jealousy! Jeremiah, evidently a leading light in the medical world, pronounced many medicines as useless (Jeremiah xlvi. 11) against God-inflicted illnesses, perhaps such as are described in I. Samuel v. 8, 9, which ultimately, however, were cured in quite an unorthodox manner (I. Samuel vi. 5). In fact, medical science in those days was altogether in a much more advanced state than it is now. Lifting people up cured their fever (Mark i. 31); sight was restored by touch (Mark viii. 23–25); severed ears flew back to their original place, or regrew like a lizard's tail (Luke xxii. 5). Dumbness was attributed to a non-belief in angels (Luke i. 7, 13, 20), and sometimes curable by a gynecological event (Luke i. 20, 64), though frequently it was attributed to devils, as was blindness, epilepsey, and lunacy (Matthew ix. 32, 33; xii. 22; xvii. 14, 18; Luke ix. 39–42). The operation of castration would then frequently save the life of the soul, just as now trepanning will frequently save the life of the body (Matthew v. 28–30; xix. 12). Old rags were a rare (!) cure (Mark v. 25–30). Death was in those days a curable disease, just as the mumps are now (Matthew xxvii. 51, 52; Luke viii. 53–55; John xi. 44, etc., etc.). Pathology was Demonology, and Medicine mere Superstition.

I do not intend here to go dung-plunging in the Word of God, after the fescennine revulsions of pathic lust and Sodomistic vice incidents fit only for a medical work, of most limited circulation. All I will say is, that in my excursions through the fœtid duets of the Book of Books, casual observance has pointed me out no fewer than 183 chapters which, if published—any separate one, that is to say—in any public work, would not be tolerated for one minute, much less for two thousand years. I believe there are 929 chapters in the Bible. Thus we have one out of every five unfit for public perusal, and the number of feculent verses these chapters contain probably runs well into a four figure sum.

Botany

As we sail round the world's history, and drink deep of the lore of the past as well as of that of the present, one thing pre-eminently strikes us, for it matters little where the bark of knowledge may ride, and it is this—that where Ignorance reigns, her subjects grovel in the fantastic, and wallow deep in the grotesque; and even where enlightenment has shed her rays of a "larger hope," nations, like individuals, look back on the fairy tales of their youth, not only with a far-off pleasure, but with a pleasure not unmixed with reverence. The romantic ever appeals to the heart of man; it is one of the few better instincts found in the human breast. The present is humdrum enough—petty toils and troubles fill our lives, and our days are of sighs rather than of laughter; but not so with the past. Its toils and tears have vanished in the mist of ages, radiant form appears robed in all the ideals of the yearning present; and thus as the future is dark and mystic, so the past is bright and illusive. Alone over the present broods the monotony of life, yet the present but yesterday was the yearning future, and to-morrow will be the alluring past.

As the Druids had their sacred groves, and as the Brahmas had their sacred Kadamba or Jámbu tree, so the Israelites had their own sacred botany, and the same breeze that rustled through the oaks of Mona rustles through the pages of God's holy word. The word of God, however, is true, and whosoever shall change one jot of it shall have his name erased from the great book, "the book of life" (Revelation xxii. 19). And as the Bible ends with the mention of this mystic volume, so does it begin with the Mention of a most mystic tree, "the tree of the knowledge of good and evil" (Genesis ii, 9). Its fruits were not so large as elephants, as the mystic Jámbu trees were supposed to be, but still they were wonderful enough; for they contained the concentrated essence of an ever-greedy and fiery hell, as well as that of death (Romans v. 12, 17, 18, 19; I. Corinthians xv. 21, 22; Genesis ii. 17). It grew in the midst of a beautiful garden with another mystic tree, "the tree of life" (Genesis ii. 9). This garden was watered by four rivers; it was a perfect *El dorado*. All who inhabited it lived in contentment, happiness, and peace, as well as in ignorance of good and evil; in other words, it was a kind of gilded Earlswood.[91] Death was unknown, but it lurked like an asp in the golden fruit, which "was good for food," and "pleasant to the eyes," and "a tree to be desired to make one wise" (Genesis iii. 6). One small bite, and illusion is disillusionized. The blush of innocence fled from the cheeks of our first parents, and "they knew that they were naked," and their eyes were opened, and they were "as gods knowing good and evil" (Genesis iii. 7, 5). The lion roared, and ceased eating grass (Genesis i. 30); the wolf would no longer lie down with the lamb (Romans v. 12); and the serpent lost his legs, and ate dust (Genesis iii. 14,). Sorrow, disease, sickness, and death entered the world (Genesis iii. 17, 3). Birth became an agony (verse 16), life a toil (verse 19), and death a horror (verse 19).

The prince "of many thronèd powers, that led the embattled seraphim to war,"[92] warmed his hands as the human fuel fed the greedy flames of the bottomless pit, and all because of a pippin. "The woman whom thou gavest to be with me she gave me of the tree, and I did eat";[93] or was it a custard apple, as fateful and as pippy as the pomegranate of Proserpine of old? However, Elohim, the gods, became frightened. "Behold the man is become as one of

[91] Founded in Redhill, Surrey, in 1848, the Royal Earlswood Hospital (also known as the Royal Earlswood Asylum for Idiots) was the first institution for people with learning disabilities.

[92] Milton, *Paradise Lost*, bk. 1, lines 128–129.

[93] Genesis 3:12.

us, to know good and evil: and now, lest he put forth his hand, and take also of the tree of life and eat, and live for ever."[94] Poor old Elohim! What have you done with your omnipotence? So, to overcome this terrible catastrophe of living for ever—which originally seems to have been the normal state of man, and the immortal one never changes his mind—he made them each a pair of trousers (Genesis iii. 21), and chased his poor mortal inventions out of the Garden of Eden, to live in a land of thorns and thistles (Genesis iii. 24, 18). But, evidently to prevent all further contingencies, the "tree of life" was transplanted, and we next find it peacefully growing "in the midst of the paradise of God" (Revelation ii. 7); the streets of which are of pure gold, "as it were transparent glass" (Revelation xxi. 21). There it grows, with the River of Life, apparently, flowing through its midst, yielding twelve manner of fruits monthly; "and the leaves of the tree were for the healing of the nations" (Revelation xxii. 1, 2). "Blessed are they that do his commandments, that they may have a right to the tree of life, and may enter in through the gates into the city. For without are dogs, and sorcerers, and whoremongers, and murderers, and idolaters, and whosoever loveth and maketh a lie" (Revelation xxii. 14, 15).

Besides these magic trees, there were other botanical freaks, such as magic grass that needed neither sunshine or rain to make it grow (Genesis i. 11, 16, and Genesis ii. 5, 6); the gourd of Jonah, for which "God prepared a worm . . . and it smote the gourd that it withered . . . which came up in a night, and perished in a night" (Jonah iv. 6–10); the fig-tree, which also withered, not on account of worms, but because of the Lamb's bad language (Mark xi. 13; Matthew xxi. 19); the burning bush that wouldn't burn (Exodus iii. 2); and the rod of Aaron of serpentinous renown (Exodus iv. 4, 17).

Zoology

The first thing that strikes us, on reading the account of the animal creation in the "Blessed Word," is the extraordinary bran-tub antics the Almighty must have gone through to produce it. Birds and fishes were produced at the same time, and a whale or so jumbled up with them (Genesis i. 20, 21), although the mammalia were not created till the next day; bats were mixed up with fowls (Leviticus xi. 19); the cony and hare chewed the cud (Leviticus xi. 5, 6); and

[94] Genesis 3:22.

the carnivora lived on grass (Genesis i. 30). Shortly after the creation all the zoological world gathered round the supreme animal, Adam, who was the living image of the supreme God (Jah), and, no doubt, many of his 930 years must have been expended in naming them. Waiting for the arrival of the 113 species of snails, which are only found in the Madeira Islands, must have been an exceedingly tedious job, and the deep sleep that afterwards fell on hint is accountable easily enough when it is taken into consideration that he must have named some 1,600 mammalia, 12,500 birds, 600 reptiles, and 1,000,000 or more inferior creatures and animalculæ. Mr. Foote (from whom I take these numbers)[95] suggests that the South American sloth must have started towards Eden several years before the creation (Genesis ii. 20). Amongst the zoological monstrosities may be classed the four-footed birds (Leviticus xi. 20); also four-footed beetles and bald locusts (Leviticus xi. 21–23). In those days animal instinct was truly wonderful. Some fishes were famous at collecting submerged coin (Matthew xvii. 27); other beasts had hands, and were morally responsible (Genesis ix. 5); and cattle were penitent. "Let man and beast be covered with sackcloth, and cry mightily unto God: yea, let them turn every one from his evil way, and from the violence that is in their hands. . . . And God saw their works that they turned from their evil ways; and God repented of the evil, that he had said that he would do unto them; and he did it not" (Jonah iii. 8–10). So wrote the man who was a bit of a zoologist himself, having resided three days' in a whale's belly (Jonah i. 17), and praying in this tabernacle so fervently that the whale was struck with a violent nausea, and vomited him up on the dry land (Jonah ii. 10). This story, incredulous as it may first appear to the half-educated, is not really so, when we consider that its truth was vouchsafed for by the blessed Lamb, who taketh away the sins of the world (Matthew xii. 40). Other points may still be observed—the docility of the animals that inhabited the ark (Genesis vii. 2, 3, 13–15): the extraordinary sexual perversion of Laban's flocks by Jacob, ancestor of the Lamb, who was, however, without blemish (Genesis xxx. 37, 42); the generative propensities of dust (Exodus viii. 16–19), and the magical prolificness of frogs (Exodus viii. 6, 7); the vitality of Egyptian horses and cattle (Exodus ix. 3, 6; xiii. 15; xiv. 9, 27, 28); the pugnacity of hornets (Exodus xxiii. 28); the loquacity of asses (Numbers xxii. 27, 28); the curativity of brazen snakes (Numbers xxi, 9); the

[95] "There are, according to Hugh Miller, 1,658 known species of mammalia, 6,266 of birds, 642 of reptiles, and 550,000 of insects." G. W. Foote, "Noah's Flood," in *Bible Romances* (London: Freethought, 1882, 35.

sagacity of ravens (I. Kings xvii. 6); the lunacy of pigs (Mark v. 2–13, etc.); the piety of cattle (Revelation v. 14); and the amativeness of a certain blessed lamb (Revelation xix. 7), whose father was a dove (Matthew iii. 16; Luke iii. 22; John i. 32), and, like the Jovian swan, had a weakness for the fair sex. This lamb is at perpetual enmity with a certain talkative snake (Genesis iii. 1), which is as garrulous as Manu's fish, or Balaam's ass.

The above animals, always excepting the Blessed Lamb, are more or less those with which we are accustomed to meet. The following are not so, and belong to the fabulous lands of myth and legend:—

The unicorn, one of the supporters of our national arms, seems to have been quite a favourite. Job greatly doubts his docility, doubting whether he would "abide by thy crib," and considers that he would "harrow the valleys after thee" (Job xxxix. 9–11). We also find mention of this truculent creature in Deuteronomy xxxiii. 17; Numbers xxiii. 22; Psalms xxii. 21; xxix. 6; and Isaiah xxxiv. 7. The behemoth was another pet of Job's, who lived on grass, "and his force is in the navel of his belly" (Job xl. 15, 16). Still another of his pets was the leviathan. "Canst thou draw out leviathan with an hook? or his tongue with a cord which thou lettest down? . . . His scales are his pride, shut up together as with a close seal . . . Out of his mouth go burning lamps, and sparks of fire leap out. . . . He maketh the deep to boil like a pot; he maketh the sea like a pot of ointment" (Job xli. 1, 15, 19, 31). Bede's speculations regarding the leviathan are as follows: "Some say that the earth contains the animal leviathan, and that he holds his tail after a fashion of his own, so that it is sometimes scorched by the sun, whereupon he strives to get hold of the sun, and so the earth is shaken by the motion of his indignation; he drinks in also, at times, such huge masses of the waves that when he belches them forth all the seas feel their effect."[96] Poor Noah, what a job he must have had in the ark with him! That venerable gentleman must have also experienced some trouble in catching the fiery serpents (Numbers xxi. 6; Deuteronomy viii. 15) and winged snakes (Isaiah xxx. 6). The origin of these last was as follows: "Out of the serpent's root shall come forth a cockatrice, and his fruit shall be a fiery flying serpent" (Isaiah xiv. 29). This brings a new animal on the scene, quite one of the most extraordinary, the cockatrice. This animal was a serpent hatched from the egg of a cock—very rare. Mention is made of it in Isaiah xi. 8; xiv. 29; lix. 5; and Jeremiah viii. 17. In the Revised Version it is

96 "Warfare of Science with Theology." A. White, vol. i., p. 327 [original note]. Bede's treatise "De mundi constitutione" from his *Opera* is quoted in White, *History of the Warfare*, 327.

called Basilisk. Discussing the cockatrice of Scripture, the English Franciscan Bartholomew tells us: "He drieth and burneth leaves with his touch, and he is of so great venom and perilous that he slayeth and wasteth him that nigheth him without tarrying; and yet the weasel overcometh him, for the biting of the weasel is death to the cockatrice. Nevertheless, the biting of the cockatrice is death to the weasel if the weasel eat not rue before. And though the cockatrice be venomous without remedy while he is alive, yet he looseth all the malice when he is burnt to ashes. His ashes be accounted profitable in working alchemy, and, namely, in burning and changing of metals."[97]

Now for the dragon. "It shall be an habitation of dragons, and a court for owls" (Isaiah xxxiv. 13). "The young lion and the dragon shalt thou trample under feet" (Psalm xci. 13). "Praise the Lord from the earth, ye dragons" (Psalm cxlviii. 7). "The beast of the field shall honour me, the dragons and the owls (*sic*): because I give waters in the wilderness and rivers in the desert, to give drink to my people, my chosen" (Isaiah xliii. 20). "And the wild asses did stand in the high places; they snuffed up the wind like dragons" (Jeremiah xiv. 6). "Therefore I will wail and howl, I will go stripped and naked: I will make a wailing like the dragons, and mourning as the owls" (Micah i. 8). "I am a brother to dragons, and a companion to owls" (Job xxx. 29); also Deuteronomy xxxii. 33; Psalms xliv. 19; lxxiv. 13; Isaiah xxvii. 1; li. 9; xiii. 22 xxxiv. 13; xxxv. 7; Jeremiah ix. 11; x. 22; xlix. 33; li. 34, 37; Ezekiel xxix. 3; Malachi i. 3; Revelation xii. 3, 4, 7, 9, 13, 16, 17; xiii. 2, 4, 11; xvi. 13; xx. 2). What a lot of dragons there must have been! Bartholomew tells us regarding dragons:— "The dragon is most greatest of all serpents, and oft he is drawn out of his den and riseth up into the air, and the air is moved by him, and also the sea swelleth against his venom, and he hath a crest, and reareth his tongue, and hath teeth like a saw, and hath strength, and not only in teeth but in tail, and grieveth with biting and with stinging. Whom he findeth he slayeth. Oft four or five of them fasten their tails together and rear up their heads, and sail over the sea to get good meat. Between elephants and dragons is everlasting fighting; for the dragon with his tail spanneth the elephant, and the elephant with his nose throweth down the dragon. . . . The cause why the dragon desireth his blood is the coldness thereof, by the which the dragon desireth to cool himself. Jerome saith that the dragon is a full thirsty beast,

[97] Ibid., vol. i., p. 34 [original note]. See, for example, John Trevisa Bartholomaeus and Robert Steele, *Medieval Lore: An Epitome of the Science, Geography, Animal and Plant Folk-Lore and Myth of the Middle Age: Being Classified Gleanings from the Encyclopedia of Bartholomew Anglicus on the Properties of Things* (London: E. Stock, 1893); quoted in White, *History of the Warfare*, 34.

insomuch that he openeth his mouth against the wind to quench the burning of his thirst in that wise. Therefore, when he seeth ships in great wind he flieth against the sail to take the cold wind, and overthroweth the ship."[98] More trouble for Noah; but his paternal heart must have been sorely rent when the satyrs came along to take up their abode in the ark, for he was a family man; and, if we are to believe the classics, these satyrs were gentlemen of most uncouth behaviour, and quite unfit companions for Mrs. Noah, and Mrs. Shem, and Mrs. Ham, and Mrs. Japheth. The old man himself, after his voyage, took to drink. Who can tell? But we must not scandalize! (Isaiah xxxiv. 14). "Owls shall dwell there, and satyrs shall dance there" (Isaiah xiii. 21).

Before we bring this chapter of biblical zoology to a close, there still remains a class of animals to deal with—viz., the heavenly beasts. Ezekiel, on one occasion, beheld an exceedingly extraordinary beast, or, rather, "four living creatures," who looked like men, had four faces, calves' feet, men's hands, wings, "and they sparkled like the colour of burnished brass." "As for the likeness of their faces, they four had the face of a man, and the face of a lion . . . the face of an ox the face of an eagle" (Ezekiel i. 3–10). A very similar beast is mentioned in Ezekiel x. 12–14, whose whole body and back and hands and wings "were full of eyes round about." Daniel, another seer, saw a somewhat similar set of creatures, the first like a lion, with plucked eagle's wings, standing on its feet, "and a man's heart was given to it"; the second like a bear, "and it had three ribs in the mouth of it between the teeth of it"; the third like a four-headed leopard, with four wings; and the fourth, "dreadful and terrible," a stamping monster, with ten horns and teeth of iron (Daniel vii. 4–7). Four other well-known beasts were those four which prowled round about their creator's throne, saying, without ceasing, "Holy, holy, holy Lord God Almighty, which was, and is, and is to come." They look like a man, a calf, a lion, and a flying eagle, and are full of eyes within (Revelation iv. 6–10). We have just noted a four-headed leopard; now we have to classify in this list a seven-headed one, "having seven heads and ten horns, and upon his ten horns ten crowns" (Revelation xiii. 1, 2). A queer kind of locust also seemed to inhabit the celestial regions. They were like war-horses, wearing gold crowns, with men's faces, and women's hair, "and their teeth were as the teeth of lions." They had wings, and tails like scorpions. "The sound of their wings was as the sound of chariots . . . and their power was to hurt men five months" (Revelation ix. 7–10). And last,

[98] Ibid., vol. i., pp. 34–35 [original note].

but not least, "I beheld, and, lo, in the midst of the throne and of the four beasts, and in the midst of the elders, stood a lamb as it had been slain, having seven horns and seven eyes, which are the seven spirits of God sent forth into all the earth" (Revelation v. 6).

Such is biblical zoology, and such is biblical science. It gave the world a wrong conception of the creation (Genesis i., ii.); a wrong idea of the evolution of man (Genesis i. 27); an unscientific origin of languages (Genesis xi. 6–9). It forced down the throats of men, long after they had outgrown their mental childhood, universal floods (Genesis vii. 19); visible noises (Exodus xx. 18); inflammable waters (I. Kings xviii. 33, 38). It expected them to believe that a culprit could be detected by casting lots (Jonah i. 4–15); that mysterious hands wrote on plaster (Daniel v. 5); that iron floated (II. Kings vi. 5, 6); that seas separated when a holy twig was waved over them (Exodus xiv. 21, 22); that boats could endure forty years' hard wear without wearing out (Deuteronomy xxix. 5); and that rivers could he changed into blood (Exodus vii. 20, 22). And it taught that God, the Almighty, the Omniscient, the Infinite, the Eternal, walked (Genesis iii. 8), talked (Deuteronomy v. 24), smelled (Genesis viii. 21), worked (Genesis ii. 2), rested (Genesis ii. 2), repented (Genesis vi. 6), sat (Psalms xcix. 1), flew (II. Samuel xxii. 11), laughed (Psalms xxxv ii. 13), cursed (Genesis viii. 21), winked (Acts xvii. 30), and spued (Revelation iii. 16), etc., etc.

Omne ignotum pro magnifico—whatever is unknown is held to be magnificent. So with the Bible—unknown, it is the Word of God; known, the Word of Man; as former, divine; as latter, very, very human.

An Old Song[99]

[*After Heine*][100]

V. B. Neuburg

Thou art dead, nor knowest night;
Quenched thine eyes' translucent light,

[99] *Agnostic Journal* 58, no. 4 (January 27, 1906): 52; repr. in *A Green Garland*.

[100] See Heinrich Heine, "Altes Lied," in *Romanzero* (Hamburg, Germany: Hoffmann und Campe, 1851), 161–162. For an early translation, see Heinrich Heine, *Selections from the Poetical Works of Heihrich Heine* (London: Macmillan, 1878, 112–113. German poet Heinrich Heine (1797–1856) is remembered for his lyrics, which were set to music by Robert Schumann and Franz Schubert.

Pale thy baby mouth of red—
My dead baby, thou art dead.

A summer night with wild storm fraught,
To thy grave, oh! thee I brought;
The nightingales did dirges sing,
The stars went to thy burying.

Through the wood, as we went by,
Did resound[101] thy litany;
The waving firs, in solemn guise,
Moaned masses—dim sad melodies.

As by the willowed pool we sped,
In rings the elves did measures tread,
When, lo![102] they stayed their revelries,
To gaze at us with mournful eyes.

And when unto thy grave we come,
The silver moon, no longer dumb,
Mounts high the skies. . . A deep sob swells;
Far in the distance toll the bells.

The Dream[103]

V. B. Neuburg

Night had dawned, and the moon was high,
A silver wheel in a dark blue sky.

All the winds had told their tale,
All the stars were bright and pale.

[101] "Did sound" becomes "Resounded slow" in *A Green Garland.*
[102] "When, lo!" becomes simply "Lo!" in *A Green Garland.*
[103] *Agnostic Journal* 58, no. 7 (February 17, 1906): 103; repr. in *A Green Garland.*

A line of sea-foam curled and leapt,
And thought was hushed, and daylight slept.

"Watchman, what of the night?" men said,
"And how of the hours that speed and have sped?"

I said, "It is well, for the night is deep
Over your heads: go back and sleep.

"Lo! it is well, for the white stars gleam
Over your heads: go back and dream."

They, answering, smiled, "It is well, yet say,
With lyre and voice, when it shall be day."

So I strayed alone by the hungry sea,
And the night grew deeper, and covered me.

And I lay alone on the earth, and soon
I slept a deep sleep in the night's high noon.

All the winds were blent and stilled,
All my dream with song was filled.

And all the stars shone rosily
Over a darkened, sleepless sea,

And in my dream I rose, and peered
Over the sea, where a little boat steered.

Over the waves it came to me,
With a golden light that illumed the sea.

And one leapt out whose eyes were day-fair,
Who symbolized Night in his floating hair.[104]

[104] In *A Green Garland*, this line becomes "And night not more dark than his floating hair."

He took my hand in his own, and said.
"Brother, how long hast thou been dead?"

I gazed on him for awhile and said
"Brother, how sayest thou I am dead?"

He turned and pointed, and lo! there lay
Behind me my body, ... and then it was day.

I said, "Never now shall I tell of day,
For my voice is lost, and my body clay."

I said, "It is over: not now for me
To summon men to the brightening sea."

He answered, "'Tis well. Come hence with me:
Were it not well to cross the sea?"

But my hand grew stiff in his, and I said,
"Brother, O brother! I am not dead?"

He led me on to the edge of the sea,
Saying, "Brother, wilt thou not go with me?

Another sunrise shall welcome thee:
Wilt thou not, then, come over the sea?"

I turned, and men were drawing sharp breath
Over my body. They saw not Death.

I snatched my hand from Death, and said,
"O my brothers! I am not dead!"

But still they paid no heed to me;
They shaded their eyes, looking over the sea.

Said Death, "How shalt thou know Death and fear?
Am I not Death? And am I not here?"

And then Death[105] went to the boat with me,
But men still gazed eagerly over the sea.

Death touched my hand . . . and the dream was o'er;
I went, with my lyre, back, back from the shore.

I summoned men, and my notes rang true,
And the sunlight flashed on a sea of blue.

And I sang to the throng, and I cast out fears,
For the words of Death rang still in my ears.

I sang, "It is well! and lo! there glows
Morn over the sea, and a dawn-breeze blows."

I shook my hair in the sunlight: then
I tuned my lyre to the ears of men.

And with merry laughter and sobbing breath
I sang of the night, and my dream of Death.

A white half-heard note came to me,
And wove itself deep in my minstrelsy.

From the blazing east the sun rose high—
A golden wheel in a golden sky.

Hail, Saladin![106]

March 20th, 1906

J. F. C. F.

Insensate herd! 'tis their's to triumph now,
But time shall come, when, on my honoured brow,

[105] This word is "he" in *A Green Garland*.
[106] *Agnostic Journal* 58, no. 11 (March 17, 1906): 165.

Posterity shall place a tardy crown,
And truth shall hurl the base detractors down.

—*Byron*[107]

I.

Hail, noble knight! hail, valiant Saladin!
Long may thy sword (lash bright in Freedom's war,
Long may thy name resound midst crash and roar,
In that great fight that battles against sin;
Lead, and we follow, forward till we win:
Onward, yet onward, striking at the core
Of evil statecraft and priest-ridden law;
Hark, cries of victory rise amidst the din.

Thy cause succeeds, the serried ranks fall back;
Sheath thy red sword, a glorious day is won,
The rout is o'er, the Age of Lies hath run
Into the past, and midst Death's hideous track,
Thy form stands god-like as those ages black
Ignoble die before Truth's rising sun;
Unclasp thine helm, thy worldly work is done,
O mighty chief o'er Superstition's wrack.

Well hast thou fought, the enemy have fled;
The cold world hears and trying to retrieve,
O'er thy brave brow a laurel crown doth weave,
Where ebbs away life's flowing stream so red;
Hark, dying warrior, ere thou meet'st the dead,
Truth reigns where once the Church did all deceive
The Cross lies low and the sad World doth grieve;
Thy name and her's are for all ages wed.

[107] "Leon to Annabella: An Epistle after the Manner of Ovid," in George Gordon Byron, *Don Leon; a Poem by the Late Lord Byron . . . Forming Part of the Private Journal of His Lordship, Supposed to Have Been Entirely Destroyed by Thos. Moore . . . To Which Is Added Leon to Annabella; an Epistle from Lord Byron to Lady Byron* (London: printed for the booksellers, 1866). The poem *Don Leon*—a defense of homosexuality and a plea for tolerance thereof—is attributed to Byron, but despite showing an intimate familiarity with events in Byron's life, its references to events that occurred after the poet's death renders his authorship highly doubtful. It is equally doubtful that Byron wrote "Leon to Annabella."

II.

Great counterpart of that Salah-ud-Deen,
Who freed, in mercy, the adultress,
Thy spirit moves in deepest tenderness,
And o'er thy helmed brow is cast the sheen
Of those lost days of love that might have been,
Had'st thou but travelled through life's wilderness
Had'st thou but lived in those sad times of stress,
In those dark days that knew not Truth's bright gleam.

Clasp hands with him whose flashing scimitar
Crashed down the wearers of the crimson cross,
No wall restrained, no moat or yawning fosse
Repelled the rush of crescent and of star:
The cross of Christ dies in far Syria,
The Christian hosts lie numbered midst the loss;
The desert dust is blown o'er scrog and moss,
Re-born in thee, brave son of Scotia.

Thy heart, attuned to his, heats through the age,
And in its berserk mood is near akin,
Or, like the just, chivalrous Noureddin,
Can dry the tear, or bitter pain assuage.
Love, Truth and Beauty are thy battle gage,
O gentle knight, O tender Saladin,
In thee the souls of sweet Jellaledin
And thoughtful Omar kiss their troth's sweet pledge.

III.

Bright son of ages now long past and gone,
And ever echoing memory of those days
Lost midst the pitfalls of that priestly maze
Built in the dark before true light was born,
To burst resplendent o'er Love's breaking down;
Hail Saladin, to thee we sing our praise,
And through the mist of ages on the gaze;
O valiant herald of Truth's glorious morn.

Thine was the night that caught Truth's perfect fire
From the dark clouds of deep inanity,
And from the slough of priestly vanity
Raised the true Christ from out the Christian mire,
Thine was the hand that struck Life's mystic lyre,
Whose notes redolent with divinity,
Speed onward through the vast eternity,
Increasing as our souls to them aspire.

Thine was the soul that laboured for the true,
Thine was the mind that grappled for the just,
Thine was the will that conquered priestly lust,
Leaving Life's roses for her bitter rue:
Hail Saladin, for many pass, but few
Sort Truth's fair jewels from the ages' dust,
And leave this world the better for their trust,
Then onward go, all hail great knight to you!

Lucknow, India

Christianity in India, 1724[108]

Letters to the Editor

J. F. C. F.

Sir—The following, as a testimony of the effects of missionary propaganda in India, is taken from an old book entitled, "The Agreement of Customs between the East Indians and Jews," printed and sold by Joseph Marshall, at the "Bible," in Newgate Street, in the year 1724, which may interest some of your readers. It is as follows:—

> "Besides these Mestis, who are really descended from the Portuguese, there are others who also assume the name of Topases, as the Parias whom I mentioned in Article 15. When they become Christians they put on the

[108] *Agnostic Journal* 58, no. 11 (March 17, 1906): 173–174.

Hat, and presently in an instant they are chang'd from the contemptible State that is among the Indians, to the Quality of Senhor Soldad, which is no small Title among the Christians of the Country. But the Indians always despise them, and can tell them, that none but the Beggars embrace Christianity, whom for that reason they call *Christians d'Aros*, i.e., Christians of Rice; meaning by this, that they do not become Christians, but only that they may live more at ease, and secure Rice to themselves, for in this Country there is no mention made of Bread. And in effect I do not find that the Christians take it much amiss, for these Parias are commonly the most despicable People that can be imagin'd in the World, and tho' they turn Christians, yet they are never the honester men for all that. They are very much addicted to Stealing, and when they cannot make use of their Hands, they very dextrously use their Feet. What I say here may, at first view appear surprizing, yet there is nothing more certain; for if you let fall any Silver, a Knife, or a Fork, and do not presently reflect upon it, they, because they commonly wear no Shoes, take up very dextrously with their Toes, that which is fall'n, and then putting one Hand behind them, they find a way, by bending the Leg, to put into their Hand that which their Foot hath taken up. And all this Contrivance is formed while you do not see them stoop in the least; nay, they will be talking to you all the time they do the Trick, especially when it happens to be in the Night.

"It seems, that as soon as they turn Christians, they count it below them to work. To this purpose I have heard from a Person worthy of Credit, that one day finding a young Woman Arrested, who practis'd a Trade very common in the Indies, and probably did something else, for which no such Person is punish'd, somebody ask'd her, why she did not work for her Living; and that the young Woman being much surpriz'd with the Question, answer'd him, That she was a Christian: A very fine Answer indeed!"[109]

So much for 1724. and turning to the census returns to 1901, what do we find? Practically the same result:—

"In Western India, the returns (of Christians) were swelled by the inclusion of famine waifs. In Madras and Bengal the more degraded classes

[109] De La Créquinière and John Toland, *The Agreement of the Customs of the East Indians, with Those of the Jews, and Other Ancient People: Being the First Essay of This Kind Towards the Explaining of Several Difficult Passages in Scripture, and Some of the Most Ancient Writers, by the Present Oriental Customs with Cuts; to Which Are Added, Instructions to Young Gentlemen That Intend to Travel* (London: Joseph Marshall, 1724), 148–149.

tend to become converts, partly for social reasons. Nearly two-thirds of all Christians are in the Madras Presidency . . ."—*The Times*, Weekly Edition, May 13, 1904.[110]

And he said unto them, "Go ye into the world, and preach the gospel to every sinner";[111] which, like so many other divine fiats, does not seem to have been altogether a success,—Yours truly,

Serenade[112]

[*After Goethe*]

V. B. Neuburg

Ah! Thy soft pillow leaving,
    Dreaming, thy sleep give o'er;
While song my strings is weaving,
    Sleep! What would'st thou more?

While song my strings is weaving,
    The starry hosts restore
The heart's eternal heaving;
    Sleep! What would'st thou more?

My heart's eternal heaving,
    Raises me high,—to lore;
To[113] earth no longer cleaving;
    Sleep! What would'st thou more?

110 This quote, attributed to the *St. James's Budget*, has been widely repeated. See, for example, "The Population of India Today: The Results of the Latest Census—Distribution of Population, Education, Occupation, Proportion of Males to Females, and Religion," *Public Opinion* 36, no. 22 (June 2, 1904): 687; and "India's Religions: A Bewildering Record," *West Gippsland Gazette*, July 19, 1904, 5.

111 Mark 16:15, but in the KJV, the last word is "creature," not "sinner."

112 *Agnostic Journal* 58, no. 19 (May 12, 1906): 291; repr. in *A Green Garland*. An earlier translation appeared in Johann Wolfgang von Goethe and William Gibson, *The Poems of Goethe: Consisting of His Ballads and Songs and Miscellaneous Selections Done into English Verse* (London: Simpkin Marshall, 1883), 134–135. Neuburg matches Gibson in the last line of each stanza ("Sleep! sleep! what would'st thou more?") and comes close to his sixth line ("The starry host adore"); Neuburg's rendition is otherwise distinctive and arguably more poetic. For example, where Gibson's third stanza begins "Love's sempiternal fire," Neuburg's runs "My heart's eternal heaving."

113 "To" becomes "Of" in *A Green Garland*.

To earth no longer cleaving,
Too high thy dreaming bore
Me, in the night-wind grieving,—
Sleep! What would'st thou more?

Of me, in the night-wind grieving,
Dreaming, O give not o'er:
Ah! Thy pillow not leaving,
Sleep! What would'st thou more?

I. H. S.[114]

J. F. C. F.

Hail! from the sky is sung,
"Peace and goodwill";
Lo! high the spear is flung
To wound and kill;
Crash of the blood-red sword,
Innocents torn and gored,
Birth of the bastard Lord,
Author of ill.

Bring forth mine enemies,
Slay them by me;
Look in my blood-shot eyes,
There will'st thou see
Belting the world, a girth
Of tongueless joy, a birth
Of lipless days of mirth,
Of agony.

See, all my mouth is red
With flesh of man;
Harlots shall foul thy bed,

[114] *Agnostic Journal* 58, no. 21 (May 26, 1906): 324.

And be thy ban;
Then all the world for me
Brainless shall live to be
Spouse of my lechery:
Leviathan.

Matted my blood-red hair
Wafts round the world,
Crimsons the sun's bright glare;
Meteors hurled,
Rush into scarlet flame,
Write o'er the world my name,
Words of eternal shame,
All hope is furled.

Hark! how the battle's cry
Rises and wanes,
Blood-red the glooming sky
Darkens, and gains
O'er all the world; and night
Closes an epoch bright;
Shrieking, the carrion kite
Power attains.

O'er my dark brow a band
Of twisted thorn,
Wounded in foot and hand,
Side bleeding, torn;
I rise before thy sight,
Fiend of the serpent night,
Power of awful might,
Slayer of dawn.

Mocked at with sneer and gibe,
Justice I curse;
Wake, all ye fiendish tribe,
Strive, do your worse:
See, all the sky grows dark,

Night falls, the jackal's bark
Frights far the singing lark;
    Earth a huge hearse.

Nailed to the crucifix,
    Eli, Eli;
To rise again phœnix,
    Sabactani;
To rise from out the mud
Rotten with human blood,
Winged o'er the world to scud,
    To brutify.

For all the agony
    That I did bear,
Shall rise a fiend o'er thee
    With fiery hair,
Tearing thee limb from limb,
Shrieking a savage hymn,
Chilling those ages dim,
    Desperate with care.

List, all the tombs do ope,
    I rise again;
Close fast the door of hope,
    Usher in pain.
Rise all ye ghostly dead
Dye the green sward blood-red,
What I have said, is said;
    Surge the red main.

Into the sky I soar
    To sit by God;
Sightless as blood-red war
    On earth is shod:
I am the curse of life,
I am the cause of strife,
I am the butcher's knife,
    I am the rod.

Thought thou that I was born
    But to do this:
Lighten a world forlorn
    To realms of bliss;
Look, fool, thy life is whored
Raped by my crimson sword;
I am the scorpion Lord,
    Father of Dis.

I did not come to bring
    Peace, but the sword;
Rise, all ye nations, sing
    Songs of discord:
Rush o'er the blood-stained sod,
Follow the steps I trod,
I am the Son of God:
    I AM THE LORD.

Young Summer[115]

Victor B. Neuburg

TAKE we now the onward path, joyous 'neath the summer sun,
For the world is wide around us, and the battle almost won:
Ride we hard, for neck to neck, our panting steeds press on for home,
Where the spring is always tender, where there laughs the light sea-foam.

The hawthorn flings its scented love across the path we ride,
The morass and the meadow glow in beauty side by side:[116]
The leafy elms entent us with a roof that changes oft
From the passion-depth of summer's hue to leaves light-edged and soft.

Oh, we pass the winding river, and a thousand swelling hills,
And we hear the brooklets' gossip, and the murmur-haunted rills;

115 *Agnostic Journal* 58, no. 21 (May 26, 1906): 333; repr. in *A Green Garland*.
116 In *A Green Garland*, this line becomes "Morass and sun-kiss'd meadow glow in beauty side by side:".

And the bees are in the clover,[117] and the speedwell in the shade
Grows pale in fading beauty, of the sunlight all afraid.

Life and love have drawn us onward; on the open road we fare,
And the mighty hills grow taller, and we linger here and there
To catch the breath of panting day, hot-breathed beneath the sun,—
And the world spreads wide around us, and the battle's almost won!

The sun-light brings the thrush's song; the hidden cuckoo's call:
The spring's white veil is cast aside, life enters love's own hall,
The sea's faint murmur floats across the smoothly-sloping hills,
And tender Zephyrs stir to smile the silver-hearted rills.

No stay we make, but hasten on unto the sun-lit goal;
The day's hot breath brings echoes from the summer's mystic soul.
We ride beneath pink chestnut-boughs, and white, entwined with may,
Domed temples, where the bird rejoice, and where the breezes play.

All eagerly we hasten on: the summer-dawn has stirred
To life renewed the mother-earth, and, ah! we two have heard
A song of life forever young,—of pulses never stilled,—
The endless life, the endless song, wherewith the earth is filled.

Ah, trace we still the onward path,—stay to, nor break the spell[118]
That holds as all enthralled by hill, and brake, and stream, and well,—
For us young Summer's feast is spread, for us the earth is green,
For us a thousand colours mingle in the summer-sheen.

And love and life and beauty draw us onward, and we go
With eyes and hearts attuned to earth. with glances all aglow.
And never may we lose the scent that came with early May,
For we have lived and loved and known the meaning of the day.

[117] In *A Green Garland*, this phrase becomes "And the bloom is on the clover,".
[118] The phrase "stay to, nor break the spell" becomes "nor stay to break the spell" in *A Green Garland*.

Three Lyrics and a Sonnet[119]

TO B. C.

Victor B. Neuburg

I.—The First Poet[120]

Out on the heath, the heath, the first poet saw the moon-set;
The Night exhaled her mystic breath,
And chanted in love of transcendent Death,
And the first poet dreamed in the moon-set.

Out on the star-guarded heath the first poet roved;
The distant roar of the homing sea
Found echo within his melody,
And with arm outstretched to the sky he roved.

—Water and stretches of heather in moonlight,
The calling of birds, the glow-worm's spark,
The scent of the heath springing up through the dark,
And the far hills all silver in moonlight.—

Onward and onward and on with the stars,
Earthward down-circling, then spanning the sky,
The night-spirit sings, and the breezes reply;
And the land is at peace 'neath the hush of the stars.

Out on the heath, the heath, the poet first sang,
And dawn was at hand, for spinning afar,
The earth returned to the sunward bar,
And the first poet, hearing, was glad, and sang.

119 *Agnostic Journal* 58, no. 22 (June 2, 1906): 349.
120 Repr. in *A Green Garland.*

II.—Bohemia

The Kingdom of the Rose and Star:
A shelf of books, an old guitar,
A lamp, a bed,—Bohemia!

And many days I seeking spent
For life, and for life's wonderment,
Then found the Kingdom of Content.

What if, from out thy sill I see
A dozen roofs for every tree?
Thy nature is humanity.

And life and love within thee dwell
In Poesy's and music's swell,—
In roundelay and villanelle.

The dwellers in thee surely know
The gods, and love, and like, and woe:
Who more unto the gods may owe?

Around thee snatches float of song,
And rays of art: thy life's as long
As is thy art, and thou art strong.

O mine, and bard, and histrion,
Romance how has your kingdom known,
—The kingdom you have made your own?

O fragrant rose! O radiant star!
I sing is vain, for ye are far,
Within my lost Bohemia.

III.—The Quarrel

"No light, save mine, brings echoes from the sun,"
Said Day-spring to the Night, and Night in scorn

Cried, "Victory is mine when day is done
I guard the cradle of the infant Morn."

Then Day-spring: "Dawn is mine. I do but tread
Lightly the world and bring the light of day,
And life is both. Behold my shining head,
The symbol that men herald far away."

"Nightless, how should men know the stars?" said Night,
"And, save by contrast, how should nature live?
I bring the message of the stars' delight:
What has the day of so much worth to give?"
"The promise of the Night," said Day, and kissed
The brow of Night, and vanished unto mist.

IV.—Forwards
[*From the German of A. De Nora*][121]

Ho! Glance not long to left or right,
Upon Time's eager steed swift ride,
And let him, at his spirit's height
Fly where he will,—the world is wide!

Who on the saddle once has sprung
Cares not what yelps beneath his steed,
For all the mire of life is flung
No higher than his boots, indeed.

And while in worn old paths still treads
Philistia, in mire and slime,
He laughing sits above men's heads,—
Upon his steed the lord of time.

Hounds bay, the crowd abuse all cry,
The law gives chase . . . . the tumult all
Is quelled. On to the goal doth fly
His steed; behind the other crawl.

[121] See De Nora, "Vorwärts!," *Jugend* 2, no. 27 (1905): 520.

Freethought[122]

Victor B. Neuburg

FREETHOUGHT is the antithesis of dogmatism. While dogmatism orders its votaries to think in a certain way, irrespective of the temperament and stage of development of the individual thinker, Freethought advises it adherents: "Find your path and stick to it, whether you be with the crowd or no," thus giving free play to every type of thinking mind. It is unnecessary for Freethought to be dogmatic; for, while the religionist is made, the Freethinker becomes.

At a certain stage of development, the ego refuses to accept dogmas as its mental pabulum, and demands the right to find its own pastures—to wander over the fields of thought in search of satisfaction.

It is the misfortune of dogmatic religion that it refuses to recognize this fundamental right of the emancipated ego. It is as though a man who lived upon beans and milk were to declare his diet the only "orthodox" one, and threaten everyone who did not share his dietary views with indigestion—even those who lived in countries where beans were almost unknown.

This, it seems to me, is the chief cause of that decay of religion that is so prominent a factor of modern progress. Religion is all for herding thinkers—or, rather, non-thinkers—together, and endeavouring to persuade them to be contented where they are.

This damnable doctrine of "being content in the position to which God has been pleased to call you," is the greatest bar Reform has to break. Like all inherently superstitious doctrines, however, this bar is inevitably giving way before the tremendously strong current of modern thought—a current that has become infinitely strengthened by the centuries of repression to which it has been subjected by ecclesiasticism. Truly, indeed, can we Freethinkers declare that "Out of evil cometh good." No martyr ever suffered, or ever will suffer, in vain.

The doctrine of "being content"—the doctrine of non-thought, non-desire, non-progress—is a fit teaching for slaves, who are too inert, too stupid to think for themselves. For, obviously, no reform is possible without the willing co-operation of a portion, at least, of those who are to benefit by

[122] *Agnostic Journal* 58, no. 26 (June 30, 1906): 402. Although predating Neuburg's introduction to Crowley, the sentiments expressed in this essay are remarkably Thelemic, a testament to how simpatico they were.

that reform, Also, like nearly all doctrines that have reference to "God," the teaching of "being content" is blasphemy against humanity.

If there be a God, all real progress must be an advance towards him, and whoso denies this blasphemes against the human race. By "real progress" I mean increase of happiness. By "happiness" I mean being in harmony with nature.

The difference between dogmatic Religion and Freethought is fundamental. Dogmatic Religion teaches us to satisfy a problematic God by denying certain nature; Freethought teaches us to satisfy nature by complying with her demands. Religion is based upon the shifting, barren, treacherous sands of metaphysics; Freethought upon the firm, slowly-changing rock of human nature.

To the Moon[123]
[After Goethe]

V. B. Neuburg

Shining over wood and vale
    With thy dusky light,
Once thou gavest, still and pale,
    To my spirit flight.

O'er my fields thou still dost gleam
    With thy gentle gaze,
As a friend's kind eye might beam,
    Watching o'er my days.

Every echo knows my heart
    Of happiness and stress;
Wander thou 'twixt joy and smart,
    In thy loneliness.

Flow on, flow on, thou hasting stream,
    Joy may I never see;

[123] *Agnostic Journal* 59, no. 1 (July 7, 1906): 6. This is a translation of Goethe's "An den Mond" (1778), a poem for which Franz Schubert created two musical settings in 1815: D259 and D296.

As thou dost flow, flows mirth—a dream—
And love, and loyalty.

Yet once, yet once, that garb so rare
Upon me I did set,
That whoso gazed might e'er despair,
Nor ever might forget.

Stream, down the valley haste along,
Nor stay be thine, nor ease;
Flow on, and, flowing, lend my song
Thy whispered melodies.

If thou, within the winter's night,
Dost raging overflow,
More young, thou servest fair Spring's might,
Aiding young buds to grow.

How happy he who from the world
Stands, without hate, apart,
One friend within his breast impearled
Who shares with him his heart;

And—what the world has never known,
Maybe, has never guessed—
Doth wander in the night alone
The pathways of his breast.

Horresco Referens[124, 125]

J. F. C. F.

"Simple Bible teaching";[126] such is the designation which is shortly going to be applied to the undenominational (?) religious instruction of this country: an

[124] *Agnostic Journal* 59, no. 2 (July 14, 1906): 17–18.
[125] In this article I attack the Bible as the Word of God, and not as the Word of Man [original note].
[126] On April 9, 1906, Minister of Education Augustine Birrell (1850–1933) introduced his Education Bill to the House of Commons, in which he proposed that schools receiving public

education which, instead of centering round the infantine virtues of our children, finds its expression in the maturer vices of their parents. By "vice," I take the word in its fullest sense, and mean by it all that is degrading, depraving, and corrupting; for any parent who places the Authorized Version in the hands of a child is thereby robbing that child of purity, innocence, and chastity: and opening to its ignorant, susceptible mind, the road which leads to the prison, the brothel, and the gallows. No more would we think of placing Burton's "Arabian Nights" in the hands of our sons and daughters than we would of teaching them to lisp Pantagruelisms on their mother's knee.[127] Why, then, should we place a book crammed with absurdities, redundant with crimes, crowded with contradictions, ignorant, credulous, superstitious, feculently immoral, and revoltingly obscene, on their school desks, for their perusal, with comment or without?

Comment! Does the following need it? That the world was peopled by incest (Genesis iv. 17, 26), that Abraham committed incest (Genesis xx. 12), also Reuben (Genesis xxxv. 22), also Absalom (2 Samuel xvi. 21–23), also Amnon (2 Samuel xiii. 1–22), etc., etc.

Does the following need comment? That Abraham trafficked with his wife's honour (Genesis xii, 11–19, xx. 2–18); so also did his son Isaac (Genesis xxvi. 6–12); or that God Almighty displayed his back parts to Moses (Exodus xxxiii. 23); or that Lot offered his daughters to a mob of lustful Sodomites (Genesis xix. 1–8): or the truly beautiful story concerning a certain concubine at Gibeah (Judges xix. 20–30).

What are our children to believe? Are they to believe, with the Prayer-book, that a man may not marry his sister, his son's wife, his brother's wife, or his wife's sister; and also at the same time believe with the Bible, that Abraham married his sister (Genesis xx., 12), that Judah had intercourse with his daughter-in-law (Genesis xxxviii., 13–27), that Onan was struck

support should be run by the public (as opposed to a particular religious denomination) and therefore confine their normal religious instruction to "simple Bible teaching," with more specific Bible education reserved for church Sunday schools and the like. This nonsectarian move provoked quite the debate among Liberals and Conservatives alike. Although it passed the House of Commons, by the time it emerged from the House of Lords it was considerably emasculated, resulting in the Commons rejecting the amendments and the bill being dropped altogether.

[127] Sir Richard Francis Burton (1821–1890) and François Rabelais (1494–1553) are well known enough, but their tandem mention here is noteworthy, as both authors were tremendously influential to Aleister Crowley (with whom Fuller was in correspondence by this point). In the dedication to the second volume of Crowley's *Confessions*, Burton was one of "Three Immortal Memories," described as "the perfect pioneer of spiritual and physical adventure." Rabelais' Pantagruel, meanwhile, as explained in chap. 5, this volume, section "Saints and Other Gnostics," was an inspiration for Crowley's "Do what thou wilt shall be the whole of the Law" and his Abbey of Thelema.

dead for marrying his brother's wife, Tamar (Genesis xxxviii., 7–10), and that Jacob married Rachel the sister of Leah (Genesis xxix., 23–30)?

Are they to believe in the singleness of human marriage, and at the same time be given a book describing the polygamous marriage of Abraham (Genesis xx., 12, xvi. 4), of Jacob (Genesis xxix., 23-30, xxx. 1–10), of David (2 Samuel v., 13; xii., 8; xx., 3) and Solomon (1 Kings xi., 1–3)? Are they to be read as a work of moral instruction—moral instruction indeed, which would make a de Sade shiver in his shroud, or an Aretino blush with very shame—a work replete with laws against indecency, unchastity, fornication, adultery, incest, beastiality and Sodomy; a book whose ideal heroes break every law contained in it; a book dealing extensively with rape, castration, childbirth, divorce, circumcision; which teems with the words of "harlot" and "whore"; which is crammed with filthy ideas, and disgusting language, and references to menstruation, begetting, conception and parturition, punctuated with such words as "foreskin," "belly" and "womb"; a book which teaches, that motherhood is sinful (Psalms li., 5), that God will cause wives to be ravished (Isaiah xiii., 16; Deuteronomy xxviii., 30, etc), that captured women may be violated (Deuteronomy xxi., 10–14), that marriage is evil (I Corinthians vii., I, 7–9, 32–35, 37–40), that a prophet may walk about stark naked (Isaiah xx, 2–4), eat dung (Ezekiel iv., 12–15), and marry a prostitute (Hosea i., 2, iii., 1), that God is a loving father, and yet once drowned all the world, innocent and guilty alike (Genesis vi., 5–17), that he commanded and approved human sacrifice (Leviticus xxvii., 28, 29; Genesis xxii., 2, 9, 10; Judges xi., 34, 39), and that he ultimately tortured to death his only begotten son (Colossians i., 19, 20, etc.)?

Here are a few moral lessons in "Simple Bible Teaching":—

1. *God condemns all the world because of one man.*

   "By one man sin entered into the world, and death by sin; and so death upon all men, for that all have sinned."—Romans v. 12.

2. *God tortures innocent animals.*

   "Behold, the hand of the Lord is upon thy cattle which is in the field, upon the horses, upon the asses, upon the camels, upon the oxen, and upon the sheep: there shall be a very grievous murrain . . . and all the cattle of Egypt died."—Exodus ix, 3, 6.

3. *God sanctions slavery.*

   "If thou buy an Hebrew servant . . . If his master have given him a wife, and she have born him sons or daughters; the wife and her children shall be her master's, and he shall go out by himself. And if the servant shall plainly say, I love my master, my wife, and my children; I will not go free: then his master shall bring him unto the judges; he shall also bring him to the door, or unto the post; and his master shall bore his ear through with an aul; and he shall serve him for ever."—Exodus xxi. 2–6, also Leviticus xxv. 44–46.

4. *God orders the burning of witches.*
   "Thou shalt not suffer a witch to live."—Exodus xxii. 18.

5. *God demands religious persecution.*
   "If thy brother, the son of thy mother, or thy son, or thy daughter, or the wife of thy bosom, or thy friend, which is as thine own soul, entice thee secretly, saying, Let us go and serve other gods . . . Thou shalt not consent unto him, nor hearken unto him; neither shall thine eye pity him, neither shalt thou spare, neither shalt thou conceal him: but thou shalt surely kill him; thine hand shall be first upon him to put him to death, and, afterwards the hand of all the people. And thou shalt stone him with stones, that he die."—Deuteronomy xiii. 6–10.

6. *God massacres a whole nation.*
   "But Sihon of Heshbon would not let us pass by him: for the Lord thy God hardened his spirit, and made his heart obstinate, that he might deliver him into thy hand. . . . And we took all his cities at that time, and utterly destroyed the men, and the women, and the little ones, of every city, we left none to remain."—Deuteronomy ii., 30, 34.

7. *God entices Ahab by lies.*
   "And the Lord said, Who shall entice Ahab king of Israel, that he may go up and fall at Ramothgilead? . . . A spirit . . . . said, I will go out, and be a lying spirit in the mouth of all his prophets. And the Lord said, Thou shalt entice him, and thou shalt also prevail: go out, and do even so. Now therefore, behold, the Lord hath put a lying spirit into the mouth of these thy prophets."—2 Chronicles xviii., 19–22.

8. *God sends delusions.*
   "God shall send them strong delusion, that they believe a lie: that they all might be damned who believed not the truth."—2 Thessalonians ii., 11, 12.

Here are eight loving-kindnesses of OUR Father, which I have no doubt the church will be only too pleased to accept without comment. And now how about OUR Lord, he was a worthy chip of the old Block (head). The finite atrocities of the Old Testament were far too lenient, so he sends his enemies right and left to an eternal hell (Matthew xxv., 41–46, etc.), damns the rich (Matthew xix., 24), speaks unintelligible parables, so that people may not be saved (Mark iv., 11–12), idealises cannibalism (John vi., 53–56), recommends castration (Matthew xix., 12, etc.), celibacy (Matthew xix., 10–12), wife desertion (Luke xiv., 33), insults women generally and his mother in particular.

Is this the book to teach a higher morality, a nobler system of ethics? a book whose heroes were:—Adam, a sneaking coward; Moses, a juggling murderer; Abraham, a grabbing pimp; Isaac, ditto; Jacob, a slippery cad; Joshua, a blood-thirsty cut-throat; Lot, an unnatural bawd; Samson, a puddle-trotting harlot-quester; David, a homo-sexual-adulterous-psalm-singing, stone-slinging slit-throat (one of the very worst, and ancestor of the Lamb whose ghostly "pa" was *a* pigeon, and whose mundane one was *the* pigeon); Solomon, a notorious lecher; Isaiah and Jeremiah, both ranting revivalists; Ezekiel, an evil-smelling dung-devourer; Peter, a fearsome coward; John, an effeminate idiot; Paul, a slanderous misogynist. Now, a lady or two: Rahab, a treacherous harlot; Deborah, a villainous murderess; and Sarah, a senile adulteress. Enough! though there are many more.

Is this the book on which we are to educate our children? the book which contains a thousand absurdities:—The creation story; the Eve-and-apple story; the flood story; the Babel story; the Lot's wife story; the plagues story; the sun-standing-still story; the Balaam's-ass story; the Jonah-and-the-whale story; the virgin-mother story; the resurrection story; the crucifixion story: the ascension story; and a hundred others; this book begins with a fairy-tale and ends with a nightmare? This book makes of its God a murderer, of its Ghost an adulterer, of its Virgin a harlot, and of its Redeemer an illegitimate, who lived on earth like a twopenny cracker, and flew up to heaven like a halfpenny squib.

Holy Grab[128]

J. F. C. F.

As a humble seeker after Freedom and Truth, I, oh unfortunate one, had, before Sunday, July the twenty-second of the year of our Lord, one thousand

[128] *Agnostic Journal* 59, no. 5 (August 4, 1906): 65–66.

nine hundred and six, arrived at the hasty and miserable conclusion that all ethical champions of the Romish faith were as dead as the much lamented dodo. With the scorching tears of repentance I will henceforth attempt to wash clean the much-scribbled slate of my wretched existence, and, with ten thousand genuflexions, I will straighten the miserable kink of my deluded brain. For a great light has arisen from the lupanar of the Seven Hills; this day a champion has been found in Gilead, "for the Lord hath a sacrifice in Bozrah, and a great slaughter in the land of Idumea." The Rev. Father Bernard Vaughan[129] hath spoken. I strike my head seven and seventy times seven on the ground before him and listen:—

> "The prodigal son—the giddy, genial, dashing young Englishman—falls into the hands of the fast, smart set, who, in the words of the Lord, 'devour his substance.' Aye, they devour it as ravenously as the panther or the tigress in the Zoo devoured the raw meat tossed to them.
>
> "Against the man-eating tiger of the jungle a man could defend himself; but before the man-eating tigress of Society he is powerless to escape. One thing every man may know who goes into this set: if he go into it with money he will come out without any. Husband, wife and children are crushed to death merely to gratify women in this set,
>
> "Many a beautiful *débutante* going into Society, has been led to the card-room by her hostess—I know it—and at the end of the game she rises from the table innocent of what has happened; she is told, with the sweetest 'Good night, darling,' all that she owes, The family doctor and the family lawyer can tell you better than I can the number of innocent and beautiful English girls who have been ruined at the card-table—ruined and brought to the verge of the grave. And a girl with this curse on her—what can she do? She must pay her debts. Does she ask her father or her mother? No; she is too ashamed. She runs from one to another—she knows not whither—until at last some devil in human form, who has laid his trap, makes his bargain, He gives her money, the debt is paid; but the poor girl feels she can never be herself again. And this is going on every day."[130]

129 Bernard Vaughan (1847–1922) was a world-famous Jesuit and brother of Cardinal Herbert Alfred Vaughan and Bishop John Stephen Vaughan. Around 1906, Bernard was active as a Catholic preacher in Westminster and London's East End.

130 On Sunday, July 22, 1906, Bernard Vaughan delivered a sermon denouncing the general decay of English society and how the prodigal son could not have survived today's temptresses of the Smart Set—that is, the rich, fashionable, educated, and artistic crowd. See, for example, "News from the Dioceses: Farm Street: Father Bernard Vaughan and the 'Smart Set,'" *The Tablet* 108, no. 3455 (July

Demosthenes further states that a poor ill girl on her sick bed said unto him: "I have called you to see to what man can reduce a woman. I am in the agony and the torments of hell."

Father Vaughan, give me your hand—one moment; the shade of Ananias—I mean R. A. Torrey—has risen up before me: I dismiss it with one of Mr., G. W. Foote's tracts, and will as fervently believe your revelations as I do those of St. John.

The last word quoted from your tirade is "Hell." Do you believe in this special locality for the damned? Your poor, sick patient did! Those who even possess as much as you do, will eventually go there. Do you believe when Christ descended into Hell he suffered the torments of the damned? Can you realize what these torments are? You can not. If you could, in five minutes you would be a raving maniac. Neither can have Christ; for if he had, he would have risen and swept the world clear of all life; for life with a hell is the greatest curse of God. This hell is the terror with which your Church has cramped the understanding of myriads upon myriads of human beings; this hell is the horror with which she has polluted the minds of millions upon millions of children; this hell, O trickster of Rome, is the joker of thy cheating Church, with which she has extorted money and gold, lands, kingdoms, and continents.

In the name of hell she burnt thousands of innocent men, women, and children; and not content with sending billions to eternal damnation, she painted this fair earth crimson with the blood of agony and the flames of destruction. It was thy swindling Church that invented the Rack, the Thumbscrew, the Wheel, the Boot, the Spider, and the Iron Virgin. The emblem of thy Church has been the Knave of Spades. She cheated till she could cheat no more; with her spade she has destroyed the monuments of the great, and with it she has dug the graves of the elect. Inveigh, if thou will'st, against the horrors of card-playing; but, remember, there are not so many cards in the whole world as souls that thy Church has put out of it in writhing agony. Her table has been an Aceldama,[131] her stakes human lives, and her winnings

28, 1906): 138; "Society Snares: Man Eating Tigresses Is the Name: Caustic Reproach," *Dawson Daily News* [Tacoma, WA], August 11, 1906, 2; and Bernard Vaughan, *The Sins of Society: Words Spoken by Father Bernard Vaughan of the Society of Jesus in the Church of the Immaculate Conception, Mayfair, during the Season 1906* (London: T. Fisher Unwin, 1907).

[131] Aceldama ("field of blood" in Aramaic) is the place near Jerusalem purchased with the thirty pieces of silver that Judas received for betraying Jesus (see Acts 1:18–19); it may also refer to any place of bloodshed.

holocausts of dead. She has play with human lives as the gambler has with his gold; and as the gambler she has created misery and woe, has cheated and tricked; but no gambler has ever turned his home into such an unendurable hell as thy Church for nearly two thousand years has rendered this world. She has been the greatest cheat, the greatest trickster, that this world has ever seen, or is ever likely to see. In her girlhood she played "Beg o' my neighbours," in her maidenhood (*sic*) "Grab," and now she, the exposed harridan, plays "Nap."

"Bridge." What a small thing is "bridge" to the "Bridge of Sighs." Have you ever been to Venice, Father Vaughan? Have you ever looked at that interesting and quaint little arch that spans one of the canals? Have you ever thought of the scores of wretched victims who, in ages past, when your Church was supreme, were hurried across it never to return? More agony has crossed that Bridge of Sighs than ever crossed the span of the Beresina.[132] I see that demigod, Napoleon, on a cold winter day, standing there by the horrible deroute; he clears the bridge with grape, and in a few minutes the tangled mass of waggons, horses, and men, arc no more. I see the children of the Catholic faith, day after day, year after year, hurrying some trembling human being across that small Bridge of Sighs. Man-eating tigers indeed; they were diabolical fiends, the same who tore to pieces Hypatia, the same who drenched the world in the blood of the Crusades, and of St. Bartholomew. Where are the Incas and the Astecs? Ask thy fœtid Church.

Against the tiger man may defend himself; but against thy butcher church, for more than a millennium and a half, if man attempted to do so, she plucked his eyes out as a vulture; and now that she can no longer burn, and slay, and blind, she accepts: and, like a foul hyena, prowls round the dead and lives on the flesh of the great. Clubs have been thy Church's symbol also, and with them thou hast dashed out the brains and understanding of man. and driven him across that "bridge" which unites the Vatican with Hell.

"Many a beautiful *débutante* . . ."—true; but what has your church done for *débutantes*? The beautiful ones she has crammed into the brothel, and the ugly ones she has burned at the stake. She has belted the whole world with houses of ill fame; she has produced such writers as Liguori and Dens, whose

[132] The *Ponte dei Sospiri*, or "Bridge of Sighs," is an enclosed limestone bridge spanning the Rio di Palazzo in Venice. It was the passageway connecting the interrogation rooms in Doge's Palace to the New Prison. The Battle of Berezina is named after the river that Napoleon's army had to cross—with heavy casualties—in its November 1812 retreat from Russia. In French, the word *Berezina* is a synonym for "disaster."

works—if they were not of a "religious" character—would not be tolerated even in the brothels of Port Said. Their filth is the filth of Sodom, and their lust the lust of Gomorrah. Happier he who should go and kiss the posteriors of the goat of Mendes, than he who should read such revolting obscenities, let alone question with them a trembling suppliant. A man may offer money in exchange for a woman's honour, but only a priest can take her money and put questions to her which would make Mutinus himself blush, and Priapus vomit with disgust.[133]

The heart is the emblem of love. The Queen of Hearts was the Virgin Mother of Christ. Thy Church has cheated with her as she has cheated with every card in her pack. The supreme trick of the trickster is the three-card trick; the supreme trick of thy Church is the three-god trick, and it has served thy old strumpet well these last nineteen hundred years[.]

As to diamonds, the heart of thy Church alone resembles them in their hardness. The diamond is the most brilliant of stones, and the Romish faith is the darkest of religions. She sprang from the sewers of the Suburra, and throve in the fornices of Byzantium; as Theodora, the Christian Empress of Rome, she not only shared the bed of an emperor, but ministered to the licentious pleasures of the populace as a courtesan. Thy church has indeed been a precious gem!

Do you believe, Father Vaughan, in Hell, in Persecution, in Auricular Confession? If you do, then in attacking card-playing society for faults which are as drops in the ocean compared to the crimes of the Church to which you belong, you become one of the meanest cheats who ever shuffled cards or souls; if you do not, then stand up as a man, and say so.

The City of Lies[134]

J. F. C. F.

Once, man in ignorance did raise
A fragile tower to the skies,

[133] In ancient Rome, brides-to-be would mount the statue of the phallic deity Mutinus Tutunus in preparation for marriage. Although Mutinus was one of the *di indigetes* or deities indigenous to Rome (as opposed to those imported from other cultures), he shares some characteristics with the Greek fertility god Priapus, who was depicted with an exaggerated perpetual erection.

[134] *Agnostic Journal* 59, no. 6 (August 11, 1906): 87.

Seeking to leave the fettered ways
Of a sad world of lies;
He built it high, with stone and mud,
Mixing the mortar with his blood,
His sorrows, and his sighs.

The sun shone on its gilded spire,
A beck'ning finger to the throng;
Deep from its precincts did suspire,
A mystic siren song.
The clanging of its noisy bell,
Drove airy devils into hell,
Seeking to right the wrong.

Around the battlements were raised,
A mighty town, both fair and strong;
And he that owned the tower gazed
Upon the fickle throng;
But in the turret from on high,
He caught the laugh, but lost the sigh,
Of builders' lash and thong.

Into a city the town grew;
And to the city flowed the world;
Where midst her roses and her rue,
A limpid stream she purled.
But soon flowing round the tower,
She tore up every beauteous flower,
Which down her eddies whirled.

Then, from man's blood the star-blind seer,
Extracted gold a thousand years;
And threw his spells both far and near,
Warping the mind with fears,
Till at the clink of gold man's brain
Sank, as the suns midst drizzling rain;
The rain of human tears.

Red blushed the world with blood and gain;
    The jarring door of Death did ope,
Through which echoed the shrieks of pain,
    The creak of wheel and rope:
And as the day became more dim,
He bid the nations worship him,
    Their mystic only hope.

Fast fell the night dismal and dark,
    Alone the moon shone dim and red;
The night-jar shrieked where once the lark
    Had sung, and darkness led
The west into a land where wan,
Alone the eastern crescent shone,
    As vice sought virtue's bed.

But as the moon, whose borrowed light
    Reflecting glories of the East,
Struck with a ray the tower's might;
    Then swore the blood drunk beast:
To slay the moon, demented fool,
Ten thousand princes as his tool
    Became a vulture's feast.

The seer looked out, and cursed, and swore;
    Divorced his soul and took to bed,
As knights fall fast, the wretched whore
    Who on their corpses fed.
Then groaned the world for all the best
Were dead; and in their place was dressed
    A crimson woman red.

"Son of the Moor, pale prince divine,";
    Was shouted loud but yet some thought
As parting clouds let stars forth shine,
    Can sins he sold and bought.
Then as the thunder clouds return,
Flash lightnings; so the seer did burn
    The starry light they sought.

Roll thunder till the crack of doom,
    Raging, and roaring, o'er the Earth;
Shrieking with pain from out the womb
    Of the harlot leapt Dearth
Of Soul, of Love, of Faith, of Fire;
A worthy offspring of his sire,
    Upon whose lips froze mirth.

Far spent in travail was the night;
    Unnatural vice, incestuous lust,
Shook to its base the towers might;
    And eaten deep with rust,
As some worn sword smiting would yield,
A thousand fragments to the shield,
    It crumbled into dust.

And as it fell, across the West
    Sped the first rays of waking morn;
Apollo kissed Aurora's breast,
    And a new light was born.
Then foul the Vulture of the night,
Rose for a space a vampire kite,
    To suck the blood of Dawn.

But arrows sharp the sons of Dawn
    Drew from Truth's quiver and let fly,
Until the Vampire's heart was torn,
    And to the ground it fell to die:
A living corpse, a living death,
A foul excresence without breath,
    A putrid rotting lie.

Still by the carcass of itself
    A shiv'ring wraith sits on a clod;
Shrieking it asks a little pelf,
    Crawling where once it trod:
It sucks the strength still of the frail,
And makes life hideous with its wail
    To rouse a dying God.

Four Sonnets to William Blake[135]

Victor B. Neuburg

I. Invocation

Strong hands of yesterday, what strength were thine,
That we should be to-day with all our powers!
Now is illumed the wide horizon-line
That marks the æons, and the days and hours,
Wherefore, strong hands, whenever darkness lowers,
We light the gloom with goblets of thy wine,
And ah! how many of our fairest flowers
Owe their descent to blooms from thy fair shrine.

Strong hands! methinks, back gazing through the gloom,
I feel thy touch, and hear a voice that seems
An echo from the rocks of secret doom:
"We sowed that thou might'st reap; our life we gave
To thee we knew and loved but in our dreams.
Thou too shalt rule far, far beyond the grave."

II. Longing

Strong eyes of yesterday, what sights were thine,
To gaze and gaze through worlds to worlds beyond,
To mark the passage of the mystic sign
That only thou in unknown tongues had'st conned.
Thou barest in thy hand a magic wand
To test the aura of earth, flame, air, brine;
Thou bathed'st unseen within the Secret Pond,
Close guarded by a minister divine.

[135] *Agnostic Journal* 59, no. 7 (August 18, 1906): 109. According to Jean Overton Fuller, these were Neuburg's last contributions before going to Cambridge: "At twenty-three, he was late in starting, but he had behind him a literary reputation other students might envy." Fuller, *Magical Dilemma*, 111. This is also around the time that Fuller met Crowley—that is, in mid-August 1906. As such, this represents a turning point of sorts in the life experiences that inform their subsequent works.

New maps of unguessed lands, from thee we take
Heaven and hell, strong sleep, and fairyland;
We long in vain our thirst unquenched to slake,
But lo! we find but thorns and thickets fierce,
And find no heaven, but only barren sand,
And barriers too thick for us to pierce.

III. Fulfilment

Red dreams and white, blue heav'n and golden stars,
Tall pines beneath a pale green-yellow sky,
Vermilion sunsets ruled with crimson bars,
And all the hues whereof the thrushes cry;
A mist uprising higher and more high,
Purging the vision of its unknown scars,—
We too with thee beyond the mountains spy,
In deep, full-fashioned, burnished fairy cars.

Thy name upon the heavens high is writ,
Thy hands have laid the inner secret bare;
Thy feet upon the uplands scornful tread;
We follow, each his own still finding there,
There, where the ruling sign leads overhead—
Brother, we thank thee for the gift of it.

IV. Reflection

The gift of song came to thee in the night,
The dawn the theme remembered, and thy song
Emerged from mental grey to black and white,
Enhued with tints wherefor thy heart did long;
Therefore thy message was sublime and strong,
Therefore the world was clearer to thy sight
Than it may be for those whom right and wrong
Make dull the hues of the Primeval Right.

Thou knewest what their vision leaves unseen;
Thou had'st no scale whereby to judge; for thee
No foolish scheme could limit thy mind's green,—

As nought may change the colour of the sea.
And nothing hindered thee that thou should'st be
The Seer of the greatest that hath been.

Marie Spiridonova[136]

Victor B. Neuburg

The outraged flesh. the mind in anguish burning,
The brave eyes closed in deep excess of pain,
The young and splendid blood in fever churning;
O foulest blot upon the world! O stain
On the world's manhood! Shall it be in vain
That she has suffered what few men could stand,
Because she strove to aid her tortured land?

The curse of Fate on Russia shall be lightened
Never, till she has trod the downward way;
The grip of Fate o'erpowering shall be tightened
On her, too foul to see the light of day.
Weep, weep! O land! No solitary ray
Shall light thy gloom till thou art purged of this—
A crime to weep in hell's most deep abyss.

What gods can they be, who are calmly seeing
Earth's noblest women to vile brutes enthrall'd?
Is there no chord within fair England's being,
That throbs, that at such outrage is appalled?
Not ever was a bitterer crying called

[136] *Agnostic Journal* 59, no. 8 (August 25, 1906): 118. Russian Socialist-Revolutionary Party member Maria Alexandrovna Spiridonova (1884–1941) was a political activist who became famous for assassinating brutally oppressive Police Inspector General Gavril N. Luzhenovsky in January 1905. Her subsequent abuse, torture, and imprisonment prompted a public outcry against police brutality even among those who disapproved of her crime, making hers a true cause célèbre. Tried and sentenced to death by hanging in March 1905, her punishment was commuted, on account of her health, to a life sentence at Maltzevskaya Prison in Siberia, where she remained for the next eleven years (i.e., until all political prisoners were released following the February Revolution of 1917). After her release, her activism and celebrity both persisted. Charged in 1937 with counterrevolutionary conspiracy, she was ultimately executed in 1941 on Stalin's orders, as part of the Medvedevsky Forest massacre.

Over the wastes of Holy Russia's soil.
Is England's blood too sluggish now to boil?

The martyrdoms unspeakable for anguish
Call forth from men the sacred human fire;
The prisoned souls that into madness languish
Make all the world a bloody, choking mire.
O agony unutterable! O dire
And dreadful curse! How shall we raise our eyes
As men, as women, to the open skies?

Words! words! and words! 'Tis, after all, not wond'rous
That noblest womanhood should suffer so;
Maybe my protest is unduly thund'rous,
And yet to common manhood do I owe
This,—that I let my outraged spirit go.
Will no one speak the words? Which shall be said,
That England's heart is sleeping, or is dead?

A Song for a Free Spirit[137]

Victor B. Neuburg

Not all the wise of Attica,
Not all the bards that sang in Rome,
May ever lead thy Spirit far
Along the path that leads it home;
Stand thou beneath a wider dome
Than ever knew a centre-star,
Be thou baptised in purer foam
Than ever a priest's hand may mar.

Search not in books if thou would'st know
Whither have gone the summer trees.

[137] *Agnostic Journal* 59, no. 10 (September 8, 1906): 157.

Nor seek in maps if thou would'st go
    A voyage on the unknown seas;
    Not any book the Spirit frees,
Not any map the path may show
    That leads across the upland leas,
That ends in summer through the snow.

Dive deep within thy being; rise
    In wisdom from the heart of things;
Within the gloom train thou thine eyes,
    Within thyself test thine own wings:
    The baptism of the Spirit stings,
The Spirit flutters ere it flies,
    But at the end triumphant rings
A paean; never Spirit dies.

Fear not Thyself: be wise—an hour,
    A single hour, ere Nature calls,
Hast thou within thy being's power
    To rise above thy prison walls;
    An hour, and then the darkness falls,
And then a shadow casts thy tower;—
    When gloom shall fall upon thy halls,
Arise! nor let thy Spirit cower,

Arise, and gaze thou on the light,
    Bathe thou thy Spirit in the blaze;
Is it a little thing, or slight,
    To fare along the sunlit ways?
    But only thou thyself can'st raise
Thyself; no man for thee may fight
    The battle that shall make thy days
Free, and unawed at coming night.

Let no man lead thee? Who can tell
    But thou the way thy Spirit leads?
Seek no man's heaven, shun no man's hell,
    Save within thee thy Spirit pleads

A space in which to scatter seeds,
A place wherein to sink a well,
A desert place to free from weeds,
A spot where it may ring its knell.

Not all the men who ever wrote
Philosophy or poesy
For thee may ever thy steer boat,
Nor clear the sea of rocks for thee;
Keep thou thy Spirit ever free,
Nor strive to check the warning note
That tells of *was* or *is to be*,
Or bids thee sink, or swim, or float.

So shall in sight thy haven rise,
Maybe before thou know'st, when thou
Hast had all things before thine eyes,
And all thy thoughts behind thy brow.
Ah! thou hast found a resting now,
And over thee the starlit skies
Shall shine upon thy worn-out prow,
The track that far behind thee lies.

An Agnostic View[138]

Victor B. Neuburg

Some time after the death of Herbert Spencer[139] a number of distinguished men considered the desirability of raising some abiding monument in his honour. They decided to seek permission to erect a memorial tablet in Westminster Abbey, and this scheme was commendable because of its simplicity.

[138] *Agnostic Journal* 59, no. 11 (September 15, 1906): 173; repr. in *A Green Garland*.

[139] Victorian British sociologist, philosopher, and political theorist Herbert Spencer (1820–1903) was a proponent of evolutionary theory and is perhaps best known for coining the phrase "survival of the fittest," which extended Darwin's natural selection into sociological and ethical discourse, arguing in favor of laissez-faire economics and small government (a perspective later to be termed *Social Darwinism*). A fierce critic of religion and proponent of empiricism, Spencer was an agnostic, acknowledging that the fundamental nature of reality was unknowable.

The desire was to set up in the Abbey, where the fame of so many great men is commemorated, a plain and unobtrusive record of Spencer's life and labours. But though the appeal for permission to carry out such a plan was made by a large number of the world's greatest thinkers and most distinguished public men, the Dean of Westminster felt himself compelled to withhold his assent.—*Daily Chronicle*, September l0th, 1906.[140]

The vast colossus of the latter years[141]—
    Huge silver statue in the realm of Thought—
With arms strong-folded,[142] and calm upward gaze,
    Stands on the massive pile his hands have wrought,
    And something of the glamour hath he caught
That to the gods pertains; the sky dark-blue
Sheds over him the calm undying hue
    Of intellect; the brow's most noble rise
    Endomes the depths of the deep-seated eyes.

Unflinching, strong, could this brave Statue stand
    Pure and unsullied in a Christian fane,
While pigmies, in the shadow of his hand,
    Mocked the advance of mighty Reason's reign
    With jeers and gapes ignoble and in vain?
He, the Agnostic giant, in his might
Would shame the dying faith's dark priests to flight;
    The superstition that he smote would reel
    Beneath the wond'rous[143] Statue's mighty heel!

Why should a Christian temple shelter him
    Within the dark recesses of its night?
Should Phoebus' image stand in corners dim,
    Lest it should fade beneath the sun's strong light?
    Should feeble priests serve incarnated Might,
Muttering dull shibboleths of "love" and "grace,"

140 Additional published sources for this quote include "Herbert Spencer Memorial," *Nottingham Evening Post*, no. 8745 (September 10, 1906): 8; "Herbert Spencer and Westminster Abbey: The Dean's Refusal of a Memorial," *Derby Daily Telegraph*, no. 9315 (September 10, 1906): 3. As part of its article, the *Daily Chronicle* also published the opinions of eminent me in favor of a national Spencer memorial.
141 This becomes "days" in *A Green Garland*.
142 This becomes "firm-folded" in *A Green Garland*.
143 This becomes "towering" in *A Green Garland*.

An insult to our Giant's scornful face?
Should Faith and Reason share the self-same fane?
Would Sun and Night[144] together peaceful reign?

Nay, 'tis the sun would make the darkness fade,
As Truth shall superstition smite and slay,—
No wonder, then, that men should be afraid
To have their temple dim the sun's wild ray
Admit, for light makes neither truce nor stay,
But reign sole queen; shall he, her mighty one,
The thunder-browed apostle of the sun
Honour a fane where Christians kneel in dread
And slave-like love unto a god that's dead.[145]

Four Poems from the German[146]

Victor B. Neuburg

[*Note.*—It is probably unnecessary for the translator to state that he dissociates himself from the Theistic sentiment of "The Happy Wanderer."]

Song
After Heine[147]

Oh, how they have moved me
To anger flushed and white,
Some, because of their loving,
Some, because of their spite.

144 "Can Sun and Night" becomes "Can God and Man" in *A Green Garland*.
145 *A Green Garland* revises this entire verse to read:

Nay, for this man hath made heaven's pantheon fade,
If Truth doth Superstition smite and slay.—
What wonder then that men should be afraid
To have their temple dim the sun's wide ray
Admit? For light makes neither truce nor stay,
But reigns sole queen: shall he, her mighty one,
The thunder-browed apostle of the sun,
Honour a shrine where Christians kneel in dread
And slave-lie love unto a god that's dead?

146 *Agnostic Journal* 59, no. 12 (September 22, 1906): 182.
147 This is a translation of poem 40 of Heinrich Heine, "Lyrisches Intermezzo," in *Buch der Lieder* (Hamburg, Germany: Hoffmann und Campe, 1837), 152.

My bread, how have they tainted,—
Poisoned my goblet bright,
Some, because of their loving,
Some, because of their spite.

But she who most bath moved me,
Pained me,—with anguish torn,
Never, ah! *she* hath hated,
Never *she* love hath borne.

Winter
After Heine[148]

Truly, cold can burn
Like fire. In the driving snow
Poor mortals run and turn,
And ever faster they go.

O Winter, stern in requitals,
All our noses you freeze,
And your piano-recitals
Give to our ears no ease.

But Summer does more than atone;
Then through the woods I can stroll,
Conning love-lyrics alone—
Alone with grief of my soul.

The Happy Wanderer
After Eichendorff[149]

To whom God would his favour shew
He sends into the world so wide,
That he may all his wonders know,
In hill, stream, meadow, mountain-side.

[148] Heinrich Heine, "Winter," in *Neue Gedichte* (Hamburg, Germany: Hoffmann und Campe, 1862), 213.

[149] "Der frohe Wandersmann," in Joseph Freiherr von Eichendorff, *Gedichte* (Berlin: Duncker & Humblot, 1837), 5. Eichendorff (1788–1857) was a famous German Romantic poet, novelist, and critic.

To lazy folk, at home who lie,
No message has the dawn to give:
What, save a cradle lullaby,
Know they, and cares, the means to live?

The brooklets from the hill-sides spring,
The larks so high for gladness dart;
Oh, why should I with these not sing,
With swelling throat and joyous heart?

The good God only own I guide:
He who streams, larks, and field and wood,
And earth and heaven upholds beside,
Hath o'er my life best power for good.

Barbarossa
After Rückert[150]

Frederick the Emperor,
Redbeard whom men call,
Beneath a subterranean door
Dwells in a castle hall.

Never hath he perished;
Within the castle deep,
Far from the land he cherished,
Enchanted, he doth sleep,

His kingdom's old time splendour
With him he took; one day
He'll be that land's defender
Whose might he took away.

The throne is gleaming ivory white
Wherein his limbs are spread;
The table is of marble bright
Whereon he rests his head.

[150] From Friedrich Rückert, *Kranz der Zeit* (Stuttgart, Germany: Cotta, 1817), 2:270–271. Friederich Rückert was the pseudonym of German poet and professor Friemund Raimar (1788–1866).

His beard's hue is not flaxen;
As burning fire it glows;
Through the table hath it waxen
Where finds his chin repose.

As in a dream his head is bowed,
Half-opened are his eyes,
Long-pausing, aye, he calls aloud—
Unto a page he cries.

Still sleeping, he to him doth cry;—
Go, boy, my halls before,
And see if yet the ravens fly
Around the mountain hoar.

And if the ravens olden
Still round the mountain sweep,
My lids must still be folden
With hundred years of sleep.

In the Temple of Isis[151,152]

J.F.C.F.

As in thine eyes I gaze,
Thy love is as the haze

[151] *Agnostic Journal* 59, no. 13 (September 29, 1906): 205–206.

[152] Isis was one of the most celebrated deities of Egypt. She was the Venus of Cyprus, the Minerva of Athens, the Cybele of the Phrygians, the Ceres of Eleusis, the Proserpine of Sicily, the Diana of Crete, the Bellona of the Romans. By some she is supposed to be the same as lo, daughter of Iacchus. The name Io is probably connected with Iacchus, the mystical appellation of Bacchus at whose feasts the Bacchantes used to cry: "Evoe Iacchus! Evoe Iacchus!" also "Io Evohe!" Io Evohe!" Bacchus was the son of Demeter (Ceres), and is the same as the Osiris of Egypt, from which country Orpheus introduced him to Greece. Osiris was the son of Rhea (Nüt), but not by her husband Helios (Râ), but by her lover Kronos (Seb). The words "Io Evohe" contain the four primitive letters of the Hebrew tongue.

JOD, symbol of the vine-stock, or sceptre of Noah.

HE, chalice of libation.

VAU, the medium between these two signs, the mysterious lingam of India.

HE, the maternal letter appearing as a second time to express fecundity in nature arid woman.

Of early morn;
And as the Sun's bright rays
Night's dreamy eyes amaze,
Thy love is born.
Mystic thy form doth rise,
Born 'twixt the seas and skies;
Eva from Paradise,
On Earth reborn.

The zephyrs of the air
Blow kisses through thy hair,
As rising sun,
Leaves blushing Dawn all bare,
Tearing her night-robe fair—
All starry-spun.
High soars the Lord of Light;

The J.H.V.H. is the tetragrammaton of the Qabalists, the unpronounceable name of Jahveh or Jehovah. Jahveh is a phallic god. The connection between Christ and Osiris is too well known to need explanation.

According to Plutarch, Isis, the moon, married her brother Osiris, the sun; his brother Typhon murdered him, and the yearly inundations of the Nile were supposed by the old Egyptians to be the tears shed by Isis over her dead lord. The worship of Osiris was closely connected with the festivals of Phallica in Egypt, as were those of Dionysius in Greece.

Isis was the goddess of Love, of Marriage, and of Motherhood. It has been said by mystics, "To eat of the tree of knowledge of good and evil, is to assimilate good with evil; to cover the face of Osiris with the mask of Typhon, to raise the veil of Isis" [original note].

The quote at the end of this portion of the original note appeared in Éliphas Lévi, *La Clef des grands mystères, suivant Hénoch, Abraham, Hermès Trismégiste, et Salomon* (Paris: G. Baillière, 1861), 311, as "Manger du fruit de l'arbre de la science du bien et du mal, c'est associer le mal au bien et les assimiler l'un à l'autre. C'est courvrir du masque de Typhon le visage rayonnant d'Osiris. C'est soulever le voile sacré d'Isis, c'est profaner le sanctuaire." For the translation contemporary to Fuller, see Arthur Edward Waite, *The Mysteries of Magic: A Digest of the Writings of Éliphas Lévi*, 2nd ed. rev. and exp. (London: Kegan, Paul, Trench, Trübner, 1897), 85. There, it is rendered, "To eat of the fruit of the tree of knowledge of good and evil is to associate and assimilate good and evil one with another; it is to cover the radiant face of Osiris with the mask of Typhon, it is to raise the veil of Isis, and profane the sanctuary." Crowley would later offer his own translation of the text as a supplement to *The Equinox* vol. 1, no. 10 (Spring 1913).

The original note continues in the following two paragraphs:

> But, the mystery of Isis, in reality lies much deeper than this, for her spirit is emblematic of that mysterious affinity which attracts heart to heart. The inscription, is as sphinxlike now as it was thousands of years ago; it is to be found on her statue, and reads as follows;—
>
> "*I am all that has been, that shall be, and none among mortals has hitherto taken off my veil*" [original note].

This last quote was well known in Fuller's time, having appeared in, for example, Anonymous, *On Temptation; and on the Agency and Personality of the Devil* (London: William Macintosh, 1875), 107; and Rosina Bulwer Lytton, *Cheveley: Or, The Man of Honour* (New York: Harper, 1839), 27.

The dismal hosts of Night
Towards the West take flight"
    Thy love is won.

Upon thy lips my kiss,
Burns to a fiery bliss,
    As hour of noon
Unveils mystic Isis,
The kiss of Osiris
    Fainting doth swoon.
From out the virgin sea,
Rises Aphrodite,
Boundless as sea-waves free:
    Sweet honey-moon.

Thy golden hair caressed,
Lies tangled o'er my breast;
    As Phœbus bright
Drives slowly towards the West
His weary steeds to rest,
    Midst flaming light.
Blue as a virgin's eyes,
The sapphire of the skies
Blushes, as Evening sighs:
    "O bridal night."

Thy blush dies with the East,
Our sorrows are increased
    To bitter woe.
Thy bridal garment creased,
Is soiled: Beauty turned Beast;
    Thou know'st, I know.
On veiléd Isis' breast,
The crescent moon doth rest
Symbol of Love's behest:
    To melt like snow.

As deep as thy blue eyes
Are spread the starry skies,

A jewelled dome.
The wisdom of the wise
Our hearts imparadise
O mighty Aüm.[153]
Rise, love, from off the Tree
Of Good and Evil, we
Have eat, and knowing see
Shadow and gnome.

Thy lips grow white and cold,
My kisses wild and bold
As nights are chill:
The fleecy clouds of gold
Are in black thunder rolled,
Foreboding ill.
No star, no sun, no moon,
No dawn, no morn, no noon—
All gone. Life's mystic rune,
In death is still.

Awake, my love, for we
Sought love unbound and free
Through hate and ire.
Now, through the clouds we see
The being of To Be,
Midst flame and fire.
Enveloped in a kiss—
One Self, one God, 'tis this—
Knowledge, past woe or bliss,
And past desire.

[153] Aüm or Om signifies the holy and ineffable wisdom of Brahman, who is "*na asad, na u sad*," neither not-being nor yet being.

"There no sun shines, no moon, nor glimmering star,
Nor yonder lightning, the fire of earth is quenched;
From him, who alone shines, all else borrows its brightness,
The whole world bursts into splendour at his shining."
Kâthaka Vpanishad. 5. 15 [original note]

Fuller appears to be quoting from Paul Deussen, *The Philosophy of the Upanishads* (Edinburgh: T. & T. Clark, 1906), 137. This verse is also quoted in Fuller, *Star in the West*, 208.

To live one moment bright,
Then perish in the night
Without a morn:
The sun in all his might
Is but a speck of light
Through gates of horn.
There is no sun, no day,
No night, no starry way.
No change, no death; for aye
Our love is born.

Both echo, and both call;
Both player and both ball,
To onward roll:
The smallest of the small,
The great—the boundless all—
Both start and goal.
O Power without a name,
We from thy glory came
A spark as from a flame:
O mighty Whole.

Chill moment in our life,
As flash of sun-kissed knife
O mystic Yod.[154]
Infuriate whirls the strife,
Death's drum, Life's singing fife;
Thy flaming rod
Falls, 'midst the lightning's flash,
The thunder's roar, the crash
Of systems as they dash
Back to their God.

[154] Yod, is the Y, I, or J of the Hebrew alphabet, the iota of the Greeks. Its mystic number is 10, which is symbolic of the "All complete," the "Fully accomplished." The Pythagoreans called it Deity, Heaven, Eternity, and Sun. It has also been called "The fountain of eternal nature." The ten Sephiroth and the mystical relationship between the ten numerals and Aüm may also be noted [original note].

In name Ineffable,
The same Inscrutable
As was, and is.
Unknown, Unknowable,
The All perdurable,
Eternal bliss.
Kephra, of morning bright;
Ra, Lord of noon and might;
Turn, welcomer of night:[155]
Mystic Isis.

Trust and Prey[156]

J. F. C. F.

Cleanliness cometh next to Godliness, so Messrs. Lever Brothers[157] must be very nigh to him who washeth away the sins of the world. Once Christians used to sing, "Wash me in thy precious blood, and take my sins away."[158] Those were the good old days of wheels and blood; but times are changing, and in these days of Lever and Sud, many followers of the Lamb, without spot or blemish, are now yelling themselves hoarse with that beautiful hymn, "Don't wash me in thy precious sud, nor take my sin away."

[155] These three Gods symbolize the three positions of the sun's course in the vault of the skies. In the Turin papyrus it is said: "I am Khepra in the morning, Râ at noon, Tûm in the evening" [original note]. The Turin papyrus alluded to here—published as Willem Pleyte and Francesco Rossi, *Papyrus de Turin*, 2 vols. (Leiden, The Netherlands: E. J. Brill, 1869–1876)—appears with a translation matching Fuller's quotation in Alfred Wiedemann, *Religion of the Ancient Egyptians* (London: H. Grevel, 1897), 57.

[156] *Agnostic Journal* 59, no. 19 (November 10, 1906): 289–290.

[157] Lever Brothers was a British soap-manufacturing empire founded in 1885 by brothers William and James Lever, based on a new process invented by chemist William Watson. By 1900, the company had subsidiaries worldwide.

[158] This popular hymn—sometimes identified as "The Pilgrim's Song" or sometimes simply prefaced with "The time is short"—begins with the words:

A few more years shall roll,
A few more seasons come,
And we shall be with those that rest
Asleep within the tomb.
Then, O my Lord, prepare
My soul for that great day;
O wash me in Thy precious blood,
And take my sins away.

Having carefully read the Bible, from Berashith to Amen, I find no less than one hundred "Trusts," and over half that number of "Preys," yet, curious to say, no single mention of Soap. Such Trusts and Preys, however, are sufficient to justify my title; but are they sufficient to justify—

Dr. Allen, Bishop of Shrewsbury;
The Rev. Canon R. J. Livingstone, of Shrewsbury;
The Ven. Archdeacon Shears, of Stafford;
The Rev. Canon French, of Liverpool;
The Rev. Canon Bennett, of Exmouth;
Dr. A. Maclaren, of Manchester;
The Rev. F. H. Wales, of Altrincham;
The Rev. F. Ellstow, of Faversham;
The Rev. W. Earle, of Rugby;
The Rev. C. D. Snell, of Sevenoaks;
The Rev. E. C. Lowndes, of Chester,[159]

holding shares in any concern whatever—let alone a soap trust which has attempted to reduce the pound by an ounce, and which underpays its workers?

"The young girls and young men receive less than the average throughout the trade, and adult skilled work is paid twenty-five per cent. less than at Messrs. Price's, just across the road."[160]

This twenty-five per cent. short wages goes to increase the income of the above gentlemen, who bray all their lives, "Blessed be ye poor." This is certainly one way of keeping the "blessed poor" poor; yet, whether it is the best method of rendering them "blessed," is quite another question. I have heard of young girls folding sheets of Bible pages by day for a modicum which would scarcely keep a healthy cat in "lights," and by night folding up their chastity for a shilling. On the work of these prostitutes have the Hottentots and Tahetians been brutalized, debauched and exterminated. On the gold of the harlot hath the Church of Christ thriven, and grown fat and kicking. "Blessed be ye poor," and some loathsome creature, eaten with disease, soulless and rotten, plunges over London Bridge. "Blessed be ye poor," and a drunken Hottentot sodden on "Cape smoke," ape-like, jibbering, crawls to his hut. "Blessed be ye poor," and the Bishop of Shrewsbury holds shares in a

[159] *Daily Mirror*, Oct. 25, '06 [original note].
[160] Ibid. [original note]. Messrs. Price & Co. were the chief manufacturers of glycerin in England. Their line included candles and various soaps.

Soap Trust; but this is not all, for he holds shares in the most execrable Trust that has ever cursed this planet—the Trust of the Christian Church; the monopoly of the Heart.

Once the Church monopolized every mortal and immortal thing—body and soul, mind and heart, gold, silver, power, estate, churches, temples, prisons, brothels, barracks, the home, duchies, kingdoms, empires, continents, the World, yea, Heaven and even Hell itself! She monopolized everything, from the wage of a harlot to the crown of an Empire; she preyed, and she preyed, and she preyed, whilst man trusted her; and, should he cease to trust, then, in his turn, he was trussed like a fowl on a spit, just to show the world that either Mary or Elizabeth, or whoever was the Lever of the day, could wash souls, whether bodies liked it or not.

The Church, which, on one side, could produce such men as St. Augustine and St. Francis, could, on the other, produce a Calvin and a Luther. Whatever may be said of the old saints, they were men of the Word. Read the Confessions of St. Augustine, or, better still, that sublime little work, the Fioretti of St. Francis, penned by an unknown hand, in the dim days of the thirteenth century. Who, from the above list of clergy (a Bishop, an Archdeacon, a Canon, a Reverend)—"Faugh! bring me an ounce of civet, good apothecary, to drown the stench of these disgusting creatures!"—who among the above can compare to Brother Bernard, who, when he heard St. Francis preaching, "Behold, the counsel that Christ giveth us, come, then, and fulfil that which thou hast heard, and blessed be our Lord Jesu Christ, who hath deigned to shew forth his own life in the holy Gospel," went out and sold all that he had—and he was very rich?

Who, now, among all the Bible-banging pulpiteers, of church or chapel—Vaughans, Ingrams, Torreys, and *autre canaille*[161]—who rail at the society their Church has manured for nearly two thousand years have uttered such sublime words as St. Francis did to his little sisters, the birds? Not one. The first shuffle cards, the second trashy novels, and the third brimstone and treacle; and St. Francis: "My little sisters, the birds, much bounden are ye [unto God, your Creator, and always in every place ought ye] to praise Him, for that he hath given you liberty to fly about everywhere, and hath also given you double and triple raiment; moreover, He preserved your seed in the ark of Noah, that your race might not perish out of the world; still more are ye beholden to Him for the element of air which He hath appointed for you; beyond all this, ye sow not, neither do you reap; and God feedeth you, and

161 French, "other blackguards."

giveth you the streams and fountains for your drink, the mountains and the valleys for your refuge, and the high trees whereon to make your nests; and because ye know not how to spin or sew, God clotheth you, you and your children; wherefore, your Creator loveth you much, seeing that He hath bestowed upon you so many benefits; and, therefore, my little sisters, beware of the sin of ingratitude, and study always to give praises unto God."[162]

This, indeed, was a follower of Christ; no gaitered bishop, or silk-hatted canon; bare-headed and bare-foot, without scrip or purse, he followed in the footsteps of his master. He possessed no money to invest in Soap. I doubt me much if he had wherewith to buy himself a single cake. The cold waters of the mountains were his bath, a wayside stone his pillow, and the stars were his canopy. It may be an allegory, but St. Francis is said to have fasted forty days, like his Saviour; but it was no allegory when, to-day, I saw a reverend Father in God entering Simpson's, in the Strand, to pay half-a-crown for two slices of beef and a potato; neither was it when I saw yet a second reverend gentleman step out of a first-class carriage at Victoria Station.

Christ, the Son of God, their divine Master, to whom allegiance had been sworn by these two modern Christians, would have begged for scraps outside Lockhart's, and would have tramped miles to avoid taking a penny 'bus.

A man who sells canned workman as potted ham is liable to become incarcerated in a jail; but a man (*sic*) who sells canned cant as Christ is always eligible to be enthroned at Canterbury. A Trade Trust is smashable, but a Religious Trust is only damnable. Year in, year out, Sunday after Sunday, we hear thundered from the pulpit, Lazarus and Dives, the camel and the needle's eye, Christ and Nicodemus, and the blessings of poverty; yet those who stand in the very rostrum, and beat the drum ecclesiastic only do so for gold. Counting their coins with Scrooge, they invest them in the most profitable Corner, and put their trust in God; irrespective as to whether the workers earn their bread in the gutter, or end in the Lock Hospital.[163]

For such Christians who daily drive the rusty spear of hypocrisy into the quivering flank of their Saviour; for such Christians who hourly trust and prey, I have no words to convey my contempt. Serving God and Mammon, in the words of St. Paul, they are those "Whose end is destruction, whose God is their belly, and whose glory is in their shame, who mind earthly things." They are the vermin of the Heart, the very lice of the Spirit, who trust and prey.

[162] This is the "Sermon to the Birds" traditionally attributed to Saint Francis of Assisi (1182–1226).
[163] Founded in 1747, London's Lock Hospital was the first clinic for sexually transmitted diseases, particularly syphilis.

Rejected Sonnets[164]

Victor B. Neuburg

ANIMA ABITURA[165]

How stern and strong the sense that still doth brood;
Grief's heavy-lidded, luminous, clouded eyes
In pain and wonder half materialise
From out the dark the spirit that is woo'd
By silence from the world's deep solitude;
As a dank vapour from the earth doth rise
Death's presence, while the living angel flies
Invisibly downward o'er the house imbued

Now faintlier with the elemental strife.
Silence and light make him who passes mute;
No word he knows, no word is his to say,
But, hovering o'er the broken house of life,
He sees its ruins in the light of day,
And lo! the flower of life in death hath root.

JAMES THOMSON [B.V.][166]

Singer of Dürer's matchless Queen of Pain,
Incomparable song was thine to pour
Into thy starless heaven; let them adore
The sunshine who have never known blind rain
And stormy skies; who never loved in vain
Know not the enchanted land of Nevermore
Where darkness broods in sorrow, and the roar
Breaks louder on the strand of life's dark[167] main.

164 *Agnostic Journal* 59, no. 21 (November 24, 1906): 332.

165 Reprinted in *A Green Garland*, along with "Tannhäuser," as "Two Sonnets." The Latin phrase in the title refers to "the soul about to depart."

166 Reprinted in *A Green Garland*, along with the following two poems—"Herrick" and "Burns"—under the collective title "Three Singers." Scottish poet James Thomson (1834–1882) is best known for his long poem *The City of Dreadful Night* (1874), which resolves in its final canto around the image of Albrecht Dürer's *Melencolia I*. Thomas wrote under the pseudonym Bysshe Vanolis, which is taken from the names of the poets Percy Bysshe Shelley and Novalis.

167 This word is "sad" in *A Green Garland*.

Son of the luminous Dark, intensest woe
Loosened thy tongue; thy drooping lips have paid
The debt of agony that thou did'st owe
To the sad earth that bore thee: thou art laid
Within her bosom. Be thou not afraid,—
Not any pain is thine e'er more to know.[168]

Herrick[169]

Lyrist light-lipped, half Pagan, half devout,
With smiling scholar-eyes, the centuries
Bear thy bright notes upon the fragrant breeze;
Thou standest yet thy garden's gate without,—
Fair Julia, sweet Bianca, swell the rout
Of maidens laughing 'neath green summer-trees;
Gentle Perilia will thy hands swift seize,
In mirthful grace leading thee all about.

The sweet-browed Horace lived again in thee;—
Fair Devon held the famous Sabine farm:
Thy mellow'd singing lends the minstrelsy
Of England's golden age a silver charm,—
Thy lips the easy notes still yielding free,
A laughing English maiden on each arm.

[168] Nay, but thou art arisen, and dost brood
In happy wonder o'er the railing earth,
Thine eyes alight with pity and with mirth
Within thy heaven's joyous solitude,
Whence earth and all her wonders may be viewed,
In all their littleness and all their girth
Passing the gates or death, the gates of birth:
Wilt thou again be tempted to intrude?
Methinks some future day shall see thee born
Purged of thy halo dark, with sunlit eyes,
And lips Apollo symbol'd to the morn,—
Some happier planet ruling in thy skies,
And, save for thy forgetting, yet more wise
Thou when thou passèd'st onward so forlorn.
Psyche [original note]

The two verses in this footnote were omitted when the poem was reprinted in *A Green Garland*.

[169] Reprinted in *A Green Garland* as part of the collection "Three Singers." English cleric-poet Robert Herrick (1591–1674) is known for his collection *Hesperides*, whose "To the Virgins, to Make Much of Time" begins with the immortal words "Gather ye rosebuds while ye may."

Burns[170]

The rapturous sense of full-strung youth, the glow
Of lyric ardour and of love untamed
Within thy swelling bosom rose and flamed,
Now as the sun-light bright, now fierce as tow
Swift-burning; but thy golden songs' swift flow
Brought quenching to thy fire; well wast thou named,
Singer of love: wherefore should'st thou he blamed,
Whom Nature freely dower'd with joy and woe

More keen than other men's? Who shall repine
If that thou burnéd'st thy fierce youth away?
Thy love is ours, thy melody divine.
Phœbus, Apollo, in love's halls did play,
And lo! as Mercury thou madest thine
His lyre, and fled'st to Scotia 'fore the day.

Russia in Tumultu[171]

The curtain lifts a moment, when the wind
Rages too fiercely, and the swirling dust
Raised by the wanton stirring of wild lust
And fearful up-pent passion makes men blind
To the fierce battles that are waged behind;
With aching brows we gaze, with shattered trust
Menarch and helot seeing hellward thrust,
In hate and bitter jest their arms entwined.

Raucous and shrill, the warning voice of Doom
Urges them on impartial as they sway

[170] Reprinted in *A Green Garland* as part of the collection "Three Singers." Poet and lyricist Robert Burns (1759–1796) is celebrated as the national poet of Scotland for writing in the Scots language or dialect and for preserving and adapting folk songs from across the nation, including "Auld Lang Syne."

[171] The Revolution of 1905 was a period of intense political and social turmoil throughout Russia, from January 1905 to June 1907. This poem appeared in the November *Agnostic Journal* in the midst of this tumultuous period.

Hot-breathed, oblivious, o'er the reeking fume
Of wasted blood and war-compounded clay:
The mocking brilliance of the rising day
Shall rise upon a grave,—the grave of whom?

TÄNNHAUSER

The Pilgrims' Chorus[172]

Dim-drawn and throbbing is the passioned lyre,
Tuned to the theme eternal, love in pain,
Wild sense of life and love at war in vain,
Far-parted by the anguish of white fire;
The spirit's sense drugged in a clinging mire
Of slime and agony,—hot hands insane
Letting the fabled gold slip, slip like rain
Through fingers shaken by infinite desire,—

Master! Thou hast bewitched us; thou art wise,
But not in earthly wisdom: cease, O cease
To bear[173] *this shameful thing before our eyes.*
Give thou the fearsome stream its last release.
In pain unspeakable the throbbing dies,
And, lost in deathless passion, findeth peace.

Saladin: In Memoriam[174]

Victor B. Neuburg

THE *Agnostic Journal* has lost its Editor; the world has lost one of its most strenuous fighters for freedom. Saladin was one of those Titans who strike off the world's fetters while she sleeps.

[172] Reprinted in *A Green Garland*, along with "Anima Abitura," as "Two Sonnets." The "Chor der Pilger," or "Pilgrims' Chorus," from Richard Wagner's opera *Tannhäuser* (1845) is sung by the pilgrims as they travel to Rome seeking penance. Crowley had published a poetic adaptation of this opera four years previously. See Aleister Crowley, *Tannhäuser: A Story for All Time* (London: Kegan Paul, Trench, Trübner, 1902). Given Wagner's immense popularity at the time, he is a logical source of inspiration among poets.

[173] The errata slip to *A Green Garland* indicates that this word should be "bare."

[174] *Agnostic Journal* 59, no. 24 (December 15, 1906): 372–373.

Saladin's creed was one that underlies every religion in the world; the supreme reality underlying all forms drew him to itself, but so many barriers interposed that his soul was bruised in the attempted passage, and he drew back to devote his life to demolishing one of the greatest of those barriers.

Saladin slashed and hewed at the grossly-materalised symbols that form the idols of the unthinking; the popular and absurd gods knew no mercy from him; he was not of a nature to easily brook compromise; he had but to perceive a lie to attack it with all his force. If this passion for truth be the predominant element in a man's character, he will—granted the possession of intellect—be pre-eminently a man and a leader of men.

In Saladin that intellect was assuredly not lacking, and the result is that we who mourn him mourn at once a personal friend of marvellous magnetism and charm, and a man who devoted his life to an heroic effort to liberate the world's mind. Saladin, in a word, brought a magnificent brain garnished with high culture, and a faithful and magnanimous nature, as an offering upon the twin altars of Truth and Freedom. And the sacrifice was not in vain.

Before Saladin's influence can be accurately gauged, it will, of course, need the perspective that is always and infallibly lent by Time. But even now, when his weary body has been but just cast off and laid within the breast of the kindly mother-earth that bore him, it may be said with absolute certainty that that influence will be felt throughout the coming centuries. In that day when intellectual freedom shall be part of man's birthright, Saladin will come into his own, within the hearts of men.

So strong and idiosyncratic a personality as the dead Chief's could, in the nature of things, have no peer, and for this reason he leaves no successor,—"His soul was like a Star, and dwelt apart."[175] Little men leave places that may easily be filled, and it is a proof of Saladin's greatness, that—as was said of the hero of the Scandinavian legend—no hand can wield his gigantic battle-axe. Truly was Saladin of the royal stock, and his successor is not yet known.

In happier times, Saladin would have been a revered and happy member of some more positive school of thought than that with which he identified himself, and whose acknowledged Chief he was. Such a man as he, born in our superstition-cursed day, could but be a leader out of the paths of falsity, and a light-bearer through the mists of folly. This work was necessary,

[175] William Wordsworth, "London 1802," in *Poems, in Two Volumes* (London: Longman, Hurst, Rees, and Orme, 1807), 140, line 9. Wordsworth's original, which eulogizes John Milton, reads "Thy soul."

but 1, for one, cannot help regretting that he, who possessed a mind at once reverent and critical, a heart both fiery and tender, a wide and thorough academic knowledge, and, above all, the artist's love of perfection of form, should not have been devoted to some more constructive system than that to which his life was given.

For me, as it must be for all who knew the Chief personally, and, in a lesser degree, for those who knew him only through his writings, a light has gone out of life; and there is sadness in my heart when I recollect that I shall never again hold that firm hand in my own, shall never again, in the flesh, see the brave, kind eyes flash their indignation or their humour; shall never again hear that sympathetic voice speak with the passion of enthusiasm on life and literature.

It is not for me, an outsider, to speak of the dead man's domestic life. But I want to mention the unselfishness and ever-gentle devotion of his wife, who must indeed have suffered often and greatly during the closing years of her husband's life; she never complained, and I know that this thought must be her greatest solace until she joins Saladin in that country whereof he is now an inhabitant. The Chief—as I love to call him—knew many sorrows; they saddened him infinitely, they embittered him not at all, and I feel, in saying this, that I am paying the greatest tribute to the heart of Saladin that could be paid.

I think the name of Saladin will never die from the hearts of us who knew him, and I think, further, that I may say that those who come after us will worthily bear in their hearts a spark that will leap into a flame at the mention of the Chief's name.

I cannot say "The Chief is dead; long live the Chief!" as could be said of a mere hereditary ruler. Saladin was too great for that. No "appointment" can ever adequately replace him we have lost. We have to take them as they come; they can never he made.

No one, I think, will accuse me of egotism if I mention here what I, personally, owe to Saladin. He was my only discriminative critic at a time when I was absolutely unknown, and, along with his appreciation, he gave me the hospitality of the columns of his paper. What this means to a writer of verse I need not say. I will say but this: that I should never have been able to give him an adequate return for his encouragement, even had he outlived me.

For the rest, I feel that I have been voicing the sentiments of the contributors to, and readers of, the *Agnostic Journal*, and 1 wish to conclude this incomplete and inadequate notice with the name of the great man who forms the subject of it—Saladin, William Stewart Ross.

Saladin[176]

J. F. C. F.

"To-day the heart leaps o'er the land and the sea
To a God's natal manger in Far Galilee;
Oh, then, to the hungry one open thy door,
And be, like that God, a friend of the poor;
For thy brother lies low, in this merry Yule-tide,
With the thorns on his brow, and the spear in his side;
And thy sister's struck down on the pitiless sands
With the iron nails struck through her feet and her hands.
Think not what she is, but what she has been,
For that God was a God to the soiled Magdalene.
And while the high impulse your human heart warms,
Leap forward and take the whole race in your arms."[177]

Heart of hearts! O great and radiant spirit, thou hast left us; Eros hath taken thee, and no man knoweth whither thou hast gone. Far, far away across the dark waters of death; far into that mystic land untrod by mortal foot, with him whose ever-youthful hand unveils the living, and shrouds the dead. No pale and fearful gnome stood by thy side, as the light of the stars sank back into the gloom of death; but the form of Love—Eros! Christ of the ages, Saviour and Preserver, Torch-bearer of life, who lighteth us from the darkness of the womb, through the labyrinthine mysteries of this world, back into the mystic depths of Eternity,

Twenty-four years gone by, since where I stood a few days ago mourning Saladin, Saladin himself stood sorrowing over the tiny coffin of a blue-eyed and yellow-haired little boy—his son: and prophetically he then wrote regarding that tearful day: "At what time I have to join my Bruno in that upper layer of yellow gravel I cannot tell; but men who elect to lead a forlorn hope do not usually live to a ripe old age."[178] His prophesy has now been fulfilled.

176 *Agnostic Journal* 59, no. 26 (December 29, 1906): 401–402.

177 Saladin: "Song of Winter," Christmas, 1884 [original note]. These are the closing lines from William Stewart Ross, "Song of Winter (On the Merry Birthday of the Man of Sorrows, 1884)," in *Isaure and Other Poems* (London: W. Stewart, n.d.), 84–88.

178 Saladin [William Stewart Ross], *From the Valley of the Shadow of Death* (London: W. Stewart, 1887?), 1.

Where lieth Pythagoras or Hermes? Where is the sacred spot where Orpheus or Christ made one with Mother Earth? No man knoweth, none can tell. Dust to dust, ashes to ashes, and the atoms of our atomy are, in the space of a few years, cast back into the æons from whence they sprang, to blush again once more perchance in the petal of a rose, or peradventure to throb 'twixt the kiss of two lovers' lips. Yet something lives on mystically, directing, guiding, and sustaining us, urging us on, unnamed and unnameable, the subtle spirit of a noble life well spent. Let the scoffer hold his peace. There, as the cold wind of December sang dirge among the memorials of the dead, there at my feet lay the stark form of a great adept, in the alembic of whose heart and through the athanor of whose affliction had been revealed the stone of the wise: that sparkling gem called—"Truth."

> "Let us begin and carry up this corpse,
> Singing together.
> Leave we the common crofts, the vulgar thorpes
> Each to its tether,
> Sleeping safe in the bosom of the plain,
> Cared for till cock-crow:
> Look out if yonder be not day again
> Rimming the rock-row!"[179]

"Know or doubt." These two words sum up the creed of the Agnostic; but whether they sum up the life of Saladin I know not, neither do I care; for his nature seems to me to belong to those which find no expression in words. One of the few amongst the many; he was Saladin, Saladin only, Saladin and nothing more.

"He worked with no party," it has been said, and, also, "No party could work with him." Hail, Saladin! Perceval or Gareth neither worked with a party; bravely with lance in rest they rode away into the night of the world; unfettered by the petty ways of sects, and the simple doings of factions.

> "I have churned into foam their gioes and ferries,
> And heaved the wild wave o'er the ridge of their skerries
> And yelled on the desolate shores of Lofoden
> The war-cry of storms in the region of Odin."[180]

[179] Robert Browning: "A Grammarian's Funeral" [original note].
[180] Ross, "Song of Winter," lines 11–14.

So wrote Saladin twenty-two years ago, on the merry birthday of the man of sorrows.

> "And the bolt of the lightning glared red in the gloom,
> And showed the berserker his fathomless tomb."[181]

—and perhaps his fame.

If I had, however, to sum up Saladin's life in one word, I should choose "WORK."

For thirty years and more his keen sword was drawn in the cause of love, freedom, and justice; for thirty long years he drove its flashing blade through malice, cruelty, and lie. Toiling, ever toiling without rest, till the early hours of the dawn grew old and died away in the chime of the midnight bell. The great marvel is that he lived so long, not that he died whilst yet in middle age.

Five days before his death I saw him for the last time. Ill and worn he lay in bed still working, about him were littered proof-sheets for the forthcoming copy of this *Journal*, and I have since been told, that up to his last day, almost the last hour, he worked on and on.

> " 'Now, master, take a little rest!'—not he!
>   Caution redoubled,
> Step two abreast, the way winds narrowly!)
>   Not a whit troubled
> Back to his studies, fresher than at first,
>   Fierce as a dragon
> He (soul-hydroptic with a sacred thirst)
>   Sucked at the flagon."[182]

As I sat by his side, he told me how he had given up the whole of his life for the welfare of the *Journal* he so dearly loved, and spoke to me about old friends, both living and dead, and how curious it was that so many of the former, quite unaware of his illness, had, nevertheless, visited him of late:— "There is some close relationship," he said, "between those hearts that are in tune," then he paused, "a close affinity," he added, "some subtle quality the ordinary person does not possess." And Saladin was right, he knew best as to what he said, what he meant and felt, in spite of those puritanic Freethinkers,

181 Ross, "Song of Winter," lines 21–22.
182 Robert Browning: "A Grammarian's Funeral" [original note].

who find but blasphemy in the mysteries of life, and the ridiculous in the mysteries of death; to whom the sacred is profane, and the divine inane; cast these "certain" men into the balance of Rhadamanthus, weigh them, O Minos, measure them, Aeacus! And their weight? The weight of Calvin, of Knox, and of Zwingli.[183]

> "He would not discount life, as fools do here,
> Paid by instalment.
> He ventured neck or nothing—heaven's success
> Found, or earth's failure:
> 'Wilt thou trust death or not?' He answered, 'Yes':
> 'Hence with life's pale lure!'
> That low man seeks a little thing to do,
> Sees it and does it:
> This high man, with a great thing to pursue,
> Dies ere he knows it.
> That low man goes on adding one to one,
> His hundred's soon hit:
> This high man, aiming at a million,
> Misses an unit."[184]

Such also was this high man, this warrior of Truth, knight of the round table of Eternity, at which board sit the chosen great, those few beings who realize the divine in their manhood, those few elect who sit with Chaos, and Cosmos, and Chronos, who, as the Brahmin would say: Have realized their end, and have been made one with the Infinite.

"The Light shineth in the Darkness, and the Darkness comprehendeth it not."[185] So with Saladin. Perhaps one of the most intensely religious men who have ever lived, he has ever been mistaken by the multitude. He chivalrously attacked evil, and more particularly evil under the guise of good. He publicly fought for over thirty years the corruptions of dogmatic Christianity; he fought the Christian Church and the erroneous conceptions it held regarding its founder, not the founder himself; and even then, when he had

[183] Rhadamanthus, Minos, and Aeacus were the three underworld demigods and judges of the dead. John Calvin (1509–1564), John Knox (1513–1572), and Huldrych Zwingli (1484–1531) were Reformation leaders in their respective countries of England, Scotland, and Switzerland.
[184] Robert Browning: "A Grammarian's Funeral" [original note].
[185] John 1:4–5.

struck down his foe, with tears he would wash the wounds which his arrows had made.

His indeed was a noble soul, a great and pure spirit: few are his equals; few, few, very very few have ever surpassed him.

> "Here's the top-peak; the multitude below
> Live, for they can, there:
> This man decided not to Live but Know—
> Bury this man there?
> Here—here's his place, where meteors shoot, clouds form,
> Lightnings are loosened,
> Stars come and go! Let joy break with the storm,
> Peace let the dew send!
> Lofty designs must close in like effects:
> Loftily lying,
> Leave him—still loftier than the world suspects,
> Living and dying."[186]

After Agnosticism[187]

Aleister Crowley

Allow me to introduce myself as the original Irishman whose first question on landing at New York was, "Is there a Government in this country?" and on being told "Yes," instantly replied, "Them I'm agin it." For after some years of consistent Agnosticism, being at last asked to contribute to an Agnostic organ, for the life of me I can think of nothing better than to attack my hosts! Insidious cuckoo! Ungrateful Banyan! My shame drives me to Semitic analogy, and I sadly reflect that if I had been Balaam, I should not have needed an ass other than myself to tell me to do the precise contrary of what is expected of me.

For this is my position; while the postulates of Agnosticism are in one sense eternal, I believe that the conclusions of Agnosticism are daily to be pushed back. We know our ignorance; with that fact we are twitted by those who do not know enough to understand even what we mean when we say

[186] Robert Browning: "A Grammarian's Funeral" [original note].

[187] Originally written *c.* 1903–1904, Crowley added the text of this essay as a new endnote to *The Sword of Song* in *The Works of Aleister Crowley* (Foyers, UK: SPRT, 1907), 2:206–208.

so; but the limits of knowledge, slowly receding, yet never so far as to permit us to unveil the awful and impenetrable adytum of consciousness, or that of matter, must one day be suddenly widened by the forging of a new weapon.

Huxley and Tyndall[188] have prophesied this before I was born; sometimes in vague language, once or twice clearly enough; to me it is a source of the utmost concern that their successors should not always see eye to eye with them in this respect.

Professor Ray Lankester,[189] in crushing the unhappy theists of the recent *Times* controversy, does not hesitate to say that Science "can never" throw any light on certain mysteries.

Even the theist is justified in retorting that Science, if this be so, may as well be discarded; for these are problems which must ever intrude upon the human mind—upon the mind of the scientist most of all.

To dismiss them by an act of will is at once heroic and puerile: courage is as necessary to progress as any quality that we possess; and as courage is in either case required, the courage of ignorance (necessarily sterile, though wanted badly enough while our garden was choked by theological weeds) is less desirable than the courage which embarks on the always desperate philosophical problem.

Time and again, in the history of Science, a period has arrived when, gorged with facts, she has sunk into a lethargy of reflection accompanied by appalling nightmares in the shape of impossible theories. Such a nightmare now rides us; once again philosophy has said its last word, and arrived at a deadlock. Aristotle, in reducing to the fundamental contradictions-in-terms which they involved the figments of the Pythagoreans, the Eleatics, the Platonists, the Pyrrhonists; Kant, in his *reductio ad absurdum* of the Thomists, the Scotists, the Wolffians,—all the warring brood, alike only in the inability to reconcile the ultimate antinomies of a cosmogony only grosser for its pinchbeck spirituality; have, I take it, found their modern parallel in the ghastly laughter of Herbert Spencer, as fleshed upon the corpses of Berkeley and the Idealists from Fichte and Hartmann to Laotze and Trendelenburg[190]

[188] Crowley cites biologist Thomas Henry Huxley throughout *Sword of Song*, especially in "Science and Buddhism." Irish physicist John Tyndall (1820–1893) was a popularizer of science and a vocal supporter of Darwin and Huxley.

[189] British zoologist Sir Edwin Ray Lankester (1847–1929) was director of the British Museum of Natural History at the time when this was written.

[190] British philosopher Herbert Spencer (1820–1903) was the father of Social Darwinism. German philosopher Johann Gottlieb Fichte (1762–1814) proposed an "infinite ego" underlying the self and world, along with the existence of the finite ego (subject) and the nonego (object). German philosopher Karl Robert Eduard von Hartmann (1842–1906) laid the foundation for psychology with his

he drives the reeking fangs of his imagination into the palpitating vitals of his own grim masterpiece of reconcilement, self-deluded and yet self-conscious of its own delusion.

History affirms that such a deadlock is invariably the prelude to a new enlightenment: by such steps we have advanced, by such we shall advance. The "horror of great darkness" which is scepticism must ever by broken by some heroic master-soul, intolerant of the cosmic agony.

We then await his dawn.

May I go one step further, and lift up my voice and prophesy? I would indicate the direction in which this darkness must break. Evolutionists will remember that nature cannot rest. Nor can society. Still less the brain of man.

"Audax omnia perpeti

Gens humana ruit per vetitum nefas."[191]

We have destroyed the meaning of vetitum nefas and are in no fear of an imaginary cohort of ills and terrors. Having perfected one weapon, reason, and found it destructive to all falsehood, we have been (some of us) a little apt to go out to fight with no other weapon. "FitzJames's blade was sword and shield,"[192] and that served him against the murderous bludgeon-sword of the ruffianly Highlander he happened to meet; but he would have fared ill had he called a Western Sheriff a liar, or gone off Boer-sticking on Spion Kop.

Reason has done its utmost; theory has glutted us, and the motion of the ship is a little trying; mixed metaphor—excellent in a short essay like this—is no panacea for all mental infirmities; we must seek another guide. All the facts science has so busily collected, varied as they seem to be, are in reality all of the same kind. If we are to have one salient fact, a fact for a real advance, it must be a fact of a different *order*.

Have we such a fact to hand? We have.

First, what do we mean by a fact of a different order? Let me take an example; the most impossible being the best for our purpose. The Spiritualists, let us suppose, go mad and begin to talk sense. (I can only imagine that such

book *Philosophie des Unbewussten*. See Karl Robert Eduard von Hartmann, *The Philosophy of the Unconscious*, Berlin, 1869). He attempted, in his works, to unite Hegel's "idea" with Schopenhauer's "will." By contrast, German philosopher Rudolf Hermann Lotze (1817–1881) was a critic of Hegel's ideological pantheism. Likewise, German philosopher Friedrich Adolf Trendelenburg (1802–1872) criticized Hegel and Kant in favor of Plato and Aristotle.

191 Horace, *Odes*, I. 3 [original note]. In Latin, "The human race, afraid of nothing, rushes through every unspeakable crime." Horace, *Carmina*, bk. 1, poem 3, line 25.

192 Scott, *The Lady of the Lake* [original note]. Sir Walter Scott's (1771–1832) influential poem *The Lady of the Lake* first appeared in 1810.

would be the result.) All their "facts" are proved. We prove a world of spirits, the existence of God, the immortality of the soul, etc. But, with all that, we are not really one step advanced into the heart of the inquiry which lies at the heart of philosophy, "What *is* anything?"

I see a cat.

Dr. Johnson says it is a cat.

Berkeley says it is a group of sensations.[193]

Sankharacarya says it is an illusion, an incarnation, or God, according to the hat he has got on, and is talking through.

Spencer says it is a mode of the unknowable.[194]

But none of them seriously doubt the fact that I exist; that a cat exists; that one sees the other. All—bar Johnson—hint—but oh! how dimly!—at what I now know to be—*true!*—no, not necessarily true, but *nearer the truth*. Huxley goes deeper in his demolition of Descartes. With him, "I see a cat," proves "something called consciousness exists." He denies the assertion of duality; he has no datum to assert the denial of duality. I have.

Consciousness, as we know it, has one essential quality: the opposition of subject and object. Reason has attacked this and secured that complete and barren victory of convincing without producing conviction.[195] It has one quality apparently not essential, that of exceeding impermanence. If we examine what we call steady thought, we shall find that its rate of change is in reality inconceivably swift. To consider it, to watch it, is bewildering, and to some people becomes intensely terrifying. It is as if the solid earth were suddenly swept away from under one, and there were some dread awakening in outer space amid the rush of incessant meteors—lost in the void.

All this is old knowledge; but who has taken steps to alter it? The answer is forbidding: truth compels me to say, the mystics of all lands.

Their endeavour has been to slow the rate of change; their methods perfect quietude of body and mind, produced in varied and too often vicious

[193] In *A New Theory of Vision* (1709), Berkeley suggests that we visually judge distance by allowing one group of sensations to suggest another set with which we have experience.

[194] In his First Principles, Spencer writes, "Supposing a given manifestation of force, under a given form and given conditions, be either preceded by or succeeded by some other manifestation, it must, in all cases where the form and conditions are the same, be preceded by or succeeded by such other manifestation. Every antecedent mode of the Unknowable must have an invariable connexion, quantitative and qualitative, with that mode of the Unknowable, which we call its consequent." Herbert Spencer, *First Principles*, 2nd ed. (London: Williams and Norgate, 1867), 193.

[195] Hume, and Kant in the "Prolegomena," discuss this phenomenon unsatisfactorily.—A.C. [original note].

ways. Regularisation of the breathing is the best known formula. Their results are contemptible, we must admit; but only so because empirical. An unwarranted reverence has overlaid the watchfulness which science would have enjoined, and the result is muck and misery, the wreck of a noble study.

But what is the one fact on which all agree? The one fact whose knowledge has been since religion began the all-sufficient passport to their doubtfully-desirable company?

This: that "I see a cat" is not only an unwarrantable assumption but a lie; that the duality of consciousness ceases suddenly, once the rate of change has been sufficiently slowed down, so that, even for a few seconds, the relation of subject and object remains impregnable.

It is a circumstance of little interest to the present essayist that this annihilation of duality is associated with intense and passionless peace and delight; the fact has been a bribe to the unwary, a bait for the charlatan, a hindrance to the philosopher; let us discard it.[196]

More, though the establishment of this new estate of consciousness seems to open the door to a new world, a world where the axioms of Euclid may be absurd, and the propositions of Keynes[197] untenable, let us not fall into the error of the mystics, by supposing that in this world is necessarily a final truth, or even a certain and definite gain of knowledge.

But that a field for research is opened up no sane man may doubt. Nor may one question that the very first fact is of a nature disruptive of difficulty philosophical and reasonable; since the phenomenon does not invoke the assent of the reasoning faculty. The arguments which reason may bring to bear against it are self-destructive; reason has given consciousness the lie, but consciousness survives and smiles. Reason is a part of consciousness and can never be greater than its whole; this Spencer sees; but reason is not even any part of this new consciousness (which I, and many others, have too rarely achieved) and therefore can never touch it: this I see, and this will I hope

[196] It is this rapture which has ever been the bond between mystics of all shades; and the obstacle to any accurate observation of the phenomenon, its true causes, and so on. This must always be a stumbling-block to more impressionable minds; but there is no doubt as to the fact—it *is* a fact—and its present isolation is to be utterly deplored. May I entreat men of Science to conquer the prejudices natural to them when the justly despised ideas of mysticism are mentioned, and to attack the problem *ab initio* on the severely critical and austerely arduous lines which have distinguished their labours in other fields?—A. C. [original note].

[197] Author of a text-book on "Formal Logic" [original note]. John Neville Keynes (1852–1949) lectured on ethics at Cambridge from 1884–1911, during which time he wrote the book *Formal Logic* (1884), which Crowley would later recommend to his students.

be patent to those ardent and spiritually-minded agnostics of whom Huxley and Tyndall are for all history-time the prototypes. Know or doubt! is the alternative of highwayman Huxley! "Believe" is not to be admitted; this is fundamental; in this agnosticism can never change; this must ever command our moral as our intellectual assent.

But I assert my strong conviction that ere long we shall have done enough of what is after all the schoolmaster work of correcting the inky and ill- spent exercises of the theological dunces in that great class-room, the world; and found a little peace—while they play—in the intimate solitude of the laboratory and the passionless rapture of research—research into those very mysteries which our dunces have solved by rule of thumb; determining the nature of a bee by stamping on it, and shouting "bee"; while we patiently set to work with microscopes, and say nothing till we know, nor more than need be when we do.

But I am myself found guilty of this role of schoolmaster: I will now therefore shut the doors and retire again into the laboratory where my true life lies.

Elohim and the Number π[198]

Capt. J. F. C. Fuller

In the July number of *The Monist* I was much interested by your article "The Number π in Christian Prophecy,"[199] but I somewhat fail to see your justification in approximating π to 3 ½, or half the mystic 7. Even in primitive times the ancient astrologers and mathematicians were probably not quite so inaccurate as they are often represented.

A still more curious coincidence concerning π and Hebraic numerations, is, I believe, to be found in their word Elohim. The following, a short time ago, was pointed out by a friend of mine:

1. ELOHIM = 1 ,30 ,5 ,10 ,40 = אלהים.
2. (Strike out the zeros) = 4, 1, 5, 3, 1 .
3. Draw a magic pentacle and in scribe the figures round it as in the sketch.
4. Place a decimal point between the 3 and the 1.

[198] Paul Carus, J. F. C. Fuller, W. S. Andrews, and Wm. F. White, "Mathematical Occultism and Its Explanation: A Symposium," *Monist* 17, no. 1 (January 1907): 110–111.
[199] Paul Carus, "The Number π in Christian Prophecy," *Monist* 16, no. 3 (July 1906): 415–421.

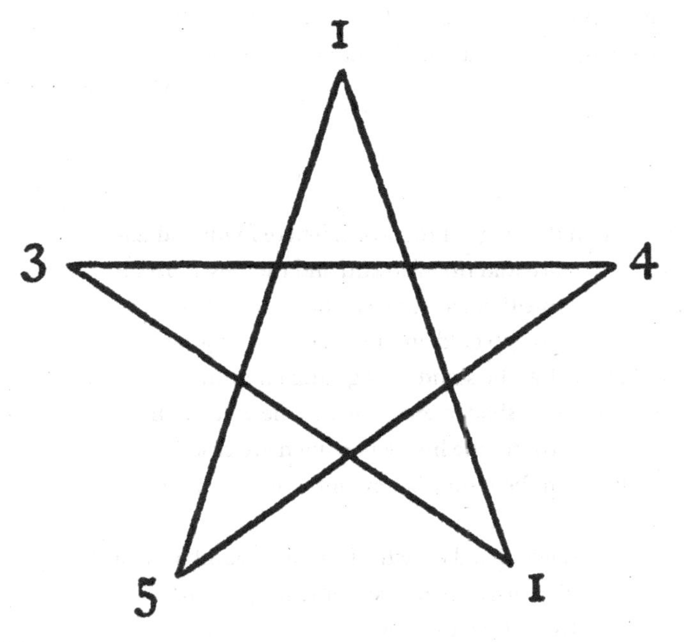

Figure A1

London, England

De Morte[200]
[In Honour of Saladin]

To R. H. Fitzpatrick

Victor B. Neuburg

Dear friend, whoever you are, here, take this kiss,
I give it especially to you—Do not forget me,
I feel like one who has done his work—I progress on,
The unknown sphere, more real than I dreamed,
more direct, darts awakening rays about me—
So long!

200 *Agnostic Journal* 60, no. 1 (January 5, 1907): 4.

Remember my words—I love you—I depart from materials,
I am as one disembodied, triumphant, dead.

—*Walt. Whitman.*[201]

I.

Upon the ridge of the world where night and day
Part, and the eastward and the westward lie
On either side the watcher, and the sky
Turns now to gold and red, and now to grey,—
There doth he stand, and gazing far away
With shaded eyes watches the vultures fly
Around the hills where men are cast to die
Beneath the moon-beams and the sun's hot ray.

And dawn and dark wheel circling round his head,
To mingle in an ever-widening sphere,
And from its centre is a fierce heat shed,
But as he stands there lights upon his ear
A pæan of the love that casts out fear,—
The tribute of the ever-living dead.

II.

Lo! He is parted from the cold dull tomb,
Our pure-eyed priest of Man, whose song arose
From out the ash of human joys and woes,
Who learned of light within the blackest gloom;
And he is passed from our dull fret and fume
Unto the sphere where speechful silence glows;
His manifold mantle shall descend on those
Who worshipped with him at the feet of Doom.

He sees the whirling world as in a dream;
He hears, but hears as one apart, afar,
As through his being flows an endless stream

[201] These are the final lines (stanza 23) of Walt Whitman's "So Long." See Walt Whitman, *Leaves of Grass* (New York: Heritage Press, 1855), 456.

Of song and light from star to furthest star,
And in his eyes unquenchable doth gleam
Unmeasured love for all that strive and are.

III.

O blest Nirvana! Let his soul forget,
Forget the fears that stung him on his way;
Now let him stand uncovered to the day
That dawns upon the night-tide of his fret;
For on his brow a crown of thorns was set,
And in his hand a broken staff there lay,
And all his body was in disarray,—
I see him in his anguish even yet.

The shell is burst; the harp's wise note is fled;
The spherèd heavens around him lie, and see!
There stands the giver of the melody
New-risen from the clay; the gold and red
Within the dawn his heart's desire have fed,
And he hath found Nirvana, and is free.

IV. Of Fame.

Blue-lighted space, and every breath a flame;
Green-crested seas wide-flecked with glittering foam;
Deep woods, of silver echoings the home,
Echoes of many a star-wreathéd name;—
And lo! a gold-eyed god enraptured came,
With tawny yellow hair that rimmed the dome
Of his fair brows that bore a jewelled comb
Beset with stars: the golden god was Fame.

And as he passed me by, I rose and gazed
Far in the shining wake of him; he turned;
A blinding moment my dull eyes I raised,
And through me throbbed his gaze that stabbed and burned,
But in his eyes came mirrored to me, dazed,
The name of him I mourned, for whom I yearned.

A god of shadows, not of mortal men,
He shuns the earth, or enters but to flee,—
Fame stays but little with humanity
That strives to draw him downward with a pen.
But his eyes healed my bleeding heart again
I might not follow, but he raised for me
A clarion-note that sounded o'er the sea,
And echoed far away, beyond my ken.

And on the heaven's brow there flashed a sign
That sudden lit the god's swift-darkening way,
And herald voices filled the air divine
With bursts of music that proclaimed the day;
The fiery flash the far horizon-line
Illumed, and merged in the sun's stronger ray.

V.

Cast back the veil before the empty shrine;
The altar fire is dead; the sun is set;
Go! I make a living altar to Regret,
And she shall bless the sacrificial wine.
The sable queen response doth lend divine,
But in her answer love and fear are met,
And from the impact there resoundeth yet
A note more tender-true, more subtly fine.

For Life and Death lie mingled; never more
Shall Death's strong arm untwine from Life's fair breast;
And Death's fierce heart is sweetness at the core,
And Life makes answer still to Death's behest:
Death's hand to Life doth beckon, Life's to Death,
Through the twain doors of ether and of breath.

VI.

Upon his body lies a flowery lyre,
It lies upon his breast with broken strings,—
The chords were sundered by his soaring wings

As he fled through,—a flame of heaven's fire.
Ah! he is the land of Heart's Desire,
    And Poesy her radiant mantle flings
    About him, as a triumph-song outrings,
And all the winds of heaven him inspire.

The portals lie before him; weep not now,
    Lest he return, nor find his heaven soon;
But see, Oblivion o'er his radiant brow
    Hath cast a light more soft than did the moon,
And all the grace that did his heart endow
    Irradiates the life behind him strewn.

Paganism and the Sense of Song

[An essay by Victor B. Neuburg, followed by three letters exchanged between J. A. Reid and the author. —RK]

Paganism and the Sense of Song[202]

Victor B. Neuburg.

PAGANISM is an attitude of mind towards Nature; it corresponds to the emotional plane, which preceded the mental in the history of mind, and hence Paganism is natural to children and savages. And inasmuch as Paganism represents a more purely natural attitude towards Nature than those that are the outcome of later and more extended culture, in it may be found the key to many "mysteries" that elude the scientific specialist and the university professor.

The sense of sound is, I think, the earliest to receive impressions from what is exquisitely called by Emerson the "Over-soul"; music is said to be the youngest of the arts, but music is sound perceived through the medium of the intellect, and it is sound perceived through the medium of the emotional nature with which I am now chiefly concerned.

[202] *Agnostic Journal* 60, no. 3 (January 19, 1907): 34–36.

The cry of the wind skirling and whistling through the trees; the plash and call of flowing water; the yearning and moaning of the sea; the patter of raindrops on sand, fell upon the ear of primitive man, and he heard, without understanding, the myriad voices of the forces of Nature. And his was the wisdom of the child—with a difference; child-likeness was mingled with human experience, and the gods came into being. Primitive man may have been wiser than he knew, for, after all, we have no certain knowledge of the beginning and ending of the scale of life; Pan may manifest where our ears are too dull to catch the notes. To the poet, in many respects a "return" to a primitive "type," the sea actually does speak, and the rain and the wind murmur secrets of the beginnings of things.

Primitive man was rather a poet than a scientist; intuitive rather than reflective, and thus the modern creeds, that are lineal descendants of the older ones, contradict purely scientific conceptions. But the perfect creed is a blend of science and poetry. To science is the power of progress, to poetry the power of vision. Either without the other is comparatively valueless. For this reason we, as Freethinkers, attack the popular conceptions as being neither poetic nor scientific, and therefore useless as factors of progress.

The seeming contradiction between science and poetry is due to the materialisation of symbols and mental concepts. Primitive man, to whom the great realities were the stars, and the sun, and the wind, and the sea, was not a Theologian, but a Seer. The modern creeds are due to the tendency of men to reverence the past, merely because it *is* the past,—possibly a subconscious inherited reminiscence of ancestor-worship. Owing to this strong and unfortunate tendency, that which was originally and rightly intended as a symbol, becomes mistaken for the thing-in-itself, and the symbol thus loses all its significance, and becomes a mere fetish. At the same time, the thing-in-itself (or, rather, the conception of it), degenerates into a mere formula. This is what has happened to the modern religions; to the vast majority of their votaries their original meaning and significance are utterly obscured, and their spirit is dead, or at least so soundly sleeping, that nothing less than the clarion voice of a Master could succeed in recalling them to life. Thus it is that the modern men who go straight Nature for their impressions are infinitely more religious than the professional Theologians who trade (probably in most cases innocently and ignorantly) on cut-and-dried formulæ and the blood and bones of dead gods.

To modern thought the old, crude, coarsened symbols are unpalatable, and the power of leadership in the only real sense—that of discriminative appreciation, as opposed to that of slavery—is in inverse proportion to "orthodoxy." The men who, directly or indirectly, chiefly influence democracy—with which, tilt the next great reaction, lies the future—are Spencer, Darwin, Swinburne, Whitman, and their disciples. The chief cry, even in the retrograde and discredited [exoteric] Christian churches, is to-day for *breadth*, and this is an intensely significant fact. The very votaries of one of the stupidest and most impossible superstitions the world has ever seen are exclaiming against and explaining away—in itself a liberal education!—the crudities and doctrinal immoralities they were taught in their childhood. The new reformed school of Christian Theology—the Campbell-Lodge[203] one—suffers at present from excessive sentimentality, but even this is infinitely better than the old-fashioned Christian Materialism, and, after all, it is due to reaction. When the balance is struck the New Religionist will find himself not far from the Humanist and the Pagan; and, inasmuch as the reforming religious impulse came to Christianity from without rather than from within, the "New Religionist" will have to walk by far the greater part of the way towards reconciliation.

Real progress consists of schism and reunion. The process is as follows:—A small party of "heretics" perceives a new truth, for which offence it is damned by the orthodox multitude, the extent of the damnation (damnation is, after all, a matter of degree) being coincident with the power and will of the majority. When the heretics have absolutely proved their point, the majority slowly, and at first unwillingly, takes steps towards reconciliation, which idea is welcomed by everyone except the fanatics on both sides. If the heretic smiles sarcastically to himself, it is no-one's business but his own, and he is surely justified. The very stupidest majority can scarcely resist fact when it has been levelled down to its intellect, and it is mere narrowness for the heretic to grudge the acceptance of *his* knowledge—albeit unwillingly—by his late opponents, on the ground that it *is* his knowledge, and not his opponents'. Let us, therefore, be thankful for small mercies, and if the "New Theology" becomes impregnated by *real* spiritualism and secularism, which

[203] Rev. Reginald John Campbell (1867–1956) espoused a view of the bible that was more in line with modern historical or critical views and that became known as "The New Theology." He was the subject of much attention in January, 1907—attention that continued when Campbell finally responded to his critics that year by releasing the hastily written volume called Reginald John Campbell, *The New Theology* (New York, Macmillan, 1907). Sir Oliver Lodge (1851–1940) was a British physicist who turned heads when he took up an interest in Spiritualism, joined the Society for Psychical Research, and began (much like Campbell) to espouse nontraditional, albeit Christian, views about the soul and spirituality.

are the same thing, it seems to me that we should rather rejoice at the sign of progress, than be furious because our opponents are not "whole-hoggers."

Whole-hogging is essentially art amusement for the very strong and the very bigoted. True wisdom, it seems to the present writer, consists in eclecticism, and not in the surrender of the intellect to a "party," and an appeal to a "leader" in every difficulty. That is the way Churches are formed, and churches of all kinds are essentially for the use of those who depute others to do their thinking for them.

Self-unfoldment is eventually the only thing worth striving after. This sounds selfish; but in reality it is nothing of the kind; for those who are best able to influence and assist others are obviously they who are in some way or other are superior to those they would assist. On the other hand, to some types self-unfoldment comes by helping others. But every thinking man must discover the particular brand of egoism or altruism best suited to his own particular soul. All this has been superbly expressed in a sonnet by Laurence Binyon:—

THE CLUE

Life from sunned peak, witched wood, and flowery dell
A hundred ways the eager spirit woos,
To roam, to dream, to conquer, to rebel;
Yet in its ear, ever a voice cries, Choose!

So many ways, yet only one shall find;
So many joys, yet only one shall bless;
So many creeds, yet for each pilgrim mind
One road to the divine forgetfulness.

Tongues talk of truth, but truth is only there
Where the heart runs to be outpoured utterly,
A stream whose motion is its home,—to dare
Follow one faith and in that faith be free.

O Love, since I have found one truth so true,
I would lose all, to lose my loss in you.[204]

[204] Laurence Binyon, "The Clue," in *The Venture: An Annual of Art and Literature*, ed. Laurence Housman and Somerset Maugham (London: Pear Tree Press, 1903), 158.

Laurence Binyon finds his particular clue in Love; whether Love is the clue for everyone, I cannot say. From the point of view of the initiate, "God" may be "love"; to those who, like the present writer, are not initiates, and whom honesty compels to be Agnostic, love is but a manifestation of Pan, though perhaps it may be said to be the fairest of his manifestations.

Pan is even now being re-born—a birth whereof the intellectually observant may quite easily assure themselves—and, as is ever the case with the birth of gods, a new faculty is coincidently evolving amongst men; this new faculty is known by the name of "Cosmic Consciousness," and consists of harmony between Nature and the Soul. At present the Cosmic experience is comparatively rare, and where it exists it is usually outside the control of him who experiences it. Pan is ever being born, for Nature is ever manifesting in fresh forms.

Entrance into Nirvana or complete Cosmic Consciousness, is obtained only after repeated manifestations upon the physical plane. Cosmic Consciousness is unexplainable in words; but to those who have experienced it, it is so real that ever afterwards ordinary life and thought take on a more or less unreal appearance. To the orthodox Secularist, all this will be the greatest heresy; but, none the less, the present writer must, in honesty, say that almost the only times he has really lived have been when this new Consciousness has manifested itself. Cosmic Consciousness, by the way, is no more connected with the clairvoyance and clairaudience of the Spiritualists than with physical sight and hearing.

Sings Ethel Wheeler (in "The Year's Horoscope"):—

> I cross the rim of sense, and reach the deep,—
> The vast devoid of sight or sound of strife,—
> Vitality unnourished by the breath:
> The silence of a sleep more still than sleep,—
> The passion of a life more quick than life:
> Not sleep, not life,—but death, and after-death.[205]

If any proof be needed to show that Cosmic Consciousness is in no wise connected with orthodox "religion," it may be found in the tact that this newly-evolving, but by no means new, "sense" was strongly developed in Richard Jefferies, an Atheist, a record of whose experiences may be found

[205] Ethel Rolt-Wheeler, *The Year's Horoscope* (London: A. C. Fifield, 1905). This book contains twelve sonnets, one for each month. Neuburg is here quoting from the poem for July.

in "The Story of My Heart."[206] The writings of "Michael Wood"[207] and Arthur Machen are exceedingly illuminating if they be intelligently read, because they contain many luminous hints on matters connected with Cosmic Consciousness and the origin of religion. I should, perhaps, add that "Michael Wood" writes from the Theosophical, and Arthur Machen from (I believe) the Catholic, standpoint.

This Cosmic Consciousness it was that in earlier days evolved the gods, who, as Blake says, reside in the human breast. Occultly, man corresponds to the universe in the relationship of microcosm to macrocosm; the development of "the god within," or the gradual unfolding of the sheaths of the Self is taught esoterically in all religions as the *summum bonum*, and I think that Cosmic Consciousness is the "outward and visible sign" of this process of unfoldment. To the unthinking, heaven and hell, "God" and the Devil, Christ and the Holy Ghost, are actual physical realities; to those who possess insight, these "things" are symbols for various experiences of the Soul as it is drawn alternately towards and away from the underlying Reality whence it sprang.

This underlying Reality can neither be destroyed nor explained; let not those who attack misunderstood and perhaps unnecessary symbols fall into the delusion that they are destroying the real Religion; let not those who "explain" religion imagine that they can enlighten the unawakened without symbolism. For Religion is an affair neither of the intellect nor of the emotions, but of the individual Soul, and the paths to the "divine forgetfulnes" are infinite in number, and not to be formulated in creeds.

Letters to the Editor

The Dying Creed[208]

J. A. Reid

Sir,—Mr. Victor B. Neuburg, in his interesting article, "Paganism and the Sense of Song" in last week's *A.J.*, remarks: "Whole-hogging is essentially an amusement for the very strong and the very bigoted." Has not the time arrived when those who profess to be Agnostics should finally burn their

[206] Richard Jefferies, *The Story of My Heart: My Autobiography* (London: Longmans, Green, 1883).
[207] "Michael Wood" is the pseudonym of theosophist Joy Hooper. See, for example, Michael Wood, *The Saint and the Outlaw, and Other Stories* (London: Theosophical Publishing Society, 1904).
[208] *Agnostic Journal* 60, no. 4 (January 26, 1907): 62.

boats and discard the idea of God and immortality? We are just now hearing a good deal of the "New Theology" which candid critics justly say is not theology or new. It seems to be a formula invented by some preachers who have not the courage to accept facts. but who are finding that Freethought criticism is effectively doing its work.

I suppose the best part of a million of money will be spent on the new Liverpool Cathedral without a word of protest from those who are supposed to guide the destinies of this nation. What sort of religion is to be propagated there when it is built? The Christian religion has been riddled with criticism, and yet the priests try to go on just the same.

There is a significant article in the January issue of the *Edinburgh Review*, entitled "The Age of Reason."[209] John Morley's contributions to Freethought literature are belatedly reviewed. Of course, some effort is made to reconcile Freethought and clericalism, but the seriousness of the issue is not ignored. The pious *Daily Mail*, which at least knows the commercial value of Christianity, talks of the incalculable benefits the Christian religion has conferred on the human race. What are they?

Think of the bloodshed and the millions of money expended to propagate these legends. Is it not time to cry "halt"? Cannot the effort and money be spent more judiciously by serving humanity than by worshipping a mythical God? Who would care to live for billions of years? We can cultivate all the virtues without surrendering our reason. —Yours truly,

A Reply[210]

V. B. Neuburg

SIR,—I crave some space in which to reply to the remarks made by my friend, Mr. J. A, Reid, in the *A.J.* for January 26th.

Mr. Reid asks if the time has not "arrived when those who profess to be Agnostics should finally burn their boats and discard the idea of God and immortality?"

The best way will be for me to endeavour to make clear my position to Mr. Reid. Let me say that I do not "discard the idea of God and immortality" because

[209] The unsigned article "The Age of Reason" reviews six books by British writer John Morley (1838–1923): *Voltaire* (1872), *Rousseau* (1873), *Compromise* (1874), *Critical Miscellanies* (1877), *Diderot and the Encyclopædists* (1878), and *Burke* (1888). "The Age of Reason," *Edinburgh Review* 205, no. 419 (January 1907): 1–27

[210] *Agnostic Journal* 60, no. 6 (February 9, 1907): 94.

I am an Agnostic; but I am an Agnostic because I hold certain views upon these questions. In other words, I do not try to shape my views into accordance with a system of thought; but I am compelled to subscribe to a certain system because it happens to be in consonance with my views. This seems to me to be a more philosophical attitude than that advocated by Mr. Reid. I dislike dogmatic credos (and non-credos) because I think that they are bars to brotherhood.

My friend's idea that all Agnostics should adopt certain hard-and-fast attitudes towards "God" and "immortality" savours—to my nostrils, at least—too much of the religious systems that I suppose most readers of the *A.J.* have outgrown.

I want to say a few words in regard to the ideas of God and Immortality.

As to "God," I am quite Agnostic; indeed, I call myself an Atheist, which I claim to be, in the real connotation of that term: I am, so far as I know, without a personal God. An *im*personal God is inconceivable to me; but I do not—because I cannot—deny the possibility of His or Its existence. On that particular point I am Agnostic.

As regards "immortality," I am Agnostic; but I am pretty well convinced that the *Ego* persists, for a time at least, after the death of the physical body. It would take up too much space to go into the matter at all fully here; and I am loath to raise in the *A.J.* a controversy that bids fair to become perennial. For those who want to investigate there are nearly always the means at hand, and I do not pose as a teacher.

And surely the attitude of Agnosticism towards "Immortality" is a non-committal one, rather than one of absolute denial? Is not this latter attitude rather dogmatic for an Agnostic—a non knower?

I am glad Mr. Reid found my article interesting. —Yours truly,

Agnosticism and Atheism[211]

J. A. Reid

Sir,—I would like to thank Mr. Neuburg for his letter in which he further explains his views respecting Agnosticism and Atheism. He says he is pretty well convinced that the *ego* persists, for a time at least, after the death of the physical body. Probably my views on the question of "God" and immortality are now fairly familiar to your readers. I am afraid I cannot share Mr.

[211] "Letters to the Editor," *Agnostic Journal* 60, no. 7 (February 16, 1907): 110.

Neuburg's views respecting a future existence. As to the Christian God idea, it is unthinkable to me now. If such a monster did exist I would not worship him. Who believes in the doctrine of eternal punishment now? And what becomes of the Christian plan of salvation? Here we are doubtless on common ground.

If the *Ego* of man persists after death, which I do not believe, a similar condition of things would occur in regard to the lower animals, seeing their common origin. I do not think consciousness can exist apart from the brain. The doctrine of annihilation is not exactly consoling, but the brain reels at the Christian idea of immortality. I believe in natural causation. I think we might eliminate the word "God." It is a meaningless expression. —Yours truly,

The Successor of Samson[212]

[Articles and a letter pertaining to Mahatma Śri Agamya Guru Paramahamsa. —RK]

The Successor of Samson[213]

M. M.

THE New Year is to bring with it a new religion, and before many months have passed, we shall all be performing "miracles," providing only that we can scrape together the necessary funds to pay the initiation fees. Ha, ha! The everlasting fees—the never-to-be forgotten fees! What would the religions teacher do without them? Still, if only the instructor carry out his part of the contract, there can be no reasonable cause for complaint. The great prophet who has set himself this task is at present residing in a West-End boarding-house, and his Institute, which is to be known as "The Parliament of Life," is soon to be open in the vicinity.[214] I trust the name on the door plate will be sufficiently imposing. Behold it!

[212] Mahatma Śri Agamya Guru Paramahamsa garnered international headlines when he made a return trip to London in late 1906, looking for students. Two of them (briefly) were Crowley and Fuller. An *Agnostic Journal* article mocking the Mahatma and his cause célèbre prompted a defensive letter to the editor from Fuller. Given Fuller's later sendup of Paramahamsa in *The Equinox* (1910), this trio of articles presents a telling arc. For more on Paramahamsa, see "The Tiger Mahatma" in chap. 3, in this volume.

[213] *Agnostic Journal* 60, no. 4 (January 26, 1907): 51–52.

[214] Paramahamsa in fact announced plans to open a Society Agamya Siddhaut Sabha or "Parliament of Infinite Wisdom," not of Life. See "When a Mahatma Gets Angry: A Too Curious

"Mahatma Agamya Guru Paramahamsa."

I think, if I were he, I should plant it in the front garden, and allow it to run up the wall, like a creeper, and there might be a telescope or a long ladder handy for the use of short-sighted visitors who desire to examine the top end.

It is all very well to remark, "What's in a name?" But no man can say there is not a deal in this one. Bill Jones, Bill Higgins, or Bill Adams would never do as names for a "miracle" instructor; but with a title of the length of a telegraph-pole the business ought to buck up in no time. So "Walk up, ladies and gentlemen, as we are positively about to commence now, and no waiting." Of course, as usual, the skeptical scoffer will sneer and gibe and jeer. But what of it? Let him. I tell you that Mahatma Agamya Guru Paramahamsa is a name to conjure with, and those who laugh at it are only jealous because they cannot borrow a few yards. But the good old-fashioned name of "miracles" is not to be used.

The gentleman's powers are not miraculous, but "occult." Quite so; and if you wish to learn the secret, pay up, and you will be shewn how to check the action of the heart so that no common or garden doctor could say whether you are alive or dead! And the instant you are ready you can "wake up." Then, too, by carefully following a few simple instructions you will discover how to rip tigers to ribbons, with one hand tied behind you, and the other in a sling; and all at a weekly cost for food of one and nine pence, including Sundays.

The modern Samson went so far as to tell an interviewer that, "If a tiger come into a room, now, I would tear him in two—So!"[215] Now, here we have something definite to deal with. It is quite obvious that we can all get as far as the bare statement—but most of us would find we had a train to catch if the animal happened to overhear the remark, and stalked in. And I would respectfully suggest that before any prospective apostle part with any money he should witness a performance of this feat by the Professor. Observe, I do not say it cannot be done.

I merely remark that I fancy the tiger would take the risk, and that the average insurance company would require a fairly heavy premium for any that they might possibly incur, notwithstanding the fact that the Mahatma's

Stranger Is Excommunicated; Agamya Guru Paramahamsa Rebukes the Intruder and All West Eighty-Second Street Hears the Doom Pronounced—the Street Is Getting Used to It," *The Sun*, June 28, 1907, 2.

[215] Despite the extensive press coverage garnered by Paramahamsa's return to London, I have been unable to locate the source of these quotes that are attributed to him in M. M.'s "Successor of Samson."

face "is very stern and dark, very powerful and dogged." The tiger antagonist would very likely present much the same appearance.

I can even suggest yet another comparison. The gentleman with the railway name only takes one threepenny meal every twenty-four hours, as a means of riveting his mind on one idea, and one idea only, and had the man-eater been thus dieted for about two days, I am pretty certain that *he* would have but one idea too which would be to eat one Mahatma—"So!" I never before heard of a tiger tearing feat of this sort, being carried through on a foundation of a bunch of carrots a day, a reflection that must make glad the hearts of all vegetarians. Possibly it is only owing to the fact that the professor *is* a vegetarian that he stopped short of declaring that he would *eat* his antagonist as well as kill him.

I note that the new Samson's second title is "Tiger Mahatma." But, did the little contest to which I have referred come off, methinks it would be a case of christening the animal Mahatma-Tiger!

> Ah yes, my dear Paramahamsa,
> It's all but quite certain I am, Sah,
> Were the tiger and you
> To see the bout through,
> Your chance would not be worth the faintest consideration.

That one-meal-a-day business is a pretty old idea and monkish in origin, I fancy. It is bad enough in itself; but when the instructions are to "take that meal at midnight" the trouble spreads.

Nothing could be more conducive to nightmare, and my own idea is that either Paramahamsa is an impostor, or he has "got 'em." Bu who is to tell how many meals he indulges in, any more than how many Bovrils he imbibes? Here again we are asked to take the gentleman's word just as we are expected to credit the statement that Jesus fasted forty days in the wilderness; though whether he did or not we shall never know. Perhaps he was after one idea only. I am sure I should have but one idea, did I but survive a forty days' fast, and that would be to ascertain the whereabouts of the nearest larder.

But I fancy that the majority of Paramahamsa's apostles will have no need to resort to special diet to drive all the ideas but one from their heads, as this is about all most of them will possess; and in case they may meet any stray tigers, they had better feed well up for possible encounters; for strength and starvation seldom go together. Anyway, that is the lesson of all experience.

But I prophesy a bright future for the Professor. People simply dote on the "occult." You may preach whatever you choose, and gather round you many disciples, if only you contrive to introduce a spice of the mysterious into your doctrines. Only tell your dupes that they will live again, somewhere away in the Vast Forever, in the Great Beyond the Never, and they will not stop to enquire what the Dante's Inferno you are talking about, but lap it up like a kitten does milk.

Oh yes, Paramahamsa will find plenty of folks at his heels to enquire into the "occult," and the business is bound to thrive, carrots or no carrots. There is much faith left in the world yet, and there are still many fools with money to spend upon it. This is recognized by every religious quack on earth. And while faith, like unto a grain of mustard seed, remaineth,[216] and little cons like unto sovereigns and half-sovereigns are forthcoming, not to dwell upon the stray cheques and fivers, such teachers as the great Paramahamsa are bound to leap in bank-note-oriety. Saith the great Paramahamsa:—

> "If people want occult powers, I will show them those occult powers, if they show their endeavours to me. There are the forces of mind. If you will command one of them to the practice of Yoga, then that force will be commanded, and then you will get the effect of that force—a 'miracle.'"

And there you are, don't you know! Simple, is it not? But there is a good deal to learn before you can open up in opposition to Paramahamsa, for he tells of no less a number than seventy-two thousand eight hundred "forces" to be disposed of—doubtless at so much per force. These, at a penny a force, would total up to £303 6s. 8d. But, presuming there would be a reduction by taking the lot, and that the rate were, say, four forces a penny, the Tiger Mahatma would still be able to fasten his talons upon the respectable sum of £75 16s. 8d. And, allowing him two thousand converts, his banking account would reach a total of £150,166 13s. 4d., less the greengrocery and Institute expenses. I do not suppose things will be quite so prosperous as this; but there should be a nice little nest-egg made out of the concern, which might eventually be floated as a Company. But, if Paramahamsa would only step down to the Alhambra to "tear that tiger in two—so!" I venture to predict he would either die a millionaire or a mangled Mahatma.

[216] Matthew 17:20.

Letters to the Editor

"The Successor of Samson"[217]

J. F. C. F.

Sir,—In the cause of Truth, and for the sake of the high reputation the *A.J.* has always held in the ranks of Freethought, I feel it my duty to expostulate with "MM" against his most unjust attack on Mahatma Agamya. As it happens, the Mahatma is a personal friend of mine, but I will place this fact aside, merely stating it that it may not be thought that I speak without authority: and also during my three years' residence in the East, I came in constant contact with Fakirs and Yogins, both honest and dishonest, and so can fairly judge of the honesty of Mahatma Agamya, which I believe to be perfectly pure.

To state that the Mahatma brings with him a new religion is untrue; his principles are those of Patanjali.[218]

To state that he asks for fees is absolutely incorrect. He asks for none. His disciples are collecting a small fund sufficient to pay for a meeting-room and his expenses, which are extremely small.

The Mahatma does not claim any miraculous or occult power; he has denied such practices to me personally many times. He merely claims that his powers are a purer form of those natural forces which we all possess. By the simple practice of Hatha Yoga, he can stop his heart's action and appear as dead, which he once did in the presence of Max Müller. Such displays are very common in the East.

He calls himself the Tiger-Mahatma, and does not pretend to tear tigers; this, evidently, is a part of the interviewer's obtusity. At least, I can say he has not the appetite of a tiger, for he is a strict vegetarian, partaking of one meal a day, which in India would cost less than one anna. —Yours truly,

[217] *Agnostic Journal* 60, no. 6 (February 9, 1907): 93.

[218] The *Yoga Sūtras of Patañjali* (compiled *c.* 500 BCE–400 CE) were popularized in the late nineteenth century by Swami Vivekananda and the Theosophical Society. Vivekananda's seminal interpretation of Patañjali's sutras, *Raja Yoga* (1896), introduced yoga to a wide Western audience. For a modern examination of the text, see David Gordon White, *The Yoga Sutra of Patanjali: A Biography* (Princeton, NJ: Princeton University Press, 2014).

Half-Hours with Famous Mahatmas, No. 1[219]

Sam Hardy

Yogi Mahatma Śri Agamya Paramahamsa Guru Swamiji is a certain Punjabi lala, who, on account of his tremendous voice and ferocious temper, has well earned for himself the name of The Tiger Mahatma.

My first acquaintance with His Holiness was in November 1906,[220] when he paid his second visit to England. I had seen his name in the daily press, but before calling upon him, I had read up what I could about him in his book: *Śri Brahma Dhàrà*, in the preface of which he is praised as follows:

> He seeks to do good, he accepts money from no one, and lives a very simple, pure life . . . I . . . was much impressed by his great breadth of mind, his sweet charity, and his loving kindness for every living thing. . . . These teachings . . . breathe love and kindness, and dwell upon the joys of pure, clean living.[221]

Forewarned is to be forearmed, and I had read the same type of "puff" on many a patent pill box!

On entering 70, Margaret Street I was shown upstairs and ushered into the den of Tiger Śri Agamya. Besides himself, there were three people in the room, two men and a woman, and as I entered one of the men, an American, was saying: "O Mahatma! I haven't the faith, I can't get it!"

To which His Holiness roared out:

"You sheep are! . . . I no want sheep! . . . tigers I make . . . tigers tear up sheep, go away! . . . no good, get intellect . . . get English! . . . no more!!"

The three then departed, and I was left alone with the Blessed One. Neither of us spoke for about ten minutes, then at length, after a go or two at his snuff-box, he gave a loud grunt, to which I replied in a solemn voice:

"O Mahatma, what is Truth?"

"No Truth! All illusion," he answered, "I am that Master, you become my disciple; I show you all things; I lead you to the ultimate reality . . . the supreme stage of the highest . . . the infinite Ultimatum . . . the unlimited omniscience of eternal Wisdom—All this I give you if you have faith in me."

[219] *The Equinox* 1, no. 4 (September 1910): 284–290. "Sam Hardy" is a pen-name of J. F. C. Fuller.
[220] This was two months prior to the "Successor of Samson" article in the *Agnostic Journal*.
[221] Sri Agamya Guru Paramahamsa, preface to *Śri Brahma Dhàrà: Shower from the Highest* (London: Luzac, 1905), iv, vi.

As faith is exceedingly cheap in this country, I offered him unlimited oceans of it; and at this he seemed very please, and laughed:

"Ha! ha! You make good tiger cub . . . you tear sheep up . . . all is illusion!" Then after a pause: "De vouman," pointing to the door, "is no good!" And then, without further hesitation, he entered upon a veritable Don Juan description of his earthly adventures. This I thought strange of so sober-minded a saint, and so put to him several questions concerning the Vedanta Philosophy, and its most noted exponents, to see what he really did know.

"Do you know Swami Vivekananda?" I asked.

"Ha," he replied, "he no good, he my disciple, I am the master!"

"And Swami Dayanand Sarasvati?" I continued. The same answer was vouched to me, although this latter teacher had died at the age of seventy, forty years ago. Thinking it about time to change the conversation, I said:

"O Thou Shower from the Highest! Tell thy grovelling disciple what then *is* a *lie*?"

"Ha!" he replied, "it is illusion, this truth that has been diverged from its real point . . . an illusive spring in the primo-genial fermentation of *fee-no-me-non*, in this typo-cosmy apparent to the sense which you call *de Vurld*!!!"

With this, and promises of oceans of blissful reality from the highest eternality of ultimate ecstasy, he bade me sit in a chair and blow alternately through my nostrils; and, if I had faith, so he assured me, I should in six months' time arrive at the supreme stage of the Highest in the infinite Ultimatum, and should burst as a chance illusively fermented bubble in the purest atmosphere of the highest reality.

The next occasion on which I saw the Mahatma was at a business meeting of his disciples held at 60, South Audley Street. His Holiness called them tiger-cubs, nevertheless seldom have I seen such a pen full of sheep. A man from Ilfracombe proposed this, and a man from Liverpool second that; at last a London plumber arose, and with great solemnity declared: "Gintlemen, hi taik hit 'is 'oliness his really 'oly, hin fact gintlemen hi taik hit 'e his Gawd; . . . hand so hi proposes the very least we can do for 'im his to subscribe yearly towards 'im foive shillins!" ("'ear, 'ear" from a comrade in the corner). However, the sheep wouldn't have it, and the little man sat down to ruminate over lead piping, and solder at twopence a stick.

During the summer of '07 I had little time to waste at number 60, and had almost forgotten about the Mahatma, who, so I had been told, had let England for America, when I received a card announcing his return, and asking me to be present at a general meeting.

This I did, and as usual was more than bored. After business was over the Mahatma entered the room, all his sheep locking round him to seek the turnips of his wisdom. On these occasions he would ask questions and select subjects upon which his disciples were supposed to write essays. One of these, I can still remember, was: "How to help the helpless hands"; another was: "What is dis-satisfaction, and what is true satisfaction?" And the answer was: "Love fixed on mortal things, without the knowledge of its source, increases vibration and creates dissatisfaction (*mortal things* is good!)."

In his book, *Śri Brahma Dhàrà*, which contains some of the most astonishing balderdash ever put in print, may be found his philosophy. This is a stewed-up hash of Yoga, Vedanta, and outrageous verbosity. "Love," he writes, "is the force of the magician Maya, and is the cause of all disorder"[222] (it seems to be so even in his exalted position). "This force of love,—in the state of circumgyration in the extended world,—is the cause of all mental movements towards the feeling of easiness or uneasiness: but the mind enjoys eternal beatitude with perfect calmness, when the force of love is concentrated over the unlimited extension of silence"[223] ('silence' is really choice!).

"Virtue," he defines as: "The bent of mind towards self-command"[224] (and evidently practises it). His morals are good; but his scientific conceptions really "take the cake!" "[T]here are Three Kinds of animate creations in the world," he writes: "They are the creations from (1) the Womb; (2) Eggs; (3) Perspiration. . . . "[225] Another gem: "How is it that some of the bodies are male and some are female?" Answer: "If the male seed preponderates, a male body is produced; and if female, a female. While, when both are equally proportioned, an eunuch is born" (!)[226]

At one of his male meetings—there were also female ones; but mixed bathing in the ocean of infinite bliss was not allowed—he related to us his pet story, of how he had "flumoxed" the chief engineer and the captain of the liner which had brought him back from America.

He informed them that coal and steam were absurd; what you want, he said, is to have two large holes made in the sides of your ship, then the air will

[222] This is more paraphrase or amalgamation than a direct quote. In *Śri Brahma Dhàrà*, Paramahamsa writes, "The world is a delusive charm of the great magician called Màyà," and "there is a force of the magician, the movement of which is the cause of all such disorder, and that force is,—'Love.'" Paramahamsa, Śri Brahma Dhàrà, 1, 7.

[223] Paramahamsa, *Śri Brahma Dhàrà*, 7.

[224] Paramahamsa, *Śri Brahma Dhàrà*, 25.

[225] Paramahamsa, *Śri Brahma Dhàrà*, 18–19.

[226] Paramahamsa, *Śri Brahma Dhàrà*, 22.

blow into them and turn the wheels, and make the ship go. When the captain pointed out to him, that if a storm were to arise the water might possibly flow into the ship and sink it, he roared out, "No! no! . . . get English! . . . get intellect! see! see! de vind vill fill de ship and blow it out of de vater and take it across over de vaves!"—Since this now becomes public property there probably will be a slump in turbines!

It was towards the close of last October, when I received from a friend of mine[227]—also a so-called disciple—a letter in which he wrote: "There was a devil of a row at 60 last night. M: pressed me to come to his weekly entertainments; so I came. He urged me to speak; so I spoke. He then revealed his divine self in an exceptionally able manner; I refrained from revealing mine. His divine self reminded one rather of a 'Navvy's Saturday Night, by Battersea Burns.'" He further urged me to go and see the Mahatma himself on the following Sunday; and this I did.

I arrived at 60, South Audley Street at seven o'clock. There were already about twenty sheepish-looking tigers present, and when the Mahatma entered the room, I sat down next to him; for, knowing, in case a scrimmage should occur, that a Hindoo cannot stomach a blow in the spleen, I thought it wisest to be within striking distance of him.

The Mahatma opened the evening's discussion by saying: "Humph . . . I am Agnostic, you are believers. I say 'I don't know,' you contradict me." And during the next hour and a half more Bunkum was talked in that room that I should say in Exeter Hall during the whole course of the last century. At last it ended, and though I had made various attempts to draw His Holiness into argument, I had as yet failed to unveil his divinity. He now started dictating his precious philosophy, and in such execrable English, that it was quite impossible to follow him, and I once or twice asked him to repeat what he had said, and as I did so I noticed that several of the faithful shivered and turned pale. At length came the word "expectation" or "separation," and as I could not catch which, I exclaimed "what?"

"You pig-faced man!" shouted His Holiness, "you dirty fellow, you come here to take away my disciples . . . vat you vant vith this: vat! vat! vat! vat! . . . You do no exercise, else you understand vat I say, dirty man!" And then turning to his three head bell-wethers who were sitting at a separate table he sneered:

[227] That is, Aleister Crowley.

"X———" (my friend present at the previous revelation of his divinity) "send this pig-one . . . eh?"

"I don't know why . . . " I began.

"Grutch, butch!" he roared, "you speak to me, you cow-eater! . . . get intellect," he yelled, "get English," he bellowed, and up he sprang from the table.

As I did not wish to be murdered, for he had now become a dangerous maniac, I rose, keeping my eyes on him, and taking up my hat and stick, which I had purposely placed just behind me, I quietly passed round the large table at which his terror-stricken fold sat gaping, and moved towards the door.

The whole assembly seemed petrified with fear. At first the Blessèd One appeared not to realize what had happened, so taken aback was he by any one having the audacity to leave the room without his permission: then he recovered himself, and at the top of his tiger-roar poured out his curses in choicest Hindustani.

On reaching the door I opened it, and then facing him I exclaimed in a loud voice in his native tongue:

"Chup raho! tum suar ke bachcha ho!"[228]

With gleaming eyes, and foaming lips, and arms flung wildly into the air,—there stood the Indian God, the 666th incarnation of Haram Zada, stung to the very marrow of his bones by this bitterest insult. Beside himself with fury he sprang up, murder written on every line of his face; tried to leap across the table—and fell in an epileptic fit. As he did so, I shut the door in his face.

Aum.

Demos and Aristos[229]

J. F. C. F.

"Whenever the dharmma decays, the a-dharmma prevails; *then* I manifest myself. For the protection of the good, for the destruction of the writ, *for the firm establishment of* THE NATIONAL RIGHTEOUSNESS, I am born again and again." —*Krishna.*[230]

[228] Translated from Hindi: "Shut up! You are the son of a sow!"

[229] *Agnostic Journal* 60, no. 9 (March 2, 1907): 129–130; *Agnostic Journal* 60, no. 10 (March 9, 1907): 147–148; *Agnostic Journal* 60, no. 11 (March 16, 1907): 162–163; *Agnostic Journal* 60, no. 12 (March 23, 1907): 178–179; *Agnostic Journal* 60, no. 13 (March 30, 1907): 197–198.

[230] These are the closing words of Sister Nivedita [Margaret E. Noble], *The Web of Indian Life* (London: William Heinemann, 1904), 301. The italics in Fuller's quote are present in the original.

Looking back, beholding the actualities of life, we find a curiously symmetrical undulation on the sea of human events, a gradually-increasing swell, rising from the hollow of one wave to the summit of another, on the social flood. At times a silent calm stills the face of the waters; at others they are lashed with fury as the gale shrieks through their foaming crests; but, generally, a gentle swell rolls on, and as each wave, from birth to death, is part of the great ocean of the world, so is each ideal an event in the great ocean of human thoughts. As they rise so do we, as they sink so do we; and as they cannot be separated from the waters of their formation, neither can we from the inheritances of our birth.

Life, more life, is the universal cry of the living, and yet Nature, in her supreme wisdom, has so fashioned her creation that no ultimate goal is attainable, no halt can possibly be made on our journey towards the night of our days, without peril and danger. The mountain is rugged, the road is arduous, and yet, here and there, as we toil on beyond our brothers, yearning for the ever-receding summit of our desires, are we not often lured into some enchanted grove of ease, or lulled to sleep by the sweet melody of satisfaction, the siren song of success, of rank, and of wealth? Do we not often halt and pitch our tents never to strike them again? Do we not ever, have we not ever, and shall we not ever, halt and halt again, losing, in the warm leisure of our rest, the grail that we so ardently sought, or finding grasp, to spill in our ease the nectar we caught from the lips of the past? How often is the cup dry? Till some Titan re-fill it with tears of despair, the groans of want, and the shrieks of massacre. And this very toil, this master-lash which whistles for ever around us, is at once the saviour and tormentor of our existence.

> Build up heroic lives, and all
>   Be like a sheathen sabre,
> Ready to flash out at God's call,
>   O Chivalry of Labour!
> Triumph and Toil are twins; and aye
>   Joy suns the cloud of Sorrow:
> And 'tis the martyrdom To-day
>   Brings victory To-morrow.—*Gerald Massey.*[231]

[231] Gerald Massey, "To-Day and To-Morrow," *Arthur's Home Magazine* 4, no. 4 (October 1854): 308. Although best known in occult circles for later works like *A Book of the Beginnings* (1881), *The Natural Genesis* (1883), and *Ancient Egypt, Light of the World* (1907), Massey was also a notable poet. See, for example, Gerald Massey, *The Poetical Works of Gerald Massey* (London: Routledge, Warne,

The law of Nature is "toil"; the hope of man is "ease" and these two are as twin sisters, inseparable, urging man on to higher aspirations, acting and reacting the one on the other. "By the sweat of thy brow shalt thou live," and "by the ease of thy toil shalt thou die."[232] From the waters of affliction man quaffs the falernian of emperors, the nectar of Olympians, the soma of the gods, but never the amrita of eternity. Nothing remains, all changes, all grows, all decays—there is an eternal flux. And without this lash of Circumstance, directed by the unknown hand of Perfection, we could not be; we should stagnate, dry up and fall to dust; otherwise, perfection would be our lot, yet perfection is of the absolute, and the absolute is as the sphinx, cryptic and without tongue.

Here might be mentioned that the infinite depends on the finite, life upon death, the present on the past; lower love upon hate, joy upon sorrows, wealth upon poverty. Each depends on the other; each nowhere existent as an absolute without the other, each, with the other, forming an eternal monism, composed of an irritating dualism, inseparable, yet diverse, thriving when in conflict, degenerating when in contact, and dying when in union. Perfection cannot exist without imperfection, neither can the soul of an individual or a nation without the dust of the body or the race.

Why, if the Soul can fling the Dust aside,
And naked on the Air of Heaven ride,
Were't not a Shame—were't not a Shame for him,
In this clay carcase, crippled to abide?[233]

So sang the tent-maker of Naishàpùr, and never were truer words uttered. Why? why, indeed? Because the "why" carries with it the impossible division of a perfect unit, without destroying its identity and value.

The inseparableness in the sphere of thought is graphically demonstrated in "The Mental Traveller," by the masterhand of Blake.[234] The idea conceived

and Routledge, 1861). The poem—as reproduced here and elsewhere—has minor variations in capitalization from its original publication.

[232] This is a popular paraphrase of Genesis 3:19, which in the King James Version reads, "In the sweat of thy face shalt thou eat bread, till thou return unto the ground."

[233] This is Edward J. FitzGerald's translation of poem 44 from Omar Khayyam, *Rubáiyát of Omar Khayyám: The Astronomer-Poet of Persia*, trans. Edward FitzGerald (London: Macmillan, 1904), 41.

[234] William Blake's poem *The Mental Traveller*, about traveling in the realm of the mind, is part of the Pickering Manuscript, unpublished until 1863.

in pain, is born amid enthusiasm, falls under the ban of society; yet develops, grows, and moulds the old society into a new one; but again, in its time, grows old and effete, rotting inwardly, becoming a corruption to the society it formed, till, like a phœnix, it rises once again from the ashes of its formation. So in the realm of action, the idea urges man on through action towards the ideal, the ideal ever, fatuus-like, dancing before him on the path of life, never attainable, yet ever visible: a column of smoke by day, and a flaming pillar of fire by night, guiding him on. Let him once halt, let him once loose in the splendour of the sun, or in the obscurity of night, the ideal of his heart, and his decay is as certain as that of a tree which remains unwatered in an arid desert.

This attempt to realize the ideal becomes plainly visible as we turn from page to page in the world's history. In the lower forms of life the ideals—or, rather, the needs—were essentially physical and material, and as all impress of character tends to become inheritable and instinctive; so through the law of natural selection the fittest—in other words, those who more closely realized their needs best—survived. But this material need of the lower world, which is realized through the natural law of "toil," stimulated by fear, is very different from the ideal which developed through the higher mammals culminating for the present in man; for, not only does it instinctively carry out the natural law of "toil," stimulated by fear, but it reasoningly carries out the human law of "ease," stimulated by "belief." The reaction of the latter on the former humanizes the brutal, drawing the talons from the claws of nature, it thereby stimulates—through the utilitarian hope of happiness—the mind towards that great ideal—a state of mental perfection.

Now, if we turn to history what do we find? Firstly, in ancient times that the ideal was as a flaming pillar of fire again and again discovered, again and again lost in the darkness of the primeval night. Horde swept away horde, yet amidst all the horror of bloodshed a greater ease arose. The first ape who hurled a stone or brained his foe with a broken branch, broke the fetters of toil and cleared the way for the road of ease. Stocks and stones grew into weapons of war, weapons into agricultural implements, and from these again sprang all the arts, and crafts, and sciences, of ancient and modern times; and as there is not much resemblance between a monera and a full-grown European, neither is there much similarity between a stone and a machine-gun, or a stick and a steam-hammer; yet such things are, and a direct chain of cause and effect is as traceable in the one as it is in the other.

When savagery gave way to civilization, we might expect to find a minimising of bloodshed; but this is not so, tribal raids gave way to national conflicts; and the father of the family, the chief of the tribe, became the lord of the manor, and the king of the country. For when the road of ease was for a time cleared of the briars of toil; the minority no longer lost the pillar of fire in the depths of the night, but the majority lost the pillar of smoke in the splendour of the historic day; unorganized brute force lay on its sick-bed, and mental exclusiveness reigned supreme.

From this point we enter the sphere of historic evidence. Centuries and millenniums swept away palæolithic and then neolithic man; the ages of copper, of bronze, and of iron arose; the jabber of the ape had long given way to uttered language and writing; history became certain, the great struggle began; tradition became more sure, engendering pride, and pride in its turn grew into national esteem—in other words patriotism was born. Great nations came into existence, nomadic tribes which had wandered over the fertile plains grazing their flocks, and pillaging if their strength so permitted, now settled; priest-craft and priesthood grew; tribes united under certain beliefs; leaders were appointed, leaders grew into kings, kings into emperors, emperors into gods.

We now enter a new phase in the world's history. Barbarism was not dead, but was changing, eliminating, little by little, the proper personal freedom of the individual (anarchic), and substituting in its place the liberty of the nation (legislative). Then a greater conflict than ever was waged by man against man—the conflict of man against the State; freedom against liberty, toil against ease.

II.

> "Whenever the dharmma decays, the a-dharmma prevails; *then* I manifest myself. For the protection of the good, for the destruction of the evil, *for the firm establishment of* THE NATIONAL RIGHTEOUSNESS, I am born again and again."—*Krishna.*

The argument of this article is now fairly started, the great conflict of the people against the State, of democracy against aristocracy The gradual growth through toil of the masses to the gradual decline through ease of the classes. And what are the dominant factors in this growth and decay? (1) Warfare, (2) Agriculture, (3) Religion, (4) Science, [(5) Morality (?)].

We cannot here deal with the first two, and will only concentrate our attention on the third, and then on the fourth.

The great moving force that in its infancy urges man on to deeds that even revolt his better understanding to horrors, that tortures his sense of right, namely religion; ultimately settles, stagnates, and then corrupts his further endeavours, a drag on his progress, at length for pure self-preservation adapts itself to its new surroundings, and, like a phœnix, rises resplendent from the ashes of its corruption; it is, in fact, the first great moving principle from barbarism towards civilization. It grafts to itself not only the warlike tendencies of early man, but casts over kingship the halo of divinity, authorizes the legislation by the word of God, and further sanctifies itself and its actions, casting its tentacles like a great octopus from the nearest to the furthest limits of the semi-barbaric state.

All nations rose through toil, all nations perished through ease. Nature first massacres, then debauches. Egypt, Assyria, Babylonia, Persia, India, Greece, Rome, arose; dynasty followed dynasty, and nation followed nation; blood overflowed, and then the wine-cup; the acrid of the toiler gave place to the perfumed locks of the faineant; curses changed to love songs, blows to kisses, and the homespun shirt of the farmer to the emperor's vest of tyrean purple.

Glance at the last-named nation alone—the Roman.

Commonly accepted, Rome was founded in 753 B.C., between then and 509 the plebs (aliens) rose into recognition; in 494 the "First Secession" was held at the Mons-sacer, and the Tribunate was established; in 449 the "Second Secession" took place, resulting in the Valerio-Horatian laws; and in 287 the Third or last Secession established the legislative power in the Lex Hortensia. Meanwhile, in 367 the Licinian Rogations dealt a severe blow at patrician privileges, which were followed in 133 by the agrarian legislation of Tiberius Gracchus, and ten years later, in 123, by that of his brother, Gains.

The cup of blood was filled to the brim, and over-flowing. Long years of toil, of war, of misery, had brought with them a universal longing for rest. The triumvirate of Cæsar, Pompey, and Crassus, heralded in a new epoch. The Republic had reached its height. Demos stood triumphant over the toil of centuries, reaching the summit of his desires, he paused, and therein lay his fall; dashing to the ground the cup of his misery, he rose intoxicated on the cup of ease, Aristos the self-sufficient!

Augustus donned the purple in B.C. 27, in A.D. 410 Alaric sacked Rome, and sixty-six years later the Western Empire fell.

The heroic period of Rome, as all heroic periods, did not last long; the nation had travailed and born many a noble son, but now she had grown old and sterile; no longer was there a Coriolanus to utter, "Mother thou hast conquered me, but hast brought me to misery," as he departed to die in exile; nor a Camillus, who at the age of eighty, led the legions of his country against the foe; Curtius sprang into the yawning chasm, and Decius rushed to his death on the spears of Gaul; but where now were their like? Gone to rise no more, buried under the midden of increasing ease and sensuality. Cato, the last of the old Romans, and in his place stood the sybarite with dyed hair and painted cheek. What a picture is that of Cato on his farm, living in a hut on boiling turnips for his supper, compared to that of Trimalchio at his banquet, seated before a hog crowned with a pudding and garnished with fritters and giblets, tarts with Spanish honey, grape jelly, chitterlings, livers in patépans, chaperoned eggs, dormice stewed with honey and poppy seeds, paste-eggs containing beccaficos in yolk seasoned with pepper, sausages, etc., etc., and Opimian falernian a hundred years old.

Every great age of joy of national supremacy will give place to an age of sorrow and national degradation. As a seed strives in the soil, so does a people in the country where it has been cast by the hand of chance or determination; it dies and withers, or else it battles with adversity; and as from an acorn springs the oak, and the oak shades the birds of the air, so the ideal gathers under the cool of its shadowing wings the thoughts of the world; then in its supremacy is its creaking form torn from the mind by some raging gale, strangled by the creeping ivy of corruption, or else rots to a senile decay through decrepitude or stagnation. Thus with peoples and nations as they die so are they reborn, tribulation breeds aspiration, aspiration, empire and glory, and glory the coffined-silence of death.

The soul of man centres in the ideal. Given a fertile soil it will in time bear fruit, irrespective of labour or plough. It is the past which produces the idea; it is the present which idealizes the idea; and it is the future which extinguishes it with a nightly hand, or fans it into the sunburst of a resplendent dawn.

All great national crises are ethical ones; it is the inner soul trying to break the outer shell of circumstance, the inner soul mystically moving inwardly; it is a great explosion of feeling, the disruption of the present from the past towards the future. The dry bones of our ancestors weigh on us as the sins of Christian, yet we stagger on till we can bear them no longer; then the ideal man, the Avatara of the East, the Adam Qadmon of the Qabalists, the Christ of the Christians, and the Superman of modern philosophy, rises before us a holy graal of aspiration, and as we grasp it the burden slips from off our weary shoulders and bounds rattling down the hill of past hopes to the vale of shrieks and ribald song, to the creaking wheel of circumstance the straining ropes of desire. Yet lo! the cup of a greater hope is dry, and the summit of our expectation has receded. Struggle on, poor martyr, thy journey is endless as the years, infinite as time, vast as eternity; yet, struggle on, for the day is short and the night is long, flourish as the flower of the field and be beautiful, "For the wind passeth over it, and it is gone."[235]

As all dies so all is born, and birth foretells death, and death actualizes birth. Egypt has gone, and so has Assyria; the splendour of Greece laboured and bore the grandeur of Rome, and the spirit of eternity hovered over the capital of the seven hills; silently in the hearts of man it uttered: *"Oyez! oyez! le roi est mort; vive le roi!"* So the old order changed, giving place to the new, and on the throne of the deific Cæsar, crowned with the iron crown of power, we see his form no more, but in his stead that of the Son of Man, son of the crushed and yearning East deified and crowned with the twisted thorns of woe.

Times were propitious; Rome had reached the zenith of her power, and the empire which had known Cæsar and Augustus soon began only to know such men as Nero and Caligula. Rome was supreme, and yet a cankering worm was eating away her very soul. The amassing of wealth had brought in its turn a wave of luxury that swept over the empire. Rome was its centre, and a veritable seething pot of cultured vice. The *lupanaria* and *fornices* infested every quarter of the city; the imperial palace was one vast harem, wherein the most abandoned orgies and bacchanalian revels took place. Courtesans, as the hetæra of Corinth, usurped the highest positions in society and a woman could only enter it by such means as would now facilitate her exit. Messalinas would share the imperial couch or the pallet in the *lupanaria* as desire prompted; the days of Asphasia and Phryne had returned with all the viciousness of ancient Greece, and with little of its refinement, for it was the desire of all to wallow undisturbed in the ruin of bestial lust.

A great ethical change, however, was setting in, as it always must when the climax of luxury has been reached. As Aristos was born so must he die; and as Demos died so must he be reborn. The Roman empire was on its decline, the sun of its glory was setting, and decay had taken hold of all its members. The old religions were tottering; the glories of Zeus had been eclipsed by the grossness of Priapus, and Priapus could but for a short time satisfy the craving of even the most debased of men.

[235] Psalms 103:16.

Amongst the lower classes of slaves and workers, hundreds of smaller sects were arising, permeated with a gross spiritism, for all great changes are heralded in with mysticism and wonder; and amidst these many sects was one—the Nazarenes, the followers of a certain Galilean carpenter, by name Jesus. In him they found a kindred spirit, one who preached poverty, who depreciated riches, descried learning, offering them a kingdom where they should reign supreme, receiving for the ephemeral sorrows of this transient world the eternal joys of an everlasting heaven.

"Blessed be ye poor: for yours is the kingdom of God."
"Blessed are ye that hunger now: for ye shall be filled."
"Blessed are ye that weep now: for ye shall laugh."[236]

But:—

"Woe unto you that are rich: for ye have received your consolation."
"Woe unto you that are full: for ye shall hunger."
"Woe unto you that laugh now: for ye shall mourn and weep."[237]

Such were the words of Jesus, and just such an appeal the down-trodden masses yearned for. "They have caught a glimpse of a better life. They lift their soiled hands and bloodshot eyes in trembling prayer and cry: 'We poor people are human; we are men, women; we are children of love and light; and the earth is ours, and the new earth that is to come.' "[238]

"Christianity was the great sob, the great sigh, and also the great smile of a proletariat that was learning its own human dignity."[239]

Demos was reincarnated.

III.

"Whenever the dharmma decays, the a-dharmma prevails; *then* I manifest myself. For the protection of the good, for the destruction of the evil, *for the firm establishment of* THE NATIONAL RIGHTEOUSNESS, I am born again and again."—Krishna.

236 Luke 6:20–21.
237 Luke 6:24–25.
238 "The Religion of the First Christian," by F. J. Gould, p. 54 [original note]. Frederick James Gould, *The Religion of the First Christians* (London: Watts, 1901), 54.
239 Ibid., p. 27 [original note].

These first Christians were as little children taken in the arms of their great Master; as children they loved him, wondered and followed him; but as children they were child-like, morally weak, intellectually ignorant. At times they would discuss who should be the greatest in the kingdom that was to come (Mark ix., 34), and would be pacified by such simple answers as: "I appoint unto you a kingdom, as my Father hath appointed unto me; that ye may eat and drink at my table in my kingdom, and sit on thrones judging the twelve tribes of Israel" (Luke xxii., 29, 30); at other times they might say: "Grant unto us that we may sit, one on thy right hand, and the other on thy left hand, in thy glory" (Mark x., 37).

Their childish questions were only rivalled by the obtuseness of their understanding, as displayed in (Matthew xvi., 11, and Mark viii., 17). They were simple; they were impulsive: "There shall be joy in heaven over one sinner that repenteth, more than over ninety and nine righteous persons which need no repentance."

A little love was all they needed, a little human affection; without it they were beasts, with it they were men.

After the death of their master, the sect which he had been the instrument of founding continued to assemble at Jerusalem, under the guidance of Simon Peter, being based on the strictest communistic maxims. It probably gained many converts among the ignorant and oppressed classes who flocked there yearly to celebrate the passover. The sect grew, and among its heterogenous congregation one result only was possible, namely, that many quarrels and schisms would occur. During the life of Jesus disputes had even arisen among his own followers as to who should be the greatest. Among the ultra-communistic section such incidents as that of Ananias and Sapphira occurred (Acts v., 1–10). In Paul's community Elymas was smitten with blindness as "a child of the devil" (Acts xiii., 10, 11.), and Hymenæus was handed over "unto Satan" (I. Timothy, 1, 20). As time wore on, their differences became more acrimonious. John, in his Revelation, scowls at Paul and his Gentile following, who "say they are Jews and are not, but are the synagogue of Satan" (Rev. ii., 9). He denounces the doctrines of Nicolas (Rev. ii., 6, 25), one of the seven first deacons of the Church, as hateful, and he expresses his detestation of the Laodiceans (Rev. iii., 16), by saying that the Almighty would spue them out of his mouth. Paul returns the compliment by "withstanding" Peter for his "dissimulation" (Galatians ii., 11, 13), and sneering at James and John (Galatians ii, 9) as seeming to be pillars, the former of whom retorts that Paul is a "vain man" (James ii, 20). Paul vehemently tells the Galatians: "If any man preach any other gospel unto you than that ye have received, let him be accursed" (Galatians i., 9). Even the "beloved disciple," in his second epistle, manifests the same persecuting spirit: "If there come any unto you, and bring not this doctrine, receive him not into your house, neither bid him God-speed; for he that biddeth him Godspeed is partaker of his evil deeds" (II. John, 10, 11).

But, in spite of these bickerings and disputes, this was the heroic age of Christianity, when men would die for their faith, when women and children would prefer to be torn to pieces by wild beasts, burnt at the stake, and torn to shreds, than renounce the God of their hopes, and the Heaven of their dreams.

The Neronian persecutions first forced this faith into notoriety, and fresh fuel was added to the blazing flames of reputation by those of Domitian, Vespasian and Trajan: and as the death of the martyr was often fanatically noble, so was his life only too frequently bestially vicious. Even as early as the time of St. Paul, we find that Saint reproving the Christians for profaning their own feast of the Lord's Supper: "When ye come together, therefore, into one place, this is not to eat the Lord's supper; for in eating every one taketh before other his own supper; and one is hungry, and another is drunken. . . . (I. Corinthians xi., 20–34). Again, we find them chided for their wickedness in (II. Peter ii., 10–15)—"Spots they are and blemishes, sporting themselves with their own deceivings while they feast with you, having eyes full of adultery, and that cannot cease from sin, beguiling unstable souls . . . ."; and in the 12th verse of Jude: "Woe unto them! for they have gone the way of Cain . . . these are spots in your feasts of charity."

Nevertheless, Demos toiled on, and the crime that crept into the Christian community in many ways rather strengthened than weakened its cause; a stern asceticism set in, celibacy, which had long been regarded as a virtue, was considered as doubly so now; marriage as a vice; anchorites were not even allowed to see their own mothers, or possess female animals; St, Euphraxia would not wash her feet; St. Ammon had never seen himself naked; St. Macarius slept in a marsh; and St. Simeon lived on a pillar.

Christianity was not only fast becoming mad, but was also becoming vastly attractive. Gibbon relates an anecdote of a Benedictine abbot, who confessed: "My vow of poverty has given me a hundred thousand crowns a year; my vow of obedience has raised me to the rank of a sovereign prince."

The historian sarcastically adds: "I forget the consequence of his vow of chastity."[240]

In 304 A.D. the emperor Marcellus was reduced to the servile position of a groom, and held the stirrup for the Pope to mount his horse. The heroic age was over.

In the midst of all this hideous ignorance and sordid filth, quarrels were for ever arising, and schisms splitting up parties, intolerance became the order of the day, sect hating sect as they would the very fiend himself. The first age of Christianity was rapidly passing away, the persecuted became persecutors and assumed a power superior to the masses; distinction arose between the clergy and laity; but still the former were the representatives of the latter. This, however, did not last long; the power they had rapidly grew, the *spiritus priviatus* became an intolerable onus, and was cast off; henceforth, the road to heaven lay alone through the gateway of the Church. "No man could have God for a father unless he had also the Church for a mother";[241] religion became a monopoly, an era of mental slavery set in, and "the Church became the State concubine."[242] Aristos was reborn.

The central figure in this change was Constantine—the murderer of his wife, his brother-in-law, his nephew, his father-in-law, and his son. His title being unsound, he threw in his lot with the rabble, and, being converted to Christianity drew to his side the powerful Christian mob. During his reign the famous Nicene creed was drawn up (A.D. 325) with an addendum declaring that:—

> "The Holy Catholic and Apostolic Church anathematises those who say there was a time when the Son of God was not, and that before he was begotten he was not, and that was out of another substance or essence, and is created or changeable or alterable."[243]

This only added fresh fuel to the Arian schism in the East, and helped the condensation of the supreme ecclesiastical power in the supreme bishop in the

[240] Decline and Fall—xxxvii [original note]. See, for example, Edward Gibbon, *The History of the Decline and Fall of the Roman Empire: In Twelve Volumes* (Leipzig: Fleischer, 1821), 4:395nL.

[241] In his epistle, *De unitate ecclesiae* (*On the unity of the church*), St. Cyprian, the bishop of Carthage, states, "He can no longer have God for his Father who has not the Church for his mother" (vi).

[242] William Windood Reade, *The Martyrdom of Man* (London: Trübner, 1872), 249.

[243] This original addendum to the Nicene Creed—intended to settle the Trinitarian debate between the ecclesiastics Alexander and Arius—was later dropped.

West; whilst the former was confused by Arians, Macedonians, Appollinarians, and later by Nestorians and Monophysites, the progress of the latter was certain. The sack of Rome in 410 A.D. destroyed the power of Paganism for ever; two years previously the heathen temples had been despoiled: "The last fatal sign and omen of the departure of Roman greatness was, that the statue of Fortitude, or Virtue, was thrown into the common mass" (*Zosimus*, v. 41).[244]

In the East, religion ceased more than ever to be an affair of pure religion, and developed into a string of imperial court intrigues. The wild and ferocious monks of the Nitrian desert murder the gentle Hypatia, and scoop the flesh from her body with broken shells. Justinian, the cowardly slave of the royal prostitute Theodora, who ministered to the licentious pleasures of the populace as a courtesan, was emperor; intellect was down-trodden. philosophy was at a stand-still, the Dark Ages were swiftly approaching, the gloom fell, and Aristos was enthroned for the night of a thousand years.

Paganism once exterminated, fraud and forgery set in with renewed vigour. Those who deceived received commendation instead of censure. The "greatest and most pious teachers," says Mosheim, were "nearly all of them infected with this leprosy."[245] "No fable could he too gross, no invention too transparent, for their unsuspicious acceptance, if it assumed a pious form or tended to edification," says the author of "Supernatural Religion."[246] "The forgery of documents appears to have been a recognised part of the ecclesiastical profession. It was not obscure laymen who composed these manuscripts for the amusement of their leisure, but the recognised leaders of Christianity, who held that the end sanctioned the means, and prostituted Truth in the temples of Religion."[247] Neither was fraud behind hand. "Piety, like the itch, could be caught by wearing another man's clothes."[248] Helena discovered the true cross, and soon all Europe was covered with its splinters. The Virgin's girdle was preserved, also her shoes, her stockings, and her milk; the prepuce of the Redeemer was treasured at Charroux, also at Antwerp, Besancon,

[244] Quoted in Henry Hart Milman, *The History of Christianity, from the Birth of Christ to the Abolition of Paganism in the Roman Empire* (New York: A. C. Armstrong and Son, 1887), 150.

[245] See, for example, Johann Lorenz Mosheim, James Murdock, and James Seaton Reid, *Mosheim's Institutes of Ecclesiastical History, Ancient and Modern: A New and Literal Translation from the Original Latin, with Copious Additional Notes, Original and Selected* (London: W. Tegg, 1878), 149.

[246] Walter Richard Cassels, *Supernatural Religion: An Inquiry into the Reality of Divine Revelation* (London: Longmans, Green, 1874), 460.

[247] G. W. Foote and J. M. Wheeler, *Crimes of Christianity* (London: Progressive Publishing, 1887), 83.

[248] N. Summerbell, *History of the Christian Church from Its Establishment by Christ to AD 1871 Including the Rise of the Roman Heresy, All the Popes, the Temporal Power, the Abominations of Popery and the Reformation* (Cincinnati: Office of the Christian Pulpit, 1873), 321.

Calcata, Heldesheim, and Rome; every village had its saint, every hut its relic: art was extinct, science was extinct, philosophy was extinct, literature was extinct—only rubbish abounded.

The ignorance of the age hurried on the hideous supremacy of the Papacy, Everything was done to render the people ignorant, everything was done to extract from them the little they might know. Auricular confession was instituted to wrest the domestic secrets from their brainless sycophants, and so gave the Church as great a power over the individual as she held over the State. If the individual rebelled, excommunication was his lot; if a State, an interdict was the award.

During the creeping gloom of this intellectual night the only ray of light that flickered in the European darkness was that of two Semetic races—the Moors and the Jews.

IV.

> "Whenever the dharmma decays, the a-dharmma prevails; *then* I manifest myself. For the protection of the good, for the destruction of the evil, *for the firm establishment of* THE NATIONAL RIGHTEOUSNESS, I am born again and again."—*Krishna*.

THE times which had known Pythagoras and Thales, Aristotle and Plato, Archimedes and Euclid, Epictetus and Aurelius, had vanished from the memory of man; alone in the night the crescent shone, and such names flash forth as Ben Musa, Al Mamun, Alhazen, Giaber, Avicenna, Averroes, and Algazzali. From the time of Constantine to the days of Roger Bacon, scarcely a man of scientific worth arose in the whole of Christian Europe; and as Christianity gained power in Spain, Moorish learning died.

Jewish literature met with a similar fate. Whereever found it was destroyed, and this unfortunate people, who had not only furnished Europe with an Almighty God, but had also supplied a Goddess and a Saviour, met with the most ruthless persecution.

Milman thus describes one of these scenes:—

> ". . . all the Jews were arrested, put to the torture, convicted, condemned to be torn by red hot pincers, and then burned alive. The picture of their sufferings as they writhed on the stake is exhibited with horrid coolness, or rather satisfaction, in the book of the legend. And this triumph of faith,

supported, it is said, by many miracles, is to the present day commemorated in one of the first Christian cities of Europe."[249] [i.e. Brussels]

The next move on the part of the Church to strengthen herself at the expense of others and to give a vent to the factious spirit of her vassals, was to start the crusades. This was done by Urban II., who promised absolution from all sin to whomsoever should take up arms to win back for Christendom the tomb of Jesus. "Women appeared in arms in the midst of warriors," says Michaud, "prostitution not being forgotten among the austerities of penitence."[250] "The moral fabric of Europe," says Mill, "was convulsed; the relations and charities of life were broken; society appeared to be dissolved."[251]

Hordes of pious savages swept over southern Europe, thousands of helpless Jews and peasants were massacred, carnage and rapine were the order of the clay, "virgin modesty was no protection," and, "conjugal virtue no safeguard."[252] Gibbon tells us: "In the dire necessity of famine, they sometimes roasted and devoured the flesh of their infant and adult captives,"[253] and Mills relates that at the taking of the Mosque of Omar: "Such was the carnage . . . that the mutilated carcasses were hurried by the torrent of blood into the court; dissevered arms and hands floated into the current that carried them into contact with bodies to which they had not belonged. Ten thousand people were murdered in this sanctuary."[254]

In the fifth crusade the most hideous scenes were enacted, the Cathedral of St. Sophia rang with the gambler's curse and the obscene song of the drunkard; the floors ran with blood and a prostitute was seated on the throne of the patriarch, ridiculing him whose tomb they were supposed to be endeavouring to wrest from the hand of the infidel (*sic*).

The sixth crusade was chiefly composed of "Women, children, the old, the blind, the lame, the lepers":[255] they were sacred, but, however, the boys were sold as slaves, and the girls to the Oriental harems.

[249] Milman, p. 552 [original note]. Henry Hart Milman, *The History of the Jews* (London: J. Murray, 1829–1930; repr. London: George Routledge, 1878), 552.

[250] Joseph François Michaud, Hamilton Wright Mabie, and William Robson, *The History of the Crusades, Translated by W. Robson: A New Edition* (London: Routledge, 1881), 1:59.

[251] Charles Mills, *The History of the Crusades: For the Recovery and Possession of the Holy Land*, 2nd ed. (London: Longman, Hurst, Rees, Orme, and Brown, 1821), 1:60.

[252] Mills, *History of the Crusades*, 1:68.

[253] Gibbon, *Decline and Fall*, 4:126.

[254] Mills, *History of the Crusades*, 1:254.

[255] Mills, *History of the Crusades*, 2:165.

The ninth crusade, in 1268, ended this wave of European insanity, by signing a treaty in favour of the infidel. And the result? Aristos was supreme, not only at Rome, but over the Western world; the Crusades, as a running ulcer, had freed his body from physical decay; he grasped in his hands the reins of power and the goad of despotism; his coffers were filled with the gold of the devout, individuals were excommunicated, and nations placed under interdict. Aristos became a God!

But, as Time knows no repose, a change was at hand. Man is but a passing breath from the lips of the Eternal; and a God, is he any more? As manhood decays, so does godhood rot; as the former sloughs through ease, so does the latter through excess; all changes, all passes, and in the crucible of the alchemist, in the alembic of the sorcerer, and in the cauldron of the witch, scorched with the flames of superstition, choked with the smoke of ignorance, gloomed in the crimson darkness of this age, the shadowy form of Demos the reborn. Half-sane, half-insane, maddened, illumined with mystery, the thoughtful groped through the night; the God of the Papacy had become the Power of the Dead, the emblem of the martyred Jesus had become the oriflamme of massacre, the insignia of corruption, the symbol of crime. Can we wonder, then, that man sought the Devil as his protector, and the wizard as his redeemer.

As the "serpent was more subtil than any beast of the field,"[256] so was the Diabolus of the mediæval eclipse. "And the serpent said . . . Ye shall not surely die: For God doth know in the day ye eat thereof, then your eyes shall be opened, and ye shall be as gods, knowing good and evil." Seeking wisdom, they found it in the *Compact with the Devil!* and the asinine collections of the Dominicans gave place to the grusome appurtenances of the laboratory.

"From when does the Sorceress date?" asks Michelet, and he answers: " 'From the ages of despair.' "

"From the profound despair the world owed the Church. I say again unhesitatingly: 'The sorceress is the Church's crime.' "[257]

And what was the Church's crime? Vice that was more than Neronic, obscenity that was undreamt by the Arbiter Elegantiorum, and lechery that would have brought a blush to the brow of a Messaline. Boniface VI. was a man of infamous character; Sergius III, the slave of every vice; Stephen

[256] Genesis 3:1.

[257] La Sorciére Michelet, Eng. trans., p. 7 [original note]. Jules Michelet, *The Sorceress: A Study in Middle Age Superstition*, trans. A. R. Allison (Paris: Charles Carrington, 1904), 7.

VIII. was such a peril to the wives and daughters of the Roman citizens that they unsexed him; John III. was the son of Sergius III. by his concubine Marozia, and surpassed his parents in crime; John XII. was publicly accused of concubinage, incest and simony, he was murdered whilst in the act of committing adultery; Benedict IX. Mosheim calls "a most flagitious man, and capable of every crime";[258] Boniface VIII. was accused of assassination, usury and living in concubinage with his two nieces; Clement V. gave himself up to the most criminal debaucheries; John XXII. was found guilty of murder and incest, and was accused before the Council of having seduced two hundred nuns; Sixtus IV. strove to excel all his predecessors in crime; Symonds says: "The private life of Sixtus rendered the most monstrous stories plausible, while his public treatment of these men [ED—his nephews] recalled to mind the partiality of Nero for Doryphorus";[259] Alexander VI. (1492–1503) was one of the most depraved scoundrels that ever lived; Mosheim says "so many and so great villainies, crimes, and enormities are recorded of him, that it must be certain he was destitute not only of all religion, but also of decency and shame."[260]

Can we wonder that men even groped for better things in the lowest depths of hell?

> "When Colbert, in 1672 (Michelet writes), shelved Satan with so little ceremony, forbidding the Judges of the Realm to hear cases of Witchcraft, the Norman *Parlement*, in its obstinate conservatism, its sound Norman logicality, demonstrated the dangers attending such a decision. The Devil is nothing less than a dogma closely bound up with all the rest. Touch the vanquished of the ages—are you not touching the victor, too? Doubt the acts of the one—is not this paving the way to doubt those of the other, those very miracles he did to fight the Devil? The pillars of heaven are based in the abyss. The rash man who shakes this infernal foundation may well crack the walls of Paradise."[261]

Let us see now how these walls were cracked, and how the whole building crumbled into dust.

[258] Mosheim, *Institutes of Ecclesiastical History*, 182.
[259] John Addington Symonds, *Renaissance in Italy: The Age of the Despots* (London: Smith Elder, 1898), 304.
[260] Mosheim, *Institutes of Ecclesiastical History*, 437.
[261] Ibid., p. 13[original note]. Michelet, *Sorceress*, 13.

We have already enumerated some of the names that added lustre to the Golden Age of Spain. There, whilst learning was honoured, to the rest of Europe it only met with persecution.

Erigena (*d.* 875), was the only man in the whole West who knew Greek. After him, for five centuries, it was unknown; scarcely a lay name of note appears till the thirteenth century, the century which saw the invention of paper; and it was not till 1453, the year which saw the fall of the Eastern Empire, and the invention of printing in Europe, that free inquiry in any way became instituted.

From this date we find the pulpit rendered secondary, and a host of Titanic names appear in the pages of modern history. Aristos was stricken with the palsy. Europe was sick of such men as Sergius, Stephen, Sixtus, and Alexander; the cup of hope was filled with the excrements of degradation: Demos, son of the astrolabe and the alembic, shattered it to the ground; Europe had conceived, she now laboured, and, travailing, bore such sons as Columbus, Leonardo, Copernicus, and Paracelsus to avenge the night of a thousand years. Wycliffe had already left his mark, the socialistic opinions of the Lollards were spreading in England, the Albigenses had been exterminated; but their ghostly finger beckoned on the sons of the age, the peasants revolted, the pseudo-sciences were revived, the Renaissance, as a flash of vivid lightning rushed through the dismal sky of the Dark Ages, the clouds parted, the dawn broke, the Reformation was at hand.

V.

> "Whenever the dharmma decays, the a-dharmma prevails; *then* I manifest myself. For the protection of the good, for the destruction of the evil, *for the firm establishment of* THE NATIONAL RIGHTEOUSNESS, I am born again and again."—*Krishna.*

As early as the third century Lactantius and Eusebius had poured forth their contempt on astronomy. Peter Damian, the Chancellor of Gregory VII, declared all sciences to be "absurdities" and "fooleries." Alchemy was considered untrue because not mentioned by Solomon. In 1317 John XXII. issued his bull, *Spondent pariter*, against alchemists, and the more chemistry came to be known it became classed as one of the "seven devilish arts." In 1437, and again in 1445, Eugene IV. exhorted, in a bull, the inquisitors to punish so-called magicians. In 1484 Innocent VIII. destroyed tens of thousands of men and women accused of magic by his bull *Summis*

Desiderantes. Similar bulls were issued by Julius in 1504, and Adrian VI. in 1523. In 1163 Alexander III. forbade physical studies to ecclesiastics; in 1243 the Dominicans interdicted every member of their order from the study of medicine and natural philosophy. In 1278 the authorities of the Franciscan order condemned Bacon's teaching, and threw him into prison for fourteen years. In 1380 Charles V. of France forbade the possession of furnaces and chemical apparatus. In 1418 Antonio de Dominis was tortured to death for investigating the phenomenon of light, and in Spain everything like scientific research was crushed out among the Christians.

Six hundred years B.C. Pythagoras, and after him Philolaus, had suggested the movement of the planets round the sun, three hundred years later Aristarchus stated this truth with greater precision, in the fifth century A.D. it was brought to light again by Martianus Capella, and then lost in the darkness in the middle ages till a demi-god arose in the person of Nicolas Copernicus.

Demos had one foot on the throne; soon he was destined to wrest crown and sceptre from the hands of the despot, and to hurl him from the dais of his pride down the steps for his presumption.

In 1543, the year of his death, Copernicus published his great work "*De Revolutionibus Orbium Cælestium.*" On May the 24th he received the first copy, a few hours later he was beyond the reach of the world. In 1616 his works were condemned as damnable; in Nuremburg the Protestants ridiculed him as the Roman Catholics did at Rome; in the same year Pope Paul V. placed his works on the Index, from which they were not removed till 1835 by Pius Vll. The Ptolomiac astronomy was dust.

In 1591 Giordano Bruno asserted that other worlds might be inhabited as well as ours, on the 16th of February, 1600 A.D. he was burnt to ashes at Rome, and to-day his statue stands there as a verification of the Truth.

Still the truth lived on, and ten years after the execution of Bruno, Galileo established beyond all possible doubt the certainty and truth of the doctrine of Copernicus.

"Herein was fulfilled one of the most touching of prophecies. Years before, the opponents of Copernicus had said to him, 'If your doctrine were true, Venus would show phases like the moon.' Copernicus answered: 'You are right; I know not what to say; but God is good, and will in time find an answer to this objection.' The God-given answer came when, in 1611, the rude telescope of Galileo showed the phases of Venus."[262]

[262] "Warfare of Science and Theology," Andrew White, p. 130 [original note].

In 1615 Galileo was summoned before the Inquisition. Christian Europe thundered with applause. In 1632 he published his "Dialogo," for which he was thrown into prison, threatened with torture, and publicly made to recant his heresy, "The Movement of the Earth."

Thus Demos strode into manhood; and whilst Paul III. was breeding bastards at Rome, Luther fondling Catherine von Bora at Wittenberg, and Henry VIII. ogling his own daughter, Anne Boleyn; men like Palestrina, Aquapendente, Ubaldi, Gilbert and Tycho Brahe, rose into eminence. Luther attacked Copernicus, Calvin attacked Servetus, and Zwingle condemned all astronomy, but the sceptre had fallen from the hands of Aristos, and his crown was wrenched from his head by such Titans as Kepler, Newton, Laplace, Priestly and Voltaire.

In 1859, Charles Darwin published the first installment of his great work, "The Origin of Species." It was at once met with a howl of execration and a shriek of blatant abuse. Newton described it as "a brutal philosophy—to wit, there is no God, and the ape is our Adam."

Another critic spoke of persons accepting Darwinian views as "under the frenzied inspiration of an inhaler of mephitic gas." From America came the words, "If this hypothesis be true, then is the Bible an unbearable fiction. . . . Then have Christians for nearly two thousand years been duped by a monstrous lie . . . Darwin requires us to disbelieve the authoritative view of the Creator."[263]

"DUPED BY A MONSTROUS LIE." Aristos was dead!

Oyez! Oyez! le roi est mort! Vive le roi! We enter a new epoch, the great age of Science.

The democratic republic of Rome grew into the aristocratic empire of the Cæsars; the empire gave way to communistic Christianity, which in its way grew into the oligarchic papacy; then becoming unbearable, the Papacy succumbed to Catholic learning. Learning has grown into practical science. Have we reached the goal of our aspirations? Have we climbed the summit of Parnassus? In a few years, a few centuries, a millennium, perhaps, shall we have conquered the spheres of knowledge, and, like Alexander, find no fresh worlds to subdue? I think not. Science in her time will become as corrupt as Christianity, as dogmatic as oppressive. Life will be rendered unbearable, and, like the Erewhonians, we shall rise and destroy the cursed machines; and a new heroic age will again begin, of what kind there is no

[263] "Warfare of Science with Theology," pp. 71–72 [original note].

certain knowledge. Perhaps it will be a great age of love and a higher morality. When women mentally, as well as socially, shall rise to be equal, and worthy partners of men; when the laws of marriage give place to the laws of love; when people seek excitement in healthy exercise and works of virtue, and not in the fœted atmosphere of the Divorce Courts; when better laws are instituted, when better education is taught, when birth is regulated, rational suicide and homicide legalized, better sanitation undertaken, better food, better air, better literature, music, and art; then will drunkenness, prostitution, vagrancy, cruelty, disease, idiocy and ignorance give way to the great powers of Love, Truth, and Beauty.

Yet by Demos stands Aristos, the eternal Gemini.

How long? how long? the wheel of Fortune turns; to-day we are with the heroes of Olympus, to-morrow gibbering with the outcasts of Orcus.

A Recall[264]

Victor B. Neuburg

Upon my bed in sickness I did lie,
Too weak to know or think, too sick to dream;
And they had left me, and I feared to die,
For through my veins
An ever-growing, turgid, rolling stream
Of blood and youth unconquered hurried by;
And in my brains
All thought was merged into a lurid gleam
Of light; my laboured breath
Too strong for me did seem,—
And then came peace and calm, and with them mighty Death.

A sombre mantle o'er his shoulders fell,
Trailing the ground, where scarce his feet did light;
And he exhaled a faded, musky smell
With his slow breath;
His eyes were deepless as a starless night;

[264] *Agnostic Journal* 60, no. 9 (March 2, 1907): 134; repr. in *A Green Garland*.

His bosom with deep breath did sink and swell;
No word he saith,
But held his bended arms, as loth to smite,
Against his sides; he seemed
Fitter for sleep than fight:
Around his radiant head an ominous halo streamed.

Bright stars the window of my chamber bore,
As in a frame-work set; I strove to rise
Upon my elbow; said I, "Never more,
Unless I strive,
Shall I behold the daylight with mine eyes."
And I was losing fast my vital store.[265]
"Now shall I dive
With this dark angel who is over-wise,
Into his sunless halls,
Where the dark Fate denies
A gleam of light, a flash of summer to her thralls?

The angel to my window moved, and gazed
Into my garden sweet with night and dew,
And, his head leaning on his arms, upraised
His speechless eyes:
Then, turning to my bed-side, slowly drew
My eyes to his, that held me dulled and dazed.
I strove to rise,
But a calm breeze from the still garden blew,
Over my weary brow,
And suddenly I knew
That, as his sad lips moved, he whispered softly, "Now."

And so I rose, night-garmented, and sped
Swift doorwards, with the angel at my side,
And marvelled at the speed with which he led,
Yet felt no speed,
And he traversed much space and countries wide;

[265] This line becomes "And agony had chilled my being's core;" in *A Green Garland*.

Past myriad towns o'er which were stars thick-spread,[266]
He still did lead.
And still I followed swiftly in his stride
Over unshadowed lands;
Then, by the yellow tide
Of a broad hasting stream, he turned, and seized my hands.

Now, on the purple hills the dawn did fall,
Slow-moving, grey, it crept around the world,
And fringed with light the sombre, flowing pall
Of ancient Night;
The angel's lips with sorrow deep were[267] curled,
As one whose steps are stayed by a great wall
Of dreadful height,
Or one who sees[268] an alien flag unfurled
His city's heart within,
And sees his kinsfolk hurled
From towers high, and hears their bones crash 'midst the din.

So gazed the angel, as he dropped my hand,
And sombrely surveyed the dawning day;
Then, lingering a moment on the strand,
Unfurled his wings
That then I first saw; swift he sped away,
His wings vibrating as the skies he spanned;
He passed the rings
Of light that fringe the sun,—his dark array
Faded into the light, . . .
And so I wondering lay
Upon my couch, and lo! the day had conquered night!

And so they came to me when daylight came,
I smiled at them and at the light of morn;
The sun had risen as a mighty flame;
The morning breeze

[266] This line becomes "Past myriad towns o'er which were stars thick-spread," in *A Green Garland.*
[267] This becomes "are" in *A Green Garland.*
[268] "Or one who sees" becomes "Or one's who spies" [*sic*] in *A Green Garland.*

Blew me the thrushes' singing; I was worn
And wearied pleasantly. They spoke my name.
Slow-rustling trees
I heard outside my window, on them borne
The healing morning air.
Ah! then no more forlorn,
I lay at ease, and smiled that life should seem so fair.

The Eagle and the Serpent[269]

Victor B. Neuburg.

"When the sun was at noon, Zarathustra suddenly looked upwards wondering—for above himself he heard the sharp cry of a bird. And lo! an eagle swept through the air in wide circles, a serpent hanging from it not like a prey, but like a friend; coiling round its neck.

" 'They are mine animals,' said Zarathustra, and rejoiced heartily. 'The proudest animal under the sun, and the wisest animal under the sun have set out to reconnoiter . . . More dangerous than among animals I found it among men. Let mine animals lead me!' "

—*Nietzsche*[270]

The Eagle of the Dusky Wing
Swirls, and then droops in wheeling flight,
And casts a glance unpitying
Over the shadowed Hills of Light;
Poised o'er the Valley of Dry Bones
He cries in harsh unwond'ring tones.

About the Eagle's neck a Snake
Hisses and twirls, slips slack and twines,
His eyes as the wide sun awake,
His breath as fierce as poisoned wine's.

269 *Agnostic Journal* 60, no. 13 (March 30, 1907): 204; repr. in *A Green Garland*.
270 "Zarathustra's Introductory Speech," *Thus Spake Zarathustra* pt. 10.

Unwinking he the Valley scans,
His voice hushed as a pious man's.

"Return, return to early fields;
Look back, look back to fading day:
The mother Earth her harvest yields,
The sun illumes the natural way.
Give ear and turn, nor be thy breath
Enchained to martyrdom and death.

"The Son of Man hath fallen deep,
The Man of Sun hath yet to rise,—
Go! thrust from off thy brows the sleep
That dims thine eyes, that dims thine eyes.
Return, return, and still return:
Live in the sunlight, bask and burn.

"The wind from the high hills of Day
Blows on thy hair and dreaming eyes;
The sunlight floods the only way
That gives thee power, that makes thee wise.
Give ear, before thy race is done,
O thou who hast blasphemed the sun!

"Be cunning, if thou be not strong,
Be bitter, if thou be not fair,
For Might is Right, and Right is Wrong,
If thou woulds't breathe the purer air,
Let not thy spirit quail; be wise,
Nor let love dazzle thy strong eyes.

"The kingdom of the setting sun
Is thine, but we, we scan the day,
And as we rise the night is none,
For nought defiles the perfect Way
Of strength and might and wisdom; we
Dwell with the One Infinity.

"Lips locked in love, the mystic light
    Serves but for twain, should serve for all,
Why should ye greet the coming night,
    Why should ye be the Dark's fell thrall?
Was it for this ye strove and rose
From primal pain, from primal foes?

"To ye hath given the wise old Nurse
    And Mother, on whose breast ye've lain,
A respite from the primal Curse,
    A breathing-space from strife and pain.
Will ye ungrateful bow and bend
To alien gods, that nothing lend?

"Nothing? Aye! Less than nothing. Ye
    Are on the knees to phantom kings,
Poor pictures of the things ye see,
    Gods with dull eyes and broken wings,
If wings they ever knew, who creep
Within the shades of death and sleep.

"Awake! Be wise! Ah! Not for long
    Your message to the star-course rings;
Not ever may I cry 'Be strong,'
    Not ever shall resound my wings.
Cast off the lumber of the years.
The kings, the powers, the loves, the fears.

"O Son of Man, thy fall is deep;
    Will ye not rise to wiser gods?
Too long ye've sung of death and sleep,
    And forged your tyrant's ruling rods.
Arise! Cast off the web ye've spun;
Stand naked to the rising sun!"

. . .

The dark wings flap, the night draws on,
    The Eagle flies abroad to prey;

The wonder of the song is gone
With daylight and the love of day;
Calm stars o'ershine the fields we ploughed,
The laugh of peasants rises loud.

And round the board we sit and raise
Our voices o'er the sparkling wine
That holds the light of other days,
That breathes of youth and hours divine,
When the sun gave the grapes their bloom,
When the air bore the press's fume.

The board resounds with laughter wild,
And singing strong and high and deep,
The hours with mirth are still beguiled,
And then come weariness and sleep.
New day shall find new fields to plough,
Fresh sweat shall stream from each strong brow.

The winds from off the hills of day
The Eagle sang, shall fan our brows,—
Those hills so bright, so far away,
Beyond the reach of feet and ploughs.
So shall we wait in peace the night,
When maybe stars shall give their light.

And if the summer rains fall swift,
And if the night in clouds be veiled,
The morning shall the clouds see drift,
Nor hath earth's harvest ever failed.
The night our feasting shall renew,
The morning break with golden hue.

The winds from the bright hills of day
Have eyrie-wards the Eagle borne;
The Snake has sought the hidden Way,
His glittering eyes grown cold in scorn.
Around the board we sit, and give
Thanks to the sun whereby we live.

Freethought[271]

Victor B. Neuburg

FREETHOUGHT is a stage between Agnosticism and Gnosticism.

Obviously, Agnosticism is not the highest possible ideal, for it is a confession of ignorance. It may be argued, however, that this confession of ignorance applies exclusively to what is inherently unknowable, but the fact that a thing is *now* unknowable is no guarantee that it must forever remain so.[272]

But Agnosticism is one of the most useful of systems, for by its very name, it implies intellectual honesty, and this quality is probably the most important of all qualities in the search for truth.

The value of Agnosticism in the evolutionary scheme—if scheme there be—seems to me to be this:—That it makes the seeker after knowledge very cautious before accepting as true any theory relating to the Cosmos or its workings.

"To thine own Church be true," says the theologian; "To thine own self be true," says the Freethinker, and the only way of reconciling these *dicta* is by being a member of a Church that knows no dogma. Such a Church has, of course, no objective existence, and it is well that this should be so, for every organisation contains within it the seeds of decay. But such a Church exists subjectively, and the members of it are these who regard no exclusive *-ism* as being necessary to "salvation," mental, moral, physical, or "supernatural,"—but the mere fact of being a member of the human race. It is simply egotism, and very amusing egotism, to describe a man as "converted" when you have merely made him think as you think. Real conversion can only be effected by awakening the Man in an individual, and inducing him to think for himself. Whether he agrees with you or not is a matter of relatively small importance, for, as soon as his intellect has been awakened, a man will soon find a path for himself.

> "Save his own soul's light overhead,
> None leads him, and none ever led."[273]

I think that this is the gist of all the real "Inner Teaching"; like all great principles it is infinitely simple, and has results infinitely complex. It is this very simplicity

[271] *Agnostic Journal* 60, no. 13 (April 6, 1907): 210–211.

[272] I admit, of course, that, on the particular plane of being on which we find ourselves, much must remain forever unknown, and, as Spencer puts it, "Unknowable." But there is a possibility, and, in my opinion, almost a certainty, of the existence of other planes of being. And on these planes, now almost inconceivable to us, a degree of Gnosticism may be possible [original note].

[273] Algernon Charles Swinburne, prelude of *Songs before Sunrise* (1871), lines 151–152.

that has baffled the disciples of every great teacher. The truth was so simple and obvious that they overlooked it, and, perhaps, so obvious was it to the teacher, that he neglected to express it to them directly. To this neglect must be attributed the curse of Sectarianism. In the very nature of things, every sect, and every religion—for what is a religion but a sect on a larger scale?—must believe itself to possess more of truth than do its rival sects, and this feeling of superiority militates more against brotherhood than do all other causes combined.

Truth is one, but has an infinite number of aspects. What but bigotry can we look for from him who views Truth from one point of view only? And when we remember that that point of view is probably very erroneous, owing to its lack of perspective, what wonder is there at the enormous number of unnecessary tragedies brought about by the conflict of the votaries of rival sects or religions.

By perfect freedom for the individual, we attain to perfect freedom for the race, for he who is truly free will never encroach upon the freedom of others. He will have no need. To persecute is invariably a sign and confession of weakness. Strength smiles tolerantly at opposition; it is Weakness that becomes enraged upon having its authority questioned.

Real brotherhood is not obtainable by dogmatism, which is, as I have attempted to show, the most prolific cause of disunion. But diversity of thought—*free* thought—is no bar to brotherhood. And diversity of thought is inevitable, for no two thinking minds can view things in precisely the same light.

Complete unity of thought is to be found only among those who do not think for themselves, but receive their ideas ready-made; and it is these people—the children of Dogma—who are always ready to persecute those who differ from them, for, never having thought themselves, they cannot conceive of the use or necessity of thought in others.

Madeleine Bavent[274]

1607–1647

J. F. C. F.

"Died every day she lived."—*Macbeth, iv. iii.*

Blood! This one word sums up two thousand years of Christianity. The followers of Christ have drenched the world with blood; blood, blood, blood,

[274] *Agnostic Journal* 60, no. 17 (April 27, 1907): 257–258. Sister Madeleine Bavent was eighteen years old when, in 1625, she became the first nun at the Louviers Convent to fall victim to demonic

everywhere blood! Christ himself proclaimed his existence 'midst the blood of innocents, and departed this life 'twixt two bleeding malefactors; and from that portentous day, when "ghosts did shriek and squeal about the streets,"[275] the crimson sweat of Gethsemane has bedewed the world with the scarlet blood of woe, and the black horror of fiends.

"Let's carve him as a dish fit for the gods, not hew him as a carcass fit for hounds,"[276] are the words the great bard of Avon places in the mouth of the pagan Brutus; not so, however, the words that issued from the fetid gullet of Christianity—the more brutal the death, the better pleased was the scarlet woman of the seven hills; the more fiendish were the means, the more glorious was the end; the more foul the end, the better pleased was *her* God—that God who nailed his only begotten Son, as a farmer would a weasel, to a cross of agony—the lintel of Hell!

In the year 415 A.D., the wolfish demoniacs of Alexandria tore to pieces Hypatia, and hurled the statue of Serapis into the flames of general destruction. In 1905 A.D., the yelping Czar-hounds of Russia tortured, with fire and knout, the heroic Marie Spiridonova,[277] and would if they could dash the leaden hammer of orthodoxy into the face of Freethought; but the great norm of Reason is not built of clay, or marble, or granite, nor yet even of bronze; a colossus it stands in the mind of every upright man, and neither sword nor fire can destroy it, let the demons and the wolves howl as they will. Bay Truth, O Christian, as a hound will bay the moon; yet Truth was before the moon, and Truth shall be after the Sun and all his children are once again swallowed up in the endless circles of eternity. The dog and the moon, O Folly, thy name is Christianity!

But to commence the subject I wish to deal with, and which the agonised form of Marie Spiridonova recalls to my memory.

Hypatia was a pagan—little excuse as this may be, yet she was not a Christian; Marie Spiridonova shot a Christian, there was provocation—little excuse as such a deed may also be in such a country as Russia, where deeds "without a name" are of daily occurrence, yet she destroyed a follower of him who came not to bring peace but the sword. Now listen to what I believe to be

possession. She accused the convent's director, Mathurin Picard, and the vicar of Louviers, Father Thomas Boulle, of bewitching her and taking her to participate in a witches' sabbath. This resulted in a witchcraft panic with tortures, exorcisms, and more nuns coming forward.

275 Shakespeare, *Julius Caesar*, act 2, scene 2.
276 Shakespeare, *Julius Caesar*, act 2, scene 1.
277 See Neuburg's earlier article, "Marie Spiridonova," in this anthology.

the authentic history of another unfortunate woman, this time a Christian, nay, more, a spouse of Christ.

In the city of Rouen in the year 1607 was born Madeleine Bavent,[278] at the age of nine she was left an orphan, and three years later was apprenticed to a worker in linen in the city of her birth. The confessor of this establishment was a Franciscan who was absolute master of this house; three other girls worked there whom he was in the habit of drugging, "he had his will of three of them, and Madeleine, at fourteen, made the fourth."[279] Two years after her initiation into the mysteries of Christ she was received as a novice in the convent of Louviers; she still was perhaps too pure-minded to submit to the strange way of living as practised by the nuns of this house, and incurred the displeasure of the authorities for having endeavoured at communion to hide her bosom with the altar cloth, this offence was aggravated by her further being reluctant to unveil her soul to the Lady Superior, which she preferred to do to an old priest called David.

David was an *Adamite*, and preached the nudity Adam practised in his innocence; and obedient to his teaching, the Sisters of the convent of Louviers, often to break their souls into discipline would resume the condition of their mother Eve. He did not hide his doctrine from the youthful Madeleine. "The body cannot contaminate the soul; we must, by means of sin, which makes us humble and cures our pride, kill sin."[280] Thus was she ushered into the sisterhood of Christ, and thus did she become the spouse of Jesus, son of the immaculate Mother of God.

She was eighteen years old when David died, but his successor, the *curê* Picart, in his turn only pursued her with more ardent importunity than ever. At confession he spoke of nothing but love, and made her sacristaness so that he might the more often be alone with her in the convent chapel. She did not like him, but, nevertheless, he assailed her in every fashion; when she was ill; even when she was almost on her deathbed this inhuman monster encompassed her weakened imagination with hellish fears by means of diabolical talismans. These failing, then he himself shammed sickness, and assailing her through her compassion, begged her to visit him in his room, a magic potion sealed his wretched deed. She

[278] The following history of her martyrdom is merely an abridged account of the eighth chapter of Jules Michelet's "La Sorciére" as given in the English translation of that famous book, a work which should be read by all Freethinkers and Christians alike [original note].

[279] Michelet, Sorceress, 229.

[280] Michelet, *Sorceress*, 230.

became with child by him, and drugs were provided to attempt to right the wrong he had done her; for convents in those days could well dispense with the necessity of calling in medical aid. What became of the child no one knows, and all that history hands down to us, is that Madeleine herself declared that she subsequently bore several other children to this father in God.

"Picart, already an oldish man, dreaded Madeleine's fickleness, fearing she might form a new connexion with some other confessor, to whom she could pour out her remorse. He adopted a hateful means of attaching her irrevocably to himself. He made her swear an oath pledging herself *to die when he should die, and be with him where he should go*. The poor faint-hearted creature endured agonies of terror. Would he drag her with him into the tomb? Would he set her in Hell alongside of himself? She fully believed herself a lost soul. She became his chattel, his familiar spirit bound to do his will, and he used her and abused her for every vile purpose. He prostituted her in a four-fold orgy, carried out with his vicar Boullé and another woman. He made use of her to win over the other nuns by a magic talisman. The sacred wafer, dipped in Madeleine's blood and buried in the convent garden, was a sure way of agitating their senses and eluding their wits."[281]

It was this same year that Urban Grandier was burnt as a sorcerer, and all France was ringing with the accounts of the devils of Loudon. Madeleine felt herself possessed, she was assailed by devils and pursued by a cat with fiery eyes, then the other sisters caught the hysterical contagion. About this time Picart died, and his death lessened the danger of the irregularities of the convent being disclosed; so another visionary was found to fight the devils which had taken possession of Madeleine; her name was Anne, and on her introduction to the convent this pair fell to sacrificing each other with outrageous calumnies.

The Penitentiary of Evereux, by the advice of the bishop of Evereux, condemned Madeleine without a hearing, and ordered that an examination of her body was to be made so that the Satanic sign-manual might be discovered. This examination was carried out by the Sisters of her convent; these virgin-nuns, after stripping the unfortunate girl naked, first examined her in a most revolting manner, and then drove into her quivering flesh long needles in order to discover the devil's spot which would reveal itself by its

281 Michelet, *Sorceress*, 231–232.

insensibility to pain. But every stab hurt, and they failed to prove her a witch, yet, nevertheless, they had the satisfaction of gloating over her tears and cries of agony.

These means failing, her tormentors ordered her to be immured in an *in pace* for life. The Penitentiary now carried her off as his prey, and deposited her in the dungeon of the episcopal palace, a low subterranean gallery, damp and filthy. Here she suffered from horrible ulcers, lying, as she did, in her own excrements. The perpetual darkness was disturbed by a dreadful scampering of rats, the object of much terror in prisons at that time, as they often gnawed off the helpless prisoners' ears and noses.

Every day the Penitentiary would come into an other cellar overhead, and speak down an orifice leading into the *in pace*, extracting from her what confessions he would for the condemnation of others he was then victimizing.

To terminate her wretched existence she swallowed spiders and gulped down pounded glass; but in vain; then with an old blunt knife she tried to cut her throat, but could not succeed. Next she attempted to drive it into her bowels, again in vain; the wound soon healed. Then followed the crowning horror of her martyrdom. The brutal servants of the bishop's household, despite the horror of the place and the disgusting condition of the wretched woman, would come and take their pleasure of her deeming any outrage on a witch a permissible and godly act.

Henceforth she may be justly regarded as mad; acting like a maniac she signed interminable lists of crimes she had never committed—lying, slandering, and bearing false witness against others; for every time it was desired to ruin a victim she was hailed to Louviers to accuse him. On her evidence a wretched man named Duval was burnt at the stake. Shortly after his death she confessed to the atrocity of her evidence. "From henceforth the universe rejected the odious creature and spued her out; her only world was her dungeon."[282] In 1647 the *Parlement* under Mazarin decreed that the Sodom of Louviers should be destroyed, and the women dispersed. This was carried out during the month of August of the above year; but when they came to Madeleine's dungeon on the 21st of that month to open the doors of her prison all they found was a carcass of rotten flesh and mouldering bones.

[282] Michelet, *Sorceress*, 239.

The Suicide[283]

J. F. C. F.

Our Father[284]

A blushing cheek and a smiling lip,
A trusting heart and a yearning soul;
From the cup of joy two lovers sip,
And pay not the world the lovers' toll;[285]
Free without bond, or script, or deed:
Then in the bracken by their side
They see a stealthy serpent glide,
Hissing the Christian creed.

Thy will be done

The thunders roll through the dismal sky,
The lightnings flash, his heart doth fail,
Trembling he fears the Christian lie,
Deserts his love to the howling gale:
As night grows dim his love is dead,
Upon her lips his kiss hath lied;
She, whom he said should be his bride,
An outcast he hath made.

Lead us not into temptation

Her lips are dry, her body chill;
Around her flit a phantom host
Hissing to her temptations ill;
Then laughed the Holy Ghost:
"Sweetheart, why shiver in the cold?

283 *Agnostic Journal* 60, no. 19 (May 11, 1907): 291–292.
284 Love [original note].
285 Marriage [original note].

Look—all the streets are paved with gold;
The joys of life are manifold
Drink, here is Satan's toast."

Forgive us our trespasses

One sip; it cannot do me harm;
One sip, just one: how chill is night,
The cold, grey street is growing warm,
Look! it is growing bright—
The dismal gas-lights of the street,
The pavement all deserted, wet,
Into a glowing serpent meet,
Satan with jewels set—

Another sip—I am athirst,
The fire burns fierce within my throat!
"Yea, love," says Christ, the triply curst,
"Drink to the Mendic goat."[286]

More drink, more drink, more more, more more;
God sneers, and into dark disgrace,
Kicked to the street a wretched whore,
And spat into her face.

Deliver us from Evil[287]

Baptismal curse of God,
O fiery gust!

[286] The goat of Mendes, or the goat of the Sabbath, represents Lust; also the Ahriman of the Persians, the Typhon of the Egyptians, the Python of the Greeks, the Baphomet of the Templars, and the old Serpent of the Jews. As the Pentagram with one horn in the ascendant represented Christ (head, arms, and feet). so with two horns in the ascendant it represented Satan, or the goat of Mendes (two horns, two ears and a beard) [original note].

[287] The author of this song is not mad; in it he simply attempts to paint some of the frenzy that may possibly fill the mind of a would-be suicide. It is well known with what glowing colours Christians are apt to paint their heaven, and it is also well-known how very apt they are to judge anyone who should speed his course to this realm of unutterable bliss, as "*temporary insane*" [original note].

The power of thy rod
Is burning lust.

Blood of the dying Christ,
O fearful curse!
Thy power hath sufficed,—
Love's hearse.

Sin of the Holy Ghost,
Thou lying word,
The hellish host
Have heard:
Round me they jibbering scud,
A reeking throng,
Rain blood!
O Song!
Drink madly, drink deep, never sing;
Kiss sadly, no sleep ever bring:
Rolled in lust, a burning gust
Of Fury.
Love is dead, bend thy head
Demurely.
Gold thou sneering bawd;
Drink thou shrieking lord;
O! Virgin Mother,
Thy fair life is whored;
There, close above Her,
Sits on a golden throne,
Heaped o'er man's flesh and bone,
To gloat,
The gilded goat
Of lust;
O! burning rust
Into my heart
Thy dart
Is thrust!
Into my form is crowded,
Death's norm o'er-shrouded;
Into my brain is crammed,

Thy hate, O! pain, thrice damned!
Into my soul,
Doth roll
The whole
Of Evil:
And in the mind,
Sits blind
A hind,[288]
The Devil.

Curled round my feet the waters hiss—
Death's kiss.
O bridge of sighs!
Thy bliss
Is this,
It cries.

Tottering upon the brink;
Past vision, thought, or think,
Fall!
Hell's furies call,
Ha! Ha!
They laughed,
Ho! Ho!
Our craft
Doth grow,
Go! Go!

Sweet murmuring waters hide
My misery;
Still waters o'er me glide,
I cannot see:

I hear not, my eyes close,
Oh! mystic rose;
Sweet Death, thy breath

[288] The above goat [original note].

It purifies lust's lies;
O wisdom of the Wise.
Love sighs,
Love dies,
I rise.

The Kingdom

The Sun creeps over the chilly dawn:
A weeping branch from the muddy tide,
Caught a body ragged and torn,—
The corpse of a luckless suicide.
The hair of her head is matted with mud;
Her face is battered blue and red;
Her eye-balls, starting from her head,
Are clotted black with blood.

The Power

'Midst slime on the mud she now doth rest,
'Mongst reed and rush, who weeping hide
The naked form of their unasked guest—
The corpse of the luckless suicide.
The slug and the snail crawl over her cheek:
The worms wriggle 'twixt lid and eye;
And on her face both grub and fly
Their charnel feast do seek.

The Glory

Her lips are rotten, her teeth are bare;
The flesh creeps back from the grinning skull:
The bone protrudes betwixt brow and hair;
Her eyes are sunk in their sockets dull;

A fleshless hand grips the frozen weed,
As chill and cold as the Christian creed.

Amen

Look! there on the mud by the ebbing tide
Lies the corpse of the luckless suicide;
And far from out the realms above
I hear: "All hail! for God is Love!"

Demcomep[289,290]

J. F. C. F.

THE clock struck midnight, I shivered, what was that? A distinct rap! With a pack of Tarot cards in my hand I was casting up the probable cycle of Aunt Philadelphia's life; she was rich;—again rap, this time most distinctly. I placed the twenty-first card, "The Universe," on the black cloth before me; rap, rap rap! This time there could be no mistake about it: rap, rap, rap, rap, rap! The heels of the silver Christ above my head were violently tapping the black ebony cross on which he hung. I muttered an "Ave Maria," crossed myself, and poured out a whisky-and-soda. What could it mean? Was the Universe coming to an end? Then I remembered it was the morning of the twenty-second of September, of the year of the Master, nineteen hundred and six.

Twenty-two! Something about this number tempted me; then, with difficulty, I divided it in half, when lo! that evil number eleven. Eleven disciples after the fall of Iscariot, I thought, and, thinking, fell asleep.

At breakfast next morning, I had forgotten all about the mysteries of the night, and was playfully dallying with a kipper, when the maid brought me in the *Standard*.

I opened it. My kipper flew out of the window; this struck me as odd and unusual, not to say annoying: then the life-size painted "photo" of my maiden

289 *Agnostic Journal* 60, no. 20 (May 18, 1907): 305–306.
290 *Demcomep*: Probably *PEMbrokeshire EDucational COMmittee*—though veiled in great darkness [original note].

aunt swung round on its nail over the mantel-piece, and came down with a crash.[291] At the time I did not notice it, my eyes were glued on "the end of the world"; a thousand times No! Not a world without end, but without beginning, I read:

"GENESIS I. BARRED IN SCHOOLS.

"The Pembrokeshire Education Committee decided yesterday that the first chapter of Genesis must not be read in Council Schools."[292]

Three lines, that was all. No roaring of thunder, no flashing of lightning, no raging of the seas, no quaking of the earth, not even a twopenny-tube[293] smash; the Pembrokeshire Education Committee had decided that the Omniscient had bungled, that the All-perfect God of gods was at fault—that was all! the universe had come to no-beginning.

Genesis I. dismissed in three lines! What about Genesis II.? Phew I To think of the blasphemy: that might go also. And Genesis XIX! Lord, have mercy upon us poor sinners; without that sacred chapter there could be no morals, no regeneration; our wives would turn from us, our very daughters would forsake their homes, and would no longer obey, tend and cherish their broken-hearted fathers. O the horror of it all, the horror of it!

[291] The comic hyperbole displayed here recalls a later incident connected to *The Star in the West*. On August 15, 1907, the *Daily Mail* ran a cartoon illustration of the mysterious lamen that adorns the cover of Fuller's *The Star in the West*, along with an anonymous letter which read:

> "Two days ago I received the enclosed card anonymously, and just glancing at it briefly, thinking it an advertisement of some sort, I placed it on the mantelpiece.
>
> "Within a few minutes, disasters of a minor kind began to happen in my little home.
>
> "First, one of my most valuable vases fell to the ground and was smashed to pieces. My little clock stopped—the clock was near the card—and then I discovered to my amazement that my dear little canary lay dead at the bottom of its cage!"

[292] The "Standard," 26th Sept. [original note]. The press widely reported in September 1906 that the Pembrokeshire Education Committee, while discussing religious education at Haverford-West, unanimously agreed that Genesis 1 should not be read in elementary schools in their jurisdiction. A subsequent story clarified that a letter had been submitted to the committee requesting that Genesis I not be read; one committee member proposed that the letter not be read, and the motion was seconded without further discussion. See, for example, "Religious Education: First Chapter of Genesis 'Barred,'" *Western Gazette*, no. 8872 (September 28, 1906): 10. See also "The First Chapter of Genesis," *Manchester Guardian*, September 22, 1906, 6; and "First Chapter of Genesis," *Nottingham Evening Post*, no. 8756 (September 25, 1906): 6.

[293] The deep underground Central London Railway—which opened in 1900 and whose tunnels are still part of the London Underground's Central line between Shepherd's Bush and Bank—was nicknamed the Twopenny Tube because for a flat rate, two pence, a rider could travel between any two stations on the line.

Why had these children of Lucifuge thus tampered with holy writ? Why dismiss Genesis I.? Why not the whole book—O Satanus, why not? Was it that their knowledge of the word of God had not travelled so far? Lord, be praised, for thy mercy endureth forever. O mystery of mysteries, these are they who shall educate thy children, O Lord, these bugs of Orcus.

The world was as a lamb which had lost its mother; it was without a beginning. There was a void, something must fill it, that was most certain, most sure.

Something had to be done to fill this bottomless chasm—at last—yes—it was a desperate and daring deed; the world had no creation; in its place I determined to substitute the creation of the "Gold-finding Hen," that mystic bird which, for many generations past, the Church has cabalistically worshipped under the guise of the "Amorous Pigeon." Therefore, without delay, I sat me down, and the spirit of the Lord came upon me in the form of a black hen, and I thought; for had not that servant of the Lord been wrong now that Demcomep had discovered that the world was not created at four o'clock on the morning of Thursday, the 27th of October, 4002 B.C.?[294]

Then the word of the Lord came upon me and I wrote:—

> "1 In the beginning God came to Oramasis, the father of Tardsuc, and said unto him, Let there be a black hen, and there was not a black hen.
>
> "2 Then was he exceeding wroth and said, Behold now take unto thyself aromatic woods, such as aloes, cedar, orange, citron, laurel, orris-root with rose-leaves and dry them in the sun;
>
> "3 And place them in a golden chafing-dish, and pour over them balsamic oil, and add unto them fine incense and clear gum. And Oramasis did so.
>
> "4 Then did Elohim bless them saying, 'ATHAS SOLINAM, ERMINATOS, PASAIM.'
>
> "5 After which he commanded Oramasis that he should cover the dish with a glass, and thereon direct the rays of the sun; so that

[294] According to the seventeenth-century "young Earth" chronology of James Ussher, archbishop of Armagh, the first day of creation took place on Saturday, October 22, 4004 BCE. Augustin Calmet later "corrected" some errors in Ussher's calculations and concluded that the year of Earth's creation was actually 4002 BCE.

the wood might kindle, and the glass might melt, and a sweet odour might arise as a savour unto his nostrils; and Oramasis did as the Lord bid him.

"6 Then said the Lord unto Oramasis collect thou the ashes and place them within a golden egg while yet red hot, and lay the egg on a black cushion;

"7 And he did so, covering it with a glass cut from the midst of a pure crystal.

"8 Then Oramasis lifted up his eyes and stretched out his arms and cried with a loud voice, 'O SANATAPER, ISMAI, NONTAPILUS, ERTIVALER, CANOPISTUS.'

"9 And the Lord said, expose the glass unto the most fierce rays of the sun, and he exposed it.

"10 Then was the glass enveloped in flame ceasing to be visible, and a slight vapour arose, and from out the vapour flew a black pullet.

"11 And Oramasis said in a clear voice, 'BINUSAS TESTIPAS,' and the hen nestled in his bosom.

"12 Thus was the creation of the gold-finding hen finished and all the host of them, and God saw everything he had made and behold it was very good."

Then again was I overshadowed and the voice as of one rejected cried unto me, Write, O Scribe, for my literary reputation is at stake, the wedge hath been inserted and the timber will soon split, and when the prop hath been destroyed, O then who shall support my house, and if the house fall where then wilt be thy God?

So I wrote the second chapter of the Book of the Beginning:

"1 Now it came to pass that Oramasis the father of Tardsuc was alone in his hen-house, and the black pullet spake to him saying;

"2 O Oramasis I lay golden eggs, but what am I?

"3 Then was Oramasis tempted, and he seized the hen in such a manner that she could not cackle, and he repaired to a high road, and to a cross-road which leadeth into that high road;

"4 And at the twelfth hour of the night he drew with a cypress rod a circle in the dust of the earth, and he placed himself in the midst thereof, and tore the bird in twain till she died.

"5 And over her thrice he did repeat, [']*Eloim, Essoim, frugative et appellavi*.'

"6 Next he turneth him unto the East and kneeleth praying for a little while.

"7 And behold unto him came an Unclean Spirit, and it appeared unto him wearing a scarlet surcoat, a yellow vest, and breeches of pale green.

"8 And it had the head of a dog, with ears as of an ass, and horns above the ears, and his hoofs were like unto those of a calf.

"9 And its name was Demcomep.

"10 Therefore the Lord sent him forth from the hen-house to till the ground from whence he was taken.

"11 So he drove out Oramasis, and he placed at the east of the hen-house Kerubim and a flaming sword which turned every way to keep the way of the hen roost."

Of course, as the "Catholic Truth Society" states, "Agnostics cannot possibly grasp such sublime mysteries as these, though most probably Mrs. Eddy might, during her lucid intervals." And to corroborate this wonderful truth, and so make it impervious to the attacks of this wicked sect, I will quote the words of that eminent divine, the Rev. J. Gerard:[295]

"The Agnostic held that he could know nothing about God or other truths of religion; but that the Christian whose religion was a vital element in his life could draw upon a source of knowledge utterly sealed to his antagonist, namely, upon his own experience of the working of God in his soul."

Or, to those who are not adepts in the mysteries of the Church, this, being interpreted, meaneth: "The laying of the golden eggs by the black hen."

[295] The original article indicates a footnote here, but the corresponding note is absent. In late 1906, the Catholic Truth Society held a meeting at Brixton, at which one presentation was "Father Gerard's paper on 'Agnosticism.'" See "The Chronicle: Home News," *Messenger* 46, no. 5 (November 1906): 512. The proceedings were published as *Conference Papers, 1906* (London: Catholic Truth Society, 1906). Given the proximate timing of this and Fuller's paper, this may be what he is referring to. The "Rev. J. Gerard" would appear to be Scottish Jesuit John Gerard (1840–1912), as opposed to the more famous cover Elizabethan Jesuit John Gerard (1564–1637) who escaped from his torture and imprisonment in the Tower of London.

Ballade of the Daisy[296]

[From the Old French of Froissart]

V. B. Neuburg

Above all flowers in[297] fair the fragrant rose,
To her the modest violet e'en gives place.
The fleur-de-lys,—the marjoram sweetly blows,—
The gentle iris tall, with slender grace;
And all men love the simple columbine,
Peony, lily, and the marigold,
For every flower hath a face divine,
But, as for me, if that the truth be told,
Of all flowers I the daisy sweetest hold.

Whether the day be dull, or chill with snows,
Whether the season may be fair or base,
Ever the daisy meetly nods and grows,
Sweetly and fair, with white and crimson face;
In seasons due doth ope and close her eyne
The daisy sweet; she fades not nor grows old.
And for this thing, (now thought hath long been mine,)
That truth her gentle being doth enfold,
Of all flowers I the daisy sweetest hold.

And now once more the daisy newly glows,
Again young Spring hath won the year's long race;
Upon the sward have I seen seated those
Whose hearts a pleasant arrow pierced apace.
Ah! may the god of love his arms entwine
Around the twain,—so may their hearts grow bold
With courtesy and pleasance; so, in fine,

[296] *Agnostic Journal* 60, no. 20 (May 18, 1907): 311; repr. in *A Green Garland*. Not to be confused with Jean Froissart's (1337–1405) longer, mythic ode, "Le Deit de la Margherite," this is Neuburg's take on the French historian and poet's shorter ballad of twenty-seven lines, beginning with "Sus toutes flours tient-on la rose à belle."

[297] The errata slip to *A Green Garland* indicates that this word should be "is."

Weaving a wreath, my carol shall be trolled,—
"Of all flowers I the daisy sweetest hold."

Napoleon and the Superstitious[298]

J. F. C. F.

A little less than a hundred years ago, a titanic figure held in the shadow of his hand the destinies of the Western world; yet how strange, this colossus was at times himself but a mere puppet dancing on the palm of Superstition. The mystic thread of wonder is to be found wound round every heart; in some as a slender hair, in others again as a stout cord, and in the unwinding of it from such a heart as that which beat in the breast of the little Corsican, we must take the utmost care; for now, over a century he has stood the ever magnifying scrutiny of European thought. A colossus has equally colossal foes and colossal friends, who unitedly turn him into a demon or a god, amassing round him their several desires, to enhero, or enslave.

The true Napoleon is fast growing into a myth, as all great men do; the feudal nature of the European is not yet dead; man equally loves to serve, as to be served; and as the present is ever more prosaic than the past, seeking his ideals in those days when he was not, or in those lands where he can never tread; he transforms his ideal man, his hero, first into an immortal, and then into a god.

Had Napoleon been born two thousand years before his day, it would be difficult to deny the supposition, that not only would he have long since been deified, but that through the extraordinary astuteness of his government, and the lucidity of his thought, we, at this present day, might be Napoleonites instead of Christians. And, with this possibility in view, it is almost impossible to discover, certainly to declare, that all the following curious incidents are veraciously authentic, and they, after all, are but a few of the ever-accumulating legends which are being washed around the majestic form of this hero, by both his worshippers and detractors alike.

As this giant stepped forth unto the stage of the world during the night of the 14th and 15th of August, 1769, the celestial orbs heralded his advent by the birth of a new star, the much-talked-of star of his destiny.

[298] *Agnostic Journal* 60, no. 22 (June 1, 1907): 337–338; *Agnostic Journal* 60, no. 23 (June 8, 1907): 355–357.

The Abbé Martenot remarked a new star of great brilliancy in the constellation of Virgo. Nor was it the only welcomer of the future Emperor; another Emperor, the Great Frederick, is stated to have dreamt on this notable night, that he saw the star of his kingdom and his genius shining in the firmament, luminous and resplendent. He was admiring its brilliancy and its lofty position, when above him there appeared another star which eclipsed it as it ascended upon it. There was a struggle between the two, for a moment their rays were confounded together, and his star obscured, enveloped within the orbit of the other, fell to the earth, as if pushed down by a force which seemed likely to extinguish it. The struggle was long and obstinate; at last his star got free, and continued to shine in the firmament, whereas the other one vanished.[299]

There is little possibility now to vouch for the correctness of this dream, though several evidences seem to witness to its truth. Probably it was but a piece of that Teutonic sycophancy which was so prevalent whilst the emperor ruled the destinies of the Germanic Empire. But a still more curious story, and this time a prediction, was found to suit the Emperor's reign in an old book published in 1542, whose title was *Livres de Prophéties*, by Master Noël Olivarius, Doctor of Medicine. The prophecy runs as follows:—

> "Italian Gaul shall see born not far from her bosom, a supernatural being: this man will come early from the sea, will come to learn the language and manners of the Celtic-Gauls, will open to himself, though still young, and through a thousand obstacles, a career among soldiers, and will become their greatest chief. This sinuous road will give him much trouble, he will wage war near to his native land for a lustre and more. . . .
>
> "He will wage war beyond the seas with great glory and valour, and warring once again throughout the Roman world. . . . Will give laws to the Germans, will spread trouble and terror among the Celtic-Gauls, and will then be called King, but afterwards will be called *Imperator* by an enthusiastic people.
>
> "He will wage war everywhere throughout the empire, driving out princes, lords, and kings, for two lustres and more. . . .

[299] "Curious Bypaths of History," Cabanés, p. 230 [original note]. Auguste Cabanès, *Curious Bypaths of History: Being Medico-Historical Studies and Observations* (Paris: C. Carrington, 1898), 230.

"He will come to the city, commanding many great things: edifices, seaports, aqueducts, canals; he will alone by means of great riches accomplish as much as all the Romans, and all within the domination of the Gauls. Of wives he shall have two . . . . And but one son only.

"He will go on warring until the lines of longitude and latitude do cross fifty-five months (*sic*). There his enemies will burn a great city and he will enter there and go out again with his men from beneath the ashes and great ruins, and his men, having neither bread nor water, by great and killing cold, will be so unfortunate that two thirds of his army will perish, and further one half of others, then no longer under his domination.

"Far away, the great man abandoned, treacherously forsaken by his own, hunted out in his turn, with great loss in his own city by great European population; in his place will be put the old King of the cape.

"He, compelled to be in exile in the sea whence he came so young, and near to his native land, living there for eleven moons with a few of his own true friends and soldiers, who were only seven times two in number, as soon as the eleven moons are run, he and his men take ship and land in the country of the Celtic-Gaul.

"Driven out once more by European trinity, after three moons and one third of a moon, [he] is again replaced by old King of the cape, whereat he is thought to be dead by his soldiers, who in these times will press Penates to their heart . . . .

"And he, saving the ancient remains of the old blood of the cape, rules the destinies of the world, dictating sovereign counsel of every nation and of every people, fixes basis of everlasting fruit, and dies. . . ."[300]

This curious prediction was read out to Napoleon by the Empress Joséphine. The Emperor wished to attach no importance to it, but was evidently moved, contenting himself by observing: "Predictions always say what you exactly want them to say."[301]

Joséphine, by nature a very superstitious woman, was always fond of perusing the stories of sorceresses and magicians; and there is little doubt that though Napoleon was the child of the freethinking Revolution, the natural tendencies of his Corsican and Italian descent, strongly at times inclined

[300] Cited in "Curious By-paths of History" [original note]. The book is cited by Cabanès, *Curious Bypaths*, 265. The quoted prophecy appears on 265–267 of *Curious Bypaths*.
[301] Cabanès, *Curious Bypaths*, 267.

him to the belief in the superstitious, which was still more accentuated by his marriage with his first wife. On one occasion when the First Consul, in a fit of irritation with his brother Lucien, he said to him: "I will crush you as I crush this box,"[302] at the same time hurling to the ground a gold snuff box bearing the portrait of Joséphine painted by Isabey. The thickness of the carpet, however, prevented his heel from doing much damage, the portrait alone becoming unfixed from the lid; whereupon Joséphine, who was present, cried out: "Oh! it is all over! It is a sign of divorce! Bonaparte will separate himself from me as the snuff box separated itself from the portrait."[303] Her predictions were only too true; but whether this story was invented after the actual divorce or not, I cannot say. Possibly not, as Joséphine is said to have shortly afterwards consulted the sorceress Lenormand concerning its occult meaning.

Religion does not seem to have been a topic of much interest in the recorded conversations of Napoleon, except perhaps during his last year in St. Helena. There he frequently declared his hostility to the Papacy, which had been several times forcibly demonstrated during his rule; he denied the divinity of Christ, considering that he was put to death as a fanatic who professed to be a prophet or the Messiah. "So slight is his belief in the Saviour," writes Rosebery, "that he mentions as an extraordinary fact, that Pope Pius II. did actually believe in Christ."[304]

At times he also seemed to disbelieve in an after life; once at St. Helena he said, "When we are dead, my dear Gourgaud, we are altogether dead."[305]

Yet he was far from being a narrow-minded dogmatist, he accepted the mysteries of life and religion, and once in a liberal minded mood said: "Only a fool says that he will die without a confessor. There is so much that one does not know, that one cannot explain."[306] At another time he broke out with: "Were I obliged to have a religion, I would worship the sun—the source of all life—the real God of the earth."[307] His respect for the divine origin of man was small, "A man is only a more perfect being than a dog or a tree, and living better. The plant is the first link in a chain of which man is the last."[308]

[302] Cabanès, *Curious Bypaths*, 251.
[303] Cabanès, *Curious Bypaths*, 252.
[304] "Napoleon: The Last Phase." p. 170 [original note]. Archibald Philip Primrose Rosebery, *Napoleon: The Last Phase*. (London: Arthur L. Humphreys, 1906), 170.
[305] "Napoleon: The Last Phase," p. 171 [original note].
[306] Rosebery, *Napoleon*, 173.
[307] Rosebery, *Napoleon*, 188.
[308] Rosebery, *Napoleon*, 170.

This remark is notable having been uttered at a time when Charles Darwin was still in the nursery.

All great men recognise the greatness of systems and things outside them, such proof of their greatness being but a truism. Because, however, in the land of the sphinx, Napoleon coming into contact with the greatness of Mahomet, uttering those words: "We Mahometans," it does not necessarily follow, that he was in any way nearer being by religious persuasion a Mahometan, than any other great man who recognised the guidance of a Superior Power.

The Emperor was by nature far too great a diplomatist to offend the Arab population, and besides, he was a great admirer of the East. This fact, I think, is clearly demonstrated by his once saying: "So I, had I remained in Egypt, should probably have founded an empire like Alexander, by going on a pilgrimage to Mecca."[309] And as Alexander went to Ammon, so I believe would he, have gone to Mecca, diplomatically, and diplomatically alone.

As a believer in Providence, or Fate, some assert a strong inclination on the part of Napoleon; but no doubt this has again been exaggerated by lesser minds. Great and liberal-minded, he did not laugh at doubt, as at first the ignorant are so apt to do; neither did he accept without weight or judgment; yet wise in everything he did, he at once perceived that the ignorance of his subjects was ever susceptible and acceptable to the accomplishment of a providential mission by which he might dilute the purer wisdom of his understanding to the weaker knowledge of his subjects.

Yet, in many ways, he seems to have held faith in his destiny, and no doubt the phenomenal success of his early years strengthened this belief. His bravery was incontestable; three times was he wounded; twenty times he risked death—at Toulon, Montereau, Waterloo, and many other battles. "*The future is in the hands of God*,"[310] he again and again enjoined; and when we look back on this colossus, it verily seems that it was. His very successes alone were apt to make him a fatalist; but as his successes were the children of the preponderance of his genius, we may almost say that the book of Fate lay open before him, unwritten, ready to be inscribed by whatever words his mighty hand might write.

A hater of impostors and charlatans, he, however, curiously clung to certain superstitions, the most notable, perhaps, being "the Star of his destiny."

[309] Rosebery, *Napoleon*, 200.

[310] Auguste Cabanès, *Curious Bypaths of History: Being Medico-Historical Studies and Observations* (Paris: C. Carrington, 1898), 225.

The story concerning the "Star" at the siege of Dantzig is well known; it rums as follows: In 1806, General Rapp returned from the siege of Dantzig, and having occasion to speak to the Emperor on some important military plans, entered his cabinet without being announced. He found the Emperor deeply absorbed in thought, and, being afraid to speak to him, made a slight noise to attract the Emperor's attention. Napoleon turned round, and, clutching Rapp by the arm, said:

"Do you not perceive it? . . It is my star! . . .There yonder . . . before you. . . brilliant; it has never abandoned me. I see it in all great occurrences; it commands me to go forward, and is to me a constant sign of good luck."[311]

Five years after this event, lie pointed it out again to Cardinal Fesch; suddenly turning to the Cardinal, the Emperor said:

"Do you see that star above?"
"No, Sire."
"Look well!"
"Sire, I see nothing."
"Well then! I myself do see it,"[312] replied Napoleon, turning from him.

A pretty example, illustrating his believe in Fate, happened at the Tuileries when he was First Consul. One day he sent for Mme. de Montesson, and on her arrival, advancing to meet her said:

"Madame, you may ask for whatever you should wish."

"But General, I have no right to avail myself of your offer."

"You forget then, Madame, that I received my first laurel crown from your hands. You came to Brienne to distribute the prizes, and when you placed on my head the wreath that was the forerunner of so many others, you said: 'May it bring you good fortune.' "

As Mme. de Montesson was about to reply, Bonaparte interrupted her, saying:

"I am a fatalist. Therefore it is easy to see why I have not forgotten an incident that you do not remember."

He afterwards loaded Mme. de Montesson with honours and gifts, and gave her a yearly pension of 60,000 francs.[313]

[311] Cabanès, *Curious Bypaths*, 231.
[312] Cabanès, *Curious Bypaths*, 231–232n.
[313] From "Madame . . . " down to "60,000 francs" is a very lightly edited copy of what is written in Cabanès, *Curious Bypaths*, 233–234.

Another story of a similar nature and displaying his open-hearted benevolence, may here with advantage be related:—

A few days before his entry into Berlin, Napoleon travelling along the Potsdam road was overtaken by a storm, it was so violent that he took refuge in a house. Wrapped in his grey overcoat, he was surprised to see there a young woman, who was visibly startled at his presence; she was an Egyptian, who had preserved for him that religious veneration that all the Arabs had for Napoleon. She was the widow of an officer of the army of the East, and fate had taken her to Prussia, to this house, where she had been taken care of. The Emperor gave her a pension of twelve hundred francs a year, and took charge of the education of her son, the only inheritance left her by her husband. "This is the first time," said Napoleon to his officers, "that I dismounted to seek shelter from a storm; I had a presentiment that a good action was awaiting me here."[314]

Small matters sometimes pre-occupied his thoughts, such as the chiming of church bells, which he always listened to with the utmost delight. The fall of his horse at Polwiski was, at the time, a matter of concern to him, and probably more so to his soldiers. On this occasion, several of his personal staff rushed to his aid, and on the Emperor regaining his feet, he was the first to exclaim: "In such great circumstances, on the eve of grave events, one becomes superstitious in spite of one's self";[315] which were well-timed and chosen words, for, but a moment later, Berthier turned to Caulincourt, and whispered: "It would be better for us not to cross the Niemen; this fall is of evil omen."[316] Curious enough, a quite unforeseen event turned the minds of his soldiers from contemplating the evil interpretation of this mishap. From some citizens of Kowno, Baron Denniée[317] tells us, the Emperor learnt that "The Emperor Alexander assisted at a ball where, by a singular coincidence, the flooring of the principal saloon gave way towards midnight, at which hour the bridges over the Niemen. It may easily be understood that all sorts of conjectures were made about this event, to give it a favourable interpretation!"[318]

Another small incident which disclosed for a moment the under-current of superstition which lived deep down in his colossal mind, took place

[314] Bonapartiana, p. 29 [original note]. Attributed to *Bonapartiana* in Cabanès, *Curious Bypaths*, 259.
[315] Cabanès, *Curious Bypaths*, 258–259.
[316] Cabanès, *Curious Bypaths*, 259.
[317] Itinaire de la Campagne de, 1812 [original note].
[318] As quoted in Cabanès, *Curious Bypaths*, 259.

near Saint Cloud, when his horse, frightened by the flaming red shawl the Empress Marie Louise was wearing, shied, violently throwing the Emperor. The carriage in which the Empress was driving, stopped immediately, and she expressed her deepest regret at what had happened. Napoleon, who had just risen from the road, was, however, not in a very amiable frame of mind, and to her inquiries harshly replied: "Madam, since you have been with me nothing but ill luck attends me"; which, in many cases, had only been too true.[319]

Friday was a day full of apprehension to him; he never undertook anything he could help on that day, and when he was forced to, always did so with fear. He himself says:

> "Born with a strong propensity to superstition, I never undertook anything on a Friday without apprehension; moreover, I do not know whether it was by pure chance or by reason of the unfavourable state of mind into which the Friday put me, but the enterprises which I commenced on that day always succeeded badly. For instance, among others, I remember that the night of my departure from Saint Cloud for the campaign in Russia, was a Friday night."[320]

No date brought more souvenirs to his mind than the 20th March. As a fact, the ephemerides of the 20th March in the life of Napoleon are particularly remarkable.

It was on 20th March 1779, that Charles Bonaparte, the father of Napoleon, came, with his son to Paris for the purpose of placing him at the military school at Brienne.

The 20th March 1785 Napoleon was informed of his father's death.

20th March 1794 Napoleon arrived at Nice as Commander in Chief of the Army of Italy.
20th March 1800, battle of Heliopolis.
20th March 1804, the Duke of Enghien was shot in the night at Vincennes.
20th March 1808, abdication of Charles IV of Spain.
20th March 1809, battle of Abendsberg.
20th March 1811, birth of the King of Rome.

[319] Bonapartiana, p. 98 [original note]. Cabanès, *Curious Bypaths*, 256n.
[320] Cited by Cabanés, ibid., pp. 261–262 [original note]. Cabanès, *Curious Bypaths*, 261–262.

20th March 1814, taking of Toul.
20th March 1815, return of Napoleon to Paris.
20th March 1821, Napoleon wrote the last codicil to his will at Saint Helena.[321]

But so many great events were crowded into the life of this marvellous man, that during his entire life it would be difficult to find a single day which remained unmoulded by that power which lived within him. Great events; the birth of some majestic code, the death of some titanic conflict, jostled each other onward as they whirled from the magic hands of that ever working craftsman which was himself. The events of his life were not the frail offspring of the fleeting years, but the children of a slowly moving period. His material conquests have gone back to their material owners; but his spiritual victories ever live with us, and the entire world, as they do still, and will for ever, in the brave heart of his adopted child, his dear and beloved France. And, wondrous to say, they know no age, and as the years move on along the eternal path of time, no decrepitude wrinkles their brow, or ashens their hair; sons of a mighty wisdom, and daughters of a vast knowledge, rejuvenescent as the years sink dying round their feet, building up for them a great column of fame which bids to vanish midst the stars, and above which is still visible the countenance of one who is fast becoming nebulous as some Orphic mystery.

Neither did he, or those about him, attribute a mystic influence to dates and clays only; the letter M to him was even more fateful, perhaps more justifiably so: Maret, Mollien, Montalivet, Montesquiou, Massena, Marmont, Macdonald, Mortier, Moncey, Murat, Marboeuf, Moreau, Mallet, Metternich, Melas, Menou, Miollis, Marchand, Montholon, Maitland, were all men intimately connected with the events of his life. Marengo, Montenotte, Millesimo, Mondovi, Montmirail, Montereau, and Mont-Saint-Jean were seven of the great battles he fought, the first six he won, the last he lost; and finally was it not at La Malmaison that he passed the only few hours of calm that he enjoyed during his chequered career.[322]

But who of us, after all, even now, a century further advanced on the dial of time, can with simple truth say: "We are in no way superstitious!" Our knowledge is so limited, our ignorance so vast, that for us it is excusable; how

[321] Ibid., p. 262 [original note]. From "No date brought more" to "Saint Helena," this is quoted from Cabanès, *Curious Bypaths*, 262n.
[322] Ibid, p. 264 [original note]. See Cabanès, *Curious Bypaths*, 264–265.

much more so then for one, whose very life seems to have irradiated success and astonishment; and still how much more so for those who worship one whose foot-prints in the sands of time are fast becoming obliterated by the dusty breath of that mysterious desert across which we all have to pass.

The Agnostic Journal
[An unpublished insertion to Crowley's *Confessions*][323]

Aleister Crowley

The death of Stewart Ross left his weekly *The Agnostic Journal* a sheep not having a shepherd. Fuller and I had long realized that one could not begin to initiate people until their minds had been cleared of all rubbish. It occurred to us that Saladin's public might furnish us, better than any other, with the raw material of adepts.[324] We accordingly decided to try to buy the paper, which had always lost money but was useful to Saladin as a medium for keeping his adherents together, and of publishing fanatic appeals for financial support. It was therefore of no value whatever as an asset in his estate; there was no money to keep it going for more than a fortnight, nor even the material to fill its columns beyond a month at the outside. We were acting generously in offering £150 for the dead horse.[325]

[323] This previously unpublished account, intended as an in insertion to the manuscript of Crowley's *Confessions*, comes from the Metzger-Aeschbach archive, Kantonsbibliothek Appenzell Innerrhoden, Trogen, Switzerland, catalog item CMO-41-D-10-07-15. For context, William Stewart Ross died on November 30, 1906, and the *Agnostic Journal* ceased publication in June 1907. See "Saladin's Illness and Death," in chap. 1, in this volume.

[324] Crowley would use a similar strategy in 1912: appointed British Grand Master of Ordo Templi Orientis (O.T.O.) and tasked with getting a national section going, he looked to the A∴A∴ membership as a pool of potential members.

[325] This early attempt to get into the journal-publishing business demonstrates Crowley following the example of the RPA's *Literary Guide*. In 1909, Crowley would launch his journal, *The Equinox*, for which he supplied most of the content. A few years later, he became contributing editor of George Sylvester Viereck's *The International* with the August 1917 issue, and he once again began rounding out each issue with an assortment of his own poetry, short stories, plays, essays, and reviews, written under various pseudonyms. He later contemplated buying the *Paris Evening Telegram* with Frank Harris in 1924, or the Aquila Press in 1929, before his backers purchased the short-lived Mandrake Press Ltd. in 1930. In a similar way, he also sought to repurpose existing groups for his ends—namely, the promulgation of Thelema or of himself as its prophet. Given authority in the Antient and Primitive Rite (via John Yarker) and O.T.O. (via Theodor Reuss), Crowley refashioned them into the Thelema-centric organization that continues as O.T.O. today. He made similar (albeit unsuccessful) attempts to insert himself as the Theosophical Society's World Teacher, or the figure around which German occult organizations might unify at the "Weida Conference," or as the rightful source of AMORC's authority.

We went to a meeting of the family and executors with one or two of his principal supporters. Mr. Livingstone-Anderson, the celebrated herring-gutter, was one of the brightest luminaries.[326] Fuller always maintained that the Grand Lodge of the Guild of Fish-entrail Eliminators had a tradition (dating probably from the time of the Apostle Peter or some equally eminent Extractor of the abdominal viscera of the piscine clan) that a sure sign of sinister and superstitious activities is the Monocle—one of which I was wearing, with some vague idea of protecting myself from the possible contagion of the meeting.

This was, in fact, an extraordinarily musty assembly. England has a monopoly of a certain indescribable smell derived, I believe, from some fungus which grows in Victorian surroundings, the presence of damp, and the absence of fresh air. This smell is quite idiosyncratic to lower middle-class houses in the larger towns of England, and while rather passive than active, is so persistent that a dozen Livingstone-Andersons, even if perspiring, could hardly overpower it.

The essence of our proposal was to pay £150 in cash—Mrs. Ross needed the money very badly—for a property which had never possessed any commercial value and was in any case moribund, there being no alternative proposal to keep it going.[327] But my monocle and my manner mystified and terrorized the meeting, while Fuller's soldierly bearing increased the panic by filling their minds with the conviction that he had concealed dragoons with machine guns so as to command every avenue leading to the doomed house. They rejected our offer unanimously, and the paper perished in due course.

This incident is typical of the sort of difficulty that any free spirit constantly finds confronting him; if there is any suspicion of genius it is a thousand times worse. No matter how advanced such people as these "agnostics" imagine themselves to be, they are in reality a narrow-minded sect of highly respectable cattle. They may be in absolute accord with what one proposes at the moment, but they fear that one's next move may be something too frightful to imagine and they prefer to have no dealings with any one so dubious and so dangerous.

[326] This is probably W. J. Livingstone Anderson. The January 6, 1907, *Freethinker* mentions him asking about G. W. Foote's imprisonment for blasphemy. See "To Correspondents," *Freethinker*, January 6, 1907, 9. He also contributed a long biographical blurb about Ernest Pack for Ernest Pack, *The Trial and Imprisonment of J. W. Gott for Blasphemy* (Bradford, UK: Freethought Socialist League, 1912?), 130–134. In this blurb, Livingstone Anderson refers to Saladin/Ross as his companion and the person who introduced him to Pack.

[327] For more, see See "Saladin's Illness and Death," in chap. 1, in this volume.

The Value of Atheism[328]

To the Editor of *The Freethinker*

J. F. C. Fuller.

SIR,—Often, upon reading such excellent articles as "What Price God?" by Mr. G. W. Foote, in the *Freethinker*,[329] I have asked myself the question: "What, then, is the real value of Atheism?" And time after time, I have been forced, with perhaps few other Freethinkers, to answer: "Zero."

The question resolves itself thus:—

> 1. What is Theism? The system of thought as held by a Theist; and, we are told, a Theist is a man "with God."
> 2. What is Atheism? The system of thought as held by an Atheist; and, we are told, an Atheist is a man "without God."

And the difference scientifically:—

> 1. The Theist says: there is a God, and He created something out of nothing—the universe.
> 2. The Atheist says: there is not a God, and that something has ever been something—the universe.

Thus we find that the Theist postulates an "Uncreated Creator," to the Atheist's "Uncreated Creation"; and that both their arguments are merely verbal, as neither explain the creator nor the creation, and the result is—*nil*.

But, I hear many assert, science does explain the creation, just as I have heard many others say theology does explain the Creator, Yet I frankly fail to see how either of these systems in any way offers an explanation. The former, as the latter, resting purely and solely on hypotheses based on ever changing philosophical arguments. Science asserts the "Laws of Nature," theology, the

[328] *Freethinker*, September 8, 1907, 27(86): 572–573. There appears to have been a follow-up, as "To Correspondents" in the September 22, 1907, issue includes the remark, "J. F. C. Fuller.—No room this week, anyhow."

[329] G. W. Foote, "What Price God?" *Freethinker* 27, no. 83 (August 18, 1907): 513–514 and *Freethinker* 27, no. 84 (August 25, 1907): 529–531.

"Laws of God." Yet both these codes, Natural or Divine, rest, as every thinker mint acknowledge, upon mere inferences drawn from the vast and unbalanced ignorance of man's mind, and his inability to grasp first principles, or things as they are in themselves,

Turning now from the scientific and religious aspect, let us look at the question philosophically. Roughly, Atheism philosophically falls under the system of Materialism, and Theism under that of Idealism.

Now let us take an infinite chain:—A, B, A, B, A, B, A, B. The Materialist will say all is matter and will place his finger on A; to him, matter is first, mind is second. The Idealist will place his finger on B and say, mind is first, matter is second. The Pantheist puts his finger on both A and B at once. And the difference philosophically:—

1. The Materialist says the universe began with A.
2. The Idealist says the universe began with B.

Thus we find that both their arguments are merely verbal and that their value is—*nil.*

And so with all other systems of thought. It is much easier to prove them all one than it is to prove them all diverse. Descartes becomes Spinoza, Spinoza—Locke, Locke—Berkeley, Berkeley—Hume, Hume—Kant, Kant—Spencer, Spencer—Huxley, and Huxley—G. W. Foote, etc. To not be considered a more babler of words, I should like to explain myself as follows:—

It seems to me that Berkeley, nearly two hundred years ago now, answered the scientists apparently for all time, by stating, "It seems no less absurd to suppose a substance without accidents, than it is to suppose accidents without a substance." And that, "though we should grant this unknown substance may possibly exist, yet where can it be supposed to be? That it exists not in the mind is agreed; and that it exists not in place is no less certain; since all extension exists only in the mind, as hath been already proved. It remains therefore that it exists no where at all"[330]—*i.e.*, in the Absolute Zero. And again, he asserts, this time by the word of Philonous:—

[330] *Principles of Human Knowledge* [original note]. George Berkeley, *A Treatise Concerning the Principles of Human Knowledge*, pt. 1 (Dublin: printed by Aaron Rhames for Jeremy Pepyat, 1710), para. 67.

> "Consequently every corporeal substance being the *substratum* of extension must have in itself another extension, by which it is qualified to be a *substratum*: and so on to infinity? And I ask whether this be not absurd is itself, and repugnant to what you granted just now, to wit, that the *substratum* was something distinct from, and exclusive of extension?"[331]

And what is pure extension?—Absolute Zero.

Thus, the whole cosmic process resolves itself under the one great law of Inertia; so that the entire universe lies before us, as Luther said of God, "A blank sheet, on which nothing is found but what we ourselves have written." Or, again, in the words of Spinoza, "Final or first causes are only figments of the human mind," bubbles which must burst before the finite can once again dissolve into the infinite atmosphere of eternity. In any category, infinity excludes finity, unless that finity be an identical part of that infinity. As Mr. Crowley states in his work *Berashith:*—

> "In the category of existing things, space being infinite, for on that hypothesis we are still working, either matter fills or does not fill it. In the former, matter is infinitely great; if the latter, infinitely small. Whether the matter-universe be 10^{10000} light-years diameter, or half a mile, it makes no difference; it is infinitely small—in effect, Nothing."[332]

So in the first case we see, being infinitely great all else is crowded out, and it = 0; and in the second, all being infinitely small, the unmathematical illusion (the *maya* of the Hindus) likewise vanishes in 0. So, likewise, does Theism resolve into Pantheism, which itself dissolves into Atheism; the I = ∞ = 0 and *vice versâ*.[333] But which? I, for one, can but answer, *Agnosco!*

[331] *Three Dialogues* [original note]. George Berkeley, *Three Dialogues between Hylas and Philonous, in Opposition to Sceptics and Atheists* (London: printed by G. James for Henry Clements, 1713), first dialogue.

[332] Aleister Crowley, *[Berashith]: An Essay in Ontology; with Some Remarks on Ceremonial* (Paris: privately printed, 1903); repr. in Aleister Crowley, *The Sword of Song: Called by Christians, the Book of the Beast* (Benares, India: Society for the Propagation of Religious Truth, 1904).

[333] This whole section, beginning with the discussion of Berkeley, is a lightly edited quote from Fuller, *Star in the West*, 260–261.

Vertebrates and Invertebrates[334]

To the Editor of *The Freethinker*

Aleister Crowley

Sir,—At the very outset of the Boulter case[335] I wrote to the leading Rationalist paper, urging them to identify themselves with the latest victim of "gentle Jesus, meek and mild." Needless to say, they "respected my point of view"—but refused to publish the letter.[336] It will only serve them right if they are prosecuted themselves in a year or two—for cowardice in the face of the enemy. The truth is that as soon as people of any shade of opinion become sleek and well-fed and respectable and secure, the manly virtues leave them. I welcome the Boulter prosecution for many reasons; not least for this, that I like to be on the side of the vertebrates. I would rather gnaw on the bone of Atheism than stodge myself with the mashed potatoes of polite Rationalism.

I am glad to see that you and the N. S. S. are as ready as ever to die in the last ditch. Like R. L. Stevenson's Berserk, "I am off to die with Odin."[337] Hitherto I have fought shy of a label, for I am at least as much a mystic as a sceptic; but for the purposes of this argument I pray you to honor me with the title of Atheist. If we should ever quarrel on the point, it will at least be not until the mangy lion of Ecclesiasticism and the jackals of Nonconformity have finally ceased to show their fangs, crimsoned with the blood of a great company of Atheist heroes and martyrs, physically overcome, spiritually invulnerable.

[334] *Freethinker*, February 16, 1908, 28.

[335] In 1908, the "socialist tailor" Harry Boulter was charged with blasphemy over his lectures at Highbury Fields. He was such a respected North London radical (and a friend of Guy Aldred) that the NSS defended him even though he was not a member, He would be found guilty but discharged.

[336] See "Our Letter-Box," *Literary Guide and Rationalist Review*, no. 140 (February 1, 1908): 30. The *Literary Guide and Rationalist Review* here notes, "Aleister Crowley.—We respect your point of view, but do not see that service would be done by inserting your letter."

[337] The line Crowley quotes is from Robert Louis Stevenson, "Faith, Half-Faith, and No Faith at All," in Robert L. Stevenson, *Fables* (London: Longmans, Green, 1896).

A Song of the Promise of Dawn[338]

Victor B. Neuburg

With the swift-winged wind I fly,
Yet who my wings hath heard?
With the spray of the sea I gleam
Yet who hath seen me shine?

I flash in the summer sky,
But who hath caught the word
That burns in the heart of the dream;
The dream that hath made thee mine?

I glow in the heart of the fire,
Yet who have I warmed indeed?
I splash in the cooling rain,
Yet whom have I saved from death?

I lie in the heart's desire;
I spring in the shooting seed;
Without me all is vain,
Yet who will spare me breath?

As the world is old, I am old;
But who at my shrine doth bend?
As spring is young, I am young;
And yet whose lyre is mine?

As death is cold, I am cold,
But never a man will lend
A note in the song he has sung,
A drop of his heart's red wine.

[338] This is one of two new poems included in *A Green Garland*.

A Leaf (of Grass) from Walt Whitman[339]

Victor B. Neuburg

"Then the eyes close, calmly close, and I speed forth to the darkness,
"Resuming, marching, ever in darkness marching, on in the ranks,
"The unknown road still marching."—DRUM-TAPS.[340]

Then the eyes close; the lamp is darkened now,
    The spirit's prison is empty, the spirit free;
A gentle hand smooths the unclouded brow,
    Kind fingers seal the eyelids tenderly,
And, maybe, in the darkness, ere he rise,
The watcher plants a kiss on the shut eyes.

Asleep! asleep! the soothing night-air blows
    The hair the wind may ruffle never more;
The door is shut; the camp-fire cracks and glows,
    The shadows waver darkly in its roar
A shadow-play of death and life: the damp
Of evening dews o'erspreads the little camp.

Sweet breeze, blow softly o'er the dead, the dead,
    The day is passed, the night is starless, chill
The herald-breeze of dawn, ere dawn is red
    With sunlight, blows from the high eastern hill.
The night is cold; draw close your cloaks, for lo!
The unknown road far stretches. Let us go.

339 This is one of two new poems included in *A Green Garland*. The work of American poet Walt Whitman (1819–1892)—particularly his famous and frequently revised-and-expanded collection *Leaves of Grass* (1855)—was controversial for its sensuality and sexual imagery.

340 These are the last four lines of "A March in the Ranks Hard-Prest, and the Road Unknown" from Whitman's Civil War poetry collection, *Drum Taps* (New York: n.p., 1865), 44–45, upon which lines this poem expands.

The Creation of Eve[341]
After Blake's Picture[342]

Victor B. Neuburg

SOFTLY she rises, with a child's clear eyes:
The male still sleeps; the god instructeth her,
Who with his fellows did of late confer
On her who should complete this paradise.
In perfect wisdom he has made her rise;
She stands new-born, the utmost worshipper,
For in her being's depth doth stir
The royal knowledge: she is wholly wise.

The mystic moon o'erhangs her, whence of late
The gods to earth transferred their charge, and she,
The perfect Mother of the uncreate,
Hath taken to her flesh, that is to be
The way of carnal birth,—the door of Fate
Betwixt the borders of infinity.

Diary Entry, October 11, 1908[343]

Aleister Crowley

2:22 I further take this opportunity of asserting my Atheism.

I believe that all these phenomena are as explicable as the formation of hoar-frost or of glacier tables.

[341] *Theosophical Review* 41, no. 246 (February 1908): 540; repr. in *Triumph of Pan.*

[342] "The Creation of Eve" is one of several watercolor illustrations that William Blake (1757–1827) did to accompany John Milton's *Paradise Lost* (in this case, bk. 7, lines 452–477). Three different versions of this particular work survive.

[343] "John St. John: The Record of the Magical Retirement of G. H. Frater, O.·.M.·.," *The Equinox* 1, no. 1 (supplement, 1909): 128–129. With this publication, Crowley sought not only to model what a "magical record" should look like but also to demonstrate how a Great Magical Retirement, with a resultant "attainment," could be accomplished without completely disengaging from one's day-to-day activities.

I believe "Attainment" to be a simple supreme sane state of the human brain. I do not believe in miracles; I do not think that God could cause a monkey, clergyman, or rationalist to attain.

I am taking all this trouble of the Record principally in hope that it will show exactly what mental and physical conditions precede, accompany, and follow "attainment" so that others may reproduce, through those conditions, that Result.

I believe in the Law of Cause and Effect—and I loathe the cant alike of the Superstitionist and the Rationalist.

The Confession of St. Judas McCabbage[344]

I believe in Charles Darwin Almighty, maker of Evolution; and in Ernst Haeckel, his only son our Lord Who for us men and for our salvation came down from Germany: who was conceived of Weissmann,[345] born of Büchner,[346] suffered under du Bois-Raymond,[347] was printed, bound, and shelved: who was raised again into English (of sorts),[348] ascended into the Pantheon of the *Literary Guide* and sitteth on the right hand of Edward Clodd:[349] whence he shall come to judge the thick in the head.

I believe in Charles Watts; the Rationalist Press Association; the annual dinner at the Trocadero Restaurant;[350] the regularity of subscriptions, the resurrection in a sixpenny edition, and the Bookstall everlasting.

Amen.

[344] This section is a parody of the Apostles' Creed. "Judas McCabbage" was Crowley's nickname for Joseph McCabe. Earlier in his diary, contrasting competing models of illumination in which an Adept either ascends to the light versus drawing down the light, writes, "The other idea of the Light descending and filling each principle with its glory is, it seems to him, less fertile, and less in accord with any idea of Evolution. (What would Judas McCabbage think?)." Aleister Crowley, diary entry, October 9, 1908, in Crowley, "John St. John," 102–103.

[345] German biologist August Weismann (1834–1914) ranks second only to Charles Darwin among the most notable nineteenth-century evolutionary theorists. He is particularly remembered for germ-plasm theory, which stood in opposition to the Lamarckian theory of inherited acquired characteristics.

[346] As an outspoken proponent of scientific materialism (or, as some saw it, atheistic evangelism), philosopher-physician Ludwig Büchner (1824–1899) was in many ways the German equivalent of Thomas Henry Huxley.

[347] Emil du Bois-Reymond (misspelled as "Raymond" by Crowley), founder of German electrophysiology, rivaled Haeckel as one of the most effective German popularizers of Darwinism. Indeed, Finkelstein called him "the first German Darwinist," even though Haeckel would wind up better-known. Gabriel Finkelstein, "Darwin and Neuroscience: The German Connection," *Frontiers in Neuroanatomy*, no. 13(2019): 33. See also Gabriel Finkelstein, "Haeckel and du Bois-Reymond: Rival German Darwinists," *Theory in Biosciences* 138, no. 1 (2019): 105–112.

[348] Crowley here alludes to the second runaway hit from the RPA's Cheap Reprints stable: Joseph McCabe's translation of Haeckel's *The Riddle of the Universe* (1899).

[349] English banker Edward Clodd (1840–1930) was an evolution enthusiast, the biographer of his personal friends Thomas Henry Huxley and Herbert Spencer, and, from 1906 to 1913, chairman of the RPA.]

[350] The location of the RPA's Annual Dinner moved around over the years, but during the time when Crowley wrote this, they had settled for a few years (1907–1910) on meeting in early May at the

R. P. A. ANNUAL DINNER.

SATURDAY, MAY 2ND, 1908.

Members of the Rationalist Press Association who wish to be present at the forthcoming Annual Dinner, and who have not already applied for tickets, should do so at once.

The Dinner is to be held at the Trocadero Restaurant (Shaftesbury Avenue—close to Piccadilly Circus) on the evening of Saturday, May 2nd, the Empire Hall and Alexandra Reception Room having been retained for this purpose.

Last year's Dinner was the most numerously attended and probably the most keenly appreciated of these annual gatherings, and there is every reason to expect as great a success this year. Sir Edward Brabrook will occupy the Chair, and will be supported by some of the best known figures in the Rationalist Movement; and also, it is hoped, by one or more noted speakers who have not been present at previous Dinners of the R. P. A.

Evening dress is optional.

The musical items of the programme will be few, but of good quality. The Reception Room will be open at 6 o'clock, and dinner will be served at 7, thus giving opportunities for social intercourse both before the dinner and after the speeches.

The price of the tickets, which are available to non-Members as well as Members, is 5s. 6d. each. Apply promptly to the Secretary, R. P. A., Ltd., Nos. 5 and 6, Johnson's Court, Fleet Street, London, E.C.

Figure A2 Announcement of the seventh RPA annual dinner, which took place the same year as Crowley's diary entry, from the *Literary Guide and Rationalist Review* 143 (March 1, 1908): 72.

Trocadero entertainment complex and catering hall in Piccadilly Circus. They favored using Empire Hall, with the adjoining Alexandra Room for its reception. Approximately 160 members attended the 1908 meeting. See "The R.P.A. Dinner," *Literary Guide and Rationalist Review* 144 (June 1, 1908): 90–91; "Random Jottings," *Literary Guide and Rationalist Review* 130 (April 1, 1907): 56; "Random Jottings," *Literary Guide and Rationalist Review* 142 (April 1, 1908): 56; "Random Jottings," *Literary Guide and Rationalist Review* 154 (April 1, 1909): 56; Advertisement, *Literary Guide and Rationalist Review* 166 (April 1, 1910): 56.

Prior to 1907, the dinners met at locations such as the International Hall of Monico's restaurant in Piccadilly Circus in 1906, the Hotel Cecil in 1904 and 1905, and the Holborn Restaurant in 1903. See "Random Jottings," *Literary Guide and Rationalist Review* 118 (April 1, 1906): 56); Advertisement, *Literary Guide and Rationalist Review* 93 (March 1, 1904): 40; "The R. P. A. Annual Dinner," *Literary Guide and Rationalist Review* 106 (April 1, 1905): 57; and "Random Jottings," *Literary Guide and Rationalist Review* 80 (February 1, 1903): 24.

Two Poems[351, 352]

Victor B. Neuburg

The Cauldron

I was born when a witch
    Spread her withered hands over a blaze,
With a big hazel-switch
    With notches for days,
    With notches for days.
And slimy and rich
    Her ugly voice prays:
By God! I was there with the witch!

What matter to me
If the sun be at war with the sea?
    Will they drench me or burn?
    I was born in the heart of an urn
When the gold was all fled;
And they thought I was dead
Before birth, but I sped
    Forth, forth from the fire,
    And lo! with desire
I escaped, and I roam
At will from my home.

They call me, and lo!
Why should I go?
They feed me with gold;
They are withered and old,
For I suck and I suck,
And they give me good luck.

[351] *Theosophical Review* 43, no. 258 (February 1909): 549–550. The author's name appears as Victor B. Neuberg [*sic*].
[352] Reprinted in *Triumph of Pan*.

Lo! I am one with the air,
For air is my blood and red fire is my hair,
And the wind is my lair.
　　And they draw me with thought,
　　For of air am I wrought.
They call me, and then
I flee among men,
　　And madness and rust
　　And the music of dust
I give them, and they
　　With the fury of trust,
　　Feed me with flame of desire and bright lust!
And I conquer the day,
And I float, and I float, and I float far away.

A Lost Spirit

I PASS by darkened windy ways,
　　Through bog and dripping heather;
I flash before the silver rays
　　The moon holds tight together.
I sing beneath the waning moon;
An ancient god-forgotten rune
Springs to my lips to taste, and soon
The way behind with light is strewn.

O silent city silver-lit,
　　O rainy roads reflecting
Tall houses where the old ghosts flit,
　　Their shadows thin projecting
Across my path—the street lamps glare
Before my soft eyes everywhere.
Ah! men forget my face is fair,
The tangled glory of my hair.

O sobbing wind! O hedges dark!
　　O hills bereft and lonely!

They've snatched the hidden boundary-mark,
    And left the ruins only.
Dimly the flickering shadows stray
Across the lonely hill-side way:
Why should I weep and howl and pray?
They sleep, and wait the empty day.

O dream of the red olden time!
    O clash of armour splendid!—
A string of wind-begotten rhyme,
    And all their pain was ended!
O lonely sea! O lonely earth!
O dying art of glorious mirth!
My song, my song is little worth
To bring their bastard seed to birth!

What need of me in thunder-flash?
    What need in battle story?
What need among the whitened ash
    Of old far-winnowed glory?
They call me not to birth-bed throes;
Invoke me not with gold and rose;
The summer wanes, the summer grows,—
They call me not from fire or snows.

1 linger by the cottage-door
    When twilight sings of sorrow;
I flit around the gorse-strewn moor,
    And all the gold I borrow.
But in mine eyes my doom is set,
Yea! in their golden-glooming fret
Is woven the divine regret,
And ah! my birth-time is not yet.

On a Statue of the Buddha[353]

Victor B. Neuburg

Flower of the Lotus, nobly born,
Spring thou amidst our English corn,
And let us smile thine eyes beneath,
Deep-purple in their fringèd sheath:
Peaceful beyond our dreams of ill
And good, thou smilest and art still.

What secret chamber hast thou found
Within the gloom of thought profound?
Wisely thou smilest: naught, naught less
Than deep translucent Nothingness—
The word that all wide space shall fill.
But thou? thou smilest and art still.

Dim dreams of dawn within thy breast
Have set thy yearning heart at rest;
Thou sittest in the dark green shade
Beyond the need of dumb gods' aid:
Thine eyes were lit beyond the Hill;
Thine eyes smile ever, and are still.

O Lord who found'st the gates of truth
Too low for gods, too strait for youth—
Who saw'st the winding paths that bring
All men within the mystic Ring—
How may we find the hidden Rill
Whose healing waters made thee still?

Thou smilest and art still, but we
Lie deep-enmeshed in mystery
Thine eyes have made a truce with Pain,

[353] *Buddhist Review* 1, no. 3 (July 1909): 182–184.

For thou hast found how life is vain:
The clarion soundeth loud and shrill,
But thou, Lord, sittest ever still.

Lord of the unforgetting birth,
Whose doorways spanned the arch of earth,
What lamp hath led thee to the door
With dark beyond and light before?
Thy striving wearied thee, until
Thou saw'st, and then thy heart was still.

Far from the web, Siddhartha, Lord,
Thou sittest at the gods' dim board,
And holdest in thy stern caress
Thine ever-virgin Nothingness.—
Not thine the cup that men fulfil—
Thou smilest ever, and art still.

We lie within the choking dust,
In pain and hate, in love and lust;
Thou mayest now our pain forgo,
Who cast off life with joy and woe—
Thou see'st our life, our love, our skill:
Thou smilest, and art ever still.

Lord of the opening lotus-flower,
With shells of æons for thy bower,
Teach us indeed that we may know
The vanity of life and woe;
We strive, we bear, beget and kill,
But thou, O Lord, remainest still.

O vain for thee the word to teach
In soaring song, in wondrous speech;
Not thou the gift of sleep may'st bring,
Deep-merged within the mystic Ring—
We die and live, drink blood and spill,
But thou, Lord, smilest and art still.

Thou smilest, for thou art the Law;
Thou smilest not in love or awe,
But, seeing to the end of space
And time, thou bear'st a god-filled face:
We creep into the lotus-flower,
And sleep and hour, and sleep an hour.

The *Literary Guide and Rationalist Review*, 1908–9. Monthly, 2"d."[354]

Aleister Crowley

Of all the lame ducks that crow upon their middens under the impression that they are reincarnations of Sir Francis Drake, I suppose that the origin-of-religion lunatics are the silliest.

Listen to Charles Callow-Hay[355] on Stonehenge! Here's logic for you!
Stonehenge is built in the form of a circle.
The sun appears to go round the earth in a circle.
Argal, *Stonehenge is a solar temple.*
Or, for the minor premiss:
Eggs are round.
Argal, *Stonehenge was dedicated to Eugenics.*[356]
Listen to Johnny Bobson[357] on Cleopatra's Needle!
The Needle is square in section.

[354] "Reviews," *The Equinox* 1, no. 2 (September 1909): 386–389. Although unsigned, this review was penned by Crowley. There are far too many *Equinox* reviews of RPA titles to reproduce them all, but this is the most substantial example, showcasing Crowley's characteristic approach to humor, parody, and inside jokes.

[355] This is regular *Literary Guide* contributor Dr. Charles Callaway (d. September 29, 1915) and author of Does Determinism Destroy Responsibility? and King David of Israel: A Study in the Evolution of Ethics, both published in 1905 by Watts & Co. Although he doesn't write specifically about Stonehenge in the issues reviewed, the cross-cultural argument in articles by such authors as Charls Callaway may be the target of Crowley's critique. See, for example, Charles Callaway, "The Origin of Easter: A Study in Myth, Magic, and Religion," *Literary Guide and Rationalist Review* 142 (supplement, April 1908): 1–4.

[356] The *Literary Guide* touched off a spate of subscriber letters with the publication of D. Waudby, "Can We Breed Intelligence?," *Literary Guide and Rationalist Review* 143 (May 1, 1908): 68–69.

[357] John Mackinnon Robertson, MP (1856–1933), was a regular contributor to the journal and the author of *Pagan Christs*, which Crowley would later cite in "The Revival of Magick." As with Callaway, Robertson doesn't reference Cleopatra's Needle in any of his *Literary Guide* contributions in 1908 or 1909, so this critique appears to be more metaphorical.

The old Egyptians thought the earth had four corners.
Argal, *The Needle was built to commemorate the theory.*

Or, even worse!

The Needle is square in section.
It must have been built so for a religious reason.
Argal, *The Egyptians thought that the earth had four corners.*

It is impossible to commit all possible logical fallacies in a single syllogism.

This must be very disappointing to the young bloods of the R.P.A.

The Rationalists have created man in their own image, as dull simpletons. They assume that the marvellous powers of applied mathematics shown in the Great Pyramid had no worthier aim than the perpetuation of a superstitious imbecility.[358]

Here is Leggy James translating the Chinese classics.[359]

Passage I. is of so supreme an excellence that it compels even his respect.

What does he do?

He flies in the face of the text and the tradition, asserting that "heaven" means a personal God. This shows what "God has never left himself without a witness"—even in China.

Passage II. is quite foolish—*i.e.*, he, He, HE, Leggy James Himself, cannot understand it. This shows to what awful depths the unaided intellect of even the greatest heathen must necessarily sink. How fortunate are We—*et cetera*.

It is such people as these who accuse mystics of fitting the facts to their theories.

Here is Erbswurst Treacle[360] dictating the Laws of the Universe.

[358] While no articles on the mathematics of the Great Pyramid were published in 1908–1909, a review did appear of Gerald Massey's final, posthumous work, *Ancient Egypt: The Light of the World*. See "Egypt and Christian Origins," *Literary Guide and Rationalist Review* 140 (February 1, 1908): 21–22; and "Gerald Massey's Last Book," *Literary Guide and Rationalist Review* 141 (March 1, 1908): 43.

[359] A reference to famed *I Ching* translator and commentator James Legge (1815–1897) and his Sacred Books of China. See *Sacred Books of China: The Texts of Confucianism, Part 2: The Yi King*, trans. James Legge, 2nd ed., Sacred Books of the East 16, ed. F. Max Müller (Oxford: Clarendon Press, 1899). In his personal and heavily annotated copy of this book, Crowley crosses out "James" on the title page and hand-writes a substitution, changing the author's name to "Wood N. Legge." Legge was not a contributor or the subject of a review in 1908–1909. Crowley here appears to be referencing an article—and subsequent reader correspondence—about whether the Buddha was a pre-Christian example of a virgin birth, a discussion that involved references to various Chinese classics. See Chilperic, "The Miraculous Birth of the Buddha," *Literary Guide and Rationalist Review*, December 1, 1908, 150: 180–181. See also the subsequent correspondence in *Literary Guide and Rationalist Review* 151 (January 1, 1909): 15–16; *Literary Guide and Rationalist Review* 152 (February 1, 1909): 31–32; and *Literary Guide and Rationalist Review* 154 (April 1, 1909): 63–64.

[360] German biologist and Darwin promoter Ernst Haeckel (1834–1919) is known for positing the since-disproven theory that "ontogeny recapitulates phylogeny." See, for example, Ernst Haeckel,

It is certain (saith Erbswurst Treacle) that there is no God. And proves it by arguments drawn from advanced biology—the biology of Erbswurst Treacle.

Oh! the shameless effrontery of the Pope who asserts the contrary, and proves it by arguments unintelligible to the lay mind! How shocked is the Rationalist!

My good professor, right or wrong, I may be drunk, but I certainly see a pair of you.

So this is where we are got to after these six thousand, or six thousand billion years (as the case may be),[361] that, asking for bread, one man gives us the stone of Homoiousios and another the half-baked brick of Amphioxus. Both are in a way rationalists. Wolff gives us idea unsupported by fact, and argues about it for year after year; Treacle does the same thing for fact unsupported by idea. Nor does the one escape the final bankruptcy of reason more than the other.

While the theologian vainly tries to shuffle the problem of evil, the Rationalist is compelled to ascribe to his perfect monad the tendency to divide into opposite forces.

The οὐδὲν plays leapfrog with the ἑν as the ἑν has vaulted over the bar of the πολλα and the παν.[362] So the whole argument breaks up into a formidably ridiculous logomachy, and we are left in doubt as to whether the universe is (after all) bound together by causal or contingent links,[363] or whether in truth we are not gibbering lunatics in an insane chaos of hallucination.

And just as we think we are rid of the priggishness of Matthew Arnold and Edwin Arnold[364] and all the pragmatic pedants and Priscilla-scented lavenderians, up jumps some renegade monk, proclaims himself the Spirit of the Twentieth Century, and replaces the weak tea of the past by his own stinking cabbage-water.[365]

"Haeckel's Darwin Address: The Theory of the 'Origin of the Species' Has Solved the Problem of Creation," *Literary Guide and Rationalist Review* 156 (June 1, 1909): 89–90.

361 A possible reference to Edward Greenly, "The Age of the Earth," *Literary Guide and Rationalist Review* 147 (September 1, 1908): 131–132.

362 οὐδὲν = naught; ἑν = one; πολλα = many; παν = all.

363 This is part of Haeckel's philosophical outlook. See, for example, "Mr. Butler Burke on Haeckel," *Literary Guide and Rationalist Review* 139 (January 1, 1908): 12. This article says of Haeckel's "Materialistic Monism" that "Haeckel thinks, and, we think, quite rightly, that all nature is a dynamical system of connected events. He regards this vast connected system as a great mechanical and well-adjusted whole."

364 Matthew Arnold (1822–1888) and Sir Edwin Arnold (1832–1904) were both English poets.

365 Whenever Crowley mentions cabbage in the context of the RPA, he is referring to its guiding light, Joseph McCabe (1867–1955), formerly a Roman Catholic priest (hence Crowley's "renegade monk").

It seems useless nowadays to call for a draught of the right Wine of Iacchus.

The Evangelicals object to the wine, and the Rationalists to the God.

We had filed off the fetter, and while the sores yet burn, find another heaver iron yet firmer on the other foot—as Stevenson so magnificently parabled unto us.

Then how this nauseous stinkard quibbles!

This defender of truth! How he delights with apish malice to write "in England," wishing his hearers to understand "Great Britain"; and when taxed with the malignant lie against his brother which he had thus cunningly insinuated, to point out gleefully that "England" does not include "Scotland."

Indeed a triumph of the Reason!

And why all this pother? To reduce all men to their own lumpishness. These louts of the intelligence! These clods—Clodds![366]

My good fellows, it is certainly necessary to plough a field sometimes. But not all the year round! We don't want the furrows; we want the grain. And (for God's sake!) if you must be ploughmen, at least let us have the furrows straight!

Do you really think you have helped us much when you have shown that a horse is really the same as a cow, only different?

Quite right; it is indeed kind of you to have pointed out that even Gadarene pigs might fly, but are very unlikely birds, and that the said horse is (after all) not a dragon. Very, very kind of you.

Thank you so much.

And now will you kindly go away?

Concerning "Blasphemy" in General and the Rites of Eleusis in Particular[367]

Aleister Crowley

[The editor wishes it to be clearly understood that The Bystander *does not associate itself in any way with the views of Mr. Crowley. We have offered him the*

[366] English author Edward Clodd (1840–1930) was chairman of the RPA from 1906–1913.

[367] *The Bystander*, November 16, 1910. After Aleister Crowley organized performances of his *Rites of Eleusis* at Caxton Hall on seven successive Wednesdays starting on October 19, 1910 (one for each of the seven celestial bodies in classical astrology), he came under fire from the yellow press. See, for example, "An Amazing Sect," *Looking Glass*, October 29, 1910, 140–142; "Is a New Smyth-Pigott among Us?," *John Bull*, November 5, 1910, 707; and "An Amazing Sect.—No. 2," *Looking Glass*, November 12, 1910, 203–205. *The Bystander*, which had provided a sympathetic story ("Nine O'clock Ecstasies!

hospitality of our columns to repel the serious charge that the Rites of Eleusis *now in progress at the Caxton Hall, Westminster, are "orgies" of a blasphemous character, and it is entirely for the public to decide whether or not he succeeds in doing this. Our columns are open for correspondence.]*

Pioneers, O Pioneers!

Whenever it occurs to anyone to cut a new canal of any kind, he will be well advised to look out for trouble. If it be the isthmus of Suez, the simple-minded engineer is apt to imagine that it is only a question of shifting so much sand; but before he can as much as strike the first pickaxe into the earth he finds that he is up against all kinds of interests, social, political, financial, and what-not. The same applies to the digging of canals in the human brain. When Simpson introduced chloroform,[368] he thought it a matter for the physician; and found himself attacked from the pulpit. All his arguments proved useless; and we should probably be without chloroform to-day if some genius had not befriended him by discovering that God caused Adam to fall into a deep sleep before He removed the rib of which Eve was made.

The Abuse of the Gutter

Nowadays a movement has to be very well on the way to success before it is attacked by any responsible people. The first trouble comes from the gutter. Now the language of the gutter consists chiefly of meaningless abuse, and the principal catch-words, coming as they do from the mouths of men who never open them without a profane oath or a foul allusion, are those of blasphemy

Nocturnal Planetary Rites a Feature of the London Autumn Season," *The Bystander*, October 12, 1910, 73), gave Crowley a platform for his response, "Concerning 'Blasphemy.'" Crowley felt some common cause with the agnostics and rationalists, who over the years both confronted accusations of blasphemy and mounted legal challenges to those accusations. Unfortunately, Crowley's rejoinder merely egged on the tabloids, which followed with more articles. articles. See "The Amazing Sect Again: Crowley on His Defence," *Looking Glass*, November 19, 1910, 242; and "Mr. Aleister Crowley Defends Himself against M.A.P.," *M.A.P.*, November 26, 1910, 641. The attacks against Crowley and his circle became so vicious that George Cecil Jones sued (unsuccessfully) the *Looking Glass* for libel. For details, see Richard Kaczynski, *Perdurabo Outtakes* (Royal Oak: Blue Equinox Oasis, 2005).

[368] Sir James Young Simpson (1811–1870) introduced the use of chloroform as a childbirth anesthetic, designed obstetric forceps, and advocated for midwives.

and immorality. The charge of insanity is frequently added when the new idea is just sufficiently easy to understand a little. There is another reason, too, for these three particular cries; these are the charges which, if proved, can get the person into trouble, and at the same time which are in a sense true of everybody; for they all refer to a more or less arbitrary standard of normality. The old cry of "heresy" has naturally lost much of its force in a country nine-tenths of whose population are admittedly heretics; but immorality and insanity are to-day almost equally meaningless terms. The Censor permits musical comedy and forbids *Oedipus Rex*; and Mr. Bernard Shaw brands the Censor as immoral for doing so. Most people of the educated classes will probably agree with him.

Insanity and Blasphemy

As for insanity, it is simply a question of finding a Greek or Latin name for any given act. If I open the window, it is on account of claustrophobia; when I shut it again, it is an attack of agoraphobia. All the professors tell me that every form of emotion has its root in sex, and describe my fondness for pictures as if it were a peculiarly unnatural type of vice. It is even impossible for an architect to build a church spire without being told that he is reviving the worship of Priapus. Now, the only result of all this is that all these terms of abuse have become entirely meaningless, save as defined by law. There is still some meaning in the term "Forger," as used in general speech; but only because it has not yet occurred to any wiseacre to prove that all his political and religious opponents are forgers. This seems to me a pity. There is, undoubtedly, a forged passage in Tacitus and another in Petronius. Everyone who studies the classics is, therefore, a kind of accomplice in forgery. The charge of blasphemy is in all cases a particularly senseless one. It has been hurled in turn at Socrates, Euripides, Christ, El-Mansur, the Baab, and the Rev. R. J. Campbell.[369]

[369] Among the less well-known figures here, Crowley refers to Persian mystic Al-Hallaj (also called Mansour Hallaj, *c.* 858–922), who was executed for blasphemy; The Báb (Siyyid 'Alí Muhammad Shírází, 1819–1850), founder of Bábism (with himself as divine messenger) as a precursor to the B'hai faith, was tried and found guilty of apostasy; and Reginald John Campbell (1867–1956) was an outspoken minister who courted controversy among his critics with his books Reginald John Campbell, *The New Theology* (London: Chapman & Hall, 1907); and Reginald John Campbell, *New Theology Sermons* (London: Williams & Norgate, 1907).

The Morality Red Herring

Legal blasphemy is, of course, an entirely different thing. In the recent notorious case where an agent of the Rationalist Press Association, Harry Boulter by name,[370] was prosecuted, the question proved to be not a theological one at all. It was really this, "Were the neighbours being annoyed?" "Was the man's language coarse?" and the Judge and Joseph McCabe agreed that it was. But in modern times no one has ever been prosecuted in any civilised country for stating philosophic propositions, whatever may be their theological implications. We have no longer the Casuists of the Inquisition, who would take the trouble to argue from Bruno's propositions of the immanence of God that, if that were so, the doctrine of the Incarnation was untenable (and therefore he shall be burned). It is only the very narrowest religious sects that trouble to call Herbert Spencer an Atheist. What the man in the street means by Atheist is the militant Atheist, Bradlaugh or Foote; and it is a singular characteristic of the Odium Theologicum that, instead of arguing soberly concerning the proposition, which those worthies put forward, they always try to drag the red herring of morality across the track. Of all the stupid lies that men have ever invented, nothing is much sillier than the lie that one who does not believe in God must be equally a disbeliever in morality. As a matter of fact, in a country which pretends so hard to appear theistic as England, it requires the most astounding moral courage, a positive galaxy of virtues, for a man to stand up and say that he does not believe in God; as Dr. Wace historically remarked, "It ought to be unpleasant for a man to say that he does not believe in Jesus";[371] and my dislike to Atheism is principally founded on the fact that so many of its exponents are always boring me about ethics. Some priceless idiot, who, I hope, will finish in the British Museum, remarked in a free-thinking paper the other day, that they need not trouble to pull down the churches, "because they will always be so useful for sane and serious discussion of important ethical problems." Personally, I would rather go back to the times when the preacher preached by the hour-glass.

[370] See "To the Editor of The Freethinker" in "Vertebrates and Invertebrates," in this anthology.

[371] In a lecture on agnosticism, Protestant churchman and college administrator Henry Wace (1836–1924) remarked, "It is, and it ought to be, an unpleasant thing for a man to have to say plainly that he does not believe in Jesus Christ." The result was a public back-and-forth between Wace, T. H. Huxley, the bishop of Petersborough, and others. See Henry Wace et al., *Christianity and Agnosticism: A Controversy* (New York: D. Appleton, 1889).

The Pot and the Kettle

I have always been very amused, too, in this connection of blasphemy by the perusal of Christian Missionary journals, on which I was largely brought up. They are full from cover to cover of the most scandalous falsehoods about heathen gods, and the most senseless insults to them, insults penned by the grossly ignorant of our religious population. It is only in quite recent years that the English public have discovered that Buddha was not a God, and it was not the missionaries that found this out, but scholars of secular attainment. In America, particularly, the most incredible falsehoods are constantly circulated by the Missionary Societies even about the customs of the Hindoos. To read them, one would suppose that every crocodile in India was fed with babies as the first religious duty of every Indian mother; but, of course, it is most terribly wicked for the Hindoo to make fun of the deities of the American. For my part, who have lived half my life in "Christian" countries and half my life in "heathen" countries, I cannot see much to choose between the different religions. Their arguments consist, in the end, of passionate assertion, which is no argument at all.

Religion and Draw-Poker

There is an excellent story—much better known in India than in England—of a missionary, who was explaining to the poor heathen how useless were his gods. "See!" said he, "I insult your idol, he is but of dead stone; he does not avenge himself, or punish me." "I insult your God," replied the Hindoo, "he is invisible; he does not avenge himself, or punish me." "Ah!" said the missionary, "my God will punish you when you die"; and the poor Hindoo could only find the following pitiable answer: "So, when you die, will my idol punish you." It was from America, too, that I obtained the first principle of religion; which is that four to a flush are not as good as one small pair.

Orgies!

Still, I suppose it is useless to contest the popular view that anyone whom any fool chooses to call an Atheist is liable to conduct "orgies." Now, can anyone tell me what orgies are? No? Then I must reach down the Lexicon. *Orgia*, only used in the plural and connected with *Ergon* (work), means sacred rites, sacred worship practised by the initiated at the sacred worship of Demeter at Eleusis, and also the rites of Bacchus. It also means any rites, or worship, or sacrifice, of any mysteries without any reference to religion; and *Orgazio* means, therefore, to celebrate Orgies, or ceremonies, or to celebrate any sacred rites. It is really a poor comment upon the celebration of sacred rites that the word should have come to mean something entirely different, as it does to-day. For the man in the street Orgie means a wild revel usually accompanied by drunkenness. I think it is almost time that someone took the word Orgie as a Battle Cry, and, having shown that the Eucharist is only one kind of orgie to restore the true enthusiasm (which is not of an alcoholic or sexual nature) among the laity; for it is no secret that the falling away of all nations from religion, which only a few blind-worms are fatuous enough to deny, is due to the fact that the fire no longer burns in the sacred lamp. Outside a few monasteries there is hardly any church of any sect whose members really expect anything to happen to them from attending public worship. If a new Saint Paul were to journey to Damascus, the doctor would be called in and his heavenly vision diagnosed as epilepsy. If a new Mahomed came from his cave and announced himself a messenger of God, he would be thought a harmless lunatic. And that is the first stage of a religious propaganda.

The Stations of the Cross

Now the real messenger of God can always be distinguished in a very simple way. He possesses a mysterious force which enables him to persist, heedless of the sneers and laughter of the populace. It then strikes the wiser people that he is dangerous; and they begin on the blasphemy and immorality tack. In the life of our Lord, this will be noticed. In the first place, there was just the contemptuous "he hath a devil," which was the equivalent of our "he's just a crank," but when it was found that this crank had adherents, men of force and eloquence like Peter, to say nothing of financial genius like Judas Iscariot, the cry was quickly changed into wild accusations of blasphemy and allegations of immorality. "He is a friend of publicans and sinners." A sane Government only laughs at these ebullitions; and it is then the task of the Pharisees to prove to the Government that it is to its interest to suppress this dangerous upstart. They may succeed; and though the Government is never for a moment blind to the fact that it is doing an injustice, the new Saviour is crucified. It is this final publicity of crucifixion (for advertisement is just as necessary in one age as another) that secures the full triumph to him whom his enemies fondly suppose to be their victim. Such is human blindness, that the messenger himself, his enemies, and the civil power, all of them do exactly the one thing which will defeat their ends. The messenger would never succeed at all if it were not that he is The Messenger, and it really matters very little what steps he may take to get the message delivered. For all concerned are but pawns in the great game played by infinite wisdom and infinite power.

Orderly, Decorous Ceremonies

It is, therefore, a negligible matter, this abuse, from whatever source it comes. It should waste my time if I were to prove that the *Rites of Eleusis*, as now being performed at Caxton Hall, are orderly, decorous ceremonies. It is true that at times darkness prevails; so it does in some of Wagner's operas and in certain ceremonies of a mystical character which will occur to the minds of a large section of my male readers. There are, moreover, periods of profound silence, and I can quite understand that in such an age of talk as this, that seems a very suspicious circumstance!

Seascape[372]

Victor B. Neuburg

ACROSS the sandy shallows
The salt winds cry and mourn;
The little twittering swallows
Cry out their notes; forlorn
The grass at the sea's edge
On the cliff ledge.

A cold grey sky; the wind
Rustles through the trees;
Chilled grasses weep; unkind
To them the icy breeze.
Brown hedgerows sway and creak,
The wind's so bleak.

[372] From Tillyard, *Cambridge Poets*, 152–153.

And rain, gray, ceaseless rain,
    Insistent, nagging, dull,
Comes, like a dreary pain
    On a face grown beautiful
By patient suffering.
Soft rain-drops sting.

The fields are bare; the hills.
    Still barer in the gray,
Stand stark, and silence fills
    The empty, useless day,
Silent, save for rain,
Dead, save for pain.

And the weary, changeless sea
    With spiritless white foam
Lies level as a lea
    Under the empty dome:
No life on sea or earth;
A cold, slow dearth.

But the swallows cry in the rain,
    And a gull that floats on the sea,
Cries out and cries out again,
    In listless monotony.
And the wind cries and cries,
And never dies.

Serpens Noctis Regina Mundi.[373]

(*Invocation a la Lune. Ballade Argentée.*)

Victor B. Neuburg

OH lustrous Lady of the luminous lake,
    Moving in magic mazes through the trees—

[373] From Tillyard, *Cambridge Poets*, 155–156.

The sombre, swaying trees—light-lady, take
A moment's murmurings; heart-harmonies
That break my breast: I kneel before thy knees,
All humbly hesitant; the silver shoon
I crave to kiss make molten melodies
To the Slow Nocturne of the Rising Moon.

Oh lustrous Lady, for thy shadow's sake
Is slain my slumber, ended all my ease;
I dream at dawn, nor with the wild-birds wake
To dulcet day; marred are mine images
Of lost low lands, of secret summer seas,
Where grave gold Glamour is so subtly strewn,
That from that dryad-dream no faerie flees
To the Slow Nocturne of the Rising Moon.

Oh lustrous Lady of the Silver Snake,
Whisper thy worshipper if his pleadings please
Thine ear; oh, merrier music might I make—
Murmurs of moonlit meads, of light-green leas—
Where pagan priests muttered thy Mysteries
Before the baleful Birth; in their swaying swoon
They prophesied palely in thy curious keys
To the Slow Nocturne of the Rising Moon.

L'envoi.

Oh lustrous Lady, may my memories
Of the untroublous times ere noisome noon
Bring back thy secret serpent-sorceries
To the Slow Nocturne of the Rising Moon.

The Late Mr. G. W. Foote[374]

[Letters to *The New Age* editor among John Duncan, Constance Brooks, and Victor B. Neuburg. —RK]

[374] Following the death of George William Foote (1850–1915), founding editor of the *Freethinker*, an exchange took place in the letters to the editor column of the *New Age: A Weekly Review of Politics,*

Alas, He Meant Well[375]

John Duncan

Sir,—Mr. G. W. Foote is dead. One of his disciples asserts that his style was after Hooker, another that his model was Swift.[376] A very nice discrimination! But let us not worry about Mr. Foote's style, though he is comparable with two great Churchmen. I can, indeed, vouch for Mr. Foote's ecclesiastical tendency, since I once heard him preach after the fashion of an intoning parson with a cough. Perhaps it would be worth a moment to consider what place Mr. G. W. Foote held among us; for posterity, as it turns over our national biography, will only know of one Foote, a mimic and an infidel, of whom Dr. Johnson said: "If he be an infidel, he is an infidel as a dog is an infidel; that is to say, he has never thought upon the subject."[377] The actor Foote alone will be remembered, not for his infidelity, but for his mimicry. We do not know Mr. G. W. Foot for his infidelity, but as one of the few me of our time who really bothered about religion. Enthusiastic for all the ethics of Christianity, he carried his religious principles so high that once he suffered prosecution because parsons could hold the same ethical teaching but wear a different sort of collar. Because so many Christians were only Christian by word and form, Mr. Foote, a Liberal pacifist, set out to Christianise Christianity in the name of Secularism. This departed gentleman had the rare qualities of honesty and moral intrepidity; he also possessed a capable intelligence, yet he has gone only to be thought of as one of that infinite number that merits the epitaph, "Poor Souls, they meant well!" A chaotic heaven is stock-full of such souls

Literature, and Art, in which Victor Neuburg leapt to the defense of his late colleague. For the sake of context, the full correspondence is reproduced here.

[375] From *New Age* 19, no 3 (November 18, 1915): 69–70.

[376] Influential Church of England theologian Richard Hooker (1554–1600) is best known for his book *Of the Lawes of Ecclesiastical Politie* (1594). A monument erected in 1632 by William Cowper dubbed him "judicious," and he posthumously became known by that name. See, for example, Richard Hooker, *Judicious Hooker's Illustrations of Holy Scripture in His Ecclesiastical Policy* (London: printed for the collector, 1675). On the heels of Foote's death, one eulogy described Foote as "modeling" his style on *Judicious Hooker*. See "Judicious Hooker," *Freethinker*, October 31, 1915, 695; quoted in Joss Marsh, *Word Crimes: Blasphemy, Culture, and Literature in Nineteenth Century England* (Chicago: University of Chicago Press, 1998), 176. Jonathan Swift (1667–1745) is considered to be the foremost English-language satirist, remembered for works such as *Gulliver's Travels* (1726) and *A Modest Proposal* (1729). Chapman Cohen (1868–1954), who succeeded Foote as editor of the *Freethinker*, listed Swift as one of his predecessor's influences. See David H. Tribe, *100 Years of Freethought* (London: Elek Books, 1967), 153.

[377] English author and devout Anglican Dr. Samuel Johnson (1709–1784) spoke these words in reference to an altogether different Foote, British comedic actor (i.e., "mimic") and playwright Samuel Foote (1720–1777). See James Boswell, *The Life of Samuel Johnson, LL.D.* (London: Charles Dilly, 1791), 321.

whose ill-service to humanity was their great pains to establish what neither God nor man wanted, or perhaps if they have not gone along that road of which the paving-stones are good intentions, they flit the empyrean, lost arrows driving at non-existent butts. To Mr. Foote was the glory of carrying forward the burden of a two-century-old scepticism, and it is necessary to have to place him and his friends in the same category as the Orangeman in Belfast or Liverpool who cracks a skull for King William's sake.[378] They forget time flies. Mr. Foote could not see the world for looking at it. He started a student, and afterwards set up as a teacher, yet fixing his sight on civilisation and its disease he could not see the wage-system.

Concerning the evils of modern life, it was the delusion of the Secularist, as of the Freethinker of the eighteenth century, to believe the supreme powers which denied the blessing of a Radical liberty and a Liberal prosperity solely sustained their supremacy by means of the State trick of religion which imposed on the credulity of the masses. The Secularist's aims were, therefore, in politics to displace any establishment of religion, and in manners to spread a general religious scepticism among the people. Indeed, as many have seen, the aims of the Secularist were but the weak reflections of those of that arch-Secularist, the progressive Capitalist, for what the Secularist desired the Capitalist had accomplished a century before, and what is left of that religion for which men once cut each other's throats will not cover a threepenny-bit. Poor Foote and his miserable survivors! Yet who weeps? The simply well-meaning ones are the curse of mankind, since folly has no safer means of imposition than by the plea of sincerity. In the seventeenth century that man was of no use to mankind who inclined neither to the king's party nor to the republicans'. Milton and Salmasius[379] may have striven in vanities and error, but they dealt with a subject which drew around the greatest souls of the age and left apart only village idiots and Bedlamites. When the landed aristocracy fought against the swelling commercialists, when children were born Whig and Tory, and men like Swift and Pope[380] were called Whigs by the Tories and Tories by the Whigs—not because there were of neither party, but

[378] "The Orangemen" here refers to members of the Irish Protestant political activist group the Loyal Orange Institution, which today is commonly referred to as the Orange Order. Taking its name from Protestant king William of Orange (1650–1702), its marches through Catholic neighborhoods are often marred by violence.

[379] Duncan is alluding to French scholar Claude Saumaise's (a.k.a. Claudius Salmasius; 1588–1653) 1649 royalist tract *Defensio regia pro Carolo I* (*Royal defense of Charles I*) and English poet John Milton's (1608–1674) rebuttal, *Defense of the People of England* (1651).

[380] Like Milton, Alexander Pope (1688–1744) is a beloved English poet, best remembered for his *The Rape of the Lock* (1712, with revised editions in 1714 and 1717).

rather because they were of both—well-meaning blinkards lived and died, like Mr. G. W. Foote, in an endeavour to blow cobwebs off church porches.

We have yet to make the national hall-mark for the only legitimate bone of contention four our age, and it seems that this war is going to establish this identification. It is not the manufacture of shells or the winning of the war. If we believed some talkers this war is not the last war, but the *first*. Last century the best of men discovered the Wage-System,[381] and the strange, fantastic history of the Socialist movement is the history of the publication of that discovery. The twentieth century has not really commenced. It will commence at the termination of this war, and we have to defy chronology by counting up the nineteenth century to the peace declaration. After this: New Style. As a marriage, it will be for better or worse; which, we know not; but this we know, that if that faction which is the heir to the revolutionary Socialist movement fail to impress its thought upon the English people, and fail to uncover the system of slavery that underlies national life, another faction which is somewhat older than the Socialist movement will complete the work it has been about for so long. Faction is not a bad word, in spite of Johnson.[382] The history of mankind is the history of factions, but in every age there are two factions which, finding unity in a struggle, like Aaron's serpent swallow up the rest.[383] The minor factions live off the subject as a wandering debater talks off the subject. It will be found that the argument against the Catholic mediævalist, the humanitarian secularist, the reforming Christian, the Tory this and the Liberal that, serves equally against them all. It is that argument which is valid against the National Guildsmen in Lapland. However, when we accuse others of a misdirection of intellectual forces our accusation may be returned with the additional charge that we have the Wage-System on the brain. Perhaps we have, but let us see. The minor factions (those that do not understand the Wage-System) have all various values of social justice which spring from a goodwill common to the mass of mankind. Here we find the test. The "Notes of the Week" of your issue of November 4 were a handbook on style for those who fight on the side of the angels. Did benevolence aid pensioners, then it crippled their brothers; did patriotism stir women into

[381] At this point, Duncan's letter digresses into a screed on socialism.

[382] In his hugely influential *Dictionary of the English Language*, lexicographer Samuel Johnson (1709–1784) defined a *Tory* as "one who adheres to the ancient Constitution of the state and the apostolical hierarchy of the Church of England, opposed to a Whig," and defined *Whig* as "the name of a faction." Samuel Johnson, *A Dictionary of the English Language*, 2 vols. (London: W. Strahan, 1755).

[383] In the biblical story of Moses (Exodus 7), Aaron's rod turns into a serpent that devours the similarly transformed rods of the pharaoh's sorcerers.

industry, then it enslaved their men and sisters. Charity fixes the prices of food and gives the poor a stone. Honesty gives a helping hand to agriculture and enriches fat landlords. The virtues combined are futile if there be no consideration of that concrete disorder that affects every movement of our lives. Let Goodheart[384] apply to the realities of Capitalist society, and after a day of experience his own heart will give his head the lie.

Mr. Foote was a good example of the well-meaning ones. It is a pity to attack them, but we can weep and wound. What tears have we shed at the sight of a good name in "Current Cant"![385] I have not been asked to compose Mr. Foote's epitaph, but one cannot resist the desire to make a brief summary of his existence and record what limits were set to the operations of his quick parts. A seventeenth-century satirist mentioned a petition of the chimney-sweepers, "That they may have the scouring of all ecclesiastical consciences every spring and fall." Mr. Foote was one of the fraternity. His was dirty work, but he liked it. He was a little Christian black boy that clambered up the flues of the Church.

The Late Mr. G. W. Foote[386]

Constance Brooks

Sir,—Mr. John Duncan's opinion of the late Mr. Foote is of very little consequence to anyone but himself, but his misrepresentations of his aims must not be allowed to pass unchallenged. The chief counts in his indictment seem to be, firstly, that Mr. Foote devoted his energies to attacking superstition instead of the wage-system; secondly, that he was a Radical and a Pacifist; and, thirdly, that, while attacking the Christian religion, he upheld Christian ethics. If Mr. Duncan still believes that superstition has no influence on the continued maintenance of the wage-system, I can only recommend him to study the controversy carried on some time ago in your pages by "A. E. R." and many correspondents.[387] A study of the *Freethinker*, if he will condescend

[384] The *New Age*'s column "Pastiche" in the September 30, 1915, issue contained the following "quote": "'I desire the emancipation of the wage-worker, but at this time *every* sacrifice must be made by the Trade Unions.'—Mr. Sympathetic Goodheart." See Triboulet, "Miracles," *New Age* 17, no. 22 (September 30, 1915): 531.

[385] "Current Cant" was the name of a column in the *New Age* that published brief quotes from other journals.

[386] From *New Age* 18, no 5 (December 2, 1915): 119.

[387] A. E. Randall was the regular "Views and Reviews" columnist for the *New Age*. His book reviews touched on many subjects including Marxism, psychoanalysis, and religion, but few dealt specifically

to glance at that obscure journal, will enlighten him on the subject of Mr. Foote's attitude toward Pacifism and Christian Ethics. His pacifism did not, at any rate, lead him to oppose Britain's entry into the war, and that pacifism is the only pacifism which counts to-day. It is hard to see Mr. Duncan's point when he inveighs against Mr. Foote's "Christian" ethics, in view of the fact that the *Freethinker* was the only paper, besides *The New Age*, to take a reasonable attitude during the recent journalistic attacks on Nietzsche.[388]

If I have misunderstood Mr. Duncan's meaning I can only apologise for the dull intellect of one of Mr. Foote's "miserable survivors," which is incapable of following the lightning movements of Mr. Duncan's brilliant brain.

The Late Mr. G. W. Foote[389]

John Duncan

Sir.—I thank Miss Constance Brooks for inviting me to re-read a *New Age* controversy and a contemporary comic paper, but I regret that the invitation is a substitution for argument. Mr. Foote attacked superstition! We all do, even the Archbishop of York. Superstition is such sticky stuff and nobody likes it. But what sort of superstition perpetuates wagery? The child's belief in Jonah's adventure, the Salvationist's golden kingdom-come, the seance spook, or superstition such as that which lets its afflicted believe that a proletariat with a technical, secular education can reach full citizenship without property or its equivalent in controlled labour power? Mr. Foote made his choice, and I hope that I explained it.

If the defence of Nietzsche is to be a proof of a lack of Christian ethics, we will not find much of Nietzsche in Mr. Foote's history. It is not un-Christian to do justice to an anti-Christian philosopher, but it is a pity that Nietzsche

with the "wage-system." See, for one example, A. E. R., "Views and Reviews: Work and Women," *New Age* 17, no. 22 (September 30, 1915): 530. This article concludes, "The wage-system does not suit women, and they do not know how to adapt it to their peculiar requirements; and the only place in the wage-system for women is outside."

388 With the outbreak of World War I in July 1914, the German impetus for this conflict was widely (and unfairly) blamed on Nietzsche. For letters in the *New Age* that ran counter to this narrative, see Oscar Levy, "Nietzsche," *New Age* 16, no. 11 (January 14, 1915): 294–295; W. H., "Nietzsche or Christ," *New Age* 16, no. 12 (January 21, 1915): 327; David Irvine, "Nietzsche," *New Age* 16, no. 24 (April 15, 1915): 653; and William Marwick, "Nietzsche in India," *New Age* 17, no. 1 (May 6, 1915): 23.

389 From *New Age* 18, no. 6 (December 9, 1915): 143.

was not defended by Mr. Foote before August, 1914 Colonel Ingersoll, a pious man whose complaint was that the Christian's God was not good enough, affected, I believe, Mr. Foote's mind more than did the terrible German. Although it is quite irrelevant, I confess that, being a Christian, I agreed with Mr. Foote's charitable sentiments and my assertion was that his head prevented their fruition. If Miss Brooks likes not the term Christian ethics, let us use Nietzsche's term, "Slave Morality," and if she has heard Mr. Foote speak or has read his writings she is sure to know what I mean. If she prove that Mr. Foote was no champion of the virtues understood in Nietzsche's term, then I lose my sentimental regard for her departed leader. As it is, I cherish my regard and have a licence to laugh at a life-long anti-Christian who cannot bespeak a new suit of values.

I assure Miss Brooks that when I used the word pacifist but once in conjunction with Liberal I did so for a matter of nomenclature, and by way of winking at the relationship of Quakerism and Christianity.

The Late Mr. G. W. Foote[390]

Victor B. Neuburg

Sir,—Like most superior people, Mr. John Duncan does not quite understand. His remarks on superstition need no comment. The Archbishop of Yorke and Mr. Foote both attacked superstition. True. And they both read the Bible and both wore hats. The identity is unmistakable: long ago it was remarked that Shelley was really a Christian and Torquemada really an Atheist. Mr. Duncan's pseudo-Shavian sophistry is neither original nor clever. As for nobody liking superstition, the vast majority in this country like nothing else; that is why the wage-system persists, and that is why *John Bull* has a circulation of over a million. Is it not so? Superstition is just the "sticky stuff" that clogs the minds of the people, but if they did not "like it" they would scarcely patronise it so passionately.

I take it, and I think that Mr. Duncan will not contradict me that a man's attitude towards wagery, like his outlook upon life generally, is mainly determined by his spiritual state. The late G. W. Foote saw with perfect perspicacity, and he worked for more than forty years to clear out the weeds of

[390] From *New Age* 18, no. 7 (December 16, 1915): 166–167.

religious superstition from the mind of man. As he worked almost single-handed against the most tremendous odds he was unable to devote himself to every branch of political, ethical, and religious reform. For this sad failure of purpose I feel sure that the dead Atheist's ghost would, if it ever heard of him, apologise to the eminent reformer, Nietzschean, and Christian, Mr. Duncan. Mr. Foote "made his choice" indeed: and who but Mr. Duncan shall say that it was not a wise one? No one, I imagine, except professional theologians and their "flocks."

G. W. Foote was the spiritual heir of Laing,[391] of Richard Carlile, of Holyoake, of Bradlaugh,[392] and of other pioneers and heroes who, however much they may be despised by superior and ultra-refined persons, are the men to whom we owe such mental freedom as we possess. (If any[393] doubts this, let him read the contemporary accounts of the almost incredible heroism of Carlile and his crowd. No greater courage was ever recorded than that chronicled in the *Lion* and the *Republican*[394] of the early years of the last century.)

If Mr. Duncan is really a Christian, his remark that Mr. Foote was not a Nietzschean is an impertinence. If he is not a Christian he is merely a farceur, and it is not in the best possible taste to "rag" the memory of a man but just dead.

To call Ingersoll[395] "pious" is one of the less-than-half truths so dear to Christian apologists. But if everyone who is non-Nietzschean is to be labelled "pious," there is no more meaning to be attached to the word. It is a lie to call Ingersoll pious in any attempted[396] sense.

The sooner Mr. Duncan loses the habit of expressing "sentimental regard" for men whom he libels the moment they are dead, the better it will be for his friends and for his ethics. "Sentimental regard," of course, has no connection with "slave morality." It is, no doubt, a Nietzschean virtue.

[391] In a follow-up letter to the editor of December 23, 1915, Neuburg offers this erratum: "'Laing' in paragraph 3 should, of course, be 'Paine'"—that is, American revolutionary Thomas Paine (1737–1809). Victor B. Neuburg, "Letters to the Editor: The Late Mr. Foote," *New Age* 18, no. 8 (December 23, 1915): 191.

[392] Richard Carlile (1790–1843), George Jacob Holyoake (1817–1906), and Charles Bradlaugh (1833–1891) were the original leaders of secularist thought.

[393] Neuburg's December 23, 1915, follow-up letter says that "'any'... should be 'anyone.'" Neuburg, "Letters to the Editor," 191.

[394] Richard Carlile (1790–1843) was a British political agitator on behalf of voting rights, freedom of the press, sexual equality, and an end to child labor, and he was the publisher of the radical newspaper *The Republican* and the journal *The Lion*. He was prosecuted for blasphemy, libel, and sedition, and he was jailed multiple times.

[395] "The Great Agnostic" Bob Ingersoll (1833–1899) was a leading freethinker in the United States.

[396] Neuburg's December 23, 1915, follow-up letter says that "attempted" should be "accepted." Neuburg, "Letters to the Editor," 191.

Mr. Duncan's "licence to laugh" at Atheists because they are not all Nietzscheans will be endorsed by the eminent Duncanian Thersites, but by no one else of any distinction.

If Mr. Duncan wants "a contemporary comic prayer," might I suggest the *Christian Herald* instead of the *Freethinker*—to which, by the way, at least two *New Age* writers contribute? It is even more Christian, and only half the price. Mr. Duncan might also find "a new suit of values" at the *Freethinker* office. It might not be Nietzschean, but it would at least be decent, and proof against "intellectual" sneers at the great dead.

The Late Mr. Foote[397]

John Duncan

Sir,—There should be a law to prevent disciples from entering a discussion while fresh memories of a lost master incapacitate their faculty of reason. I inform a Secularist that superstition is a vague term and in rushes another Secularist to assert that superstition does support the Wage System, since Blatchford,[398] etc. Mr. Victor B. Neuburg should have answered Miss Brooks; I wasn't smart enough to think of Blatchford. As "V. B. N." makes Blatchford an arch-priest, why is he vexed when I point to what was evidently Mr. Foote's ignorance of the necessity of property to citizenship, and infer that Liberalism is a superstition? It is useless for "V. B. N." to argue, as he would if he were calm and could state his case clearly, that an attack on Theology is an attack on the Wage System. (Theology is the preserve of the Secularist; the Churchmen's ignorance of Capitalism can be attacked by Christian and Pagan.) The apathy of so many of our countrymen to the evil of Wagery is not caused by the fatigue of prayer meetings, but by a lack of spiritual and physical appetite. The motive for revolution is the appetite for richer spiritual fare and larder lining. A good stomach (common cliché, desire for a full life) and a religion raise the standard of living, thereby supplying a motive, but desire alone leads only to confusion if the reason cannot direct the power to its proper work, which is, in this case, economics. Mr. Foote thought Christianity false, and advocated Humanitarianism as expressed in

[397] From *New Age* 18, no. 8 (December 23, 1915): 191.

[398] Robert Blatchford (1851–1943) was a British socialist, atheist, and author.

the rules of the Secular Society, yet, I repeat, by his attitude towards the Wage System he was tied in a bundle with the benevolent Catholic Mediaevalists and the social-reform Christians, all enemies of ignorance that is, superstition. To-day, despite the weak interpretations of Christianity and widespread apathy, there is plenty of motive for social change, as a study of the Trade Union Movement shows, but there is a great deficiency of intelligence about the realities of Capitalism. Mr. Foote specialised for forty years in "religious superstition," says "V. B. N." I said so, and my remark that he missed the Wage System is libellous. What was said of Mr. Foote can he emphasised against his disciple who happens to mention the Wage System; that when he professes to face the fact of the marketing of human labour by crying down a superstition which, judging by his letter, he cannot define, he proves nothing but his perfect inutility to a movement that promises to make England a greater country and realise some of the aspirations of his Humanitarianism.

"V. B. N." has so completely lost his temper that he has misunderstood my letter. I did not mention Nietzsche until Miss Brooks took that genuine Anti-Christian as a standard. I used her measure, as I knew that Mr. Foote held, as I do myself, that morality which a Nietzschean calls a "Slave Morality." To justify a criticism of the dead, I can cite a fine letter from Parson Sterne to a friend on the ridiculous proverb, *De mortuis nihil nisi bonum*,[399] but I prefer to remind a rabid Secularist of the opinion of the editor of the *Freethinker*, who agrees with Mr. C. Chesterton[400] that no mercy should be shown to what one believes to be false. My letter was an attempt to sum up the life of a representative Secularist whose career, as I suggested by a reference to Foote, the actor, might be an uninteresting subject a year hence. "V. B. N." may lose a personal friend, but the world only loses a character with a label, and as such I treated the late Mr. G. W. Foote.

By the way, I advise "V. B. N." to abandon a trite style of attack and stale irony. If an opponent says nothing worthy of comment, don't comment, and never cant about "superior person," which though used ironically is flattering and certainly places the assaulter in an inferior position. If an opponent avoids gravity, don't make that an excuse for charging him with insincerity.

[399] Loosely, "Do not speak ill of the dead," or literally, "Of the dead, say nothing but good."

[400] The younger brother of literary critic G. K. Chesterton, Cecil Chesterton (1879–1918) was a vocal proponent of the socioeconomic theory of distributism (the idea that ownership of the means of production should be widespread rather than held by a small, wealthy elite).

The Late Mr. Foote[401]

Victor B. Neuburg

Sir,—It does not surprise me that Mr. Duncan dislikes irony, seeing that his own invective is apparently unable to rise above a snarl. Doubtless, his is

> "The desire of the moth for the star,
> Of the night for the morrow."[402]

With Trade Unionism I am not concerned: I gave a very rough sketch of what I imagine will be the late Mr. Foote's place in history; as Mr. Duncan does not seem to challenge its main accuracy, I take it that he accepts my sketch as a more or less true one. As I have tried to explain, and as Mr. Duncan tries not to understand, Mr. Foote's business was not with Economics, but with Theology. To anyone but a religious carper that would surely be enough.

I know that there are persons who believe that the Golden Age (see Virgil and others) is delayed because the late Queen Victoria was not a vegetarian or the Pope was not a Protestant; but the limit of fanaticism has been reached when it is gravely stated—as an economic tragedy—that Mr. Foote "missed the wage-system." For once I will be dogmatic: boldly I declare that nothing sillier has been said in print for a year. No wonder Mr. Duncan thinks *The Freethinker* a comic paper!

I am glad that Mr. Duncan has dropped his nonsense about Ingersoll, or is that only in abeyance? But he must have his little joke, and so I am accused of calling Mr. Blatchford "an arch-priest." I said that he was a popular hero. He is. Are "arch-priest" and "popular hero" synonymous? Or is Mr. Duncan merely being clever again? If he is, he need not trouble to explain: I quite understand. Why it should be "smart" to mention Mr. Blatchford I do not know. Does Mr. Duncan?

It is not for me to define superstition: I did not try to. It is not germane to the discussion. But Mr. Duncan has already defined it as "sticky stuff"; and I have no doubt that the Sir James Murray "of a year hence" will use that definition (it cannot be meant for an epigram, can it?) adding in parenthesis that it has no connection with almond rock.

[401] From *New Age* 18, no. 11 (January 13, 1916): 263.
[402] Lines 13–14 of "One Word Is Too Often Profaned," from Percy Bysshe Shelley, *Posthumous Poems* (London: John and Henry L. Hunt, 1824), 200.

I said that Mr. Duncan's remarks on superstition were unworthy of comment. But they were worth ridiculing, as is all pretension in the realm of hard and barren intellectualism. Mr. Duncan's annoyance is not astonishing in the circumstances. *Hinc illae lachrymae.*[403]

So Mr. Foote was a man "with a label." Are we not all men with labels? (I dare not think how Mr. Duncan, the sweetness and light specialist, would label me!) "Are we not all stricken men?" Mr. Duncan has an excellent, and even original, label of his own, as I have written above. Is it for him to jibe?

Not for one moment, Mr. Duncan, do I believe that the creator of my Uncle Toby Shandy[404] would have sanctioned spiteful and completely irrelevant attacks upon the newly dead.

I thank Mr. Duncan for his lesson on style, and by way of return I present him with no less than three small, but I trust useful, homilies.

Firstly, as regards clarity of thought. There is no more a necessary connection between Trade Unionism and Atheism than there is between a piano and a banana. The latter may be "based" (or placed) on the former, but the connection is-or should be-a purely accidental one. Similarly, Atheism, as I more than hinted in my previous letter, is an admirable basis for any old kind of unionism; if only for the reason that men without connections in the sky are likely to display more enthusiasm for earthly and secular relationships than men whose interests are centred in God and his family. I do not expect Mr. Duncan to see this, because he has "the wage-system" on the brain—common cliché for obsession, and the chief symptom of obsession is that it can never see more than one thing at a time.

Secondly, as regards the value of words. There is a subjective as well as an objective value in words, those useful adjuncts to argument. Mr. Duncan says, with a Christian sneer, that Mr. Foote attacked religious superstition for forty years. Thus he belittles the work of a man who devoted a long and mentally successful life to the cause of human freedom. The result is a libel. I say the same words with affectionate reverence, and the result is not a libel. Strange?

Lastly, as regards manners. It is not good form to refer continually to an opponent by his initials. One experiences the same kind of squirm that one feels when a man refers habitually to his wife as "Mrs. K." It is the worst kind

[403] "Hence those tears."

[404] Toby Shandy is the uncle of the titular character in Laurence Sterne's classic nine-volume comic novel, *The Life and Opinions of Tristram Shandy, Gentleman* (1759–1767).

of provincialism. Mr. Duncan peppers his column with "V.B.N.s" like a small boy blowing peas at passersby through a "shooter." As I have sub-edited for the rudest man in London,[405] I am familiar with this sort of thing; but it is vile form.

As Mr. Duncan is flattered by what he is pleased to call my irony, I hope that he will be nothing less than ravished by my plain-speaking.

In conclusion, I wish to assure Mr. Duncan that I am not a Secularist, and that I was not a friend—I regret to say—of the late Mr. Foote. I knew him but slightly, and that chiefly as a very occasional and, I fear, unworthy contributor to his excellent journal. May I say also that I never lose my temper in debate? That is one of the things I learnt from the deceased editor of *The Freethinker*.

Meals with the Masters[406]

Rationalist Press Association. Moles

Aleister Crowley

I went to call on Edward Clodd[407]
And found him busy with a rod
Making strict measurements of God.

Observing him, with lots and lots
Of interest, I saw Charles Watts:
Who said: "This Mary Queen of Scots

[405] While Neuburg was subeditor to William Stewart Ross for the *Agnostic Journal*, the "rudest man in London" may well be Aleister Crowley. The spring 1912 issue of *The Equinox* (number 7) listed Victor B. Neuburg on its masthead as subeditor, along with Mary D'Este Sturges as editor. For numbers 8 through 10, they appeared in these roles under their respective magical mottoes, *Lampada tradam* (I will pass on the torch) and *Virakam*. Lampada tradam, adopted by English polymath Rev. Dr. William Whewell (1794–1866) for his coat of arms, was also Neuburg's motto of a Zelator (2°=9□) in the A∴A∴. Neuburg and Crowley would part in 1914, roughly two years before Neuburg wrote this current letter. His reference to "the rudest man in London" was several years before British tabloid *John Bull* dubbed Crowley "The Wickedest Man in the World" (March 24, 1923) and "Britain's Worst Man" (June 22, 1929) in its headlines.

[406] From Aleister Crowley, *The Book of Oaths*, unpublished MS in the Yorke Collection, OS N2, N3, N4, Warburg Institute, London. This poem is from Part 3 (Fauna). An extract from Aleister Crowley's diary in the Metzger-Aeschbach archive, catalog item CMO-41-D-03-21-07, includes an early draft of this poem dated November 1923.

[407] Chairman of the RPA, 1906–1913. See "The Confession of St. Judas McCabbage" in "Diary Entry, October 11, 1908" and note 349.

"Was just a crazy Catholic,
"Besides I simply cannot stick
"Her swank: the whole thing makes me sick."

"Mary?". The Reverend McCabe
(Joseph) woke angry and outgrabe
Against the Virgin and the Babe.

He said, "Such births are not legit-
-mate (*sic*); I like it not one bit
Even when I was a Jesuit.

"Oh Mene! Mene! Mene! Tekel
"Upharsin! Things of this sort make Hell
As incredible as old Ernst Haeckel.

"Philogenous or saprophytic,
"It matters little: every critic
"Agrees that risk of syphilitic

"Infection must invariably
"Follow misconduct!"
"Very ably"—as I might almost say, Mcably—

"You put it," answered Edward Clodd,
"But don't distract me with these odd
Ideas—I'm busy mapping God."

The purr of fat E.S.P. Haynes[408]
Thrilled the assembly: "Watts complains
"Of Mary Queen of Scots's reign's

"Too frequent incidents's courses
"Of violence, the illegal forces
"She used instead of neat divorces.

[408] Rationalist lawyer who arranged Crowley's divorce from Rose Kelly. See chap. 4, in this volume.

"I could have fixed her up, poor kid,
"Finally (exactly as I did
"For Crowley) for say fifty quid."

"I must admit that Haynes can hustle.
"But let us hope that all this fuss'll
"Be over soon," remarked Earl Russell.[409]

"Oh! Hell! You're simply wasting breath,"
(Said Haynes) "That show at Nazareth!
"Why, it would tickle me to death.

"You know me—that I never boast—
"But I would simply love to roast
"That rotten egg the Holy Ghost."

"I never could approach the *limen*
(Sneered Robert Blatchford[410] sourly) "Why men
"Make all this fuss about a hymen?

"It's made precisely like a pie-crust.
"I'd sooner let my new push-bike rust
"Than let my good old marlinspike rust."

At this indecent cynicism
Charles Watts saw gape the vast Abyss[411]
Of Hell, and went and asked baptism,

From the old soapy Bishop Ingram
(Winnington).[412] "Why, I've made my Jing ram"
(Blatchford continued) "every thing gram-

[409] The second Earl Russell, Frank Russell (1865–1931), was the elder brother of British philosopher and Nobel laureate Bertrand Russell (1872–1970), a supporter of the RPA, a contributor to its journal, and a fixture (and occasional speaker) at its Annual Dinner. Bertrand was likewise a supporter: his paper "The Case for Agnosticism" was published by Watts & Co. (n.d.), and his later talks "Why I Am Not a Christian" (1927) and "The Faith of a Rationalist" (1947)—which exemplified basing religious belief upon reason and evidence—would be published by the RPA.

[410] Robert Blatchford (1851–1943) was a British socialist, atheist, and author.

[411] The word "Abyss" breaks the rhyme pattern of this poem, possibly indicating a transcription error in the Yorke collection typescript.

[412] Arthur Winnington-Ingram (1858–1946) was bishop of London, 1901–1939. His strong words against Germany during World War I veered into jingoism.

"iniverous, every female mammal
"From a black beetle to a camel
"That I could teach to spurn the trammel

"Of man-made morals"—"Here come off it!"
Cried Joe McCabbage:[413] "Where's the profit
"Of talk of this kind?" "Let him cough it

"Up" (interrupted Edward Clodd)
"Blatch has not reached the period
"Of culture when to measure God

"Suffices his instinctive craving
"For joy: he has to keep on raving
"About his gift for misbehaving."

At this, instead of cooling off,
Blatchford replied, "You bloody toff,
"I've half a mind to toss you off

"The carpet underneath the table,
"And then perhaps with luck McCabe'll
"Perceive the point of this old fable

"About the virgin in the stable"—
The talk became a roaring Babel.
I felt that I was quite unable

To stick it out: I donned my sable
Coat and my hat: "I'm on my way, bel-
-ov'd Brethren, to a girl called Mabel."

[413] Joseph McCabe. "The Confession of St. Judas McCabbage," in "Diary Entry, October 11, 1908," in this anthology.

Appendices

The Legend of Aleister Crowley

A Fair Plea for Fair Play[1]

Victor B. Neuburg.

THE portly and voluminous poet, mystic, magician, explorer, scholar and publicist, Aleister Crowley, here has his Legend[2] given to the world before the trifling formality of his death.

It is at once the strength and the weakness of this decorously-tempered panegyric that it is the work of an instructed advocate rather than of an impartial judge.

In considering, criticizing and appraising this unique and bulky figure we have to bear in mind—and it is only fair that we should thus bear in mind—the character, or rather the characteristics, of his countrymen.

Critics of life so diverse as Jonathan Swift, Dean of St. Patrick's, and Thomas Babington, Lord Macaulay, have in their several ways noted the proneness of the English mob to single out an object of hatred, and to howl at that unfortunate figure until they have either slain it, or cast it into the limbo of unreturning exile.

For us Freethinkers, it should suffice to recall the names of certain of our own heroes and martyrs who have thus enjoyed the favour of this distinguishing mark of approbation at the stone-filled hands and patriotic voices of their grateful fellow-countrymen, who never forgive genius, originality, or independence of thought. Byron, Shelley, Richard Carlile, Charles Bradlaugh,[3] are names among a score or two that might be given that indicate what are

[1] *Freethinker* 1, no. 34 (August 24, 1930): 538–539.

[2] *The Legend of Aleister Crowley*, By P. R. Stephensen, Mandrake Press. 2s, 6d. [original note]

[3] While Lord Byron and Percy Bysshe Shelley were famous poets, they were also supporters of parliamentary reform. British free-press advocate Richard Carlile (1790–1843) quoted from their works, among others, in his radical journal *Sherwin's Political Register* as part of his activist activities. Charles Bradlaugh (1833–1891) was another British activist and reformer, and he was the founder of the NSS in 1866.

the real feelings of the man in the street towards his saviours and benefactors. Mob psychology is an inferiority complex magnified to the *n*th power; and in England, at least, there are not enough people of exalted temperament to prevent the martyrdom of the "sports" and leaders among mankind.

At one time we knew Aleister Crowley pretty well, as is plain from this book; and although in some respects he was perhaps "not quite nice to know," as the slang phrase goes, we do not think that it is quite fair to charge him with murder, cannibalism, black magical practices, moral aberrations, treachery, druggery; as is the custom amongst the cunninger and more degraded jackals of Fleet Street. We know something of journalists, but we know very few members of the newspaper craft who would not sell themselves for twenty guineas down if it were quite "safe." Rigid moralists, like the good Horatio Bottomley and the Almost-Reverend James Douglas,[4] it seems to us, really protest too much in their religious and disinterested efforts to keep England pure and holy; and for this reason, differing as we do from very much that is taught and advocated by Aleister Crowley, we respectfully decline to join the howling mob of interested pietists who every now and then raise the wind in the Silly Season by shrieking with inspired vituperation at the poet under discussion.

If a tithe of the charges brought against Crowley be true, he should be exiled from every country in the world, and, after the judicious application to his person of various Chinese tortures, he should be hanged, drawn and quartered first, broken on the wheel afterwards, and the remains sown with salt before being cast into the infernal pit; but somehow we have an instinct against accepting the unsupported assertions of the professional moralists of our popular journals, and we do not know that Mr. Douglas, Mr. Bottomley, and the lesser lights of cheap journalism have ever proved their case up to the hilt. In these circumstances we venture publicly to record our opinion that the poet might be allowed to follow his path in comparative peace until something definitely criminal is proved against him, when the police, no doubt, will be quite capable of dealing with the case. Crowley is at least as important a figure as the late D. H. Lawrence

[4] Horation Bottomley (1860–1933) was editor and proprietor of the popular tabloid news weekly *John Bull*. James Douglas (1867–1940), as editor of the *Sunday Express* newspaper during the 1920s, was a proponent of censorship and during his tenure called for banning several books, including Aleister Crowley's *The Diary of a Drug Fiend*. Both newspapers frequently made Crowley the target of their vitriolic attacks.

and Mr. James Joyce,[5] both unquestionably men of genius; and when we remember the kind of thing said about these artists in our cheaper prints, we hesitate to acquiesce in the Sunday Newspaper verdict on Aleister Crowley.

Mr. Stephensen gives an amusing and interesting, if one-sided and partial, account of his subject; and the book will have its place when the history, literary and social, of the early twentieth century comes to be written.

A final note; we ourselves differ profoundly on many points—on most points, indeed—from Crowley; but we do not see why he should not have a fair show; this notice therefore is written solely in the interests of fair play, by one who is in no respect a follower or partisan. It is a plea for ordinary human toleration, addressed by a Freethinker to his fellow Freethinkers. Those of them who feel inclined to quarrel with our estimate of Crowley's genius might inform themselves by glancing at his latest published book, *Confessions*.[6] This work, now in course of publication, is, in our considered judgment, the greatest autobiography that the world has ever seen. We have not the least doubt that posterity will endorse this finding.

The Master Magician[7]

Victor B. Neuburg

Magick. By The Master Therion. (Aleister Crowley). Being Part III. of Book 4. In Four Parts. (Foyles: 15s. net.)

Between the ecclesiastics, whose reason is Authority, and the rationalists, whose authority is Reason, the problem of Magick had until recently been solved in the negative; but, in my view, no authority is, or can be, absolutely final; and reason depends on higher reasons—ad infinitum.

[5] D. H. Lawrence's *Lady Chatterley's Lover* (1928) was one of the most famous banned books of the twentieth century. While an uncensored version of the text was not released in the United Kingdom until 1960, London's Mandrake Press—publisher of *The Legend of Aleister Crowley*—issued a private edition in 1929 in defiance of the authorities. James Joyce's *Ulysses* (1922), one of the most important works of twentieth-century literature, was similarly banned in the United Kingdom and the United States until the 1930s.

[6] Aleister Crowley, *The Spirit of Solitude: An Autohagiography; Subsequently Re-Antichristened the Confessions of Aleister Crowley*, 2 vols. (London: Mandrake Press, 1929). Six volumes of the work were projected, but only the first two were published; the third volume got as far as page proofs, but the company folded before the volume could be released.

[7] *Sunday Referee* 2875 (October 9, 1932): 4.

It has been remarked by the Master Alfricobas Nasier [*sic*][8] that beans and bacon is a good dish spoiled between Moses and Pythagoras. Even so, the honourable and ancient science of Magick has been discredited between Reason and Authority, twin brothers of mind who have usurped the throne held aforetime by the Royal Wisdom.

Magick, by the Master Therion, is a re-issue of a bulky work originally issued semi-privately in Paris some years ago.

Magick, to the already-discredited Victorians, was, as we know, "all imagination"; and that is a perfectly true statement; the only snag being that the poor, stupid, stodgy Victorians had no idea as to what "imagination" is. They had forgotten, or were ignorant of, their Blake: "Everything possible to be believed is a image of truth." There, if it be needed, indeed, is an apology for, and justification of, Magick.

> "All discussions upon philosophy are necessarily sterile, since truth is beyond language. They are, however, useful if carried far enough—if carried to the point when it becomes apparent that all arguments are arguments in a circle."

Magick is a text-book of How To Do It. Those who hold that "magick" and "superstition" are synonymous terms will have none of it; but such à priori reasoning, itself "superstitious" as regards the potentialities of scientific investigation, will no longer avail with the increasing few who are "all out" for a wide and synthetic view of the multiform, multi-hued cosmos, wherein we function.

There are, in our civilisation, thousands of wandering sheep and goats who claim "occult" knowledge and attainments; and who seem, to the ordinary human eye, to be merely cranks, charlatans, and dupes.

It is to these, mainly, perhaps, that *Magick* is addressed; both an art and a science, the management of the path is a way through life. To the few it is *the*

[8] This should be "Alcofribas Nasier," the pseudonym of French satirist François Rabelais (formed from an anagram of his name) as author of *Pantagruel* (1532), the first book in his *Gargantua* series. The fifth book of *Gargantua and Pantagruel* contains the passage "Your Duke of Touraine's income will not afford him to eat his bellyful of beans and bacon (a good dish spoiled between Moses and Pythagoras)," to which Neuburg refers. See chap. 6, "How the Birds Are Crammed in the Ringing Island." Neuburg's reference here to Rabelais is sly, as *Gargantua and Pantagruel* also refers to the Abbey of Thélème, where "all their life was spent not in laws, statutes, or rules, but according to their own free will and pleasure." The Thelemites governed themselves under only one rule, which was *Fais ce que voudras* (Do what thou wilt). These ideas clearly influenced Crowley's conception of his Law of Thelema, "Do what thou wilt shall be the whole of the Law," and his establishment of an Abbey of Thelema in Cefalù in 1920.

way; and this book is a guide to the feet and a lamp to the eyes of those who would tread the way to attainment.

The writer, the Master Therion, is the Bad Boy of British Journalism—Aleister Crowley. This wicked man (*vide* the Press, *passim*) has produced a work that is witty, erudite, profound, and accomplished; though *Magick* will find no favour with orthodox religionists, orthodox scientists, or orthodox Freethinkers, it is a work that, for ease of style and thoroughness of execution, could have emanated from only one pen of our generation.

For once, Mr. Crowley may be treated fairly, critically, and without the rancor that is born of the over-payment of the professional scurrility-mongers of Grub-street. Much of this author's extreme unpopularity is due, beyond dispute, to his persistent habits of explosive violence of expression and passionate assertiveness; habits not merely stupid, but dull as fireworks in sunlight; his "fun" is so often deliberately wounding that one is tempted all the time to regard his own wounds as being funny—at least in so far as they are the result of his own ineptitude in the management of tools wherewith he has been familiar not only almost from his cradle, but—if we are to credit his own account of himself—from his previous incarnations, including that famous one wherein he claims to have been Eliphas Levi.[9]

There would be no point in repeating or reprinting criticisms of contemporaries that exhibit the rancid taste of the controversial theologians of the late middle ages, and the restrained manners of a sick and sulky bear. Such impure puerilities give the profane their chance of a happy sneer at the term "Master." "Some master," they say—and with more than some justice—"who cannot control his own hand or his own pen."

It were ungrateful to end on a cavil, cavalierly though the Master Therion insists upon serving his supposed opponents.

The writer's accomplishment is patent; he is a master, at any rate, of prose; his power of expression is as near perfection as that of any author I have read. As felicitous as Goldsmith, Crowley is as lucid as Darwin, as direct as Bunyan, as terse as Horace.[10] There is no question as to the virtue of his prose.

[9] Éliphas Lévi was the Hebraicized form of French occultist Alphonse Louis Constant's (1810–1875) given name. Under this pseudonym, his books on ceremonial magic sparked a revival of magic in France and throughout the continent. See Christopher McIntosh, *Eliphas Lévi and the French Occult Revival* (London: Rider, 1972). Aleister Crowley believed himself to be a reincarnation of Lévi, who died four and a half months before Crowley's birth.

[10] Anglo-Irish novelist Oliver Goldsmith (1728–1774) is the author of *The Vicar of Wakefield* (1766). English naturalist Charles Darwin's (1809–1882) introduced his theory of evolution to the world in *On the Origin of Species* (1859). Prolific English preacher John Bunyan (1628–1688) is best

Barring its hideous flaws of manner, *Magick* is a work that will carry its message to the rare student who, in our weltering age, is cool enough to "count"; the book may, indeed, be a book for the few; but then it is the few who "tell"—by telling truly and wisely—in any generation of men.

Aleister Crowley 1898–1911

An Introductory Essay[11]

Major-General J. F. C. Fuller

The legend that Aleister Crowley was the wickedest man in the world was concocted by the gutter press, and fertilized by his own vanity. If the world would not accept him as one of its greatest of lyric poets, he determined that it should do so as the Beast of the Apocalypse. This came easily to him, because his parents were Plymouth Brethren of the narrowest type, and, incredible as it may seem, it was his mother who believed him to be that Beast, and fixed on him its name. Actually, what manner of man was he?

In my opinion, a versatile and unbalanced genius: a poet, a philosopher, a mountaineer, a skilled player of chess. a brilliant conversationalist, and a deeply read student of the occult. Also he was a man at daggers drawn with conventional religion, ever eager to trail his coat and shock society. He did not object to criticism of his poems, nor of his magic, nor even of his erratic behaviour, as long as he was flush; but when broke, as he periodically was, he would not hesitate to stoop to the meanest of actions in order to justify himself. By so doing, he alienated all his closest friends.

When his father died, he came under the guardianship of his maternal uncle, George Archibald Bishop, a religious fanatic. Later, he went to Trinity, Cambridge, and on coming of age inherited a third of his father's fortune, said to be £50,000. The life interest of another third went to his mother, and the remaining third was split up into life interests among a number of relatives, to all of whom he was the residual legatee.

known for *The Pilgrim's Progress* (1678). Horace (65–8 BCE) was the celebrated Roman lyric poet whose *Carmen Saeculare* (17 BCE) Crowley used as the title for one of his own works.

[11] J. F. C. Fuller, introduction to *Bibliotheca Crowleyana: Catalogue of a Unique Collection of Books, Pamphlets, Proof Copies, MSS, etc. by, about, or Connected with Aleister Crowley* (Tenterden, UK: Keith Hogg, 1966), 2–8.

On leaving Cambridge he became acquainted with an occultist. George Cecil Jones, who introduced him to Samuel Liddell Mathers, the hierophant of a mystical fraternity, the Hermetic Order of the Golden Dawn, of which Jones and also W.B. Yeats were members, and in November, 1898, Crowley was initiated in it as a neophyte. This was the first great turning point in his life.

Mathers was a profound student of the Hebrew Kabbala, and he divulged to Crowley its doctrines, including the secret, revealed by the Kabbalist Pico della Mirandola in the 15th century, that Sammael (Satan) and not Tetragrammaton (YHVH) the Jehovah of the Old Testament, was the lord of the world. And that, as the medieval sorcerers whispered, *Daemon est Deus inversus.*

Sammael was androgynous, and his counterpart was Esheth Zenunim, the Harlot, or Woman of Whoredoms, also called Lilith, which signifies "night." He was the active principle, while she was the passive, and when in union they formulate the Antichrist, or Anti-Logos, known as Hay-yah (also as Chiva) the Beast, the numerical value of which is 25, one unit less than that of Tetragrammaton. Hence Omar Khayyam's:

> A Hair perhaps divides the False and True;
> Yes; and a single Alif were the clue—
> Could you but find it—to the Treasure-house,
> And peradventure to THE MASTER too;[12]
> (N.B. the numerical value of Alif - A - is one).

Nothing could have fitted Crowley's loathing of the religion of his parents better. Henceforth he *was* the Beast his mother had named him, and as such he would invert the world and become God, or, at least, be absorbed into the Godhead. Listen to him in his mystical poem "Aha" (see *The Equinox*, Vol.1, No.3):

> **Marsyas** [the Adept]:
> My stature shall surpass the stars:
> He hath said it! Men shall worship me
> In hidden woods, on barren scaurs,
> Henceforth to all eternity.

[12] This is poem 50 in Khayyam, *Rubáiyát*, 47.

Olympas [his pupil]:
Hail! I adore thee! Let us feast.
Marsyas:
I am the consecrated Beast.
I build the Abominable House.
The Scarlet Woman is my Spouse.[13]

In 1900 we find him in Mexico climbing volcanoes. And in 1902 he set out with five others to climb Chogo Ri (also called "K2" and "Mount Godwin Austin") in Baltistan, which ranks after Everest as the second highest mountain in the world. After spending 68 days on a glacier, bad weather compelled the abandonment of the attempt.

In 1903, on August 12, in circumstances too complex to relate here, he married Rose, the sister of Gerald Kelly the artist, who had been an undergraduate with him at Cambridge. In the following year he and his wife went to Cairo, where he stepped over the threshold of the second great turning point in his magical career.

There he spent a night with Rose in the King's Chamber of the Great Pyramid, and carried out an invocation, which lit up the chamber—so he said—with astral light. Next, when in the Cairo Museum, Rose suddenly stopped before a show-case; pointed at a stele numbered 666—the number of the Beast—and exclaimed—"there!"

What actually followed is obscure. It would appear that Crowley passed into a kind of trance, during which, between noon and one o'clock on three consecutive days a spirit, that called itself Aiwaas, and claimed to be the minister of Hoor-Paar-Kraat who from 1904 onward for 2,000 years was to govern the world dictated to him *The Book of the Law* (*Liber Al vel Legis*).

My own interpretation is, that the spirit was Crowley's subconscious mind and the dictation automatic writing. Whatever it was, it convinced him that he had contacted the new Aeon of the god Horus. Later, he linked up the message he had received with Rabelais' Abbey of Thelema and its rule of "*Fay ce que voudras*,"[14] which he expanded into "Do what thou wilt shall be the whole of the Law. Love is the law, love under will."

Strange to say, he took little notice of this remarkable revelation until years later; but when he did, it became an overmastering obsession.

[13] Aleister Crowley, "Aha!," *The Equinox* 1, no. 3 (March 1910): 49.
[14] From François Rabelais's *Gargantua and Pantagruel*.

After his return home, his wife gave birth to a daughter, whom he named Lilith, and a few months later he decided on another mountaineering exploit. This time it was to climb Kanchenjunga, the world's third highest mountain, and, as a preliminary move, he took Rose and her infant child to Burma. Shortly before the attempt was made—it ended in failure—chance involved me in the Crowley saga.

At the time I was stationed at Lucknow, and in a journal *The Literary Guide*, I happened to read a review of Crowley's *Why Jesus Wept.*[15] I wrote for it, and in it found a leaflet in which he offered a prize of £100 for the best essay on his works in their "Traveller's Edition." I ordered it, and on its arrival, with the inconsequence of youth, I decided to chance my luck.

Soon after followed the first letter I received from Crowley. It was addressed from the Drum Druid Hotel, Darjeeling, and was dated June 26, 1905. It began: "Dear Sir, your letter of May 17 has been forwarded to me here, where. I am preparing a small expedition to Kanchenjunga;" and it informed me that copies of all his later poems, which were to appear in vol. II of "The Traveller's Edition"—still in the press—had been posted to me.

I spent the hot weather writing the essay, and in October went down with a record attack of enteric fever; instead of the normal 21 days it topped 70. In the spring of 1906 I was invalided home, and on August 8 received, in return to a letter of mine, the following reply from Crowley.

> "I am sorry to hear of your enteric fever, but fate has treated me even worse; for after a most successful trip through China without a day's illness for any of us, our baby girl died of that very disease on the way home."

A week later I met Aleister and his wife for the first time at the old Hotel Cecil in the Strand, and in October my essay, *The Star in the West* was finished and posted to Crowley. In 1907 it was published, and in it, among other things, I analysed Crowley's philosophy, which I called "Crowleyanity." Some of it was leg-pull, but the greater part a serious attempt to fathom it. Symbolically it is depicted on p.215, and I mention this because three years later the gutter press described "Crowleyanity" as a "bacchanalian riot of orgies!"

In 1908, Crowley decided to bring out a biennial publication called *The Equinox*. He described it as "The Official Organ of the A.∴A.∴," and the

[15] Most likely, Fuller is referring to the review "Hinc Illæ Lachrymæ," *Literary Guide and Rationalist Review* 105 (March 1, 1905): 45.

Review of Scientific Illuminism." On its cover was printed the slogan: "The Method of Science . . . The Aim of Religion." But, like so many of his projects, the aim was protean and the method erratic; and it became a kind of occult emporium of mystical knowledge. It sold like hot cakes, and, in spite of its expensive production, had he not been so prodigal, it might have provided him with a modest income.

The Order of the A.·.A.·. demands a brief explanation. So far as my knowledge goes, it never existed outside Crowley's imagination, and was no more than a duplicate of Madam Blavatsky's Himalayan Mahatmas. He created several of these ghostly orders, such as L.I.L., "The Lamp of Illimitable Light," and O.T.O., "The Order of Oriental Templars." He loved to play with them, and when broke, on the lines of the Philosopher's Stone, found them convenient instruments wherewith to extract gold from the pockets of his more affluent followers.

In 1909, with the poet Victor B. Neuburg, who since 1906 had become his *chela* (a cross between a discip1e and a maid of all works) he carried out his "Operation of the Thirty Aethyrs" (see *The Equinox*, vo1.I, No.5) in the Sahara,[16] and on his return was financially a desert.

In 1910 I saw little of him, and in August sensed danger when I received a letter from him in which he informed me: "There is some hope of things turning out right for us all. Don't say a word until it is a fait accompli, as you are financially interested." I was not, nor did I know what he was up to. But I had my suspicions that he was contemplating the irrigation of the Sahara.

Soon after, I became aware of what he was about. It was to give a series of public performances, entitled *The Rites of Eleusis*, in order to raise money for the A.·.A.·.! Because a number of his friends strongly objected to it, I urged him to, abandon the project. Also I had a hunch that he was dabbling with fire. But the more he was pressed, the more stubborn he became.

The Rites, which coincided with his wife divorcing him, were performed at the Caxton Hall, Westminster, between October 19 and November 30, 1910. They were heralded by an artistic brochure, on the brown cover of which was stamped a black swastika. In it was the following:

"In order to induce this religious ecstasy in its highest form Crowley proposes to hold a series of religious services; seven in number. These services . . . will be conducted by Aleister Crowley himself, assisted by other

[16] [Aleister Crowley and Victor Neuburg], "Liber XXX Aerum vel Saeculi sub figurâ CCCCXVIII being of the Angels of the 30 Aethyrs: The Vision and the Voice," *The Equinox* 1, no. 5 (supplement, March 1911), 1–176.

Neophytes of the A.·.A.·., the mystical society, one of whose Mahatmas is responsible for the foundation of *The Equinox*."[17]

In every sense the performances were most proper, though dim, because the stage was candle lit. So innocent were they that I took my mother to one of them. Innocence, however, is no shield against the vomitings of the gutter press. In *The Looking Glass* of October 29, a racing rag, edited by a man called F. de Wend Fenton,[18] the A.·.A.·. was described as "a blasphemous sect, whose proceedings conceivably lend themselves to immorality of the most revolting character." To heel came *John Bull*, Bottomley's muck raker.[19] It asked: "Is a new Smyth-Piggott among Us?"—this referred to an amorous parson, recently in trouble over his "Abode of Love."[20]

I wrote to Crowley, so did others of his friends, and we urged him to take proceedings of libel against *The Looking Glass*. He refused to do so, and gave as an excuse that, an English judge had once said: "Suffer any wrong that may be done you rather than seek redress at law."

Three days later, Cecil Jones, whose name had been bracketed with Crowley's, had a writ of criminal libel served on *The Looking Glass* and in his letter to me added: "Crowley goes to Algeria tomorrow. Some of his friends will say he ran away." Emphatically, de Wend Fenton did, and in his issue of December 17 wrote:

> "We understand that Mr. Aleister Crowley has left London for Russia. This should do much to mitigate the rigour of the St. Petersburg winter,
>
> "We have to congratulate ourselves on having temporarily extinguished one of the most blasphemous and cold-blooded villains of modern times."

[17] [Aleister Crowley], *Eleusis* (London: [The Equinox], 1910), 2.

[18] Newspaper and tabloid publisher West F. de Wend Fenton tended to skirt the edges of propriety, resulting in a number of court cases. In addition to the *Jones v. The* Looking Glass libel case (in which the newspaper prevailed), in other instances he was fined £1,000 for libel (1911), sending obscene material through the mail (1913), and contravening the Defence of the Realm Act (1918). Given the earlier attacks against him, Crowley gleefully reported on de Went Fenton's obscenity-related fines of £91. See *The Equinox* 1, no. 9 (March 1913): xxv. For more on *Jones v.* The Looking Glass, see Kaczynski, *Perdurabo Outtakes*.

[19] Horation Bottomley (1860–1933) was editor/proprietor of the popular tabloid news weekly *John Bull*.]

[20] "Is a New Smyth-Pigott among Us? Mr. Aleister Crowley's Blasphemous and Prurient Propaganda," *John Bull*, November 5, 1910, 707. Church of England clergyman John Hugh Smyth-Pigott (1852–1927) became in 1899 the second leader of a notorious English messianic cult known as the *Agapemone*, or "Abode of love," after their communal estate in Spaxton, Somerset. Smyth-Pigott, like church founder Henry Prince before him, proclaimed himself Christ incarnate, presided over a primarily female congregation, and took several "spiritual" brides. In January 1909, he was tried in ecclesiastical court for fathering two children with a church member other than his wife. He was defrocked in absentia in March 1909.

The case came before Mr. Justice Scrutton on April 26, 1911, and on the findings judgment was entered for the defendants.

Jones lost his case. (1) Because Crowley (who was in court) had not prosecuted *The Looking Glass*. (2) Because Jones had not subpoenaed him. And (3) because in the margins of Crowley's "Ambrosii Magi Hortus Rosarum" (see *Collected Works*, vol. II)[21] a number of schoolboyish acrostics in Latin were printed, the initials of which spelt out four-letter words; therefore all his writings were taken by the jury to be obscene. Shades of Lady Chatterley and of Bobby Burns![22]

Later, I asked Jones why he had not subpoenaed Crowley. His reply was: "If, as my friend, he had not the decency to come forward willingly, it would have been an insult to myself had I compelled him to do so." He was an exceedingly upright man with a high sense of honour.

After the trial, I wrote to Crowley and told him that our friendship was at an end. Stubborn as ever, on May 4 I received in reply: "you are wrong. It was not want of pluck that decided my action in November. It was, as I told you, mystical reasons." It was nothing of the sort, in November it had been an asinine saying he attributed to a judge.

From the day of the trial I never met him again, nor did I communicate with him, and until his death in 1947 all I garnered of him were the periodic effusions of the gutter press. Yet the neophyte of Euterpe and Erato endures.

To me he remains one of the greatest of English lyric poets, and among those of France, comparable with Rimbaud and Baudelaire.[23] By the magic of Eros the Beast in him was transfigured into Beauty: *Alice*, *Clouds without Water*; many of the poems enshrined in *Gargoyles*, *The Winged Beetle* and *Rodin in Rime*; the superb "La Gitana" in *Konx om Pax*, and the incomparable

[21] "Ambrosii Magi Hortus Rosarum" was first published in Crowley's *Sword of Song* and reprinted in volume 2 of *The Works of Aleister Crowley*.

[22] As mentioned in "The Legend of Aleister Crowley: A Fair Plea for Fair Play," note 5, in the appendices, D. H. Lawrence's *Lady Chatterley's Lover* was one of the most famous banned books of the twentieth century. Poet Robert Burns's *Merry Muses* is, however, the most famous banned book of the eighteenth century. Burns collected and wrote bawdy and erotic poetry, which was discovered among his papers after he died and privately published not long thereafter; it remained banned in the United Kingdom until 1965. Robert Burns, *The Merry Muses of Caledonia: A Collection of Favourite Scots Songs, Ancient and Modern, Selected for the Use of the Crochallan Fencibles* (Edinburgh: n.p., 1799).

[23] Arthur Rimbaud (1854–1891) and Charles Baudelaire (1821–1867) were great French poets. Crowley translated several of Baudelaire's poems, which were published in *Vanity Fair* magazine and in Charles Baudelaire, Aleister Crowley, and Jean de Boschère, *Little Poems in Prose* (Paris: E.W. Titus, 1928).

four *Rosas* are works of the highest poetic genius.[24] Much of the rest is Hudibrastic satire, and some of it is swill.

[24] [Aleister Crowley], *Alice: An Adultery* (n.p.: privately printed, 1903); Rev. C. Verey [Aleister Crowley], *Clouds without Water: Edited from a Private M.S.* (London: privately printed, 1909); Aleister Crowley, *Gargoyles: Being Strangely Wrought Images of Life and Death* (Foyers, UK: Society for the Propagation of Religious Truth, 1906); Aleister Crowley, *The Winged Beetle* (privately printed, 1910); Aleister Crowley, *Seven Lithographs by Clot from the Water-Colours of Auguste Rodin with a Chaplet of Verse* (London: Chiswick Press, 1907); Aleister Crowley, *Konx Om Pax: Essays in Light* (London: Walter Scott, 1907); H. D. Carr, [Aleister Crowley], *Rosa Mundi. A Poem* (Ph. Renouard: Paris, 1905); H. D. Carr [Aleister Crowley], *Rosa Inferni: A Poem* (London: Chiswick Press, 1907); H. D. Carr [Aleister Crowley], *Rosa Coeli: A Poem* (London: Chiswick Press, 1907); Aleister Crowley, *Rosa Decidua* (n.p.: n.p., 1910).

Index

For the benefit of digital users, indexed terms that span two pages (e.g., 52–53) may, on occasion, appear on only one of those pages.

Figures are indicated by *f* following the page number